FUTURE SCIENCE

About the Editors

JOHN WHITE is an author, editor, and teacher engaged in the exploration of consciousness. He is an editor of *New Realities* (formerly *Psychic*) and *Human Dimensions* magazines, and is on the editorial boards of the *Journal of Altered States of Consciousness* and *Re·Vision Journal*.

Mr. White's books include *The Highest State of Consciousness*, *What Is Meditation?*, *Frontiers of Consciousness*, *Psychic Exploration* (which he edited for Edgar D. Mitchell), *Other Worlds, Other Universes* (co-edited with Brad Steiger), *Relax* (co-edited with James Fadiman) and *Everything You Want to Know about TM*. More than one hundred fifty articles and reviews by him have appeared in popular magazines such as *Reader's Digest*, *Saturday Review*, *Human Behavior* and *Science Digest*, in professional journals such as *Journal of Altered States of Consciousness*, *Journal for the Study of Consciousness* and *Fields Within Fields*, and in major newspapers such as the *San Francisco Chronicle*, *Chicago Sun-Times*, and *National Enquirer*. His articles have been reprinted in textbooks on linguistics, education, biology, psychology and yoga.

STANLEY KRIPPNER, Ph.D., is program planning coordinator for the Humanistic Psychology Institute in San Francisco. He has also served as president of the Association for Humanistic Psychology, as vice president for the western hemisphere of the International Association for Psychotronic Research, and as director, from 1964–73, of the Dream Laboratory at Maimonides Medical Center. In 1972 he chaired the First Western Hemisphere Conference on Acupuncture, Kirlian Photography, and the Human Aura. Subsequently, he co-edited (with Daniel Rubin) the proceedings as *Galaxies of Life* (later published in paperback as *The Kirlian Aura*). He is also co-editor (with Daniel Rubin) of *The Energies of Consciousness*. He co-authored (with Montague Ullman) *Dream Telepathy* and (with Alberto Villoldo) of *The Realms of Healing*. His career in parapsychology is described in his own words in *Song of the Siren: A Parapsychological Odyssey*. He has written more than three hundred articles appearing in psychological, psychiatric, educational, and scientific journals.

FUTURE SCIENCE

*Life Energies
and the Physics
of Paranormal Phenomena*

EDITED BY
*John White
and Stanley Krippner*

ANCHOR BOOKS
Doubleday & Company, Inc.
Garden City, New York

The Anchor Press edition is the first publication of *Future Science.*

Anchor Press edition: 1977

Library of Congress Cataloging in Publication Data
Main entry under title:

Future science.

Bibliography
1. Occult sciences—Addresses, essays, lectures.
2. Psychical research—Addresses, essays, lectures.
I. White, John Warren, 1939-   II. Krippner,
Stanley, 1932-
BF1411.F87   133.8
ISBN: 0-385-11203-3
Library of Congress Catalog Card Number: 76-23808

To our children, the future

Sandy
Tom
Sharon
Tim

Carie
Bob

with love

The editors wish to express their deep gratitude to Dr. William A. Tiller for his help in preparing this book by making a technical review of all selections. His guidance has been invaluable.

CONTENTS

VI. THE SOCIAL DIMENSION
The Impact of Science on Society

VII. APPENDIXES

INTRODUCTION

The expanding perimeter of human knowledge has brought pioneering scientists in many frontier areas face to face with events that cannot be easily explained in terms of present scientific concepts of reality. Psychic abilities, UFOs, strange energy effects from human-made devices—these are some of the unusual phenomena that have puzzled and intrigued those explorer–scientists. But upon reporting their observations from the borderland territories, the all-too-frequent reaction by other scientists has been to disregard these unusual occurrences or to discount the reports as "pseudoscience."

This is not a new situation, of course. The observation of meteorites in the 18th century was greeted with derision by the scientific establishment of the day, including such representatives of the Age of Enlightenment as Antoine Lavosier and Thomas Jefferson. More recently, Nobel Prize winner Alexis Carrel, a French surgeon and pioneer investigator of paranormal phenomena, said in his classic *Man the Unknown* that most scientists "willingly believe that facts that cannot be explained by current theories do not exist." Likewise, in *The Personality of Man*, which considers the question of life after death, G. N. M. Tyrrell wrote: "The major part of the scientific world does not *wish* to examine the evidence, but endeavors only to evade and escape from it. It is not animated by a scientific desire to know the truth but is in the grip of a psychological urge to disallow what is distressingly unfamiliar."

This regrettable attitude is a debasement of true science. It conceives of science as a body of knowledge rather than as a method of knowing. In doing so, it becomes dogmatic, doctrinaire, and has been properly labelled "scientism." A firm rejection of this attitude was made by physicist P. W. Bridgman when he said in *The Logic of Modern Physics:* "It is difficult to conceive anything more scientifically bigoted than to postulate that all possible experience conforms to the same type as that with which we are already familiar, and therefore to demand that explanation use only elements familiar to everyday experience."

From scientism's narrow viewpoint about what is possible and impossible, what is real and unreal, the paranormal events with which this book is concerned are examples of pseudoscience, and are explained—if explained at all—as due to poor observation, uncontrolled experimentation, delusion, deception by the experimental subject, or falsification of data by the experimenter. Failing that, they are simply ignored or labelled "anomalies," as if so naming them disposes of them. The scientists who investigate these phenomena are dismissed as members of the "lunatic fringe."

It is true that the history of science has documented many cases of faulty observation, uncontrolled results, irrational belief, and even fraud. But there is another theme weaving through the history of science in which the "lunatic fringe" has proven to be the "leading edge." It is that theme which provides the substance of this book and the reason for its title, *Future Science.*

Years of patient work by scientists in many countries have established the reality of a wide variety of strange events that have been categorized under different and competing general classifications. We prefer to use the term "paranormal phenomena" here because paranormal means "not scientifically explainable." (We would modify that definition by adding "yet." We would also emphasize that paranormal does *not* mean impossible or absurd.)

Others, however, prefer terms such as "fortean events" and "anomalistics." We feel that "anomalistics" lacks wide usage while "fortean events" is too broad for the focus of examination intended here. (Fortean, incidentally, is an adjective derived from the name of Charles Fort, an early 20th century researcher into unusual and unexplained events, ranging from the Loch Ness monster, abominable snowmen, and mysterious rainfalls of fish and frogs to celestial hints of extraterrestrial life and even interpenetrating universes. A fortean event, therefore, is any event that does not have a scientific or rational explanation.)

The true spirit of science is *scire*, "to know." It is a desire for knowledge coupled with a reliable method of knowing— not just assimilation of data from others so that one can smugly wear the label "scientist" with a sense of superiority about being able to regurgitate more facts than most others.

Seen that way, the scientific method has much in common with mysticism. Both are concerned with understanding ultimate reality. Both are systems of knowing that have proceeded along different lines but which seek knowledge of the final truth. Although one focuses on outer events, while the other turns inward, both operate on the basis of "cleansing the doors of perception," as the mystic poet William Blake wrote, and aim at wisdom, final truth.

Unfortunately, to those whose ability to understand is self-limited by an attitude of know-it-all scientism, the mystic method of knowing seems merely mystification, and is considered pseudoscience. Yet Lawrence LeShan has demonstrated in his book *The Medium, the Mystic, and the Physicist* that statements about the nature of ultimate reality made by certain renowned scientists and mystics alike, when not identified by the speaker's name, cannot be distinguished. They are virtually identical in content and expression. This suggests that science and mysticism, while using radically different methods in their search for truth, may sometimes end up at the same place. And it is interesting to note that LeShan's book grew out of an earlier work of his entitled *Toward A General Theory of the Paranormal*.

This book takes the position that many so-called paranormal events are not beyond science—they are only beyond presently accepted models of science. In almost every sphere of activity, science is abutting in some way upon events that have heretofore been considered either occult nonsense or sheer delusion. But the onrush of materialistic, technological investigation has brought an ironic revelation: There are dimensions of experience known to prescientific traditions and esoteric thought which are now apparent and accessible to empirical objectification.

Prejudice dies hard, though. Max Planck observed: "A new scientific truth does not triumph by convincing its opponents and making them see the light, but rather because its opponents eventually die and a new generation grows up that is familiar with it." Many people in the scientific community will probably dismiss this book as an updated version of those fantastic tales in *The Arabian Nights*. This is because in scientism, or institutionalized science, there sets in an outlook based on the "infallibility syndrome," which assumes it knows everything, and the "null hypothesis syndrome," which tends to reject everything unknown, and thus also everything new. Our hope is that *Future Science* will help to reduce this knee-jerk reaction operating so powerfully today.

It has operated just as powerfully in previous decades, of course, when scorn and ridicule by the dogmatic scientific establishment of the day greeted those who advanced radically new ideas. Copernicus is the best-known example. The development of non-Euclidean geometry (see Sec. III) also met extreme scientific prejudice. Gauss, the most respected mathematician of his period, developed such geometry, working on it for thirty years, but kept it secret until his death because he was afraid to publish such a radical new idea, even with the developed mathematical proofs. The Russian mathematician Lobachevsky developed the subject thoroughly and published it in a series of papers. For his brilliance and daring he was driven from his position at the University of Kazan, despite many years of outstanding performance.

Einstein's life offers another example of the reception given to someone who challenges entrenched scientism. His original paper founding special relativity theory contained only elementary mathematics and developed no fundamentally new equations, since Lorentz had already developed the same simple transformations. Einstein's work was largely ignored for several years because he was regarded as an upstart Swiss patent clerk who had only injected some unscientific metaphysics into Lorentz' equations. Had it not been for his explanation of the photoelectric effect and his classic explanation of Brownian movement (the rapid motion of microscopic particles suspended in fluids or gases resulting from the impact of molecules surrounding the particles), his work may well have gone unnoticed. But his theory of general relativity raised a furor, and he was bitterly attacked by some of the leading scientists of his day. In a letter from several leading German physicists recommending Einstein for membership in the Prussian Academy of Science, Max Planck wrote: "He should not be judged too severely for occasionally losing sight of the objective in his logical reasoning, such as in his theory of light quanta. For in even the most exact of the natural sciences one must take risks to achieve anything really new." Ironically, Einstein was not granted a Nobel Prize for founding the theory of relativity. Instead, it was the very theory of light quanta that Planck disparaged, a theory that explained the photoelectric effect, that won the Nobel Prize for him.

We hope that this book will stimulate those open-minded scientists who are willing to investigate the "impossible" and the "absurd." This is not incompatible with the scientific method. Professor J. G. Taylor of King's College, London, and author of the recent book about psychic children *Superminds: An Enquiry into the Paranormal,* maintains that scientific objectivity does not have to be disregarded in order to study paranormal phenomena. According to the *Journal of Parapsychology** (September 1975), he feels that repeatability "allowing the possibility of many investigators observing the event at different times" is a key to the scientific investigation of extrasensory perception. If, says Taylor, an investigator uses patience and ingenuity, employs the highest level of scientific controls possible, and is prepared to devote a great deal of time to the task, paranormal events can be investigated scientifically.

The implications of the paranormal could shake contemporary scientific models and their related technology to their foundations. These phenomena may force us to take a new

* This periodical, along with the *Journal of the American Society for Psychical Research* and the *Journal of the Society for Psychical Research* are the most prestigious publications in psychic research. Because these publications are available to readers in libraries or through subscription (see Appendix III), we have selected articles for this volume that generally fall outside their scope.

and revolutionary view of the cosmos, of how reality is structured, of how matter, energy, and consciousness interact. In its theoretical aspect, the paranormal leads us into the most profound questions humans have ever asked, and we consider these in Section IV. In its applied aspect, the paranormal leads us to the possibility of new forms of energy (considered in Sec. II) and a new technology (see Sec. V) by which those energies can be measured and controlled. Last of all, the question of values arises. If mind and matter can be manipulated and controlled remotely—a possibility already suggested from research thus far—there is enormous potential for good and evil in a mastery of the operational mechanisms of paranormal phenomena. Thus, the book ends with Section VI, an examination of the social dimension of this investigation. The appendixes contain suggestions for further exploration.

The time has long since passed when investigators of the paranormal can be referred to as "true believers" or as examples of "human gullibility" bedazzled by illusions. The existence of psychic phenomena and a host of related events has been established by the scientific method, using sensitive instruments and careful observation to gather data, conduct experiments, and formulate hypotheses and theories. It is now time to get on with the business of explaining them and elucidating the place which they occupy with regard to the body of presently accepted knowledge.

Readers should approach each chapter of this book with open-minded skepticism. They should ask themselves if the chapter presents reliable data or if it is speculative in nature. If data are presented, are they laboratory experiments or observations? If they are observations, were controls imposed to insure reliability of what was observed? Science proceeds from observation of unusual phenomena to controlled observation, to experimentation, to replication of the experiments, to speculation and hypothesis building, to the testing of hypotheses, and finally to the construction of theories which are consistent with the newly acquired facts.

In evaluating this research, it is well to bear in mind the words of the English naturalist Thomas Huxley, who said when the great debate about evolution arose: "God give me strength to face a fact, though it slay me." His contemporary, the physicist Lord Kelvin, echoed this by saying: "Science is bound by the everlasting law of honor to face fearlessly every problem which can be fairly presented to it." It is interesting to recall that a similar piece of advice comes to us from Buddha: "Believe nothing which is unreasonable and reject nothing as unreasonable without proper examination."

I SETTING THE PERSPECTIVE

*From Pseudoscience
to Superscience*

1

The Introduction demonstrated that an investigation of paranormal phenomena is justified both on grounds of logic and the spirit of true scientific inquiry. However, something can be reasonable without necessarily being true. That is, if no data support the argument—no matter how logical or appealing it appears—the subject is in *fact* only an illusion, a fanciful invention of unbridled imagination or wishful thinking.

Is there evidence, as well as logic, to support the argument in favor of investigating the paranormal? Yes, and this short transitional section will set the perspective from which we will later review some of the evidence. Thus it will be clear that the investigation is both valid and warranted—not a chimera chase or a hunting of the snark.

We will begin by taking an overview of the subject and attempting to define its domain. We must bear in mind, however, that any attempt at definition is necessarily tentative because the accumulation of scientific knowledge is an endless process, and every new answer raises a dozen new questions. Any one of those questions, when answered, might contain the seeds of still another revolution in science that could eventually lead to a redefinition of what we offer here.

Our overview starts from the year 1882, when the Society for Psychical Research was founded in England. The American Society for Psychical Research began three years later. These organizations were initiated in order to look scientifically at a group of phenomena collectively called psi, from the first letter of the Greek word, *psyche,* meaning mind or soul. Parapsychology is the term for the laboratory approach to psi phenomena, stressing controlled experimentation and rigorous statistical analysis to establish the reality of normally imperceptible events and processes. J. B. Rhine, L. E. Rhine, and William McDougall developed this approach at Duke University in the 1930s and are widely regarded as the founders of contemporary parapsychology.

The Duke experiments led to the definition of parapsychology most often used: the branch of science that deals with psi interactions, i.e., behavioral or personal exchanges with the environment which are extrasensorimotor—not dependent on the senses and muscles. "Psychical research" is a synonym for parapsychology; it was especially popular at the turn of the century when societies for psychical research were founded. ("Psychic research" means the same thing and is preferred by some writers for grammatical purposes.)

Psi phenomena are classified into three categories: extrasensory perception (ESP), psychokinesis (PK), and survival phenomena (i.e., evidence of life after death). Each of these categories has many specific forms. ESP, for example, includes telepathy, clairvoyance, precognition, and retrocognition. PK is studied through its effects on living objects, nonliving objects, and moving objects; it includes telekinesis, materialization and dematerialization, levitation, thoughtography, and psychic healing (although not all investigators accept each of these as a real phenomenon). The category of survival phenomena involves research into mediumship, hauntings, apparitions, poltergeists, and reincarnation memories (again, with some researchers not accepting all of these phenomena as real). There is considerable overlap among these areas. Psychic healing, for example, may involve ESP as well as PK; likewise, some poltergeist phenomena may be manifestations of a person's unconscious PK rather than the effects of a discarnate entity.

In recent decades, some investigators have come to feel that even the traditional domain of parapsychology needs to be expanded in the scientific search for understanding unusual phenomena. They have begun to take an interdisciplinary approach to many kinds of unusual events that seem to challenge traditional scientific notions of time, space, matter, energy, and causality.

Notable among these was the psychologist Carl Jung, who

had a deep interest in psychic phenomena and paranormal events. He himself had many experiences with psychic phenomena, which reinforced his interest in alchemy, the *I Ching*, oriental religions, and UFOs. His concept of synchronicity or meaningful coincidence was developed in an attempt to make rational what otherwise defied all notions of reason and cosmic orderliness. But providing a label is not the same as providing an explanation. Thus, in his later years Jung came to look upon physics as the field that could most profitably link with psychology to elaborate upon these concepts, such as synchronicity, that he himself had been unable to articulate adequately. In fact, according to Arthur Koestler in *The Heel of Achilles* (containing his excellent essay "Science and Para-Science"), it was Nobel laureate Wolfgang Pauli, one of the chief architects of quantum theory, who collaborated with Jung in his further development of the synchronicity principle.

Many other investigators of the paranormal now recognize the need for a convergence of psychology and physics. This occurred because paranormal events of the sort we are concerned with here represent a meeting ground in space-time between inner and outer reality, between subjective and objective knowing. The paranormal turns out to be an entry point into the larger question: what is reality and how can we know it? As noted in the Introduction, this has been the traditional question of both science and mysticism over the years.

There have been many terms proposed for the burgeoning field that studies the physics of paranormal processes. Among them are paraphysics, parascience, psychoenergetics, psychophysics, and psychotronics. These terms are not synonymous, although they have a great degree of overlap. All of them, however, can be distinguished from both parapsychology and psychic research (with which they are fully congruent) by the wider spectrum of purportedly paranormal phenomena allowed within the scope of investigation—phenomena such as firewalking, plant perception, UFOs, acupuncture, psychic surgery, "pyramid power" and other energetic effects from geometric forms, and geological/archeological mysteries involving "power points" and "ley lines." (The latter will be discussed in Sec. III.)

Paraphysics is sometimes defined as "the investigation of

the nature, and modes of action, of forms of energy not described in traditional Western physics." These forms of energy are additional to, and possibly fundamental to, those forms or expressions of energy hitherto discovered. The concept of energy—the capacity to create an effect, to do work, or to produce activity—is a critical one in this book and will be examined more closely in Section II.

Perhaps the most articulate advocate of the term "paraphysics" is Benson Herbert, editor of the *International Journal of Paraphysics* (see Appendix III) and founder of the Paraphysical Laboratory in Downton, England (see Appendix III). In an article entitled "Ufology and Paraphysics" (Vol. 1, No. 4, 1967), Herbert defined paraphysics as:

> The study of anomalous physical effects apparently not to be explained by current physical theories; its method is by scientific controls to eliminate all known physical causes, and the residue, if any, not so explained is defined as a paraphysical effect. If paraphysical events can be shown to exceed chance or random variations, having regard to the number or quality of their occurrences, then physical theories must be modified, in accordance with standard scientific practice, so as to embrace these anomalous phenomena.

Another term for the study of the physics of paranormal phenomena is psychotronics, which Zdeněk Rèjdák, president of the International Association for Psychotronic Research discusses in this book. In personal correspondence with the editors, Rèjdák defined the term as follows:

> Psychotronics is an independent, interdisciplinary branch of science dealing with the interaction at a distance among people and between people and the surrounding world, animate and inanimate. These distanced interactions are connected to energetic forms proper to the higher organized living matter and are still subject to research. Psychotronics holds that these phenomena are latent in every living individual, and studies the psychic and physical components of the phenomena in their natural unity. It studies also the energetic substance of traditional phenomena known under the designation of telepathy, telekinesis, and the like.

The term "parascience" was used in a special 1974 issue of

Impact of Science on Society, official publication of the United Nations Educational, Scientific, and Cultural Organization. "Psychophysics" is used by many conventional psychologists to denote physical measurements of psychological phenomena; the EEG, for example, is a psychophysical tool. This term was first applied to the study of psi phenomena by Charles Honorton, who is director of research at the division of parapsychology and psychophysics at Maimonides Medical Center in Brooklyn, New York.

"Psychoenergetics" is used by some Soviet parapsychological investigators to describe their field of research. Again, it implies that the researchers are especially interested in the energetic aspects of psi phenomena, although there is still no absolute proof that energy, as physicists use the term, is involved in these unusual events.

Whatever the term that ultimately gains common usage, it will denote a field of inquiry that is "para" or outside conventional scientific models, but definitely *not* outside psychology or physics or science in general *as a method of knowing.* It is only, as William Tiller has pointed out, beyond presently accepted models of physics, psychology or science—and perhaps it will always be beyond those with mental blinders who hold that present models represent the ultimate development of science.

The thrust of Tiller's article is given in its succinct title, "New Fields, New Laws." This is followed by an excerpt from "New Horizons in EMC" by Rexford Daniels, who was part of a federal government task force to study electromagnetic compatibility. The committee, reporting to the White House, also included Robert O. Becker (noted for his pioneering work in the use of electrical fields to enhance healing), Henry L. Logan (an expert on weather and its cycles), and Luther Monell (who compiled a frequency spectrum chart, now widely regarded, to accompany his part of the report). The last article in this section is by Rèjdák, who discusses psychotronics and its relation to science.

Although the words "new" and "revolutionary" may occur frequently in this and following sections, bear in mind that many of the phenomena themselves have probably been known to humanity for millennia, and that Western science is only now "catching up" to what various other traditions have recognized in different ways from early times. The phenomena are only new to science—not to the totality of human knowledge. And revolution, which comes from "revolve," means to turn back or come again to the starting point. Let that be part of our perspective as we proceed to look at the data and concepts in this section.

2.

New Fields, New Laws

WILLIAM A. TILLER

The flux of worldwide investigation and activity in the area of psychoenergetic fields and phenomena has been such that it has exceeded the "critical mass" condition for a self-sustaining reaction. Since we presently have some ability to monitor this aspect of nature, we can anticipate continued growth of awareness and perception relative to it.

Such an activity does not deny the validity of our present knowledge of the universe, nor does it pose a threat to what I shall call conventional physics. Rather, it calls for an extension or expansion of present laws to reliably model behavior in variable space that circumscribes psychoenergetic fields.

Acceptance of the psychoenergetic findings is difficult for those who have had no experiential awareness of these "other" energies of nature and it is understandable when they are vehemently rejected in many quarters as violating our collective picture of the universe. In fact, some of the criticism about sloppy experimental procedures is justified because it is extremely difficult to develop completely "clean" protocol for these experiments.

However, the body of experimental data in support of this field is so vast that it cannot be denied much longer. One may be able to quibble about the quality of a single experiment or about the veracity of a given experimenter but, taking all the supportive experiments together, the weight of evidence is so strong as to readily merit a wise man's reflection.

Research in this area usually follows two main paths: (1)

"New Fields, New Laws" by William A. Tiller is an original article written especially for this volume and is printed by permission of the author.

that which is designed to illustrate the existence of phenomena, and (2) that which tries to distinguish the important variables and to quantitatively measure the significant parameters of this domain of nature. The former is needed to awaken the human community to awareness of this aspect of nature; the latter is needed to build a reliable foundation of scientific understanding and its extension to an exciting new technology.

We may liken conventional scientific understanding of the universe to the visible tip of an iceberg. We have come to know that exposed tip very well. However, like the iceberg, most of nature is still hidden from us. History contains references to, and speculation on, many aspects of the hidden iceberg and very recent research suggests some fascinating possibilities.

A. From experiments on telepathy,[1] psychokinesis,[1-3] manual healers[4] and traveling clairvoyance,[5] we seem to be dealing with *new energy fields* completely different from those known to us via conventional science.

B. The universe seems to organize and radiate information in *other dimensions* than just the physical space-time frame with which we are familiar. From experiments on PK,[1-3, 6] radionics,[7] materialization–dematerialization,[8] etc., the cause–effect relationships seem to follow a different path or "field line" than we have been used to dealing with in the conventional space-time frame of reference.

C. At some level of the universe, we are *all interconnected* to each other and to other things on this planet. We see this in the Soviet telepathy experiments with rabbits[1] and in the Backster experiments with plants, eggs, and assemblies of living cells[9] (yogurt, blood, etc.).

D. *Time, space, and mass are deformable*, i.e., they are not as immutable and confining as we have tended to think. Experiments on precognition,[10] out of the body projection,[11] materialization, and dematerialization,[8] etc., point to this.

E. With our physical sensory systems, we *cannot perceive reality*. From modern information theory,[12, 13] we deduce that we cannot know reality but can only gain some information about reality. We settle for a set of consistency relationships. Slater's experiments on the "upside-down" glasses[14] strongly support this view.

F. Finally, a *biological transformation* seems to be taking place in humanity at this point in time. From the author's personal experiential feelings and from those of others, from observations of the rapid rise of endocrine dysfunction (hypoglycemia, etc.) in humans plus from observations of the manifesting instability of the human sector of our planet, new energies appear to be circulating in man that, on one hand, cause internal tensions and subliminal fears and, on the other hand, cause manifestation of psychic experiences and abilities.

Mankind seems to be voyaging into a new world of perception and does not yet have reliable tools to cope with this apparently new environment. Just as most of the key ideas upon which our presently accepted science is based were known to the Greeks and lay fallow for almost 2000 years before development, most of the key ideas upon which this new science will be based seem to have been known to the Eastern cultures for even longer. Now seems to be the time for transforming these ideas into an accepted science!

Here, one should reflect on the example of Newton and Einstein. Newton's work on gravitation was not shown to be wrong by Einstein but merely limited to a domain of variable space in nature far removed from speeds approaching the velocity of light. The laws of Einstein reproduce the laws of Newton in the appropriate limit of small velocities. In the decades and centuries ahead, we should hope to follow and extend Einstein's example and develop quantitative laws which reliably model nature in the psychoenergetic domain and which simplify, in the appropriate limit, to our present physical laws of nature.

As an example to illustrate the point, let us look at the life sciences. Up till now, medicine, biology, and agriculture have viewed living organisms as operating via the following sequence of reactions:

$$\text{function} \leftrightharpoons \text{structure} \leftrightharpoons \text{chemistry} \qquad (1)$$

Thus, flaws in the function area were traced to structural defects in the system that arose out of certain chemical imbalances. The rectification procedure was usually via an adjustment of the chemical environment with more and more sophisticated chemical complexes being utilized to trigger the organism's defenses and repair mechanisms. The dilemma that arises is that as both the organism and its threatening invaders adapt to the new chemical complex, they become progressively less sensitive to it and so the escalation of potency must continue. One very deleterious aspect to this procedure is that the unnatural chemical content of the organism increases and begins to influence other levels of functioning of the organism than the one being corrected. This effect is particularly serious in the agricultural area where the method of application of the chemicals is via the soil. As a chemical equilibration develops between the plants and the soil, percolation of water through the soil spreads the chemicals over a large area and the whole ecosystem begins to suffer from chemical pollution. In addition, there is some question concerning the long-term effects on other organisms associated with the intake of these chemicals residing in the plants. Clearly, mankind must find a better way of understanding and dealing with flaws of function in living organisms.

In searching out alternative procedures for influencing the well being of living organisms, one must first question the validity or completeness of equation (1). Are there effective physical, as distinct from chemical, techniques for modifying organismic functioning? Are there potential techniques for doing likewise in the domain of what would presently be called "nonphysical energies"? We know that osteopaths have had considerable success with human functioning using physical techniques and for the last two hundred years there have been serious reports of various types of nonphysical phenomena which suggest the naivete of equation (1).

In neuropsychiatry studies, one sees that small electric currents between certain specific points in the brain give rise to the same behavioral changes as observed with certain chemical intakes.[15] In other studies, Becker[16] has shown that small dc electric currents $(1-10^3 \ \mu\mu A/mm^2)$ cause cell regeneration, tissue repair, and fracture rehealing, whereas dc currents greater than $10^4 \ \mu\mu A/mm^2$ cause cell degeneration. Studies of acupuncture show that the application of either mechanical or electrical energy at certain specific exterior body points cause changes in the structure and function of certain specific body organs. Studies in the alteration of enzyme activity (trypsin) by placing solutions in either a strong magnetic field or between the palms of a healer have shown the influence of nonchemical fields on what we think of as essentially a chemical aspect of certain molecules.[17] In modern psychotherapy, we see chemical treatments influencing mental states.[18] Present biofeedback studies abound with results which indicate that human mental states and states of visualization significantly alter the physiological parameters of the organism. Likewise, under hypnosis or in the aikido, Zen, or yoga disciplines, the human body has been found to exhibit remarkable feats of strength and endurance.

All the foregoing examples and many more indicate that equation (1) should be replaced by

$$\text{function} \rightleftarrows \text{structure} \rightleftarrows \text{chemistry} \rightleftarrows \begin{matrix} \text{electric,} \\ \text{magnetic, and} \\ \text{gravitational} \\ \text{fields} \end{matrix} \rightleftarrows$$

$$\begin{matrix} \text{nonphysical} \\ \text{space-time} \\ \text{fields} \end{matrix} \rightleftarrows \begin{matrix} \text{mind} \\ \text{fields} \end{matrix} \rightleftarrows \qquad (2)$$

At this point, we are unable to specify the components in the categories "nonphysical" space-time fields[19] and "mind" or nonspace, nontime fields. We merely need to recognize that they exist and need to be clearly delineated by future research. We thus see that the door begins to open to alternate pathways for stimulating healthy growth of biological organisms. Of course, the same physics that operates in living systems operates in the inanimate domain of nature and great benefits will ultimately be discovered and utilized in this sphere as well.

It is clearly arbitrary to partition nature into the domains labeled (a) physical space-time, (b) nonphysical space-time, and (c) nonspace, nontime. In our very distant future, we are likely to find that there is only *one* energy which has manifold expressions depending on the state of consciousness which interacts with the energy. However, we presently have a scientific foundation which has already segmented and delineated uniquely different energy characteristics as perceived by our biological senses and by our extended instrumentation senses. Thus, we must continue along the path already laid down by our scientific forebears until we have reached the level of consciousness where the unity can be known.

Let us go forward with care, courage, and enthusiasm, performing our work thoughtfully and rigorously. It is far too important to deserve any less than the very best of our abilities to provide a firm and reliable foundation of understanding in this area. The techniques of analysis and experimentation and the standards of quality synonymous with conventional science serves as a meaningful guide to us. Let us be open minded and flexible in our seeking, but let us also require extensive proof before we rest to enjoy the satisfaction of a completed task.

REFERENCES

1. S. Ostrander and L. Schroeder, *Psychic Discoveries Behind the Iron Curtain* (Englewood Cliffs, N.J.: Prentice-Hall, 1970).
2. W. A. Tiller, "A.R.E. Fact Finding Trip to the Soviet Union," *A.R.E. J.* **7**, 68 (1972).
3. H. Forwald, *Mind, Matter and Gravitation* (New York: Parapsychology Foundation, Inc., 1969).
4. A. Puharich, "The Search for a Common Denominator in Medicine and Healing," in *Proceedings of The Dimensions of Healing Symposium* (Los Altos, Calif.: Academy of Parapsychology and Medicine, 1973).
5. S. Karagulla, *Breakthrough to Creativity* (Los Angeles: De Vorss and Company, Inc., 1967).

6. W. A. Tiller, "A Technical Report on Some Psychoenergetic Devices," *A.R.E. J.* **7**, 81 (1972).

7. W. A. Tiller, "Radionics, Radiesthesia and Physics," in *Proceedings of The Varieties of Healing Experience Symposium* (Los Altos, Calif.: Academy of Parapsychology and Medicine, 1972).

8. A. Puharich, private communication of some experiments by U. Geller.

9. C. Backster, "Evidence of Primary Perception in Plant Life," *Int. J. Parapsychology* **10** (1968).

10. R. Targ and D. B. Hurt, "Learning Clairvoyance and Precognition with an Extra-Sensory Perception Teaching Machine" (New York: IEEE Symposium on Information Theory, January 1972).

11. I. Swann, *To Kiss Earth Goodbye* (New York: Hawthorn, 1975).

12. L. Brillouin, *Scientific Uncertainty and Information* (New York: Academic Press, 1964).

13. P. J. van Heerden, *The Foundation of Physics* (Wistik-Wassenaar, The Netherlands: R. V. Uitgeverij, 1968).

14. J. Rock, *The Nature of Perceptual Adaptation* (New York: Basic Books, 1967).

15. D. E. Wooldridge, *The Machinery of the Brain* (New York: McGraw-Hill Book Company, Inc., 1963).

16. R. D. Becker and D. G. Murray, "The Electrical Control System Regulating Fracture Healing in Amphibians," *Clinical Orthopedic Related Research* **73**, 169 (1970).

17. M. Justa Smith, "The Influence of Enzyme Growth by the 'Laying-On-of-Hands'," in Dimensions of Healing Symposium Proceedings (Los Altos, Calif.: Academy of Parapsychology and Medicine, 1972).

18. D. Hawkins and L. Pauling, *Orthomolecular Psychiatry* (San Francisco: W. H. Freeman and Company, 1973).

19. W. A. Tiller, "Devices for Monitoring Nonphysical Energies," in Edgar D. Mitchell's *Psychic Exploration*, edited by John White (New York: G. P. Putnam, 1974).

3.

The Possibility
of a New Force in Nature

REXFORD DANIELS

In 1963, the scientific advisor to the president and acting Director of Telecommunications Management asked the Joint Technical Advisory Committee[1] to look into the present use of the electromagnetic spectrum and make any recommendations needed for improvement and any possible new uses of the spectrum in the future. The 1968 final 1200 page report, "Spectrum Engineering—The Key to Progress,"[2] was the first public document to mention the importance of "side effects of electromagnetic energy" and to suggest that serious consideration be given to their effects in all disciplines and the establishment of a central interdisciplinary clearinghouse of such information for the immediate use by all science. A Frequency Spectrum Chart was included in the report to show the interdisciplinary relationships of frequency, as a common denominator, between all branches of science and as a simple method for data retrieval. This study triggered the establishment of an Advisory Council to the Executive Office of the President known as the Electromagnetic Radiation Management Advisory Council (ERMAC) which is now just beginning to function and will be the overall coordinator of problems in this field. I had the honor of being chairman of Task Force 63.1.4 of the JTAC 63.1 Subcommittee which compiled the side effects section of the report. The instructions to this Task Force, at the start, were to investigate any,

"The Possibility of a New Force in Nature" by Rexford Daniels is reprinted, with permission, from the 1970 IEEE Regional Electromagnetic Compatibility Symposium Record, October 6–8, 1970, Texas (70 C 28 EMC). Copyright 1970 by The Institute of Electronic Engineers, Inc.

and all, phenomena in nature which might use, or interfere with the use of, the spectrum now or in the future. No limits or restrictions were placed upon us, and nothing should be omitted because of its bizarreness. We were thus able to avoid the men in white coats and gathered some interesting information which was jocularly called "The Chamber of Horrors."

We found eight different individuals, or groups, who had happened upon an unknown force which penetrated everything; could not usually be measured by conventional electronic instrumentation; did not attenuate according to recognized formulas; and could cause instantaneous reactions at incredible distances. Because of the diversities of use of this force, it appeared that it might even have a spectrum of its own. Each group interested in it had a name descriptive of its use, such as: a second force of gravity (gravitons), hydronics, eloptics, orgone, Backster's phenomenon, dowsing, radionics, and radiesthesia.*

Because of the intangibility of much of the information as to its uses and no satisfactory explanation as to just what it was itself, no mention was made of it in the JTAC report. However, a continuing investigation of this force is now being done by the Spectrum Study Committee of G-EMC which contains many of the members of the original JTAC 63.1.4 Task Force. We are no closer to the final answers but we are continually adding to our information.

Probably the most common use of this force is in dowsing, which is a controversial method of finding water, but which is now gradually becoming respectable through its use by the United States Marine Corps in Vietnam to locate underground tunnels, buried ammunition, and other materials. The Marines have found that only approximately one person out of seven comes by this ability naturally although others may be trained. A common civilian application of this force is called "map dowsing" from which it is claimed it is possible to locate a desired object by dowsing a map of the location by means of a pendulum or other instrument. We found during

---

* The author confuses terms here. *Radiesthesia* is sensitivity to radiations in general. *Dowsing* is a form of radiesthesia. *Radionics* is an instrumental form of radiesthesia. *Editors.*

World War II that the British and Australian Navies used this method successfully to locate German submarines, while the American Navy knew better, and would not even try it. The Southern California Edison Company has a man who dowses wells for use with their electric pumps. Over a period of twenty years, he claims to have found over eight thousand.[3]

There seems to be a certain amount of ESP associated with the efficiency with which dowsing is used. This naturally introduces variables which make it difficult for individuals to get similar measurements which cautions a too strong dependence on the results. A good book on this subject is *Henry Gross and His Dowsing Rod* by Kenneth Roberts.[4] Map dowsing as done by Henry Gross, who found three fresh water wells on Bermuda by dowsing a map of Bermuda at his home in Maine, might conceivably be an eventual requirement of electrical and electronic engineering for locating good and bad areas for grounding and other purposes. European countries are way ahead of us in using this method. . . .

A study of dowsing, however, leads into the study of another aspect of this force which is called radionics or radiesthesia. The first worldwide conference on this subject was held in London in 1950, for which the Proceedings of the Scientific and Technical Congress of Radionics and Radiesthesia[5] may be obtained. This Congress had to do with the human electromagnetic field which appears to have a spectrum of its own based on the frequencies given off by molecular emanations. An impetus to this work was given, ten years previously, when Dr. I. I. Rabi of Columbia University was awarded the AAAS prize for his researches on nuclear resonance. An Associated Press release of December 30, 1939, described his findings as follows:

> Atoms can act like little radio transmitters broadcasting on ultra short waves. . . . Man himself, as well as all kinds of supposedly inert matter, constantly emit rays. The existence of such rays coming from man and all living things, and probably from the inanimate, has been suspected by a few scientists for many years. Today brought experimental proof. . . .

Two Frenchmen, Jules Calte and Andre Coatrieux, went

into more detail in a United Press dispatch, July 7, 1949, under a Paris dateline, as follows:

> Every metal and every person sends out short waves of different lengths. Personal wave lengths are as individual as fingerprints.

Since then, a principle of resonance absorption has been established and described in the following manner:

> In every frequency band (or for specific frequencies within a band) there exists one or more natural or man-made resonators that absorb within that frequency band. This principle is known as the principle of resonance absorption. The effects produced by the energy absorbed by a particular resonator depend on the characteristics of the resonator. . . .[6]
>
> The interaction of electromagnetic radiations with matter is basically similar although different materials are affected at different wave lengths . . . The resonating structure thus determines the energy quantum which can be absorbed and hence the frequency of the radiation which will affect it. . . .[7]

As you can understand, it took quite a bit of courage, on the parts of certain members of the Task Force, to show an active interest in these phenomena, yet they persevered to the point where they determined that there should be a practical basis for further investigation. In this search, several patented instruments were discovered as well as experimental equipment not patentable.

A group in Georgia† obtained a patent[8] on instrumentation both to transmit and receive this energy which they called *eloptics* from a combination of the words "electricity" and "optics" because the energy obeys some, but not all, of the laws of electricity and the laws of optics. It is described as energy which radiates from, or is in some manner given off from, or forms a force field around, everything in our material world under normal conditions, at ordinary room temperature and without any treatment of any kind. Each element and combination of elements gives off this energy; however, the energy from each element differs in frequency from the

† See Advanced Sciences Research and Development, Inc. under "Organizations" in Appendix III. *Editors.*

radiation coming from every other element. Eloptic energy can be conducted along light rays, focused with lenses, refracted with a prism, and its effects implanted upon photographic film. No opportunity was available, however, to check on these claims.

A group in Florida‡ had tried, with no success, to get the government to consider a phenomena which they called hydronics. It was an energy which was demonstrated could be conducted through everything, appeared to radiate from the ends of an antenna instead of from the length, was not attenuated according to Maxwell's laws and could not be measured by conventional electrical test instruments. Government engineers, who witnessed demonstrations, reported that it was nothing new yet they could not seem to duplicate it. Subsequent research revealed that fish talk could be recorded by this method, scuba divers could use it for underwater communication and students could win first prizes in school science competitions by thinking up new applications, but still nobody has found out what kind of energy it is, and there are no reports yet available from responsible scientists.

Another manifestation of the existence of a source of energy, about which little seems to be known, is in connection with tornadoes and hurricanes as well as with the little "dust devils" which are often seen on dirt roads. It is rotary in motion, can exhibit wave action and seems to have electromagnetic frequencies such as the 50 MHz signal which can appear on TV sets at up to thirty miles distance from the phenomena. Scientists are now trying to find a relationship between the rotary motion of atom structures and the rotation of the planets in our solar system. This force may be an attribute of our presently known gravitational force or it may be a separate gravitational force which could be called "the second force of gravity." It has been recently ascertained that France is very interested in this phenomena and has proposed a special laboratory to study it. A French inventor has also patented instrumentation which, he claims, can emit and transmit these gravitational waves, which he calls gravitons.

‡ See Sarasota Research and Development Corp. under "Organizations" in Appendix III. *Editors.*

The industrial applications of such an invention, he claims, are essentially telecommunications through both electrically conducting and nonconducting solids, such as terrestrial crusts, mountains, sea water, etc. It also appears to be another possible aspect of hydronics.

Anyone delving into these unidentified forces soon runs into the work of the late Dr. Wilhelm Reich, who claimed to have discovered a force which he described as "life energy" or "biological energy" and named it "orgone." It controls biophysical emotion, again penetrates everything and has a wavelike motion. Some people refer to it as the ether in nature which electromagnetic energy modulates. Dr. Reich ended his days in jail and all his works were ordered destroyed by the judge who sentenced him. Yet there seems to be an increasing international revival of interest in his work and a number of his burned books are being republished.

The last aspect of unidentified forces investigated has been called the Backster phenomena and deals with the accidental discovery by Cleve Backster of the influence of thought upon plants. Mr. Backster* is considered the outstanding authority on the use of the polygraph for lie detection purposes. One day he wondered how long it would take the watering of a plant in his office to reach the top leaf. He attached the galvanic skin response section of a polygraph instrument, which tests the emotional reaction of people, to the top plant leaf and then followed the reactions on the polygraph machine. Tracings soon began to appear, which he recognized as emotional reactions, and he began to experiment further.

He tried several physical experiments, with little results, and it was only when he thought of burning a leaf that the needle on the chart jumped upwards. Subsequent tests by him, over a period of years, have revealed that plants can respond to human thought with distance no consideration. His plant, back at the office, once registered instant pleasure when he decided to return to his office from as far as twenty miles away. The interest of the electromagnetic compatibility engineer, in this phenomena, would seem to center around the influence of thought on the results of experiments with plants

* See Backster Associates under "Organizations" in Appendix III. *Editors.*

and animals, and introduces still another variable into the electromagnetic compatibility field, known as TLC—tender loving care.†

The foregoing examples of new horizons, resulting from the research of certain individuals and groups into the characteristics of an unknown force, are more or less speculative. Nonetheless, they may yield important data if intensively studied.

REFERENCES

1. The Joint Technical Advisory Committee is made up of representatives of the Institute of Electrical and Electronics Engineers and the Electronic Industries Association to help the United States Government solve problems in the electronic field.
2. *Spectrum Engineering—The Key to Progress* (New York: Joint Technical Advisory Committee, IEEE, 1968), 345 East 47th St., New York, N.Y. 10017.
3. "Water Dowsing—An Underground Story," *Los Angeles Times,* Sunday, December 7, 1969.
4. Kenneth Roberts, *Henry Gross and His Dowsing Rod* (New York: Pyramid Books, 1951).
5. *Proceedings of the Scientific and Technical Congress of Radionics and Radiesthesia* (London: Markham House Press, Ltd., 1950), 31 King's Road, London SW 3, England.
6. L. J. Baranski, *The Frequency Spectrum and the Principle of Resonance Absorption,* North American Aviation, 1963.
7. U. Slager, *Space Medicine* (Englewood Cliffs, N.J.: Prentice-Hall, 1962).
8. "Detection of Emanations from Materials and Measurement of the Volumes Thereof," Patent No. 2482773, September 27, 1949.

† At its 1974 annual convention, the American Association for the Advancement of Science held a seminar on electrical responses in plants, where two scientists reported negative findings in their attempts to replicate Backster's one experiment and numerous reported observations. *Editors.*

4.

Psychotronics:
The State of the Art

ZDENĚK REJDÁK

Psychotronics is the science which studies interactions over distance, interactions bound by an energetic form as yet not understood. This form of energy is a property of living matter, and the interactions manifest themselves between "subjects," as well as between subjects and "objects" (including living objects).

Workers in various branches of science have long been aware of a range of phenomena which, although they interact individually with existing branches of science, cannot be understood with the means at the disposal of organized science. This is why the problems related to these phenomena have been sidetracked from the main line of scientific research. Despite this, however, parapsychology came into being to deal with some of the unexplained phenomena; the rapid progress made in scientific research has also shown that the phenomena in question really exist.

The last ten years have been marked by many changes in the field of psychotronics. The overall problem has been, in some respects, one between generations. Researchers of the older generation actively interested in psychotronic questions conceived their approach to the problem mainly in its philosophical and psychological aspects. Most frequently, they concluded that very complex psychic processes were involved which, besides, were regulated only with difficulty and were therefore not reproducible. These older persons saw as their

"Psychotronics: The State of the Art" by Zdeněk Rejdák originally appeared in *Impact of Science on Society*, Vol. 24, No. 4, 1974. Copyright © 1974 by The Unesco Press and reprinted by permission.

main task the proof and defense of the existence of these processes. As far as the collection of facts and the conducting of great numbers of experiments are concerned, their work is evidently worthy of respect.

Younger scientists began to believe, during the same period, that the approach of their elders was one-sided. They preferred to model, intensify, formulate, and calculate. Psychotronics has been deemed by the younger generation to be too attractive to overlook, especially since the milestones along its path of development are emblazoned with names like Jan Evangelista Purkyne, Crookes, Lodge, Babak, Richet, Driesch, Bekhterev, Vasilyev, Rhine, Tenhaeff, and others. Their efforts to grasp the more technical problems caused them to abandon the earlier view of psychotronics as a borderline interdisciplinary branch. To the unipolar philosophical–psychological conception, the younger breed of researchers added a second pole of technical and physical conception.

The Degrees of Belief

In the vast ground between these two poles, we should be concerned with the relationship between the scientific public and questions of psychotronics. At present, a qualitative change is taking place; a basic turning point has been reached in the minds of many scientific workers. Not only have they shown growing interest in psychotronic matters, they have begun active research in the domain. To illustrate the scale of interest of the scientific world in regard to psychotronics, the degree of relation would look something like this: 1, positive; 2, neutral; 3, indulgent; 4, expectant; 5, indifferent; 6, negative; 7, *a priori* negative.

The attitudes of the majority of scientists are described by the first four adjectives on the scale. You will note that there is a stepping up of the critical attitude manifested toward psychotronic questions. (I do not assume any uncritical enthusiasm among scientists.) Rather, there is a constructively critical attitude which could be expressed as follows: in principle, they favor investigating these problems, they are interested in the existence of the phenomena investigated in psychotronics, but it is essential that there be available properly elaborated and precise methods of research corresponding to the importance of the problems involved.

I do not want to imply, for my part, that the methods used thus far have been unscientific; they were adequate at the time they were selected, whether to prove the existence of the phenomena, to classify them, or determine the conditions and periodicity of their occurrences.

Let us look now at the scientists listed on our scale as Nos. 6 and 7, beginning with the "negative" attitude. These believe that psychotronic phenomena do not exist or are the product of the imagination; or if they admit their existence, they come to the conclusion that the phenomenal events occurred by chance, or that the conditions obtaining at their occurrence were falsely interpreted; or else that the specific phenomena really exist but, because they cannot be reproduced at any time in approximately the same conditions, the "negative" scientists see no clear reason why they should deal with the phenomena. In the last case, they pose the question: is there any sense in investigating phenomena which can occur even intensively (e.g., spontaneous psychokinesis) if we cannot take hold of them firmly enough to be able to describe them adequately?

The Czech academician, Josef Charvat, in his *Life, Adaptation, and Stress,* gives an unequivocal response to the requirement to apply mechanically the positivist methodology to living processes: "primum movens of the central nervous system is spontaneous activity, inquisitiveness, creativity. We have no model in the physical world for biological behavior, after all. Therefore any comparison of a stabilized state in living matter with similar states in chemical systems is but approximate and even further removed from psychism."

A scientist with a negative spirit, once he has decided to examine problems in psychotronics, wants to see for himself, to experiment. There is the case of the British mathematician S. G. Soal. He had attacked the statistical proof confirming certain phenomena and reproached the researchers for not having improved their statistical method. Only after he had met two of the experimental subjects himself was he convinced of the reality of the phenomena. And yet we, the practitioners, admit freely that we much prefer scientists who show a negative attitude and a skeptical approach as long as possible to uncritical and naïve enthusiasts.

Hard-core Resistance

In quite a special category belong the *a priori* negativistic scientists. There was, in Czechoslovakia, a well-known psychiatrist and hypnologist who repudiated entirely the field of psychotronics. It happened once that an experimental subject seated with his face turned toward a blackboard, yet in a deep hypnotic trance, began to read what the psychiatrist had written on the board; the subject then read a text the physician had written in pencil on a sheet of paper. The specialist was unhappy about the incident for an entire week, but soon concluded that the subject was able to read because he could analyze the sound of chalk scratching on the board and of the pencil moving over paper. Rather than admit the possibility of some unconventional transfer of information, this scientist preferred to invent a "substantiation" of an entirely speculative character. He became, in fact overnight, a specialist in subliminal hearing. Noteworthy here is that *a priori* negativists can make incursions, without scruple, into fields alien or incomprehensible to them.

Still, we can consider this speculative brand of *a priori* negativism as being within the bounds of decency. Worse is the case of the scientist who dips into negativism so deeply that he abandons the ethics of scientific work, and even resorts to misrepresentation and falsification. . . .

What are the motives behind negativism *a priori?* There are several. First, there is the negativism of persons unconcerned with whether paranormal phenomena exist or not; scientific fact to them is only that which is already regarded as scientific fact. Academician Petr Kapitsa, on the other hand, does not divide phenomena into the possible or impossible; he prefers the discovered and undiscovered distinction. "It is enough to read the works of Newton and his contemporaries" (Kapitsa has written) ". . . they believed that the knowledge of inanimate nature was completed . . . we must not make again the old mistake and believe that there will be no more new discoveries in the future." The Soviet physicist adds, "I want to pay attention to one basic question concerning the study of living nature . . . the majority of phenomena are explained by existing laws, but it still seems to me that one of the fundamental properties of living nature, the ability of reproduction, can be the manifestation of some natural forces which we do not yet know and which we cannot explain by the rules known so far."

Second, their attitude is motivated by fear. The field is unknown, and whatever might be observed could lead to mysticism. The opposite is true, however: avoiding the unknown area gives free rein to charlatans, and broad scope to rampant prejudice. Their fears are fostered further because the negativists cannot imagine how any new knowledge could be integrated with the sciences to which these scientists have become accustomed. They stop being impartial in their science. Their apprehensions are groundless: all knowledge can be broadened, complemented, and made more precise.

Third, to be negative *a priori* reflects a motivation of conservatism and indolence. After having become the master of scientific territory, engaging in something new requires learning how to think in a new way. The desire to have understood everything is not a trait shared by all.

Breaking Down the Resistance

How should those dealing with psychotronics join hands with those still distrustful of this discipline?

They should, first, accelerate elaboration of an adequate methodology in the research on psychotronic phenomena. They should pattern their experiments, second, in such a fashion that these can be repeated at any time. Practical experimentation in psychotronics must be one of our main targets. And third, the scientific public should be enlightened by way of appropriate publications. This task is complicated by the flood of information available to scientists today; it is difficult to keep up in one's own field, but scientists in general should be made aware of the growth of literature during the past twenty years in what they consider to be the paranormal fields. Last, of course, there is the continuing job of keeping the lay public informed; there the spread of progressive thinking must play a decisive role.

All branches of science are of interest to laymen, but ours has attracted particularly many because it deals with both psychic and somatic questions—what makes people live and be themselves. Laymen dealing with our branch do so, however, as rank amateurs bringing their personal problems into the picture, sometimes even distorting and discrediting the work done. Pressing is the question of how to enlighten properly the nonscientific public. The sensational stories about houses haunted by ghosts, about astral projections and the like attract the layman but do immeasurable harm otherwise. Psychotronics is not the same as spiritism, which of late has become an opiate to certain elements of the general population throughout Europe, the Americas, and elsewhere.

In an age when scientific advance is taking giant strides, the assumption of an interdisciplinary approach is the cardinal condition for the orderly investigation of psychotronic phenomena. Only this will help us extricate ourselves from the current conjecture, uncertainty, and disputes—by combining the scientific method peculiar to physics, communication techniques, mathematics, cybernetics, psychology, psychiatry, medicine, neurophysiology, and physiology, bionics, geology, anthropology, sociology, and space biology.

It is readily apparent that there is no need to retain the term "parapsychology." It fails not only to reflect the multidisciplinary character of the field, it fails too to convey the existence of the energetic component without which none of the phenomena we are concerned with is imaginable. The combination of both psychic and energetic components has been pointed out repeatedly: by the Russian physician Kotik (1908), later by Hans Berger in the 1920s and 1930s, and by the Dutch geologist Tromp (1949). We specialists in the field decided to adopt the term "psychotronics" proposed, by the French engineer Fernand Clerc, in the radio-technical journal *Toute la Radio*. "Parapsychology" thus reverts, like mesmerism or metapsychology, to the description of a stage of development of psychotronics.

Enriching Biology and Physics

The main task of psychotronics, now, is to coordinate the laws governing the living and inanimate worlds and complement them with new increments of knowledge from physics, biology, and psychology; this knowledge will derive from specific manifestations of the human psyche, with man or an appropriate model of man serving as the interlink.

The psychotronic branch of knowledge possesses, today, as voluminous a literature as the entirety existing in other branches. But the sources of the literature of psychotronics are such that a second task of psychotronic specialists is to revaluate the existing documentation. An analysis of past laboratory experiments will help us, also, to define clearly the methodology of the discipline. A reassessment of this kind will serve, too, to prevent the division of psychophysical phenomena into discrete psychic and physical segments. It is not by mere chance that some physicists in the Federal German Republic involved in plasma research believe that new knowledge of the interactions between living organisms will enrich both biology and physics.

Parapsychology dealt mostly with rarely occurring phenomena, trying timidly to indicate that these incidents probably will affect everyone to a small degree. Psychotronics, through its pluridisciplinary approach, seeks to establish that psychophysical phenomena affect ninety percent of humankind. Refraining from examining the exceptional prodigies psychotronics purposely shapes its experiments in such a way that they can be reproduced substantially at any time. This purpose applies whether we are concerned with the action of the human organism on an easily movable system (e.g., an indicator of negative pressure or vacuum, an easily movable system on a liquid's surface, or the possibility of visual influencing) or using a device (say, a plethysmograph) to determine remote, synchronous neurophysiological processes.

Test results so far are not necessarily sensational, but they show a certain stability. It is now that we realize that all of us observe psychotronic phenomena (such as spontaneous telepathy between mother and child) in our daily lives, that these have been associated with humans, even with living matter, since time immemorial. They are comparable to electrical or chemical processes, although it may still be impossible to reduce them neatly into either one. If parapsychology functioned as the model

$$individual \rightarrow output$$

then psychotronics takes as its model

$$living\ organism \rightarrow \frac{energetic}{work} \rightarrow output$$

The introduction of automation control and electronic information processing machines to all walks of life about twenty years ago caused us to proclaim the scientific–technical revolution. After the first flushes of delirium with what these marvels of machinery could do (compose music, write poems, pour forth advertising design), came sober reality. People began to doubt themselves, suffering from an inferiority complex vis-à-vis the all-powerful, all-controlling technology they had created. Contemporaneously, the qualitatively new investigations into psychotronics came at the right time. This research is helping rehabilitate the basic human values, revealing that the person is not so helpless after all.

Psychotronics may lead us to the very brink of a new revolution in science. It is here that we must give substance to that second pole of which I spoke: a scientific–human conception to counterbalance the scientific–technical revolution we are experiencing. Otherwise, we shall flood the world during the next century with both mechanical and human robots, thereby stepping up estrangement and social disintegration.

II THE OCCULT FORCES OF LIFE

*Ancient Mysteries,
Modern Revelations*

5

From the viewpoint of those who see only a material universe operating mechanically through random processes, life itself is the ultimate paranormal event. Modern science recognizes four basic field forces or forms of energy: the electromagnetic, the gravitational, and the weak and strong nuclear forces. All phenomena, including life and mental activity, are presumed to be explicable in terms of these energies and their associated physico-chemical mechanisms. And although organic micromolecules and "proteinoids" with attendant life-like properties have been synthesized in the laboratory, the two decades of research since S. L. Miller's 1955 production of organic matter from a mixture of gases have not created life per se or identified the energies of life. Neuroscientist Wilder Penfield, for example, in his book *The Mystery of the Mind,* concludes that mind—the hallmark of life—"will always be quite impossible to explain on the basis of neuronal action within the brain . . . The mind is peculiar. It has energy. The form of that energy is different from that of neuronal potentials that travel the axone pathways."

The word "energy" comes from the Greek *energeia,* meaning "active." It is generally understood as the capacity to do work or to be active. But in its original sense it meant *vital* activity, that which can move or quicken inert matter. En-erg-y means literally "of (itself) motivational-ness."

Thus in earlier times there was a distinct and publicly acknowledged sense of a fundamental life force. Although recognized, however, it was not easily understood. It was apprehended but not comprehended. In that respect, it was occult —that is, normally hidden, undetected, secret.

In recent years, an increasing number of people seeking to understand paranormal phenomena have come to feel that science would do well to re-examine an overlooked principle in nature—the same principle of vitality or livingness that ancient traditions considered primary. This principle introduces what may be called a psychic factor. One researcher summarized his views on the subject by saying that there is an energy in living organisms that is weak and unpredictable, but it can be refracted, polarized, focussed, and combined with other energies. It sometimes has effects similar to magnetism, electricity, heat, and luminous radiation, but it is none of these. Attempts to control and employ the energy have met with little success; investigators have not even begun to define the laws governing its operation.

Addressing himself to the same topic, the fortean–naturalist Ivan Sanderson, founder of the Society to Investigate the Unexplained (see Appendix II), wrote an editorial in the SITU journal *Pursuit* (October 1972) on the nature of what he called this "new force" in physics.

> This fifth force is certainly involved in various aspects of SSP (meaning supersensory proclivities) and it would now seem to be the major force operative in the true psychic field and possibly the only one acting therein. Its manifestations are in no way affected by any of the other known forces; and, while doubtless universal in nature, it can be observed, measured, and investigated only in the biological field. The presence of a living thing is necessary to bring it to light. Although we have not yet defined it or its parameters, it has now been demonstrated that it, and it alone, can explain a whole raft of what were previously thought to be mysteries or pure imagination, such as mental telepathy, SSP (supersensory projection), and SSR (supersensory reception), the two PKs—psychokinesis and pyrokinesis—and possibly the whole group of things clustering around clairvoyance. It would explain all that has puzzled the psychologists about things like the so-called subconscious, hypnotism, and the like.

Sanderson pointed out that psychics such as Peter Hurkos, who once demonstrated telepathy while inside a Faraday cage, show that these abilities probably do not function along electromagnetic lines. Eileen Garrett, the celebrated medium, did the same. Uri Geller's recent performance of the same feat, reported by Stanford Research Institute physicists Harold Puthoff and Russell Targ in the prestigious scientific journal *Nature* (October 1974), if valid, reconfirms this phenomenon. "Is it not time," Sanderson asked in his editorial, "that we stopped just ignoring all these things, or blithely relegating them to that vague field of the psychic, and got the technicians to work, trying to define the nature of this force and, by both theory and experimentation, give us a set of laws for it such as govern the other four forces? There is ample published material to get started on, so that at least a basic pattern might be assembled almost immediately. There is then the matter of seeking its parameters and fitting new observations into this pattern, rejecting them, or altering the pattern."

This force seems to have been recognized many times in history by various prescientific traditions. As we show in a survey of those traditions (see Appendix I), accounts of a mysterious X force run through ancient occult and spiritual documents. For example, the French magus Eliphas Levi, in his book *Transcendental Magic*, described the properties of the magician's "astral light": "There exists an agent which is natural and divine, material and spiritual, a universal plastic mediator, a common receptacle of the vibrations of motion and the images of form, a fluid and a force, which may be called in some way the Imagination of Nature . . . The existence of this force is the great Arcanum of practical Magic." W. E. Butler presents a useful survey of this topic in this section.

In the orient, the Chinese conception of ch'i (ki in Japanese) was thought to be the intrinsic vital force throughout all creation. It is this life energy which acupuncture manipulates to maintain health and which can be concentrated through disciplines such as tai ch'i and aikido to perform paranormal acts. According to Confucianism and Taoism, without ch'i, nothing can exist, and from it spring the yin and yang forces that are present in all living things. Paralleling this in the yogic tradition of India and Tibet is the notion of prana, which Gopi Krishna examines in his chapter.

Within modern times there have also been people who claim to have identified through science a fifth and fundamental force in nature. Wilhelm Reich is perhaps the most notable—and controversial—figure. His purported discovery of the orgone energy is considered by orgonomists to be at the heart of future science. In the Reichian view, as expressed primarily by the American College of Orgonomy (see Appendix III), orgonomy is a basic branch of natural science. Orgone is the all-pervasive life energy—primordial, massless, preatomic—from which all other forms of energy are derived. Some writers, observing parallels with Franz Anton Mesmer's notion of animal magnetism and Karl von Reichenbach's concept of odic force, feel that Reich's experiments should be replicated by outside investigators. W. Edward Mann, in his article on Reich and orgone, tells why he thinks that such an investigation is justified.

A parallel between orgone and the Soviet concept of bioplasma, as presented by Viktor M. Inyushin, is made by other writers. The *Eden Bulletin* (see Appendix III) in January 1975 attempted to link the Soviet work in psychoenergetics with the purported sale of Reich's publications to scientists in the USSR before an American federal court ordered the books burned.

This section, therefore, presents articles describing various traditions, ancient and contemporary, that claim to have identified an unusual form of energy as the key to understanding paranormal phenomena. Laurence Beynam, an American engineer living in Turkey, recently surveyed this vast subject and reported his findings in an article entitled "Quantum Physics and the Paranormal" that appeared in the journal *Astrologia* (Vol. 1, No. 2, 1975). According to Beynam, some of the characteristics of this hypothetical energy are:

(1) It is observed in the operation of heat, light, electricity, magnetism, and chemical reactions, yet is different from all of them.

(2) It fills all space, penetrating and permeating everything, yet denser materials conduct it better and faster, and metal refracts it while organic material absorbs it.

(3) It is basically synergetic. It has a basic negentropic, formative, and organizing effect, even as heat increases, and therefore is the opposite of entropy (that is, disintegration

and disorganization of matter) set forth by the Second Law of Thermodynamics, which it thereby violates.

(4) Changes in the energy precede observable physical changes, and it is supposed to create matter, energy and life. This is also observed in certain psychokinetic phenomena where metals continue bending long after the initiating agency or psychic sensitive has touched them.

(5) It has its opposite number. Seen clairvoyantly by psychics as red and yellow, this opposite form of the energy is opposed to the life-giving energy outlined above. This occurs when the life-giving energy is leaving, instead of entering (emerging into) a region. While the blue, synergic energy gives a cool, pleasant feeling to the sensitives, the yellow–red entropic energy creates a feeling of heat and unpleasantness.

(6) In any structure that is highly organized (e.g., crystals, plants, humans), there is a series of geometrical points at which the energy is highly concentrated (e.g., chakras in the yogic tradition, acupuncture points in the traditional Chinese medical system).

(7) The energies will flow from one object to another. According to the Hawaiian Huna tradition, it is "sticky" so that an invisible stream of energy will always connect any two objects that have in any way been connected in the past (thus providing the basis of sympathetic magic). The energy is subject to exponential decay, radiating outwards in the course of time from an inert material, but always there is a residue (since decay goes on to infinity). The density of energy varies in inverse proportion to the distance, which sets it apart from electromagnetic and gravitational laws, but for which a theory of potentials may be applicable.

(8) The energy is observable in several ways: as isolated pulsating points, as spirals, as a cloud or "aura" surrounding the body, as a flame, as a tenuous web of lines (the Yaqui sorcerer don Juan's "lines of the world" and the occultist's "etheric web").

Despite the foregoing, we should not ignore the possibility that some paranormal phenomena result from little-known or imperfectly understood effects of recognized forces. Research engineer James Beal, speaking at the American Anthropological Association's 1974 symposium on parapsychology and anthropology, surveyed the data dealing with electrostatic fields and brain/body/environment relationships. After describing bioelectric field effects in the context of extraordinary events such as paranormal healing, he noted that the effects should not be construed as the cause behind unexplained psychic events. Rather, he said, they may serve as "weak indicators, precursors, or stimulators in regard to effects filtering down from a higher system." In other words, a fifth type of energy—if it exists—would have to interact with the other four types.

The late Harold Saxton Burr of Yale University developed techniques to study an indicator system such as those proposed by Beal. His electrodynamic theory of life, first announced in the 1930s but still largely unknown to orthodox scientists, offers a possible link between electromagnetism and psi—a potential bridge between the physical and the paraphysical. It has been said that the work of Burr and his colleague Leonard Ravitz deals with the prephysical foundations of life.

The Burr–Ravitz work indicates that there is a guiding field of electromagnetic energy—generally termed a life field or L field—that performs a directive, organizing function on the physical structure of an organism. Burr and Ravitz demonstrated that the state of health of an organism could be determined far in advance of the least observable physical sign by using a microvoltmeter to inspect its L field. Ravitz himself has informally reported that the L field as a whole disappears *before* physical death. Sensitivity to the L field might explain much about how psychic healers function in diagnosis and cure.

The data suggest, however, that L fields are themselves affected by other forces. Ravitz made the further discovery that the state of the mind affects the voltage gradients of the L field. Edward Russell, who describes the Burr–Ravitz work in this section, refers to this power of thought as a T field, meaning thought field. He notes that although L fields are ordinary electromagnetic phenomena, not a new force in nature, they are nevertheless of immense importance for showing how mind or T fields can *measurably* affect L fields and thus the physical body. Therefore the study of L fields may give science an opening into that critical area where physics and psychology interface.

We will begin this section with a look at the "fields of life" which have already been investigated by science and then move into an examination of the inadequately explored forces which various traditions hold to be the occult answer to the riddle of existence. The chapters differ in their orientation. The material in Russell's chapter on the Burr–Ravitz work can be easily investigated and replicated because the scientific literature contains details of the experiments and the technology. Reich's work, as described by W. Edward Mann, is described in detail by Reich and his followers. Those who would replicate his experiments, however, will have to examine the various Reich archives for his unpublished material. A different problem exists in regard to Inyushin's research; most of his voluminous writings have never been translated into English. Gopi Krishna has urged a scientific test for his theories and in his other writings has offered provocative ideas for researchers. W. E. Butler's article belongs to the esoteric tradition and needs to be translated into scientific terms. Langston Day's paper is a presentation of various experiments; however, the reader should be warned that he combines the respected writings of Schroedinger, Rutherford, and Millikan with the highly controversial and somewhat dubious reports by Mesmer, Abrams, and von Reichenbach. This is an interesting chapter, but one to be read with a skeptical and a discriminating eye.

6.

The Fields of Life

EDWARD W. RUSSELL

I.

"A new scientific truth," wrote the great scientist Max Planck, "does not triumph by convincing its opponents and making them see the light; but rather because its opponents eventually die and a new generation grows up that is familiar with it."

How many must die before the importance of the great discovery of the fields of life is *generally* accepted by biologists?

Over forty years have passed since Dr. Harold Saxton Burr and Dr. F. S. C. Northrop, distinguished members of the Yale University faculty, first advanced the Electrodynamic Theory of Life—a theory rapidly confirmed by countless published experiments. But it is only in recent years that some younger biologists have realized the immense significance of this discovery. This suggests that Max Planck's depressing dictum was only too true.

What was Burr's discovery and why is it so important? Briefly, he found a previously unknown, higher order in the process by which all living things are organized and keep their form through constant changes of material.

It had long been known that we constantly renew our skin, hair, and blood. But, until some biochemists learned how to introduce radioactive elements into the body—which can be photographed after they have been incorporated in the body

"The Fields of Life" by Edward W. Russell is an original article written especially for this volume and is printed by permission of the author.

cells—nobody realized that most, if not all, of the human body is being perpetually renewed.

All the protein, of which our bodies are so largely composed, is constantly being discarded and replaced with fresh protein derived from our food. This, of course, does not happen suddenly—it happens continuously. Liver and serum proteins are turned over every ten days; the proteins of the lungs, brain, skin, and principle muscles are turned over every 158 days. Even bone is constantly replaced with fresh material. Only the *design* of our bodies, changing slightly with growth and age, remains constant.

What preserves that design? What literally "keeps us in shape" through constant changes of material? This was a mystery to biologists until Burr and his associates demonstrated that all living forms are organized and maintained by an electrodynamic or, if you prefer, electromagnetic field. He called these organizing fields "the fields of life" or "L fields" for short. And he found that there is an L field for every kind of living form—from men to mice, from trees to seeds.

We cannot see a field. But, as most school children know, we can see what it does if we place a magnet under a card and scatter iron filings on the card. The filings will assume the pattern of the field of the magnet; and however often we substitute fresh filings, they will always assume the same pattern.

L fields do the same thing. No matter how often the molecules of the body are renewed, the L field preserves their pattern and arrangement. L fields, however, are infinitely more complex than the simple field of a magnet; in fact, the body contains countless subfields, all under the control of the overriding L field. There is also feedback from the subfields of the various organs which interact, to some extent, with the L field. Despite this feedback, however, the overall L field of the body is primary and controls its component fields.

II.

There is nothing "psychic" about L fields. Though far more complex than the fields known to conventional physics, they are of the same nature and can be measured and mapped with the highly sensitive modern voltmeters which are used in any electronic laboratory. These instruments are not used to measure skin resistance, as in a lie detector. Rather, they measure fields. These fields are revealed by different voltage gradients between different parts of the body. These gradients are simply differences of electrical dc *potential* and are not to be confused with the electrical *currents* to be found in the brain or on the skin. If the instruments are sensitive enough, the field can be measured without contacting the skin at all.

Burr and his associates found a characteristic L field in every kind of living form they examined with their voltmeters. They found L fields in rabbits, mice, salamanders, plants, trees, seeds, and even slime molds.

When they measured the L fields in frog eggs, they found that these revealed the *future* location of the frog's nervous system—an indication that it is the L field which organizes the body of the frog. By measuring the L fields of seeds they found it possible to predict how strong and healthy the future plants would be. When, over a period of many years, they measured the L fields of trees, they found that these were influenced by such external forces as sunspots and phases of the moon—an indication that all life on Earth is a part of and subject to the influence of the great forces of the universe.

Burr established that L fields are true fields and that he was not measuring skin resistances, as some suggested. He did this by demonstrating that it is possible to measure the voltage gradients with the electrodes spaced a small distance from the surface of the body and not in contact with the skin. He also demonstrated the same thing when he rotated a salamander floated in a dish beneath—and out of contact with—electrodes connected to a voltmeter and recorder. As the creature was rotated, the recorder showed a tiny alternating current as the head and tail of the salamander passed in turn under the electrode.

These and countless other experiments demonstrated beyond all doubt that L fields are an important step in the organization of life—a "tool" that nature uses to build, maintain, and repair all living forms. This discovery, therefore, is of fundamental importance to understanding what life is, especially for biology and medicine.

III.

We can visualize the human L field as an electromagnetic corset. Unlike women's corsets, however, L fields control the *whole* body, not merely some parts of the figure; and we cannot take them off at night! We are controlled by our L field from the moment of conception until we die.

When a sperm fertilizes an ovum, the right conditions are created for an L field—presumably from some spatial reservoir—to take over and to start building an embryo. In animal experiments, Burr was able to detect the L field of a growing embryo, because the field properties of the embryo radiate through the liquid environment in which it lives.

Since the L field is the organizer of the body, it is obvious that changes in the L field can warn us that there are, or will soon be, physical changes in the body. Sometimes changes in the L field *precede* physical symptoms. On the other hand an injury to the body can produce changes in the L field. By L-field measurements, for instance, it is possible to measure the rate of healing of wounds, even internal ones. This, of course, is of great potential value to surgeons.

Since the L field is an integrated organizing unit, any physical injuries or changes affect the field as a whole. Thus it is possible to detect these injuries or changes in some convenient part of the body at a distance from the affected part. And one of the most striking—and useful—examples of this is the detection of ovulation by voltage changes in the L field.

Burr discovered that ovulation in the female is preceded by a sharp rise in voltage—a fact which he confirmed by an experiment on a female rabbit. First he stimulated ovulation in the rabbit. Then he anesthetized it, opened the abdomen, and placed an electrode in a salt-filled chamber around the ovary. The ovary was continuously scanned with a microscope and the voltage changes recorded on a recording galvanometer. At the moment the egg was released, as seen through the microscope, the galvanometer recorded a sharp change in voltage.

To measure the moment of ovulation in a woman, however, it is not necessary for the electrode to be close to the ovary, since this physical event affects the whole field. All that is necessary is for the woman to dip the index finger of each hand in two little dishes filled with saline solution and connected to the voltmeter.

By such measurements on many women, Burr was able to establish the important fact that "there is no necessary relationship between ovulation and menstruation, for either may exist without the other; ovulation may occur without menstruation and menses without ovulation."

This explains why the "rhythm method" of birth control has been found to be unreliable for about thirty percent of the women who use it. If suitable instruments were generally available, it would be possible for women who, for religious or other reasons, do not use contraceptives to avoid conception by merely taking regular measurements of the voltage in their L fields. This would be of great practical utility in planning parenthood.

L-field measurements can also be useful to women who want to conceive but have had difficulty in doing so. Such a woman was a married patient of Burr who had longed for a child. She went daily to his laboratory and took her own voltage measurements and, when she saw the voltage rising, went home to her husband. A much-wanted child was the result.

L-field measurements can also be used to determine the best time for artificial insemination.

IV.

As noted earlier, changes in the optimal L field sometimes precede overt physical symptoms. For this reason L-field measurements can sometimes be used to give warning of, say, cancer before the physician can observe any physical signs. They are particularly useful for the rapid detection of malignancy in the female genital tract.

This has been demonstrated by Barton, Musselman, and Langman, who first became interested in Burr's detection of ovulation. After using L-field measurements for artificial insemination, Langman carried out a long and meticulously controlled series of experiments on nearly one thousand women, mostly at New York's Bellevue Hospital.

Langman measured the L fields of his patients by introducing one electrode into the vagina until its tip came to rest in the posterior fornix. The other, or "reference," electrode was bandaged to the lower abdominal wall. In the vast majority of cases he found that, if the potential between the two electrodes was negative, the patient was suffering from some malignancy, which was later confirmed by normal tests.

His results were subjected to a most careful statistical analysis. To summarize them, in nine out of ten cases of malignancy a negative potential was recorded. A negative potential does not always mean malignancy but ninety-five percent of all malignancies can be uncovered by these "electrometric" tests. They can be carried out by qualified technicians at the rate of five per hour per instrument. As a screening procedure to detect malignancy in large numbers of women, therefore, electrometric tests are far quicker and cheaper than the microscopic examination of biopsy material. Thus they offer an important technique for the *early* detection of malignancy.

Some of this work by Langman and Burr was published as long ago as 1942. But, to the best of this writer's knowledge, none of the commanders of the much-advertised "war on cancer" have so far paid the slightest attention to the valuable "weapon" that this research offers—further striking confirmation of Planck's dictum.

V.

In the future it may be possible to use L fields for treatment as well as for diagnosis. For since the L field controls the body and abnormalities in the L field often precede physical symptoms, it would seem logical to attack disease through the L field. So far, little consideration has been given to this possibility. There are, however, some indications that it is worth pursuing.

Around the time of World War II, for instance, some German scientists researched the effects on the body of what might be termed the "electronic environment." They found that this differs with the nature of the surface of the Earth. With a porous, sandy soil the earth "breathes" air in and out with changes in atmospheric pressure. When the earth "exhales" air it is negatively charged, and this charge, they found, has definite effects on the body. They did not know about L fields, but if they had, they would undoubtedly have concluded that the negative charge affected the L field, rather than the body directly. They noted that these effects do not occur over rocky ground because it cannot "breathe."

It has long been known that electrical storms, which induce powerful currents in the earth, have a most depressing effect on some people. And it is now known that the electrical conditions which accompany certain winds in the form of positive ions, rather than the winds themselves, have a depressing effect, no doubt on the L field and thus the body. Well-known examples of such winds are the *mistral* of the Mediterranean, the *foehn* wind of Bavaria, and the *santana* of southern California.

Some years ago, a German scientist reported some striking successes in treating patients, suffering from various problems, by placing them on a couch in the middle of a powerful electrostatic field. Apparently he had not heard about L fields but it seems probable that in some way he was revitalizing them electrically.

Another indication of the possibilities is some research by Mr. George De la Warr, who applied mild alternating magnetic fields of specific frequencies to different parts of the body. He found that these would cause a reflex action at some distance from the spot where he applied the field, which suggests that he was treating the L field as a whole. With the same treatment he was able to reduce cholesterol levels and white cell counts, which suggests the same thing.

These things at least suggest that the possibility of treating the L field electromagnetically is worth pursuing.

If such research is undertaken, Kirlian photography, which is arousing such interest, may well play a useful part. There is some dispute whether this technique makes it possible to photograph a part of the L field or whether Kirlian photographs are of some more subtle "aura"; and it may be some time before this dispute is resolved. In the meanwhile, Kirlian photography might be used to examine the effects of electromagnetic fields of different frequencies.

VI.

While measurements of L fields can be useful in diagnosing such physical conditions as cancer, ovulation, or the rate of healing of internal wounds, they can be equally valuable in assessing the condition of the mind.

As long ago as 1948, Dr. Leonard J. Ravitz, Jr.—referred to by Burr as his "most brilliant pupil"—made a discovery of the utmost significance. He found that the state of the mind is reflected in the L field. In other words, certain mental conditions can be measured or detected with a voltmeter; and it is hard to overestimate the importance of this discovery. To quote Burr:

> Perhaps the most remarkable result obtained in our laboratory by Dr. Ravitz was when he found a significant electro-metric correlate of hypnotism that was astonishing to watch: *a continuously recording voltmeter showed evidence of marked changes in voltage gradient during the hypnotic process.*
> . . . If anyone needed objective evidence of the results of hypnosis, one needed only to look at the charts recorded under these conditions. Needless to say, this suggests an enormous range of studies which could be made paralleling those of Dr. Ravitz and, wherever possible, extending them.

In other words, Ravitz was the first man in history to measure the depth of hypnosis electrically and thereby to demonstrate that mind can influence the L field—an electromagnetic phenomenon.

Good doctors have always known that the mind can influence the body for good or ill. A strong "will to live" can often defy the medical probabilities. Conversely, worry can produce ulcers. But until Ravitz made this discovery, nobody knew *how* the mind does this. It now appears that the mind produces "psychosomatic" symptoms—as it is now fashionable to call them—by interfering with the organization of the L field. If this inference is correct—and Burr did not disagree when the writer suggested it—"psychosomatic" symptoms can best be attacked by trying to change the attitude of mind of the patient.

In other words, L fields are the "bridge" or intermediate link between the mental and the physical. Thus they offer evidence that mind and body are quite separate, which is contrary to the belief of some modern biologists. In this writer's view, too, L fields at least partly explain how radionic therapy achieves its results—by acting on the L field of the patient through his mind (see Chap. 29).

In later experiments on many thousands of patients, Ravitz made another important discovery: the voltage gradients in human beings are not constant but vary rhythmically in time.

If the voltage gradients of a healthy person—taken between the forehead and the palm of a hand—are taken every day and plotted as a graph it will be found that they appear as a series of sine waves which reflect the mental and physical ups and downs of the patient. If the peaks of these curves happen to coincide, the individual will be "at his best"—at the maximum point of physical energy and mental alertness of which he is capable. But if two "valleys" in these curves happen to coincide, the individual will be at his lowest ebb, and therefore specially susceptible to accidents.

Such knowledge can be of great importance to those engaged in hazardous occupations, such as airline pilots. Even ordinary situations, such as driving a car, can be made more safe. Since these curves follow a regular pattern in all healthy, normal people, it is possible to predict highs and lows some weeks ahead and thus to give ample warning of dangerous periods for the individual concerned. Thus forewarned of an impending "low," they can either try to avoid hazardous duties or, if that is impossible, they can exercise special care and vigilance.

These curves slightly resemble those used in studies of "biorhythms," which are attracting the attention of industry at the present time. But there are important differences: biorhythm curves are usually determined by going back to the date of birth, while the curves discovered by Ravitz can actually be measured and plotted accurately for the individual *as he is at the time.* This is important as individuals may have changed since they were born.

There is some evidence, too, that the phases of the moon, along with other meteorological factors, must be taken into account if an individual's curves are to be plotted to the utmost utility.

There is another important use for Ravitz's discovery. He found that while the curves of healthy people display a steady rhythmic pattern over long periods, curves of those suffering from instability are erratic and irregular. By measuring the L fields of people, therefore, it is possible quickly to detect those who are psychologically unstable and also those who are likely to crack under stress.

In this way recruiters for the military, education, industry, etc., will be able to weed out applicants before time and money are spent on training them for duties for which they are unsuitable. Though there may be no obvious symptoms, psychotics can be detected in only a few days of measurements, though borderline cases may take a little longer.

One of the great advantages of this method is that it is entirely objective. Voltage readings can be taken by a technician, who need not say a word to the individual; and the charts can then be inspected and interpreted by someone qualified to do so, who need never see the individual. Most of the tests and subjective questions by psychiatrists can thus be dispensed with. In other words, much psychiatric testing can be replaced by a completely impersonal voltmeter—which may not be welcomed by the psychiatric profession!

VII.

There is an even more important use for L-field measurements of mental patients: they can help to decide whether inmates of mental hospitals are fit to return to the world outside.

As everyone knows, a high proportion of the hospital beds in the United States is devoted to mental patients, at enormous cost to the community. Anything, then, which can help to decide how many of them can safely be released cannot only lessen this burden but may also make life happier for many of these unfortunate people.

Conversely, L-field measurements can help to minimize a real danger to the community—the release of patients who have not been cured, even if they seem to be better, and who in fact are dangerously violent and even homicidal.

At present all that the authorities have to go by is the opinion of the psychiatrists who all too often are disastrously wrong. Newspapers frequently record these tragic cases. This writer has personal knowledge of three men, pronounced "cured" by the psychiatrists and released from institutions. Shortly after release two of them committed brutal murders and the third became so violent that he had to be locked up again.

If such tragedies are to be avoided in the future it is obvious that we need some more reliable yardstick than the personal opinions of psychiatrists. Regular L-field measurements can supply this. Electrometric tests should be given at regular intervals to all candidates for release from mental institutions for a period of months, before release can be considered. And all those released should be required to take regular electrometric tests for some months, at least, *after* release to detect any possible relapse.

Such tests would be far more reliable—and far less expensive—than psychiatric examinations.

In short, L-field measurements offer a new and precise tool to psychiatrists; and it is appropriate that they should have been discovered by Ravitz who is, himself, an outstanding psychiatrist with long, varied, practical experience.

Another and more pleasant aspect of L-field measurements is that they can be used to measure the intensity of emotion, which also may be useful to psychiatry. Ravitz has been able to measure in millivolts the strength of an emotion recalled under hypnosis. And this can also be done with a conscious emotion and without hypnosis.

For instance, when the writer was experimenting with a voltmeter he happened to think of something hilarious. Immediately the voltage between his forehead and the palm of one hand shot up by ten millivolts. This is perhaps the first time that such an elusive and intangible form of thought—a humorous idea—has ever been measured with a voltmeter!

There are many today who do not distinguish between mind and body and still confuse thought with its instrument, the brain. Many scientists, too, refuse to admit the reality of anything that cannot be measured. Ravitz' discoveries *should* cause such people to reconsider their notions.

VIII.

Apart from its value to biology and medicine, Burr's discovery of the fields of life has important philosophical and theological significance. For it shows that man is an inseparable part of the universe and subject to its precise and inexorable laws. For Burr demonstrated that the fields of life are embraced and influenced by the greater fields of space.

He did this with his historic experiments with the L fields of trees which he used to record long-term effects of the fields and forces of the universe. It was necessary to use trees because it is obviously impossible to keep human beings continuously connected to recording voltmeters for years. For what he termed his "antennae to the universe" he chose a young maple tree outside his house in New Haven, Connecticut, and a magnificent old elm outside his laboratory at Lyme, Connecticut.

Here again he was breaking entirely new ground, and it took him a long time and many experiments before he was able to develop a technique which proved satisfactory through several decades of experiment. First, he carefully removed the bark down to the cambium layer. Against this he applied the open face of small plastic containers filled with physiological salt jelly in which his special silver–silver chloride electrodes were embedded. These containers were held in the opening in the bark and the electrodes connected by special cables to recording voltmeters indoors.

After much experiment he found it best to place the containers holding the electrodes on the trunk of the tree, one above the other and about three feet apart. The lower electrode was placed high enough on the trunk to avoid interference by marauding animals. This technique was so stable that he was able to take almost continuous records over a period of nearly thirty years.

It was fascinating to see this majestic "antenna to the universe" deep in the woods of Lyme, and the pens of the recording voltmeter in the laboratory nearby, quietly inscribing what man had never seen before—the effects of the great fields and forces of space on a living thing on this planet. And it was obvious that if these can affect the L field of a tree, they must also affect the L fields of all living things, including man.

These voltmeters also recorded the effects on the two trees —one in New Haven and the other in Lyme—of such mundane factors as the changing seasons and day and night, and also variations of voltages in the air and the earth. They indicated effects which roughly followed the lunar cycle which, wrote Burr, "does not mean that the moon affects the living systems as the old wives' tale held, but rather that both the moon and the living systems respond to some more primary characteristics of the cosmos."

Though the two trees were in different environments and about forty miles apart, the records showed a remarkable correspondence which demonstrated that the effects recorded were not the result of purely local conditions.

Records of both trees showed an "extraordinary" correlation between the potentials in the trees and sunspot activity, as recorded in Zurich. And Burr—ever modest and cautious in his claims—wrote: "There is a hint . . . although this is by no means valid and final evidence—that the changing potentials of the trees follow, by a predictable amount of time, the changing relative sunspot numbers."

He goes on to say: "It would seem reasonable to conclude . . . that a study of longer duration . . . might make it abundantly clear that the field properties, not only of living systems but of the universe, interact in characteristic fashions and produce results of great significance."

Dr. Ralph Markson of the Department of Aeronautics and Astronautics at MIT, made a meticulous statistical analysis of these tree records. He concluded that "tree potentials respond either to geomagnetic activity directly, or that both parameters may be under the influence of some other geophysical factor or factors."

He also concluded: "Statistically, both the sun and the moon seem to influence tree potentials, the sun apparently through an electromagnetic mechanism, the moon through a gravitational or gravitational—electrical mechanism."

Many years of research will be needed fully to explore the new territory of knowledge which the tree records have opened up. But already they show beyond all reasonable doubt that man and all his fellow living creatures are subject to the influence—and inflexible discipline—of the great forces of space.

This is a salutary lesson for an age in which violence and indiscipline seem widespread and increasing. For, as one of Britain's most brilliant and far-seeing politicians recently observed to the writer: "Unless we can somehow instill into more of the electorate a belief in a higher power, our system of democracy is doomed."

Burr's great discovery, however, also offers an anxious and troubled age some much-needed reassurance. To quote his own words:

> The universe in which we find ourselves and from which we cannot be separated is a place of law and order. It is not an accident, nor chaos. It is organized and maintained by an electrodynamic field, capable of determining the position and movement of all charged particles . . . Law and order prevail from the biggest to the smallest; and to suggest that there is any chaos is merely to display our lack of information. In short, the universe has meaning and so have we. Though we do not understand it, the meaning is there . . .

These words—written a year before his death in 1973—epitomized the life's work of a great gentleman and scholar who, one day, will be recognized as an outstanding pioneer of science.

7.

Radiations Known and Unknown

LANGSTON DAY

Most of the radiations which figure in the scientific textbooks are represented as forming part of the electromagnetic spectrum, which is usually shown as a graduated table of all the known frequencies or rates of vibration . . .

Are there any other forms of radiation, radiations which are not listed in the textbooks? . . .

Where living matter is concerned, persons possessing a certain kind of sensitivity, or an extra sense of perception, can become aware of emanations emitted by human beings or animals. Perhaps when we come down the evolutionary scale to insects, molluscs, and plants the emanations are not so obvious, though they are clear enough in the case of glowworms and fireflies which happen to emit radiations falling within the visible lightband. Many of the mysteries of nature, such as the migration of birds, might be explained by the presence of radiations which are received in some unexplained fashion.

A. M. Gurwitsch has recorded what he calls "mitogenic radiation," which is said to come from the growth process of living cells, namely cell division in the roots of growing plants; and more recently in Columbia University I. I. Rabi, P. Kusch and S. Millman, using a new kind of apparatus, gave scientific proof of rays or vibrations which pass between one molecule and another. They showed that each cell, living or inert, is a tiny radio transmitter and receiver which gives a

"Radiations Known and Unknown" by Langston Day is excerpted from *New Worlds beyond the Atom* by Langston Day, with George De la Warr. Copyright © 1963 by The Devin-Adair Company and reprinted by permission of The Devin-Adair Company.

continuous broadcast, and that the waves range in length over the whole of the electromagnetic spectrum. . . .

There is reason to believe that some of the ancient races were familiar with this idea of radiation from living creatures; but this knowledge seems to have been lost and rediscovered after the lapse of millenniums. In more recent times it was Goethe who first suggested studying the vibrations emitted by the human body. Newton regarded the universe as a dead mechanism, but Goethe with his poetic insight saw it as filled with life and color.

About a quarter of a century later, Goethe's idea was taken up by another famous German. Baron Karl von Reichenbach was one of the most distinguished chemists of his day and the discoverer of creosote and many other chemical compounds. But his heart was not in coaltar; it was in the curious experiments which had been made by Mesmer. Towards the middle of the 19th century he began to carry out experiments of his own in this direction, using as his subjects people who [purportedly] possessed some form of extrasensory perception. Many of them suffered from various kinds of nervous disorders, but some were in good health. He called them "sensitive subjects," and with their aid he accumulated a wealth of evidence indicating that there existed in nature a peculiar kind of energy which he named the odic force. He found it in magnets, crystals, light, heat, and living cells; he found it manifesting itself wherever any kind of chemical reaction was taking place.

This energy could be accumulated or conducted along wires, focused by a lens, or distorted as a candle flame is distorted by blowing on it. It seemed to be a vital energy since he discovered that certain people could transmit it to others—for healing, the relief of pain, or even to produce anesthesia. In 1844 Reichenbach published his *Researches* and the book created a considerable stir in this country. But doctors and scientists were skeptical and could not accept his claims. Yet the great Humboldt said of his work: "The facts are undeniable: it now becomes the task of science to explain them."

Even more scorn was heaped on the head of the American

doctor, Albert Abrams,* who held the view that all matter emitted radiations and that the human body could be used as a receiver for them. Each of the organs, he found, acts as a separate broadcasting station, emitting waves of a certain frequency when not diseased or weakened. He drew up a table of frequencies which he believed represented the correct vibrational rates of the various organs. Disease, he said, was an altered rate of vibration. He claimed to be able to correct wrong vibrational rates by means of a device of his own invention, and he also claimed to be able to diagnose a patient's physical condition from a specimen of his blood.

Doctors regarded him with the greatest misgiving, and in the medical world the term "Abrams' box" is still a term of scorn and derision. Abrams' great mistake was to be somewhat bombastic about his powers to diagnose, so that he appeared in a ludicrous light when he was tricked in a test in which rabbit's blood was substituted for human blood.

The work of Abrams was carried on by Ruth Drown of California, who in 1939 published an account of her work in *Theory and Technique of the Drown Radio-Therapy and Radio-Vision Instruments.* She developed instruments for diagnosis and treatment and found she was able to treat patients through a "link" such as a blood specimen. Her work still continues in America, though it is not officially recognized in medical circles.

In England, Abrams' work was taken up by Dr. Guyon Richards . . . and by Drs. Dudley Wright, Ernest Martin, and others. Richards was much impressed by the results achieved by homeopathy, a therapeutic system which consists in administering so-called "potentized" dilutions of minerals and herbs.

Hahnemann, the originator of homeopathy, was ridiculed by the medical profession of his day. How, it was asked, could one-millionth of a grain of belladonna possibly cure scarlet fever? He and his followers knew that the almost magical effects of these microscopic doses depended upon potentization. Some subtle form of radiation entered into the dose. If you are an allopathic doctor, you pin your faith on chemistry

* See Chapter 29. *Editors.*

and administer doses of drugs, but if you are a homeopath you diminish the chemical action and rely on the radiative force in the potentized dilution.

At the moment of going to press [1963] there is news that fifteen years of research work carried out by the Boyd Medical Research Institute in Glasgow has shown that this potentization is a reality. In the experiments a crude drug was added to a diluting fluid in the proportion of one to ninety-nine drops. After vigorous shaking, a single drop of the diluent was added to a further ninety-nine drops, and so on.

When this process had been repeated thirty times the fraction of the original drug remaining was about one divided by an integer with sixty noughts. Not one molecule of the drug remained, yet more than one thousand carefully controlled experiments proved beyond any doubt that these high dilutions will affect living cells.

Richards thought that this radiative force in homeopathy was the same force which had been discovered by Reichenbach, Abrams, and others. He improved on Abrams' work and tried to prove that his table of rates bore a definite relationship to the table of atomic weights. He also confirmed Reichenbach's discovery that the human body radiates a form of energy which had not hitherto been detectable by instruments. Towards the end of his life he formed the London Medical Society for the Study of Radiesthesia and began to make use of a pendulum for diagnosis. This is "dowsing" applied to medicine.

What is water divining, or dowsing?† *The Divining Rod* by Sir William Barrett and Theodore Besterman, an authoritative book published twenty years ago, describes the work of some of the best-known dowsers and proves beyond doubt that water divining is a genuine art. Not only can water be discovered by its aid: minerals, metals, archaeological remains and many other things have been traced in this way.

Some people believe that the rod with which Moses struck the rock was a divining rod and the term "Mosaical rod" occurs in literature. Ancient Egyptian bas-reliefs show diviners at work with bells held in their extended hands. In the reign

† See Chapter 28. *Editors.*

of James I a certain John Scott "who pretended to the use of the Mosaical rods" was engaged by David Ramsey, a clockmaker, to dowse for buried treasure in the cloister of Westminster Abbey. Unhappily he failed, but the chronicler records: "The true miscarriage of the business was by reason of so many people being present at the operation; for there was about thirty, some laughing, others deriding us."

This looks as if our ancestors regarded dowsing as a psychic operation, and in fact the authors of *The Divining Rod* suggest that knowledge of the object searched for enters the operator's subconscious mind and usually shows itself by a slight involuntary twitching of his muscles. Some diviners even believe that the gift is telepathic, but it seems more likely that the dowser's neuromuscular system is affected by this same radiation which is emitted by all forms of matter and that his mind acts as a selector or tuning-in apparatus. Some dowsers get a reaction not only when they are immediately over the underground stream, or whatever it may be, but at regular intervals away from it—rather like a series of diminishing ripples.

This hardly seems like the work of mind, and yet mind enters into it in no uncertain way because in radiesthesia, of which dowsing forms a part, we are passing beyond the frontiers of matter into another sphere where mind is a demonstrable force. So when a dowser sets out in search say of coal, he must have coal in his mind; or if he prefers, he may take a sample of coal which acts as a "witness" or link. It not only helps him to focus his mind on "coal underground," but being coal it emits radiations similar to those of the substance he is seeking. Some dowsers find samples more effective when they hold them against the solar plexus.

Since dowsing works with inanimate matter it is not surprising that it can be used to detect the still more powerful radiations from living substances. Just as dowsers have discovered concentric rings of reaction at regular intervals from say, an underground stream, so they have found circling the body of a patient similar rings which vary with his state of health.

Most medical dowsers use miniature pendulums consisting perhaps of a small piece of ivory or amber suspended on a length of thread, and these pendulums are found to gyrate when placed in one of these rings emitted by the patient, the manner of the gyration giving a clue to his state of health.

Pendulists also make use of samples of diseased tissue, bacterial cultures, and so forth, which emit their own particular radiations, and by various techniques they attempt to diagnose the cause of the trouble. They are also able to check any proposed remedy, whether homeopathic or otherwise, by placing a sample of it near the patient and observing if its radiations bring the gyrations of the pendulum nearer to normal.

It may be that there has been too much loose talk about "human vibrations," "personal radiations," and so forth on the part of people with little or no scientific training. However it may be, doctors are suspicious of such ideas and medicine is apt to lean rather heavily on chemistry. But chemistry, as we have said earlier, is not very far back in the line of causality. What lies behind it?

Here and there even among the most orthodox you find an admission that there may be something more at work than chemistry. Joseph Needham, who cannot be accused of undue credulity, says [in *Order and Life*]: "It is possible to picture a single molecule or molecular aggregate (perhaps of a paracrystalline nature) exerting an influence around itself in all directions of space for a considerable distance, even into microscopic dimensions."

There are in fact formative forces in nature which cannot be pinpointed in the electromagnetic spectrum. E. Pfeiffer has produced patterns of some of them in rather the same way that many of us produced patterns of magnetic forces in iron filings when we were at school.

He covered a smooth plate of glass with a thin film of copper chloride which crystallizes when it cools. By adding the juices of various plants, human or animal saliva, urine, or diluted blood, he found that the radiations from these substances draw characteristic designs in the crystals. Lily juice, for instance, draws a sort of "lily picture," while agave produces a strange design which appears prickly.

Blood, he concluded, possesses a strong radiative energy and each person has his own peculiar blood crystallization pattern. By using sodium sulphate instead of copper chloride, he found that those forces which build up and maintain the shapes and proportions in nature depend to a great extent upon radiations from the Sun. The patterns are much less distinct at night or during a solar eclipse. His latest work seems to indicate that crystalline formations obtained from certain solutions can be affected by thought processes.

We must also take note of the work of J. C. Maby who with T. B. Franklin and others tried to record radiesthetic vibrations with delicate electronic apparatus. He found that his instruments were upset by oncoming gales, thunderstorms, snowstorms, fog, heavy clouds, and also by nearby moving objects such as aircraft, cars, and human beings; but in these latter cases only when they were at certain critical distances, suggesting a parallel to the "rings" known to dowsers.

Among other men who have contributed something towards our subject are George Crile, an American doctor, and Georges Lakhovsky.

Crile, as others have done, formed a view that the human body is an extremely complex electronic apparatus in which both shortwave and longwave radiation play important roles. Each living cell he saw as a tiny electric battery generating its own current by chemical action, and the nervous system as a network of highly specialized electrical conductors.

Lakhovsky developed the study of radiations from living matter on rather different lines. He regarded each of our [350 trillion] living cells as a tiny battery with the nucleus acting as an oscillating circuit and giving off radiations. In disease the frequency changes.

He drew an interesting analogy between human bodies and radio sets. Our radio sets work because our aerials are placed in a variable electromagnetic field created by the waves emitted by the broadcasting stations. The cells of our bodies work in a similar way. They move rapidly with the Earth's rotation and revolution through a variable electromagnetic field generated by radiations from the Sun, the Milky Way, and the distant galaxies. Like all living matter, they are balanced on a knife edge, for they are constantly under the influence of radiations of higher and lower frequency which may compel them to alter their vibrational rate and so produce one of the many diseases whose root cause is so baffling.

Lakhovsky quoted Albert Nodon's experiments which

showed that the radiation from plants is as great as that of radium or uranium. That of insects is from three to fifteen times greater, while the vital cells in human bodies radiate still more powerfully. He showed that every living thing is a delicate and complex radiative apparatus depending upon chains of interlocking processes within and supported like a fish in water by a sea of vibrations without. In his view the whole universe is knit together by a "universal plexus of cosmic rays," and all forms of matter, ranging from rarefied gases to solid rock are simply varying degrees of condensation in this plexus. In radiation everything lives, moves and has its being. . . .

In earlier days when an explorer reported having seen nuts the size of a man's head with hair on them he was laughed to scorn. Europeans could not imagine a coconut. Perhaps we shall have difficulty even in imagining some of the things described [in Day's book], but that is no reason why they should be rejected. Any Victorian scientist who had been bold enough to forecast radar or television would have been derided as an irresponsible visionary. In these days it is as well to preserve an open mind. . . .

8.

Prana:
The Traditional and the Modern View

GOPI KRISHNA

Kundalini is the ancient Sanskrit word for a form of bioenergy, the life force in humans which drives evolution and leads the race to a higher state of consciousness. Often called the serpent power, this esoteric concept can best be understood when we refer to the traditional portrait of Lord Vishnu, a familiar sight in many Hindu homes and places of worship.

Vishnu is one of the Hindu Trinity—Brahma, Vishnu, and Shiva. They represent the three essential phases of a cyclic creation. Brahma is the Creator, Vishnu the Sustainer, and Shiva (in the form of Rudra) the Destroyer. They are merely the three aspects of the attributes of Brahman itself. The picture is of tremendous significance and for that reason has come down almost unaltered through an enormous span of time. It seems incredible that so profound a knowledge of an inscrutable, complex phenomenon could be available in the so-called dark ages of the past. But the author or the authors of the presentation displayed truly amazing knowledge indeed of the various aspects of the serpent power.

In the classical portrait Lord Vishnu is shown reclining on the body of the multiheaded serpent, known as Shesha-Naga or Ananta. The body of the serpent floats on the heaving ocean of milk which surrounds it on every side. The thousand heads of the serpent make a canopy over the reclining frame of the god. The eyes of Vishnu are half-closed in samadhi

"Prana: The Traditional and the Modern View" by Gopi Krishna is excerpted from a forthcoming work, *The Dawn of a New Science* by Gopi Krishna, and is printed by permission of the Kundalini Research Foundation, New York City.

and from his navel there springs a large lotus with a long stalk on which appears the form of Brahma with four faces and four arms. By the side or at the feet of Vishnu is the lovely form of the Goddess Lakshmi. She sits close to him, touching his feet. The most remarkable feature of the picture is that the face of Vishnu is shown to be sky blue in complexion.

For the inquiring mind the representation raises certain issues which need an explanation, and many attempts have been made to answer the riddle by scholars both in the East and the West. The image of Vishnu, the Lord of Creation, reclining on Shesha-Naga, afloat on the ocean of milk, is an unmistakable pictorial representation of the effects of consciousness caused by the arousal of the serpent power. In one bold symbolic sweep the authors of the picture and the myth on which it is based have attempted to portray all the esoteric features of the awakening of kundalini.

Every human body is a "Kshir Sagar" or ocean of milk, because each of its billions of living cells is a self-charging battery of living electricity or prana. This pranic force abides in the form of an extremely subtle organic essence in all the tissues and substances of the body and is readily convertible into psychic energy. This is the bioplasma described by Soviet scientists who are conducting important experiments in this field. This work is described by Ostrander and Schroeder, who write: "From what we had seen, the Soviets appeared to have evidence that there is some sort of energy matrix in all living things, some sort of unifying invisible body or luminescence penetrating our physical bodies. But just what exactly is this energy body? How does it function? Where does it come from?"

"The exploration that answered those questions began near Soviet space centers in far off Kazakhstan," the two authors report. "A group of biologists, biochemists, and biophysicists clustered around a huge electron microscope. The Kirlians' equipment . . . was hooked up to this sophisticated, intricate electronic instrument. The scientists . . . saw in the silent high-frequency discharge something once reserved only for clairvoyants. They saw the living 'double' of a living organism in motion. . . . What was this double? Some sort of elementary plasmalike constellation made of ionized excited electrons, protons, and possibly other particles, they said. But at the same time, this energy body is not just particles. It is not a chaotic system. It is a whole unified organism in itself. It acts as a unit, they said, and as a unit the energy body gives off its own electromagnetic fields and is the basis of biological fields."[1]

At another place, referring further to the Kazakh scientists, Ostrander and Schroeder writes: "The bioluminescence visible in the Kirlian pictures is caused by the bioplasma, not the electrical state of the organism, they say. One of the most distinctive features of this vibrating, colorful energy body in all living things, according to the Kazakh scientists, is that it has a specific spatial organization. It has shape. Inside the energy body, say the scientists, processes have their own labyrinthine motion absolutely unlike the pattern of energy in the physical body. The bioplasmic body is also polarized. The biological plasma of the energy body is specific for every organism, tissue and possibly biomolecule, they said."

This bioplasmic body is a primary object of observation in the heightened states of consciousness induced by an awakened kundalini. In fact, for the first time consciousness now becomes aware of its own subtle world.

My own inward study of bioplasma or prana has revealed to me that there is a special pranic spectrum for every class of life on Earth and a specific one for every individual of each class. The real actor in our corporeal frame manipulates the gross tissues by means of subtle energies of which we have no knowledge at present. There is nothing in the wonder-exciting movement which is constantly going on in an atom to compare with the marvelous interplay of intelligent forces in the pranic body of a human, an animal, or a plant.

Plainly speaking, the study of bioplasma is yet in its infancy. However advanced might be the position of science in its investigation of the material universe, the efforts made now in the direction of the subtle forces of nature are still in a nascent state. The investigation done so far, however, denotes a change in attitude which was absolutely necessary for the study of life. The awakened individual becomes as perceptive of the bioplasma sheath as he is of the physical body.

The awareness of the latter comes about through the senses, while the former is directly apprehended by the mind. This presupposes a radical change in the very mechanism of perception. This is a point which the students of mysticism and altered states of consciousness often fail to grasp. The observer in the human is changed.

In its cosmic form prana is a highly diffused intelligent energy spread everywhere. But in the individual it takes a specific form as the bioplasma or individual prana composed of an extremely subtle organic essence drawn from the elements and compounds forming the body. It is this essence which, transformed into psychic energy, becomes the fuel for thought. The bioplasma, sustained by the cosmic ocean of prana, permeates each and every cell of an organism. In fact, it is the life of the cells as also of the organism itself. The nervous system with its countless extremely fine threads floats like a serpent on this pool of bioenergy, which is itself surrounded and permeated by the boundless ocean of universal life.

There is no agreement among psychologists about the nature of psychic energy. Broadly speaking, scientists as a class have not yet awakened to the realization that mind and thought are forms of a cosmic energy as subject to perennial laws and as capable of empirical proof as the various forms of material energy with which they deal. Only a few decades ago no biologist had any idea about the electrical activity of the brain. The fresh insights gained into the working of the most complex organ during even the last two decades were not available to the older generation of scientists.

While Wilhelm Reich's ideas concerning bioelectrical energy, which he called orgone, come closer to the concept of prana of the Indian savants than do those of other Western scientists, there is still a fundamental difference to be resolved. It is necessary to quote him at some length to grasp their significance:

> The color of the orgone is blue or bluish gray. . . . The orgone contains three different kinds of radiation: bluish-gray foglike formations; deep blue violet expanding and contracting dots and whitish, rapidly moving dots and lines. The color of the atmospheric orgone is

apparent in the blue sky and the bluish haze which one sees in the distance, particularly on hot summer days. Similarly the blue-gray northern lights, the so-called St. Elmo's Fire and the bluish formation which astronomers recently observed during a period of increased sunspot activity, are manifestations of the orgone energy.[2]

Coming from the cosmic aspect of orgone energy to the individual, Reich says:

The living organism contains orgone energy in every one of its cells, and keeps charging itself orgonotically from the atmosphere by the process of breathing. The red blood corpuscles, at a magnification of over two thousand, show a bluish glimmer: They are vesicles charged with orgone energy which they transport from the lungs to the body tissues. The plant chlorophyll, which is related to the iron containing protein of the animal food, contains orgone which it takes up directly from the atmosphere and the sun radiation.

That every individual organism is surrounded by an aura or a sheath of bioenergy is affirmed in these words: "The human organism is surrounded by an orgonotic field which varies in range according to the individual's vegetative motility." There is a gulf of difference between Reich's conception of bioelectrical energy and the prana-shakti of the Indian savants. This difference also exists in the case of all other concepts about bioplasma or life force currently held among many of the scientists in the West. For them this energy, whatever the manifestation by which it can be identified, assumes the same position as other material energies in the universe. The underlying idea in the minds of the investigators is often the same as that which influences their study of physical energies, namely to understand their nature and laws to harness them for pragmatic purposes.

But for the ancient Indian adept, bioenergy or prana is the superintelligent cosmic life energy to which he owes his own existence and the existence of the world around him. He considers himself to be no more than a transient bubble, blown up by the action of this almighty force, which continues to work day and night through all the period of his life, to maintain the ego-bound flicker of consciousness which he knows as himself.

"O youthful spouse of Shiva," says the ancient Vedic text *Saundarya Lahari*, "Thou art the mind, Thou art the ether, Thou the air, Thou the fire, Thou the water, and Thou the earth. When Thou hast transformed Thyself (thus) there is nothing beyond. Thou, with a view to manifesting Thyself in the form of the universe, inwardly assumest the form of consciousness and bliss."

This is how another ancient text, *Panchastavi,* expresses the same idea in other words: "Thou art the source of all sound of the universe. Thou art also the origin of all speech and (hence) art called by the name of Vageshwari (the goddess of speech), Vishnu (creator), Indra (the lord of the elements), and others (other divine beings) issue from Thee and at the end of the world cycle verily are again absorbed into Thee. It is in that (highest) form, full of majesty which is beyond conception, that Thou are sung as Para-Shakti (supreme energy)."

The reason for this attitude of utter surrender and submission is simple. Research on bioenergy implies entry into the realm of the spirit, into the subtle plane housing the energies and forces of life.

Obviously it is due to some unalterable feature of yogic perception that Vishnu is invariably shown to be sky blue in complexion. His incarnations, Rama or Krishna, are also depicted in the same color. In fact, one of the most popular words used to describe Krishna is shyama, that is, bluish in color. What is the significance of the blue complexion or its association with the color of clouds or the gathering shades at dusk?

Heinrich Zimmer himself admits that the Indian myths are meant to express in a popular form the lessons or experiences of yoga. He says: "The aim of the doctrines of Hindu philosophy and of the trainings in yoga practice is to transcend the limits of individualized consciousness. The mythical tales are meant to convey the wisdom of the philosophers and to exhibit in a popular, pictorial form the experience or results of yoga."[3]

But the yogic experience itself is based on kundalini. The amazing phenomena attending the arousal of the serpent power creates a revolution in the human mind that has no parallel in the mundane world. Both Indian philosophy and mythological lore are a product of this revolution. The manuals on yoga are explicit on this issue. The whole adventure of yoga is but a play of the pranic force or, in other words, bioenergy. The aim of pranayama (breathing practices) is the regulation and control of prana. The coldness of the body of a yogi in samadhi is associated with the experience because a highly enhanced measure of prana flows to the head of the successful yogi, thus reducing external temperature.

All that is encountered in samadhi is the state of consciousness radically altered by the action of pranic radiation on the brain. The experience can be so intensely absorbing and extensively varied that even the voluminous literature devoted to it in India—Vedic, puranic, or tantric—does not suffice to portray even a fraction of it.

Why Lord Vishnu is depicted sky blue in color and his spouse, Lakshmi, white or golden hued, is clearly explained in the esoteric treatises on the serpent power. The illuminated sage, when turning his attention on himself, is lost in the immensity of his now highly extended world of awareness, shining like the starlit sky at night, infinite and unfathomable, fed by the milky ocean of prana in the body. But when the same sage looks out, he perceives the external world bathed in a living luster of silvery hue or snowy whiteness, tinged with gold, forming part of a mighty presence which encompasses all.

Hence kundalini or Durga or Shakti or Lakshmi (spouse of Vishnu) or Parvati (spouse of Shiva) is shown white or golden in color, and Lord Vishnu (universal consciousness experienced inwardly), sky blue in complexion.

For the worshipers of Shakti, the samadhi of yoga represents her withdrawal from the world of name and form and absorption or laya in universal consciousness of Shiva. The world which she creates is dissolved as she ascends by stages from the muladhara chakra at the base of the spine to the topmost chakra in the head. The ponderous outer world seems to fuse with consciousness, when Shiva and Shakti unite in the sahasrara, the seventh center in the brain. In the higher dimension of consciousness induced by samadhi, on the awakening of kundalini, the cosmic scene appears to be a projection of the observer, a gigantic reflection mirrored by the mind in an inexplicable way. When the samadhi grows deeper even the image melts, leaving consciousness the sole actor on the scene.

The skylike aspect of kundalini is described in the *Panchastavi* in these words: "In the mind of fortunate devotees, O, Mother, Thou manifestest Thyself as the glowing sky, as Bindu (infinity), as Nada (the cosmic sound), as the crescent of the moon, as the fount of expression (genius), as Mother, and as the source of the nectar of Jnana (supernal knowledge)."

The same idea about the blue aspect of the inner manifestation is expressed by *Saundarya Lahari* thusly: "O, Spouse of Shiva, may Thou graciously bathe even me, who stands helpless at a far off distance, with Thy far-reaching glance, beautiful like the slightly blossomed blue lily. This (mortal) will derive the sumnum bonum of existence from such action. . . ."

At another place it says: "O Spouse of Shiva, may Thy lock of hair, which resembles an expanse of blue lilies in bloom, and which is thick, shining and soft, drive away our (internal) darkness." The esoteric writings on kundalini contain a mine of information about the potentialities of kundalini. With exhaustive study they can prove of immense value to scholars engaged in research on consciousness. Brahma, whose seat is on the lotus springing from the navel of Vishnu, is ruddy in complexion as compared to the inscrutable deep blue of twilight color of the latter. He has four faces and holds the Vedas in his hands.

The four faces of Brahma cover the four quarters of space. He holds the four Vedas in his hands because the Vedas are "Shruti," that is, revealed. Revelation is a part of the creative play of Shakti. Brahma is kundalini in her creative aspect. Like her, he is lotus born; like her he is red in color; like her he is the bearer of revelation; and, like her, he is the creator of the phenomenal world. Shakti as Lakshmi is in every way associated with the lotus. She is "lotus born," "seated on a lotus," "lotus colored," "lotus eyed," and the like.

The ascent of kundalini from the muladhara to the head center is known as laya krama or the process of dissolution.

As she pierces each chakra, the world image of ordinary perception recedes further and further, dissolving as it were into the ever-expanding pool of consciousness, until it completely fades away from vision at the seventh center in the brain. After a spell of intense absorption and bliss the Shakti descends again, recreating the world step by step in the same way as she had dissolved it at the time of her ascent. This is known as srishti krama or the process of creation.

In the ascending scale the various tattvas (elements) associated with the six chakras from muladhara to ajna chakra are: earth, water, fire, air, ether, and mind. The ponderous physical world passes from its grosser to subtler constituents after the third or navel chakra associated with fire and sight. The remaining three tattvas, air, ether, and mind—are invisible to the eye. From this stage the world image begins to melt into its subtler components until in the seventh center it vanishes altogether.

On the descent of kundalini the world picture begins to form again in its gross, visible form from the navel center where, on the body of the sleeping Vishnu, Brahma the creator emerges with the three-dimensional world of matter, space, and time. The recumbent giant form of Vishnu depicts the Turiya or transcendent plane of universal consciousness beyond the mortal sphere of time and space.

Lakshmi is sitting at the feet of Vishnu because as Shakti she is the earth, the matrix from which life is born. In the individual body she lies coiled at the muladhara chakra, associated with the tattva of earth. With one of her hands she strokes his leg, an office sometimes performed by loving Hindu wives towards their husbands. Here again, the significance runs deeper. The stroking or caressing betokens the intensely pleasing sensations arising from the touch of a beloved person. This denotes the transportingly blissful nature of the sleep caused by the rapturous flow of the supernal prana into the brain, leading to the ecstatic union of Shakti (Lakshmi) with the conscious principle (Vishnu) in the sahasrara or the thousand-petaled lotus in the head. The serpent, Shesha-Naga, has a thousand heads, denoting the mechanism of kundalini terminating in the multipetaled lotus in the brain.

The ocean of milk, honey or nectar refers to the unlimited pranic content of the body. "The Shakti resides in the center of the ocean of nectar," says *Lalita-Sahasranaman*. The allegoric representation of Shakti as the ocean of milk is unmistakably brought out in *Panchastavi* in the following verse:

> Those devotees who, in all humility, meditate on Thee, dwelling in their minds on Thy form like the orb of the full moon, or a vast ocean of milk (heaving) with waves of elixir, resembling globes of concentrated nectar, (white) like snow, they (even though) afflicted by sorrows and calamities attain to spiritual and temporal prosperity (by Thy grace).

Modern scholars have omitted to take cognizance of the important fact that there must be a vital fuel to sustain the activity of life. All the billions of cells in the body of an animal or a plant are connected to each other and act in unison in the various organs and limbs towards a common end, always motivated by a common purpose. When disorganization occurs in this unity among the parts or tissues of an organism it ceases to exist. The vital force that keeps our body alive and whole is prana, life energy, bioplasma, orgone, or odic force —call it what you will—which is still unknown to science.

Every organic cell in a living body is a mighty storehouse of psychic energy. We rarely take cognizance of this fact, when we reflect on the mechanism of life, just as we never took cognizance of the awful force present in every grain of matter before the discovery of the energy structure of the atom. This is a point which modern scientists and thinkers completely lose sight of in their speculations about mind and consciousness.

The extremely dim glimmer of sentience that regulates the conduct of a single cell, when combined and magnified with the marvelous mechanism of the human cerebrospinal system, gives rise to the wonderful world of awareness present in us. The pattern and volume of the mental activity exhibited by a human being or an animal depends solely on the pattern and volume of the bioenergy supplied to the brain. When this supply fails, the connecting link between the organism and the world of life is cut off and death ensues.

Milk denotes the primary form of nourishment on which

the human infant or the young of an animal lives and grows. In this sense, prana is the nourishing substance on which the brain depends for its life. The latest researches on the brain reveal no perceptible differences in the cranial structure of a genius and a man of ordinary or low intelligence. The examination of an unidentified brain can afford no clue to a scientist about the degree of intelligence exhibited by its owner. What can then be the cause of such wide divergence between the intellectual level of man and man and the fluctuations in the efficiency level of a particular brain at different times or during different periods of life?

There must be certain highly complex and sensitive substances which in an organic structure combine to give rise to awareness in the form in which we see it exhibited in animals and humans. The special substances used in the formation of brain matter and the nerves confirm this view. But what energy is used by this specially constructed organ and its vast network of nerves to sustain the play of our imagination and thought in man or the instinct-conditioned mental activity in animals? To what do we owe the prodigious leaps taken by certain specially gifted individual brains which even the combined thinking of a million average heads cannot match?

What is the mystery behind this remarkable phenomenon, repeated through history, which provided the one single unpredictable natural stairway by which mankind has climbed to its present height—genius and revelation?

The traditional portrait of Lord Vishnu contains an answer to this problem. It is the thousand-headed snake, floating on the ocean of milk or, in other words, the ocean of bioplasma in the human body. This bioplasma, culled from each and every cell of the organism by the ubiquitous nerves which, when aroused, can enhance the supply of the life fuel to the brain to an almost unlimited extent in a constant stream flowing up through the spinal cord. The stream is gathered from the endless pranic fuel contained in each cell, collected by the nerves. Since, like the atom, each cell is a dynamo of flowing life energy, there is no fear of diminution of the stream to the brain till the end of life.

The male generative fluid, semen, bears a resemblance to milk. According to the notions of the Indian masters, the essence of the reproductive substance pervades the whole body. Since the ancient systems of yoga were mainly oriented for men, it is not surprising that in the concept of the ocean of milk, only the male reproductive secretion has been kept in view. Considered in a metaphorical sense, the belief is in harmony with the current view. The whole cellular structure of the human body has the genetic principles present in it. From the point of view of the bioplasma also, every cell is a radial center of this energy. The activation of kundalini merely makes use of a potential already present in the body. The evolutionary mechanism is constructed in a way that, by stimulation through certain disciplines or of its own accord when ripe for the experience, it can be activated in a manner that makes the human body a virtual dynamo of live electricity or psychic energy which can stream into the brain with shattering effect.

In fact, it is this transition of the human organism from the normal condition to the state of a powerful generating plant of high-grade bioplasma which is designated as the arousal of kundalini. Every neuron in the brain, every nerve, and every nerve filament becomes a participant in this whirlwind activity that starts in the body on the awakening of the serpent power.

It is to this special aspect of kundalini that I wish to draw the attention of the world of science. The body of an individual in whom the power has been activated presents such a marvelous picture of extraordinary nervous activity in all the tissues and fibers that no physiologist can fail to notice it. The tornado of psychic forces sweeping through the organism becomes clearly perceptible to the initiate subjectively and objectively both. It is for this reason that from remote times the phenomenon has been ascribed to the operation of supernatural forces on which one could have no control. That is why an untameable colossal serpent forms the seat of Lord Vishnu interposing its huge body between him and the ocean of milk.

This symbolic image of Vishnu has been discussed to show the antiquity of the science and the stupendous implications of what it portends for mankind. If kundalini is the basic factor responsible for human evolution as also for the growth of intellect, talent and genius in individuals, then the incalculable value of the knowledge and magnitude of the research that would demonstrate the existence of this psychic power reservoir can be better imagined than described. It would then clearly mean that with the proper direction of life, earnest seekers can reach not only these rare heights of genius and talent, of which we have had a few illustrious examples in the past, but also a surpassing state of transcendent consciousness by voluntary cultivation that has no parallel in the ordinary life of man.

REFERENCES

1. Sheila Ostrander and Lynn Schroeder, *Psychic Discoveries Behind the Iron Curtain* (Englewood Cliffs, N.J.: Prentice-Hall, 1970).
2. Wilhelm Reich, *The Function of the Orgasm* (New York: Farrar, Strauss & Giroux, 1973).
3. Heinrich Zimmer, *Myths and Symbols in Indian Art and Civilization* (Princeton, N.J.: Princeton University Press, 1971).

9.

The Energy Behind True Magic

W. E. BUTLER

The term "magnetism" is an unfortunate one when we are considering the subtle force which is one of the principle factors in magical work. The use of the word comes from the experimental work of the followers of Mesmer, and though they did attempt to make it clear that the subtle energy which, according to their philosophy, permeated the whole universe was *not* the phenomenon which the scientist terms "magnetism," the misuse of the word has persisted up to the present day. The mesmerists termed this subtle force "animal magnetism" since they stated it was the power which accompanied physical magnetism, but which was also found in all living things.

At a later date the German, Baron von Reichenbach, studied the subject exhaustively, and his findings have much of value for the practical magician. As far as it has been possible for the present writer to check his results, they appear to be correct, and as they certainly enter into all magical work, it may be helpful if we give here a general outline of them.

Briefly, von Reichenbach stated that there was a force which, without being identifiable with them, yet seemed to underlie the physical forces of electricity, magnetism, light, and heat. To this force he gave the name of "od."

Through his researches, he came to the conclusion that this "odic force" was, as he put it, "the odic garment of the universe," present everywhere, but manifesting most strongly in certain things.

"The Energy Behind True Magic" by W. E. Butler is excerpted from *The Magician: His Training and Work* by W. E. Butler and reprinted by permission of Thorsons Publishers Limited.

Such things are the light radiations from the stars and the sun, all crystalline bodies, "permanent magnets," and "electromagnets," chemical action of all kinds, and most important of all, living vegetable, animal, and human organisms.

In some magical lodges, a great deal of experimental work has been done upon this particular subject, and we may here indicate some of the conclusions reached. It must be remembered that thousands of experiments have been made and the results tabulated in the lodge archives. Dr. J. B. Rhine and his followers are not the only, or even the first, workers in this field!

All living animal forms appear to have two vertical definite "poles," to use the magnetic term. The right side of the body is of one polarity and the left side of the reverse odic polarity. There is also a horizontal polarity; the upper part of the body being of one polarity and the lower half of the opposite polarity. The same applies to living vegetable forms.

The vibrations of sound have the power of liberating the odic force, and combustion which is, of course, a form of chemical action, does the same.

All substances radiate their own quality of "odic" force, as do also all electrical manifestations. In connection with this latter, a very interesting series of experiments was made at the Theosophical Research Centre, using the clairvoyant faculty of one of the members: Mr. Geoffrey Hodson. It was found that he could correctly indicate when a current of electricity was flowing in a wire placed before him, the pushbutton controlling the current being actuated by someone in another room.

It is of interest to note that it was the sensations experienced by a Bishop of the Protestant Episcopal Church in America when, even in total darkness, he accidentally touched anything made of brass, which led to investigations by Professor Buchanan and Dr. Denton into the phenomenon now known as "psychometry."

In certain magical work, use is made of the breath of the operator, and in the Catholic ritual used every year for the consecration of the "Holy Oils" the Bishop and his attendant priests breathe over the oils in the sign of the Cross. This particular use of the breath, apart from the symbolism as explained by theologians, is based upon the fact that the breath is strongly charged with the odic energy.

But the whole body radiates this energy . . . and the odic field of force around every person has received the name of the "health aura," since its appearance indicates to the trained seer the health conditions of the physical body.

Vital energy *of all types* is drawn into the etheric body and specialized for use therein. The surplus is radiated out and forms an energy field around the body. The late Dr. [Walter] Kilner* by the use of dicyanin screens observed and recorded the health indications given by the "etheric aura," as this field of living force is called.

It has been established that the "auric fields" of human beings tend to affect each other in various ways. Some auras unite easily with certain other auras, but are strongly repellent to others. Since such attraction and repulsion induces certain subconscious and conscious reactions, it is essential that the operators in a magical ceremonial should be magnetically in harmony, as the blending of their auras is one of the foundations upon which the ceremony rests.

It is of interest to note in this connection, that there are certain people whose auric energy seems to act as an "enzyme" or ferment, and in their presence even opposing auras seem temporarily to blend. Such people are invaluable in lodge working, since the lodge phenomena work through such a blended aura.

They are of the greatest value in spiritualistic "seances," when their presence will often turn what would have been a failure into a successful sitting. It has been noted, in this connection, that many of these human "enzymes" are of the auburn and redheaded types.

It is obvious that each individual brings his own unique potentialities into magical lodge and psychic circle alike, and the unfoldment of these powers, and their interaction with the powers of others in the lodge, not only opens up many possibilities, but also presents the lodge with new problems. It is true that the lodges have through the centuries built up a fairly comprehensive body of knowledge by means of which

* See his book *The Human Aura*. Editors.

they can meet such problems, but at the same time, since these powers are emerging under modern conditions, and new types of psychic make-up are coming into the lodges, there will always be forces and combinations of those forces which will tax the powers of the rulers thereof.

It is important to remember that the operation of any power or force in the human personality has its *subjective* side, and the subjective expression of "magnetism" is "emotion." For the purposes of the magician, magnetism and emotion are the same.

Stir the emotions, and the magnetic flow increases. Induce the magnetic flow, and emotions arise.

This is very apparent in the relationship between the sexes; indeed a certain debased form of the *tantric* magic deliberately makes use of this for its own not very exalted purposes, and this not in the East alone![1] Physical movements of a rhythmic type also tend to liberate magnetism, and certain forms of musical sound do the same.

To the clairvoyant vision, the psychic atmosphere of a dance hall presents a most interesting spectacle, particularly when certain forms of music of negroid origin are used.

It is clear that many people would seem to possess very little emotional force indeed. They appear to be, and often are, frigid both in their everyday life and in their sexual outlook. Psychologists know, however, that in many of these cases, the lack of emotional drive is the sign that the greater part of the emotional power of the personality has for some reason or other been locked up below the threshold of the conscious mind, and is therefore not available for conscious use. The methods of psychoanalysis are said to disperse the repressed emotional forces, and allow them to rise freely into consciousness, there to be integrated into the normal emotional circuit. Such a release of suppressed energy supposedly restores normality, and the abnormal frigidity of body and mind disappears.

In the magical lodge, this redirection of the emotional energies also takes place, partly due to the emotion-stirring ritual, and partly due to the inclusion of the individual in the general magnetic circulation of the lodge. Under the graded system of the Western lodges, as also under the *guru-chela* relationship existing in the East between the teacher and his pupil or apprentice, this redirection of the emotional energy and its accompanying magnetism takes place gradually and under control. When, however, one is working alone, or with only one or two fellow-workers, care has to be taken that the magnetic energy does not escape from control.

There is, as a matter of psychic observation, a constant circulation which goes on in the finer bodies of humans, and this process is easily affected by the mind. This mental control is exercised involuntarily and pathologically in the cases of suppression and mental dissociation, but it is part of the magical training for the aspirant to gain the power of conscious control of the magnetic energies. If these energies are aroused or liberated or increased (all perfectly valid lines of action), their corresponding mental channels and physical expression must be so directed and adjusted that the turbulent stream of energy may be safely diverted into the fertilizing irrigation channels instead of sweeping chaotically over all the mental and emotional field.

Such enlarged and controllable channels are provided by the magical ritual if it is properly carried out, and for this reason alone, ritual magic can be a safer and more efficient method than any amount of Freudian psychoanalysis.

As we have pointed out, the psychomagnetic flow of energy can be controlled by the mind, and in this way the available magnetism may be increased not merely by the release of suppressed energies but by an increase in the actual intake of those energies. One of the methods, and when properly employed one of the best, is the exercise which we have described more fully elsewhere: the key exercise of the Interwoven Light.

Now the human personality receives energy from two sources, and one of these, "elemental energy," flows in through the etheric body. It is to be remembered that this magnetic force, though it has many effects upon the physical body, circulates in, and through, the etheric body. There are, of course, detectable electric currents in the physical body, but this still more subtle force is not part of the physical forces, though its operation may be determined by the position and action of the physical vehicle, since the etheric body and the physical are interlocked most closely. This is the basis of so many of the yogic *asanas,* or postures; they determine the circuit in which the magnetic energies may flow.

It will have been noticed that we have used a special term "elemental energy" to describe this subtle force. This has been done for two reasons. It is the term used in the particular occult fraternity in which the present writer received much of his training, and by using the term one covers all the various names, magnetism, odic force, prana, etc.

There remain two points to be borne in mind by the magical apprentice. The first is that this elemental energy in one of its forms is the underlying "prematter" from which physical matter as we know it is condensed or "materialized." It therefore equates with the prana of the Hindu systems. Many Western students, misled by some of the popular presentations of the Eastern systems of yoga, limit the term prana to that aspect of it which is utilized in the exercises of *pranayama,* or breathing-control.

But in the philosophy which underlies the yoga systems, the term prana is much more comprehensive. The earthly prana, which manifests in all the living beings and organisms found on Earth, is a modification of the solar prana, which in its turn is a modification of the cosmic prana which is the undifferentiated cosmic matter termed *prakriti.*[2] This is mentioned here in order to maintain the correct perspective in the student's mind. In one of the cryptic texts of the *Sepher Yetzirah,* it is said that "the Tenth Path (*Malkuth*) causes an influence to emanate from the Prince of Countenances, the Angel of *Kether* (the highest point of the Tree of Life)." In other words, by our actions in earthly matter and prematter we are also acting on and reacting to the highest spiritual levels.

All magical work must be seen in this perspective if the magical apprentice is to become anything more than a mere "sorcerer," a meddler with occult forces. It is for this reason and as a potent reminder of it, that the magician, during his operations, wears upon his breast what is known as the "lamen." This is a symbol which represents the spiritual aspect of the work in which he is engaged, and it is by virtue of this spiritual intention that he asserts dominance and control over the creatures of the elements.

To return to our consideration of the elemental energy. The key to its use is that it can be "tied," mentally, to the breath, which in itself is said to be an expression of the dual energy of the eternal, the outbreathing and inbreathing of Brahman. The actual exercises are simple and tedious! The ones which form the foundation of such control of prana are given [elsewhere] but, of course, there are many variants and specific adaptations of the basic exercises. Before the student attempts any of them, it is imperative that *he learns to do them without any strain.* This is the most important rule, and any infringement of it may lead to most unwelcome results.

In practical training, therefore, the apprentice magician learns to release the body mechanism from the convulsive grip of the conscious mind. This is done by the exercise known as the "relaxation exercise. . . ."

Once control over the intake of the elemental energy has been obtained, such energy may be dealt with in various ways. It may be used within the student's own etheric and physical bodies, and very real self-healing may be brought about thereby. Or it may be directed outwardly on to people and things, producing very real effects thereby.

When considering its use in the physical and psychic bodies, it should always be remembered that it is quite possible, if the student is careless or pays no attention to instructions, to disorganize seriously the subconscious psychological workings of the body, and many students have found this out, to their cost. Undue concentration upon any one of the psychic centers or *chakras* should be avoided for this reason, if for none other. The great psychic centers lie close to, and directly influence the endocrine, or ductless, glands, which play such a great part in the chemistry of the body. To stimulate the centers in a balanced way is one thing; to disorganize the entire physical economy is quite another!

When the elemental energy is projected outward towards others or towards other objects, then it may be used for healing, for the spiritual illumination and initiation of those persons, or for hurt and deceptive illusion, according to the spiritual status and intention of the magician. These are, of course, the two poles of such activity.

In practical experience, most of the magicians with whom we have come into contact seem to work somewhere between these two opposites, veering one way and the other as they react to their own inner nature.

Although, theoretically, the elemental energy can be projected without any physical action, i.e., by mental effort alone, it has been found in practice that this projection is far more thorough and efficient when certain gestures and signs are employed, and certain definite thoughtforms built up. . . . They are designed to act as vehicles for the elemental energy, and may be so used.

It is important that the magician keep ever before him the key idea that though he may draw down spiritual power from the heights, he must, if he is to give that power full expression, draw up from the earth soul that elemental force which, as it ascends within him, changes its nature of manifestation from crude sex energy, as it passes through the center attributed by the Cabbalists to *yesod*, to a radiating and harmonizing force as it passes through the center of *tiphareth*.

This harmonized energy may now be discharged into the mental forms which have been built, and will truly serve as an effective link between the spiritual forces invoked, and the thoughtforms through which they manifest.

Most thoughtforms partake of the nature of the sparks from the smith's anvil. These fly upwards for a foot or so, and are extinguished. So most of the thoughtforms created by the average person never leave the aura of their creator. Only when they have already been charged and vitalized by the elemental energy have they sufficient power to go forth. And in this connection we would again repeat, emotion and magnetism go together. A long continued emotional "brooding over" some problem will generate and charge some pretty effective thoughtforms. Though such emotional brooding is usually employed in the wrong way, it can and *must* be used in a constructive spiritual way by the aspirant to the magic of light.

REFERENCES

1. It will be noticed that we refer to a debased form of Tantra. This philosophic and occult system has also its heights as well as its depths, a point often forgotten by many occult students.
2. This is more fully worked out in the Sanskrit work, the *Shivagama,* one chapter of which deals entirely with this energy and its modifications.

10.

Wilhelm Reich and Orgone Energy

W. EDWARD MANN

Wilhelm Reich (1897–1957), the discoverer of orgone energy, evolved his theory from observations made first on human sexual functioning and, later, biological experiments. Born in Austria of Jewish parents, he studied medicine, and then specialized in psychoanalysis under Freud.

Four of Reich's early works are worth brief outline here. The first, *The Function of the Orgasm*, explored the bioenergetic aspects of neurotic and healthy sex behavior. It claimed that the biological function of the orgasm was to discharge pent-up emotions and energies, some due to frustrations, and therefore help restore the organism to a healthy biological equilibrium. Another, *Sexual Revolution*, dealt with the repressive character of sexual norms in Western society, their links with the authoritarian family and how a self-regulative sex economy (or system) ought to be structured. Throughout this book he showed an unusual sensitivity to the necessary association between sexual satisfactions, love and tender feelings, and familial and social pressures with respect to feelings and one's self-expression.

The third book, written in Scandinavia after having fled Nazi Germany, was the *Mass Psychology of Fascism*. This was a brilliant attempt to explain how the German nation, with its illustrious humanist tradition, could have succumbed to Hitler. Reich pointed the finger at Germany's authoritarian social patterns, especially the authoritarian sex-repressive family system. He claimed that Hitler mobilized the repressed energies,

"Wilhelm Reich and Orgone Energy" by W. Edward Mann is an original article written especially for this volume and is printed by permission of the author.

focused by the economic depression, through various symbols and techniques that channeled these energies into mystical identifications.

The most widely acclaimed book of this period was *Character Analysis*. This set forth Reich's original thinking regarding basic character types, and specifically dealt with the relation between character defenses (discovered in therapy) and what he called "character" or "bodily armor." Basically, his theory maintained that bioenergy, traveling normally through the body in a specific circuit, gets trapped wherever muscles —e.g., in the neck or pelvis—have become chronically tight, hard, and spastic. Holding in emotions rather than expressing them can cause a tightening of specific muscle groups—"armoring"—so that the flow of energy gets blocked in these regions. Continued for years, chronic armoring not only greatly reduces the bioenergy at the disposal of the organism, but can lead to poor health and even specific physical diseases. Reich's conclusion was that to be successful, psychoanalysis had to tackle character defenses head on and dissolve them and the patterns of bodily armoring with which they were associated. Reich's theory of orgone energy flowed directly from these earlier writings, beginning with the *Function of the Orgasm,* which stressed the necessity of natural orgasm.

From clinical experience he believed that inadequate orgasmic discharge left surplus energy in the body that could power secondary and often unhealthy drives. Ola Raknes sums up Reich's insights on orgasm as follows: "A healthy sex life depends on a complete convulsive discharge of sexual energy in the embrace of a beloved partner . . . with momentary loss of consciousness. The capacity for such an experience Reich termed orgasmic potency." Continued work led Reich to postulate an orgasm formula—later called the "formula of biological tension and charge." This formula pinpointed the energy process in the orgasm, as having four beats: mechanical tension, bioelectric charge, bioelectric discharge, and relaxation.

After leaving Germany, Reich's researches on the bioelectrical components of sexuality led to a new set of inquiries which by 1939 revealed the existence of the orgone. Experiments conducted at the Institute of Psychology of the University of Oslo (from 1934 to 1936) had measured on an oscillograph the variations in the skin's electrical potential when it was touched in a way that provoked pleasure or anxiety. Results showed that skin potential climbed with pleasurable feeling and fell with anxiety.

Other experiments with various sexual acts of animals and humans indicated that the movement of a specific bioelectrical energy was actuated by such acts as kissing or petting. Reich now spoke of "bioelectricity" and this concept became the forerunner of the biological energy, orgone, a term that took its name from "organism," and "orgasm," since it was the study of sexuality that led to its discovery.

Experiments conducted in Oslo, designed to identify the basic qualities of life, led directly to the discovery of the orgone. In these experiments Reich took organic material such as dry moss or grass, heated it to a high temperature and allowed it to swell in sterilized water. Microscopic examination showed that small vesicles would develop, detach themselves from the grass, and that they were capable of spontaneous expansion and contraction like protozoa. After a while, they would gather in heaps, surround themselves with membranes, and start moving like protozoa. In other experiments, inorganic materials such as coal, dust, or rust were heated to incandescence in a gas flame and, while aglow, were put into a sterile nutritive solution. While in this solution some of the particles would swell into vesicles that moved like those particles of more organic origin. Although critics thought these vesicle movements were well-known molecular Brownian movements, Reich and his associates denied this and claimed they were soft and organic and showed inner pulsation, while the latter were angular and mechanical. Reich labeled these energy vesicles "bions," and in their tendency to organize into cells like protozoa, he saw a demonstration of the very origin of life.

Certain bions were produced from beach sand, and the resulting growth, when inoculated on egg medium and agar, consisted of large, intensely blue packets of vesicles. Under microscopic investigation ($2,000-4,000\times$) these bions seemed to consist of 6–10 vesicles. They refracted light and possessed great energetic strength: they killed or paralyzed nearby cancer cells. Reich labeled them "SAPA (from *sand packet*) bions," having a sand base, and began to study them intensely. He found out that daily microscopic examination produced eye inflammation, and if a culture of them was held in the hand, it caused skin irritation. A strange new radiation was apparently at work!

Other tests were made. While they did not directly affect an electroscope, rubber gloves left near these SAPA bions did produce a strong reaction on an electroscope. Organic substances like cotton or cellulose similarly absorbed SAPA energy, according to the electroscope test. Looking at SAPA bions at night in an enclosed space, Reich saw foglike emanations and bluish dots and lines of light. After prolonged exposure the blue glimmer would then be visible as a slowly moving gray-blue vapor around one's body and objects in the room. Other experiments—e.g., leaving rubber gloves in direct sunlight or on the stomach of a vegetatively active person for fifteen minutes—seemed to charge them with the same energy. Reich concluded that the energy was present in organisms, that it comes from the sun, and is present everywhere.

Reich began to study the SAPA bion culture, placing it in a box lined with metal and an outer layer of organic material. This outer layer was supposed to inhibit the emanation to the outside. However, after removing the SAPA culture and washing the metal walls, he still perceived the same bluish emanation. In brief the boxes which began as observation chambers were found to "draw in" orgone and eventually were labeled orgone accumulators. Experiments proved that the greater the layering of the walls, the greater—up to a point—the concentration or amount of orgone. In time, accumulators of up to twenty layers were built.

Convinced now of orgone's existence in the atmosphere, Reich began to look for it visually. He used a wooden tube fitted with a magnifying glass, which he called an orgonoscope, and observed the sky. At night he noticed a flickering especially pronounced in the darkest spots between the stars. The same flickering was visible on white clouds in the daytime, and could even be seen by looking relaxedly at a white table or door. Since the orgonoscope magnified it, he felt it was not subjective. Looking at the blue sky in the daytime, one could see dancing dots of light, pinpricks which seemed to assume an arclike configuration. (Some have called these the vitality globules that yogic tradition speaks of and see them as evidence for *prana*, a Sanskrit term for the basic life force.) Among other things, these visual phenomena were considered evidence for the atmospheric orgone. Another manifestation was the blue haze commonly observed over wooded areas.

In the late 1940s, Reich began a series of tests to demonstrate this energy scientifically. The first of these was focused on the production of heat inside the orgone box. Originally he built small orgone accumulators about one foot square, made of alternating layers of metal (galvanized iron or steel) and cellulose or other organic materials. For a control he would construct a box of the same size but made simply of wood. A finely graded thermometer placed just above the box within an enclosure or inside the box through a hole recorded higher temperatures for the orgone box than the control box. Observed throughout the day, it was noticed that this temperature difference was small at sunrise, perhaps $0.2°$ C, and would rise to around $1°$ or $1.5°$ C by 2 or 3 p.m. when the Sun's heat was maximal, and then decline by evening to a fraction of 1 degree. If the boxes were inserted into earth, the temperature difference rose from five to ten degrees. On wet humid days the heat difference was minimal, perhaps reaching a maximum of $0.3°$ C. This confirmed Reich's observation that the flickering in the sky was much less clear on wet or humid days. And he realized that water had a special affinity for orgone, drawing it to itself. These thermal tests of the orgone have been duplicated a number of times by followers of Reich who have published their findings in journals such as the *Orgone Energy Bulletin* and the *Journal of Orgonomy*.*

Another demonstration of Reich's showed that vacuum tubes left inside an orgone accumulator for a few days turned a deep blue in color when excited by electricity. This confirmed the visual impression that the orgone's color—as seen, for example, in the orgone box and in SAPA bions—is blue. Dr. Bizzi, an Italian psychiatrist and mental hospital vice-director, has, among others, duplicated this experiment. Un-

* See listings in Appendix III. *Editors.*

der specific conditions, a vacuum tube excited by body orgone or orgone from a secondary coil system showed lumination. These Reich called vacor tubes; they were used in experiments discussed later in this article, with the orgone motor.

In 1947, in order to determine whether orgone energy is identical with cosmic ray radiation, Reich purchased a Geiger–Muller portable field set, used to measure x rays and gamma rays, and experimented with the effect of orgone on the geiger counter. He carried it through the orgone laboratory and put it in orgone accumulators. At first there was no difference in reaction to the usual background of several clicks per minute. On the second or third day the number of clicks heard decreased a little. After the third day no clicks were heard, something unheard of in a properly functioning geiger counter. This suggested to Reich that concentrated orgone extinguishes electromagnetic energy. This confirmed an observation made earlier when a glass plate coated with radium was put near SAPA bions, and the typical glow was replaced with a vivid glimmering.

After the geiger counter had looked dead for a number of weeks, it suddenly began giving off a strong reaction of one hundred clicks and then thousands per minute. The impulse counter was turning sixty or more times a minute. These observations were most unusual and Reich had a number of observers sign a notarized affidavit that it actually happened. Orgone energetic reactions could now be objectified by the use of geiger counters whose tubes had been changed by "soaking" in an orgone atmosphere.

Reich realized that any energy which could turn the geiger counter so fast had motor potentials. He succeeded in getting 200,000 impulses per minute by June of 1948 and set a motor (Western Electric model KS-9154, Serial No. 1227) in motion. The article about this mentions that he used an activated filament of electronic amplifiers, with a low voltage, to get his orgone motor going. It had a secret component which he labeled "Y," and the demonstration of its power was seen and attested to by five co-workers. Reich maintained that the speed of this motor could be regulated and that its action depended upon the weather conditions prevailing (and the number of vacor tubes used) so that it had more potential on bright sunny days. Until very recently it appears that no orthodox Reichians have bothered to work at or perfect this ingenious device that draws on the free energy of the atmosphere, but now a group is attempting to duplicate what Reich accomplished.

A crucial issue, still not fully resolved, is the connection between orgone and static electricity. A number of crucial experiments were carried out to elucidate this question, and these and Reich's conclusions were set forth in a long article published in October 1944, in his *International Journal of Sex Economy and Orgone Research* under the title "Orgonotic Pulsation." This article was ingeniously set up as a discussion between Reich and an electrophysicist. Near the beginning of the article, Reich sets forth certain simple and basic differences between electricity and orgone: (1) electricity is bipolar, while orgone is unitary; (2) the slow, wavelike motions of living tissues (produced by orgone) are at variance with the rapid angular motions of electricity; (3) electrical stimuli result in body sensations, but these are alien to the organism, they have a disturbing effect, and they are at variance with organic sensations; (4) orgone's motion through the body is quite slow compared with the speed of electromagnetic radiation.

The article notes that orgone can take three different forms. In an orgone accumulator at night it has a bluish-gray color. There are also small bluish dots which seem to fly by. Reich described how the bluish dots "seem to come out of the [accumulator] walls at rhythmical intervals. As they move they seem to contract and expand. When flying by sidewise, they take a trajectory similar to a parabola. This trajectory is interrupted by looplike forms. Then if one uses a green bulb for light, one sees both a blue-violet light and yellowish-white rays which move very rapidly in all directions. It looks like miniature fireworks." In short, various experiments indicate that the orgone can appear as "blue-gray vapors, blue-violet dots which float slowly and form loops at regular intervals, and rapid, straight yellowish rays." Other experiments indicated that the orgone disturbs voltmeters and magnetic needles. For example, if a polystyrene rod is drawn through one's hair and moved past a voltmeter slowly, at a distance of two to five centimeters, the pointer is deflected according to the way the rod is moved.

Reich then argues that static electricity is fundamentally different from the electromagnetic energy discovered by Volta and Faraday, and that it is equivalent to the orgone. Thus the electroscope, which tests for static electricity, he renamed an orgonometer. Many of these tests have been successfully repeated by current orgonomic scientists (see the *Journal of Orgonomy,* 1969 and 1970).

By the early 1940s, Reich—now living in the United States—had begun to make orgone accumulators of various sizes to experiment with the curative powers of the orgone they concentrated. Small accumulators were made for tests with cancerous mice. The large accumulators, made for human beings, were not unlike a phone booth in size. Whether large or small, the principle was simple: layer metal (but not aluminum) with an organic material like cellulose or fiberglass. The more layers in the box, the greater the amount of orgone concentrated. The inside layer was always metallic, and the animal or human had to have part of his body within a few inches of the sides. Reich theorized that the animal or human body gave off an orgone field, and this had to interact with that given off by the box for any charging to be effected. Humans usually sat in the box for up to an hour at a time.

Tests demonstrated that orgone accumulators had definite but limited therapeutic effects. Cancerous mice with implanted tumors lived on the average several months longer than controls. (Double blind tests were not conducted at this time because their importance was still not widely recognized.) With humans, the pain accompanying cancer or arthritis was relieved and the disease seemed retarded. Some breast cancers shrank noticeably in size after orgone box treatments of one hour per day for a number of weeks. While these patients and others with cancer lived beyond regular medical prognosis, they usually died from liver or kidney breakdown, as these organs were unable to handle the extra toxins in the system from the disintegrating cancerous tissue.

A more portable and cheaper device is the orgone blanket, which Reich began to utilize in the early 1950s for less serious illnesses. It is usually made to any reasonable size (perhaps 2×3 ft^2) of steel wool and either wool, silk or cotton. Alternately layer the materials—wool, steel wool/wool, steel wool/etc.—for four or five layers of each, and then sew around the outside. These are placed over the body, usually over the area of the physical disturbance. A full discussion of these blankets and their uses is given in my recent book, *Orgone, Reich, & Eros*.

Another simply constructed device made in the late 1940s was called the orgone shooter. The aim was to "shoot" a good deal of orgone at a small area of the body and hasten the healing of burns or cuts. This was made by constructing a small orgone box perhaps $2 \times 1\frac{1}{2}$ ft^2—three layers of metal and organic material—and then inserting into its top a neck (about 3 feet long) of BX cable. BX is a flexible kind of metallic cable. At the end of the neck is affixed a funnel perhaps 5 inches across at the wide end. In theory, the orgone moves from inside the box through the BX cable out to the funnel and from there to the injured place on the patient's body. According to Dr. Eva Reich, daughter of Wilhelm Reich, the orgone shooter can be used to demonstrate the way in which orgone speeds up healing of burns and alleviates pain.

Reich worked first in New York, but around 1946 he moved his laboratory and research to a farm in Rangeley, Maine, far from urban civilization. He began to have constructed a number of orgone accumulators, usually two- or three-layered, and these were rented out to physicians and patients under medical supervision. He built a sizeable laboratory on this property, carried out further experimentation on the orgone, held annual conferences, and published his books and journals while doing decreasing amounts of actual psychiatric orgone therapy with patients.

In 1950 he experimented with the potential power of orgone energy to limit or negate atomic or nuclear energy. This was called the oranur experiment. According to his observations, the nuclear energy excited the orgone, making it spread many yards from the laboratory and affect both rocks and the weather.

By May of 1952 strange weather conditions, later labeled

DOR, for "dangerous orgone," began to hang around the laboratory. The salient visible effect was peculiar black clouds that drifted over the area and seemed to get stuck there. The landscape went grayish black and people, especially sensitive people, felt there was something wrong in the air or more heat than usual. The reaction of the geiger counter to the overhead passage of the black clouds was variable and strange: it was raised up to 100,000 clicks per minute and then fell rapidly or faded to nearly zero and then raced up again. Whether these were unusual weather conditions or early signs of industrial smog is still uncertain.

It is significant that Reich felt called upon to disperse these DOR clouds. In so doing, he invented a new device, a "cloudbuster" which can be viewed as another application of the orgone theory.[†]

Remembering an unexplained phenomenon from 1940, when the casual pointing of long metal pipes at the surface of a lake seemed to affect the movement of the waves, Reich experimented in April 1952 by pointing long thin metal rods at the black clouds. His aim was to disperse them. So he linked the metal pipes, 9–12 feet long and 1½ inches in diameter, through BX cable to a deep well on his property, theorizing that, as water is a great absorber of orgone, it might draw and absorb the DOR.

He pointed these pipes at the black clouds and claimed: "The effect was instantaneous: the black DOR clouds began to shrink. And when the pipes were pointed against the OR (orgone) energy flow—that is, toward the west—a breeze west to east would set in after a few minutes' 'draw' as I came to call this operation; fresh, blue-gray OR energy moved in where the nauseating DOR clouds had been a short while before. Soon we learned that rain clouds too could be influenced, increased and diminished, as well as moved, by operating these pipes in certain well-defined ways."

In the fall Reich constructed two cloudbusters aimed at the construction of clouds and the making of rain. Eventually he even went to dry parts of Arizona to bring more moisture to this desert region and apparently had some success.

[†] See Chapter 31. *Editors*.

In its final form, the cloudbuster consisted of a number of hollow metallic tubes which, by a telescopic arrangement, could be lengthened or shortened. These were attached to a stand and could be turned in any direction, vertically or horizontally. The upper ends were fitted with caps so they could be closed or opened at will. The lower ends were joined to flexible BX tubing which led into water or moist earth. To explain how metal pipes could draw energy from cloud formations, Reich pointed to the known functioning of the lightning rod. This is a metal rod, usually mounted on a building, but not necessarily so, which attracts the lightning discharge and conducts it through heavy wires into the ground.

In the next few years Reich began to experiment with a new device, somewhat similar to the cloudbuster, aimed at facilitating individual psychiatric orgone therapy. It was called a DOR buster, and its aim was to withdraw DOR from the human organism. Reich saw DOR as an energetic condition which results from the damming up of orgone in the body. Serious tension areas in the body owing to tight musculature are productive of this DOR. The device works on the principle of drawing off DOR (through water's affinity for orgone) and consists of a metal funnel attached to BX tubing leading to nearby flowing water. One recent (homemade) version has the individual sitting or lying under an orgone blanket; a metal funnel perhaps a foot or two long, connected with BX cables is placed near supposed armored areas of the body. The therapist passes the head of the device back and forth over the patient's body for about fifteen minutes in a treatment. When successful, this device draws off DOR and excites energy movement. At times it can result in outbreaks of strong emotions locked in by the bodily armoring and thus facilitates therapy.

In 1954 Reich became convinced of the existence of UFOs, having seen one near his farm that January. Various accounts of their operation by ufologists referred to a background radiation effect. Observations such as their silent movement, the quality of their lights, and their spinning movement led Reich to speculate that they were powered by orgone. After some observations and thought, he came to the conclusion that perhaps they had hostile intentions.

In late 1954 Reich directed a cloudbuster at a UFO and claimed to observe a change in the object's brilliance. Reich speculated that the UFOs were drawing energy from the earth and exuding a DOR-producing substance. In 1955 he tried to strengthen the power of the cloudbuster by adding to its base a milligram of radium that had become "transmuted" in the original oranur experiment. He believed that by its use he was able to raise the energetic level of the surrounding atmosphere, increasing the level of the charge. This procedure apparently enhanced the effect of the cloudbuster, which he now called a space gun. It was used in Arizona to scare away UFOs, whose presence was revealed to Reich visually and by the appearance of noxious clouds and a significant increase of the atmospheric radiation count on the orgone-sensitive geiger counter. (Jerome Eden has written about this work at some length in his *Orgone Energy*.)

From about 1947 onward Reich's manufacture and rental of orgone accumulators greatly upset the medical and psychiatric establishment, and they persuaded the Food and Drug Administration to investigate this device. This organization spent some years spying on Reich and getting various institutes to test many aspects of the orgone theory. Reich was brought to trial in 1954 on various charges concerned with renting the accumulators which the FDA was convinced were fraudulent. Reich's suggestions that the accumulator might facilitate healing, including such diseases as cancer, was held to be "going too far."

The trial against him dragged on for almost two years while Reich conducted his own defense and claimed the court had no right to try a scientific theory in a court of law. (The full story of this trial is now to be found in Jerome Greenfield's *The U.S.A. versus Reich*.) Nevertheless, Reich was convicted of contempt of court, fined $10,000 and given a two-year term in jail. The court also ordered that all his books which referred *in any way* to orgone energy must be destroyed. So the books and journals in his publishing house were burned. He was imprisoned and nine months later died of a heart attack. It would be years before his followers and associates recovered from his trial and death, and began to do research and publish journals and books about his work.

11.

Bioplasma: The Fifth State of Matter?

VIKTOR M. INYUSHIN

Scientists refer to four states of matter: solids, liquids, gases, and plasma. The latter is a gas that has had all the electrons stripped off the nuclei of its atoms; it exists in outer space but can be experimentally produced at very high temperatures in physics laboratories. In 1944, the Soviet scientist V. S. Grischenko raised for the first time the possible existence of a fifth state of matter—one which exists in living organisms. In 1966, he named this proposed fifth state of matter "biological plasma" or "bioplasma." In our laboratory, we have proceeded to conduct experiments to determine whether or not bioplasma actually exists.

We know that every living organism is a system that radiates energy, thus creating a field around itself. But we know little about the organism's energy network, especially during telepathy when two organisms appear to interact at a distance so great that the phenomena cannot be explained adequately by conventional means.

A living organism can be described as a "biological field" or "biofield," a "field" being a region consisting of lines of force which affect one another. The biofield has a clear spatial formation and is shaped by several physical fields—electrostatic, electromagnetic, acoustic, hydrodynamic, and quite possibly others still inadequately explored. It is likely that bioplasma represents one of the fields within the biofield of living organisms.

Our experiments indicate that bioplasma consists of ions,

free electrons, and free protons—in other words, subatomic particles which exist independently of a nucleus. Our experiments also indicate that the biofield owes its structure to bioplasma which is more stable than the other components of the biofields. This is due to the equivalence of positive and negative particles in bioplasma. We call this equilibrium "stereobioenergostasis." Under the impact of various internal and external factors, stereobioenergostasis might break down. Usually this is only temporary and the equilibrium is reasserted. However, if the equilibrium is not restored, the organism may suffer serious damage.

Bioplasmic particles are constantly being renewed by chemical processes within the cells, especially the mitochondria among which direct transfers of electrons from one molecule to another occur. The mitochondria are tiny rod-shaped bodies in the cytoplasm of most cells. They contain many cell enzymes, particularly those involved in the citric-acid cycle.

In addition to the bioplasmic particles produced by processes in the mitochondria, there is a direct absorption of charges from the environment. The lungs play an important role in the absorption of environmental charges. There is a constant interplay between the organism and its environment; some bioplasmic particles are absorbed from external sources while other bioplasmic components are radiated into space.

Kirlian Photography

Our original experiments with bioplasma utilized the high-voltage photography procedures developed by Semyon Kirlian and his wife Valentina. The basic procedure is to generate a high-frequency field between two electrodes and to place an object directly on a film resting within the field. This enables a photograph of the object to be taken without using a camera or a lens. The object will be pictured with a corona surrounding it; this corona discharge represents the air that is ionized and the electrons torn from the object when the high-frequency field is created. However, living objects show a greater variation in the size of the corona than do nonliving objects. We think that this variation is due to the bioplasmic field which interacts with the artificially created field and, perhaps, sets the limits for the corona. Therefore, bioplasma can be indirectly studied through Kirlian photography.

In experiments with rabbits, it was noted that the corona discharge varied greatly whenever the rabbit was frightened by something. The intensity of the reaction increased two- or threefold at the moment of shock but there was a return to the corona's ordinary size after several minutes. By introducing a sensor into the rabbit's brain, an intensity of radiation ten times greater than that observed on the skin and muscles was noted. These experiments, and others like them, indicated that the accumulation of bioplasma is most intense in the brain; less bioplasma is found in connecting tissues and the soft tissues of body organs.

More detailed investigations were carried out with human beings in various psychological and physiological states. It was found that the center of the spinal cord, with its large clusters of nerve cells, seems to be a center of bioplasmic activity. Bioplasmic activity is strong at the fingertips as well as in back of the solar plexus. Blood does not contain as much bioplasma as nerve cells. However, blood resembles a liquid-crystal system in which energy transfer can take place. Thus blood, too, can conduct energy; the circulatory system is a conductive energy system just as is the bioplasmic system.

Bioplasmic activity was found to depend, in part, on mood. Artists, for example, demonstrated a very bright corona when thinking of painting. A depressed person often has a very thin corona which contains several dark spots.

We are currently attempting to photograph bioplasma directly without relying on the supplementary electrical fields produced in Kirlian photography. Our preliminary data are encouraging.

Other Experiments with Bioplasma

Several other lines of experimentation support the hypothesis of the bioplasmic field. There is a large output of heat when tissue disintegrates. This phenomenon indicates the organism's ability to change mass to energy. In addition, living

organisms are able to absorb large amounts of radiation—a
feat that dead tissue cannot perform. Several other scientific
findings lend support to the concept of a biological plasma:
(1) the presence of delocalized electrons in the form of pi
electrons; (2) the existence of semiconductor properties in
cell membranes; (3) the high concentration of unpaired
electrons in biologically important molecules such as DNA
and RNA; (4) the presence of electrical polarities in organisms; (5) the semiconductor properties of chlorophyll and
the independence of the photosynthesis process on temperature; (6) the collective character of the changes in the density of quantum processes under the effect of physical factors,
as when mitogenic radiation is created in visual fields when
light hits the retina of the eye; (7) the creation of electrical
fields by frictional charges concentrated on the surface of
bodies—fields that can be detected at distances away from the
body.

Alexander Dubrov has proposed that living organisms emit
gravitational waves. If so, bioplasma could be involved in
these waves. Gravitational interaction is the weakest of all
known reactions in physics, and thus difficult to identify. Despite the small intensity of the gravitational waves, however,
they may play a definite role in the different ways living organisms have been noted to interact with their environments.
These interactions change from day to day and the variations
are difficult to explain by conventional means.

Bioplasma experiments need to be carried out under constant atmospheric conditions, such as humidity and heat. An
approaching storm, for example, can drastically influence the
results. Thus it can be surmised that the bioplasmic field is
unstable when there is a sudden alteration in environmental
forces of an electrical nature.

In spite of its sensitivity to electrical changes in the environment, bioplasma appears to be relatively stable. This seems
to reflect a balance of positive and negative particles in the
bioplasma. If there is a severe shift in one direction or the
other, it may be reflected in the health of the organism.

In spite of the relative stability of the organism's bioplasmic field, a significant amount of energy is radiated into space
by means of bioplasma. This may occur in the form of

"microstreamers" or "bioplasmoids." Microstreamers are channels of bioplasmic particles forming through the air, while bioplasmoids are fragments of bioplasma which have broken away from the organism. It is possible that the Kirlian photography process facilitates the development of micro-streamers and bioplasmoids which can be captured on film. These microstreamers and bioplasmoids may also be involved in telepathy, psychokinesis, and other instances of distant inter-action among organisms.

In an attempt to investigate the distant interaction between a person and a plant, a sensor with a liquid crystal was implanted with a thermostat and shielded by aluminum disks. The bioluminescence of the plant was measured by a sensitive tube which recorded the light leaving the plant. As a person in a distant room had his skin stimulated with a needle, the light leaving the plant increased to a remarkable degree. Similar re-sults were obtained when a different subject purposively imag-ined that he was in great emotional strain.

In other experiments, we have found the eyes to be a source of intense radiation. In several instances, the effect of the eyes could be observed even when they were separated from the measuring device by a metal screen. Our experi-ments with light indicate that bioplasma is especially conduc-tive for photons in the ultraviolet range.

Our group has hypothesized that an organism's bioplasma is an important factor in biochemiluminescence, more com-monly shortened to luminescence—the emission of light from an organism from causes other than high temperatures. Other scientists have suggested that an organism's breathing, or respiration, is the key factor involved with luminescence. To test our hypothesis, we inhibited the respiration of geranium leaves by placing them in a solution of mercury cyanide. Respiration decreased to about thirty percent of a control group of geranium leaves not placed in the solution. The leaves' luminescence also decreased to about thirty percent of the control leaves. Then we immersed a third group of leaves in a solution of methylene blue. Again the respiration rate was thirty percent of the control leaves. But the luminescence decreased to nineteen percent of the controls. We think that the discrepancy was due to the severe inhibition of bioplasmic activity caused by methylene blue which is known to be a strong acceptor of free electrons—one of the components of bioplasma.

We are also investigating the influence of light from a laser on living organisms. There is some indication that laser technology will offer a productive way in which bioplasma can be studied.

Conclusion

In summary, we have obtained evidence that a fifth state of matter, bioplasma, exists as a part of each organism's biofield. Bioplasma consists of ions, free electrons, and free protons. It is highly conductive and provides opportunities for the accumulation and transfer of energy within the organism as well as among different organisms. Bioplasma appears to be concentrated in the brain and spinal cord. At times, it may extend considerable distances from the organism, raising the possibility of its involvement in telepathic and psychokinetic phenomena.

III THE GEOMETRY OF THE PARANORMAL

Other Dimensions, Higher Planes

12.

The previous section presented the idea of an unknown energy as the motive force behind various paranormal phenomena. This section presents another concept: the multidimensional, dynamic structure of space.

Is space only the absence of matter, merely "nothingness"? Is it just a never-ending vacuum—empty distance that must be traversed from point to point, even by field forces that "propagate" themselves at high velocity? Or are there other aspects of space that provide a means for instantaneous transmission of energy and information over great distances, and for living but nonphysical entities to exist? Does space have definite properties that can be investigated and formulated into laws?

The latter possibility is becoming more and more likely in the view of certain theoretical physicists and astrophysicists who speak, for example, of hyperspace, "wormholes" in space that connect interpenetrating universes, and multidimensional states of being beyond our three-dimensional space-time continuum. Some suggest that these hypothetical aspects provide likely vehicles for the appearance of various paranormal phenomena.

The selections in this section support this position, and do so in several ways. First, they demonstrate that the concept is logically tenable. Second, they present information from non-scientific traditions that suggests avenues of exploration for testing the concept of geometric hyperspace. Last, they present several means—theoretical and applied—for carrying out the investigation.

The logic leading to this concept is presented by a philoso-

pher, Steven Rosen, who demonstrates that a radical reformulation of the paradigm of traditional science leads to
a representation of certain psi phenomena and, further, to a
realization of Jung's goal: the union of psyche and physics,
mind and body. He suggests that synchronistic phenomena
yield to definitive representation when certain new approaches to physics are followed. Moreover, his model shows
that the physical and nonphysical not only interpenetrate each
other, they *are* each other. Although seemingly different, they
paradoxically share a single reality.

The concept of nonphysical planes or supersensible realms
coexistent with physical reality is an ancient one. In metaphysical and mystical tradition, space is not a vacuum but a
plenum. In other words, space is not merely a geometrical abstraction, but rather is, as Maharishi Mahesh Yogi terms it,
the creative field of intelligence from which all knowledge
and all possibilities for physical existence is manifested. The
occult scientist Rudolf Steiner, founder of Anthroposophy,
remarked in a lecture about knowledge of higher worlds:
"Space is not a haphazard chaos but is organized in all
directions in such a way that these directions themselves
have different values." The Anglican canon, A. P. Shepherd,
described these higher worlds in his biography of Steiner, *A
Scientist of the Invisible:*

> These "worlds" are not separate regions, spatially divided
> from one another, so that it would be necessary to move
> in space in order to pass from one to the other. The
> higher worlds completely interpenetrate the lower worlds,
> which are fashioned and sustained by their activities.
> What divides them is that each world has a more limited
> and controlled level of consciousness than the world
> above it. The lower consciousness is unable to experience
> the life of the higher worlds and is even unaware of their
> existence, although it is interpenetrated by them. But if
> the beings of a lower world can raise their consciousness
> to a higher level, then that higher world becomes manifest
> to them, and they can be said to have passed to a higher
> world, although they have not moved in space.

The most commonly mentioned "other world" is, of
course, the kingdom of the dead. Many traditions maintain
that death is an altered state of consciousness and that the

soul or spirit of an organism continues to exist after physical demise, passing from the first plane to still-higher planes as the soul evolves. Recent studies of the dying by Raymond Moody, author of *Life After Life*, by American Society for Psychical Research investigators Karlis Osis and Erlendur Haraldsson, authors of the forthcoming *At the Hour of Death*, by Charles Garfield of the University of California at San Francisco, and by thanatologist Elisabeth Kubler-Ross support this view, at least to the point of dealing with the possibility of a first plane of the afterworld. Working independently, each found that the dying and those undergoing pseudodeath (near-death, with cessation of all vital signs) frequently have out-of-the-body experiences in which paranormal information is obtained and the dead (usually friends and relatives) are contacted.

That being the case, the next step for science is to begin "mapping" this interpenetrating vital world and formulating the laws of topological transformation between space and hyperspace by which higher-dimensional events manifest in our three-dimensional space-time. Is there anything already known to physical science which offers a direction or guidelines for scientifically bridging the two worlds?

We have already seen the likelihood in the Burr–Ravitz work that there is an "energy field blueprint" underlying organic physical forms. The structural configuration of the field—its geometry—is more fundamental than the material it directs into visible form.

How can we conceptualize this higher state of living geometry? We are familiar with matter in the three forms of solid, liquid, and gas. Matter in the fourth state—plasma—is less familiar (fire is an example). Nevertheless, the Soviet conception of bioplasma—living plasma—is a simple and logical extension of the solid-liquid-gas progression. Might there be still another state beyond bioplasma, a state in which living beings might normally exist just as we do in the solid state? And if we presently recognize living organisms as consisting of solid, liquid, and gaseous matter (and possibly bioplasma), might this hypothetical state also be an element of a physical organism's vitality and/or intelligence—its soul or spirit?

One indication of this comes from research in the 1930s done on food metabolism with radioactive tracers by Rudolf Schoenheimer of Columbia University. Schoenheimer demonstrated the dynamic state of body constituents. He found that molecules or part molecules in food pass into a cell and replace some part of the cellular structure previously there. After a while the replacement part is itself replaced. Through a system of complicated chemical reactions, the entire physical structure of the body was shown to be "turned over" at varying rates for different parts of the body.

Commenting on this in an article entitled "Is There A Non-Physical World?" in *Does Man Survive Death?*, survival researcher Julius Weinberger (see Chap. 36) writes:

> This raises a very important question: If this is the case, what is there about a human being that is permanent? His personality, of course. His thoughts, his character, his emotions, his memories. Also, the plan or the design, but not the material of the body.
>
> The material comes and goes, but the plan remains the same. If this is a scientifically verifiable fact, isn't it logical to step further and say that even if all the material that forms a visible human body were to be removed from it, its plan or design, and the personality, would still continue to exist? If this is admitted, it is equivalent to an admission of continuity of existence after death.

From this perspective, there is no death. There is only a change of state like H_2O passing from water to steam. Life, seen by materialists as the ultimate paranormal event, is ubiquitous. Even "empty space" may be filled with lifeforms invisible to the physical senses. Leaving aside the question of livingness, Einstein himself declared in a 1935 lecture (reported in the *Physical Review*, July 1935) that "space will have to be regarded as a primary thing with matter derived from it."

For some, the primacy of space goes beyond even the concept of nonphysical lifeforms (which theoretically could include angels and other so-called "mythical" beings) inhabiting it. Charles Musès, writing in various issues of the *Journal for the Study of Consciousness* (see Appendix III), has proposed a theory of consciousness–matter interaction termed "CM quantum theory." Musès maintains that all matter is alive in a protobiological sense. He further states (in his book *Consciousness and Reality,* co-edited with Arthur M. Young) that there are forms of living substance far subtler than our relatively crude polarized (i.e., electron–proton) matter–forms already hinted at in the mysterious physical effectiveness of the so-called "vacuum state" as revealed by modern quantum physics.

The inherent energy of the vacuum (which Musès terms noetic energy) provides the link between matter and consciousness, in Musès' view. To go "through the vacuum," he has enunciated a theory of consciousness expressed in hypernumbers and metadimensions. This is presented with some detail in his article in Section IV. Here we will simply note that Musès' work (and that of E. H. Walker, also presented in Sec. IV) identifies consciousness or noetic energy as the key to understanding paranormal phenomena, all the way from psi events through ufology to mystical experience.

It is interesting to note parallels in all this to certain ancient concepts. The ether, for example, is widely considered to be thoroughly discredited metaphysical nonsense. The term was introduced into science by Michael Faraday in the early 19th century to account for the forces between electrically charged bodies, although earlier scientists, among them Newton, had also raised the question of the ether. When James Clerk Maxwell discovered that light was an electromagnetic disturbance, Faraday's ether became the "luminiferous ether" because of its light-bearing qualities. And so it remained—an accepted but undemonstrated pillar of science—until the Michelson–Morley experiments apparently disproved the existence of the ether.

Now, however, it appears the disproof itself was faulty and the ether is being rediscovered. H. C. Dudley of the University of Illinois Medical Center presents a modern concept of the ether as an omnipresent, energy-rich neutrino sea. The implications of this all-pervasive subquantic medium for science and society are enormous.

The neutrino sea, as a modern reformulation of an ancient concept, is still far short of satisfying the descriptions of the ether presented in occult and metaphysical works, however. Among the more lucid of these presentations is that of

Guenther Wachsmuth, a follower of Steiner who writes from the Anthroposophical perspective. As described by Steiner, the ether has four aspects—the warmth, light, chemical, and life ethers. This division has interesting affinities with both the ancient Hindu concept of prana (traditionally said to have five forms) and with the modern concept of orgone (which, in the view of orgonomist Trevor Constable, is the same as Steiner's chemical ether—see Sec. V).

The ether concept might well have been presented in Section II. We felt, however, that it was better left until now because our intention in this section is to examine a number of intimately related ancient ideas that purport to explain a wide variety of paranormal phenomena. The ether is one such idea. Others are the polarities of space–counterspace and gravity–levity.

Counterspace is a term describing the nonphysical realm in which the etheric formative forces arise. One approach to the investigation of counterspace is mathematics—specifically, projective or counter-Euclidean geometry. (Musès' hypernumber theory is another mathematical approach—see Sec. IV.) Its importance for understanding living nature, which according to occult science originates in the etheric realm, is that it offers a mathematical conception of space and morphology. If Euclidean geometry is appropriate for describing the physical world, counter-Euclidean geometry opens a window into the nonphysical. If matter and spirit are the two faces of existence, then the world of spirit–counterspace may be penetrated through the creative polarity of point and plane derived from projective geometry.

Levity is held to be not merely negative gravity or the absence of gravity but rather a *primary force* characteristic of counterspace, resulting from the etheric formative forces arising in the nonphysical world. Gravity thrusts outward from the earth, pulling matter downward; levity streams inward to the earth from the cosmos, supplying the means, for example, of getting Newton's apple up in the tree in the first place. (Is this not one of biology's great mysteries: how did the apple get *up* there?)

These and other concepts are presented here because, in their totality, they offer both logical and experimental reasons for considering the structure of space in our investigation of paranormal phenomena. Thus, Rosen's article on representing the irrepresentable logically precedes the traditional occult view of space, as presented by Hermine Sabetay, a member of the Theosophical Society (founded by Helena P. Blavatsky, reportedly a gifted psychic and medium). Then Olive Whicher demonstrates a mathematical approach—projective geometry—which allows a theoretical exploration of counterspace. This is followed by Guenther Wachsmuth's brief description of the occultist's ethers and by H. C. Dudley's modern interpretation.

The last article by Serge V. King looks at specific research into geometric forms relating to the concept that space is dynamic, energetic, and has higher-dimensional geometric properties that can transform themselves into three-dimensional space. This is an area where many puzzling phenomena are met. Perhaps the best known goes under the name "pyramid power." It has gained wide attention, even appearing on the cover of *Science Digest* (February 1975) as a feature article.

A pyramid, however, is only one-half of a crystal shape. We have already seen that von Reichenbach's crystals (indeed, all crystals) apparently are natural transformers or generators of nonphysical energy. Is the crystal structure a key to controlling energy through form? Is this also the reason that wizards traditionally wear conical hats? Is this the rationalizing concept behind the "sacred geometry" of true magic and arcane religions?

In the last few decades, primarily in Europe, there has been a steady output of work under various terms: *ondes de forme* (French), *formenstrahlen* (German), form energy or waves from shapes. The scope of these investigations has ranged from laboratory experiments with geometric forms to worldwide searches, and they touch upon knowledge ranging from quantum physics to archeology.

One example of a large-scale phenomenon is the geographical feature called ley lines. These perfectly straight lines, only a few feet wide, stretch across a landscape for miles—in some cases, hundreds of miles—and form a network or grid upon the surface of the Earth. First noticed and named by Alfred Watkins in England at the turn of the century, it was soon found that these lines of great antiquity were associated with ancient sacred sites such as pagan temples, burial mounds, and terrestrial zodiacs, or the churches and cathedrals later built above them. These constructions were invariably built at intersections in the ley network. Often ley lines had been overlaid with roads or stone walls or nearly effaced by civilization. But once visually recognized at a given point, it is possible to trace them. This has been done both in Britain and more recently in North America, where Indian serpent mounds are said to be a principal feature of ley lines. According to John Michell in *The View Over Atlantis,* which surveys reports of a mysterious natural energy said to be important for maintaining prehistoric civilization, the so-called "dragon lines" of China may be the same thing as ley lines.

The paranormal aspect of ley lines, however, is the assertion that they can be dowsed, according to an article in *The American Dowser* (August 1974). In this way it is claimed that they have been found to have a corresponding underground energy flow of great speed—a flow that at certain intersections and terminal points appears to be at right angles to the surface of the earth. Along these lines underground water domes and mineral deposits are said to have been found and, on the surface of the ground, ancient stones which local traditions maintain are "charged with power."

Links between ley lines and other mysteries have been suggested. The etheric web encircling the globe that occultists speak of (and which both Carlos Castaneda in his book *Journey to Ixtlan* and William Irwin Thompson in his *Passages Around Earth* report seeing) has obvious parallels. According to *Pursuit* magazine (July 1973), it is now widely felt among ley line researchers that "the ley lines may in fact follow invisible lines of power crisscrossing the countryside, and that early Man was aware of this power, which he harnessed for his own spiritual and physical benefit (and also for the benefit of nature and the earth) by erecting his 'temples' at certain significant points along the power lines."

These power lines and power points composed of the X energy may be harmonics of a still-greater network. In an article entitled "Planetary Grid," appearing in *New Age Journal* (No. 5, 1975), Christopher Bird describes a Soviet theory involving a lattice or matrix in the planet. The Russians claim to have found evidence from fields as widely separated as archeology, geochemistry, ornithology, and meteorology, that "the earth projects from within itself to the surface a dual geometrically regularized grid."

The first part of this grid is said to form twelve pentagonal slabs over the sphere—a dodecahedron—in accordance with both Buckminster Fuller's geodesic map and Plato's statement that: "The earth, viewed from above, resembles a ball sewn from twelve pieces of skin." The second part of the grid is composed of twenty equilateral triangles, making an icosahedron. Bird writes: "By superimposing the entire dual grid over the face of the planet, the researchers say they have discovered what possibly may be the earth's energy structure or skeleton."

This gridwork is said to coincide with a wide range of natural and paranormal phenomena, including the following: the "Bermuda Triangle" and its purported corresponding eleven areas of strange disappearances ("windows" into hyperspace?) equally spaced around the globe above and below the equator; the planet's tectonic plates; the overlapping of the center of all world magnetic anomalies at the nodes and edges of the crystallike lattice; the occurrence of all global centers of maximal and minimal atmospheric pressure at the nodes of the grid; paths of hurricanes, prevailing winds, and global currents follow the ribs of the grid; the large deposits of mineral ores which lie along faults or folds in the Earth's crust, which in turn often follow the grid's ribs; and the frequent location of birth places of ancient cultures at the intersections of the grid.

This gridwork concept has been extended above the surface of the planet by the Russians and is said to coincide with certain effects in the cloud mantle, as revealed by satellite photos. Also, dark streaks on the surface of the ocean (not cloud shadows) fall in line with the cloud phenomenon with exact regularity.

Nor is this energy structure limited to the Earth and its atmosphere. The lattice, the Soviet investigators say, exists throughout the cosmos and accounts for the creation of planets, stars, and galaxies. This material, at first glance, appears to be highly speculative, but the evidence cited in Bird's article could be rechecked by other investigators.

From crystals to galaxies is a great leap, but if clear and reasonable linkages can ultimately be shown, or if both crystals and galaxies can be demonstrated as particular cases of an underlying principle, then our probe into cosmic mysteries may have uncovered a unifying concept—the dynamic structure of higher-dimensional space—for bridging science and religion. "Pick a flower and trouble a star," say the mystics. Is science about to demonstrate this? The articles presented here give indications of it. But they also demonstrate the massive amount of work that needs to be done if esoteric philosophy is to be examined through modern scientific procedures.

13.

Toward a Representation
of the "Irrepresentable"

STEVEN M. ROSEN

Introduction

C. G. Jung's life-long struggle with the problem of *psi* culminated in his monograph "Synchronicity: An Acausal Connecting Principle." Here he came to the conclusion that psychic experiences are "irrepresentable" within the framework of traditional Western thinking, for when they occur we enter a domain in which "space is no longer space, nor time time."[1] Yet Jung well knew that such events were *not* alien to the Eastern vision of the world. Indeed, we shall see that the synchronicity idea, only half understood by Jung himself, was a "spice" brought back from his intuitive excursions in the Orient, beyond the realm of Western logic.

I believe that if Jung's challenge can be met, a far-reaching synthesis of Eastern and Western tradition is promised. The urgency of the need to somehow represent the "irrepresentable" has been most recently articulated by Chari,[2] Pratt,[3] and Whiteman.[4] All agree that the answer lies beyond the orthodox conception of space and time (that orthodoxy including the Einstein–Minkowski world view as well as the Newtonian).

Pratt's view of the dilemma is especially revealing. He argues that psychic happenings cannot be accommodated in an explanatory system seeking to determine the location of events in space-time. Consequently, the physicalistic space-time approach must be discarded. But if psi can be dealt with

"Toward a Representation of the 'Irrepresentable'" is excerpted from *Cosmic Existentialism* by Steven M. Rosen and is printed by permission of author.

only *outside* the physical world, it cannot be dealt with at all, for we must then resign ourselves to an absolute dualism which is, in essence, an admission of our inability to explain.

Pratt's difficulty, at its base, was Jung's difficulty. Both writers appear to see only two alternatives: an event can be either located in conventional space-time or it must occur outside space-time entirely. On the other hand, a third alternative is suggested by Whiteman. Renouncing the notion that entities must be "simply located" in space-time, he proposes that a "hierarchical," multilevel analysis be substituted for the classical, single-level conception. However, after discussing the analogy of psi to modern physics (i.e., the quantum theory) and outlining a set of axioms on which a hierarchical theory might be built, Whiteman strikes a note of pessimism. He concludes that no extension of mathematical–physical theory will accommodate psi which is rightly regarded as *non*physical. Then is he not recommending an absolute dualism after all? Must we accept the irreconcilability of psychical and physical spheres?

Let us suppose that a unitary but open geometric structure could be described which generates higher orders of space-time continually through a process of *self*-evolution. Could this not lead us toward a representation of the "irrepresentable"? Though we would have multiple levels of reality, the levels would not be separated by void but would grow out of each other. I will present such a geometry, bringing it to bear specifically on the phenomena of clairvoyance and precognition. At the same time I shall attempt to demonstrate its fundamental harmony with the world view of the East, an outlook always accepted by Jung, if only on an intuitive basis.

Identity, Causality, and Synchronicity

The law of identity is perhaps the deepest presupposition on which the classical, single-level view is based:

$$A = A \text{ and } A \neq \bar{A}$$

The idea that bodies are simply located in space and time is a variation on the theme of identity. A given body cannot be in two places at the same time nor can different moments of time overlap in the same space. This principle is built into the special theory of relativity by the specification of "spacelike" and "timelike" space-time intervals. Two events in Einstein–Minkowskian space-time are separated in a spacelike way if the space between them is so great and the time so short that an observer could be present for both events only by traveling from one to the other at the velocity of light or greater. The theory assumes that no material body can travel that fast. Events are separated by a timelike interval if the time elapsing between them is so great and the spatial disjunction so small that an observer may be present for the onset of both events but will not experience them as occurring simultaneously unless he travels at negative velocity. The theory states that no body can travel that "slowly."

If the spacelike hiatus could be bridged, one would be violating the spatial aspect of the principle of simple location by, in effect, being in two distinct places at once. If the timelike separation were overcome, one would be in violation of the temporal aspect of the principle of simple location by encountering, as it were, two different times in the same place. Having seen what the violation of classical relativity implies, we are able to formulate our understanding of clairvoyance and precognition more specifically. Clairvoyance is the experience of an event so distant in space and so nearly contemporaneous that the relativistic barrier of the spacelike interval is surmounted; in this sense, the classical conception of space predicated on the idea of simple location is destroyed. Precognition is the experience of an event so remote in time and nearly coincidental in space that the limitation of the timelike interval is transcended, and so too the orthodox notion of simply located time.

In his struggle with the "irrepresentable," Jung framed his deliberations more in terms of the principle of *causality* than that of identity. Yet it is possible to argue that the objection to causality violation is based on essentially equivalent grounds. To appreciate this, we must understand the close relation between causality and temporal order. Russell,[5] for instance, invoked Robb's theory of time whereby we can say that event A definitely precedes event B only if it can be shown that *A* has some influence on *B*. In other words, the causal relation between *A* and *B* is suggested as the criterion of their temporal ordering: if *A* causes *B*, then *A* precedes *B*. Obviously, the statement "*A* causes *B* and *A* precedes *B*" is not a contradiction. But neither is it contradictory merely to say "*B* precedes *A*" unless one would add "*A* causes *B*," which would be tantamount to saying "*A* precedes *B*," according to Robb. The violation of causality therefore reduces to the statement "*A* precedes *B* and *B* precedes *A*." This is the same difficulty raised by Flew when he dismissed the notion of a second dimension of time (as an explanation of precognition) because it leads to the "contradiction" of claiming "that the *same* event occurred *both* before *and* after another event."[6] Here the causality-violating sequence *BAB* is rejected on the grounds that it violates the principle of simple location which states that events separated by an intervening event must be distinctive—they cannot overlap.

Jung's tacit acceptance of the causality—identity principle built into classical relativity led him to the judgment that phenomena like clairvoyance and precognition are irrepresentable. He thus stated that: "it would be absurd to suppose that a situation which does not yet exist and will only occur in the future could transmit itself as a phenomenon of energy to a receiver in the present."[7] On the other hand, he was well aware of considerable empirical evidence substantiating such "impossibilities." What is more, Jung *knew* intuitively of their validity. Hence he was drawn to postulate his principle of "synchronicity," defined as the meaningful co-occurrence of a subjective experience and an objective physical event in a manner transcending the laws of causality and identity, as in precognition and clairvoyance. And while a physical representation of synchronicity eluded him, he found an expression of his acausal principle in the Eastern way of the Tao.

The mantic procedure of sorting yarrow stalks (or, in modern times, tossing coins) is regarded essentially as a means of generating synchronistic occurrences. The hexagram constructed from the "chance" throw of the coins is the product of an objective, physical event. Nevertheless, it is presumed to be in intimate correspondence with subjective matters of deep significance (if the individual concerned

approaches the procedure with the appropriate attitude).
Thus, in the *I Ching,* for each of the sixty-four possible hex-
agrams, far-reaching and detailed interpretations are offered
involving the personal conduct of the coin tosser's life, though
the outcome of the throw is a purely random event to the
Western mind.

To fully understand the Taoist outlook, we must dismiss
the idea that objective and subjective aspects of experience
are basically separate categories of existence which are
brought together. From the Eastern standpoint, it is quite the
other way around:

> The Tao begot one.
> One begot two.
> Two begot three.
> And three begot the ten thousand things.[8]

And Jung quoted from the teachings of Chuang-tzu:

> The sages of old, says Chuang-tzu, "took as their starting
> point a state when the existence of things had not yet
> begun . . . The next assumption was that though things
> existed they had not yet begun to be separated. The next,
> that though things were separated in a sense, affirmation
> and negation had not yet begun. When affirmation and
> negation came into being, Tao faded. After Tao faded,
> then came one-sided attachments."[9]

The Taoist, of course, would not view the "fading" of Tao as
ontological, but only as a fading from personal consciousness.
To the Taoist, the "one-sided attachment" is thus both illusory and undesirable. To achieve fulfillment, we must return to the Tao, or rather, rid ourselves of the illusion that
cosmic unity itself has ever dissolved or that it never existed.
So the Eastern thinker *begins* with the assumption of universal oneness. As a consequence, he has no difficulty accepting
the idea of synchronicity, though this conception might seem
entirely nonsensical to one presuming the radical disconnect-
edness of diverse phenomena.

The unified way of viewing the world is not peculiar to
Chinese philosophy but appears as a dominant theme in Indian thought as well. In the *Rig Veda,* for instance, all substance and life is seen to emerge by a process of differentia-

tion from a unitary field of pure potentiality (*Asat*) which is primary and undifferentiated (thus "nonexistent" in the sense of not yet being actualized).[10]

We should recognize that while Asat or Tao express primordial universality, the particularities that crystallize from the eternal are just as essential to the scheme of existence. Thus Watts,[11] in his treatise on oriental metaphysics, repeatedly insisted that it is *the nature* of the infinite to abandon itself again and again to the finite. And noting with Watts that the infinite quality is not actually surrendered with this abandonment, we return to Jung's exposition wherein the Platonic notion that "all things are in all" is of central importance. That is, when the infinite whole differentiates itself into its finite parts (as by nature it will do), no part ever really ceases to embrace the whole. Differentiation is not to be regarded as a process of breakage and isolation but as a means of *displaying a face or aspect*. The particularity formed by differentiation, instead of being cut *from* the infinite whole, continues to be tied to the whole in multiple ways. Indeed, this theme of multiple connection arises in another tradition antithetical to the Western establishment. For the existentialist (at least for Heidegger):

> *Being-in-the-world* . . . (involves) a much richer relation than merely the spatial one of being located in the world . . . This wider kind of personal or existential "inhood" implies the whole relation of "dwelling" in a place. We are not simply located there, but are bound to it by all the ties of work, interest, affection, and so on.[12]

In Jung's essay on synchronicity, the most extreme implication of the multiple connection of the part to the whole is considered: that which appears least significant—the table crumb, the speck of dust—is nonetheless a microcosm of all that there is. By the same token, each individual mind, though finite, may embrace the whole of objective reality and thus may transcend time, space, and causality. Jung cites an additional passage from Chuang-tzu which is definite on this point:

> "Outward hearing should not penetrate further than the ear . . . thus the soul can become empty and absorb the whole world. It is Tao that fills this emptiness . . . use

your inner eye (and) your inner ear to pierce the heart of things. . . ." This is obviously an allusion to the absolute knowledge of the unconscious (on which psychic phenomena depend), and to the presence in the microcosm of macrocosmic events.[13]

In sum, the Eastern system of thinking presupposes a reality in which the one becomes the many and each of the many is the one. This fundamental attitude is reflected in the *internal* duality of the yin and yang. The finite way is the way of diversity, of the opposition which is an inevitable part of life. Indeed, the yin–yang symbol of Taoism is intended as a representation of all opposites (good and bad, man and woman, dark and light, etc.). Yet because every particularity encompasses the universal, finite opposites are inextricably intertwined with *each other* as well as with the infinite. A last illustration of this notion can be given in surprisingly simple terms.

Consider the Necker cube, a well known visual "illusion."

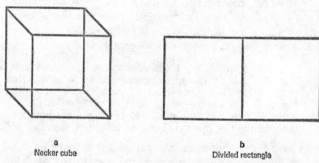

a
Necker cube

b
Divided rectangle

FIGURE 1

The cube [Figure 1(a)] is a two-dimensional projection into the third dimension. It may be viewed from either of two perspectives. But since each perspective uses the entire cube to express itself, neither should be thought merely to be contained *in* the cube as the squares are contained in the divided rectangle [each square in Figure 1(b) uses only half the rectangular surface]. A perspective embraces the whole cube and, therefore, though it is distinct, it swallows its counterpart entirely. On the other hand, the two parts of the divided rectangle are subordinated to the whole in a simple fashion (neither encompasses the whole) and are separated from one another except for a single common edge.

The Incubating Synthesis of "Psyche" and "Physis"

It is clear from Jung's own seminal statement of the synchronicity concept and Progoff's[14] lucid commentary on it that Jung's chief goal in proposing his notion was the union of "psyche" and "physis," or mind and body. It is equally apparent that he did not entirely succeed. The analogy he drew to the wave–particle duality of quantum physics[15] is revelatory. Causality and synchronicity are seen to complement one another in the manner of the wave and particle interpretations of light in Bohr's dualism. Of course, for one who wishes to *synthesize* opposites, the problem lies in the very circumstance of mere duality. For it is insufficient to simply postulate two parallel domains—one in which the orthodox laws of identity and causality prevail, the other in which classical space-time is enveloped by Universal Mind. A solution to the mind–body problem requires that the interpenetration of these realms be specifically exhibited. The complementarity must be shown to be internal—Einstein–Minkowskian space-time must be *drawn into* the fundamental interplay of yin and yang, thus displaying the physical and psychical as aspects of a single reality. This is the only way the "irrepresentable" can be made to yield.

In presenting "a case of non-Euclidean visualization,"[16] I commented that the limitation of the classical (special) theory of relativity (and thus Jung's limitation, since it was this aspect of the relativity idea that held him captive) is rooted in its adoption of the geometry of Euclid. Owing to the Euclidean character of the Einstein–Minkowskian system, the absolute future is stretched taut in a cone of light that widens upward from the point of the immediate present ("now") while the absolute past is extended below the now in an equally rigid manner (Figure 2).

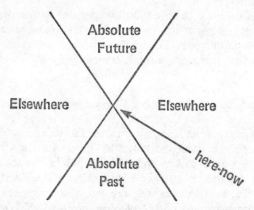

FIGURE 2   *Einstein–Minkowski light cones.*

Such a formulation renders the phenomenon of precognition quite impossible because the temporal ordering of events inside the cones cannot be reversed. All events in the cone of the absolute future are definitely *after* the now, whereas all those in the cone of the absolute past are definitely *before* it. Hence, the future cannot be experienced now.

In spatial terms, the vertex point of the cones is the immediate *here*. The spatial ordering of events prohibits the conjunction of here with *elsewhere*, the area outside the cones. Therefore, the clairvoyant experience is ruled out. Events outside the cone, being definitely elsewhere, cannot be here.

Evidently, the stretching of space-time on Euclid's "Procrustean bed" is merely a means of upholding the laws of identity and causality intimately associated with his geometry. The relativistic separation of the fore- and after-cones could be annulled (Chari's recent remark to the contrary notwithstanding[17]) if we were permitted to indulge in some bending of Euclidean flat space. We would then be able to bring a point in the "absolute" future into contact with the now, though this would defy the orthodox notion of simple location in time; likewise, the here and elsewhere could be spatially united. To the individual who argues that it is not physically possible to travel at negative velocities or faster than light, we point out that these prohibitions are not ontological imperatives in themselves but simply follow from the long-cherished Aristotelian notion of identity–causality underlying Euclidean reality.

While the geometric properties of the Einstein–Minkowski light cones conform to the postulates of Euclid, in making the transition from the special to the general theory of relativity, compliance with that postulational system is relaxed. The consequences of this for transcending identity–causality are only now beginning to be appreciated. Working with special solutions of the field equations of general relativity, mathematical physicists are starting to speak seriously of the causally "bad" behavior of certain physical systems and even of the possibility of time travel in the regions of space-time occupied by these systems.[18] Some recent efforts are directly based on Schwarzschild's original solutions of Einstein's equations generated only a year after the publication of the general theory (in 1916). Carter attributes the long delay of nearly fifty years to the fact that:

> many people thought that the region of space-time with the Schwarzschild horizon (the threshold beyond which time and space begin to behave peculiarly) could have no physical meaning. As a result of the interest which has developed in problems of gravitational collapse it is now generally realized that this view was mistaken.[19]

A massive body in a state of gravitational collapse is popularly known as a "black hole." The implications of blackhole physics are startling indeed and, in the current efforts to bring these to light, Tobin, Sarfatti, and Wolf[20] are among the most intrepid explorers. The ordinary view of space-time as Euclidean, linear, and continuous derives from restricting our vision to the middle ranges of the scale of magnitude. However, at scale extremes, linearity breaks down and space-time displays marked curvature eventuating in the formation of black holes. The distortion of space-time thus not only occurs in relation to bodies of cosmic proportion (e.g., stars in a state of gravitational collapse) but microcosmic entities as well. Sarfatti can therefore speak of both the massive black holes of astrophysics and "miniblackholes"[21] which, in relation to Wheeler's[22] conception of the fine grain of space, are the mouths of "wormholes."

What do cosmic black holes and miniscule wormholes (or miniblackholes) have in common? Euclidean space-time is *simply connected*. This is but another way of saying that the principle of simple location is upheld: different points in space-time cannot overlap. But cosmic or microcosmic black holes, in distorting Euclidean space-time, transform the simply connected continuum into one which is *multiply connected*. This means that regardless of the degree of separation of points in conventional space-time, they may be geometrically identified so that being at one implies instantaneous presence at the other. It is as though a "shortcut" has been created between distant regions of the manifold, but to take the abbreviated route, one must leave the Euclidean realm.

Wheeler offers an elementary illustration in which we are asked to punch two holes in a sheet of paper, one in the upper portion, the other in the lower. The distance between these points represents their separation in conventional space-time. Now we bend the paper so that the holes are brought back to back. The two holes are to be thought of as the mouths of a wormhole which connects remote regions of space-time. While the disjunction of points remains as great as before for the traditional journey along the surface, the traveler may reach his objective immediately by going *through* the surface via the wormhole. In this way, if the conventional space-time separation is spacelike, distant points are superimposed. And if the Euclidean separation is timelike, definitely successive points are rendered simultaneous. Hence, the classical law of simple location is surmounted.

Were the geometry of sensory perception to become non-Euclidean and develop multiple connectedness, it would be easy to see the possibility of clairvoyance and precognition. But events taking place in Wheeler's submicrocosmic domain or in regions of the universe where stars are in a state of gravitational collapse seem far removed from the direct experiences of organisms in the middle scale of nature. Here is Sarfatti's contribution: he proposes an entire *hierarchy* of space-time continua or gravitational fields that bridges the chasm between the remote extremes of magnitude. He is thus able to speak of a *biogravitational* field which is well within the reach of human experience:

There might indeed be a hierarchy of finite-range gravitational fields . . . of which the conjectured biogravitational field is of the most immediate interest. The bubbles (wormhole mouths) in the biogravitational field are quite large . . . and can, therefore, directly affect our sensory perception. Indeed, I suspect that many paranormal phenomena may be explicable in terms of biogravitational wormholes . . . providing direct multidimensional links between living systems.[23]

And, more specifically:

(an organism) in a high state of consciousness can artificially create blackholes . . . in his local biogravitational field. This would produce . . . very large distortions in his local subjective space-time environment . . . (so that) working within his local light cone (he) "sees" into the probable future. . . . This is the likely biogravitational mechanism for precognition. . . . The participator can also make use of . . . modes of the biogravitational field that act outside the light cone. In this way he can . . . (receive) at a distance actions of the type reported in experiences of . . . clairvoyance.[24]

"All Is Consciousness"

A major theme of Toben, Sarfatti, and Wolf's exposition is that "all is consciousness." At every level of organization in the hierarchy of space-time domains, singularities or holes develop at the fringes destroying the continuity that prevailed in the middle regions. Consciousness is identified as the "hidden variable" that creates the holes and then fills them, restoring continuity. In the process, the next level of the hierarchy is produced. Thus the secret thread with which plural realities are sewn together is consciousness. An "unmanifest universe" exists, as Reiser[25] would say, a "cosmic field" guiding the hierarchical unfoldment of all subfields, and it is *pure consciousness*. Therefore, in his opening statement, Sarfatti offers "the idea that consciousness is at the root of the material universe,"[26] and later, he is prompted to say that his explanation of psychic phenomena requires accepting the "additional postulate" that the distortion of the biogravitational field associated with precognition and clairvoyance is created by consciousness.

Let us examine more closely the relation between "material" space-time and the field of cosmic consciousness or "subether" (to again quote Reiser). Carrying Wheeler's illustration a step further, imagine space-time to be riddled with wormholes or miniblackholes so that every point is immediately accessible to every other point. What is the role of cosmic consciousness here? Essentially, we have been told to think of the union of remote points as a movement through the higher dimension from one side of the Euclidean plane to the other. It was by bending the two-dimensional space through the third dimension that we were able to identify "distant" points, to line them up back to back. Thus I can be in two separate places *here,* or in the future *now,* by taking a "shortcut" to the other side of the two-dimensional space.

The problem, however, is that my journey would seem to be physically prohibited by the topology of a *two*-sided reality. The other side of a two-sided continuum does, after all, appear inaccessible to the traveler on one side in the sense that there is no continuous path leading from one to the other. For this reason it becomes necessary to imagine a *rupture* in the continuum. And, alas, having broken the continuity of space-time, the hole must be regarded as *outside* the material world, as though "infinitely distant."[27] But the hole *is* created, we are told! By entering it, clairvoyant and precognitive experiences may be had, eventuating in the formation of a higher level of space-time organization.

The difficulty arises in supposing that holes are *literally* produced in the physical continuum. Consequently, they would have to be *non*physical, leading us to postulate an ethereal medium, an unmanifest field of pure consciousness existing *in addition to* the physical world and providing hidden continuity for the quantum leaps from point to point in space-time.

Do we have any choice? The idea of multiple connectedness, though mathematically legitimate, seems to suggest a physical impossibility and so warrant the dualistic supposition of a *non*physical continuum. Yet a mathematician might insist that the notion of "wormholes" or "black holes" in space-time is just an analogy, that the mathematics of multiple connectedness simply generate the *effects* of holes and that no actual holes need exist in the fabric of reality. If the mathematician is correct, the task then becomes this: to bring the mathematical description of the world into line with its physical description, to show that higher-order mathematical continuity can be given concrete, physical expression. By achieving such a goal, the need to propose a nonphysical medium for the hierarchy of physical realities would be obviated. The purely psychical medium would become unified with the mediated, the physical. With psyche and physis thus synthesized, we would be truly entitled to say that "all is consciousness" but could just as readily say "all is physis," for the fusion of mind and matter envisioned by Jung would have come to pass.

"Holes Without Holes"

Though the astonishing implications of general relativity were largely ignored until recently, we must now admit that one mathematical physicist *was* quick on the uptake. I note elsewhere[28] that as far back as 1922, Hermann Weyl offered a tantalizing clue to the potential ramifications of the non-Euclidean approach. He speculated:

> it is certainly possible in the present case (i.e., the case of non-Euclidean topology as opposed to the Euclidean geometry of the special theory) for the (light) cone of the active future to overlap with that of the passive past; so that, in principle, it is possible to experience events now that will in part be an effect of my future resolves and actions.[29]

Sarfatti also cited Weyl's enigmatic proclamation. But he did not mention that the suggestion proposed by Weyl was made after considering a topology with the surprising property of "onesidedness." The band of Möbius is the most commonplace example of this sort of structure.

The scientific–philosophical significance of the Möbius strip is discussed in three other papers.[30] Traditionally regarded as a mathematical curiosity, the strip can easily be constructed by twisting one end of a narrow band of paper before joining it to the other. The central focus of my 1973 article was the comparison of the Möbius strip with an ordinary cylindrical ring, made *without* twisting. The ring is topologically classified as two sided. It is possible to identify any point on one side of the ring with a corresponding point on the other. But this pairing process is superficial in a mathematical sense. *You* must do the matching, for the fusion of points on opposite sides is not inherent to the geometry of the ring. Consequently, they may be regarded as insulated from and external to one another. On the other hand, point pairs are connected intimately on the Möbius surface—they can be thought of as twisting or dissolving into each other through the higher dimension, as being bound up *internally*. Hence, the topologist defines such pairs of points as *single* points and the two sides of the strip, which comprise all pairs of points, as but one side. Can we not already begin to see the Möbius band as a geometric articulation of the yin–yang relation embraced by Jung?

Now it is evident that the problem of perforated space-time stems from the assumption of two sidedness. Disjunctions in orthodox space-time are clairvoyantly or precognitively surmounted by the action of linking up with points on the *other side* of the continuum. But we have seen that when the continuum is presumed to be simply two sided, the movement through the higher direction (perpendicular to conventional space-time) would have to carry the traveler *outside* of the material universe, *through a hole*.

But why not consider the space-time continuum to be topologically *one* sided like the Möbius strip? This would make synchronistic linkages quite continuous with physical reality. It is true that *locally,* at a cross section of the Möbius band, it is indistinguishable from the cylindrical ring whose two sides are segregated from each other. Hence, it appears, to the contracted consciousness, that the here-now point is absolutely separated from points temporally and spatially remote, as though void lay between them. Yet we may ask: is this impression of reality's structure (which may be identified with the traditional metaphysics of the West) not the outcome of an imprudent generalization from that narrow cross-sectional focus? As soon as the scope is broadened beyond the immediate locality, we see how one side of the Möbius band commences its hyperdimensional twist, encompassing the other side (and thus the whole). By supposing another side of conventional space-time, the effect of a hole is created; but when the continuum is regarded as topologically one sided, physical continuity is recovered. In this way, conceiving wormholes or black holes to actually be Möbius structures, we achieve an ultimate Wheelerian ideal: "holes without holes!" Or, we could alternately say that the Möbius strip models the interior region of Wheeler's wormhole for, in his illustration, the traveler is simply seen to enter one wormhole mouth and come out of the other. However, through Möbius transport, we witness the *continuous* pathway taken in the instantaneous concatenation of back-to-back points.

To avoid the possibility of being misunderstood, let me stop to emphasize that the restoration of physical continuity by no means implies the *reduction* of psychical phenomena. The reductionist does not seek to explain such occurrences but to *explain them away*, as Mundle[31] recommended we do in the case of precognition. However, rather than reduce the psychical to lesser reality status, I am proposing here an accommodative expansion of the *physical*. Thus, the restoration of physical continuity is not viewed as a return to the orthodox space-time framework but as establishing a higher order of continuity. Actually, in what we are about to see, if any "reducing" is to take place it will be a reduction of the *physical*, at least in the old, mechanistic sense of that word. Physical reality is about to take on a decidedly organic complexion. Twisting, growing, changing from within, we will begin to see it infused with the inner glow of living consciousness.

To begin, let us recapitulate the notion that multiple connectedness leads directly to a pluralistic conception of reality. A multiply connected topology promotes an expansion of the here-now point by bringing it into immediate contact with all other points at a given level of space-time, creating the effect of an elevated sense of here and now. If this broadened awareness is imagined to be embedded in its own, higher realm of multiply connected space-time, a whole hierarchy of domains suggests itself. Sarfatti thus speaks of an ascending order of gravitational fields for each level of organization of matter. Whiteman's viewpoint, stated at the outset, is in harmony; we can comprehend the phenomena of *psi* only by abandoning the single-level outlook (where simple location is the only mode of being) for a hierarchical world paradigm. Other parascience writers have expressed equally consonant positions.[32] However, it seems to me that the unity underlying the diversity cannot be clearly appreciated from these previous visions precisely because they did not address themselves to the limitations of a two-sided topology.

No void separating the strata of reality can be tolerated if unity is to be as fundamental as multiplicity. Even filling the void with an etheric mediating substance is inadequate for it gives us the impression that physical evolution is guided simply by a *non*physical and, therefore, external agent of change. The notion of a nonmaterial "cosmic midwife" thus functions to *preserve* the old, mechanistic conception of matter. What is required instead is a *synthesis* of the physical and the nonphysical wherein reality, working through matter, continuously transforms itself and, in so doing, takes on organic or "spiritual" properties. Reiser's hope of a "spiritual materialism" would then be realized. The strip of Möbius, when properly generalized, can lead us toward this goal. It can show that the physical and nonphysical spheres are interpenetrating, inextricable aspects of the *same* reality.

"Synsymmetry"

The significance of the Möbius model is entirely dependent on the critical question of *symmetry*. A body or spatial configuration satisfies the general symmetry criterion if it can be superimposed on (brought into point to point correspondence with) its mirror image. The symmetry of a figure is further specified in relation to a dimensional frame of reference. In Figure 3, the full-faced, two-dimensional figure is judged symmetric with respect to the plane of the paper because it can be carried into its mirror image without being removed from that plane. On the other hand, the two-dimensional profile cannot be superimposed on its mirror image unless it is lifted from the plane and properly turned over in the higher (third) dimension. Therefore, the profile is con-

MIRROR

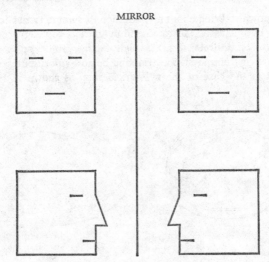

FIGURE 3 *Mirror reflection of symmetric and asymmetric two-dimensional figures.*

sidered asymmetric with regard to the plane. But we can, after all, perform the operation necessary to superimpose right- and left-hand profiles; the asymmetry of the profile is thus strictly relative. A hyperdimensional rotation out of the plane of the paper achieving the necessary superimposition may be said to restore symmetry.

The two-dimensional forms appearing in Figure 3 furnish us with alternate models of the inner structure of space-time. The full-faced figure is a representation of the here-now point "blown up" to reveal its symmetric character. Or, if we suppose the point structure of space-time to be asymmetric, this condition is represented by the profile. The Möbius continuum was found to identify distant points in space-time mathematically. Now we shall see that this identification produces a transformation of space-time that carries a point through the higher dimension into its mirror image; i.e., it accomplishes a mirror reflection as a *continuous rotation* by establishing a higher order of continuity. If the asymmetric model of the point is adopted, the Möbius topology can thus be shown to bring about a restoration of symmetry not achievable by means of the two-sided cylindrical topology.

To demonstrate, draw a right-facing profile on a small square of transparent material and begin by positioning it upright at the base of the cylindrical ring, as shown in Figure 4(a).

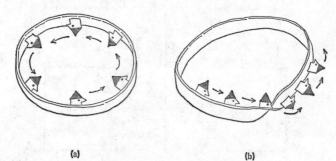

(a)   (b)

FIGURE 4 (a) *Counterclockwise rotation of profile about cylindrical ring compared with* (b) *Möbius rotation.*

You can rotate the profile indefinitely around the inside surface of the ring, but it will never leave its two-dimensional plane of rotation. As a consequence, its orientation remains unaltered, for the movement through the higher dimension necessary to transform right into left does not occur. It is true that the profile is turned upside down in the course of cylindrical rotation, but still it can be superimposed on its uninverted counterpart by merely sliding it down the page and turning it around. Because the right-facing form has been inverted, it does appear superficially to be facing left. However, from the profile's viewpoint, no change in orientation has occurred—it continues to face right.

Now consider the progress of the profile when it is rotated from the base of the Möbius strip [Figure 4(b)]. By moving it into the twisted portion of the strip, it is turned out of the two-dimensional plane of rotation and thus turned around. The twist through the higher dimension transforms the right-facing profile into a left-facing one and, in so doing, transports the profile to the other side of the surface. The crucial property of the Möbius band is here revealed. In the process of uniting spatially or temporally remote points (i.e., points situated on opposite sides of a space-time continuum), the Möbius structure transforms them in such a way that the symmetry condition is recovered at a higher level—a higher-order continuum is defined in which right is superimposed on left (or left on right) without leaving the surface.

But what if the alternate assumption is made about the inner structure of space-time, namely that points are symmetric? For the full-faced two-dimensional form of Figure 3, the question of symmetry restoration does not arise. A hyper-dimensional rotation is not needed to superimpose such a figure on its mirror image since, by definition of its symmetry, superimposition is achievable in the *same* plane. Since the full-faced figure is simply identical to its mirror image, whether it is rotated on the cylinder or on the Möbius strip, it remains unchanged. The topological connectedness of the surface (whether two sided or one sided) would hence be superfluous to the status of its points.

By conventional standards, points situated on opposite sides of a surface are understood to be temporally or spatially remote from one another. We are now discovering that their space-time separation is merely arbitrary if they are assumed to be simply self-symmetric. For whether or not the gap is bridged, the consequence is the same: the result of transporting the full-faced figure to the other side of the surface is indistinguishable from that of restricting it to the same side. Perhaps we can say that a certain "electromagnetic" factor is missing from the symmetric scenario. Distant points in space-time need to be imbued with a kind of "difference potential," their disjunction must constitute a form of *active* opposition. In other words, the separation of points must be given force by presupposing them to be enantiomorphic complements (mirror images of each other like the right- and left-facing profiles) rather than self-symmetric uniformities; otherwise all talk of "separation" will ring hollow.

In any case, we will see presently that it is not really necessary to assume the asymmetry of space-time points since this is *implied* when our geometry is expanded to its full scope. The restoration of symmetry achieved by Möbius rotation is not a final "closing of the circle." The higher continuity established is not the ultimate continuum wherein all duality is destroyed. Rather, the interplay of yin and yang continues, the dialectical tension of opposites is conserved because the Möbius strip is itself asymmetric! When the strip is formed, the right-hand end of the paper can be twisted to produce a right-facing strip, or the left-hand end, to create a left-facing one.

We next encounter a higher-order topological structure called the Klein bottle, after the German mathematician, Felix Klein. The Klein bottle superimposes the right-twisted Möbius strip on the left-twisted strip just as the strip superimposed the oppositely facing profiles. However, while the strip requires three dimensions to perform its function, the Klein bottle would entail the fourth. This is why Klein bottle operations can be conceived only by exercising topological imagination; the Klein bottle cannot be constructed in three-dimensional space. When we employ such imagination, we realize that the Klein bottle, like the Möbius strip, must be asymmetric. If there is a right-oriented Klein bottle, there must be a left-oriented counterpart, and the existence of these opposites suggests a still higher geometric form, the "hyper"-Klein bottle, which would require a fifth dimension to accomplish its fusion of opposites. Clearly, the process being described is endless. We may say, in general, that the completion of hyperdimensional rotation in dimension n (e.g., the formation of the Möbius strip by rotating a two-dimensional band through the third dimension) signals the commencement of rotation in $n+1$ (the formation of the Klein bottle by rotating a three-dimensional Möbius strip through the fourth dimension).

Higher dimensions emerge in this manner through the ceaseless dialectic of symmetry and asymmetry elsewhere referred to as "synsymmetry."[33] Here is the hierarchical conception of reality envisioned by Tobin, Whiteman, Reiser, and many others. It is a view of existence that transcends the classical dictum of simple location, thus bringing the phenomena of psi within the purview of natural description, rendering them *representable*. Moreover, in synsymmetric reality, not a hole can be found (though we might say that the effects of holes are created when the asymmetry of a given space-time domain is recognized). It is therefore unnecessary to attempt to imagine the unimaginable—we need not think of the transition from one level of reality to another as a leap through void, nor even postulate a field of pure consciousness as the cosmic facilitator of these voyages between physical strata. Consciousness and physical substance are welded together in the Möbius–Klein geometry. The physical world, being thus embodied, is seen to be a living organism, one which possesses mind. Physis and psyche, in their old connotations, do not survive this metamorphosis. Hence, we discover the synchronistic world, a world in which physis and psyche are synthesized; one in which clairvoyance and precognition are comprehended as natural occurrences in that they express the ongoing process of self-transformation, the unbroken growth from *within* of higher orders of space and time.

Finally, the opening hierarchy produced from the generalization of Möbius–Klein suggests the relation between the point structure of space-time and its global connectedness. While the Möbius strip modeled the overall connection of the two-dimensional world whose point elements (the profiles) were assumed asymmetric, the expansion of that world following the restoration of lower-order symmetry thrusts the Möbius strip into a new role: it is the point element of the three-dimensional world whose connectedness is now modeled by the Klein bottle—and this point element is asymmetric, just as we had earlier assumed that of the Möbius world to be. Thus we see that Möbius–Klein geometry describes the manner in which a cosmical twist at level n becomes an infinitesimal twist at $n+1$. I am reminded of Reiser's conjecture that "the atom is a galaxy turned inside out, rotated through a higher dimension."[34] And how nicely this harmonizes with the synchronistic interplay of microcosm and macrocosm articulated by San in his introduction to the *I Ching*: "The essence of mysticism is to *feel* . . . that $0 = \infty$ and $\infty = 0$."[35]

REFERENCES

1. C. G. Jung, "Synchronicity: An Acausal Connecting Principle," in *The Interpretation of Nature and the Psyche*, Bollingen Series LI (New York: Pantheon Books, 1955), p. 90.
2. C. T. K. Chari, "The Challenge of Psi: New Horizons of Scientific Research," *J. Parapsychology* **38**, 1, 1 (1974).
3. J. G. Pratt, "Some Notes for the Future Einstein for Parapsychology," *J. Amer. Soc. Psychical Research* **68**, 133 (1974).
4. J. H. M. Whiteman, "Quantum Theory and Parapsychology," *J. Amer. Soc. Psychical Research* **66**, 341 (1973).
5. Bertrand Russell, *The ABC of Relativity* (New York: Harper & Bros., 1925).
6. A. G. N. Flew, "Broad and Supernormal Precognition," in *The Philosophy of C. D. Broad*, edited by P. A. Schilpp (New York: Tudor, 1959), p. 425.
7. Jung, *op. cit.*, p. 27.
8. Lao Tsu, *Tao Te Ching*, translated by Fen and English (New York: Vintage, 1972).
9. Jung, *op. cit.*, p. 100.
10. Antonio de Nicolas, *Four Dimensional Man* (Bangalore, India: Dharmaram College, 1971).
11. Alan Watts, *The Supreme Identity* (New York: Pantheon, 1950).
12. J. Macquarrie, *Martin Heidegger* (Richmond, Va.: John Knox Press, 1968), pp. 14–15.
13. Jung, *op. cit.*, p. 100.
14. Ira Progoff, *Jung, Synchronicity, and Human Destiny* (New York: Julian Press, 1973).
15. Jung, *op. cit.*, p. 101 footnote.
16. S. M. Rosen, "A Case of Non-Euclidean Visualization," *J. Phenomenological Psychology* **5**, 1, 33 (Fall, 1974).
17. Chari, *op. cit.*, p. 2.
18. Brandon Carter, "Global Structure of the Kerr Family of Gravitational Fields," *Phys. Rev.* **174**, 1559 (1968); J. G. Taylor, *Black Holes: The End of the Universe?* (New York:

Random House, 1973); F. J. Tipler, "Rotating Cylinders and the Possibility of Global Causality Violation," *Phys. Rev. D* **9**, 2203 (1974).

19. B. Carter, "Complete Analytic Extension of the Symmetry Axis of Kerr's Solution of Einstein's Equations," *Phys. Rev.* **141**, 1242 (1966).

20. B. Tobin, J. Sarfatti, and F. Wolf, *Space-Time and Beyond* (New York: Dutton, 1975).

21. *Ibid.*, p. 127.

22. J. A. Wheeler, *Geometrodynamics* (New York: Academic Press, 1962).

23. Sarfatti, *op. cit.*, p. 136.

24. *Ibid.*, p. 153.

25. O. L. Reiser, *Cosmic Humanism* (Cambridge: Schenkman, 1966).

26. Sarfatti, *op. cit.*, p. 126.

27. According to Capek, this is Weyl's characterization of the physical inaccessibility of hypothesized gaps in the Euclidean continuum. M. Capek, *The Philosophical Impact of Contemporary Physics* (Princeton: van Nostrand, 1961), p. 226.

28. Rosen, 1974, *op. cit.*

29. H. Weyl, *Space-Time-Matter* (New York: Dover, 1922), p. 274.

30. S. M. Rosen, "A Plea for the Possibility of Visualizing Existence," *Scientia* **108**, 9–12, 789 (1973): "The Unity of Changelessness and Change: A Visual Geometry of World and Man," *Main Currents* **31**, 4, 115 (March–April, 1975a); "Synsymmetry," *Scientia* **110**, 539–49 (1975b).

31. C. W. K. Mundle, "Strange Facts in Search of a Theory," *Proc. Soc. Psychical Research* **56**, 1 (1973).

32. John W. Dunne, *An Experiment with Time* (New York: Macmillan, 1938); and Reiser, *op. cit.*

33. Rosen, 1975b, *op. cit.*

34. Reiser, *op. cit.*, p. 412.

35. Charles San, "How to Consult I Ching," in *I Ching*, translated by J. Legge (New York: Causeway, 1973), p. 4.

14.

Space: The All-Embracing Container

HERMINE SABETAY

Until recent times astronomical space was thought to be an immensely vast emptiness where the stars figured as relatively small islands of matter. Newton sustained the idea of a universal void, in contradiction to the ancient dictum, "nature abhors a vacuum." Later, in order to explain the transmission of light, scientists assumed that space was filled with an all-pervasive subtle medium called ether. As a consequence of Einstein's theory of relativity, and as rigorous experiments failed to reveal the existence of such an agent, this hypothesis too was discarded.

Interstellar space is no longer considered a void, as with the help of powerful telescopes clouds composed of fine dust and gas have been observed outside the celestial bodies. And according to modern field theory, even seemingly empty space is not completely devoid of content, being the playground of potential forces and elementary particles such as electrons and photons.

The investigations of modern astronomy certainly deserve our deep admiration; yet beyond doubt the occult science presents us with an incomparably greater panorama of a stupendous cosmos. For in this ancient teaching, space is a plenum or fullness. "There is not one finger's breadth of void space in the whole boundless universe," says *The Secret Doctrine*. (I:330)[1]

This wholeness comprises all the levels of manifestation, extending from the divine abstraction down to the physi-

"Space: The All-Embracing Container" by Hermine Sabetay originally appeared in *The American Theosophist*, Vol. 63, No. 5, May 1975 and is reprinted by permission of the journal.

cal world; space is called "the seven-skinned eternal mother–father" and described as "the absolute container of all that is, whether manifested or unmanifested." (I:75) In a cabalistic treatise, space is qualified as "the all-containing uncontained . . . the unknown container of all, the unknown first Cause," a statement which is, says H. P. Blavatsky, a most correct definition. (II:56)

A subtler state of space is referred to in esoteric philosophy under the name of akasha, which is described as having many aspects. *The Secret Doctrine* sometimes calls it higher "aether," being the noumenon of the lower "ether," this latter appearing also under the name of "astral Light." In the commentary on the first stanza of Dzyan, akasha is said to be a radiation of *mulaprakriti*, the primordial cosmic root-matter. Furthermore we are told that:

> Akasha is the universal soul, the matrix of the universe, the mysterium magnum from which all that exists is born by separation or differentiation. It is the cause of existence, it fills all the infinite space, *is* space itself, or both its 6th and 7th principles. (IV:81)

In other connections, akasha is designated as "the divine space," "the primordial ocean of space," "the celestial virgin-mother," etc.

The true nature of akasha is veiled in secret and known only to adepts of higher occultism. But the various hints disclosed for students let it appear as a fascinating subject. Akasha is described as containing an infinite amount of potential energy and as the source of various kinds of vibration, especially those of sound and light, which are the basis of the created universe. Divine sound, also called the divine word, gives the impulse to creation; and light condenses into matter, as modern science has shown. Thus akasha continuously supplies the energy by which the universe is evolved and maintained. In its depths are hidden the noumena of all things; it is "the great storehouse of creation." (V:234)

Moreover akasha is the divine screen recording in a permanent picture every thought, deed, or event, and these are indelibly impressed on this enigmatic medium. The wholeness of past, present, and future is contained on its imperishable tablets, which can be examined only by highly developed spirits.

According to occultism, space as an objective reality apart from the mind has no true existence. On the different levels of being the perception of space is modified; therefore these impressions are said to belong to *chidakasha* or mental space, while *mahakasha* designates the eternal absolute space of ultimate reality.

Another consideration related to the nature of space implies the idea of higher dimensions. Theosophical teachings assert that these are characteristic of superior planes and belong to the corresponding states of consciousness. A great deal of speculation has taken place about the existence of a fourth spatial dimension in addition to the three which are familiar to our perception, often in order to explain certain phenomena of spiritualism, such as materializations and the passage of physical objects through matter. H. P. Blavatsky mentions the question: ". . . in passing it is worthwhile to point out the real significance of the sound, but incomplete, intuition that has prompted . . . the use of the modern expression, the 'fourth dimension in Space'." (I:295) She goes on to declare that the term is based on a confusion of several conceptions and that the next higher dimension belongs to a sixth sense or clairvoyance. The common sense cannot imagine more than the three dimensions of length, breadth, and thickness. Nevertheless mathematicians operate with higher spaces and an unlimited number of dimensions.

On the other hand, Einstein's theory of relativity postulates a space-time continuum, introducing time as the fourth dimension, adding thus a dynamic factor to the static expanse of space. Movement is conceivable only as a function of both time and space.

Einstein has rediscovered an old truth of archaic philosophy. *The Secret Doctrine* asserts that "space and time are one . . . they are the incognizable THAT" (IV:183); "space and time being simply the forms of THAT, which is the absolute ALL." (III:166)

This latter statement seems to allude to the fundamental duality called in Hindu esoteric philosophy the *shiva-shakti-tattva*, often mentioned in Dr. Taimni's writings (*Man, God,*

and the Universe as well as in various articles in *The Theosophist*). Shiva, the principle of consciousness, is related to
space, which is stable and contains potentially everything that
has been, is, or will be. As to time, this unceasing flow is an
attribute of shakti, the principle of power. Movement is always associated with time within the background of space.

In the physical world the reflections of shiva and shakti appear as matter and energy. And as it is known that atoms are
formed of "bottled-up" energy, manifestation is viewed as an
unfolding of divine power or shakti, the mighty source of all
vibratory potencies, while the aspect of shiva or consciousness
is present in every form, however deeply veiled in the mineral
kingdom.

Such fundamental teachings of occultism are of course unknown to modern science, which is concerned only with the
lowest plane of existence. Furthermore, the space-time concept
with its mathematical developments ignores the qualities of
life and the mystery of the organization of living forms. This
category of beings has its own laws which are not those of
physics. The life force which works against decay and entropy and constructs forms of ever greater complexity, has
been called, by the French scientist–philosopher Jean Barraud,[2] the "fifth dimension"; it is the dynamic energy giving
the impulse to biological evolution.

This fruitful idea rejoins the occult doctrine that space, far
from being a lifeless receptacle of matter, as conceived by
materialistic science, or an extension unrelated to things, is a
living Entity:

> . . . the one eternal root of all, the playground of all the
> forces in nature. It is the fountainhead of all terrestrial
> life and the abode of those (to us) invisible swarms of
> existences . . . that surround us on all sides. (V:382)

For a so-called rational mind, the belief in the existence of
invisible beings as those described by folklore and fairy tales
is no other than a childish superstition; that there is an order
of devas and nature-spirits, as well as the reality of subtler
worlds, the abodes of these ethereal populations, is denied or
simply ignored.

Nevertheless, such invisible worlds do exist. Inhabited

as thickly as in our own, they are scattered throughout apparent space in immense numbers. . . . The fact that our physical eye does not see them, is no reason for disbelieving in them. (II:330)

Viewed as the dwelling of multitudes of tenuous beings, space appears as a plenum, fullness, or wholeness throbbing with life. The plenum of occultism has the same meaning as the gnostic concept of "pleroma," which is "the sum total of all the divine manifestations and emanations." (V:462) It constitutes the synthesis of all the living entities, a ladder extending from the highest spirits to the numberless inhabitants of the etheric plane.

Space is not only the container of the totality of things, considered as unrelated to each other. It is a recognized truth of occult science that there is no separation or isolation in the wholeness of the universe. As said in *The Mahatma Letters to A. P. Sinnett:*

Nature has linked all parts of her empire together by subtle threads of magnetic sympathy, and there is a mutual correlation between a star and a man. (p. 267)

According to this statement, the smallest action of a human being gives an impulse to vibrations propagated through the whole cosmos.

Space is an expression of divinity. In Vedantic terms, parabrahman contains the whole universe and is that boundless expansion. In the *Vishnu Purana,* Vishnu is shown pervading the universe, being identified with its wholeness: which is an expression of pantheism. In the Cabalah, the manifestation or the visible world is called "the garment of God."

The relation of the supreme to manifested totality is that of unity and multiplicity. The first fundamental proposition of *The Secret Doctrine* strikes the note of oneness, evoking "an omnipresent, eternal, boundless, and immutable PRINCIPLE," equated with both absolute abstract space and the root of consciousness. While the second proposition asserts the absolute universality of the law of periodicity or alternation, an aspect of time, the third is related to the two poles of being: the one and the multitude: the universal oversoul embracing all individual souls, pictured as the many sparks of one mighty flame. All particular selves are contained in the wholeness of the universal self, and each one may discover his identity with the indwelling divine reality.

The binding link between unity and multiplicity is harmony, a state of order and organization, by which the many are held together in a wholeness of greater significance than the sum total of the composing parts. This is the natural law underlying the immense diversity of living forms, all sustained by the One Life animating the whole creation.

This mighty stream of life descends from absolute being, filling the whole universe. The aim of this inconceivably powerful outpouring is expressed in this passage of *The Secret Doctrine:*

> The universe manifests periodically for purposes of the collective progress of the countless *lives,* the outbreathings of the one life. (I:310–11)

Considering the astronomical space with its innumerable stars and galaxies, we are struck with inexpressible admiration for divine order and harmony. For the Pythagoreans, the heavens formed a "musical scale and number"; and these ancient philosophers listened to "the harmony of the spheres" which they conceived as based on the sevenfold scale.

While the visible universe with its myriads of brilliant suns is in itself a stupendous phenomenon, the idea that the celestial vault shows only the outermost shell of hidden splendors in successive depths of subtler spaces, transcends human imagination.

REFERENCES

1. Quotations not otherwise specified are from *The Secret Doctrine,* by H. P. Blavatsky, 6 Vol. ed. (Adyar: Theosophical Publishing House.)
2. J. Barraud, *La Cinquième Dimension* (Paris, 1952); *La Philosophie de la Qualité* (Paris, 1956).

15.

The Idea of Counterspace

OLIVE WHICHER

At a time in history when contemporary social and economic thinking has been dominated by the idea of an expanding economy, scientific thinking has taken a similar direction—especially as regards theories of an expanding universe. It is important to note this trend, for the ways in which men have at varying times in history conceptualized the universe in which they live—the forms of thought in which their science or their religious beliefs are expressed—have a direct effect on their ways of living and upon their social forms. The prevailing "thought forms" (*denkformen*) of a time are reflected in the social organism.

For example, when the space of Euclid, with its rigid and right-angled three dimensions emanating from a central point, was taken absolutely for granted, social forms were organized in accordance, strictly graded around a central source of power, whether religious or secular. A dominion or kingdom is a finite area; the means of communication radiate quite naturally to and from the hub or capitol, relating it to the outskirts or frontiers. The area under rule may be large or small—it may expand or contract according to the exigencies of war—but the essentials remain the same. The ideal thoughtform behind this type of picture is Euclid's circle: a center with radii relating it to a more or less distant periphery or circumference—an outer limit.

When one comes to think of it, the thought-picture of the

"The Idea of Counterspace" by Olive Whicher originally appeared in *Main Currents in Modern Thought*, Vol. 30, No. 4, March–April 1974 and is reprinted by permission of the author and journal. Copyright © 1974 by The Center for Integrative Education.

Euclidean circle, or its three-dimensional counterpart, the sphere or globe, has been for centuries—and still is—a powerfully formative image or ideal, both in science and sociology.

In the 1820s and 30s, the non-Euclidean geometries were discovered. Spaces of more than three dimensions were thought out, thus shaking the absolute nature of classical conceptions of space, and of the uniform flow of time. The result was the conjoining of what had been thought of as two radically different entities into one: space-time. In the 19th century, the unceasing efforts of scientists to adapt then-current forms of thought to the new phenomena led still further away from the old, hitherto unquestioned, framework, into which researches concerning "real" objects in space and time could no longer be made to fit. The result, of course, was the theory of relativity and subsequent developments, which so radically changed our picture of the world. As a result of these new concepts of matter and energy, the old ground with its familiar landmarks appeared to dissolve away. Yet in practical, day-to-day matters, the space of Euclid is still valid—even if theoretically it is no longer finite but has, in the new understanding, acquired an "infinitely distant plane" or "absolute."

During the second half of the 19th century, Arthur Cayley and Felix Klein discovered that the specialized and rigid forms of geometry in which some specific measure appears could all be based on the more general and mobile projective form. In this way the ordinary space of Euclid, answering to our everyday experience in the physical world, and also the different non-Euclidean spaces, could *all* be approached from their appropriate points of view, which are embraced in projective geometry. (In Cayley's words: "Projective geometry is all geometry.") As Adams wrote in 1949: "Projective geometry has discovered that the ideal structure of three-dimensional space does not proceed one sidedly from the point alone, but from two opposite entities—point and plane—which play a fully equivalent part in the fundamental structure."[1]

Amid all the possibilities of variation and change in relationships between the fundamental geometric entities in projective space (points, lines, and planes) according to the definitions of this geometry, it was only necessary to propound an unique entity, as it were cosmically or absolutely given, whereby the measures of a particular type of space could be determined. This entity is called "the Absolute" of any space.[2] In projective geometry, the infinitely distant line of the plane functions just as any other line does, and it contains the infinitely distant point of every line in the plane. In the special case of Euclidean space, the absolute is the plane at infinity and the measures become equal and symmetrical around a central point. The absolute, in the full sense of the word, is the ruling factor in projective processes taking place between points, lines *and planes* in the full three dimensions of projective space. (However, for the sake of simplicity, the example given below is restricted to a two-dimensional plane figure.) When in the full three-dimensional space the absolute plane is the infinitely distant plane, then the forms take on the characteristics of what may be called *positive or Euclidean space*. It is the type of space necessary for the right-angled symmetries and parallelisms of architectural creations and the expansive and contractive rigid measures of plus and minus in the material world.

An elementary or imaginative pictorial approach to projective geometry is sufficient to introduce us to the vast range of possibilities of formative relationships between the simple elements of point, line and plane which come about by introducing *movement* into a configuration. This geometry used to be called the geometry of position (*analysis situs*), which may be interpreted as saying that no amount of movement in the relative positions of the geometrical elements would destroy the underlying law of a configuration.

Let us now take a simple example. Define a triangle as follows, dispensing entirely with any attribute concerning measurement: *A triangle is determined either by any three points in a plane, but not in a line; or by any three lines in a plane, but not in a point.* In other words, it matters not where any of the members (points or lines) of a triangle are positioned in the plane in which it lies, whether in the finite or infinitely distant. Dispense with measurement, but include the concept of the infinite, and a triangle is a triangle wherever its parts are located in the plane, even if one of its points or one of its lines is in the infinite and it does not therefore look like a conventional triangle; in thought it nevertheless *is* one. We are led to realize that points or lines at infinity function just as any other points do, and in fact are indispensable to the whole. Old distinctions resting on measurement cease to have any great significance; right-angled, isosceles, or equilateral triangles are all included in the archetypal idea of a triangle.

Projective geometry rests on beautiful and harmonious truths of coincidence and continuity, and provides us with a realm of unshakable mathematical validity in which to move about freely in thought. The creative process can be continuous and sustained, passing through the infinite point or plane and returning again. The very fact that the creation of forms in this geometry is not dependent in the first place on any kind of measurement, but is concerned primarily with *relationships* between geometrical entities, gives access to processes of creative thought entirely different from those used, for example, in building a house. In the latter case, a beginning is made from, say, a cornerstone, some predetermined measure is laid out from corner to corner and so the building grows. In projective geometry, on the other hand, the actual measures of the once completed form may be quite fortuitous and appear last, not first; yet the form, however it may arise—however it may, so to speak, crystallize out in the process of construction, and however bizarre its appearance—will always remain true to the archetypal idea underlying it.

Let us take as an instance the theorem of Pascal (1623–1662) concerning the hexagon inscribed in a conic: *The common points of opposite pairs of sides of a hexagon inscribed in a conic are collinear* (i.e., lie on the same line).[8] The theorem deals with six points in a plane and the remarkable fact that, provided *all* six points are points on a conic (*any* conic will suffice), then the "opposite" pairs of sides of the hexagon determined by these six points—three pairs of them—will each have a common point, and all three of these points will always be in line! Of course, the term "opposite" is a spatial one and correctly refers to the regular, Euclidean hexagon in the circle. This turns out to be a special case of the far more general, projective form, and the three points common to its pairs of opposite sides are all infinitely distant. The inclusion of the concept of points at infinity pro-

vides the clear thought that, in this special case, the three
points are points of the infinitely distant line of the plane in
which hexagon and circle lie. The variety of possibilities in
the positioning of the points on the conic and also the choice
of the cylic order in which to join them, added to the fact
that the conditions still hold for a hexagon inscribed into *any*
of the projective forms of a circle, fills the mind with wonder
at the mobility of the spatial interpretation of the all-relating
concept as expressed in the statement of the theorems. (See
Figures 1–4.) In this example, the line of three points or Pas-

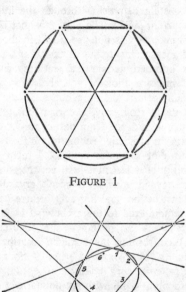

FIGURE 1

FIGURE 2

cal line, as it is called, may be regarded as the absolute of the
configuration, in the sense in which this term has been used
above.

Because this is a realm which contains the archetypes and
also the actual laws of forms as yet uncreated, it is important

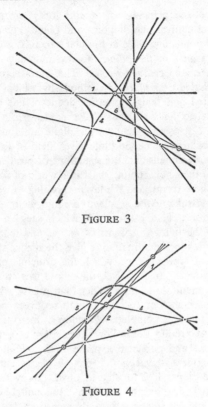

FIGURE 3

FIGURE 4

to understand and to become creative in the development of projective geometrical relationships. It is a realm of clear mathematical thought with its own remarkable laws, among which the laws of Euclidean geometry are one of the particular cases. The British scientist George Adams called the domain of protective transformations "archetypal space"; Louis Locher-Ernst used the German word *urraum* to describe what we might conceive to be an ever-moving, fluid continuum of projective possibilities, containing the seeds or potentialities of all types of form.

In addition to the all-pervading element of movement in projective geometry, there is a fundamental principle of great significance—the principle of *duality* or *polarity*, the ideal and mutual equivalence of point and plane. Polar to the geometry of points and lines in the plane there is a *geometry of lines and planes in the point;* the two mutually complement one another. As Cremona wrote: "There are therefore always two *correlative* or *reciprocal* methods by which figures may be generated and their properties deduced, and it is in this that geometric *duality* consists."[4] Laws at work in the "extensive" two-dimensional field of the plane are found again in polar opposite form in the "intensive" field of the point. So, too, the three-dimensional constructions of positive Euclidean space have their polar counterpart in a world of forms held in a point. These forms, and the laws according to which projective transformations take place among them, are of significance for a field of research which seeks a deeper approach to the living kingdoms of nature and man.

The figures included here may give the reader some idea of the different types of form which the principle of duality or polarity provides. In Figure 5, the ellipse was created projectively as a manifold of lines rather than points, without reference to any center or focus and with no preconceived measures. The tangents completely envelop it, interweaving in the infinite area around the hollow form. Figure 6 shows a pattern of lines and points in a plane, and in Figure 7 the attempt is made to awaken the idea of planes and lines in a point. The planes in both figures must, however, be thought of as infinite in extent; they continue indefinitely on all sides, and it would be impossible to draw a complete picture of them. Just as the lines and points in Figure 6 are parts of members of the plane, so, too, the lines and planes in Figure 7 are considered to be parts or members of the point. In the intensive world of the point, the part would seem to be greater than the whole; something which can never be said of forms in the familiar world of the plane.

The Austrian philosopher Rudolf Steiner, taking up the methods of scientific investigation begun by Goethe, was the first to underline the importance of projective geometry for a methodic approach to the phenomena of life. He held that it is not enough to return to vague, traditional ideas concerning phenomena, the full secrets of which do not readily open

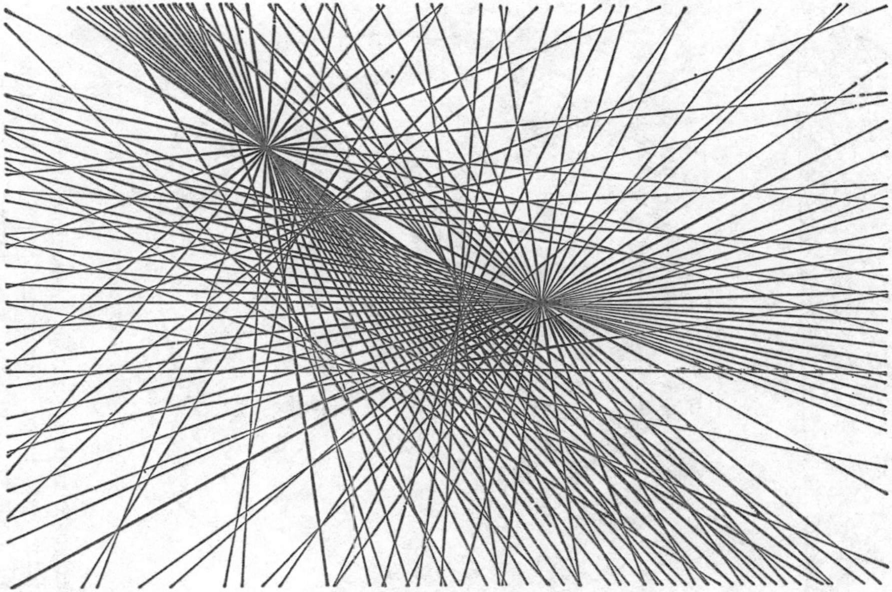

FIGURE 5

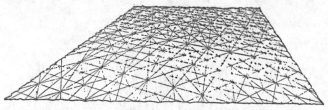

FIGURE 6

FIGURE 7

themselves to modern scientific methods. He pointed rather to
the necessity to redefine in modern terms the realm and nature of the forces that shape living forms. The kind of training in thinking which projective geometry provides makes it
possible to conceptualize such forces and their movements.
Steiner called for a mathematical approach to the laws of the
living world, and assigned to this realm the very qualities one
would expect to find in the kind of space which is mathe-

matically the exact opposite of Euclidean space, wherein the physical–mechanical forces of nature have their field of action.

The first to work out in detail the properties of such a "negative space" was George Adams, who published essays simultaneously in German and English in 1933 on what he called "physical and ethereal spaces." He and Louis Locher-Ernst, working independently, thought out and formulated the forms and laws of the negative or counter-Euclidean type of space, which Locher-Ernst described in 1940 in a book entitled *Raum und Gegenraum* ("Space and Counterspace").

This kind of space—the polar counterpart or, in a sense, the "negative" of Euclidean space—has indeed been conceived, at least as a possibility, by geometricians from time to time.[5] But from a physical point of view, its properties appeared too paradoxical, while in the purely formal sense it promised nothing new, being to the space of Euclid, so to speak, as the mold is to the cast in every detail. So far as we are aware, no one has taken the trouble to investigate it further. Scientists, interested in the interpretation of the real world on merely physical terms, have paid little or no attention to this other type of space. Yet if we allow the gestures of form in the living kingdoms to speak to us, and are not too exclusively biased in the direction of quasiphysical or atomist explanations, we awaken to the fact that precisely this type of space-formation confronts us throughout the living world. Indeed, the transformations taking place in the forms of living organisms speak eloquently of that type of transformation which we now see is possible between positive (Euclidean) and negative type (counter-Euclidean) spaces through the mediation of projective transformations in the archetypal space which includes them both.

In this connection, Professor H. V. Turnbull, who was a close friend of D'Arcy Thompson and editor of Newton's correspondence, suggested that in the realm of growth and form the planewise and not only the pointwise approach should be significant. He wrote: "In the realm of growth and form, both analyses are significant. The seed, the stem and the leaf of a plant suggest two ways of studying the three-dimensional shape, the one pointwise microscopically and the other planewise." He also drew attention to the fact that the relative completedness of a pointwise analysis, reached at a certain scientific stage, neither excludes nor is vitiated by the polar opposite aspect which may still be awaiting discovery. "This mathematical duality is not a case of competing theories, where one is right and the other is wrong. . . . The characteristic description of their relationship is that of in and through but not of for or against."[6]

Let us now try to picture the properties of the negative or counter-Euclidean type of space. The first thing to observe is that such a space is determined by a *point-at-infinity* (the counterpart of the *plane-at-infinity* on which Euclidean space depends). A point-at-infinity is, then, the absolute of this space, by which is meant a point *functioning* mathematically as infinitely distant—but not necessarily (and this is important) in the infinitely distant plane of ordinary Euclidean space. Conceivably, no doubt, the point-at-infinity of a negative space might also be infinitely distant in the space of Euclid, but it need not be so; above all, it will not be so in our present context, where this geometry is related to the living, germinating processes which develop on the Earth.

Passing from ordinary space to its polar counterpart, we interchange the roles of point and plane. As noted previously, in Euclidean space the absolute is a plane, but in this familiar space of the physical—material world, points and point-like entities predominate. The absolute is infinitely distant and unattainable, and yet all the relations show that for this very reason the space determined by it will be predominantly "pointwise." Points, or at least point-centered volumes, will be the spatial entities "inhabiting" such a space. In negative or counter-Euclidean space, on the other hand, depending as it does on a *functional infinitude* in a point, the exact opposite will be true. The constituent entities are planes—planes which are all of infinite extent and have, not a point-centered but rather a peripheral, enveloping quality. In the physical world, materials (even the living materials in plants) cannot carry out in full the planar formations characteristic of counter-Euclidean space; but in the enveloping gesture so peculiar to the living forms of the higher plants, for instance—a gesture shown often by a single leaf or by many leaves together—nature reveals before our very eyes the kind of space in which the plane, not the point, is primary. Such a space will be found to be endowed with definite orientation, form and measure, for there will be somewhere an innermost point acting as the "infinitude within" (the point at infinity), just as the outermost plane gives form and measure to the space of Euclid.

There can be no question, in a short, elementary statement such as this, of doing justice to all the work which has been done on the basis of this new mathematical development. Published work has been primarily in plant morphology and metamorphosis, related also to the work of Goethe.* There is abundant evidence to suggest that the form-giving life of nature is determined not only in the Euclidean universal space, in which matter qua matter (as it is usually understood) is at home, but also by the polar opposite type of space formation. In respect of time duration, and in respect of "one" and "many," this other kind of space plays quite a different role. It is a *type* of space-formation, not a single universal space given once and for all. Spaces of this kind come into being and pass away again with the life cycles of living creatures or of their several organs. Wherever, in effect, there is a living seed, a germinating point, a special focus of life or growth—whether within the watery substance of a living body or hovering just outside it as at the growing point of the higher plant—there we may look for the "infinitude within" of such a "time-space." We find evidence of the planar formative activity around the point in question, or in the gesture of the leaflike organs that envelop it and thence unfold. The higher plant creates its living, counter-Euclidean spaces as it develops, and grows from thence outward into three-dimensional Earth space.

The concept of the two types of space also requires another approach to the concept of forces. Here, too, the primary polarity of space has been the guide in George Adams' work on the planar counter-Euclidean aspect of force fields. The idea of force in classical Newtonian mechanics (no longer, in-

* See *Man or Matter* by Ernst Lehrs (Harper & Row, 1957) and *The Etheric Formative Forces in Cosmos, Earth and Man* (Anthroposophic Press, 1932). *Editors.*

deed, the only idea of what a force can be) is, if we reflect, in harmony with the pure geometry and kinematics of the space of Euclid. The primary characteristic of this kind of force is that in its spatial activity it is directed along a line, from point to point. We may describe the typical forces of the inorganic world as "centric forces"—forces working from center to center, that is, from point to point along the line that joins them. The archetypal instance of such a force is gravity; allied thereto are all the characteristic forces of pressure and contraction.

What kind of "force," then, will be at work in the negative-Euclidean realm? The clear conclusion is that the primary force of such a space will be levitational, suctional, planar. The balanced duality of spatial theory will express itself also in the organic balance of a living form.

In our times, it is of paramount importance to transcend the idea of a *onefold*, point-centered, material world, in which man (one of many similar units) lives his life automatically accumulating substance and losing it again. The material world of Euclidean space is, after all, not the only aspect of the universe, though perhaps of necessity man has had to become so deeply immersed in this aspect that he has not been able to see clearly beyond its limitations. As we have seen here, in the perspective of projective geometry, the universe may more adequately be seen as *three*fold, material and spiritual, with life sustained between these polar realms. A truer picture of such a cosmos reveals polarities which interplay and interweave to create the diverse forms in nature.

When man in his conscious activity of thinking has taken a more profound step in the understanding of *polarity*, as distinct from mere contrast, he will come to a creative and fundamental use of the imagination in many fields. Contrasts such as expansion and contraction in physical space take on quite another aspect in the realm of the living. To the extent to which we can learn to understand the laws of the interweaving polarities and how to put them into practice, we shall perhaps be enabled to sort out the complicated tangle of modern life.

Current methods of investigation into substances and the

forces to which they are subject do not yet gain access to the whole of the living process; biochemistry and biophysics lean heavily on concepts which rest on quantitative mathematics and apply in the physical–mechanical realm. The impetus given by a quantitative mathematics has led to the development of a quantitatively minded world; it is an essential task for the future to develop the *qualitative* aspect of mathematics, so that the generations to come may in time achieve a true science of the living, conscious aspect of the world.

REFERENCES

1. *The Golden Blade,* p. 66.
2. It is more complete and mathematically exact to say that the absolute of Euclidean space is an infinitely distant plane with an "imaginary circle" inscribed therein, and that the absolute of counter-Euclidean space is a point-at-infinity containing an "imaginary cone." "The conception of elements lying at an infinite distance is due to Desargues, who in 1639 explicitly considered parallel straight lines as meeting in an infinitely distant point, and parallel planes as passing through the same straight lines at an infinite distance . . . Poncelet [1822] arrived at the conclusion that the points in space which lie at an infinite distance must be regarded as all lying in the same plane." L. Cremona, *Elements of Projective Geometry* (New York: Dover, 1960), p. ix.
3. A conic is any curve which is the locus of a point which moves so that the ratio of its distance from a fixed point to its distance from a fixed line is constant. (*Mathematics Dictionary,* edited by G. & R. C. James [Princeton, N.J.: Van Nostrand, 1968].)
4. Cremona, *op. cit.,* p. 26.
5. In this connection, it is interesting to note that in a short article published in 1910 (*Proceedings of the Edinburgh Mathematical Society,* Vol. 28), Professor D. M. Y. Sommerville enumerated no less than twenty-seven conceivable geometries of three-dimensional space. Among them are the Euclidean and the two well-known non-

Euclidean geometries. One of the twenty-four others is the geometry of "antispace." Somewhere in mathematical literature there may be further developments in this direction: I have not found them. Interest has generally centered on such spaces as are more nearly in accord with the conditions of physical imagination; or else, alternatively, the geometry of abstract spaces of any number of dimensions has been worked out, quite without reference to the imagination or to the forms of nature.

6. "Mathematics in the Larger Context," *Research* 3 No. 5 (1950).

SUGGESTED READINGS

George Adams, *Physical and Ethereal Spaces* (London: 1965); *Von dem Aetherischen Raume* (Stuttgart: 1964); *Universalkrafte in der Mechanik* (Dornach: 1973).

G. Adams and O. Whicher, *Die Pflanze in Raum und Gegenraum* (Stuttgart: 1960).

Olive Whicher, *Projective Geometry* (London: 1971); *Projektive Geometrie* (Stuttgart: 1970).

Louis Locher-Ernst, *Projektive Geometrie* (Zurich: 1940); *Raum und Gegenraum* (Dornach: 1957).

Rudolf Steiner—The references are to many books and lectures, but three fundamental works are:—*Philosophy of Freedom* (London: 1964); *The Theory of Knowledge Implicit in Goethe's World-Conception* (New York: 1968); *Riddles of Philosophy* (Spring Valley, N.Y.: 1973).

Georg Unger, *Grundbegriffe der modernen Physik* (Teil III) (Stuttgart: 1967).

Ernst Lehrs, *Man and Matter* (London: 1958); *Mensch und Materie* (Frankfurt: 1966).

16.

The Etheric Formative Forces

GUENTHER WACHSMUTH

What we perceive in nature by means of our sense organs—as every person trained in science and philosophy knows—is not in reality substances and forces but states and the changing of these into one another. Rudolf Steiner states: "The senses inform us in regard to states. If we speak, then, of something other than states which undergo transmutations, we are no longer restricting ourselves to the bare facts of the case, but are adding concepts to these." When we go beyond the states and their metamorphoses given to us by the senses, a twofold question then forces itself upon our thought: (1) What maintains the given states in the form in which they now exist? (2) What in given instances causes the metamorphosis from one state to another?

If we begin, not like Newton from the standpoint of matter, of the bodies, but like Goethe from that of the primary forces, we must reply to both these questions: *The etheric primal forces (formative forces). In so far as they are united with bodies in the phenomenal world, these bodies continue in that state induced by them, until such time as free etheric forces of another sort, or stronger ones of the same sort, bring about a metamorphosis of the existing state.*

We shall be able to pursue this idea in the most varied examples in nature. But at this point we must first give a conception of the nature and the action of the etheric forces. Lenard writes: "Because of the identity of electric waves and

"The Etheric Formative Forces" by Guenther Wachsmuth is excerpted from *The Etheric Formative Forces in the Cosmos, Earth and Man* by Guenther Wachsmuth and is reprinted by permission of the Anthroposophic Press.

light waves, we are sure that the same ether which brings us
light, heat, and all energy from the sun also conducts the electric and magnetic forces. . . . A single ether for light, heat,
and electricity—thus did Lord Kelvin express the great
achievement of the electrical researches of Hertz." This error
Dr. Steiner combatted as early as 1888, in the words already
cited: "When we seek to discover what happens in that which
is extended in space when the entities under consideration are
being transmitted therein, we must conclude that it is always
a motion. For a medium in which motion alone is possible
must react to everything by way of motion, and all kinds of
transmission which it must perform will be carried out by
way of motion. When, therefore, I seek to discover the forms
of this motion, I shall not learn what the thing is which is
being transmitted, but only in what manner it is conveyed to
me. It is sheer nonsense to say that heat and light are motion.
Motion is merely the reaction of matter capable of motion to
the action of light."

The conclusions which were arrived at from the researches
of Hertz led not only to the error that from the mere effects
which are produced in the ether, a medium capable only of
motion, too much was concluded regarding the very nature of
the ether itself, but also to the erroneous assumption that—
because of the uniformity of the reaction of the perceptible
medium (that is, substance) to the actions of the ether—
therefore a single ether calls forth all the effects. But this
error is fundamental and has blocked the way to reality before all further researches in ether.

*As a matter of fact there are altogether seven etheric pri-
mal forces, formative forces, active in the cosmos; of these,
however, only four reveal themselves in the space-and-time
processes of our present phenomenal world. In what follows,
therefore, we shall deal only with these four etheric formative
forces.*

Anthroposophical spiritual science* designates these four
kinds of ether as:

> warmth ether,
> light ether,

* As developed first by Rudolf Steiner. *Editors.*

chemical ether (or sound ether), and
life ether.

In characterizing the differences among the four kinds of ether we cannot restrict ourselves to the ascertained fact that they are distinguished in comparison with one another by the wavelengths—that is, the degree of motion—which they call forth in the world of substance. Such merely quantitative distinctions of modern science do not at all suffice to explain the phenomena, qualitatively so utterly unlike, which the different kinds of ether produce in the world of substance. The relationship existing among the etheric formative forces is, rather, the following: The four etheric formative forces have proceeded phylogenetically one out of another, and proceed now ontogenetically one out of another; and, in reality, warmth ether has been metamorphosed—that is, has evolved into light ether; light ether into chemical ether; chemical ether into life ether. Further, the mutual relation between the etheric forces is such that the later ether, more highly evolved, always contains in itself the attributes of the earlier, yet always develops, as a new entity, an activity clearly distinguishable from that of the other. Thus the life ether contains in itself the warmth ether, light ether, and chemical ether; the chemical ether contains the light ether and warmth ether; etc. Nevertheless, each ether acts in the manner characteristic of itself alone; and only when, through having penetrated into the substance-world, it has been modified, may a higher ether, for instance, be reduced, as it were, to the action of a lower. Warmth ether, from which the other ether forces have evolved, has in turn come into being out of purely spiritual states outside of time and space.

The four kinds of ether may now be classified in two groups, and this distinction is of fundamental importance for the understanding of all that is to follow:

The first two, warmth ether and light ether, have the tendency to expand, the impulse to radiate out from a given central point; they act centrifugally; whereas the other two, chemical ether and life ether, have the tendency to draw in toward a center, the impulse to concentrate all in a given central point; their action is suctional, centripetal. This polarity of the two ether groups—the centrifugal, radiating, self-expanding will, and the suctional, centripetal will to draw inward, to concentrate—is an ultimate elemental principle lying at the bottom of all natural phenomena. This will be indicated hereafter for a great many fields of natural science.

Individually, the four ethers have the following characteristics. The etheric commences with the first state of ether, that of warmth ether. Present-day physics views "heat," not as an objective state, but only as a subjective quality called forth by a form of motion. Here also, however, the results of the theory of relativity have within a very recent period greatly modified or completely transformed many conceptions long held to be unassailable. Professor L. Graetz in his work "Der Äther und die Relativitätstheorie," which boldly denies many conceptions hitherto in constant use, thus states the problem (p. 62): "Whereas heat was considered at an earlier period to be a substance, something material, this substance theory has been abandoned since the middle of the last century, and heat and energy in general are considered as something kinetic. The second conception of the law of energy, according to the theory of relativity, conflicts with this purely kinetic theory; it conceives energy as something material. Mass is, of course, something material; and, since every change in energy is bound up with a change in mass, the theory of relativity views energy as something material, as an energy-substance, not as a motion, or at least not as motion alone. Thus it appears that energy must be conceived in the theory of relativity as energy-stuff." To future observation of nature, heat, embraced by such observation in its totality, will, in its essential nature, be just as objective a state as the gaseous, liquid, and solid states of aggregation in substance. "Heat" processes are a transition stage from the purely etheric to the so-called "substantial," and *vice versa*. We shall be able to convince ourselves of this fact from many points of view in the further course of these reflections. It will be shown later on that only through the action of warmth ether do heat phenomena arise, whereas the other phenomena, light, chemical processes, etc., possess quite different qualities for the reason that the etheric forces themselves which call forth these phenomena are marked by quite different qualities.

Warmth ether tends towards the *spherical* form. If it were merely a conveyer of "motion," then it could in turn call forth only motion in a substance-medium in which it works. Since, however, the tendency to create spherical forms is inseparably linked with its action, therefore it calls forth, wherever it enters into nature and is not obstructed in its action, spherical forms. We are here dealing—and this must again and again be emphasized—not with abstract dead oscillations of unknown origin, but with concrete formative forces.

The second ether state is that of *light ether,* or, more simply, of that which is given to the physical perception of man as "light." As Lenard says, light gave us the first intimation of the existence of ether, and he thinks: "Light is undoubtedly a transverse wave motion: that is, in a beam of light and perpendicular to its direction—never merely backward and forward displacements in the same direction with the beam, as is the case in sound waves—there are present periodically shifting states. Optical researches by no means recent—for instance, those in regard to polarization of light, have already shown the transverse character of light waves. In the course of time we have learned to recognize still other ether waves which are invisible: ultraviolet, ultrared, and electric waves; but these as a group have the same characteristics as light waves, differing only in their lengths." That the "characteristics" are similar, the lengths different, may satisfy us so long as we are testing in a one-sided and arbitrary fashion the quantitative-mechanical action in the substance-medium; but in this way we learn nothing whatever in regard to the natures and the concrete distinctions of the different kinds of ether. The light ether to which we refer, which calls forth for the human eye in the manner to be explained later the phenomenon of light, does in fact induce among other things a transverse oscillation; but in addition to what has been said above we must add that this occurrence describes the figure of a triangle, so that light ether, as we shall see, when it can exert its effect unhindered in nature, also produces there *triangular forms,* whereas warmth ether produces spherical forms.

We agree entirely with Lenard when he says: "We must take the characteristics of ether just as we find them in order to base these upon experience and seek to harmonize them in a conception free from contradiction; and we must not permit ourselves to be disturbed in this—a serious error which, I think, has often been made—if we find that *these charac-teristics are entirely different from those of matter in solid, fluid, or gaseous forms.* For ether is simply not matter." When, however, he proceeds further, saying: "and it is legiti-mate for us only by way of comparison to draw upon matter at all, in order that, proceeding from our knowledge of the motions induced in matter, we may endeavor to reach a con-ception of the motions in ether," we must remark in regard to this . . . that we shall never be able to reach a true concep-tion of ether by transferring the forms and laws of motion in matter to the ether itself. If, however, we conceive of ether, or the etheric formative forces, as formative forces void of any quality of substance, as active principles which come to living expression in the phenomenal world only through their active tendencies to definite motions, to shaping definite forms with definite qualities, then this difficulty disappears. We may say, then, that an oscillation, a form which is caused by light ether in a substance-medium, takes the shape of a triangle.

The third ether is *chemical ether* or *sound ether.* Its forces, that is, cause the chemical processes, differentiations, dissolu-tions, and unions of substances; but also—though, as it were, through activities in another field—its forces transmit to us the tones perceptible to the senses. The inner kinship of these two spheres of action will be clear to us from the phenome-non of Chladni's sound-forms. For it is tone which causes the uniting together, the orders and forms, of substance and bod-ies of substance. Steiner says: "That which the physically au-dible tone produces then in the dust is happening everywhere in space. Space is interpenetrated by waves produced by the forces of chemical ether," which, in the manner of the Chladni dust figures, dissolve and unite substances. But chem-ical ether has in reality "a tone-and-sound nature of which sensible sound, or tone heard by the physical ear, is only an outward expression: that is, an expression which has passed through air as a medium."

We shall discuss more thoroughly [elsewhere] the origin of tones audible to the senses; here we must only establish the fact that tone and chemical processes are to be attributed to the same ether in the manner explained.

Chemical ether, when it can exert itself unhindered in nature, produces, as we shall be shown concretely, *half-moon* forms.

In contrast with the expansive kinds of ether—warmth and light ether—chemical ether, as we have said, tends in its action to be centripetal.

It may also be proved that the phenomenon of cold is one of those attributes which are to be ascribed to chemical ether, a fact which is essential for an understanding of the relation between processes of cold and of contraction.

The fourth ether is *life ether*. It is phylogenetically the most highly evolved ether, and therefore in its qualities most varied and complicated, as we shall later show in connection with the most varied phenomena. It is, as we shall see, that which is rayed out to us, among other things, from the sun and then modified in its action by the atmosphere of the earth in a manner to be described . . . Life ether, together with chemical ether, belongs to the group of suctional forces, those which tend to draw inwards. We shall also be able to prove its relation to that which is called "gravitation" and to the phenomenon of magnetism.

Its form-building tendency, when it can exert its effect unhindered in substance, leads to *square* shapes, expressed, for instance, in crystallizing salt.

By way of résumé then, we may say:

There comes into existence phylogenetically and ontogenetically out of the nonspatial state:

	Spatial tendency	Form tendency	State induced
Warmth ether	Expansive or centrifugal	Spherical or triangular	Heat
Evolved therefrom, light ether			Gaseous
Evolved therefrom, chemical ether	Suctional drawing inward	Half-moon shaped	Fluid
Evolved therefrom, life ether	Centripetal	Square	Solid

17.

The Rediscovery of the Ether

H. C. DUDLEY

The growing interest in psychic phenomena became a topic of conversation for a colleague and me several years ago. We were at a conference where one symposium was given over to a discussion of ESP. My colleague asked if I believed in such approaches to science. I replied that I neither believed nor disbelieved because I knew little about the topic. "However," I said, "if psi phenomena were ever proven to be valid, I could write an equation which would define the medium by which the information might be transmitted."

I had in mind the ether—or, to put it in modern terms, an energy-rich subquantic medium composed of extremely small neutral particles called neutrinos, pervading all space and interpenetrating all matter. This concept, which has developed in the last 15 years, primarily in Europe, of a neutrino sea filling interstellar space is the modern revival of an ancient concept that began to go out of fashion after Einstein's special theory of relativity proposed that the ether did not exist. With all due respect to Einstein, it is now time for all scientists to say that Newton may well have been right after all.

This is indeed ironic, but not unprecedented. When new information enables one to penetrate deeper into old problems, then those theories—which after all are only interpretations of experimental results that have assumed the status of "self-evident truths"—have to be altered or abandoned. Science must readjust, even when concepts once branded "pseudoscience" reappear with renewed support. Failure to do so is

"The Rediscovery of the Ether" by H. C. Dudley is an original article written especially for this volume and is printed by permission of the author.

intellectual dishonesty, intellectual inertia. It turns true science itself into pseudoscience.

Pre-1930 science theorized that there must be some mechanism, tangible albeit extremely refined, present in all space through which heat, light, radio, x rays, etc., were transmitted. The source of this concept in science can be traced back to Newton, who received it from much earlier sources, including the Greeks. In 1704, Newton asked in his classic work *Opticks:*

> Is not the heat of a warm Room convey'd through the Vacuum by the Vibrations of a much *subtiler Medium than Air,* which after the Air was drawn out remained in the Vacuum? And is not this *Medium* the same with that *Medium* by which Light is refracted and reflected, and by whose Vibrations Light communicates Heat to Bodies? And is not this *Medium* exceedingly more rare and subtile than the Air, and exceedingly more elastick and active? And doth it not readily pervade all Bodies? And is it not (by its elastick force) expanded through all the Heavens?

In 1912 the following appeared in a prominent textbook of physics, and continued to appear in later editions until 1932:

> *The Ether.* To account for the transmission of waves through space containing no ordinary matter it seems necessary to assume the existence of a *universal medium* filling all space and even interpenetrating matter itself, as shown by the existence of transparent substances. That this *medium* can react on matter is shown by the fact that radiant energy is transmitted from ether to matter in the case of absorption, and from matter to ether in the case of emission of radiation by material sources.
>
> In recent years doubt as to the necessity for assuming the existence of an ether has been expressed by some who believe that it is sufficient to attribute the power of transmitting radiation to space itself. It may be doubted whether this is more than a dispute about terms. We cannot discuss the question here, but pending the settlement of the controversy it seems wise to continue the use of the word ether as at least denoting the power of space, vacant or *occupied by matter,* to transmit radiation. (Italics added)

The null results of the famed Michelson–Morley experiments (1881–1889), coupled with an assumption by Ein-

stein (1905), had by 1940 resulted in the abandonment of
any concept of the ether as a medium necessary for the transmission of light or x rays. The notion of an "ether," "aether,"
or "luminiferous ether"—some type of medium existing in all
space—disappeared from physics textbooks. Anyone who attempted to seriously discuss this subject was looked upon as
ignorant, if not a pseudoscientist.

Why, then, is it necessary to reopen this seemingly esoteric
question? What is the practical significance of such a return
to the views of bygone days? I have proposed answers to
these questions, showing how recent developments in physics
suggest: (1) a new conceptual model of the atom is required, involving the entire atom as the basic unit system
rather than reactions involving essentially mass/energy
changes of only the nucleus; (2) the real possibility of a nuclear detonation leading to "the ultimate catastrophe" of
planetary annihilation.[1-3] Perhaps this medium is also a
physical mechanism for transmission of energy underlying
certain psychic phenomena; its characteristics would seem to
make it a likely candidate.

Recent astrophysical studies show that the orientation of
the Michelson–Morley apparatus foreordained the null results. Yet their conclusions are now graphically used in all
current physics texts to "prove" the lack of an ether or of the
necessity of such a medium for the propagation of light.
Ironically, Michelson, an experimenter *par excellence* and the
first American to win a Nobel Prize in science (1907),
could not bring himself to accept as final the results of his
own work. He felt there must be something wrong, but didn't
know what.

Michelson and Morley centered their attention on the
Earth's orbital velocity (30 km/sec). They had no knowledge of the existence of galaxies, of galactic motions in relation to each other, or of the motion of our solar system in our
galaxy. Orientation of their interferometers tangent to the
Earth's surface insured that the angle of approach of an
"ether drift" would be nearly perpendicular to the plane of
the interferometer. Rotation of the instrument in this plane
would only slightly alter the effective velocity of the ether at
the two arms of the interferometers.[4] The null results are thus

explainable on the basis of pre-1900 classical mechanics. The limited information available to Michelson and Einstein is emphasized by the following:

(i) By referring to stars in this galaxy, the Earth's velocity, with respect to the galactic center, is in the range of 200–220 km/sec, as determined by several astronomic studies conducted since 1930.

(ii) Since 1960, the existence of a nearly isotropic 3.5-cm electromagnetic radiation flux has been demonstrated by several studies. This is postulated to result from the "big bang," a celestial primordial event. E. K. Conklin's experiments, conducted at Stanford University in 1968–1969, estimated the Earth's absolute motion, with this flux as the generalized frame of reference, at about 160 km/sec.[5]

This determination of the Earth's movement in our galaxy is of the greatest importance because these data disprove one of the basic portions of the theories of both Newton and Einstein. For both assumed that absolute motion could not be shown experimentally. But Conklin's experiments did just that. The direction of the Earth's motion and its speed around the galactic center were determined without reference to any other star or planet (which has put philosophers into a tizzy). All things considered, Michelson's hunch was right: there was much missing from his studies of the ether.

The modern development of an ether concept began in 1951 when Nobel Laureate Paul Dirac, now professor of physics at Florida State University, asked "Is there an ether?" as the title of a paper.[6] He answered his own question in the affirmative and stated that the ether he thought existed was essentially an all-pervasive sea of electrons (e^-) in random motion. In 1959 another Nobelist, the French physicist Victor de Broglie, suggested that this ether is "a gas made up of leptons [a class of subatomic particles of small mass] and probably neutrinos [leptons with no charge and almost no mass]."

In addition to these speculations, astrophysics has extended its studies in the past thirty years to include the space *between* the planets and the stars, and as a result has discovered dust clouds, radio signals, x rays, and electric and magnetic fields in supposedly "empty" space.

Finally, our space program efforts since 1957 have made all textbooks on astronomy published before 1965 so dated that they may as well have been written in Sanskrit for all their present usefulness.

Out of all this information explosion has come the realization that there is as much mass between the stars as there is contained in them and in the planets as well. In short, empty space is in fact crowded with interlocking magnetic and electric fields, plus neutrinos.

In contrast with these discoveries, nuclear science assumes that empty space is inert, free of mass and energy. And it is this assumption that makes it diametrically opposed to the new astronomy. On this basis there is a real battle of ideas going on between astrophysics and nuclear physics. With the mass of new evidence of how much now fills outer space, the case for the astrophysicist becomes increasingly stronger.

During the past two decades there has been developing in astrophysics the concept of a generalized neutrino sea. This flux of uncharged particles arises from the nuclear fusion reactions taking place in the countless stars scattered throughout the universe. Because the stars are almost randomly distributed, neutrinos bombard us in nearly equal quantities from every direction. These minute bits of matter pass through our bodies at a rate estimated at one million to one billion per square inch per second.

This subquantic medium has been defined as an energy-rich substrate, the common denominator in all particle reactions. The neutrino, a very small particle of matter (perhaps smaller than a quantum of light—hence the term subquantic) having no electric charge, was experimentally proven in 1953. It had been invented as an imaginary particle about twenty-five years earlier by the Austrian physicist Wolfgang Pauli. In 1932 Enrico Fermi used it to explain certain radioactive decay systems. Three decades later, the nature of this particle began to be clarified. It was not a single particle, it seemed, but a pair of particles, with mass about 1/2500 that of the electron. By 1971 the two nearly equal particles had become two sets of particles: two electron neutrinos (v_e) with mass about equal to 1/10,000 that of the electron, and two muon neutrinos (v_u), with mass about equal to the electron.

Muon neutrinos have a rest mass of about 0.6 MeV; electron neutrinos have a rest mass of about 60 eV. Their particle velocity ranges over a continuum from near zero to near the speed of light. Particle density appears to be about 10^{12} per cm^3 and their energy density has been estimated at 10^8–10^{19} eV/cm^3.[2] The subject is extensively reviewed in B. Kuchowicz' *Cosmic Neutrino*.[7]

When Einstein's famous equation $E = mc^2$ was first proposed, it was considered an interesting speculation, not a proven theory. Over the years, and especially since the first atomic bomb detonations of 1945, this equation has been accepted without question since there was no other explanation for the prodigious amounts of energy released by the atomic and hydrogen bombs. Official science now feels comfortable with this equation; it is an old friend.

Einstein himself said that Relativity must be accepted as a complete theory. If any part was proven false, he said, the whole theory is invalid. But Relativity *requires* an energy-free, mass-free space. It requires that there be no ether (particulate or otherwise), no neutrino sea, no subquantic medium. Likewise, quantum mechanics requires that the interactions of subnuclear particles and atoms take place in spaces which are free of energy and free of mass. The space in which these reactions occur *must not* contribute anything to the reaction—or else so much of modern physics is wrong.

Thus the two systems of theory which govern the thinking of modern nuclear physics—relativity and quantum mechanics—*require* the absence of the ether. Yet we are now finding this new framework and beginning to define it and characterize it with remarkable accuracy. It therefore seems imperative that we sweep away the cobwebs of time and look for a new explanation for the energy obtained from uranium and plutonium bombs and reactors. It is of no consequence to the generations of today that this requires the passing of an old friend, $E = mc^2$. Einstein developed this theorem more than a half a century ago. Such is the course of science and the challenge to this generation. We must move on.[8]

REFERENCES

1. H. C. Dudley, "Radioactivity Reexamined," *Chemical and Engineering News* (April 7, 1975).
2. H. C. Dudley, "Is There an Ether?," *Industrial Research* (November 15, 1974).
3. H. C. Dudley, "The Ultimate Catastrophe," *Bulletin of the Atomic Scientists* (November 1975).
4. H. C. Dudley, "Michelson's Hunch Was Right," *Bulletin of the Atomic Scientists* (January 1975); see also *Phys. Today*, 73 (February 1975).
5. E. K. Conklin, "Cosmic Radiation," *Nature* 222 (1969).
6. P. M. Dirac, "Is There an Ether?," *Nature* 168 (1951).
7. Br. Kuchowicz, *Cosmic Neutrino* (Poland: University of Warsaw, 1972—in English).
8. H. C. Dudley, *Morality of Nuclear Planning—??* (New Jersey: Kronos Press, 1976), available from RadSafety Associates, Box 452, Hinsdale, Ill. 60521.

18.

Neoenergy and Geometric Forms

SERGE V. KING

In the world of nature we see many examples of energy acting in particular ways through specific forms. The vortex or whirlpool shape is one natural form that seems to guide the action of energy, and one which must have been evident to people from the earliest days. Dust devils, tornadoes, waterspouts, and hurricanes are dramatic examples. It would be understandable for people to try imitating that power, to tap its universal source, as it were. Possibly this was the origin of such things as whirling dances and the spiral designs found all over the world. Both are associated with religious or magical rites intended to draw power from or transport oneself to a world beyond our ordinary sense perception.

The curious thing is that both do achieve apparently inexplicable effects. Whirling, as practiced by dervishes or shamans for instance, induces altered states of consciousness which sometimes includes deep trance states. Spirals, or flat coils, seem to emit a form of energy due to their shape alone. The special effects of electricity running through coils is well known, but even without electrical connections phenomena are produced which indicate or suggest an energy emission of some sort. The exact nature of the energy is still open to question, but it exhibits the same properties associated with other forms to be mentioned later. It very decidedly affects organic and inorganic matter, produces tactile sensations in most people and visual in some, and emits continuously as long as the form retains its shape. If a spiral is unwound, for

"Neoenergy and Geometric Forms" by Serge V. King is an original article written especially for this volume and is printed by permission of the author.

instance, the above effects seem to disappear. It is as if the form itself provides a structure through which an ever-present energy is intensified. A variety of forms induce the same effects—all without an apparent power source—which leads one to conclude that a common energy is operating through a common principle.

For the purposes of this presentation we shall call this manifestation of energy "neoenergy," to distinguish it from electricity, magnetism, light, etc., and to avoid any favoritism among the dozens of researchers who have given it their own name. Neoenergy, according to the reports of its researchers, has the current flow properties of electricity, some field properties of magnetism, some reflective properties of light, and some of the properties of heat. Yet, it seems to be independent of each of these. In association with the varied forms it demonstrates the same fundamental and unique properties. Among these are: a tendency toward vertical flow (when not guided in other ways by a material conductor); the stimulation of enzyme activity; the stimulation of all natural cell processes; certain fairly standard tactile sensations (tingling, pressure, coolness, or warmth); dehydration and retardation of oxidation; and neutralization of acidity (qualified as an apparent effect for the time being, the present evidence being mostly subjective). Let us note that these are the most consistent effects reported by researchers around the world, who are admittedly seldom experimenting under laboratory conditions. Yet their very consistency and the volume of reports would seem to merit a closer look by those with the facilities to make more accurate investigations.

The common principle governing neoenergy in relation to form, at least as we are able to determine it now, is concentration or intensification. Each of the forms which display neoenergy effects—spirals, cones, pyramids, cylinders, tetrahedrons, and others—produce greater or lesser effects, depending on their size and/or complexity. In general, the larger or more complex the form, the more intense the energetic effects. At this stage it would be premature to state that there is "more" energy present. In the absence of adequate measuring devices we can only confirm, through observation, a qualitative difference, but not necessarily a quantitative one.

By looking at some specific examples of form energy it will be easier to notice the commonality of the energy and the relationships of the various forms. Let us first examine the pyramid, the most well-known form connected with neoenergy. As a form, the pyramid is psychologically satisfying. It seems to strike a responsive chord deep within the human psyche. It is found worldwide in religious art and architecture and is utilized in many occult rites and rituals. Even the esoteric side of America's great seal has a representation of a pyramid. This does not mean that the energy effects of a pyramid are purely subjective, but more probably that the subconscious mind of man recognizes the energy latent in the form.

Man's inventions and structures generally seek to imitate or improve on something found in nature. At first glance, a pyramid on the order of those in Egypt or Central America might seem to resemble a mountain, but the painstaking regularity of the sides could indicate that another object was the source of inspiration. It is permissible to assume that the first builders of pyramids were aware of its energy properties, since it cannot be proven one way or the other. With that viewpoint in mind, the pyramid resembles nothing so much as a gigantic crystal, or a portion thereof. Crystals of gold and fluorite, for instance, have the form of two pyramids base to base—an octahedron. We know that crystals, especially certain types, have peculiar electromagnetic properties, and there is a persistent tradition that crystals are a source of healing and psychically stimulating energies. The step from a natural crystalline form to a human-made pyramidal one does not seem too lengthy if energy production were their common link.

Lest the above reasoning seem too fanciful, we have before us the *fact,* based on experimental observations, that pyramids of all sizes and materials demonstrate neoenergy effects (see *Pyramid Guide* listed in Appendix III). One of the pioneer researchers in this area, Karel Drbal, who also pioneered radio and television in Czechoslovakia, was granted Patent No. 91,304 in 1959 by the Czechoslovakian Patent Office for a pyramid razor blade sharpener. To prove that this was not based on whim or fancy, the chief patent examiner personally tested the pyramid for *ten years* before supporting the claim before the patent commission. The pyramid in question was a cardboard model based on the dimensions of the Cheops pyramid in Egypt. Later, Drbal achieved sharpening effects as well as mummification effects with plastic and styrofoam models, and with pyramids with dimensions other than that of the Cheops model. One sentence in the patent description approved by the commission states: "This invention was specially tested for a specific pyramid-shaped device, but is not restricted only to this one specific form."

Further emphasizing that form itself is a primary consideration is the additional fact that pyramid frameworks, i.e., pyramids without side panels but retaining the complete pyramid form, work about as well as full-sided models.

The claim that the pyramid can sharpen razor blades invariably brings a skeptical smile to those unacquainted with this area of study. Yet this has been demonstrated thousands of times around the world. It cannot be refuted that a razor blade retains its sharpness when kept under a pyramid between shaves—reports of a hundred or more shaves are common—but no one yet knows how the sharpening occurs. There is a report that photographs were taken of a razor blade before and after treatment under a pyramid with an electron microscope, and that the pictures showed no change in the edge of the blade. However, such reported results are only as valid as the experimental conditions. The pyramid is not a magical device. You do not just put a blade in it and— "Presto!" have it sharpened. Neoenergy, different as it may be, does follow its own natural laws which are still being uncovered. Regarding the electron microphotographs, one is justified in asking whether the test blade were new or used (used blades may take up to three weeks to sharpen) and how long a treatment the blade had (it usually takes twenty-four hours for a new blade to resharpen). Further adding to the difficulty is the phenomenon of "regression." Most serious researchers have found that the pyramid does not sharpen equally as well all the time. In other words, there are apparently outside forces sporadically influencing the neoenergy of the pyramid. A blade may be resharpening well for weeks when suddenly it may be dull for one day or several, and then will resharpen again.

Cogent arguments have been advanced to show that the neoenergy is demonstrating its properties of dehydration and anoxidation, thus strengthening the blade by forcing out water molecules. This is, in particular, the explanation proposed by Drbal, who has cited the works of several scientists to support his idea (Dr. Carl Benedicks, *Metallkundliche Berichte* [Berlin: Verlag Technik, 1952], Tome II, which deals with the weakening effect of water on steel; Born and Lertes, *Archiv. Elektrischen Uebertragung,* Heft I, 33–35 [1950], dealing with the driving effect of microwaves on water dipole molecules). Drbal and other researchers are of the opinion that microwave resonance is the key to pyramid effects and he refers to scientific works describing pyramid-shaped microwave devices. At any rate, it does seem reasonable that the effect of driving water molecules out of metal could result in dehydration and anoxidation.

If that is so, we should be able to apply the same principle to other metallic objects and achieve similar effects. Interestingly, it has been done. When oxidized metals such as silver coins and rusty nuts have been kept in a pyramid for a period of time it has been found that the tarnish or rust seems to "loosen" and can easily be wiped off with a finger or cloth. The loosening is not perfect, and primarily affects the areas of highest relief. Here we have a good case of two outwardly unrelated phenomena united by a common functioning principle.

Commonality is again evident in neoenergy effects on liquids. One of the most practical and pleasurable uses to which pyramids have been put is to "mellow" such things as coffee, tea, and wine. When left under a pyramid for a few minutes these liquids will lose most of their bite or bitterness. The change is most remarkable when low-quality liquids are used; they begin to taste like their more expensive counterparts. Even ordinary tap water quickly loses its chemical taste when treated under a pyramid. To some it then resembles fresh spring water, to others it tastes flat.

It has been suggested that in this case the neoenergy is neutralizing acidity and/or alkalinity. In testing other liquids we find this same roughly stated principle in operation. Apple cider loses its tartness to become more like apple juice. Carbonated beverages go more or less flat in minutes, and freshly squeezed lemon juice loses much of its sharpness in an hour or so. The above statements are based on the taste reactions of numerous individuals. More objective tests are presently being undertaken by the author (at Huna International—see Appendix III) and others to determine whether the neutralization of acidity or alkalinity takes place under standard laboratory procedures.

Dramatic claims have been made regarding the human health benefits of pyramids. Rejuvenation of skin tissue, headache and pain relief, revitalization, relaxation, and the actual healing of certain conditions have all been mentioned. These are not just the claims of promoters, but of users. Discounting the probable cases of autosuggestion, something is happening within the pyramid that affects health. Successful experiments with animals, who should not be influenced by the *idea* that a pyramid can help them, tend to confirm certain effects. One notable effect is the relief of pain due to cuts and bruises and the subsequent speeding up of the healing process. With daily treatment under a pyramid, cuts frequently close in less time than normal with little or no scab formation, and bruises heal more quickly and less colorfully. In the case of cuts where bleeding results, coagulation also takes place in record time. If neoenergy is compatible with or the same as the energy which governs our life processes, then the pyramid might be acting as an amplifier, providing us with an additional supply of energy to speed up or enhance natural processes. Supposing it to be an amplifier, we should run across cases where the effect is to overload a person with energy, rather than be beneficial. Sometimes this is exactly what seems to happen.

Often, a pyramid placed on the head will relieve a headache in moments. But with certain people on certain occasions it will actually induce a headache or intensify an existing one. It happens, too, that some people become quite nervous or anxious under a pyramid, as if it were supplying more energy than they could freely absorb. Sleeping under a pyramid has been recommended as a means of gaining restful, relaxing sleep, but there are people who simply cannot sleep under a pyramid. It will keep them awake all night. The more work that is done with people and pyramids, the more clear it becomes that dosage is a very important factor. Whereas one person might derive benefit from eight hours under a pyramid, there are those for whom five minutes is quite sufficient, and probably there are those for whom one minute might be more than enough, at least at certain times in their life.

The effects of pyramids on plants parallel in many respects the effects on humans. Plant growth is enhanced . . . often. Germination is more rapid . . . frequently. Ailing plants are revived . . . sometimes. Actually, some apparently healthy plants will wilt after a few minutes under—or even near—a pyramid, while others thrive in full-time habitation. The factors involved seem to be the type of plant and its size. In general, the larger and more sturdy the plant, the more energy it seems to be able to absorb, exactly as if an amplifying effect were taking place.

With the pyramid form we find correspondences between the effects on different metals, among liquids, and between humans and plants. The common thread linking all these effects, however, is still elusive. Partial theories abound and it is not the intent here to add to the confusion by proposing another theory. Nevertheless, a few observations are in order which might serve to throw some light on the mystery.

The pyramid form has its greatest effect when combined with another factor—orientation. Pyramids work best when the apothem of one side directly faces magnetic north. At the maximum disorientation of forty-five degrees the effect is quite weak. The obvious conclusion is that there is an interaction with the magnetic field of the Earth. What is more, the razor blade sharpens best when it, too, is oriented with its long axis in a north/south direction. Nothing presently known about magnetism can explain this. Granted that the pyramid may be exerting a dehydration effect on the blade, what has this to do with magnetism? Furthermore, the anomalies in pyramid operation—i.e., those times when it suddenly doesn't seem to work—have, according to some studies, been correlated with certain alignments of the moon and other planets. This would seem to indicate an interaction with gravity. But what has gravity to do with dehydration (or any of the other properties of neoenergy)? Interestingly, it has been found that planetary alignments do have an indirect effect on the Earth's magnetic field. It seems that certain alignments influence the generation of sunspots, which affect the intensity of the "solar wind," which affects the magnetic field of the Earth. But this curiosity merely brings us back to magnetism. What clues lie there?

Some little known research on magnetism in the United States and Canada shows that ordinary magnets can produce health effects on humans that are virtually identical to those produced by a pyramid. As an example, we can mention the work *Magnetism and Its Effect on the Living System* by Albert Roy Davis and Walter C. Rawls, Jr. The same research also duplicates the pyramid effects on plants and some research duplicates the pyramid effects on liquids as well. No one has yet reported the sharpening of a blade with a magnet, but that may yet happen. Is it possible that magnetism is more than what it seems to be? Could it be causing a side effect that has hitherto not been attributed to it? Of course, we can also ask whether magnetism itself might not just be an effect of something else.

The solar wind was briefly mentioned, and we bring it up again because it is a stream of ionized particles sent out by the sun. Ions may give us another clue. Ions are either positive or negative. Positive ions (cations) are atoms with one or more electrons missing. Negative ions (anions) are atoms with one or more electrons too many. What is most interesting about ions in relation to pyramids is the strong similarity in effects on humans. Anions produce analgesic, tonifying, and relaxing effects, while cations intensify pain, produce headaches, anxiety, and sluggishness. These symptoms correspond to the various reactions experienced by people under a pyramid. Perhaps the pyramid form is also associated with ionization. The action of ions may just be the key to the whole puzzle of form energy.

But before we overreach ourselves in speculation, let's look at the way other forms besides the pyramid seem to manifest neoenergy. In early pyramid research it was thought that only a form corresponding to the proportions of the Great Pyramid of Egypt would exhibit the effects. This has now been disproven by Drbal and other researchers. Not only will equilateral pyramids do the same thing, but so will tetrahedrons. A tetrahedron is a four-sided figure, as opposed to a five-sided pyramid. In appearance, it resembles a pyramid, but with only three upright sides instead of four. This means that only one side of a tetrahedron can ever be properly aligned to magnetic north. An advantage, however, is that there is no condition in which all sides are as much as forty-five degrees off orientation. That is to say that a tetrahedron at its worst is always better aligned than a pyramid at its worst. Experimentation with tetrahedrons is still fairly recent, but a growing number of researchers report even better results than with a pyramid. And it is true that companies in two countries, Italy and France, use tetrahedron containers to preserve milk and yogurt.

Often described as "a pyramid with an infinite number of sides," the cone is another form associated with noticeable effects of neoenergy. Most of the cone research in this country was done by the well-known dowser Vern Cameron, and very little more has been done since his passing. Cameron claimed that the neoenergy of a cone moved vortex style around the exterior with a strong beam coming off the tip, and that there were practically no interior effects. Having experimented with cones of different apex angles, Cameron determined through his professional dowsing techniques that a ninety-degree apex angle would give off a straight beam about one inch in diameter measurable up to a half-mile away. A more acute angle seems to disperse the beam, while an obtuse one tends to focus it a short distance away.

A fascinating discovery of Cameron's was that the energy beam of a cone could be "tapped" by running a wire from the tip to another site. The neoenergy flows along the wire and emanates in a tiny beam out the free end, though there is apparently a field emanation along the length of the wire as well. Those well acquainted with neoenergy research will notice the similarity to certain findings of Baron Karl von Reichenbach in the 19th century. This tapping phenomenon has been duplicated with pyramids, as has the additional Cameron discovery that cones connected in series seem to amplify the energy effect in the wire. A big difference between cones and pyramids is that the former seem to work better when suspended by one edge so that the apex points in a horizontal direction, while the latter seem to work better with the base in a horizontal position.

Two experiments of Cameron are worth noting for the commonality they show with pyramid effects. In one, a wire connected to three cones in series was buried a few inches underground, and a half-package of radish seeds was planted over it. The other half-package was planted ten feet away as a control. The test radishes were highly retarded in their growth, while the controls grew quite normally. The effect appears to be one of energy overload, which was previously mentioned in regard to pyramids and plants. In the second experiment, Cameron used a similar setup and directed the end of the wire to a long-standing trichina infection on his arm. After twenty minutes of treatment the infection was gone, with no apparent effect on the living tissues. Here the neoenergy seems to have given his body the necessary additional energy to rid itself of the infection. It must be admitted, however, that Cameron's experiments can only be considered suggestive because it is not known whether he used sufficient controls or was able to repeat the same results.

Baron von Reichenbach was a well-known scientist of the 19th century who discovered creosote and other things. Among those other things was a strange type of energy that he called "od" or "odic force." Though he detected the presence of this force in many ways, of significance here are his claims of this force emanating from crystalline forms. Reichenbach tested the reactions of both ill persons and healthy ones to crystals. One of his most common tests was to pass the crystals through glasses of water and, using untreated glasses as controls, see whether groups of people could tell the difference. The results were spectacular, for nearly all could taste a distinct difference and the ill subjects had the strongest reactions. Some would feel powerful tingling sensations in their hands or head by merely holding the treated water. Reichenbach conducted hundreds of tests and eventually found that while crystals of certain types emanated a field, the greatest intensity of energy emanated from the poles of the primary axes of the crystal. The emanation from either end affected the water and the people in the same way, but one end was always more intense than the other. Also, one end, usually the matrix end, apparently emitted a soft, gently warm current of air while the other end apparently emitted a cool current. It wasn't air, of course, but subjects' descriptions likened their feelings to such phenomena.

It should be obvious from these results that Reichenbach was dealing with the same force we have termed neoenergy. Some of his conclusions are worth quoting. The following is from John Ashburner's 1851 translation of his *Physico-Physiological Researches On The Dynamics Of Magnetism, Electricity, Heat Light, Crystallization, And Chemism In Their Relations To Vital Force:*

"So far as is at present made out, this property does not belong *to matter, as such, but to its form, and in fact to its condition of aggregation* [original italics]. Pouillet, in Muller's translation of his *Manual of Physics,* p. 167, says expressly, that 'it has never yet been observed in ponderable matter, that the form, the arrangement of the molecules, can be the cause of new forces acting at a distance.' But this is exactly the case here." The experiments of Reichenbach should be given serious consideration because here was a scientist who did use controls and who did a tremendous number of experiments under varying conditions.

Up till now we have discussed neoenergy in relation to regular geometric or crystalline forms, but such forms are not necessarily the only ones associated with this force. At least that is the import of the experience related by Dr. Derald Langham of Genesa in Fallbrook, California (see Appendix II). A plant geneticist and instructor of botany, Langham brought a variety of sesame seeds from Venezuela to Yale University where he transferred them from brown envelopes to some bottles given to him there. For three years they were kept in cold storage and then for about ten more years they were left at ordinary room temperature as he made several moves. Over this period seeds were sent to sesame breeders around the world, with germination tests made before shipment. Under good storage conditions, Langham had previously been able to keep the seeds for as long as three years, but with weak germination and subsequent weakening of the seedlings. This time, however, he found to his surprise that the seeds were germinating at a higher percentage than when he had first placed them in the bottles.

Langham finally showed the bottled seeds to a laser specialist, Dr. Florent Bailey, who accepted the results as a matter of course because his laser work had demonstrated that related forms strengthen each other. It seems that the bottles had about the same shape as the sesame seeds. The concept he put forth is that the seeds received additional energy peculiarly suited to them by being stored in a similarly shaped container.

Langham has since suggested that research be carried out on shaping containers to suit the product for increased shelf life and perhaps even better taste. It makes one wonder what the effect would be, for instance, of bottling wine in containers shaped like grapes. Langham has suggested further that hospitals might be built in human form for better results. Although it sounds farfetched at first glance, the idea does correspond in a way to the old herbal concept of "signatures." According to this belief, parts of plants having the shape of various organs of the body alleviate the ills of that organ. That is one reason why the Chinese considered ginseng, whose root is shaped like a man, as a cure-all. Interestingly, the correspondence does frequently apply. The whole field of form energy is so out of the ordinary that the "resonant shape" idea should probably be seriously investigated.

In this brief article we have only been able to highlight some of the aspects of form energy, and it should not be thought that the manifestations of neoenergy are limited to the forms mentioned. The spiral was used to introduce neoenergy, but little was said about the different intensities resulting from increasing or decreasing the number of spirals and their spacing. Much interesting work has been done with simple hoops or rings of various materials. Curious effects are reported by people who stand within them. Also left out for lack of space are the reported effects of the "seed crystals" of Genesa, of hemispheres in series, of cylinders with and without coil wrappings, and much, much more. The fact is that form energy is a burgeoning field and new discoveries are being made every day. We are surrounded by an ocean of energy of which we have been barely aware and which probably holds potentials that haven't yet entered our imagination. Even so, the potentials already uncovered are enough to keep many of us busy for several lifetimes. The promise of neoenergy is manifold. Its applications in health, in agriculture, in electronics and, based on some recent research, even transportation, may radically transform our lives in the next few decades.

The main objection to neoenergy is that it shouldn't exist. But it nevertheless does. The manner in which it operates goes against commonly accepted theories of physics, and unfortunately this is enough to cause its rejection by many who call themselves scientists. Theories, however, are meant to explain observed effects and predict future ones. They should never be used to condemn clearly observable effects that they cannot explain. The essence of a desirable scientific viewpoint was well expressed by Berzelius: "In science, nothing may be built upon uncertain possibilities; science may not be a tissue of conjectures: it must consist, as far as possible, of a system of demonstrated realities." In keeping with this dictum, neoenergy can be demonstrated.

SUGGESTED READINGS

1. Albert Davis and Walter Rawls, Jr., *Magnetism and Its Effects on the Living System* (Hicksville, N.Y.: Exposition Press, 1974).
2. Karel Drbal, "The Pyramid Patent," in *Pyramid Power*, edited by Max Toth and Greg Nielsen (New York: Freeway Press, 1974).
3. Bill Kerrell and Kathy Goggin, *The Guide to Pyramid Energy* (Santa Monica, Calif.: Pyramid Power V, Inc., 1975).
4. Serge V. King, *Mana Physics* (Los Angeles: Huna Enterprises, 1975).
5. ———, *Pyramid Energy Handbook* (New York: Warner Books, 1977).

6. Karl von Reichenbach, *Physico-Physiological Researches* (Reprinted) (Mokelumne Hill, Calif.: Health Research, 1965).

7. Bill Schul and Ed Pettit, *The Secret Power of Pyramids* (Greenwich, Conn.: Fawcett, 1975).

IV FROM PHYSICS TO METAPHYSICS

Toward a Creative Synthesis of Knowledge

19

Today we know more. But what do we know about what we don't know? Forty years ago there was no quantum mechanics, somewhat over half a century ago there was no atomic nucleus, no electron. At the end of the last century, Wien advised Planck to become a pianist, rather than a physicist, because physics was a closed subject. How many Plancks are there now who are playing the piano rather than doing physics? And how much new physics is there to be discovered? . . . We must try everything we can. There is still lots and lots to explore.

Albert Szent-Györgyi's words, uttered in 1966, are still true: there is much to be learned. But it is also clear that science—knowing—is an endless process. Every answer obtained, every bit of information gleaned, raises a dozen new questions. The accumulation of knowledge never ceases.

The real key to scientific progress, therefore, is not simply fact gathering. Rather, it is visionary conceptualization and theorizing that gives a new, holistic organization to otherwise separate facts. In Thomas Kuhn's terms, it is restructuring of the belief system within which knowledge acquisition takes place. Einstein's observation on the matter is worth remembering: "The mere formulation of a problem is far more essential than its solution, which may be merely a matter of mathematical or experimental skill. To raise new questions, new possibilities, to regard old problems from a new angle requires creative imagination and marks real advances in science."

In spite of enormous amounts of data, no satisfactory theoretical framework covering the varieties of paranormal phenomena has thus far been advanced to correlate data or predict new experimental outcomes the way, say, Maxwell's equations did for electromagnetism. A Maxwell or an Einstein who will give us a unified theory of paranormal phenomena is greatly needed. Even if history shows that such a person was not among the authors presented here, we feel that their contributions will eventually be recognized by the person as instrumental to his or her conceptual breakthrough.

This section's purpose, then, is to assist in the breakthrough by synthesizing knowledge and presenting new organizing concepts. Analysis alone is not enough. There must be synthesis. There must be a consolidation of information in order for an investigation of the paranormal to achieve the radical extension of science that is inherent in it. This consolidation is urgently needed because large bodies of data are being amassed in highly specialized disciplines that, first, are unaware of similar or correlating data in other fields and, second, have made no attempt to step outside their domain and relate their work in a comprehensive fashion with other investigations.

The neurosciences offer a useful example here. The consolidation and dissemination of data *within* the field of neuroscience has been highly efficient and great advances have been made. But neuroscience has failed to interface with other fields, such as parapsychology, which can offer extremely relevant data. We have already seen in the commentary introducing Section II that one eminent brain scientist, Wilder Penfield, felt at the end of a long career that the mind cannot be explained on the basis of brain matter and neural processes. This is a radical (but not unique) position among neuroscientists—and a heartening one for those investigating paranormal phenomena—because it recognizes once again the reality of the psyche. Roger W. Sperry, famous for his split brain studies, recently supported this view by telling *Science of Mind* magazine (December 1975) that current mind—brain theory "allows in principle a scientific treatment of subjective mental phenomena . . . and recognizes mental forces as the crowning achievement of evolution . . ." This view restores the psyche to psychology, a field which has become largely reduced to the study of observable behavior and the properties of the nervous system. Once the psyche be-

comes respectable again, it seems logical to say that the next
step will be to make the *psychic* respectable.

A unified theory of the paranormal must include the data
from neuroscience as well as the data from parapsychology
and any other field of science touching on the paranormal. It
must take into full account the established facts from the natural and behavioral sciences. It must also deal in a comprehensive fashion with those traditions that have recorded varieties of paranormal phenomena, including religion and various
esoteric paths. In fact, if life itself—characterized by
mind—is the primary paranormal phenomenon, then such a
theory must explain the vital awareness we all self-evidently
have. It must explain our most profound intuitions, our
deepest longings, our greatest questions—such as that question asked by Sir Bernard Lovell in a *New York Times Magazine* article entitled "Whence" (16 November 1975): "What
is man's connection with the universe of atoms, stars and
galaxies?"

Lovell went on to comment:

> Today we cannot evade this deepest problem of our ex-
> istence by an escape into philosophical idealism or re-
> alism. On the contrary, we are forced to recognize that,
> although in our daily lives we can investigate problems
> as though the object of our investigation existed inde-
> pendently of us, this is not possible when we search for
> answers in the depths of the natural world.
> Indeed, I am inclined to accept contemporary scien-
> tific evidence as indicative of a far greater degree of
> man's total involvement with the universe.

All of the articles presented here attempt in varying degrees to answer Lovell's question. E. S. Maxey, for example, relates human brain waves to terrestrial elec-
trophysiology. E. H. Walker and Nick Herbert go even
further and examine the substratum—called "hidden variables" in physics—out of which all material events proceed, even Dudley's subatomic ether of the previous section.
Their paper is important for several reasons. First, it is quantitative, predicting, in the case of psychokinesis, the *actual numerical distances* that dice will move under pure human voli-
tion. Second, in contrast to Section II, Walker's theory does

not postulate a new form of energy (although it has an even more novel assertion, namely that the hidden variables substratum is consciousness itself and as such is animating, vital, the cosmic essence of life).

In another paper, "The Nature of Consciousness" (see his suggested readings), Walker has related the nonphysical field of consciousness to the brain and provided a testable clarification of the mind–body problem. Independently adding to this investigation is the work of A. P. Dubrov, who reports the work supporting his hypothesis that living systems are capable of generating and detecting gravitational waves. Dubrov calls this phenomenon biogravitation, and shows how it may be one link or level in understanding psychokinesis and other paranormal phenomena. This hypothesized property of living organisms combines data from biology, physics, and psychoenergetics in a novel synthesis. Changes in the conformation of biological protein macromolecules from an unordered liquid state to a solid crystalline state is the basis of the biogravitational field.

The next chapter, written by William A. Tiller, proposes positive and negative space-time frames as conjugate systems and presents data from some preliminary experiments with a biomechanical transducer. In "The Convergence of Psychology and Physics," J. H. M. Whiteman puts forward a world view that could subsume psychic phenomena at both a qualitative and a quantitative level. Laurence M. Beynam's article draws from quantum theory, and the magical and mystical traditions to create a model of the universe. Beynam holds that for each major state of consciousness there is a corresponding reality.

The title of this section indicates that as science expands the perimeter of knowledge, abstract metaphysics becomes concrete reality, albeit "concrete" in a highly rarefied or subtle way. As Arthur Koestler points out in his essay "Science and Para-Science," modern physics has dematerialized matter, and therefore "the unthinkable phenomena of parapsychology appear somewhat less preposterous in the light of the unthinkable propositions of modern quantum physics."

This position is supported in an article by J. B. Rhine, worthy of mention here. In "Can Parapsychology Help Religion?," which appeared in *Spiritual Frontiers* (Vol. 4, No. 1, 1974), Rhine summarizes the findings of parapsychology over a century of inquiry. More important, he synthesizes. He shows how two divergent traditions—science (in the form of parapsychology) and religion—now complement one another. Parapsychology, he says, has helped to "naturalize" the mental world. It has found "a set of principles underneath certain hitherto unprovable claims of miraculous or supernatural happenings among the unexplainable phenomena in the legendry of religion." Rhine goes on to suggest that the discovery of psi as a possible explanation of religious miracles should no longer be called supernatural but *superphysical* because the principles involved, which have been empirically demonstrated, reach beyond the human sensorimotor system and its space-time limits.

We agree, and might well have used the term "superphysics" in place of "metaphysics" in this section's title. However, as Teilhard de Chardin once pointed out with regard to evolution, discontinuity is continuity. The quantum leaps in understanding that scientific revolutions bring nevertheless have their precursor indications. Likewise, radical shifts in paradigm do not immediately eradicate the past, but often bring much of the past along because it has the stamp of truth. Thus we chose to use "metaphysics" because the word has a long and honorable tradition which science is now beginning to discover as a rich, fertile ground for investigation —the very ground that has contributed so much to the coming revolution in science which this book foresees.

As physicist Jack Sarfatti points out in his *Psychoenergetics Systems* journal article "Implications of Meta-Physics for Psychoenergetics Systems" (Vol. 1, 1974), an application of Gödel's theorem to physics means that no theory of physics which deals only with physics will ever explain physics. "Therefore," he writes, "*meta*physical statements are absolutely vital for the evolution of physics. . . ."

Historian of science Theodore Roszak describes the attitude of synthesis called for here in a letter to *Science* (13 December 1974). Roszak, who uses the term *gnosis* to describe the new mode of knowing that will characterize future science, describes it as "a kind of knowledge other than reductive, that honors and invites the aesthetic, sensuous, compassionate, and visionary possibilities of experience as well as the rational and technical. The term is not meant to exclude scientific knowledge, but to embrace it within the program Abraham Maslow called 'hierarchical integration'."

How might gnosis, the new knowledge based on synthesis, be achieved? We reply with the words of physicist Henry Margenau in *Science and ESP*. Although spoken to the parapsychological community, the importance of his statement extends to the entire field of science:

> . . . why, I should like to ask, is it necessary to import into any new discipline all the approved concepts of an older science in its contemporary state of development? Physics did not adhere slavishly to the Greek rationalistic formulations that preceded it; it was forced to create its own specific constructs. . . .
>
> The parapsychologist, I think . . . must strike out on his own and probably reason in bolder terms than present-day physics suggests.

Where might science be led by "striking out" in search of gnosis? We have already explored several areas in the previous sections. Here we shall find a blend of modern physics and ancient metaphysics from Eastern and Western world views. Philosopher of science Oliver Reiser, author of *Cosmic Humanism,* created a phrase to describe people such as those presented here: avatars of synthesis. Through their efforts, the received scientific notions of matter, energy, space and time are being reexamined and reformulated in ways that extend science and set it on a course of convergence with mysticism. Books such as LeShan's *The Medium, the Mystic and the Physicist* and Fritjof Capra's *The Tao of Physics* present the experience of space-time and matter-energy in modern physics, showing parallels with esoteric/spiritual/mystical traditions and showing useful avenues of investigations relevant to both.

An irony is emerging from these investigations. It is this: as science "dematerialized" the world, its much vaunted objectivity also vanished, revealing that all knowledge is subjective. That is, knowledge is dependent upon the state and quality of consciousness in the knower—his or her ability to

perceive or "know" without preconception, prejudice or un-
recognized assumptions that distort through interpretation.
Moreover, the recognized fact of consciousness-matter interaction (as in psychokinesis) calls into question the
vaunted "objectivity" of scientific instruments.

Esoteric psychology in both the East and West has recognized this for millennia. People in this century such as
Sri Aurobindo Ghose, Rudolf Steiner, and Maharishi
Mahesh Yogi have redirected our attention to the fact that
knowledge is structured in consciousness. Muddled consciousness produces confusion, uncertainty, doubt—i.e., low-
grade knowledge.

To overcome this problem, Charles Tart, a psychologist
and author of *States of Consciousness,* recently proposed
"state-specific sciences." He calls for scientists to undergo
training such as that which psychics, shamans, yogis, mystics,
etc., undertake to enter various states of consciousness. By
becoming familiar with different modes of perception "from
the inside," so to speak, they will qualify themselves to evaluate the knowledge obtainable in these states but otherwise inaccessible to a scientist's ordinary mode of perception. Likewise, with such perception comes a new ability to understand
and reinterpret nonscientific documents and descriptions dealing with "knowledge of the higher worlds," as Rudolf Steiner
put it.

We support Tart's proposal and, in their own way, so do
the other articles in this section. They demonstrate that the
organic view of the cosmos common to the esoteric/spirit-
ual/mystical traditions of East and West may provide the
conceptual breakthrough science needs to go beyond the dead-
end of mechanistic Cartesian dualism.

Such a breakthrough will undoubtedly draw heavily from
modern science and technology for metaphors and terminology with which to express itself. Thus, information theory,
holography and quantum mechanics will probably figure as
prominently in the articulation of new insights based on state-
specific investigations as will the language of mysticism and
spiritual philosophy. This is the direction set here by our con-
tributors. In their totality, they demonstrate the spirit of sci-

ence leading to a science of the spirit—a grand synthesis transcending boundaries of scientific discipline, spiritual tradition, historical period and cultural preference. It is a consummation devoutly to be wished.

20.

Biopsychophysics—The Proper Study of Man

E. STANTON MAXEY

> Gentlemen, I have a confession to make. Half of what
> we have taught you is in error, and furthermore we can-
> not tell you which half it is.
>
> > Sir William Osler, speaking to a
> > graduating medical class

What is man? Biological man originates as a unicelled organism within the mother's womb. As an adult he is an extraordinarily complex organism consisting of 350 trillion highly
specialized cells affixed to an internal skeleton permitting
great mobility within his geographic environment. His sense
organs permit him wide environmental contact by way of
touch, taste, hearing, smell, and sight—none of which are
well understood. But the most basic sense, awareness, seems
to lie within a nonphysical matrix upon which all other senses
register their data.

Man is aware that he is aware. Personal experience and
common sense reveal this to each of us, although science has
no explanation at present. Nor does science know of any
other creature which demonstrates that it is aware of its own
awareness. This seems to be a primary characteristic distin-
guishing *Homo sapiens*.

But physical science, in searching for an answer to the
question "What is man?", has been unable to recognize this,
let alone account for it. Instead, in analyzing increasingly
smaller "building blocks" down through the subatomic level,
the awareness factor has become progressively more elusive.

"Biopsychophysics—The Proper Study of Man" by E. S. Maxey is
an original article written especially for this volume and is printed
by permission of the author.

On the surface, this is all very rational and objective. Beneath that appearance, however, science has become as mystical as Nostradamus. Consider the following.

In studying light, the behavior of photons (light particles) could not explain all observed phenomena and thus the wave theory came into being. Electrons (negatively charged particles which form atomic "shells"), when caused to flow through crystalline structures, also behave as if moving in waves. Physicist Louis de Broglie approached atomic structure from a waveform viewpoint, and science subsequently evolved two convenient ways of looking at all matter—particulate structure and waveform composition. Yet, question a physicist as to what it is that waves inside a vacuum jar through which a beam of light is traveling and he may reply: "Why do you suppose that anything is waving?"

James Clerk Maxwell evolved yet another viewpoint for physical reality. Albert Einstein, in commenting on it, said: ". . . after Maxwell they conceived physical reality as represented by continuous fields, not mechanically explicable . . . This change in the conception of reality is the most profound and fruitful one that has come to physics since Newton."[1]

Thus the modern scientist rides three oftentimes mutually antagonistic conceptualizations with great dexterity: particles, waves, and fields. Like the circus stunt rider, he jumps from one concept-horse to another, depending on his need to comprehend one phenomenon or another. Physics has even formalized this process into the law of complementarity, but obligingly admonishes that it should be indulged in only as a sort of court of last appeal.

Curiously, physics, while admitting that its laws provide no insight, or at most very little, into the origin of life, yet affirms that all life's energies *must* derive from a conglomerated intermix of science's particle, wave and field theories. But biology is now threatening physics even more severely than Galileo's pronouncement on the heliocentric solar system once disquieted Pope Urban VIII's Roman Catholic Church.

This is because physics allows that elemental atoms can be transmuted one into another, that the relatively large energies required for such reactions are precisely known, and that normally transmuting radioactive substances have absolutely constant decay rates. Physicists affirm such constants to be as unchangeable as the speed of light. Yet their own observations have revealed that radioactive half-life varies with changes in pressure, temperature, chemical state, electric potential, and the stress of monomolecular bonding. Living systems, from bacteria through Homo sapiens, are now known to have been ubiquitously alchemizing such elemental transformations throughout untold eons—at energy levels considered impossibly low! The physical scientist fears for the edifice of his conceptual castles should living systems so perform. And living systems, not having received their instructions from physicists, do indeed perform that way.

Woe unto physics. Life is a thorn unto its side, pricking more painfully than Bruno and Galileo's pronouncements in the 13th and 14th centuries.

Man is among such living systems. Let us examine one of his 350 trillion cells, say, a leucocyte. This cell will have a negative charge at the nucleus with respect to the cellular protoplasm and cell membrane. It is as if the cell mimics in a microscopic way the charges of the terrestrial surface as compared to the Earth's ionosphere. Cellular metabolism and oxygen consumption seem to have a primary purpose: the function being that of pumping sodium, thus maintaining a high potassium concentration on one side of the cell membrane and a high sodium concentration on the other with an associated marked ionic charge differential. Indeed, as long ago as 1943, Dr. George Crile, founder of the Cleveland Clinic, stated that: ". . . each living cell [is] a tiny electric battery generating its own current by chemical action."

Precisely correct. Yet this concept, both confirmed and expanded by contemporary research, was laughed at in Crile's time. Dr. Max Carson, called by Dr. Albert Schweitzer "a medical genius who walked among us," remarked on the essential life-sustaining qualities of the photon. With the advent of the electron spin laboratory came the brilliant and illuminating work of Nobel Laureate Albert Szent-Györgyi who revealed the biological work functions of the cellular electron transfer in the following language:

> The fuel of life is the electron or, more exactly, the energy it takes over from photons in photosynthesis; this energy

the electron gives up gradually while flowing through the cellular machinery.

Thus we have in man an astoundingly complex electrical being. Some of the isolated electrical qualities of man as a whole can be demonstrated in acupuncture point determinations. A field meter can be used to demonstrate man's total electrical field qualities. Indeed, Dr. H. S. Burr was measuring various skin potentials in the mid-1930s and at that time correlated abnormal potentials with cancer of the female reproductive tract with a reported accuracy of ninety percent. In physiological sleep, man's skin resistance may suddenly go up by an order of magnitude and the electrical charge of the head versus the foot level may completely reverse itself. During dreaming there is a distinctive electrical brain rhythm and an associated penile erection.

Puzzling indeed is man from the electrical point of view, but when one associates cognitive processes with electrical functioning, the puzzle deepens. Dr. Andrija Puharich demonstrated that persons can be taught to hear with electrical devices attached to the skin in areas unrelated to the acoustic nerve and thus we see that orthodox notions of the hearing mechanism come into question in much the same way that perception of colors with one's fingers challenges present optical neurological concepts.

All people are, by experience, aware of their five senses but where cognition of these senses takes place must, for the present, be left open for further study. Let us additionally posit that man is also aware, though subtly, of his own soul. Psyche, derived from Greek, means "the soul." Indeed, may we not question whether conscious awareness is not more properly to be viewed as a timeless soul-function manifesting periodically in life incarnate? Surely those of us laboring in the human sciences must, like the physicists, be permitted our "complementarities."

Clearly, any student examining seriously the phenomenon of cognition must question whether that function is a product of brain substance any more than all light phenomena are products of photons. Has a scientific measurement of cognition ever been accomplished? One must answer "no." Yet each of us is aware of the "I" within himself. The question must be formulated: "Is awareness itself less a fact than that of which we are aware?"

Is awareness a field phenomenon? Is the mind of man—the aware cognitive portion of his being—a function of brain matter or is it a field phenomenon associated at times with the brain but capable of transcending, in a cognitive way, all usual space and time barriers? Examples of this transcendental mode may be found in the "past life" phenomenon, Dr. Ian Stevenson's collection of some 1,300 cases "suggestive of reincarnation" and Dr. Denys Kelsey's practical use of hypnotically recovered preincarnational psychic stresses as causes of his patients' contemporary emotional or mental disorders. Dr. Stevenson is at the University of Virginia Medical School, and Dr. Kelsey practices in England. Few psychiatrists seem aware of their work or of Dr. Kelsey's clinical success.

What about "out of body" experiences in which certain persons can voluntarily will their consciousness to travel through walls, over long distances—even into foreign lands—and while there accurately perceive events occurring in real time? More commonly, in cases of acute trauma or illness, individuals not normally having this free traveling mental faculty may similarly transcend the usual physical limitations of the mind's function. One neurosurgeon known to the author was nonplussed when a patient with a head injury "hallucinated" in lucid archaic Spanish, a language to which the patient had never previously been exposed. Obviously, either such reports over many years result from some curious mass hysteria, or the mind can function apart from its usual connection with the cerebral cortex under some circumstances.

Consider the mystifying capacities of clairvoyants, mediums and sensitives. These people "see" diseases and illnesses, perceive events at great distances, name persons unknown to them and precisely depict events of the past and of the future with uncanny accuracy. At times, like the Biblical Witch of Endor (a medium), they evidentially communicate with minds of persons long dead and buried.

At this juncture some readers may have become as apprehensive over such cognitive functions as contemporary physicists are over the contemptuous bacteria's irreverent alchemical transmutation of elemental atoms. And some reassurance may be in order. Consider how frightened you might be had you lived all your life in a gray-shaded colorblind world . . . when, perhaps with some head injury, you abruptly achieved full color vision. How strange and confused would your life be . . . because how could you describe your perception of rainbow colors to your truly colorblind friends and neighbors? The likelihood is that you would be judged to have gone mad.

Common experience is a great pacifier and one need not remain colorblind in the matter of paranormal cognitive experience. Dreaming is a normal human function. Anyone following the example of J. W. Dunne, author of *An Experiment in Time,* in observing his own dreams will soon clearly recognize their frequently exact predictive content. Discovery of one's own precognitive dream scenarios generates a feeling of kinship to the fully color-visioned psychic person. That dreams have value is further confirmed by noting that physicist Niels Bohr, upon receiving the Nobel Prize, revealed to the world that his dreams had depicted the structure of the atom. And August Kekule, the chemist, was likewise honored for the great advances made possible through his dream of the structure of the benzene ring. As a result of Edwin Rickman's recurring dreams a gyroscopic device has been fabricated in England which, when spinning, weighs twenty-five percent less than when at rest. We can only wait to confirm whether or not a new comprehension of gravity will ensue and whether we will have another dream-related Nobel Laureate. We can, however, affirm that dream awareness permits each of us, albeit only intermittently, a decreased "psychic colorblindness."

The advent of complex computers has led many to feel that the brain behaves as a biological computer with similarities in control circuits, memory banks and programming processes. There are essential differences, however. No computer can solve a problem without the essential data having previously been programmed. Computers have absolutely no parallel to human clairaudience, clairvoyance and precognition. Computers have no ESP.

Therefore, let us consider the brain as an organ that both

programs the mind to some degree by transmitting information to it and through interrogating the mind receives instructional controls from it. Let us allow to the mind a field function capable both of receiving information from other than brain pathways and of exerting influences on the material realm via pathways other than through the central nervous system. Grant us the privilege allowed the physicist in his law of "complementarity" and the difficulties of memories of past lives, nonocular clairvoyant visualization of distant places, and clairaudient perceptions from the minds of nonliving persons dissolve into orderly phenomena normal to a higher-ordered system. Then the problems of plants responding to a person's mental/emotional states (as purportedly observed by Cleve Backster and others) and of natural objects defying physics' laws in response to minds of gifted psychics (e.g., Uri Geller, Ingo Swann, and Sai Baba) are more revealing of our higher-ordered system than they are destructive of contemporary physical concepts. The "out of body" travels of people such as Robert Monroe and Sylvan Muldoon may then be conjectured as their "mind fields" functioning in realms dissociated from physical brains.

But what bodily measurement can reveal to us those subtle variations accompanying these curious psychic capacities? Lacking visual perception of the auras said to surround saints and true magicians, how may we proceed?

Acupuncture has burst into the consciousness of the Western medical world and greatly disquieted accepted neurophysiological thinking. Let us see what, albeit conjectural, answers may be found here.

Acupuncture points have diminished electrical resistance and hence are readily detected with high impedance ohm meters. About 1,200 such points are distributed over the skin surface and they are said by the ancient orientals to be organized into twenty-eight different meridian systems approximately half of which transmit positive energy while the remainder are negative energy systems.[2] Energy called "chi" in Chinese ("ki" in Japanese) is said to be derived from the cosmos for these systems; moreover, the energy is said to be positive ("yang") and negative ("yin").

Let us see whether positive aerions, formed in our upper atmosphere and drifting earthward, may be equated to the "yang" energy of acupuncture theory and whether negative aerions, drifting upward from the terrestrial surface, may be equated to "yin" energy. And let us inquire whether the "nadis," said by some interpreters of yogic tradition to be points at which energy flows from more subtle bodies into the physical body system, may in fact be acupuncture points which fulfill such functions in terms of electron flow according to the laws of physics.

A voltage gradient exists in the outdoor environment which is predominantly negative at the Earth's surface and positive up to and including the inner Van Allen belt. This gradient varies from about 150 volts to as much as 3,000 volts per meter.

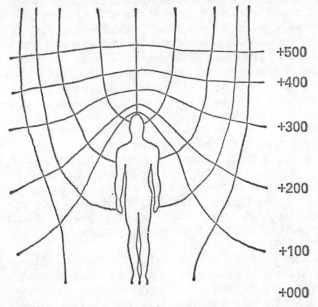

+500
+400
+300
+200
+100
+000

FIGURE 1
Voltage gradient outdoors. Current flows of equal value depicted by generally vertical lines.

This natural electrostatic field is normally modulated in response to many astronomical factors, but has a basic frequency spectrum known as the Schumann resonance, which power peaks at 7.2–8 and 14–15 hertz (cycles per second). R. Wever of the Max Planck Institute in Germany recently reported studies which revealed that 10 Hz electrical fields control human circadian rhythms and he suggested that this component of the terrestrial environment is the pace setter for such biological phenomena. Circadian desynchronization is commonly experienced by air travelers; it is called "jet lag."

In passing one may note with interest the fact that these same frequency spans are found both within the Earth's electromagnetic environment and in human brain waves as recorded by the electroencephalogram (EEG). The magnetic component of low-frequency EM waves is extremely penetrating, as shown by the U. S. Navy successfully using 45-Hz electromagnetic waves in communicating between Wisconsin and a submerged submarine off Norway. The Russian V. N. Mikhailovsky in 1969 showed that 0.01–5-Hz waves of 1,000-gamma magnetic intensity (2% of the terrestrial magnetic field) remarkably altered human EEGs. A replication of that experiment by this author revealed direct brain wave coupling at 3–13 Hz and only 30-gamma strength. This was observed in only two of thirteen subjects but it poses a question: "Are clairvoyants and mediums so gifted because their minds can tune into and lock onto penetrating magnetic waves normally existent in our environment?"

A person standing outdoors is subject to his environment, and physics dictates that aerions being propelled within the environmental electrostatic gradient would flow to the body as lightning to a lightning rod, though less intensely. Because acupuncture points have decreased resistance, electric currents derived from such traveling aerions must necessarily flow predominantly through these points.

Both the oriental literature and particle theories of physics infer that environmental electrical energy flows via acupuncture points into positive and negative meridian systems. Interestingly, positive meridian systems are located predominantly on dorsal (back) surfaces while negative meridians run over the abdomen. Could man in his early quadripedal evolution have been thus equipped to receive positive aerion energy through his back from the positive upper atmosphere and negative energy via his abdomen, palms and soles from the negatively energized Earth's surface?

An electrophysiological innovation has been achieved by Dr. Hiroshi Motoyama of Tokyo, who worked with seiketsu points. These are the meridian end acupuncture points existing at the tips of the fingers and toes. Dr. Motoyama observed that after application of three volt electrical potentials current flow measurements followed a curve with high immediate and then decreased amperages. The immediate values he termed "before polarization" and the amperages after one second "after polarization." These values were observed to vary with different seiketsu points and with different people, depending on their age and degree of homeostasis (harmonious body functioning without illness or imbalance).

Guided in part by psychic information, Motoyama developed a computerized program to record and analyze "before polarization" and "after polarization" values from the twenty-eight seiketsu points. He also showed that these phenomena could not be accounted for through the sensory, sympathetic, and parasympathetic nervous systems.

In the Motoyama device (see Section V) red numerical values from the computer indicate abnormal values. How astonishing it is to observe, for example, such red values from the left thumb (seiketsu point on the lung meridian) in subjects with known disease in the left lung. Presently, these computer analyses portend a valuable medical diagnostic tool.

But they do more. By observing instabilities of chakra-related organs in the computer readout, Motoyama is able both to recognize psychic persons and to predict something of what their paranormal capacities may be!

Chakras are said in yogic physiology to be part of the subtle etheric anatomy of man. Let us briefly consider this esoteric subject. Science discarded the "ether" after the famed Michelson–Morley interferometer experiments determined the speed of light to be constant. Presently it appears they were in error on two counts: first, there is an "ether" and second, when the solar systemic etheric flow is factored into new in-

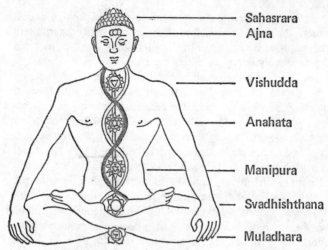

FIGURE 2
Symbolic diagramming of the chakras.

terferometer studies, the speed of light will in all probability be found not constant.

Dr. H. C. Dudley, professor of radiation physics at the University of Illinois Medical Center, has authored a number of papers equating the ether to a presently recognized and ubiquitous neutrino sea. Professor Dudley warns that energy fluxes within this neutrino sea (ether) may well account for the energy yield variations, not explained by calculations, but observed in atomic bomb tests. His explanation demands that extreme caution be employed in the use of atomic energy lest man unwittingly ignite our entire globe.

Dr. Olivier Costa de Beauregard, of the Laboratoire de Physique Théorique in Paris, has explained how energies derived from this neutrino sea theoretically might enable living organisms to alchemically transmute elemental atoms. And his explanation is entirely within the confines of physics' presently recognized and accepted laws. Thus does the biological alchemical transmutation of elemental atoms, described by Von Herseele, Pierre Baranger, and Louis C. Kervran, both conform and elucidate orthodox science's recognition of the ether. It is a recognition of the very greatest moment and promises to effectively link the physical, biological, and spiritual sciences.

Chakras, then, may be viewed as etheric fields of multiple lobes or petals, and they are said to be both organ and psychic capacity related as follows:

Chakra	Location	Organ affected	Psycharacteristic
1 Muladhara	Spine base	Adrenals	
2 Swadhisthana	Sacral	Gonads	
3 Manipura	Solar Plexus	Pancreas	Trance clairaudience and clairvoyance
4 Anahata	Heart	Thymus	
5 Vishudda	Throat	Thyroid	
6 Ajna	Forehead	Pituitary	
7 Sahasrara	Crown	Pineal	Concious clairaudience and clairvoyance

Thus, when the acupuncture meridian analyzer reveals instabilities of kidney, bladder, large intestine, and spleen meridians the manipura chakra is inferred to be active, and some clairvoyance and clairaudience is expected. And it is seen. We may hope that an apprehension of the electropsychophysiology of acupuncture will, someday, unbar the door separating the twin "complementarities" of Western medicine's time-dependent mechanistic view of life and occult Eastern wisdom's depiction of a conscious governing principle that functions independently of time and geographic barriers.

We may also hope that the evolving discipline of biometeorology (the science of meteorological mechanistic links to living systems) coupled with an apprehension of the physiology of acupuncture, will provide insights into the curious ways of yogis. Breathing is ubiquitously stressed through yogic instruction. Since the lungs present vast surface areas, possibly one thousand times that of the skin, it is logical to suspect that aerions (said in occult literature to be etheric in nature) readily dispatch their energy through respiration. It has been shown, experimentally, that mouth breathing of air rich in negative aerions results in the elevation of the blood's alkalinity and an increased bodily resistance to surgical shock. Test pilots, if breathing such air while in positive electric fields, display faster reaction times and a significant improvement in light discrimination. Does it not seem that yogis, in their breathing patterns, may simply be electrically recharging their cellular systems and that other aerions, dispatching their electrical charge through acupuncture points, assist in this charging process? Biological data favors this conjecture.

Yogis equally stress vegetarian diets as essential to bodily health and the unfolding of one's psychic perception. Aside from religious conviction, why is this so? Szent-Györgyi, utilizing sophisticated electron spin laboratory apparatus, has provided one answer. He demonstrated that red meat has the effect of absorbing electrons in bodily metabolism; thus carnivorous habits tend to discharge cellular electrical systems. Fresh fruits and vegetables on the other hand, storing the photon energy of photosynthesis in their complex chemical structures, are electrically charging to cellular "batteries."

Perhaps an analogy will clarify the concept. Our electrical terrestrial environment in relation to living systems behaves somewhat like the generator in a car; it tends to charge the battery. The chemicals within our cellular batteries indirectly derive from our food. Bad acid in automobile batteries means the car won't start. Defective chemicals in our cellular batteries mean, in addition to poor health, that our psychic radios function poorly—or perhaps not at all. How strange it all seems to the neurophysiologist.

Stranger still is the ida-pingala-sushumna kundalini system pictured both in yogic pictographs and in the Hermetic caduceus.

Serpents, always the symbols of knowledge, are found intertwined in both figures. Positive psychic energy is said to flow through one serpent, the "pingala" while negative energy flows through the other, the "ida." At each intertwining, a chakra is found and it is said that as one chakra after another becomes "opened"—i.e., activated—the individual manifests increasing psychic capacities. When all chakras are fully developed and active, we have a master with energy flowing upward actively via both serpentine figures and returning through a central shaft, the "sushumna." Thus a master such as Jesus or Buddha is said to have a fully awakened kundalini. Yet, in harmony with the observations of Dr. Ian Ste-

FIGURE 3
Caduceus, staff of Hermes.

venson and Dr. Denys Kelsey, this chakra kundalini system is said to evolve through many incarnations. Why not, if such systems picture simply a vivifying mind field which lives in its own domain?

FIGURE 4
Caduceus, staff of Aesculapius.

American medicine, in contrast, functions under the symbolic staff of Aesculapius with but one serpent and recognizes no conscious or subconscious continuity throughout multiple sequential lives. The Book of Genesis likewise portrays one serpent—*but two trees.* The fruit of one tree conveyed a "knowledge of good and evil." Could a second serpent, as pictured in the Hermetic caduceus and yogic pictographs, have been associated with Genesis' second tree of "everlasting life"? And could that secondary serpent simply have gotten lost in the myths of time?

It has been said that the proper study of man is man. True enough, for how else may we come to know ourselves? The physiological intricacies of atomic spin resonance and biometeorologically paced circadian rhythms reflect phenomena resulting from solar systemic magnetic and electric links within which conscious man is found. Religion and history, queried humbly, both invoke insights confirmable by sophisticated computer technology, and evoke recognitions of man's potentially boundless conscious capacity. Someone has said: "To define God is to deny Him."

May not one say the same of Man?

REFERENCES

1. J. Bernstein, "Profiles: The Secrets of the Old One," *The New Yorker* (17 March 1973).
2. H. Motoyama, "Chakra, Nadi of Yoga and Meridians, Points of Acupuncture" (Tokyo: Institute of Religious Psychology, 1972).

21.

Biogravitation and Psychotronics

ALEXANDER P. DUBROV

Since it thinks, one form of the development of natural science is the *hypothesis*. If we were to wait until material was ready in *pure form* for a law, this would mean suspending conscious research until then, and in any case we would never obtain a law by this means alone.

(Friedrich Engels)

Scientific and technical progress is pushing back the frontiers of our knowledge farther and farther and has already gone far beyond the boldest predictions made in the past, with the launching of the first satellite, man's first space flight, the landing of men on the Moon, the flight of spacecraft to Mars, Venus, and Jupiter, and space laboratories. These research programs have had a major public impact.

Scientific and technical progress has covered every branch of knowledge and every field of interest. A similar development has occurred in the various branches of biology, biophysics and quantum physics, but one noteworthy feature of this latter development is that the new, revolutionary scientific ideas cut across and contradict the familiar, traditional, established, classical conceptions in these branches of knowledge.

For example, a biophysicist specializing in biological thermodynamics points out that the celebrated second law of thermodynamics, unconditionally accepted as one of the

"Biogravitation and Psychotronics" by Alexander P. Dubrov originally appeared in *Impact of Science on Society*, Vol. 24, No. 4, 1974. Copyright © 1974 by The Unesco Press and reprinted by permission.

foundation stones of science, is in fact inapplicable to energy transformation processes either in the living cell or in the functioning biological macromolecule.[1] A well-known biologist has demonstrated how reactions involving the natural transmutation of elements outside the radioactive series—in other words, reactions which until now were thought to take place only inside nuclear reactors—can take place in living things.[2] Many more examples of similar work could be given.

One of the ways in which scientific and technical progress shows itself is in a clean break with previous scientific concepts and laws. This can be easily understood through materialist dialectics and is in accordance, in particular, with the law of the "negation of the negation," the new being brought forth by the old, arising in the depths and on the foundation of the old, and taking its place. In time, it in its turn will have to make way for something new, as yet only gestating within it. This is what has happened in the case of psychotronics, a new scientific discipline which studies the particular physical and biophysical phenomena occurring during human mental activity and during interaction between various living beings.

A New Biological—Physical Field

Psychotronics can also be thought of as a science which has duly come into being as a result of scientific and technical progress and which, in our opinion, has extremely promising prospects of development. For those interested in further details of this subject, we can recommend R. A. McConnell's guide,[3] intended in the main for the university-level student, and a bibliography on the subject.[4]

What is so special about this new-born science? Psychotronics carries within it the negation of the scientific disciplines from which it sprang and is the logical continuation and development of those disciplines. None of the phenomena with which it deals (i.e., the well-established scientific facts of psychotronics) can be explained in terms of the traditional concepts of physics, chemistry, biology and psychology. The book by D. Ellis entitled *The Chemistry of Psi* may be mentioned as an outstanding illustration of this.[5]

The present study gives detailed consideration to the possible role played by protons and electrons, quantum-mechanical effects and the uncertainty principle in psi phenomena, but the essence of such phenomena remains hidden. A fundamentally new approach to the facts is required, and we believe that our hypothesis concerning biogravitation provides that approach.[6]

This hypothesis claims that a special "biogravitational field" exists in living things and in man in particular. It is called a biogravitational field because its properties are in some ways akin to those of living matter and in others to those of a gravitational field.

By the term biogravitation, we designate a field-energy system. The biogravitational field is universally convertible—i.e., it is capable of transition into any form of field and energy—and therefore a unified field theory must be worked out especially for it. Many facts reported in the literature of psychotronics give evidence of this property of the biogravitational field. The biogravitational field thus reflects in microcosm the problem of the unified field, which is the cornerstone of the physics of the future. It will be clear to the unbiased reader that the work published in 1965 by the Soviet physicist K. Stanjukovic on the interdependence of gravitation and elementary particles[7] has made a fundamental contribution to the development of these ideas. This theory has now made great headway,[8] but at the time when it was published there were of course no grounds to suppose that the real solution to this problem could be found primarily in biology on the basis of facts also observable in psychotronics.

For any hypothesis to be accepted and for it to become the foundation of future theory, experimental findings which fit in with the new theory are needed. Such findings have been made at various levels in the scheme of living matter, pointing to the universal nature of the field we have discovered. The existence of a biogravitational field at the level of complete organism can, for example, be seen from the fact that the human brain has been found capable of thought transference almost regardless of distance and of the type of screening device used.[9, 10] We find this property of transference only in a gravitational field.

It has further been discovered that man is able, with special mental effort, to move any kind of object (the phenomenon of telekinesis).[11] The latest research fully corroborates telekinesis and provides considerably more detailed information about it, as evidenced by experiments with individuals possessing this kind of field to a very high degree (N. Kulagina, B. Ermolaev, T. Dadasev, U. Geller, I. Swann, and others). It is well known that the only force which acts equally on any kind of substance and causes it to move is gravitation. It should be noted that experimental research on telekinesis led H. Forwald to think that gravitation might possibly play a part in these phenomena[12]; he did not think that human biogravitational forces were involved and believed that the necessary energy was liberated from the mass of the subject under experiment by a psychokinetic triggering effect. To be fair, however, it should be said that Forwald has come closer than anyone else to a correct understanding of psi phenomena and made the first strict quantitative measurements in the field of biogravitation, even though he was wrong about the mechanism involved.

Biological Basis of Biogravitation

Mention was made earlier of the occurrence of biogravitation at the level of a complete organism, but as we said above, it is universal, and evidence of biogravitation can thus be found throughout the whole biological scale. At cell level, for example, there are a number of processes in which there are grounds for believing biogravitational forces to play a part. Let us take the example of cell division (mitosis). A remarkable stage in this process is the migration of the chromosomes towards the poles.[13] All the painstaking research carried out on this phenomenon so far has failed to explain it by means of electrostatic, magnetic, hydrodynamic, reaction, and other physical forces.[14] A number of facts, however, point to the possible role of biogravitational forces in this process. For example, it is noted in mitosis that chromosomes of different sizes move at equal speed, their movement tending to be in a straight line and to be uniform, sometimes retarded but never accelerated.[15] This would seem almost to exclude the possibility of a gravitational influence on the chromosomes' movement but it should be remembered that chromosomes move because the centriole (the "pole" of attraction) and the kinetochores of the chromosomes are linked by the fibers of the spindle, which have special elastic properties. That gravitational forces are here at work in the living cell follows also from the fact that cell division is arrested when centrifugal forces of 300,000–400,000 g working in the opposite direction are set up.[15]

Other peculiarities of the dividing cell also merit our attention. Simultaneously with the formation of a specific kind of mitotic apparatus having a strictly ordered crystalline structure, the emission of various photons, both in the ultraviolet and the visible range of the spectrum, can be observed in the dividing cell.[16, 17] It was recently observed that, during mitosis, ultrasonic oscillations with a frequency of from 10^6 to 10^7 hertz[18] and other forms of energy and fields were produced.

These unusual facts are further evidence of the possible role of biogravitational forces in this process since gravitational waves may be quantized and may change into other forms of field and energy.[7, 8] It has been reported, in particular, that gravitational waves can be detected by the sound waves generated in the photon dispersal process. This so-called photon-graviton dispersal is a characteristic of the emission of gravitational waves by any source.[19] An interesting phenomenon observed in the course of research is that when a coherent light source (laser) is directed on a semiconducting crystal, the ultrasonic waves produced cause gravitational waves to be generated having an intensity 10^{23} greater than with Weber's resonator and 10^{40} greater than with the rotating rod envisaged by Einstein.[20] Consequently, as these effects may be the basis of gravitational radiation in the cell, they cannot be excluded from consideration, since it is considered quite feasible that the biocrystalline structures of living cells may have semiconductive properties.[21] There are quite a number of other examples at cell level (muscular contraction, the transmission of nerve impulses) and at the level of a complete organism (psi photography, levitation) which point to the presence and role of biogravitation in these phenomena.

We should mention here, if only briefly, the particular properties of biogravitational forces: (a) they must act at close or long range; (b) they can be directed and focused; (c) they can be positive or negative (and cause attraction or repulsion, respectively); (d) they can carry information; (e) they are able to convert the energy of a field into matter with weight; (f) a field of such forces can persist in the absence of the source which originally gave rise to them; (g) they can undergo transition into any form of field and energy; and (h) they are closely bound up with change of symmetry groups and with distortion of space at the submolecular level of biological structures.

It can thus be seen that biogravitation possesses qualitatively new properties as well as the general properties possessed by gravitational fields in the physics of nonliving matter, and this is apparently where the difference between living and nonliving matter lies.

Thus far I have developed this hypothesis about biogravitation only from the qualitative point of view since not enough strictly defined quantitative measurements have yet been made on which to base a fully developed theory. It is only a supposition that a general field theory can be constructed from the particular properties observed in studying biogravitation. The qualitatively new properties of biogravitation, as against ordinary gravitation, raise many new and important matters of principle which are reviewed in the box on the following page.

We may thus conclude that a living organism can be both a receiver and a transmitter of gravitational waves over considerable distances since the power potential is $P^1 = 10^{-18}/10^{-23} = 10^5$, and even 10^{10} according to a less strict evaluation.

The mechanism outlined is possible since, in the cell, the protein molecules together with the layer of intracellular water adjacent to them can be in coherent, high-frequency oscillatory states.[23]

We should mention in this connection that a number of researchers have studied gravitational radiation in respect of

How the Biogravitational Field Is Formed

The occurrence of biogravitation in a living organism cannot be understood in the framework of present-day conventional biology and physics. From certain data, it may be inferred that a biogravitational field arises in consequence of changes in the conformation of protein structures as a result of the transformations which occur with polypeptide molecules. These changes in conformation induce a strictly ordered, structured crystalline state in the hydrated protein molecules and their oscillations are synchronized, as a result of which a qualitatively new physical situation is established, affecting the atom's symmetry groups and the nature of the sub-molecular space. For this reason, the biogravitational field could equally well (and correctly) be called a "conformation field," the waves could be called "conformation waves" and the wave particles "conformons." The resemblance to traditional conceptions of particle–wave dualism ends here, however, since the above-mentioned properties of the conformation field also enter into play.

Analyzing psi phenomena on the basis of traditional methods of calculation, one could hypothesize as follows about the mechanism involved. For a variable biogravitational field, according to V. Bunin, it may be accepted that gravitational radiation is contingent on the phased oscillations or rotations of hydrogen electrons or atoms in water molecules. Evaluating the magnitude of the gravitational radiation possible in that case and taking 1 g of hydrogen (i.e., 9 gs of water), we arrive at a mean quadratic velocity of hydrogen atoms at 0 °C of 1,840 meters per second, a moment of force

$$l = mr^2 = 1\text{g} \cdot 10^{-8} \cdot {}^2\text{cm}^2$$
$$= 10^{-16} \text{ g} \cdot \text{cm}^2$$

and a circular frequency
$$\bar{\omega} = 2\pi f = 2\pi \frac{1840 \cdot 10^2 \text{ cm/sec}}{2\pi 1 \cdot 0 \cdot 10^{-8} \text{ cm}}$$
$$= 1 \cdot 8 \cdot 10^{13} \text{ Hz}$$

The power output of the gravitational waves is calculated by the formula given in Braginskij's article[22]

$$P = l^2 \cdot \bar{\omega}^2 1 \cdot 73 \cdot 10^{-66} \text{ W}$$
$$= 10^{-16} \text{ g} \cdot \text{cm}^2 1 \cdot 8 \cdot 10^{13} \text{ Hz}$$
$$\cdot 1 \cdot 73 \cdot 10^{-66} \text{ W} \approx 10^{-18} \text{ W}$$

We use the same author's calculation[22] in evaluating the minimum level of a receivable signal:

$$P_{min} = \frac{2kT \cdot t^2}{\tau(n-1)}$$

where: $k =$ Boltzmann's constant;
$T =$ absolute temperature;
$n =$ number of measurements;
$t =$ coefficient equal to 2;
$\tau =$ signal accumulation time.

In actual conditions $P_{min} = 10^{-28} \text{ } W$, but a more sober evaluation would be $P_{min} = 10^{-23} \text{ } W$, which corresponds to an accumulation time of 2 hr and is considerably less than the power of the calculated gravitational wave (10^{-18} W).

rotating particles. This radiation has been examined, for example, by quantum theory methods in respect to the approach of a weak gravitational field in the case of the gravitational radiation in a synchrotron of a particle moving along a circle.[24] The most interesting thing for us in this research is the author's conclusion that the major part of the radiation is concentrated in a small angular region near the particle's plane of rotation and can, therefore, be directed.

After the Variable, Then the Constant Field

The process by which a constant biogravitational field is formed can be hypothesized in a similar way using traditional notions. Considering that, during the change in conformation of the protein molecules from a state of random aggregation to an ordered crystalline state, not only does a phased oscillation of the atoms occur but the atoms move closer together, it is to be expected that a considerable constant biogravitational field will appear, owing to the great increase in the density, at micro-level, of the biostructures. There are grounds for thinking that, in the human organism, a constant biogravitational field may be established by specialized brain structures when they are strongly excited (epiphysis, hypophysis). The feasibility of such an occurrence can be seen from the following calculation. We know that the force of the gravitational interaction of two masses is inversely proportional to the square of the distance between them: $F = k\, m_1 \cdot m_2 / r^2$. As regards the interaction of parts of a cell structure which are brought closer to each other (atoms in a water or protein molecule), the gravitational forces in this case increase considerably. It is also possible that when changes in conformation occur in a cell, there may be a temporary, local accumulation of elementary particles and the cumulative effects in the crystallized structures manifest themselves in the form of a constant biogravitational field. It is possible that a similar situation may arise at micro-level when the brain structures receive a specific stimulus during psychotronic phenomena.

Nevertheless, as has already been said above, the process by which a biogravitational field is formed may be completely different from the one arrived at by the calculations of classical physics. The two approaches should nevertheless not be seen as conflicting. We may, for example, mention yet another physical approach to the phenomenon of the constant biogravitational field. One researcher has described the theoretical calculations of the force acting on a prestressed body in a curved space.[25] These calculations were made on the basis of assumptions which are very important for us—that the diameter of the body being studied is small and the velocities at which it moves are low. The calculations lead the author to the conclusion that in the case of a stressed or "self-deformed" body, Newtonian mechanics and the general theory of relativity admit of the existence of gravitational fields and their detection.

In another article which describes the unusual surface tension of microstructures in biological systems,[26] the author shows, on the basis of thermodynamic calculations, that biocrystals are metastable equilibrium systems with a negative surface tension at the biocrystal's interface with its environment. Unique conditions obtain in the case of the polypeptide molecules contained in biocrystals: on the one hand, the macromolecule chain becomes an ordered structure and acquires elements of symmetry (corresponding to the lattice of a polypeptide crystal), but the flexible lateral substituents have the properties of molecules in liquid and the increased entropy of molecules in solution. This shows the complex nature of the physics of the state and thermodynamic properties of biocrystals, the molecules of which form part of a crystal lattice and at the same time possess the properties of molecules in solution. Thus, in biological systems, a change in the symmetry groups and a distortion of the geometry of space at molecular level are possible and, consequently, the formation of a gravitational field, with all its attendant consequences, is also possible. In this way, theoretical calculations support our hypothesis that a biogravitational field may result from changes in the conformation of protein molecules subjected to compression, tension and deformation.

Biogravitation and Contemporary Science

The difficulties of studying biogravitation are, at the moment, that its manifestations are visible but that there are no reliable physical instruments to measure it and new principles are required in order to build them. The efforts of physicists in psychotronics should be directed towards the development of just such an instrument. This is an extremely complex process since biogravitation has properties which are contradictory and mutually exclusive, e.g., close- and long-range action, and attraction and repulsion. It is nevertheless necessary to develop an instrument for measuring this form of energy, which has still not been studied in a way conforming with modern scientific practice. There are grounds for thinking that an instrument of this kind could be developed on the basis of piezocrystal sensors.[6]

Whatever the mechanism by which a biogravitational field is produced, it is a reality, and the forces it brings into play lend themselves to strict evaluation and calculation; but the further investigation of this problem requires, as usual, public interest and financial support for research.

We thus hope that in the near future, the idea of the biogravitational field as an inherent property of living systems will come to be universally acknowledged, which will lead to a reappraisal of basic tenets in various fields of science. One way to contribute to this process would be to set up (a) scientifically controlled experiments in which the "effector" (someone with extraordinary abilities similar to those of Kulagina, Ermolaev, Geller, Swann, or Pavlita who can cause any psychotronic effects) will bend the trajectory of a beam, reduce or increase the weight of an object, produce the Mössbauer effect; and (b) experiments to investigate biogravitation at cellular and subcellular level.

Let us now consider briefly the scientific implications of our hypothesis concerning biogravitation.

In psychotronics, the scientific discipline immediately concerned, a feasible explanation is provided for many phenomena known in this field, from telekinesis to clairvoyance, since all these phenomena are connected with man's ability to create his own gravitational field with all the unusual properties thereof, e.g. the distortion of space, the possibility for other dimensions to assume spatial characteristics, and the like. Although this sounds fantastic to most people, it is not very difficult for specialists in psi phenomena to provide examples in support of this view. The recognition of biogravitation frees psychotronics from many unnecessary and unscientific accretions and from mysticism and makes it a genuine scientific discipline, a science of the future. All the phenomena of this field of knowledge which hitherto seemed extraordinary and supernatural will be seen by researchers as actual manifestations of a new and previously unknown property of living systems and of man as the summit of creation.

Is It Fair to Say "Para"?

Incidentally, I think it incorrect to employ such terms as "paraphysics," "parapsychology," "parascience" (para = near, beside). These terms came into use when the real significance of psychotronics and its place in modern science were not known, and were indicative of its limitations at that time and of the difference between it and genuinely scientific disciplines like physics, psychology and other branches of knowledge. Then, it seemed to stand outside scientific knowledge, but the position has changed considerably over the last fifty years and now leading scientists throughout the world have, as a result of the enormous quantity of documentary evidence which has accumulated, recognized psychotronics as a completely new sphere of human knowledge, a science concerning a unified physical field which embraces all previously known fields and forms of energy. Psychotronics reflects in microcosm the major problems of physics and biology, the two fundamental sciences which study the world and shape our conception of it. Psychotronics is opening up new paths for modern science and pointing to new directions for the development of world science as a whole. The evolution of psychotronics will have a decisive influence on the emergence of new philosophical concepts and ideas about unity in nature, the difference between living and nonliving matter, the specific nature of thought and consciousness, and many other important epistemological problems. In this connection, we may welcome the desire shown by leading contemporary physicists to give attention to the development of instruments for painstaking research in this new field of knowledge.[27]

In biology, the discovery of this property of living systems will further our understanding of the universal relation and interaction between terrestrial and extraterrestrial living organisms. The influence of cosmic factors (planets and stars) on living beings will be clarified, since the possibility of gravitational forces altering the parameters of the space-time continuum of genetically important molecules (distortion of their micro-space) and influencing the readout of this information in ontogenesis and phylogenesis, will have to be taken into account.

Going further, biogravitation will facilitate the explanation of such complex phenomena as the various radiations from cells and from the complete organism, heat exchange, muscle contraction, enzyme catalysis, and, in particular, the formation of the enzyme substrate complex. With the assistance of the theory of biogravitation, it will be possible in biophysics to find a practically useful explanation for the mechanism of muscular contraction and the transformation of the energy of adenosine triphosphate (ATP) into mechanical work in this process. The movement of thick and thin protofibrillae and the characteristic displacement of the transverse connections between them occur as a result of biogravitational forces brought about by changes in the conformation of protein molecules. New insights into the mechanism of the permeability of biological membranes, the transmission of nerve impulses and the formation of biopotentials will be possible.

In psychology, new light will be thrown on one of nature's greatest secrets, the workings of the brain. A better understanding of mental processes, the brain's integrating activity, the coding of information and particular states of consciousness can be achieved only with the aid of the biogravitational hypothesis. More detailed information about this can be found in the writings of the well-known Soviet psychologist, V. Pushkin, who is working on contemporary psychological problems using the biogravitational hypothesis.[28, 29]

In medicine, psychotronic treatment has shown itself to possess exceptional power and possibilities, first because several very serious ailments like psoriasis, paralysis, endoarteritis and cataracts lend themselves to treatment through the influence of a biogravitational field and, second, because recovery is exceptionally quick. The biogravitational theory opens up new prospects for the understanding of psychotronic treatment and its practical application, driving out the mystical and superstitious conceptions which have hitherto prevented these methods of treatment from being accepted by the medical profession. Nevertheless, the new type of biological field and its action on living organisms requires careful all-round study.

The Infinity of Knowledge

It is a fundamental tenet of our biogravitational hypothesis that, for the first time, it is becoming possible in physics to observe and study a completely new phenomenon, that of relativistic effects at the level of small masses. At the same time, the study of phenomena whose existence in the universe was previously only a matter of conjecture, such as antigravity, antimatter, and the annihilation of particles, is becoming a real possibility. The living cell functioning on the basis of a biogravitational mechanism surpasses anything that astrophysicists have imagined existing in the distant galaxies of the universe. Kahuda's hypothesis and demonstrations of "mental time"[30] are clear evidence in support of our claims.

Fully conscious as I am of the possibilities of the biogravitation hypothesis, I should nevertheless like to end by quoting the words of the great French physicist Louis de Broglie: "Does not such a growth in our knowledge, occurring at everincreasing speed, lead us to presume that we shall soon have discovered all the secrets of the physical world? It would be a great mistake to think so, since every advance in our knowledge creates more problems than it solves."[31] These words fully apply to the hypothesis of biogravitation. The world is infinite and knowledge about it is limitless. . . .

REFERENCES

1. K. Trincher, "Die Informationenergetische Analyse der Konformationarbeit des Haemoglobinmoleküls," *First International Conference on Chemical Thermodynamics*, Baden bei Wien 5, 193 (1973).

2. C. Kervran, *Transmutations à Faible Énergie* (*naturelles et biologiques*) (Paris: Librairie Maloine, 1972).

3. R. McConnell, *ESP Curriculum Guide* (New York: Simon & Schuster, 1971).

4. E. Naumov and L. Vilenskaja, *Bibliographies on parapsychology* (*psychoenergetics*) *and related subjects* (Springfield, Va.: Department of Commerce, 1972). (JPRS 55557.)

5. D. Ellis, "The chemistry of Psi," *Parapsychol. Rev.* 6, 5 (1975).

6. A. Dubrov, *Biogravitacija* [biogravitation]. *Proceedings of the First International Conference on Research into the Problems of Psychotronics* (Prague, 1973), p. 45.

7. K. Stanjukovic, *Gravitacionnoe pole i elementarnye casticy* [the gravitational field and elementary particles] (Moscow: Nauka, 1965).

8. . . . edited by K. Stanjukovic and G. Sokolik. *Problemy teorii gravitacii i elementarnyh castic* [problems of the theory of gravitation and elementary particles], Nos. 1–5 (Moscow: Atomizdat, 1966).

9. L. Vasiliev, *Eksperimental'nye issledovanija myslennogo vnusenija* (Leningrad: 1962). *Experiments in Distant Influence*, translated by Anita Gregory (New York: E. P. Dutton, 1976).

10. D. Dean, "Pletismograph recording of ESP responses," *Intern. J. Neuropsych.* 2, 5 (1966).

11. J. Pratt and H. Keil, "First-hand observations of Nina Kulagina suggestive of PK upon static objects," *J. Amer. Soc. Psych. Res.* 67, 4, 381 (1973).

12. H. Forwald, *Mind, matter, and gravitation*, 1969 (Parapsychological monograph, No. 11).

13. A. Bajer and J. Mole-Bajer, *Spindle Dynamics and*

Chromosome Movements (New York: Academic Press, 1972).

14. A. Gruzdev, "Kriticeskoe rassmotrenie nekotoryh gipotez o mehanizme anafaznogo dvizenija hromosom [A critical examination of some hypotheses concerning the mechanism of the anaphase movement of chromosomes]," *Citologija* **14**, 2, 141 (1972).

15. D. Mezia, *Mitoz i Fiziologija Kletecnogo Delenija* [Mitosis and the physiology of cell division]. (Moscow: IL, 1963).

16. A. Gurvic, *Problema Mitogeneticeskogo Izlucenija kak Aspekt Molekuljarnoj Biologii* [The problem of mitogenetic radiation as an aspect of molecular biology] (Leningrad: Medicina, 1968).

17. B. Tarusov et al., *Sverhslaboe Svecenie Biologiceskih Sistem* [The super-weak luminescence of biological systems] (Moscow, Izd. MGU, 1967).

18. A. Mosolov and V. Kamenskaja, "Vibracionnye processy v kletke v period delenija [Vibration processes in the cell during division]," *Radioelektronika, Fiz. Matematika v Biologii i Medicine* [Radioelectronics, physics and mathematics in biology and medicine]," *Novosibirsk,* 166 (1971).

19. U. Kopvillem and V. Nagibarov, "Generacija gravitacionnogo luca v nepreryvnom rezime [The generation of a gravitational ray in a continuous regime]," *Zh. Teor. Eksp. Fiz.* **52**, 1, 201 (1969).

20. H. Seki et al., "Evaluation of the directivity of gravitational wave radiation," *J. Appl. Phys.* **44**, 5, 2401 (1973).

21. A. Pullman and B. Pullman, "Quantum biochemistry. The structure of proteins (and their constituents) and the problem of semiconductivity in biopolymers," *Compreh. Biochem.* **22**, 35 (1967).

22. V. Braginskij et al., "O vozmoznosti postanovki laboratornyh opytov po izmereniju skorosti rasprostranenija gravitacionnogo vzaimodejstvija [On the possibility of staging laboratory experiments to measure the speed of dissemination of gravitational interaction]," *Zh. Teor. Eksp. Fiz.* **38**, 3 (1960).

23. K. Trincher and A. Dudoladov, "Spin-lattice interaction

of water and protein membranes in cell metabolism,"
J. Theoret. Biol. **34**, 557 (1972).

24. V. Khalilov et al., "Gravitational radiation of relativistic
particle moving along a circle," *Phys. Lett. A.* **44**, 3, 217
(1973).

25. E. Pechlaner, "The force on a prestressed body in a
curved space," *J. Phys. Math. Nucl. Gen.* **6**, 5, 264
(1973).

26. O. Poltorak, "Otricatel'noe poverhnostnoe natjazenie kak
faktor stabilizacii biologiceskih struktur [Negative surface tension as a factor in the stabilization of biological
structures]." *Zur. fiziceskoj himii* **36**, 12, 2777 (1962).

27. J. Jungerman, "A nuclear physicist looks at psychotronics." *1 kon. o vyzkumu psychotroniky* (Prague, 1973),
Vol. 1, p. 17.

28. V. Puskin, *Autogravitacija* [Autogravitation]. *Socialistice-
skaja industrija* (Moscow, 9 September, 1973).

29. V. Puskin, "Psihologija i obscaja teorija otnositel'nosti
[Psychology and the general theory of relativity]," *Idei
Tocnyh Nauk* **3** (1974).

30. F. Kahuda, "Metoda mereni mentálni zralosti cloveka [A
new method of measuring mental age]," in *Sbornik
vedeckych praci ústavu sociálniho vyzkumu máldeze a
vychovneho poradenstvi* (Prague: University of Korlova,
1972).

31. L. De Broglie, *Sur les sentiers de la science* (Paris: Albin
Michel, 1960), p. 181.

22.

Hidden Variables: Where Physics and the Paranormal Meet

E. H. WALKER AND NICK HERBERT

The greatest need in the field of paraphysics is for a theory that will (1) aid in designing and interpeting experiments, (2) integrate different experimental results, and (3) more important, be powerful enough to suggest novel experiments leading to currently unexpected phenomena. One of us (E. H. Walker) has advanced a theory of consciousness* that has achieved agreement with certain experimental data, and that has aspects suggestive of the most striking properties of psi phenomena. This article will summarize that theory (called the hidden variable theory of consciousness), outline its connections with the foundations of quantum mechanics, and show how this leads naturally to a mechanism for certain types of psi phenomena. The theory will be applied to the Forwald cube-displacement data to calculate the quantitative relationships observed in this classic psychokinesis experiment.

Our view is that psi phenomena are some sort of extension of the conscious state. In other words, psi is connected with sentient beings, and any theory of exceptional operations of consciousness must be firmly grounded upon a good model of *ordinary* consciousness. Since psi is so tightly linked to our own consciousness, the significance of a successful understanding of psi phenomena should not be underestimated. Achieving this understanding will affect the substance of

"Hidden Variables: Where Physics and the Paranormal Meet" by E. H. Walker and Nick Herbert is an original article written especially for this volume and is printed by permission of the authors.
* See Dr. Walker's publications listed at the end of this article. *Editors.*

human existence as much as Newton did in laying the foundation of the physical sciences.

The various sciences have a central conception which is their guide toward greater understanding of ultimate reality. In mathematics, it is consistency. In physics, it is completeness. All things that have a real existence must ultimately become part of a unified formulation, with nothing that does not reflect reality.

The significance of paraphysics is clear. Paraphysical phenomena go counter to our physical concepts. Since these phenomena are associated with sentient beings, we are confronted not only with the most fundamental aspects of physics but also the relation of psychic processes to the most complex of physical systems, the human brain. We are confronted with deep problems that span physics, psychology, physiology, philosophy and parapsychology.

Quantum Mechanics and Hidden Variables

In the usual commonsense view of reality, we think of the world as being made up of rigid bodies having an independent existence in complicated interaction with one another. This is the viewpoint of classical physics—the so-called billiard-ball model of the physical world.

Quantum mechanics makes three fundamental changes in this picture:

(1) It points out that the only time a particle is actually manifest is when it is interacting. You cannot really say anything about it between interactions. This distinction seems at first merely philosophical but, as we shall see, becomes important when trying to visualize quantum processes.

(2) There is no such thing as a "smooth" interaction. All interactions take place in abrupt jumps—the famous "quanta"—which are scaled by Planck's universal constant h. If energies, masses and velocities are large compared to h, these jumps will hardly be noticed and interactions will appear quite "smooth." For automobiles and basketballs, the quanta are inconsequential; for atoms, they are all that there is.

(3) These quanta appear in an unpredictable way (the Heisenberg uncertainty principle), seemingly at random. Yet when occurring in large enough quantity, they can be described by statistical methods (the "state vector") which correctly describes the average behavior of a large collection of quanta.

From the behavior of the state vector, we can map out the average behavior of the particle's interactions. But if we try to work back from this map to try and deduce what an individual particle must have done to help produce such a map, we find that it must have been able to do things that no "particle," in the usual sense, should be able to do (such as go through two doors at the same time).

This paradox makes statement (1) above more than a philosophical nicety. Since we cannot actually verify that particles exist, as such, between interactions, and since, if we assume that they really do exist between interactions, we run into odd paradoxes—i.e., we can't fit them in a commonsense way into the statistical map—we are better off (as pragmatic physicists) declining to speak about what goes on (whether particle, wave or something else altogether) between events. Instead we should just be content to develop (in a necessarily statistical manner) the mathematics that describe the behavior of aggregates of events. Physicist Werner Heisenberg summarized this odd situation succinctly: "Atoms are not *things*."

In recent years, a theorem due to physicist J. S. Bell, based on an experiment suggested by Einstein in 1935 (the Einstein–Rosen–Podolsky experiment), has shown that if the results of this experiment are correctly described by conventional quantum mechanics, any subquantal structure—i.e., any more fundamental description of matter that would account for the strange behavior of atoms and nuclear particles, and explain the individual events—must be "nonlocal." In this case, nonlocal means that two events, though happening at distant points in space, must be instantly connected at the moment of their occurrence. Though they are quite separate spatially, they must be considered in some sense to be a *single* event.

To a physicist, accustomed to dealing with information

traveling only at finite velocities and the absolute nonsimul-
taneity of spatially separated events, "nonlocal" hidden variables sound like nonsense. This is one of the reasons that little
effort has been spent on the development of a subquantal mechanics. To a parapsychologist, however, such nonlocal
events sound remarkably like the operation of Jung's concept
of synchronicity, and he wonders how he can bring these
events into his system of thought. Telepathy, clairvoyance, ac-
tion-at-a-distance, even precognition, seem technically possible if nonlocal hidden variables in some sense can call the
tune.

It is an attractive feature of the hidden variable theory of
consciousness that Bell's theorem not only allows but *demands* that the hidden variables which would constitute any
postulated subquantal reality be nonlocal in character, and
hence suitable as a medium for otherwise baffling paraphysical phenomena.

The hidden variable theory of consciousness asserts: (i)
There is a subquantal level beneath the observational/
theoretical structure of ordinary quantum mechanics; (ii)
events occurring on this subquantal level are the elements of
sentient being. This being the case, we find that our consciousness controls physical events through the laws of quantum
mechanics. Furthermore, we find the laws of quantum mechanics possess precisely those qualities required for
us to understand the most striking properties of paraphysical
phenomena.

The speculative existence of a subquantal level and the
constraints on such an underground level (Bell's theorem)
are part of conventional quantum mechanics. Most physicists
believe that Bell's theorem forces such subquantal hidden variables to have such bizarre properties that such a level does
not in fact exist. Nonetheless there is a minority of physicists
who are trying to construct a theory of quantum mechanics
based on the subquantal level.

The novel content of the hidden variable theory of consciousness is not the assertion of the real existence of a hidden subquantal level, but the assertion that this level is the
locus of all subjective experience. In addition, this theory is
not merely limited to the vague identification of awareness

with hidden variables, but is specific and detailed enough that many quantitative predictions can be made even at this early stage.

Except in a few special cases, quantum mechanics does not predict the behavior of individual events. It only describes the average or statistical behavior of similarly prepared experiments. Whether there is an invisible dynamics behind quantum mechanics that controls the occurrence of each singular event is the concern of hidden variable theorists. A successful hidden variable theory would form a conceptual basis for quantum mechanics in somewhat the same way as the kinetic theory (mechanical laws) of molecules undergirds the theory of heat and thermodynamics. At first glance it would appear as though any statistical description could easily be given some kind of hidden variable underpinning, some imaginative hidden machinery to explain in a nice mechanical way how experiments conducted exactly the same way can give differing results. But quantum mechanics is a peculiar statistical theory and has steadfastly resisted such deeper reformulation.

So, though the world, in this view, consists of individual interactions, and only interactions, quantum mechanics is silent about the origin of these singular happenings. Quantum mechanics is only a *statistical* theory of the behavior of large numbers of individual, unpredictable and fundamentally mysterious events. It has not escaped the attention of physicists and philosophers that this puzzling situation at the core of their science might afford an opportunity for introducing "mind" into their physical world, but on the scale of Planck's constant, the brain and even the synapse (gap between nerve endings) have always seemed so "large" that significant interactions would be "smooth" and practically quanta-free.

However, the calculations of the hidden variable theory of consciousness show that a properly detailed treatment of the operation of the synapses of the central nervous system allows fundamental quantal transitions to play a determining role in their operations. Most physicists, considering quantum events to be fundamentally random, would view a quantum-mechanical model of synapses as just one more source of neural noise. According to the currently prevailing viewpoint, quantum events are random and that is that. Einstein was one of the few who attempted to extend physics to include a picture of the origin of the events themselves. Neither he nor his followers have been able to construct a plausible structure out of which the interactions would emerge in other than a "purely random" way.

At present, three alternative positions are possible:

(a) There exists a subquantal level described by presently hidden variables, but it is conceivable that these variables will some day become technically accessible and will give more information about physical processes than is available from conventional quantum theory.

(b) There exists a subquantal level governed by presently hidden variables, but there is no conceivable way that these variables could be the object of a physical measurement.

(c) A subquantal level that cannot in principle be physically observed is a metaphysical extravagance that can play no proper role in physics.

A small minority of physicists (especially David Bohm in England and his collaborators) appear to hold position (a)—that a presently incomplete quantum theory will at some future date be supported by a viable subquantum dynamics. However, most physicists (the establishment view) hold position (c)—that there is no subquantal level and hidden variables do not exist. Contrary to the views of practically all physicists, the hidden variable theory of consciousness [position (b)] asserts that there is a subquantal level whose variables will remain forever hidden to physicists (as physicists, but not as sentient participants).

Consciousness as a Hidden Variable

Let us now turn to a discussion of a problem which seems to be a philosophical one—the question of the nature of consciousness. As mentioned above, the guiding conception in physics is completeness—fundamentality, if you prefer. The question of the nature of consciousness is one omitted from that part of philosophy that became the natural sciences.

Consciousness (self-evidently) does exist but it is not incorporated into the basic structure of the physical equations or any of their elements. Nor is it derivable from them. As its subject matter, physics treats the interactions of elementary bodies as represented in space and time. The concept of the interaction as self-experiencing is not explicitly included in the equations of physics that describe the interaction. To extend the language of physics to include consciousness, two fundamental postulates are introduced:

(1) Consciousness is a nonphysical but real quantity.
(2) Physical reality is connected to consciousness by means of a single physically fundamental quantity.

To say that consciousness is nonphysical is to say that its presence is not measurable using the usual physical measurement techniques. This is another way of saying that it is not already defined as an explicit part of, or construct of, physical interactions. We will see below that this property of unmeasurability parallels the concept of hidden variables in quantum mechanics.

The second postulate is simply the most parsimonious assumption for the connection between the operations of a physical system such as the brain and the ongoing conscious experience of that brain. It is another way of saying that consciousness is a fundamental thing and not a construct.

For reasons that involve a long argument that must ultimately be justified by the fact that it works, this quantity is identified with the "state vector" in quantum mechanics.

Now let us show how consciousness as a real entity can be quantitatively characterized, even though not directly measured. It occurs in association with certain conditions of the brain's functioning. Most significant of these is the sudden onset character of consciousness—that is, normal waking self-awareness. Much as the condensation of water vapor is a process that carries a gas into a liquid when physical conditions are only slightly changed, the conscious state takes place in association with only a slight change in the brain's functioning. The change from vapor to liquid signals an enhanced collective interaction of the water molecules. Similarly, consciousness onset signals a collective interaction of the basic elements in the brain, the synapses. In the condensation analogy, we can, in principle, measure both the microscopic interactions while watching the gas become a liquid. In the brain, we can, in principle, measure the synaptic potentials but the observation of the analogous macroscopic "condensation" is denied us by conventional means. It can nevertheless be experienced through "introspection"—a decidedly nonphysical observational technique.

The firing of synapses has been compared to the switching of logic elements in a computer. The peripheral synapses and neuromuscular junctions are reliable redundant switches, but the central nervous system, unlike the computer, is composed of trillions of jittery, individually unpredictable synapses whose patterns exist primarily on the collective level rather than the individual level. Sir John Eccles has described this labile jungle of neurons as "the sort of machine a ghost might operate." This is where the information processing goes on, and that is what must be brought together in the consciousness. As mentioned above, quantum mechanics was identified as the only candidate that seemed to offer any potential here, the only part of physics in which quantities are introduced that are not already fully delineated.

It was decided by Walker that some quantum-mechanical process must be fundamental to the synaptic switching. Quantum-mechanical electron tunneling was identified as the process. It was also found to provide the mechanism whereby separate synapses could interact: by a process of "hopping conduction" which actually involves fast sequential quantum-mechanical tunneling. Thus at a low synaptic firing rate the synapses fire separately—i.e., in isolation. As the rate is increased, more and more fire simultaneously so that ultimately this hopping conduction leads to a collective physical behavior (and an associated nonphysical experience). Properly described, this collective state involves a single ongoing quantum-mechanical interaction which is described by a state vector Ψ. The consciousness is identified as interacting with the physical world through this state vector and further as serving as the hidden variables that determine the development of that state vector as time passes.

The most striking result to come from this model is a prediction of the average neural firing rate necessary to sustain consciousness in animals. In order to avoid unconsciousness (sleep, coma, syncope) the average total cortical neuron firing rate ν must be greater than a certain threshold which depends on the total number of cortical neurons N and the synaptic delay time T in the following simple manner:

$$\nu > \frac{N^{2/3}}{T} \quad \text{for consciousness to be possible} \qquad (1)$$

This relationship has been roughly verified by measurements of sleep thresholds in cats and humans.

Forwald's Psychokinesis Experiment

Beginning in 1949 and continuing for a period of twenty years, Haakon Forwald, a retired electrical engineer and inventor, performed a remarkable series of experiments to measure the mind's ability to influence the spatial pattern of falling cubes. Small cubes of various materials were mechanically dropped down onto a long inclined gangway and allowed to come to rest. A mental effort was made to "will" the cubes to move to one side or the other of the gangway's centerline. Measurements of cube positions when compared with the recorded pattern of "willing" seemed to show that the operator could indeed influence the sidewards motion of the cubes and that the effective strength of this influence depended in a systematic way on the construction and material of the cubes (see Forwald reference suggested below). Let us look at the data and see how it fits into the hidden variable theory of consciousness.

Quantum Mechanical Calculation of the Placement Effect

In the hidden variable theory of psi phenomena, conscious beings are able to manipulate elementary quantum events to bring about a strongly desired consequence. This approach may work to influence radioactive decay events as in the work of Helmut Schmidt since these events are wholly quantum events, but how can it hope to describe the manipulation of large objects such as metal and wooden cubes?

The scale of quantum events is determined by Planck's constant h. For a cube moving about on a plane, the average angular deflection due to one quantum of action has been calculated by Walker. The calculated quanta of angular deflection turns out to be only 10^{-17} degrees, one part in a hundred million billion. This quantity is an estimate of the maximum scope of the mind's action on the initial position of the rolling cube. For orientation, 10^{-17} degrees is approximately the angle that a *herpes simplex* virus on the surface of the Moon would subtend for an observer on Earth. The extent of the mind's action is small, but it is not zero. By controlling that small orientation of the cube now, the exact roll of dice can be determined one second from now.

A rolling cube is an unstable mechanical system in the sense that any initial small difference in orientation between two otherwise identical cubes is likely to be magnified at each bounce. The tiniest singular orientation at the beginning of a roll may be translated into a large cube displacement. Walker has carried out the calculation for this amplification effect and finds that, on the average, this angular deviation is increased fifty percent at each bounce of the cube. That deviation is again increased fifty percent at the next bounce, and so on.

The process of successive compoundings of small increments is a familiar problem in banking, where we must compute compound interest. It is also familiar in population growth studies. These and other such systems are conveniently characterized by their doubling times. This is the time needed to double your money, population, etc., and it depends only on the interest rate K. At a three percent annual interest rate, the doubling time is $N = 24$ years. At a six percent growth rate, the system will double in size in twelve years. At a fifty percent increase at each bounce, doubling time for cube orientation is about 1.7 bounces, which takes about a hundredth of a second. It takes less than a second for a bouncing cube to build this initial mental investment into the control of the cube's position and orientation. Walker has carried out a detailed calculation for Forwald's experimental results and has shown that the theory and experiments are in agreement.

This successful analysis of Forwald's placement data represents the first paraphysical theory that has produced quantitatively verified results. If these results can be extended and confirmed by better experiments (now in progress) designed with the help of the theory itself, we can look forward to an explosive development of paraphysics. It would not be too much to say that just as Bohr's model of the hydrogen atom was a giant catalytic step which hastened the onset of the quantum revolution, so this hidden variable description of Forwald's placement experiment may be regarded as the fulminating event in the development of a new science of sentient life.

SUGGESTED READINGS

F. J. Belinfante, *A Survey of Hidden-Variables Theories* (New York: Pergamon Press, 1973).

H. Forwald, *Mind, Matter and Gravitation* (New York: Parapsychology Foundation, 1969).

E. H. Walker, "The Nature of Consciousness," *Mathematical Biosciences,* **7** (1970);
"Foundations of Paraphysical and Parapsychological Phenomena," to appear in *Parapsychology Rev.;*
"Consciousness in the Quantum Theory of Measurement, Part I." *J. Study Consciousness* **5** (1972);

"Quantum-Mechanical Processes in Synaptic Transmission," to appear in *Int. J. Quantum Chemistry;*
"Consciousness and Quantum Theory," in Edgar D. Mitchell's *Psychic Exploration,* edited by John White (New York: G. P. Putnam, 1974).

23.

The Positive and Negative Space/Time Frames as Conjugate Systems

WILLIAM A. TILLER

In my initial model of substance,[1-4] the universe was projected as a sevenfold-dimensional construct consisting of four nonspace/nontime dimensions, two space/time dimensions, and one transitional dimension. The space/time dimensions interpenetrate each other and are embedded in the collective nonspace/nontime frame with the interfacing occurring via the transitional frame. In the initial description, they were referred to as physical and etheric; now they are referred to as the positive and negative space/time frames. The potentials existing at the nonspace/nontime levels are thought to act as force fields which directly influence event coincidence in space/time. Through human intention changes, the nonspace/nontime potentials are altered which, in turn, alter the imposed boundary conditions on space/time, thus shifting the pattern of wave flow and the details or form of events in space/time; i.e., space/time is clearly a domain of appearance rather than reality.[4] In this model, the nonspace/nontime frame is the "world of reality" and the space/time frame is the "world of appearances." The former is not perceived with our physical senses; the latter is.

At the "world of appearances" level, all we can meaningfully seek to find are consistency relationships that can be thought of as the set of natural laws connecting changing forms. These consistency relationships are not trivial. Our sci-

"The Positive and Negative Space/Time Frames as Conjugate Systems" by William A. Tiller is an unpublished address delivered to the Association for Research and Enlightenment Medical Symposium, January 1975, and is printed by permission of the author.

ence of the last four hundred years has been deeply committed to revealing such relationships and their utilization towards technological development has not only enhanced man's understanding of nature and of himself but has also allowed him to control his environment and nourish his life. Thus far, this science has been largely directed at only one of the two space/time dimensions—that perceived by the physical senses. The other interpenetrating space/time frame is largely unknown to present science.

This article is devoted to a qualitative description of a model for this companion space/time dimension and a description of the property relationships between the two space/time dimensions. The model allows rationalization of a number of psychic phenomena. Some experimental support for the model will be presented. However, the quantitative aspects of the model will be left to a later paper.

Positive Space/Time and Negative Space/Time Characteristics

My major criteria for the conceptualization of negative space/time substance were (1) its construction should be an analogue of physical or positive space/time matter, (2) it should have special symmetry relationships with positive space/time substance, (3) the negative space/time frame should counterbalance the positive space/time frame, and (4) the negative space/time substance should be nonobservable by the physical senses. It was also felt that (5) if the model can fill in some gaps in our present science, then so much the better.

Using these guidelines, we start with (4) and postulate first that the particles at the negative space/time level are superluminal; i.e., they travel faster than the speed of light ($v > c$). It is of interest to note that, in the extreme relativistic limit, quantum mechanics predicts the possibility of a spectrum of negative energy states extending to $-\infty$. Thus, the electromagnetic interaction allows a particle in a positive energy state to make a transition to one of negative energy and to cascade downward to lower and lower negative energy states while radiating unlimited quantities of energy. These states also have negative mass and are *nonobservables*. However, special defects or "holes" in this sea of negative energy states have positive mass and positive momentum and thus are *observables*. These "holes" are called *antiparticles* and the whole spectrum of such defect particles is called *antimatter*, which our science has already observed. In fact, for every particle, we have discovered a corresponding antiparticle.

Let us now go further and postulate that the particles at the negative space/time level are not only superluminal but that they are primarily magnetic in character in contrast to the electrical character of particles at the positive space/time level. Now, we not only satisfy (4), but also (5). Science has searched unceasingly for the *magnetic monopole* because the symmetry of Maxwell's equations demanded that they exist. However, we have searched in almost all conceivable areas at the physical level and have come up empty-handed. This would be understandable if these monopoles existed and were nonobservables at the physical senses level.

This proposal also satisfies (1)–(3) of our list. The magnetic monopole is indeed analogous to the electric monopole and we could expect atoms, molecules and substance to be built up from magnetic charges at the negative space/time level in an analogous fashion to our electrical structures at the positive space/time level. We note a symmetry relationship of a mirror type in that positive mass and energy at the positive space/time level have their negative mass and energy at the negative space/time level. The counterbalance is noted by considering that, by a fluctuation process in the ground of the nonspace/nontime frame, space/time polar substances of electrical ($v < c$) and magnetic ($v > c$) nature are formed whose collective energy is *zero*. Likewise, the collective momentum can be *zero*. In this case, the polar character is thought to relate to a norm level of coherence of the primary wave functions in the particles. The electrical polarity corresponds to a specific high level of coherence and the magnetic polarity corresponds to a specific low level of coherence; i.e., 1 and 0 for the electrical and magnetic monopole, respectively.

Following this tack, a broader range of correlations be-

tween these two classes of substance has been developed and
the main results are presented in Table 1 where χ and χ^* represent positive and negative space/time substance, respectively. The first five items have already been discussed. Number 6 arises from a symmetry relationship. Obviously, if all
parts of the magnetic atom or molecule are travelling faster
than EM light, c, then, as their particles go through different
energy states, a radiation will be emitted which must have a
velocity greater than c; otherwise, there would be no communications between the different parts of the atom or molecule. By symmetry, it is presumed that this magnetoelectric
(ME) light velocity, c^*, will be $\sim 10^{10} c$; i.e., the negative
space/time sensing frame in the human will have a velocity
as far beyond the velocity of electromagnetic (EM) light, c,
as the positive space/time sensing frame is below it, and c^*
will be as far above the negative space/time sensing frame velocity as c is above that of the positive space/time sensing
frame. This leads to c^* being a very large number relative to
c and the factor of 10^{10} is intended to qualitatively express
that aspect.

Both Nos. 7 and 8 in Table 1 are represented in Figure 1
for the energy of a particle as a function of its velocity. Thus,
if we take an electrical particle and increase its velocity, v, its
kinetic energy increases and thus its total energy increases
and, as v approaches the velocity of electromagnetic light, c,
the relativity factor causes the energy to increase sharply towards $+\infty$. When v is within about 0.1 percent of c, it is
thought to be possible for the particle to change its state of
coherence from I to II and become of magnetic character
with a large negative rest mass, so that the electrical particle
tunnels through the light barrier dematerializing in positive
space/time and materializing as a magnetic particle in negative space/time—as viewed by our sensory apparatus. Further
increasing the velocity of the particle increases its kinetic energy and thus its total energy becomes less negative. If we
decrease the velocity of the particle, it retraces the path to
more negative energies until we reach $v \approx 1.001c$, and then
the fluctuation of coherence may occur so that the magnetic
particle dematerializes from the negative space/time frame
and materializes in the positive space/time frame as an elec-

SPACE/TIME SUBSTANCE MANIFESTATIONS

	X	"MIRROR" RELATIONSHIP	X*
1	Electric monopole		Magnetic monopole
2	Forms atoms, molecules, etc.		Forms atoms, molecules, etc.
3	Coherence state I		Coherence state II
4	Positive mass		Negative mass
5	$v < c$		$v > c$
6	Electromagnetic radiation at c		Magnetoelectric radiation at $c^1 >> c\,(\sim 10^{10}\,c)$
7	Positive energy states		Negative energy states
8	E increases as v increases		E increases as v increases
9	Positive time flow		Negative time flow
10	Gravitation		Levitation
11	Frequency ν_x		Frequency $\nu_x^* \sim 10^{10}\,\nu_x$
12	Faraday cage screening		Non screening by Faraday cage
13			Magnetic cage screening
14	I_e generates H		I_M generates E
15	Space I		Space II

TABLE 1

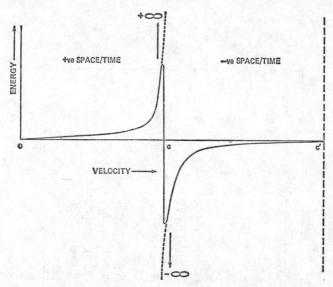

FIGURE 1   *Energy/velocity relationships between particles at the positive space/time and negative space/time levels.*

trical particle of large positive energy. We see here the analogue of black hole and white hole phenomena in conventional cosmology. We see further that *dematerialization* and *materialization* phenomena are accounted for and note that matter does not actually disappear from space but it changes its character to become a nonobservable relative to the physical sensory system and all apparatus based upon that logic. It only *appears* to be dematerialized, the object only *appears* to change its form!

Jumping to No. 11, we recall that the energy of a wave is proportional to its frequency ($E = h\nu$) and that a wave-particle duality exists so that, as the energy of a particle increases, its frequency, ν, increases. Thus, in Figure 1, as we increase v towards c, we are actually increasing the vibrational frequency of the particle up to a critical value ν_c before it dematerializes to become a negative space/time particle. As a magnetic particle, its energy will still be proportional to its frequency ($E = h^*\nu^*$) so that h^* must be a negative constant and, depending upon its magnitude, ν^* must be much much higher than ν_o so that $\nu_o^* - \nu_o$ represents a large jump in frequency; i.e., the negative space/time frame represents a higher-frequency band of substance than our physical substance. In addition, if we compare magnetoelectric light (ME) with electromagnetic light (EM), then, since $c^*/c \sim 10^{10}$, for the same wavelength the ME light has a frequency ten orders of magnitude larger than EM light. This means that the energy content of ME light is vastly larger in magnitude than that of EM light and should provide an abundant future energy source if we can effectively transduce it into positive space/time energies.

Turning to No. 9, the negative time flow relates to what we think of as the normal direction of time flow between cause and effect at the physical level. As an example to illustrate the point, consider Figure 2. Here, we represent an event occur-

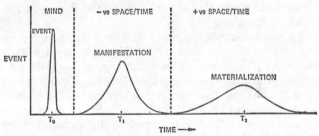

FIGURE 2 *Representation of an event at the cause level (mind level), its manifestation at the negative space/time level $\tau_1 - \tau_0$ later, and its materialization at the positive space/time level $\tau_2 - \tau_1$ later.*

ring at the level of Mind as our origin of time. The wave patterns representative of that event (thought) impinge upon negative space/time and propagate complex waves in this medium at characteristic velocities between c and c^* producing the required wave coincidence at time $\tau_1 - \tau_0$ later. This represents event manifestation at that level and is an effect derived from the initial cause. In addition, waves are propagating directly in positive space/time at much slower characteristic velocities between 0 and c. However, a much speedier and surer path for influencing positive space/time is via the event manifestation in negative space/time. This wave coincidence stimulates wave motion in the medium of positive space/time, which flows at a slower rate but produces an eventual coincidence at a later time τ_2 representing the *event materialization* as perceived by the physical senses.

If we had well-developed sensory apparatus at the negative space/time level, we would have had *precognitive* awareness of the event at a time $\tau_2 - \tau_1$ before its materialization at the positive space/time level. Thus, the event at the negative space/time level would be noted to have occurred before the recognized cause at the positive space/time level and, relative to that identified cause (not the *real cause* which actually occurred at the Mind level), it would *appear* as if time flowed in a negative direction to produce the event at the negative space/time level and in a positive direction to produce the event at the positive space/time level. Then, what we call the future coexists with the present but at a different level of substance in the universe.

Turning to No. 10, because of the mirror relationship existing between the two space/time frames, we must anticipate that every force present at the positive space/time level has a conjugate or counterforce manifesting at the negative space/time level. Thus, the force of gravitation at the physical level is balanced by the force of levitation at the negative space/time level. This will have obvious manifestations for future technology. Although it is not listed in Table 1, another characteristic that will have important implications for technology is that dealing with entropy. We obtain positive increases in entropy in positive space/time as the temperature is raised; however, we have a decrease in entropy in negative space/time as the temperature is raised.

We find that many clairvoyant and telepathic abilities are enhanced when a subject is placed in a Faraday cage which screens out electrostatic and electromagnetic waves in the long-wavelength range (radio waves and longer). This seems to diminish the external noise level and they can "tune in" more completely to the negative space/time sensing system. In support of this, if the subject is then placed in a magnetic screen room, the subject generally loses these abilities. Some few subjects seem to be able to regroup, so to speak, and to tap another sensory network that allows them to perceive beyond this magnetic screen (probably a mental level sensory system or a nonelectromagnetic or nonmagnetoelectric system). This again tends to support the postulate of magnetic substance at the negative space/time level.

From the conventional Maxwell's equations for electromagnetic energy we know that the flow of electric charge, i.e., a current I_e generates a magnetic field H. Likewise, at the negative space/time level, the flow of magnetic charge, i.e., a current I_m generates an electric field E. Thus, at the negative space/time level, a corresponding set of Maxwell's equations exist in terms of magnetic charge and magnetic current and involving the velocity, c^*, of magnetoelectric energy. Combining the EM and ME equations leads to a complete symmetry; however, using only one sensory system, the usual unsymmetrical set of equations is observed. Only when both sensory systems are utilized does the full symmetry appear.

The last item in Table 1 can only be touched upon here as a proper description of Space I; Space II is beyond the scope of this article and must be dealt with more fully in a separate paper. I merely wish to state that, although the positive and negative space/time frames are interpenetrating frames and occupy what is essentially the same space but at quite different frequency levels, the way in which they interact is via a type of spatial mapping transform. The consequences of this relationship is that there *appears* to be two types of spaces wherein the interior domain at the Space I level is interactive with the exterior domain at the Space II level, and vice versa. By connectivity relationships, this means that every point in positive and negative space/time is energy coupled, in agreement with the predictions of quantum mechanics. It is this type of interaction that generates the *"remote* viewing" capability presently being studied by many investigators[5, 6] and is at the core of "nonlocal" forces.[7]

One piece of the overall picture that has been neglected thus far, because it makes it even more complex and difficult to deal with, is the requirement of an introduction of a third type of space/time substance of a non-EM and non-ME character. Its full description is also beyond the scope of this article. The requirement for such a substance arises because it is not possible for substance traveling faster than EM light ($v > c$) to interact *directly* with substance traveling slower than EM light ($v < c$). No resonant vibrational modes are possible for the exchange of energy because there is no overlap of vibrational frequencies. A third substance must be present to serve as a connecting fluid for energy transfer and which does not suffer from the singularity phenomenon occurring at the velocity of EM light. Thus, its basic nature must be very different. In my modeling, this third energy is called "deltron" energy.

There are a few other interesting correspondences between the χ and the χ^* substances. Some of these will be introduced below and others will be presented in a later paper. Let us now turn to a listing of some of the predictions of the model and some tentative experimental support for the model.

Predictions and Support

Thus far an explanation has been given for (a) materialization–dematerialization, (b) precognition, and (c) remote viewing. In addition, it has been suggested that (d) magnetoelectric energy would be a good candidate for telepathic communication, (e) symmetry can be generated in Maxwell's equations, and that (f) item (a) above may relate to black holes and white holes in cosmology.

Some tentative experimental support comes from the following:

(1) For the last two centuries, psychics have talked repeatedly about magnetic forces and magnetic substances as being the cornerstone of ESP phenomena. The enhancement of psychic abilities inside a Faraday cage and their diminution inside a magnetic screen room also lends support to the magnetic monopole postulate. It has been found that dowsers are sensitive to the gradient of a magnetic field for dc or ac fields and to the horizontally polarized magnetic vector of an electromagnetic wave.[8] This sensitivity can be lost when the adrenal glands or the pituitary gland is properly shielded with

a magnetic screening material.[9] We note also the correlation between magnetism and healing. Careful studies of the enzyme trypsin have shown that its activity can be altered by placing solutions of it between the poles of a strong magnetic field or between the palms of a healer.[10] The effect of the healer's hands was comparable to that found with fields in the range of 10^4 gauss. A more recent study[11] showed these two influences to have measurable and comparable effects on both the surface tension of water and upon the enhanced growth rate of plants.[11] A variety of other postulated magnetic effects on living systems have also been reported.[12-15]

(2) In a variety of psychic events, one notes a spatial transposition or mirror image effect. This has been especially apparent in (a) some of the telepathy results of Uri Geller,[16] (b) Soviet experiments,[17] on communication between cells in adjacent hermetically sealed chambers separated by a quartz wall which showed that a pattern of sickness in the cells of the untreated chamber occurred and developed in a mirror reflection relationship of the pattern in the inoculated chamber on the other side of the quartz separator, and (c) some of the Pavlita psychotronic generator experiments which exhibited reversal effects when the generators acted upon the object image as seen reflected in an actual mirror.[18, 19]

(3) If we consider the behavior of magnetoelectric light versus electromagnetic light on passing through lenses, an interesting prediction can be made. Because of the mirror relationship in Table 1, ME light should speed up in passing from air to glass whereas EM light slows down. Thus, the index of refraction, n^*, for ME light should be less than unity in contrast to the case for EM light where the index of refraction, n, is greater than unity. A convex lens causes EM light to converge and should cause ME light to diverge. A concave lens causes EM light to diverge and should cause ME light to converge. This means that, if one takes a simple Galilean telescope, which contains a single concave and a convex lens, and observes an object via EM light, the experimenter will see (i) a magnified image and (ii) an erect image (the eye inverts the actual image). This is our common experience with such viewing. If one next observes, at the same location,

a negative space/time object via ME light, then the result is quite different—one sees (i) a *demagnified* and (ii) an *inverted* image. Such a result is not our common experience! However, some experiments have been carried out by Carlton[20] using young children who can see certain auric manifestations. Independent of the above predictions, he conducted such an experiment and his subjects observed (i) a demagnified image of value M_R, (meaning demagnification ratio) (ii) an inverted image, and (iii) the value of M_R was different for different subjects. The first two observations exactly fit the predictions and the third is expected as well if we make the reasonable postulate that the different subjects have somewhat different spectral sensitivity to different wavelengths of ME light. Since the value of n^* will depend upon the wavelength λ, the effective value of n^* will differ for the different subjects. Thus, the effective focal length, f^*, will also differ for the different subjects and this requires that the demagnification ratio, M_R, differ for the different subjects. These observations are strong support for the present model. Further predictions have been made and experimental studies with these children are under way. Results will be reported in a later paper.

(4) Studies carried out by Cook and the author[21] using a biomechanical transducer appear to indicate the presence of another energy than EM energy functioning in man. Whether it is the ME energy is not yet certain but it appears to have enough characteristics corresponding to ME energy that it will be useful to discuss it in the following section.

Nonlocal Forces Via Magnetic Capacitive Coupling

Let us begin by considering two high-tension lines about two hundred feet in the air and about fifty feet apart. Let us apply a dc electrical voltage across these wires and note what happens as we increase the voltage. Because of the insulation on the wires and the electrical impedance of the air, the system is well behaved until one gets up into the 1,000-kV range. At very high voltages one will begin to note electrical discharges occurring between the lines across the air gap and they become short-circuited. Now, let us do the same experiment with ac voltage at different frequencies. This time, we find that short-circuiting between the lines occurs at lower voltages and that the higher the frequency of the applied voltage, the lower is the voltage at which lateral discharges occur between the lines. The reason for the foregoing behavior is that the air between the wires has an electrical capacitive impedance, Z_e, which varies inversely as the frequency, ν_e ($Z_e = \frac{1}{2}\pi \ \nu_e c_e$, where c_e is the electrical capacitance of the air). Thus, as the frequency, ν_e, is increased, the insulation characteristics of the air decrease and it becomes a reasonably good conductor so that the short-circuiting phenomenon is a very natural process.

Now, let us consider the situation at the negative space/time level with magnetoelectric energy. From what has been said earlier, we are dealing with frequencies $\sim 10^{10}$ higher than EM energies of the same wavelength. Thus, the magnetic capacitive impedance, $Z_m{}^* = \frac{1}{2}\pi \ \nu_m{}^* c_m{}^*$, between objects will be very small and we must anticipate microcurrents of magnetic charge flowing very readily between objects even at small magnetic voltage differences. In fact, unchanging environments should quickly come to magnetostatic equilibrium. Dynamic intrusions into such an environment would give rise to magnetic voltage differentials and magnetic charge redistribution via environmental magnetic current flow. In an ever-changing environment, magnetostatic equilibrium is never reached so that ME fields will be continuously fluctuating and magnetic charge distributions will be continuously changing. Humans, acting in part as generators of such fields at a certain magnitude level, will obviously influence their local charge distribution. Flowing underground streams will also generate such fields and perhaps it is this which activates the dowser's sensitive circuits.

We will extend this line of discussion later, but at this point let us consider some experimental results obtained with the use of a particular biomechanical transducer.[21, 22] In this case, the device is a type of wand held in the hand. It consists of a $\frac{1}{16}$-in.-diam spring steel about 26 in. long with a half-nut epoxied on one end and a $\frac{1}{2}$-in.-diam, 5-in.-long, thick-walled steel or aluminum tube epoxied to the other end. It is the type of device that some dowsers use for indicating the depth of an underground stream, its linear rate of flow, its volume rate of flow, and the direction of water flow. The motion of the wand tip is the output stage of the information conversion properties of the device. The proposed mechanism is that ME or another nonphysical energy stream enters the body as a carrier wave plus information ripplings. Some organs or sensory networks of the body guide this information to that aspect of the brain or mind that registers and interprets the information. To reveal the information at a conscious level, the brain or mind sends the appropriate signal train down to the hand holding the wand, causing it to move in an information coding fashion. Our initial experiments[21] suggested that it is the small muscles of the wrist and hand that generate the specific mode of wand motion. For proper functioning, this muscle movement is to be carried out at an unconscious level with the conscious mind remaining totally neutral.

The general mode of wand tip motion is elliptical with different aspect ratios and with either clockwise or counterclockwise steady rotation or oscillatory rotation. In the extremes, this leads to five distinctive periodic modes of motion —clockwise circular rotation, counterclockwise circular rotation, oscillatory circular rotation, vertical linear oscillation, and horizontal linear oscillation.[21] It has been observed that different chemical substances produce different modes of motion of the wand. Likewise, different regions of the human body yield different modes of wand motion. However, although an individual investigator, who is sufficiently sensitive to obtain wand motion, may observe definite and specific motions of a reproducible nature for a specific set of materials, a different investigator may find some of his wand motions to be different for the same set of materials. From this we conclude that one sensitive human has slightly different internal circuitry or different spectral sensitivity from another so that the wand motions will be different for some materials. Thus, the particular motion is meaningful only when the individual's "code" or sensitivity pattern is known. However, when an experiment is performed and a before-and-after change occurs in the wand motion, then we can say that a definite energy change has occurred, no matter what the specific code of a given investigator.

The foregoing has been largely background to understand what is to follow. However, one further piece of data must be given first. Our early experiments[21] indicated that, for this energy-causing wand motion, three energy circuits exist in the body. For a right-handed energy structure (wand held in right hand), energy enters the body via (a) the sole of the left foot, (b) the left palm, and (c) the left eye, and exits the body via (d) the sole of the right foot, (e) the right palm, and (f) the right eye. Although it can enter via either a, b, or c, and exit via either of d, e, or f, strong circuits seem to be (1) a to d via the legs and pelvic area, (2) b to e via the arms and trunk area, and (3) c to f via the skull and base of brain area. Certain experiments can be performed which temporarily (about four to five minutes) block the energy flow in circuits 1, 2, or 3 (as determined by absence of wand motion at sole of foot, palm, or eye), and other experiments have been performed to reinstate the energy flow. These will be discussed in a later paper. It is relevant here only to realize that this can be used as a technique for investigating energy changes at a subtle level. Now, I will describe a few of these experiments that seem to bear on the proposed model of magnetoelectric energy.

(1) The first of these relate to the healing of oneself or another and involves either the two-handed technique or the one-hand plus wand and discharge jar technique.[21] Suppose we have a lower back stiffness that is troubling us sufficiently that we are contemplating a visit to the chiropractor. By placing our hands on either side of the spine, we cause ME energy to circulate through our arms, the trunk of our body, and the area of the back. The better a conductor of this energy we have become, then the greater will be the ME current flow through this region of the back.

This ME current seems to stimulate the flow of other currents at the physical level so that nourishment goes to that region of the back and the muscles relax. By starting as high up on the back as can be reached, holding for five to ten minutes, etc., on down to the coccyx ("tail bone"), this region of the back relaxes and seems to receive nourishment so that the severity of the problem diminishes and eventually disappears. In my own case, a yearly sequence of visits to the chiropractor of about one to two months' duration was the norm but, having used the above technique every morning for the past three to four years (about five to ten minutes total time), there has been no need to seek outside assistance. In this technique, the hands are placed on the clothes and the energy passes through the clothing. Of course, some people are better conductors than others and will note a greater benefit in a shorter time.

Using the wand and discharge jar technique, one places the left hand (for those whose circuitry is such that the energy enters the left side) on the sore region of the back (on the clothing) and the wand, held in the right hand, is placed close to the discharge jar which contains a combination of oscillating polarity materials.[21] The amplitude of wand motion indicates the severity of the condition and the wand is held there until the amplitude drops to zero. This indicates that the incompatible energy causing the sore back has been temporarily drained from that region and the back generally feels better after one has treated all the affected regions.[21] Once again, the energy travels through clothing and the rate of discharge of the condition depends on how good a conductor one is of this energy. In addition, the rate of discharge is greater if one touches the acupuncture points of the local area, especially those that are sore. In this case, the key point to be made is that energy changes, as detected by changes in wand motion, occur in a systematic way that are not consistent with EM energy and the subject feels physically better after the treatment. Of course, any person can develop himself to do this, both for his own body or another's body.

(2) As an extension of (1), suppose we take an apple that has been sprayed with insecticide. If we check its polarity with the wand, we will find it to be oscillating which means that it is incompatible with and not beneficial for our body.[21] Next, if we hold this apple in our left hand and the wand in our right hand close to the discharge jar, we will observe oscillating motion of the wand tip which, from the experience of (1), we have come to feel denotes a withdrawal of incompatible energies from the apple and passage through our

bodies to finally reside in the discharge jar. This procedure is continued until no further wand motion occurs no matter what portion of the apple is touched. At this stage, if one checks the polarity of the apple, he will find that it has been altered. Now it will exhibit a bipolar character or perhaps even a unipolar character.[21] Here, the important point is that a change in the type of wand motion occurred, which is tentative support for the proposal that there is another level of chemistry or energy than that normally perceived to be operating in materials and that its content and character can be altered by certain specific practices.

(3) Insights relating to nonlocal forces have come from a number of experiments. The first came early in my experience with Wayne Cook, the dowser who introduced me to this work. On many occasions, Wayne would be at one side of the room performing an experiment while I was on the other writing notes, and the particular experiment would knock out one or more of his energy circuits. Often, I would subjectively note a feeling of something having changed in me. Next, Wayne would notice his condition and utilize a technique for correcting it. He would then walk over and check my circuits with the wand and generally find that the same circuits were also knocked out in me. My circuit balance would be restored and we would then proceed with the experiment. We later found that the condition of my circuits had an influence on the detailed results that he would find in an experiment with the wand from across the room.

A more specific experiment occurred when my son Jeff and a friend turned up at the laboratory during one of my days with Wayne. We decided to test the energy linkage idea by sending Jeff and his friend down the hall about fifty feet away. Then we "knocked out" my eye circuit (by my looking at the end of my nose for about twenty seconds) and quickly brought Jeff and his friend back into the room. Checking the eye circuit of the friend showed no change but checking Jeff's eye circuit showed that his was knocked out. Next, while Wayne continued to check Jeff, I followed the technique needed to restore my eye circuit and Jeff's was immediately restored—as was mine. Here, we noted not only a nonlocal force interaction but also that it was sensitized by a family linkage. Our general experience has been that either an emotional or mental linkage between people enhances the nonlocal energy interactiveness of their circuits.

(4) Another stage in the study of nonlocal forces occurred when we noted that (a) looking up at normal fluorescent lights knocked out the eye circuit and (b) holding the palm of the left hand up to these fluorescent lights knocked out the hand circuit. In searching to rectify this serious influence in our research environment, we found that the placement of a specific substance within about eighteen inches of the middle of the light fixture eliminated the effect. This substance was a positive polarity substance consisting of some beneficial herbs and other materials.[21] The important point to note here is that, by merely placing a suitable material in the field environment rather than in the actual electrical circuit, an energy change was noted. After this change, it was subjectively noted that less eye fatigue seemed to occur while working in the treated room.

A similar effect was noted with television sets. When they are off, the screen exhibits a bipolar type of wand response. However, when they are on, the screen exhibits an oscillating polarity which can knock out the eye, hand, or leg circuit if one either looks towards, holds the left palm towards, or holds the sole of the left foot towards the screen. Hanging a package of the neutralizing substance from the back of the TV chassis or just setting it on top of the set alters the screen polarity back to a bipolar character and those circuits are no longer knocked out. Once again, the subjective feeling is a reduction in eyestrain while watching TV with the set in the neutralized condition. Some similar effects have been noted with other electrical equipment in the laboratory but a detailed study has not yet been made.

A few experiments have been run using a Faraday cage and the most pertinent one for us here is the following. With a material just inside the wall of the Faraday cage and the wand holder outside the closed cage, the same type of wand motion was found as when the material was also outside the cage. The reverse experiment of the material being located just outside the wall of the cage and the wand holder inside the closed cage gave identical results. The conclusion drawn from the experiment is that we are not dealing with electromagnetic energies in these wand responses.

(5) *Disclaimer.* The reader should be aware of the fact that the wand holder can influence the type and degree of wand motion with his conscious mind. Thus, if he strongly thinks that a certain result should be obtained, he can unintentionally create that result and delude himself. Whether or not such errors have crept into the experiments reported above is not known. It will take more tests by other investigators before we can be certain of the correctness or flaw in these reported observations. Thus, for the time being, we should accept these conclusions only as tentative albeit interesting, and go on from there. We will continue to be faced with this dilemma so long as humans are part of the measuring circuit.

At this point, I wish to accept a good fraction of the general conclusions that can be drawn from (1) through (4) above and return to our earlier discussion at the beginning of the last section concerning the long-range interaction of ME energy. One main deduction is that we live in a type of *integrated energy circuit* with some very interesting consequences.

The Human Integrated Circuit

In the area of semiconductor technology, a major development of the past decade has been the integrated electrical circuit. This consists of a total electronic system being constructed in and on a silicon wafer smaller than a quarter. This advance has shrunk the size of equipment over the past three decades from several cubic feet to less than the volume of a quarter. This has been achieved by recognizing that the proper spatial distribution and sizes of different types of conductors, having specifically tailored levels of conductivity, yields an electrically interactive kind of device having predictable and reliable properties. Some of these properties relate to frequency-dependent filtering of electrical signals, frequency-dependent amplification of electrical signals, frequency-dependent delay lines for electrical signals, etc. They are devices for transforming the character of electrical information. Significantly, it is found that if the spatial location of these conductive regions is shifted slightly (by as little as 0.001 cm) or their conductivity shifted by only a fraction of two, the properties of the output information from the devices can be grossly altered. This is because the active elements of the circuits are so closely spaced relative to the range of the important electrical forces involved that a slight shift produces a synergistic perturbation of the entire electrical field structure of the device. At that level, everything is electrically interactive with everything else in the circuit. This is why it is called an integrated circuit—only the integral effect is relevant.

Switching now from the EM level of materials to the ME level of materials, we have postulated, and found some support for, the idea of nonlocal forces operating at the ME level. We may thus conclude that, at this level, man lives in an integrated circuit all the time. Via a magnetic capacitive coupling, he is in interactive communication with the walls, the furniture, the books, the other people, etc., of the room he is in. Albeit a subtle force and influenceable by his mind, his energy circuits at the ME level are being supported or perturbed by everything around him—leading to exhilaration, neutrality, or exhaustion as the range of possible effects. Thus, the results of a group meeting in a particular room is to produce an integrated circuit effect at the ME level which, in turn, influences our personal energy structure at the EM level and thus our observable behavior as detected by positive space/time instruments.

We have all noted such a synergistic coupling between a group of actors performing a play and an audience viewing the play. Likewise, we have all heard about the individuals who can perform certain psychic feats in private or in the company of an emotionally supportive group but who, in the presence of an overly critical audience, fall flat on their face. I propose that the ME integrated circuit effect in operation is responsible. The energy structure of one or more severe critics so alters the frequency response of the total local environment that the psychic is no longer in frequency spectrum that allows for a successful performance. Recognizing this integrated circuit effect, investigators who wish to have psychics perform before severe critics should take the precaution of developing a group of energy-supportive people who would be present during such demonstrations. Their presence and spatial distribution would be used to maintain the needed spectral distribution of ME energy in spite of the energy field loading by the severe critics.

Investigators need to be aware of the fact that they are part of the system being studied at the ME level. Thus, their particular temporal properties of emotion, mind, etc., can tune the system under study into a slightly different region of the relevant frequency spectra. This makes it extremely difficult to achieve the kinds of reproducible results that are found in conventional physical science; i.e., the act of performing an experiment sufficiently perturbs the environment that it is almost impossible to return to the initial state for a repeat test. Within this framework we can note the importance of personal attitude on the outcome of a study or event. Positive versus negative attitudes seem to alter our state of ME charge generation which changes the ME field distribution and frequency spectrum of the local environment, thus shifting the domain of possible results.

The foregoing has only scratched the surface of this topic which will be dealt with more fully in later papers. There we will deal with the structural elements of our bodies that are a necessary linkage between the external energy fields of our environment and the internal energy fields of the body. There, we will also deal with the mechanism whereby very subtle and weak units of force can superimpose to give rise to very large magnitude and very long-range spatial and temporal effects.

REFERENCES

1. W. A. Tiller, "Radionics, Radiesthesia and Physics," Academy of Parapsychology and Medicine, The Varieties of Healing Experience Symposium Proceedings, Los Altos, Calif., 1972.
2. W. A. Tiller, "Consciousness, Radiation, and the Devel-

oping Sensory System," Academy of Parapsychology and Medicine, Dimensions of Healing Symposium Proceedings, Los Gatos, Calif., 1973.

3. W. A. Tiller, "Disease as a Biofeedback Device for the Transformation of Man," Proceedings of A.R.E. Medical Symposium, Phoenix, Ariz., 1973.

4. W. A. Tiller, "Three Relationships of Man," Proceedings of A.R.E. Medical Symposium, Phoenix, Ariz., 1975.

5. H. Puthoff and R. Targ, "Psychic Research and Modern Physics," in *Psychic Exploration*, edited by E. D. Mitchell and J. White (New York: Putnam, 1974).

6. R. Targ and H. Puthoff, "Information Transmission under Conditions of Sensory Shielding," *Nature* 252, 602 (1974).

7. D. J. Bohm and B. J. Hiley, "On the Intuitive Understanding of Nonlocality as Implied by Quantum Theory," *Foundations Phys.* 5 No. 1, 93 (1975).

8. Z. V. Harvalik, *The American Dowser* 13, 85 (1973).

9. Z. V. Harvalik, *The American Dowser* 14, 4 (1974).

10. Sister Justa-Smith, "The Influence of Enzyme Growth by the 'Laying-On-of-Hands'," Academy of Parapsychology and Medicine, Dimensions of Healing Symposium Proceedings, Los Altos, Calif., 1972.

11. R. N. Miller, Science of Mind Symposium, Los Angeles, Calif., February 1975.

12. G. W. De la Warr and D. Baker, *Biomagnetism* (Oxford: Delawarr Laboratories, 1967).

13. A. S. Presman, *Electromagnetic Fields and Life* (New York: Plenum Press, 1970).

14. A. R. Davis and W. C. Rawls, Jr., *Magnetism, and Its Effect on the Living System* (Hicksville, N.Y.: Exposition Press, 1974).

15. F. Nixon, *Born To Be Magnetic* (Chemainus, British Columbia: Magnetic Publishers, 1971), Vols. 1 and 2.

16. J. Taylor, *Superminds* (London: Macmillan, 1975).

17. V. Kaznacheyev, S. Schwin, and L. Mikhailova, "Communication Between Cells," *J. Paraphysics* 7, 67 (1973).

18. S. Ostrander and L. Schroeder, *Psychic Discoveries Behind the Iron Curtain* (Englewood Cliffs, N.J.: Prentice-Hall, 1970).

19. W. A. Tiller, personal observation in Prague, June 1973.

20. J. Carlton, "Experimental Techniques in Human Aura Analysis," Proceedings of A.R.E. Medical Symposium, Phoenix, Ariz., 1974.

21. W. A. Tiller and W. Cook, "Psychoenergetic Field Studies Using a Biomechanical Transducer, Part I," Proceedings of A.R.E. Medical Symposium, Phoenix, Ariz., 1974.

22. W. A. Tiller, "Devices for Monitoring Non-Physical Energies," in Edgar D. Mitchell's *Psychic Exploration,* edited by John White (New York: G. P. Putnam, 1974).

24.

Paraphysics:
A New View of Ourselves and the Cosmos

C. MUSÈS

The word paraphysics is recent and some scientists still shun it or act as though it does not exist. Other scientists who are seeking to enlarge the scope of scientific thinking use the term paraphysics to denote the field of phenomena covering interactions of nonphysical things (such as consciousness) with physical bodies and objects. Terms such as psychotronics and parascience have also been suggested. Disregarding terminology for the moment, the question remains: Aside from its inherent excitement, what has paraphysics to offer by way of models and explanations?

Showing, as I did in 1969, and Walker did later,[1] that Heisenberg indeterminacy energy in a biological context is enough to provide free energy usable for paraphysical effects is not enough. We must find and analyze the processes in the principal site of interaction in the body. Clearly, the synapses outside the brain are not that site, for they require the brain as their source region. And the integration of memory does not necessarily mean a field/field interaction, as some have too quickly assumed. Even the field itself is not as fundamental as is often imagined. In fact, a deeper analysis shows that all fields are ultimately generated by singularities such as radio antennas, electrons, protons, and, in the case of gravitational fields, concentrations of mass.

This is a key finding, bearing repetition: *the singularities generate the fields.* Thus, in seeking paraphysical interaction sources, we should go deeper than fields and consider the singularities themselves. What are singularities? In general, they are the sources of waves, characterized by marked individuality. Selves, for example, are singularities generating noetic (consciousness) energy fields. This principle and the essential properties of selves in relation to time will become clearer in what follows.

The Uri Gellers of this century, like the amazing D. D. Homes of the last, have shown that something is indeed there, but their example is not enough. Geller and the "wonder children" in his wake bend and dematerialize metal without touching it. Teleportations have also been reported around Geller. D. D. Home levitated himself and proved repeatedly impervious to fire before reliable witnesses. The prime question for paraphysics in all this, however, remains: How can we understand these things? Thus far it seems to me that, with all due respect to paraphysicists, little more than empty verbiage has by and large been put forth, furnishing no new or workable tools or concepts.

I suggest that the key to unlocking paraphysical mysteries lies in what I have called hypernumbers, the strange arithmetics of consciousness and time that include and lie beyond $\sqrt{-1}$. These powerful operators are a class of numbers beyond ordinary numbers, and refer to nonordinary reality and higher dimensionalities.

Hypernumbers are an entire (but finite) range of new species of number, each with its distinct arithmetic. They are the core of mathematics, and the basis of all advances in algebra, function theory, and higher projective metaspaces in geometry. Their significance for understanding changing states of consciousness and their interaction with bodies and events is profound. They offer the means for developing a genuine science of the interaction between consciousness and matter—or, to express it variously, the paraphysical, psychoenergetic, neotic interactions with matter.

We shall examine hypernumbers later in this chapter. For now, let me simply state that what emerges from this constitutes a new world view in which, as physics Nobelist Eugene Wigner[2] dreamed, advanced psychology and advanced physics become one science, closing the circle of the sciences in a

ring that generates a source and degree of power as yet but
dimly conceived. I term it C-M quantum theory (i.e., Consciousness-Matter).

In a sense, mine is a protobiological view which goes farther by basing randomness on the fact of the exercise of
choice. The uniformity of natural law, in other words, depends ultimately on a uniformity of desire on the part of
primordial living forms in nothing less than a universal sym-
biosis. At the Locarno conference on biosimulation in 1960, I
proposed that protons and electrons were actually primitive
life forms. The data of the intervening years have made that
proposal seem ever more reasonable.

It is now clear from the quantum physical nature of the
fundamental bioenergetic transductions that lie behind brain
function, that the brain is no more a mechanism than quantum physics is mechanistic. Indeed, the very notion of a fundamental determinateness or mechanism in this field is rendered obsolete by the most profound studies of the physical
world that the human mind has made. And we have found
that the physical world leads through the nature of space itself into a realm of nonphysical yet physically effective reality
whose barriers we are just beginning to cross.

On the one hand, the principle of "no absolute life-
lessness" emerges, telling us that no substance, including the
kind we call matter, exists without possessing consciousness
of some kind. This produces protobiology below us in the
evolutionary scale and reveals that protons, electrons, and
other "fundamental particles" of quantum physics are in fact
primitive life forms.[3] And above us, too, life stretches to in-
conceivable ranges of insight and performance. Indeed there
is a hierarchy of life forms extending as far beyond humanity
as below us. There are unimaginable vistas. The interest in this
new evolutionary direction has been irreversibly awakened in
humanity.

To better understand these new vistas, let us begin with the
selves which are singularities generating noetic energy fields.
An essential property of a self is an ever ongoing and
recoverable memory. That in turn requires a retainable reference point of awareness, which at the very least is always
aware of duration. Such cognizance transcends the waking

conscious state and extends through the "unconscious"—a misnomer in that *it* is often conscious of much more than the so-called "waking consciousness."

A salient fact of modern brain research should be stated here: *The brain is not the source of its own primary motivational impulses.*[4] Thus even in the hypothalamus, often thought as a prime "center," what we have is not a source but only a concentrated bundle of fibers. When impulses have been traced further than even concentrated bundles, we end up with specific neurons. But these are specialized amoebas, and by accepted evolution theory, protozoan sensibility cannot be regarded as the executive suite of human intelligence! The neurons are, however, *transducers* which use quantum electromagnetic effects depending ultimately on the polarizing ability of the vacuum. The vacuum itself thus becomes a transducer into physical state-energies for consciousness—energy in nonphysical states. The vacuum is the physically effective yet nonphysical transition state that leads to and from the domains of consciousness which do not act directly on physical entities but which can influence them indirectly by triggering cascade energy effects via the properties of space itself, as this author first pointed out.[5]

These views also imply a survival of individual entities or selves after the dissolution of their temporary carbon-based bodies or vehicles of expression in our space-time of three-plus-one dimensions. The distinction implied by this partitioning is essential, for time is actually a negadimension as we have shown elsewhere, and which Hermann Weyl realized as long ago as the first edition of his *Space, Time, Matter* (*Raum-Zeit-Materie*) in 1918.

What tools are available to us for exploring hyperspace and metadimensions? Hypernumbers provide one of the finest and most sensitive tools. The first such hypernumber (as I termed them in 1966)[6] was based on the square root of minus one and is usually called *i*. Then, in the latter half of the 19th century, the creative mathematician William K. Clifford conceived of a number (let us call it epsilon, ϵ) which is the square root of plus one and yet is not either $+1$ or -1. In mathematical symbols, we can put it like this: $\epsilon^2 = 1$, $\epsilon \neq \pm 1$. Yet neither Clifford nor those after him developed the mathematics of this number to the point of arithmetic usability. That development took until early 1968, when I showed how to calculate any of its roots, its sine or cosine, and its logarithm. In short, it was shown for the first time that this epsilon was a bona fide number and not merely some abstract operator standing simply as a shorthand symbol for a set of arithmetically inexplicable operations.

Moreover, epsilon is the "number of teleportation" in that its powers involve rotation from a two-dimensional (2-D) space, or plane, through a four-dimensional (4-D) space, and back again into the plane. If the rotation is through 180°, then right- and left-hand sides interchange; if through 360°, there is no change. With the hypernumber "epsilon" we thus can begin to see how, without breaking the laws of any more profound logic than that we ordinarily use, an object may teleport from one region of our space to another by traversing a path through a higher space during its temporary disappearance from our world.

The previously mentioned hypernumber i is, I also showed,[7] fundamental in any theory of precognition and of time changes in general that are induced by presently little understood processes of consciousness, such as time changes in trance states.

It is interesting that ever since Werner Heisenberg's matrix approach in 1926, as elaborated by Paul Dirac, modern quantum physics has had to use i hypernumbers explicitly and also ϵ hypernumbers (less awarely, in their matrix form) to represent nature accurately and to explain delicate experimental observations.

One of the most significant and epoch–heralding findings of 20th century physics was that of the discovery in the laboratory, primarily through the so-called anomalous Lamb effect (see any good modern physics text), of the existence of *inherent* energy in the so-called "vacuum" or space void of both matter and radiation. This energy may amount to the equivalent of waves of frequency above 1,000 cycles per second, and this is only a fraction of the tremendous energies involved. In a conversation with quantum physicist David Bohm in December 1975, Professor Bohm cited for me some of his yet unpublished work to the effect that the miniscule volume of space given by a cube which measures only 10^{-33} cm along its edges contains some 10^{140} ergs of energy, about 10^{60} (1 followed by 60 zeros) *times as much as all the matter in the universe.* Remember that 10^{-33} means the tiny fractional number given by 1 over a denominator expressed by a thousand million followed by 24 more zeros!

The astounding fact of the inherent energy of space is of tremendous significance for paraphysics. It means nothing less than this: *physics reaches into the nonphysical, and space itself is endowed with inherent energy that can have physical effects observed by the senses.* Thus the etheric substance so ill advisedly and unwarrantedly dismissed by relativists during the first half of the 20th century is being restored in our remarkable second half of the 20th century through the back door of the "self-energy of the vacuum."

That so-called "empty" space (which is paraphysically quite full!) is the obvious candidate for the prime transducer or mediator between matter and consciousness, was the hypothesis I put forth in the early 1970s and more specifically discussed in an article on consciousness–matter interactions.[8]

There is overwhelming evidence for the existence, beyond the dimensions of known space and time, of another realm having its own special energies and phenomena; it is a domain interacting all the while with the physical world, functioning in even so simple an act as deciding to move a certain finger, and then doing it.

The technicalities are not for discussion here. What is more important is the concept itself, for it is the most likely candidate for pointing out the path of paraphysical research in the future.

Hypernumbers offer an obvious way to mathematicize these otherwise well nigh ineffable notions. We have already discussed the unit of ordinary numbers, 1, and two units of more nonordinary reality, namely i and ϵ. All three have the property that their zero powers are 1 and that some successive product of any of these units by itself is also 1. Thus, $\epsilon \times \epsilon = \epsilon^2 = 1$ and $i \times i \times i \times i = i^4 = 1$.

Now we come to the highest and last of any hypernumber which yields 1 when multiplied by itself a given number of times. Let us designate it by the symbol w. If we ascribe to w

the following properties: $(\pm w)^2 = -1 \pm w$, and $(\pm w)^6 = 1$, it turns out that w is the hypernumber that expresses the interchanges between consciousness and physical energy or the phase alterations and interactions with matter of what might be called pure noetic energy, both conscious and unconscious. We may call it the number of noetic energy. Note that, unlike 1, i, or ϵ, the negative form of w behaves differently from its positive form, and hence the equation $(+x)^2 = (-x)^2$ is no longer true if x is w.

There is much more to be said on the significance of w-algebra to paraphysics. But even when introduced into ordinary quantum physics, w makes a vast difference. In ordinary quantum physics there are quantities inescapably manifesting as unmanageable infinities that have to be exorcized with the unsatisfactory artifice of "renormalization," which amounts to arbitrarily making them finite. But when the hypernumber w is introduced as one of the fundamental coordinates, then no such infinities appear. That is, by admitting into physics the paraphysical reality of the consciousness–matter transducing energy connoted by w, or in other words, by thus introducing a paraphysical coordinate, the previous infinities become finite. So, it was only because a part of reality was being *neglected* that the unmanageable infinities appeared, as a symptom of that neglect—much as symptoms of illness appear when a factor essential to health has been neglected.

A short list of other hypernumbers beyond epsilon is: p, having to do with the focus of attention and its cueing; *omega*, concerned with memory storage and recall processes, including associations; m, concerned with feedback on all levels and also with processes of proliferation (fission) and synthesis (fusion); v, with the relations between consciousness in the body and consciousness independent of the biophysical body; *sigma*, having to do with the differentiations and integrations of situations in and through time; and, finally, C, having to do with hypergravity (maintaining the integrity of our universe) and the transition from our type of universe to another. I am presently preparing more detailed treatment of these hypernumbers.

With hypernumbers and their concomitant higher or metaspaces, a whole new set of tools to implement paraphysics is being forged—tools that will translate previous dreams into future reality: a reality wider and deeper than humanity has ever dreamed before or deemed possible. We stand at the door of nothing less than a new era—drastic in many respects, but inalienably wondrous and exciting.

REFERENCES

1. See my "On the Modification of Random Fluctuations by a Target-Seeking Process Utilising Random Energies," *Intern. J. Bio-Medical Computing* **1**, 1 (January 1970). See also E. H. Walker's more implicit "The Nature of Consciousness," *Mathematical Biosciences*, **7**, 131 (1970); and his "Consciousness in Quantum Theory," *J. Study Consciousness* **5**, 2, 257 (1972–1973), especially the critical remarks on p. 277.

2. See, for example, E. Wigner, in *Consciousness and Reality*, 2nd ed. edited by C. Musès and A. Young (New York: Avon/Discus, 1974), Chapter 9.

3. For further details, see *Progress in Bio-Cybernetics* (II), edited by Norbert Weiner and Joseph Schadé, pp. 252–253; and *J. Study Consciousness* **1**, 2, 77 (1969).

4. One of the finest contemporary brain researchers, Dr. James A. Olds of the California Institute of Technology, holds this absence of motivational impulse sources in the brain as a fundamental fact that we must reckon with. It is extremely significant, and a direct consequence of the deeper fact that the self is not the brain.

5. See K. Demys' discussion of CM (consciousness/matter) interaction in *J. Study Consciousness* **5**, 2, 239 (1972–1973). See also my "Psychotronic Quantum Theory," in the Proceedings of the June 1975 Monte Carlo Conference of the International Association for Psychotronic Research; and in the 1973 IAPR Proceedings of the Prague Conference.

6. In a pioneer study given before the New York Academy of Sciences and published in *Annal. N.Y. Acad. Sci.* **138**, 646 (1967). This material, as in any newly burgeoning and ongoing field, has been continually updated. See

"Hypernumbers and Their Spaces," *J. Study Consciousness* **5**, 2 (1972–1973). See also the chapter by me in the NATO advanced study volume *New Concepts . . . in Parallel Information Processing,* edited by E. Caianiello (Leyden: Noordhoff, 1975), p. 337 ff.

7. "Trance States, Precognition, and the Nature of Time," in *J. Study Consciousness* **5**, 1, 77 (1972).

8. See *J. Study Consciousness* **5**, 2, 239 (1972–1973).

25.

The Convergence of
Physics and Psychology

J. H. M. WHITEMAN

Psychological phenomena are normal, abnormal, or paranormal. Customarily, the normal and abnormal are included in the science of psychology, while the paranormal is "beyond" or "besides." Unfortunately, this way of looking at things suggests that the paranormal has been excluded from scientific psychology because it conflicts with established science. The next step is then to suppose that the paranormal must be reconciled with the "basic limiting principles" of science,[1, 2] above all, with physics, if we are to justify parapsychology's claims to be a true science.

Such a view, though widespread, reveals a lack of comprehension of the state of contemporary physics and its philosophy. Consider, for instance, how one might argue that telepathy conflicts with established scientific principles. The argument might begin with the assertion that thought originates and becomes conscious in a brain. The thought must then take the form of some physical property or "field vector" which can travel through space to the other brain, where it must be converted back again to thought. But, the argument might conclude, no such localized field vector exists, capable of carrying every detail of sensation, feeling, conceptual formation, memory, and will, which is needed to make up the structure of thought.

Arguments of this kind are clearly *metaphysical*. They depend on assumptions that are not, and never could be, experimentally established. The "basic principles" of science

"The Convergence of Physics and Psychology" by J. H. M. Whiteman is an original article written especially for this volume and is printed by permission of the author.

thus prove to be only the "obsolete tenets of an antiquated metaphysical school."[3] For "the development of natural science has gradually discarded every single feature of the original commonsense notion [of mechanistic science]. Nothing whatever remains of it."[4] "The very concept of a material system . . . ceases to be justified."[5]

One can see how crude mechanistic ideas gained their foothold in the 17th century. "Galileo and the physicists 'peeled off'" the sensory properties from material objects, "without caring much what became of them."[6] They also "peeled off" concepts, intuition, imagination, feeling, will, reason, and law, and reduced all science to the manipulation of mathematical measures—a manipulation which presupposes, but sidesteps any accounting for, the very awareness of objectivity, reason, and law which was taken as "peeled off."

Until very recently, therefore, psychology and physics have been split apart, except so far as psychology has adopted techniques of physics for the attaching of measures to overt behavior.

Today it is clear that we must start afresh and aim to build an integral science—psychology and physics together (in complementary aspects)—and not "forget about the tools used for the consideration of one when thinking about the problems of the other."[7] The paranormal need not, then, be in conflict with science. For nature, truly seen as a whole, cannot contradict itself.

Beyond Matter–Mind Dualism

One of the first lessons we have to learn in philosophy is that everything we can know about the external world, as about our internal world, is resolvable into awarenesses which seem to be exclusive to us—as we say, "subjective" or in our own "minds." Whether we see an object, feel it, kick it, or walk around it, what we experience and know consists of our own perceptions and cognitions. Yet the object is similarly experienced and known by other people. How can this be, if all the knowledge is "subjective"?

The answer given by matter–mind dualism is that there is

an *unknowable substratum* in objects. Because this is unknowable, it has not the character of any awareness or possible awareness to any particular person, and so can be common to all. But then the mistake is made of attaching ideas of position and movement and other distinctions of quality to the unknowable objects. Clearly, if nothing whatever is knowable about them, nothing can be said about them, and no science can be built on their existence.

The early scientists, in spite of protests from Leibniz and Berkeley, tried to escape the dilemma by postulating that positions and motion are absolute. That is to say, the apparent variations in appearance to different observers can be related by fairly simple mathematical formulas. Obviously the motion of a man walking in a train does vary according to whether we measure it from the train itself or from a point beside the track. But because a formula covers both cases, it was thought that the condition of the observer could be ignored, and the world could thus be treated as independent of mind. (It was overlooked that the formula is itself a structure of *reason*.)

Hence arose the myth of the *container of space* with dead matter placed in it, and all living awareness merely an effect of dead and unknowable "matter." But perhaps it will be said: "What else can we do? And anyhow the method works!"

The reply to this is, first, that it does *not* work in the theory of relativity and quantum theory, the two corner stones of modern physics; and second, physics itself has forced upon us a new world view, which corresponds in an astonishing way with what famous philosophers and mystics, from direct insight and experience, have been declaring over a period of two thousand years at least (Buddha, the Upanishads, Plato, Plotinus, Leibniz). We have today reached the point where all these currents of research have begun to merge.

Let us consider some of the new "basic principles" which physics has now taught us. First in importance, perhaps, comes the principle that a distinction must be made between *potentiality* and *actualization* or, in psychological language, between the *unconscious* and the *conscious*. Even though another person is not in sight, his existence has to be allowed for. He might shoot at us with a gun; he might come into view five minutes later. But, it could be said, he can see himself and observe his own actions, and if we put together his and our observations we get a single observed world. Against this sort of argument, it must be pointed out that he can see only shifting and partial views of himself according to *his* circumstances at the time (not ours), and that no one can see his motivation when he decides to shoot at us, or the disposition which leads him to do it.

Thus every person, and likewise every object, has "potentialities" to be observed or to act in an infinite variety of ways according to circumstances. And none of these potentialities, in itself, is physically observable.

Have we then an "unknowable substratum" after all? No, because the substratum (or more correctly, superstratum) which we are pointing to here *is* knowable in a certain way; otherwise we could not point to it. It is knowable, either as a *structure of possibilities in reason,* or (in the case of motivation) as a *necessary supplement in reason,* without which our observations do not make sense. And in particular circumstances (discerning our own motivations, for instance) the potentiality *can* be observed by *nonphysical* means.

In the theory of relativity, the potentiality of an object's existence is expressed by means of what are called "transformation group" laws which connect the various possible appearances to people observing it from different positions or while moving in any way with respect to it (the measured shape alters according to the relative velocity of object and observer). In quantum theory the potentiality of a radiation field is expressed by means of a field vector which causally relates a source with the probable rate at which absorptions of quanta of energy would be observed.

This leads to consideration of another "basic principle" of contemporary physics, namely that causation resides, not in causal chains of physically observable objects or materials, but in a three-tiered *hierarchy* of operations concerned with the *whole* circumstances.

To illustrate this in the simplest way, let us suppose that a physicist has set up apparatus to produce a narrow beam of light so excessively weak that it cannot be seen as such. As is known, energy can only be absorbed from radiation in "chunks" called *quanta*. So if the eye (or some more sensitive detecting apparatus) is placed in the way of the beam, it may be that the absorption of a quantum will be detected, like a sudden flash, at some unpredictable time.

Must we then say, with Einstein, that quantum theory supposes a "dice-playing God," to specify arbitrarily when and where the absorption is to occur precisely? On the contrary, if we accept that an actualization or manifestation to the senses occurs by an integration of the *whole* circumstances, it is clear that physics must ignore the subjective and microscopic conditions of any particular occasion and deal with *overall* effects. As in the throw of dice, mathematics can predict the overall probability of a 6 on one out of six trials on the average, but it cannot predict to what particular result the infinite *small-bias* potentialities will lead on any particular occasion.

It follows that causation must be dealt with at three "levels." First, there is the devising of the experimental setup, depending on some purpose previously decided on. Then there is the level on which the physicist proposes an "overall" wave function or field vector but on which he should really include also the subjective potentialities of the experimenters and the objective potentialities of details with which the mathematics cannot deal. Last, there is the level on which all the potentialities are integrated and a particular observation is actualized.[8, 9]

The particular observation is therefore unpredictable in physics because the necessary potentialities have not all been included in the calculations.

As already commented, potentiality is a superstructure rather than a substructure. Causality is wholly in the *universal reason,* from the "top downwards." It proceeds from a universal purposive level; then there is what may be called a "thought image" level where potentialities work out the purposes, partly automatically (by the field equations) and partly subjectively or through small-bias effects; and last there is actualization at the level of observed physical phenomena, resulting from an integration of the whole of the potentialities on that occasion.

Even if we were to stop at this point it is clear that a kind of telepathy, better perhaps called *koinonoia* ("mind sharing"), is implicit in modern physics. For the potentialities of minds, as well as of physical objects, have to be integrated when an observation is made.

Physical Laws and Universal Reason

Along with belief in matter–mind dualism there arose a greatly oversimplified view of scientific method which became dominant in the 19th century and still is dominant today, in spite of cogent objections made by philosophers and scientists of repute.

Put uncompromisingly, it is the doctrine, in Popper's words that "all theories are, and remain, conjectures, as opposed to indubitable knowledge."[10] That is to say, the scientist can propose an hypothesis, make deductions from it, and so build a theory or "conceptual system," finally checking that a large variety of deductions square satisfactorily with observation. But the theory stands only so long as another one does not turn up and fit better.

This view of scientific theories—as never having any element of certainty—is at once seen to be false in the case of Euclidean geometry. This is a conceptual system whose logical coherence has never been doubted. How then did it get into nature? For it is certain that the lengths of the three sides of a right-angle triangle do agree with Pythagoras's theorem, to a degree of accuracy depending on how accurately we have constructed the straight lines and right angle. They cannot do otherwise without offending against logic. Likewise, we may ask, how did the conceptual system of electromagnetic theory, or of elementary particle theory, get into nature?

In the case of geometry it is clear that nature provides the opportunity for us to copy the concepts by a process of successive approximation. The concepts take actual physical form by virtue of additional small-bias potentialities which convert the *a priori* exact into the empirical uncertain. Nevertheless the overall effect is according to reason.

The truth seems to be, therefore, that nature is full of opportunities for the actualization of concepts. In fact, it is hardly too much to say that nature is nothing but concepts ac-

tualized; for without concepts, it would not be intelligible.
Hence it is to be expected that if we can find concepts which
are "primordial" enough, all natural law could be developed
from them by a kind of deduction. And this is what has
proved to be the case in mechanics (classical or relativistic),
and also, as we shall see, even in electromagnetic theory and
elementary particle physics.

As might be expected, however, the buried conceptual possibilities in nature are exceedingly various, abstruse, and
difficult to unearth. Only a few of the simpler instances can
be briefly referred to here, apart from the analyses to be
offered in the next two sections.

One of the simplest instances of the reason inherent in
physics was discovered by the 14th century Paris philosopher,
Buridan, and concerns the fall under gravity of bodies of
different masses. If we take three equal balls falling side by
side in a vacuum, and then repeat the experiment with two of
the balls stuck together with a minute spot of glue, the body
of double mass must clearly keep step, as before, with the
remaining ball. There is therefore a logical compulsion in nature, ensuring that bodies of different masses keep step with
each other when they fall in a force field.

The phenomenon of "equal fall" has been experimentally
verified to an accuracy of one part in a hundred thousand
million. But even if experiment had shown some difference,
we should have been obliged to accept the principle and introduce some interfering cause, such as air resistance, to account
for the departure from what logic requires. For science cannot be built on a contradiction. Here, then, we have one kind
of certainty in science.

Assuming now, what is true, that Euclidean geometry and
special relativity are forced on science in a similar way,[11] let
us consider the classical approximation in which time is taken
as "absolute," and derive Newton's laws of motion for a particle in a force field.

If the motion of the particle is not to be haphazard and nature in consequence mere chaos, there must be some *law of
motion*. But it is clear that in any system of dynamics a particle may be started moving in the field with any speed, and the

motion must *then* be prescribed. I shall call this the "teleological principle."

Let us now consider motion in a straight line and suppose the field given at each point. The law might conceivably connect the force with the velocity of the particle (i.e., rate of change of distance), the acceleration (second-order rate of change of distance), or higher-order rates of change, or any combination of these. But if the velocity were involved explicitly in the law, our arbitrary choice of initial velocity could not be reconciled with the fact that the field is not arbitrary. On the other hand, it is easy to show that if third or higher order rates of change were involved, the motion would not be uniquely determined. Hence the law must relate the force to the acceleration alone, and thus we can take the acceleration as providing our measure for the force per unit mass (this being, as we have just seen, the same for all masses).

As regards reaction, given the qualitative fact that reaction occurs, the quantitative fact follows that it must be "equal and opposite" to action, because no other way of determining the reaction uniquely presents itself.

It is common knowledge that the law of gravitation was logically derived by Einstein from the tensor calculus. This tells us what kinds of law will be logically consistent when various observers with different positions and orientations apply it to their own measures. As it happens, only one tensor is suitable, and this gives the inverse square law as an approximation.

We are not to think that something in nature carries out these complicated reasonings every time some motion has to occur. Rather, the potentialities for motion which are logically inherent in teleological demands and the qualitative possibilities in nature must be thought of as being already present in a timeless way, as the result of Pythagoras's theorem must be timelessly inherent in the group logic of translations and rotations. So, on any occasion, the possibility which alone is permitted by logic comes automatically into actualization.

Categories and Cycles

We come now to a concise examination of the structures of reason which seem to be primordially involved in psychology. The method to be used has been called phenomenological analysis, essential insight, or mystical recollection and disclosure. The broad features of the world view presented may be confirmed in "higher" kinds of separative experience ("out of the body"). More detailed supporting evidence, including that of scientific research in the psychological field, is referred to below and elsewhere.[12, 14] Finally, the deduction of physical theory and exact formulations in correspondence with this psychological analysis provides an indirect but scientifically very compelling kind of confirmation.

We first distinguish three primordial categories of concepts or "ideas," making up the "building bricks of knowledge":

(1) ideas of *purpose,* e.g., love of truth, beauty, possessions, etc., or hate, hope, fear, etc., of these. Such "ideas" are characterized by means of

(2) *relational concepts,* e.g., association, attachment, cause, change, future, and are made finally definite by

(3) ideas of *perception and fulfillment,* e.g., sensations, images, feeling-impressions, pleasure, pain, etc.

All these can be described as *timeless ideas* or units of "essence," and the three categories correspond, respectively, to the good, the true, and the beautiful. But none can be actually known without three *timelike objectivities,* or categories of "existence":

(1) actual impulsion or motivation (not merely the "idea" of it);

(2) actual changes (not merely the "idea" of change) in regard to

(3) actual objects (and not merely the "ideas" of them).

These correspond, respectively, to force, motion, and mass, and may be simply described as *drive, time,* and *objectivity.*

They are as if known from the way ideas "actually behave."

A seventh and in fact primal category is also needed: of consciousness, will, and choice, to direct the others. It must be capable of individualization (as a single "I am") and also of multiplicity. It can know or not know, and understand or not understand, particular ideas, structures of ideas, or existences.

A second stage in analysis reveals that some primordial "organization" must be provided to give meaning to the fitting of means to motives. This will have the consequence that degrees of perfection of fitting, or "harmony," are possible. *Values* thus arise, and the possibility of development of the individual consciousness. Motives and means which conduce to such harmony can be called "good," according to degree.

In mystical teaching, the primordial "organization" is called archetypal or divine human, whose sacrifice and descent into multiplicity and conflict make possible the actualities of creation, in worlds and individual lives.

A further consequence is that there must be a hierarchy of "spheres of consciousness," so that "trial means" and "perfect patterns" may coexist with "normal" consciousness and so give meaning to "wisdom." It then follows that potentialities at one "level" must be connected with those of other levels by *correspondence* and *emergence,* as the expression on the face *corresponds* with and *emerges* from the feeling which it expresses.

Another fundamental mystical teaching is that three *quasi-spatial* concepts, subject to degree, correspond to the three categories of essence, when these characterize an individual state of consciousness in regard to wisdom. In reverse order they are:

(3) height and depth   ("fulfillment")   : z 3
(2) right and left   ("openness to means")   : y 2
(1) before and behind   ("acceptance of purpose") : x 1

The allocation of symbols x,y,z and 1,2,3 will be found convenient for reference in the later analysis, as well as agreeing with accepted terminology in physics.

We can also identify three *quasitemporal causations* as follows:

(3) actualization : τ 4
(2) change and flow : t 5
(1) impulsion : T 0

As we shall see, an emergent *world* is "projected" by the infinite possibilities for the orienting of axes for x,y,z at right angles and for positionings with respect to them, all these being provided by "rotations" of the x,y,z,t and τ axes, two at a time. The corresponding psychological life thus similarly requires combinations of the categories two at a time.

This conclusion can also be drawn more directly from the fact that any one category of ideas or existence—*purpose*, for example—is quite abstract and general unless associated with means, end, impulsion, or some other category.

Since there are six primordial categories to be associated in pairs, there are fifteen resulting psychological "functions," to which one can add the actualization itself as a sixteenth. The sixteen will be found to proceed logically in a cycle of four "quarters" or major directions of creative activity, the first being as follows:

E $\begin{cases} \text{impulsion of purposes} & \text{(enthusiasm)} & : & Tx & 01 \\ \text{flow of purposes} & \text{(inspiration)} & : & tx & 51 \\ \text{actualization of purposes} & \text{(illumination)} & : & \tau x & 41 \\ \text{consideration of adaptive means and fulfillment:} & & & yz & 23 \end{cases}$

In the mystical teachings this "quarter" is likened to the East, where the Sun rises. The second, or *responsive*, quarter, is as follows:

S $\begin{cases} \text{impulsion of means} & \text{(response)} & : & Ty & 02 \\ \text{flow of means} & \text{(working out)} & : & ty & 52 \\ \text{actualization of means} & \text{(judgement, approval)}: & & \tau y & 42 \\ \text{consideration of fulfillment and purpose} & : & & zx & 31 \end{cases}$

The third and fourth quarters, though of extreme importance in self-development, can here only be indicated by the most obvious features: 54, *application*, i.e., movement to actualization, "going out"; and 03, *nonattachment*, i.e., impulsion to (the state of timeless) fulfillment.

Apart from confirmation by mystical teachings which have been widespread from four thousand years ago, there are two versions of the fourfold "creative cycle" which have been described in scientific research.

Henri Poincaré, in his analysis of mathematical invention, names the four chief stages (beginning with the third or "Western" quarter, i.e., the "going out"): preparation, incubation, illumination, precising. The course of artistic creativity in general is obviously the same.

Freud describes the *releasing* form of the cycle, by which one passes from rule by the "pleasure–pain principle" to rule by the "reality principle."[13] The unthinking attachment or fixation to which "application" leads in earlier years, so that frustration often results, gives place to a voluntary checking. In other words, the third quarter or function, which Freud describes simply as "action," is succeeded, not by an immediate and unthinking reaction of pleasure or displeasure, but by "restraint upon action," a "raising of the level of the cathectic [attaching] process," and Denken ("recollection").

The various functions in the cycles under discussion, though sharply distinguished, have a generality which is capable of giving rise to infinities of variant modes and developments. A general purpose (e.g., to satisfy hunger) may be particularized in an infinity of contemplated ways. These may come into focus, shading into one another, occasionally undergoing abrupt changes, and eventually passing into the unconscious. Processes of change and interaction between one mode of the cycle and another thus continue ceaselessly on the background of another mode or state of consciousness more or less stabilized by other means.

These and other considerations point to the "horizontal" composition of fluctuating modes of the cycle, resulting in a *field* of consciousness, and the "vertical" composition of such fields to provide meaning and causation. The individual consciousness, like a searchlight, will keep exploring the whole structure, but remain chiefly focused on one "level" of actualization (e.g., physical awareness, dream, thought images) till a change is more or less abruptly caused.

Actualization for an individual in the physical world has two aspects: (a) the "projecting" of the object into the world, in conformity with physical law and thus also with what other individuals may observe; and (b) the sensory perception as if in the body and occurring through bodily processes in correspondence with psychological ones. The former may be described as the effect of *objective* functions at the physical level, and the latter as the effect of *bodily subjective* ones there.

Similar conclusions follow in regard to phenomena of the "inner worlds" of thought and images, since there also one is aware of (mental) objects which are presented to the (inner) senses, and perceptions occurring still more inwardly, in correspondence with psychological processes.

The fact that the inner observation of thought and images is usually "hazy" and seems as if it occurs in the physical body is easily explained. For the *bodily subjective* functions at that level would have to be themselves of a thought-image character. But obviously few people are ever aware, outside dreams, of a thought-image body from which they see the nonphysical objects. Hence the *physical* body and eyes tend to take its place, and the objects seem to be seen by the physical eyes and "located" accordingly. This is what is called the *mergence* of nonphysical objects in the physical world.

The further conclusion then follows, that if the *bodily-subjective* functions at the "inner" level are sufficiently developed, the thought-image body (or perceiving organism at that level, whatever it may be) will no longer escape observation in its own sphere of life. And when it does come to observation, there will be no compulsion on it to appear as if in the place of the physical body, or even on its copying the physical body (unless the observer has a fixed idea that it must do so).

Thus the possibility of "out of the body" experience presents itself as necessarily involved in our new scientific world view.

Foundations of Physics

Problems concerning the causal origination of physical experience from potentialities in the universal reason are greatly illuminated by the phenomena of collective apparitions.[14] Such an apparition may be seen and even felt by the various percipients, in perspectives, including those presented by a mirror, subject to the same geometrical laws as hold in the physical world. But the phenomena are undoubtedly of a nonphysical nature, and are moreover of a purposive origin, insofar as their appearing is explained by memories, thoughts and intentions and not by the presence of physical objects.

A purposive structure of ideas can thus instantly produce manifestations of an object to different people, simultaneously yet so that the different perspectives are related as the laws of geometry and physics require.

From what has been said concerning the primordial origin of all creative laws, physical observation by different people must come about in essentially the same way, this being the reason why the inner and physical worlds both manifest Euclidean geometry and the laws of geometrical optics. The difference appears to be simply that the physical "level" is the ultimate ground of fulfillment for purposes in every individual mind and at every level of conscious life. Hence the physical potentialities constitute a *universal* ground for all existence. What was at its source a power of reason becomes, in physical actualities, something absolutely final and independent of the will of any individual.

We can also conclude that while *objects* are in all cases instantly actualized from purposes, by elaborate laws of correspondence, their various appearances and positionings are related one with another according to the laws of reason by the field structures of light or other "radiation." Here we have, in simple form, an instance of the distinction between "boundary conditions" (or "bound systems" in quantum theory) and the "free field." The "bound systems" are concentrations of fields. Hence we may confirm our previous conclusion that sixteenfold structures must be causally at the origin of all actualizations at every level, physical or nonphysical.

Without attempting to examine the case where "bound systems" making up solid bodies must themselves be taken as subject to change, we may deduce the general character of the field laws at any level from the possibilities which tensor analysis reveals.

The sixteen (objective) components projected to each point x,y,z,t of the field can be taken as constituting the field itself if they are "functions" of x,y,z,t which vary from point to point and instant to instant. Tensor analysis then shows that a field equation specifying first-order rates of change in the field components can give logically consistent results only if it has the form of the *gradient operator* plus an additional constant, operating on the full sixteen-component "field vector," and with the whole equated to zero: $(\gamma + k) P = 0$.

"Operation" means here a "tensor product," of which three kinds exist. Rather surprisingly, the inclusion of all possible products results in another sixteen-component tensor field. The projected field equation thus requires that the total for each component on the left should be zero, and so we obtain sixteen equations in sixteen components.

If six of the components are put equal to zero, the other ten components are found to satisfy Maxwell's equations for the electromagnetic field in empty space, along with the continuity equation for the electric current density. Moreover, the fact that the variables τ and T are not subject to transformation, i.e., different points of view (see the next section), results in all the components transforming as physical theory requires—as a rank-two tensor with six independent components, two vectors with four components, and two invariants. Hence the ten components of the field in empty space behave in every way exactly as do the electric and magnetic field vectors **E** and **H** and the current density **J**, and so can be identified with them.

According to this derivation, the waves of uniform velocity which are the solution of the field equations are "as if" structures of potentiality, making the only causal connection logically possible in empty space between cycles at the various points.

There is another method of solution of the sixteen field equations, very elaborate and artificial, which does not require putting any of the components equal to zero, and thus which does not imply empty space. We can add the components all together, with directional symbols σ_{81}, σ_{51}, σ_{23}, etc., alongside, substitute "matrices" for these symbols so that the tensor products work out correctly, and then "factorize" the total result. What is obtained then is Dirac's linear wave equation for the fermion field (electrons, positrons, etc.), the field then being represented by only two components making what is called a *spinor*. One can then combine spinors so as to obtain the original components (a generalized "current density," for instance). This method of "primordial" deduction is quite different from the method of trial hypotheses which led to elementary particle theory in its present form.

The Logic of Paranormal Phenomena

If the world view here presented is accepted as basically correct, there is no conceptual difficulty over the occurrence of telepathy and clairvoyance. All potentialities at the thought-image level have to be integrated upon actualization, whether they are of objects or of the observer and whether the "objects" are physical ones (clairvoyance) or thought images (telepathy). The connections which result in one "object" being actualized rather than another (we may call them "resonances") clearly have the character of thought governed by character tendencies and interests, and have nothing directly to do with physical distance, which is not actualized at that level.

Further consideration must be given, however, to (a) the *structure of personality* (this leading to conclusions concerning survival and mediumship), and (b) the manner of securing the *finalization of a plan* according to universal wisdom at the ideal-purposive level, i.e., the setting up or controlling of "boundary conditions," (this covering also effects of PK and the possibility of memory, retrocognition, willed action, and precognition).

We must distinguish between (1) the case where all objects are allowed to continue as part of the field, virtually uninterfered with from the purposive level, e.g., the solar system; and (2) the case where there is interference by which the positions or motions of certain objects are controlled or new "boundary conditions" are set up, e.g., by muscular action in response to desire.

Case (1) is, strictly speaking, unrealistic. There is indeed interference both from outside the solar system and from small-bias causes within, which could result, by chain reactions, in a cosmic disturbance. In either case, therefore, an ideal-purposive level has to be admitted if a hiatus in physical theory is to be removed. And we have to admit also possible "life interference" from the "lower level" of *unconscious motivations* outside the universal plan but controllable by it, or else permitted as part of the plan. For there is no doubt that such motivations do occur; but the plan would be brought to nought, and events left to chance, as it were, if they were not controlled.

Purposive motivation implies *conscious* thinking; for "unconscious thinking" is a self-contradictory expression (the term "unconscious" applied to "motivations" in psychoanalysis means unconscious to the *patient*). Hence to admit purposes and a universal plan worked out by them is to admit a level of individual *intelligences* transcending the physical condition; and to admit unconscious motivations is to admit at least the potentiality for a thinking mind, which is not that of a physically embodied person, to actualize the effect of such motivations in us without our knowledge or control. Freud, indeed, speaks of the Id as being sometimes "malicious."

We thus arrive again, by an analysis of physics, at the *monadic* or *corporate* structure of personality strongly urged by McDougall and Gerald Balfour on the ground of psychological or parapsychological evidence, and explicitly stated by many great mystics, including Gotama Buddha, St. Paul ("you are members one of another"), and Swedenborg, as well as being essential to other systems of teaching such as Hasidism. To reject the teaching under all these circumstances would suggest the psychological "disorganization" into which so many conservative scientists have lapsed when brought up against evidence contrary to the world view subconsciously assumed by them.

It is of considerable interest to check that the mathematical formalism in terms of three spacelike variables and three timelike ones provides, as it should, for a possible change in boundary conditions, and thus a suspension of the field equations and conservation laws deduced from them, if the higher purpose or plan requires it.

In terms of this world view, we evidently have to admit a *fulfilled* potentiality of past events (since they remain causally operative), a *provisional* potentiality of future events (without which various alternatives could not be contemplated before the plan is finalized), and a *developing* potentiality of real existences, including individual living beings.

A percipient who has a physical body but is observing a fulfilled potentiality in his thought-image sphere could take his present physical time as t_1, and the time of some event of the past (experienced by him in his thought-image sphere at physical time t_1) as t_0. Then if $t_0 - t_1$ is negative, the effect is (individual) memory or (cosmic) retrocognition. For example, an event at 3 o'clock, remembered at 4 o'clock, means a time-shift backwards of one hour.

Similarly, if $t_0 - t_1$ is positive, the effect is (individual) will-determined action or (cosmic) precognition. The two spheres have to be correlated in some way, and the normal would be when an event of the plan, at t_0 in the thought-image sphere, is actualized at t_0 in the physical sphere. But nothing prevents a time shift.

Although these are simple time shifts, it has to be remembered that the shifted thought-image pattern of events can be contemplated backwards or forwards from the higher purposive level, which is not subject to these time variables or field equations. The power so to contemplate is called "recollection" in mystical teachings.

There does not seem to be any one right way to allocate values to the "planning" or "cosmic" time variable T, except that the values allocated may change only if the plan is changed. The reason for this is that the field equations can be deduced only if T is not subject to different points of view (or the rotations 01, 02, 03, 04, 05 are suspended). When the plan is changed, so that T is changed in certain regions, the field equations no longer hold, so we are free to change the boundary conditions, i.e., the behavior of specified objects in that region of the field. It follows that T could be suitably identified with $t_0 - t_1$, in the notation above.

This seems to complete a satisfactory verification that

parapsychological phenomena as well as physical phenomena are in accord, quantitatively as well as qualitatively, with the world view here being presented. The classical world view, on the other hand, agrees with neither.

REFERENCES

1. C. D. Broad, *Religion, Philosophy, and Psychical Research* (New York: Humanities Press, Inc., 1953).
2. C. E. M. Hansel, *ESP, A Scientific Evaluation* (New York: Charles Scribner's Sons, 1966).
3. C. Burt, *Psychology and Psychical Research* (London: Society for Psychical Research, 1968).
4. J. H. M. Whiteman, "Parapsychology and Physics," in *Handbook of Parapsychology,* edited by B. B. Wolman (New York: Van Nostrand Reinhold Co., 1976).
5. A. Messiah, *Quantum Mechanics* (New York: John Wiley, 1962), Vol. II.
6. C. A. Mace, "Some Trends in the Philosophy of Mind," in *British Philosophy in the Mid-Century,* edited by C. A. Mace (New York: Humanities Press, Inc., 1966).
7. E. P. Wigner, "The Role of Invariance Principles in Natural Philosophy," in *Proceedings of the International School of Physics "Enrico Fermi," Course XXIX,* edited by E. P. Wigner (New York: Academic Press, Inc., 1964).
8. J. H. M. Whiteman, "Quantum Theory and Parapsychology," *J. Amer. Soc. Psychical Research* (1973).
9. J. H. M. Whiteman, *Philosophy of Space and Time* (London: George Allen and Unwin Ltd., 1967).
10. K. R. Popper, "Three Views Concerning Human Knowledge," in *Contemporary British Philosophy,* edited by H. D. Lewis (London: George Allen and Unwin Ltd., 1956).
11. J. H. M. Whiteman, "A Three-tier Ontology for Parapsychology and Modern Physics," in *Parapsychology in South Africa,* edited by J. C. Poynton (South Africa: South African Society for Psychical Research, 1975).
12. J. H. M. Whiteman, "Parapsychology as an Analytico-

Deductive Science," in *Quantum Physics and Parapsychology*, edited by Laura Oteri (New York: Parapsychology Foundation, Inc., 1975).

13. Sigmund Freud, "Formulations on the Two Principles of Mental Functioning," in *Collected Works*, Standard Edition (London: The Hogarth Press Ltd., 1911), Vol. 12.

14. G. N. M. Tyrrell, *Apparitions* (New York: Macmillan, Inc., 1970).

26.

Quantum Physics and Paranormal Events

LAURENCE M. BEYNAM

> Occurrences which, according to received theories, *ought not* to happen, are the *facts* which serve as clues to new discoveries.
>
> Sir John Herschel

> The truth is not only stranger than you imagine; it is stranger than you *can* imagine.
>
> J. B. S. Haldane

One aspect of the universe which has never fitted in too well with Western science is that of paranormal events. The reasons for this, one suspects, are several. One, probably, is the problem of measurement, which was given a beautiful exposition by mathematics professor William Garnett many years ago,[1] and which may be summarized as follows: If space is not Euclidean, i.e., does not have a frozen, static structure, any distortion in said space will influence any object within it *and* at the same time, by implication, the measurement apparatus itself, so that the distortion does not show up in the measurements. If similar distortions of space-time are involved in paranormal events, and they may indeed be involved in certain phenomena of the poltergeist class, insistence upon concrete measurement results may be not a help but a hindrance in our understanding of such events.

Another aspect of the measurement problem is that we cannot build instruments to measure processes or energies which we cannot imagine in the first place. Faraday, Ampère, and

"Quantum Physics and Paranormal Events" by Laurence M. Beynam is an original article written especially for this volume and is printed by permission of the author.

the rest had at least an idea about what they were going to measure and how to measure it. Denying the reality of electromagnetic phenomena would have been, not the pathway to the discovery of electromagnetic fields, but rather the very method by which this discovery might be effectively blocked. The proper procedure in measuring something is, first, acceptance of the possibility that there is something to measure, and, second, a more or less definite idea about how this measurable entity functions. One can then go on to construct the proper measurement apparatus. Nor is excommunication of scientists claiming to have measured unknown, and therefore generally unacceptable, energies a viable solution.

There seems to be, however, a deeper reason why paranormal events have been banned from widespread scientific discussion, and this is afforded by the Western mode of thinking. As psychologist Carl G. Jung has pointed out, we in the West tend to separate, isolate, analyze, dissect, and generally miss the forest for the trees. (This is not to deny the reality of trees; but does acceptance of their reality detract from the reality of the forest?)

An historiography of this development would require a volume in itself. Suffice it to say here that in an individualistic society, whose culture is determined by the largely subconscious root assumptions of its members, those of its members engaging in scientific research are constrained to follow its value judgments *without even realizing* that they are doing so.* Such things as telepathy, confluential events, and psychokinesis are then seen to be naturally inexplicable in terms of individuality and separateness. One needs to posit the opposite—and typically Eastern—notion of connectedness if one wishes to explain such phenomena. Psychotherapist Jan Ehrenwald has neatly summarized this necessity as follows:

In short, we have to give up the idea of a punctiform,

* As William Irwin Thompson has observed (though in a different context): "All the computers in the world won't help you if your unexamined and unconscious assumptions on the nature of reality are simply wrong in their basic conception."[2] Those who accuse psychic researchers of "escapism" would do well to remember that the argument is double edged: If paranormal events are real, then it is themselves who are avoiding reality, just because they cannot accommodate such events within their world view.

egocentric, unicerebral localization of "consciousness" and adopt the theory of a potential *multicerebral* or *scattered* localization of mental processes. . . . We have to conceive of human personality in terms of a potentially open system . . . or rather of a personality field sweeping across the boundary lines of strictly isolated individual units.[3]

The psi-field theory of William G. Roll et al.[4] would seem to be one step in this direction. The Western paradigm of individuality seems to have outlived its usefulness, and a fresh infusion of guiding principles is necessary if science is to help humankind to survive, and to survive itself.

This latter point is becoming obvious especially in the fast-moving field of high-energy physics. Although the recent discovery of several new particles has been hailed as the dawn of a new era, I want to suggest that the "grand synthesis" in physics, sought after by so many, may be found, not in the models currently under discussion, but in the direction pointed out by some of the world's greatest physicists. As the British journal *New Scientist* has commented: "What is becoming clear is that simple particle hunting—naming the parts—isn't taking us any nearer the elusive goal of elemtarity."[5] Werner Heisenberg, one of the founding fathers of quantum theory, recently suggested that "what is really needed is a fundamental change of concepts; we will have to abandon the philosophy of Democritus and the concept of fundamental elementary particles."[6] The necessary changes have likewise been indicated: According to Wolfgang Pauli: "It would be the more satisfactory solution if mind and body could be interpreted as complementary aspects of the same reality."[7] Similarly, Heisenberg and Niels Bohr have both stressed the importance of consciousness. Bohr comments:

> . . . consciousness must be a part of nature, or, more generally, of reality, which means that, quite apart from the laws of physics and chemistry, as laid down in quantum theory, we must also consider laws of quite a different kind. . . . Here we obviously have a genuine case of complementarity, one that we shall have to analyze in greater detail. . . .[8]

It is quite possible that the problem posed by the proliferation of elementary particles cannot be resolved without first solving the problem of consciousness; that elementary particles are the lure of *maya,* leading us on by the nose; and that this matter can be settled not on the level at which it is being attacked but only on a higher level, a level which may necessitate taking paranormal events into account.

Can we, then, accommodate paranormal events within our present level of scientific knowledge? The answer, I think, is both yes and no. We can, but only if we shift our viewpoint; we need to look at the data afresh. A gestalt switch seems to be required.

Now that paranormal events are being investigated scientifically, the present tendency is towards finding an electromagnetic explanation.[9–12] Electromagnetism was insufficient, however, to explain quantum physical and relativistic phenomena, and it seems of doubtful value in explaining certain classes of paranormal events, such as OOBEs and dematerializations. John B. Hasted, David J. Bohm, Edward W. Bastin, and Brendan O'Regan state that in experiments with Uri Geller: "part of an encapsulated single crystal of vanadium carbide apparently vanished . . . there is no known way of producing this effect within the closed capsule and no possibility of substitution."[13] Hasted et al. have suggested the possibility of "some at present unknown force, energy, or mode of connection"[14] being involved. In that case, measurable electromagnetic effects may be secondary phenomena, arising merely as side effects of a more fundamental process; due, perhaps, to some sort of breakdown or decay. Such a process is clearly indicated if dematerialization and teleportation indeed occur, for in that case an explanation depending only on one of the four physical forces (electromagnetic, gravitational, weak nuclear, and strong nuclear) is obviously insufficient, when even all these forces taken together cannot afford a clue. As John G. Taylor remarks: "No feasible physical explanation [of dematerialization] can be given in present terms."[15] Friedbert Karger and Gerhard Zicha have likewise found it necessary to postulate a fifth type of interaction[16] in addition to the above four.† The British au-

---

† Actually, a fifth force, the "weak neutral current," was recently isolated and identified, but there appears to be little ground for equating this force with the energy in question.

thor Colin Wilson, in his monumental work on the occult, states that some such notion is "the fundamental proposition of magic‡ and occultism, and perhaps the only essential one."[17] Thus, an unwitting synthesis of two *apparently* contradictory systems, magic and science, may be at hand. Anthropologist James George Frazer was farsighted enough to see this when he said: "The dreams of magic may one day be the waking realities of science."[18]

In view of all this, if electromagnetism is ultimately found to be the underlying cause behind paranormal events, it will have to undergo changes in its basic conception which will unavoidably result in a structure very different from what we now understand by the term. In addition, any "unified field theory" or "grand synthesis" in this day and age should attempt the union of physics, paraphysics, psychology, parapsychology, and mysticism in order to be worthy of the name, a task clearly beyond the present range and scope of electromagnetic theory.

While more than one process may be involved in paranormal phenomena of various kinds, the more powerful and elegant solution would be to find a process capable of generating different results under different circumstances. This is also necessitated by Occam's razor; one unknown energy is enough for the time being. As Hasted et al. have noted: "If a piece of metal can respond to the brain in an unknown way, the brain may similarly respond to the metal."[19] Thus, one type of energy may be sufficient to explain both ESP and PK. Moreover, as will be seen shortly, the basis for such an understanding already exists. All that is necessary is to pull the strands together. This leads to a simple model which seems capable of rendering paranormal events explicable within a wider framework. The model outlined below is by no means a perfect one; it serves to demonstrate, however, that such models are not inherently impossible. (Only the main points can be outlined here; part of a more detailed treatment has been published elsewhere,[20] which this paper summarizes and supplements.)

‡ Emphatically not that kind of "stage magic" characterized by sleight of hand and illusion.

Theoretical Aspects: General

> Your theory is crazy, but it's not crazy enough to be true.
>
> Niels Bohr

> For any speculation which does not at first glance look crazy, there is no hope.
>
> Freeman J. Dyson

The correspondence of various states of consciousness (SCs) to various states of reality (SRs) has been demonstrated in recent years. Psychedelic substances were only a small junction along this road[21]; the subsequent research on the induction of trance states[22] has shown that chemical or electrical explanations fall short of covering the full complexity of such states. The objective–subjective distinction, an obsolete remnant from the mechanistic world view of the 19th century, has finally been dissolved, and the public mind has finally caught up with the earth-shaking discoveries of quantum physics, which first saw the light of day half a century ago. In addition to psychedelic and trance-state research, the notion of a single, unchanging and unchangeable reality independent of the perceptor has been challenged on several other grounds.

One of these is the epochal tetralogy of a young anthropologist, Carlos Castaneda.[23-26] The fictive experiences (both drug induced and sober) of Castaneda with his mentor, Juan Matus, merely served to underline what had earlier been inherently obvious but not explicitly stated in anthropological research—namely, that reality is a more or less arbitrary construct geared to the metaphysical presuppositions of a culture, social group, or individual. Another step in the same direction is provided by the science historian Thomas S. Kuhn, who has analyzed the structure of scientific revolutions. According to Kuhn, every scientific revolution brings about such a profound change in world view (in terms of theories, experiments, etc.) that the pre- and postrevolutionary scientists seem to be living in entirely different worlds. Commenting on the Chemical Revolution, for instance, Kuhn says:

> Chemists could not . . . simply accept Dalton's theory on the evidence, for much of that was still negative. Instead, even after accepting the theory, they had still to beat nature into line, a process which, in the event, took almost another generation. When it was done, even the percentage composition of well-known compounds was different. *The data themselves had changed.*[27] (Italics added.)

All this, however, is but a prelude to the findings of quantum mechanics. Heisenberg's uncertainty principle leads directly to the conclusion that, to use the words of physicist Dietrich Schroeer, "the observer cannot be separated from the experiment,"[28] and while this is generally held to be true for microcosmic phenomena, there is evidence for its truth in the macrocosmos as well. "To put it bluntly," says Henry Margenau, "science no longer contains absolute truths."[29] The very act of and the very intention behind observing disturbs the observed.

This point needs further elaboration. In quantum physics, a particle can be anywhere in the universe before it is observed; the probability of its being too far away from a certain localization is very small, but cannot be entirely ruled out. When it is observed, only one probability is actualized from an infinite number of "probability amplitudes." The "state vector" (or "statistical ensemble") is the superposition of these probability amplitudes, and is said to have "collapsed" upon observation to leave only one probability as the actualized one.

At this point, differing interpretations arise. The Copenhagen interpretation holds that the collapse of the state vector occurs in a completely probabilistic (or random) fashion. On the other hand, those physicists such as David Bohm who are not satisfied with this interpretation have postulated "hidden variables" that collapse the state vector.

It is found, however, that any measuring instrument introduced to determine what is going on enters an undecided, or "schizophrenic," state, for it, too, is a collection of probability amplitudes. For the same reason, the same thing hap-

pens with any chain of instruments brought in to monitor the
first one, this being known as "von Neumann's catastrophe of
infinite regression."[30] The regression is terminated only with
the introduction of an observer's consciousness. Thus, it is
consciousness itself that collapses the state vector and makes
the selection from an infinite number of probabilities. To
quote Margenau again: "Consciousness is the primary medium of all reality. Even the external world is initially a posit,
a projection of consciousness."[31] According to another great
physicist, Eugene P. Wigner, consciousness is the ultimate
referent of reality, and Wigner has developed this viewpoint
in a mathematically sophisticated manner.[32, 33] Finally, Bryce
S. DeWitt states: "The Copenhagen view promotes the impression that the collapse of the state vector, and even the
state vector itself, is all in the mind."[34]

All of the above serves to indicate that a state of consciousness (awareness) and its corresponding state of reality
cannot be meaningfully separated from each other. Psychologist Charles T. Tart has called for the development of
"state-specific sciences" in order that states of reality radically
different from ordinary physical reality may be investigated.[35]

One fact that seems to emerge from the present discussions
on the nature of consciousness is that it is nonlocal (i.e., not
confined to a certain region of space-time, such as our heads).
Starting from a study of mysticism, psychologist Arthur J.
Deikman finds that "awareness is not localized"; in addition,
awareness is organization, or rather its mental or psychological counterpart.[36] Approaching the question from the
physical side, Evan Harris Walker[37] has applied Bell's criterion of nonlocality for Bohm's hidden variables (i.e., any hidden variable must be nonlocal) to Wigner's concept of consciousness. In this view, nonlocal and nonphysical (i.e.,
nonmeasurable) hidden consciousness variables collapse the
state vector. Walker finds that every process in the universe,
down to the tiniest particle, possesses consciousness.[38] Indeed,
if nonlocality is to be accepted, things cannot be otherwise.
Every point in every reality must be conscious, though each
one projects (or "perceives") a different reality or a different aspect of the same reality. It seems, then, that every
point possesses a dual nature of consciousness and reality, this

duality not being confined to physical reality or "matter" alone, since there can be other SCs and SRs. Physical reality may, however, be considered to be a special case, and searching for a nonlocalized process that might be both a subset of a more general range of SCs, and a possible complementary to matter in the form of mind, we find that superluminal processes lend themselves as a promising candidate, at the same time providing a means whereby paranormal events may be explained.

Theoretical Aspects: ESP

Precognition may be singled out as the factor providing the key clue. The fact that precognition involves information transfer in the reverse time direction necessitates, due to the theory of relativity, the adoption of faster-than-light (super- or supraluminal) processes as a possible explanatory cause allowed for by the laws of physics. One such process is provided by the de Broglie wave (or matter wave), this entity being indispensable to an understanding of modern physics. (Here we are not concerned with the wave *group*, which has a velocity equal to that of the physical matter it is coupled with.) Physicist Gerald Feinberg[39] and mathematician Adrian Dobbs,[40] on the other hand, have theorized superluminal particles of (mathematically) imaginary mass. While Feinberg's derivation is quite rigorous, Dobbs' conception covers the "objective probabilities" encountered in quantum theory. Here it must be remembered that in terms of quantum theory, all matter consists simply of probability waves, densities or amplitudes. According to Dobbs, future probability states emit "psitrons" in direct proportion to their possibility of realization. Since normal concepts of time and velocity are suspended for superluminal processes, Dobbs has introduced a second time dimension along which objective probabilities are strung out.

On the other hand, Feinberg's "tachyons" have the interesting property that their momenta periodically emerge into and submerge out of the space-time continuum, thus presumably producing an effect akin to an impulse at regular space-time intervals. In between, tachyons would appear to be completely nonlocal, spread out across the entire complex plane.

Tachyons can be viewed either as carrying negative energy backwards in time or positive energy forwards in time.[41] This interchangeability allows us to view a tachyon as a bidirectional discontinuous field line, microminiature "warp," "wormhole," or short-circuit that carries information across space-time regardless of direction, somewhat as light photons carry information within ordinary space-time. Taken collectively, they would function as a warp directly connected to the original object–event and seen somewhat as a hologram projection ("tulpa" or "apparition"; see next section).

We have, thus far, two kinds of superluminal processes, one of a wave and the other of a particle nature; the existence of the former is established, while the existence of the latter is in doubt. However, the complementary wave–particle or "wavicle" nature of infraluminal and luminal processes is a good precedent for the possibility of the same in the case of superluminal processes as well, although the latter will most likely have strikingly different characteristics from the former ("laws of quite a different kind"–Bohr). (Note also that speaking of the wavicle nature of matter is a simplification; it is actually neither a wave nor a particle, but exhibits characteristics we can summarize under the conceptual models of "wave" and "particle.")

The immense utility of a supraluminal field model is that it allows us to satisfy Bohr's and Pauli's notions of the complementarity of mind and matter in an unexpectedly fruitful way. The small step of equating supraluminal processes with consciousness enables us to view mind (supraluminal) and matter (infraluminal) as two complementary regions with an energy (luminal) interface; also, the equations show that there is a mutual and instantaneous interaction. Further, the supraluminal field was derived from the necessity to explain precognition; yet since the time constraint is dissolved, the field is of a nonlocal and nontemporal nature, enabling a basis for telepathy, clairvoyance, and retrocognition to come into view.

Thus, each point in space-time should be topologically connected, through the supraluminal field, ultimately with every other point; yet this interconnection does not result in a meaningless jumble of chaos. Obviously the connectivity is *organized*. The situation is exemplified in an application from luminal processes, namely holograms. Several researchers have independently drawn attention to the importance of the holographic model; it may be a spirit of the times. For the holograph, at each and every point, contains all the information contained in the whole; subdivision into individual parts does not directly lead to a loss of information; *information, or structure, is conserved*. The holographic model is thus inherently synergic (informational, organizational, and non-random) as opposed to entropic (disorganizing, disintegrative, and randomizing). This implies impartibility; the whole cannot be meaningfully separated into parts isolated from each other without changing its very identity in the process.

Applying the holographic model to the supraluminal field, it is immediately obvious that the infinituple connectivity—which, however, is organized within a stratified structure of successive levels—implied by the field shows it to be of a synergic nature (note the connection with Deikman's consciousness as organization). The utility of equating consciousness with this field now becomes apparent: Each point in the field immediately obtains information from ("reacts to") any change at any other point; it is, for all practical purposes, "aware" of what is happening at other points. Such a concept can be applied with telling effect to biology, where the hormone theory of cellular differentiation seems a cumbersome and mechanistic device at best, and the notion of a "biohologram" is much closer to reality; it can be applied not only to intercellular but to interorganismic communications, investigated by Cleve Backster, where some kind of "primary consciousness" has been claimed to reside even in the smallest of cells; finally, when we realize that the dictum "everything is connected with everything else" is one of the four ground rules formulated for ecology by Barry Commoner, the full implications of the picture begin to emerge. But this is by no means the end; for we next encounter physicist David Bohm, who tells us that the primary emphasis in quantum

theory is now on "undivided wholeness," and that the "sep-
arability of the world into distinct but interacting parts is no
longer valid or relevant."[42] This is such an order of unity that
even the concept of a signal loses its meaning; indeed, even
the tachyonic or psitronic models that have been invoked may
be rendered obsolete, serving merely as stepping stones for
our minds which cannot span the gap so fast.* ESP is, in this
analysis, a natural by-product of a field required by biology,
ecology, and quantum physics; as Brendan O'Regan has
noted: "Psychic research, if it did not already exist, would
have to be invented to fully explore the 'new' experimental
paradigm of 'undivided wholeness'."[43]

When we next turn to anthropology and history, in order to
see whether this idea has any precedent, we are at once faced
with an *urgrund* concept, an *urfeld* (ultimate field) of existence postulated not only by almost all primitive people but
also by luminaries such as Paracelsus and by physicists, such
as Lancelot Law Whyte. (See Appendix I for a partial listing of such theorizers and/or discoverers.) This "energy," as it
may loosely be called ("synergy" may be more accurate) is
almost always a "life" energy; it is formative, negentropic, intelligent, conscious, etc., providing a connective substratum
for all things in the universe. Such connectivity requires superluminal processes, since the speed of light cannot afford
non-time-consuming information transfer; and because there
are principles, such as the Mach principle and the Pauli
exclusion principle, which are operative at any instant throughout the entire universe, thus necessitating instantaneous con-
ductance of information (see also the subject of "exchange
forces" in the next section). It remains to be seen, of course,
whether even the word "transfer" is a relevant one.

In contrast to those physical forces governed by the second
law of thermodynamics, the synergic field would seem to
work inwards toward the center from the periphery. Schroedinger points out that the organism "sucks in" negative en-

* Perhaps one could alternatively hypothesize a hyperspace
model in which all points are equidistant from each other; in the
case of dimensionlessness (void) this distance would be zero. Also,
the de Broglie wave seems better suited to a field model from which
the concept of a conventional signal has been excluded.

tropy from its environment.[44] In fact, since organism and environment (or any object and the rest of the universe) cannot be meaningfully separated from each other, it would be strange if their interaction occurred only in one direction (outward from the organism or object) and not the other. It is interesting in this connection that whereas the retarded potential solution in electromagnetic theory describes a wave traveling outward from the origin, the advanced potential solution describes one traveling inward to (converging toward) the center.[45] Perhaps there is a mechanism whereby the consciousness field thus forms and maintains infraluminal matter, possibly by means of an inversion relationship, although the field itself is of a nonlocalized nature.†

This synergic, formative "energy" was called "prana" by the ancient yogis and "psychic ether" by some contemporary researchers. Physicist Carl Friedrich von Weizsäcker[47] draws attention to the similarity between *prana* and the probability amplitudes in quantum physics, and indeed one might go so far as to equate this principle with the state vector in the most general sense.‡ However, in considering the physical world as a subset of a more general set of realities, a supraluminal picture for this formative energy may, in this restricted range, prove more meaningful. In other words, this prephysical energy would have supraluminal properties for physical matter in particular and would be equivalent to the state vector in general.

As for the mathematical treatment of such a holistic or "holographic" field, it will likely require the utilization of the higher-order hypernumbers, theorized several years ago by Charles A. Musès.[48, 49] Due to their recent discovery, hyper-

† For those who find it difficult to conceive of such a relationship, the work of artist Maurits C. Escher provides a graphic example. "Circle Limit III" is a mandala of interlocked fishes. "Outside it, however," says Escher, "is the 'absolute nothing'. But the spherical world cannot exist without this emptiness around it, not only because 'inside' presumes 'outside', but also because in the 'nothing' lie the strict, geometrically determined, immaterial middle points of the arcs of which the skeleton is constructed."[46]

‡ This implies, of course, that properties adhere to the state vector which have yet to be recognized. The reasons for equating the two will become clearer in the following section.

number mathematics is still in its infancy, and much work will have to precede a qualitative exposition. (Note also that mathematics, in the very process of quantitative description, has moved further and further towards qualitative modes of analysis.) Such an exposition will necessarily be exceedingly complex, which is why more powerful tools are needed than those presently available within the conventional framework of higher mathematics.

Theoretical Aspects: PK

> Imagination can not only cause that-which-was-not, to be; it can cause that-which-was, not to be.
>
> Harold C. Goddard

> A thing can both *be, not be,* and be anything else.
>
> Robert Heinlein, *Waldo*

> Beside the actual universe I can set in imagination other universes in which the laws are different.
>
> J. L. Synge

> Thoughts are things.
>
> Huna saying

In this section we return from the specialized analysis for physical matter to the more general norm of all realities; restricting ourselves to a supraluminal model is no longer necessary, although the concept of an all-ordering *urfeld* or Ultimate Consciousness must be retained.

The accounts of magic among primitive peoples and throughout history have always seemed to make some kind of perverse sense to those investigators who were inclined to take such things seriously. Most of magic, of course, is just what it seems to be: Nonsense. There remains a core, however, which we will now attempt to tackle.

First, in the light of the previous section, it is seen that primitive peoples had, and still have, a soft spot for the concept of undivided wholeness. Thus, all things in the universe were in interaction, and the time and place for particularized magic working had to be chosen with care; the astrobiological situation had to be taken into account; there were "power points" in the *urfeld* where connectivity was concentrated on a higher order, etc. Once the proper place and time were selected, it remained for the magic worker to enter a trance state in which he could contact and "bring down" a nonordinary SR. Following Frazer[50] in part, the laws of magic may now be summarized as follows:

(1) The law of contagion, or sympathy. Things (objects, concepts*) which have once been in contact or have in any way been connected will from that moment onwards remain connected and continue ever afterwards to act on each other. (According to the Hawaiian Huna, the "mode of connection" is "sticky" and can stretch almost indefinitely as things are removed from each other's state space.)

(2) The law of similarity, or homeopathy. For any two things that have thus been connected, action of one kind upon one will lead, due to the pure and noncontaminative nature of the "mode of connection," automatically to change of the same kind in the other. Like produces like, like attracts like into the same information state space.

(3) The law of contiguity. The part, due to laws (1) and (2), represents the whole.

The fact that (3) is an accurate statement of the holographic model's primary characteristic forces us to consider the other two items more seriously.

Since magic, when shorn of all its window dressing, appears to be more or less equivalent to PK, it will be necessary, in our treatment of PK, to explain the laws of sympathy and homeopathy as well.† It will be seen that the state vector constitutes, to borrow Don Juan's term, the "cubic centimeter

---

* The two can be distinguished only on lower levels of consciousness integration.

† The more recent "black boxes" of Abrams, De la Warr, Hieronymus, Campbell, etc., also seem to be connected with the "holographic energy" and to be based on unconscious PK.[51, 52] These serve merely as symbolic props or prostheses for the inexperienced mind (they are, in fact, extensions of the mind) and become unnecessary after a while. Their utility stems from the symbolism necessary to alter one's SR, just as in a less technological age such symbolism was provided by more exotic paraphernalia.

of chance" through which "quantum magic" may be introduced.

Several researchers into the paranormal have pointed to the
difficulty of separating extrasensory perception (ESP) from
psychokinesis (PK). For instance, Ehrenwald remarks:

> . . . the possibility could not entirely be ruled out that a
> psychokinetic effect, involving all the paraphernalia of
> an ESP experiment—including the method of ran-
> domization, of shuffling cards, of recording procedures,
> etc.—may ultimately be responsibile for the semblance
> of precognition obtained [by various experimenters].[53]

Physicist Helmut Schmidt, famous for his research in these
areas, states that "the relationship between PK and precognition seems to be generally rather close, to the extent that a
rigorous separation between PK and precognition might in
the statistical laboratory tests not be possible."[54] Walker explains the experimental evidence for telepathy in a similar
way: "A message in the usual sense is not being transmitted,
but a future state is being selected"[55]; also, "PK involves the
same basic process as clairvoyance . . ."[56]

Recently, two leading physicists have offered their views
concerning PK, each with reference to the most fundamental
entity known to quantum physics, namely ψ, the state vector
(or, as it is otherwise known, the wave function).

Now the wave function is subject to two kinds of change.
As long as it is left alone and unobserved, it changes in accordance with the Schroedinger wave equation, where an operator called the Hamiltonian determines how the wave function evolves. Alternatively, the Hamiltonian changes drastically and discontinuously (the state vector collapses)
upon observation.

Brian D. Josephson‡ speculates that one can control the
Hamiltonian itself:

> That is to say, perhaps one can modify the laws of na-
> ture. This may be the way in which psychic phenomena
> take place. One could make a force to act on something
> merely by modifying the Hamiltonian so that the object
> had more energy in one position than another. Psychic
> phenomena might thus be connected with altering the

‡ Nobel Laureate in physics, 1973.

Hamiltonian which determines the equation of motion in a system. Perhaps also some kinds of psychic phenomena can be considered as establishing a coupling energy between oneself and the thing one wants to influence.[57]

Evan H. Walker has given much thought to the subject, and assigns the function of collapsing the state vector to a subset of the consciousness (c_i) variables which he calls *will* (w_i).[58] In Walker's view, such effects as dematerialization, teleportation, and metalbending are not inherently impossible; all that is needed is a highly sustained willpower, which results in the collapse of the state vector on the macroscopic level at an extremely improbable state.

If these views are correct, as they seem to be, physical reality is much more fluid (amenable to direct mental influence) than has been hitherto believed; in fact, it is as fluid as we like. The deep involvement of the subconscious in paranormal phenomena would then lead one to the conclusion that subconscious levels and ultimately the collective consciousness is reacting to and changing the "world line" each of us follows in ways of which we are unaware. Parapsychologist Rex G. Stanford calls this "psi-mediated instrumental response" (PMIR); he notes that this can "occur without the person's being aware that anything extraordinary is happening."[59] In that case, Walker's w_i variables must have subconscious components as well; each SC would have a w_i subset. In this conception, reality is determined jointly by conscious and subconscious strata.

Walker's view is based on the orthodox collapse of the state vector. Hugh Everett III,[60] John A. Wheeler, and R. Neill Graham, on the other hand, have proposed a different interpretation of quantum mechanics, one known shortly as the EWG interpretation, in which the state vector is not collapsed at all (or rather, from the point of view to be outlined below, we should perhaps say collapsed at all its values). In this view, based on flawless mathematics, each point in the universe splits or branches off into myriads of probable universes each micro-micro-second; the "world line" we follow is but one of the countless probable ones that really exist. Wheeler conceives of a "superspace" in which any one point is an entire universe, while neighboring points are slightly different universes.[61] It is a far cry from the sober treatment of EWG to the colorful language of Fredric Brown, yet his statement of the case is an accurate one:

> If there are infinite universes, then all possible combinations must exist. Then, somewhere, everything must be true. . . . There is a universe in which Huckleberry Finn is a real person, doing the exact things Mark Twain described him as doing. There are, in fact, an infinite number of universes in which a Huckleberry Finn is doing every possible variation of what Mark Twain *might* have described him as doing. . . . And infinite universes in which the states of existence are such that we would have no words or thoughts to describe them or imagine them.[62]

Now it so happens that one psychic research group has come up with a very interesting result. Taking after the Toronto S.P.R. research group (who gave us "Philip," an imaginary "ghost" or communicator having no relationship with historical reality), this group has, it seems, netted a host of Dickensian storybook characters, including such favorites as the Artful Dodger, Oliver Twist, Fagin, Bill Sykes, and Nancy. These fairytale communicators have produced a range of physical phenomena.[63]

Crazy? Perhaps—and perhaps not. Whether Dickens' creations, Huckleberry Finn and anything ever imagined by anybody has its respective probable universe or "parallel continuum" in which it actually exists, remains to be seen. Of course, were one to trust the concepts of "primitive" peoples, concepts which are rapidly being approached by ultramodern physics, one would at this point be reminded of the Tibetans, who, according to Alexandra David-Neel, tended to believe that everything one can imagine can be realized. They claimed that *if the imagined facts corresponded to no external reality, one could not conceive of them or their images*.[64] However, whatever the case may be in this respect, a tentative analysis would seem to indicate that, if we are to avoid falling into solipsism (which would imply that members of a race of creatures among a million others inhabiting a random dust speck in the universe are the *sole* claimants of consciousness, and would play havoc with the nonlocality of consciousness), other states of reality, geared to other states of consciousness, *already* exist. Psychologist Robert Masters' experience with a trance subject in which the Sekhmet* archetype was activated, would seem to show that such archetypes, if nothing else, possess an existence quite apart from either that of the subject or of the experimenter.[65]† It is here that the EWG interpretation lends itself as an immensely powerful tool to sifting sense out of all this seeming outrage.

If we apply Walker's concept of a consciousness-collapsed-state vector to the EWG interpretation, it becomes clear that every nonordinary state of consciousness is coupled to a nonordinary state of reality (or probable universe), diverging from our ordinary reality as its probability in our terms diminishes. There is an ultimate connective tissue for all these universes, and that is the infinite-dimensional consciousness (c_i) field (or, to take up the more restricted argument of the last section, superluminal psitrons which connect each probability with each other one). The connection through a collective consciousness of these universes dissolves the barriers preventing their interaction; the noninteraction concept had been based on a consideration from which the subject of consciousness had been excluded. Just as, in Walker's conception, consciousness collapses the state vector, in the modified EWG interpretation it can choose one universe or another. A change of SC would therefore cause a "transverse acceleration of probability amplitudes," by which a different probable universe is actualized. The evidence for the actual, instead of only virtual, existence of parallel continua stems from out-of-body experiences (OOBEs), where events seem to follow a course determined not just by the experiencer but by the collectivity of consciousnesses geared to that reality, just like in the everyday world we are familiar with. As was pointed

* An ancient Egyptian goddess.

† Oxford philosopher H. H. Price has suggested that once an idea has been formed in the mind, it possesses "an independent life of its own . . . it not only exists but operates independently, apart from the consciousness in which it originates." (In this case, "by which it is tapped" would be a better expression of what happens than "in which it originates.")

out before, this view is also less solipsistic and anthropocentric.

Rearrangement of the proximity of probabilities is thus possible. Imagining a certain thing would connect that thing in its respective universe with present reality by means of what, for the lack of a better word, we are forced to call a "warp." Tulpas (materializations) would be created in this manner. Note that such a "warp" is necessitated simply by an unconventional collapse of the state vector.

Note also that this warp or "space-time annihilation" may not be unidirectional; for instance, Ted Serios' thought-ography[66] is best explained by a "personality fragment projection" providing a short-circuit between the camera and the locality under consideration. This also shows why damage directed at the "astral body" may lead to damage in the physical body. A warp of this kind would be the basic element of connectivity, at the same time providing a basis for Homeopathy and Sympathy. This is not far from Gertrude Schmeidler's hypothesis: "We can think of ESP or PK as making a fold in the universe* and producing contact between two things ordinarily separated,"[67] except that this "fold" or connection is now expanded to cover all possibilities; once made, it can be used by others. Whether, of course, the number of parallel universes is infinite we do not, at the present level, know; if not, there would be restrictions to what can be imagined and/or actualized—that is, restrictions to PK.

On the other hand, the reality one lives in is conditioned and constrained by one's cluster of SCs (subconscious strata). The reality in this case will be more probably than not a linear continuation of previous realities. This model may provide an understanding of dreaming and psychopathology. In the first, the subject is in an alternate reality while asleep, but in the second, alternate realities of a generally unpleasant nature are projected in the waking state.

These concepts help us to understand other aspects of the world as well. As Aldous Huxley wrote to J. B. Rhine: "Any religion, if intensely enough believed in, creates the objects of

---

* In this connection, it is interesting to note that the Sufic term for OOBEs, *tayy al-makān*, means "folding of space."

its worship—gods, defunct saints, and the like. These objectifications or projections may become centers of energy reinforcing the energies of individual prayers, desires, and imaginations, and these may assist the worshiper in getting the result he desires."[68]

One prediction from this model would be, returning to high-energy and particle physics, that any particle searched for with enough zest has a high probability of being found. Indeed, the discovery of many particles during the past half-century was preceded by hypotheses and *expectations* concerning their existence. The giant accelerators are not instruments that detect what "really" exists but expensive machines that "create" or actualize the conscious and subconscious expectations of physicists, a fact which, among other things, dovetails quite well with Stanford's PMIR concept. As Thompson remarks: "When we build a cyclotron to search for elementary particles, we do not observe elementary particles; we observe what happens when we try to search for elementary particles."[69] Josephson is quite explicit on the subject, and deserves being quoted at length:

> The wave function, it seems, cannot control the observer's intention. We may ask therefore whether the observer's intentions can influence the outcome of an experiment. Quantum mechanics only tells us the probability distribution of observed values of physical quantities. If the observer was emotionally involved in the outcome of the experiment and particularly wanted one result to come out rather than another, perhaps that would shift this probability distribution. . . . [Physicists might] have an influence in causing the experimentally determined probability distribution to come out just as they expected it ought to be.
>
> Currently in physics there's the strange phenomenon that the laws of nature seem to keep on changing. New symmetry violations are being discovered, the velocity of light is found to be different from what people thought it was, and so on. An odd thing, which may or may not be significant, is that sometimes when a new observation is made different people get different results. In one instance a particular symmetry was broken on one side of the Atlantic, but not on the other; *however, after a while everyone got the same results.* The conventional explanation would be that errors were being made on one side of the ocean, but conceivably the true explanation is that

the discrepant results were genuine, and that it was the process of communication of knowledge from one side of the Atlantic to the other which caused a kind of phase transition or ordering process, as a result of which identical results were subsequently found in both places.[70] (Italics added)

To sum up, then, the model would look something like this: In n-space (with some reservations, Wheeler's superspace) all points can, and do, take on an infinite number of qualitative–quantitative values, while at the same time retaining a consciousness by and through which any reality is projected or perceived. The sum for any point of the values and their corresponding antivalues it can take on would be a null set, giving the supracosmic void or hyperspace which is identical with the universal mind, which in turn creates the universes of the modified EWG model. What cannot be overemphasized, however, is, first, that the state vector and the EWG model are merely constructs employed to render the truth partially intelligible in terms of ordinary consciousness. Second, and even more important, is that all these realities are interwoven by the absolute consciousness at such an incredible level of complexity that any lesser consciousness, due to its incomplete perception of reality, tends to find fault with various aspects of the lesser reality it perceives. It is only in mystical states of consciousness, characterized by infinite existence, intelligence and bliss (the *sat-chit-ananda* of the Hindus) that the ordering is seen to be perfect and faultless. This interweaving would seem to be accomplished mainly through the exchange forces in quantum physics, where the very substance of anything is extinguished and reappears simultaneously elsewhere as something else, limitations of size, kind and space-time being immaterial[71] and in a manner of ordering which beggars the imagination. (The exchange forces, by the way, are still another candidate for the holographic field's mode of operation.) Thus it is that, to paraphrase Shabistari,[72] the universe is contained in a mosquito's wing, and within a single point in space unimaginable heavens roll.

Social Implications

Let us pass over the implications for science, one of which, as astronaut Edgar Mitchell has pointed out, may be the replacement of expensive spaceflight by free OOBEs. Commenting on the applications of a "holographic energy," Jean Houston remarks:

> . . . we may have the guidelines for the learning and application of a metatechnology hitherto known only among shamans and other specialists in nonordinary realities. . . . It would be a supreme, but delightful, irony if these alternate, but presently largely inexplicable energy systems . . . were to provide dominant world governments with resources and energies sufficient to help them free themselves of their bondage to the now destructive and limited dynamics of the scientific–industrial paradigm, with its inevitable predilection toward doomsday.[73]

The real question we must ask, however, might be the following: Between $E = mc^2$ and the A-bomb there are forty years; how long between psychic research and Armageddon? For if history is any guide, and if any credence is to be lent to the various versions of the Atlantis myth, such a meta- or paratechnology, "in the hands of the dominant world governments," could lead to disastrous results.

The best safeguard against this seems to be the development in every individual of a personal feeling for "undivided wholeness." In addition, if the "law of karma" is to be taken seriously, every action is equal to its (instantaneous or delayed) reaction. The only sensible choice would then be the dissolution of selfishness and the cultivation of love, love for everything that comes—and does not come—within one's range of consciousness. Like the relativistic light beam that circumnavigates the universe to return to the point it started from, such love (and, indeed, any other feeling) *cannot* but go anywhere except back to its origin.

If enough people take up this view, we may in our time be approaching something far beyond expectations, a giant evolutionary step. As Thompson remarks: "The next step will be like the transformation that altered an ape into a man."[74] In *Childhood's End,* first published in 1953, that prophetic science-fiction writer, Arthur C. Clarke, envisioned the development of humanity into an "overmind." Starting from one child, the development proceeded somewhat as a crystallization in a saturated solution, rapidly spreading throughout the children. One can only marvel at the way in which Uri Geller's powers have spread, during television performances, to other people, the overwhelming majority of whom are children; it is not without reason that Clarke, who was earlier a skeptic believing that "any illiterate peasant can pull the wool over any parapsychologist's eyes," upon seeing with his own eyes the demonstrations of Geller at Birkbeck College, London University, on that fateful day of June 21, 1974, is reported to have exclaimed, in effect: "My God! It's all coming true! This is what I wrote about in *Childhood's End.*"[75]

Another Clarke first, as many readers will be aware, was, with Stanley Kubrick, the novel and movie *2001,* in which humankind reached "Beyond the Infinite" through the Stargate.

But "The Stargate," said William Irwin Thompson, "is in our foreheads." I wonder . . . could it be? . . . that the time has come for each of us to call out . . . instead of "Open, Sesame" . . . "Open, Stargate"?

REFERENCES

1. William Garnett, "Presidential Address," *Mathematical Gazette* 9 Pt. 1, 135 (1918), 237; 9 Pt. 2, 136 (1918), 249; 9 Pt. 3, 138 (1919), 293.

2. William Irwin Thompson, *At the Edge of History* (New York: Harper & Row, 1971), p. 118.

3. Jan Ehrenwald, *New Dimensions of Deep Analysis* (New York: Grune & Stratton, 1955), p. 212.

4. William G. Roll, *The Poltergeist* (New York: Signet, 1974), ca. 1972, pp. 143–152.

5. "Monitor," *New Scientist,* July 24, 1975, 196.

6. *Ibid.*

7. Quoted in Arthur Koestler, *The Roots of Coincidence* (New York: Random House, 1972), p. 55.

8. Werner Heisenberg, *Physics and Beyond* (New York: Harper & Row, 1971), pp. 114–115.

9. E. Douglas Dean, "Precognition and Retrocognition," in Edgar D. Mitchell, *Psychic Exploration*, edited by John White (New York: Putnam, 1974), p. 172.

10. Harold Puthoff and Russell Targ, "Psychic Research and Modern Physics," in Mitchell, *op. cit.*, pp. 525–529.

11. Michael Persinger, "ELF Waves and ESP," *New Horizons* **1**, 5 (1975), 232.

12. John Taylor, *Superminds* (London: Macmillan, 1975), pp. 236 ff and 167–169.

13. *Nature* **254** (1975), 470.

14. *Ibid.*, p. 471.

15. *Ibid.*, p. 473.

16. Quoted in Alister Hardy, Robert Harvie, and Arthur Koestler, *The Challenge of Chance* (New York: Random House, 1974), p. 198.

17. Colin Wilson, *The Occult* (New York: Vintage, 1973), p. 52.

18. James George Frazer, *The New Golden Bough* (abridged), edited by Theodore H. Gaster (New York: Mentor, 1959), p. 740.

19. *Nature, loc. cit.*, p. 471.

20. L. M. Beynam, "Quantum Physics and the Paranormal," *Astrologia* **1** Pt. 1, 2 (1975), 12.

21. Robert E. L. Masters and Jean Houston, *The Varieties of Psychedelic Experience* (New York: Delta, 1966).

22. Masters and J. Houston, *Mind Games* (New York: Delta, 1972); *New Ways of Being* (in press).

23. Carlos Castaneda, *The Teachings of Don Juan* (New York: Pocket Books, 1969).

24. Castaneda, *A Separate Reality* (New York: Simon & Schuster, 1971).

25. Castaneda, *Journey to Ixtlan* (New York: Simon & Schuster, 1972).

26. Castaneda, *Tales of Power* (New York: Simon & Schuster, 1974).

27. Thomas S. Kuhn, *The Structure of Scientific Revolutions*

    (Chicago: University of Chicago Press, 1962), p. 134.
28. Quoted in *Time,* April 23, 1973, 84.
29. Henry Margenau, "ESP in the Framework of Modern
    Science," in *Science and ESP,* edited by John R.
    Smythies (London: Routledge & Kegan Paul, 1967), p.
    213.
30. Bryce S. DeWitt, "Quantum Mechanics and Reality,"
    Phys. Today, September 1970, 32.
31. Margenau, loc. cit., p. 215.
32. Eugene P. Wigner, "The Place of Consciousness in Mod-
    ern Physics," in *Consciousness and Reality,* edited by
    Charles A. Musès and Arthur M. Young (New York:
    Outerbridge & Lazard, 1972), pp. 132–141.
33. Wigner, "Remarks on the Mind-Body Question," in *The
    Scientist Speculates,* edited by Irving J. Good (New
    York: Capricorn, 1965), ca. 1962, pp. 284–302.
34. DeWitt, loc. cit.
35. Charles T. Tart, "States of Consciousness and State-Spe-
    cific Sciences," *Science* **176** (1972), 1203; also in *The
    Nature of Human Consciousness,* edited by Robert E.
    Ornstein (San Francisco: W. H. Freeman, 1973), pp.
    41–60.
36. Arthur J. Deikman, "The Meaning of Everything," in
    Ornstein, *loc. cit.,* pp. 317–326.
37. Evan H. Walker, "Consciousness in the Quantum Theory
    of Measurement," *J. Study Consciousness* **5** Pt. 1, 1
    (1972), 46; **5** Pt. 2, 2 (1972), 257.
38. Walker, "The Nature of Consciousness," *Mathematical
    Biosciences* **7** (1970) 175.
39. Gerald Feinberg, "Possibility of Faster Than Light Parti-
    cles," *Phys. Rev.* **159** (1967), 1089.
40. H. A. C. Dobbs, "Time and Extrasensory Perception,"
    Proc. Soc. Psych. Res. **57** (1965), 197.
41. John G. Taylor, "Particles Faster Than Light," *Sci. J.*
    September 1969, 45.
42. Quoted in Brendan O'Regan, "The Emergence of Para-
    physics: Theoretical Foundations," Mitchell, *Psychic Ex-
    ploration,* p. 460.
43. *Ibid.,* p. 462.
44. Erwin Schroedinger, "Heredity and the Quantum The-

ory," in *The World of Mathematics,* edited by James R. Newman (New York: Simon & Schuster, 1956), Vol. 2, pp. 992–995. See also Marcel Vogel, "Man–Plant Communication," in Mitchell, *loc. cit.,* p. 295.

45. Dean, *loc. cit.,* p. 172; Puthoff and Targ, *loc. cit.,* p. 529.
46. *The World of Maurits C. Escher* (New York: Harry N. Abrams, 1971), p. 40.
47. C. F. von Weizsäcker, Introduction to Gopi Krishna, *The Biological Basis of Religion and Genius* (New York: Harper & Row, 1971), p. 42.
48. Charles A. Musès, "Hypernumber and Metadimension Theory," *J. Study Consciousness* 1, 1 (1968), 29.
49. Musès, "Working with the Hypernumber Idea," in *Consciousness and Reality,* edited by Musès and Young, pp. 448–469.
50. Frazer, *op. cit.,* p. 35.
51. Thomas G. Hieronymus, "Detection of Emanations from Materials and Measurement of the Volumes Thereof," U. S. Patent Office, Sept. 27, 1949, Patent No. 2, 482, 773; John W. Campbell, Jr., "Psionic Machine—Type One," *Astounding Science Fiction,* June 1956, 97; Campbell, "Unprovable Speculation," *ibid.,* Feb. 1957, 54.
52. Denys Parsons, "The Black Boxes of Mr. De la Warr," *J. Soc. Psych. Res.* 41, (1961), 12. Note the unwitting (and unnoticed) Serios effect on p. 28.
53. Ehrenwald, *loc. cit.,* p. 113.
54. Helmut Schmidt, "Psychokinesis," in Mitchell, *loc. cit.,* p. 190.
55. Evan H. Walker, "Consciousness and Quantum Theory," in *ibid.,* p. 562.
56. *Ibid.*
57. Brian D. Josephson, "Possible Connections Between Psychic Phenomena and Quantum Mechanics," *New Horizons* 1, 5 (1975), 226.
58. See Ref. 55, pp. 560–565.
59. Rex G. Stanford, "Clairvoyance," Mitchell, *loc. cit.,* p. 148.
60. Hugh Everett III, " 'Relative State' Formulation of Quantum Mechanics," *Rev. Mod. Phys.* 29, 3 (1957), 454.
61. Quoted in Hardy, Harvie, and Koestler, *loc. cit.,* p. 243.

62. Fredric Brown, *What Mad Universe,* quoted in *Sci. Amer.,* May 1974, 123.

63. Iris M. Owen, "'Philip's' Story Continued," *New Horizons* **2,** 1 (1975), 18.

64. Alexandra David-Neel, *Magic and Mystery in Tibet* (London: Corgi, 1971), pp. 7–8.

65. Robert Masters, "Consciousness and Extraordinary Phenomena," in Mitchell, *loc. cit.,* pp. 603–614.

66. Jule Eisenbud, *The World of Ted Serios* (New York: Pocket Books, 1968).

67. Quoted in Alan Vaughan, *Patterns of Prophecy* (New York: Hawthorn, 1973), p. 148.

68. Letter dated Dec. 30, 1942, quoted in Wilson, *loc. cit.,* p. 490.

69. William Irwin Thompson, *Passages About Earth* (New York: Harper Perennial, 1974), p. 95.

70. Josephson, *loc. cit.,* pp. 225–226.

71. Banesh Hoffmann, *The Strange Story of the Quantum* (New York: Dover, 1959), pp. 184–186.

72. Mahmud Shabistari, *The Secret Garden,* translated by Johnson Pasha (New York: E. P. Dutton, 1974), p. 27.

73. Jean Houston, "Myth, Consciousness, and Psychic Research," in Mitchell, *loc. cit.,* p. 582n.

74. See Ref. 69, p. 149.

75. Uri Geller, *My Story* (New York: Praeger, 1975), p. 86.

V THE NEW TECHNOLOGY

*Harnessing
the Energies of Life*

27

The search for new forms of energy and the discovery of new ways to harness previously known forms has always engendered a new technology, which in turn produces a "revolution." The word "harness" itself is a case in point. It reminds us of that period in history called the Agricultural Revolution when people first learned to domesticate animals and employ their power for human purposes such as plowing.

Consider the consequences of atomic power, electricity, and prior to them, steam power. In 1807, for example, during the war between France and England, a mechanic named Robert Fulton offered Napoleon Bonaparte the chance to power ships of the French navy with steam engines. The emperor called Fulton a madman and threw him out of court. Eight years later, as the vanquished Napoleon was being taken to St. Helena on an English battleship, the American steamer *Fulton* steamed briskly by the English vessel. Napoleon, gazing at the departing steamer, confided to a companion: "I forfeited my crown when I chased that man Fulton from the Tuileries."

Undisputed proof of the X energy would have the same potential for far-ranging scientific and social consequences, both benevolent and destructive. In fact, some researchers consider the case for the X energy to have been made, and have already taken strides in the direction of technological invention and refinement based on that presumed energy. (Others, such as R. N. Miller, who has contributed a chapter to this s͟ have used current technological devices—such as the mber, biofeedback instrumentation, and water sur- n measures—in unconventional ways.) The history of science shows that invention has often preceded full scientific demonstration and understanding of the invention's energy source. Such may be the situation here. This section, therefore, will look at some of the efforts to produce new classes of technology that operate on principles arising from the nature of the X energy, and to utilize conventional technology for novel ends.

A new technology brings new terminology. You have already encountered the word "psychotronics." Here it will assume the form of "psychotronic generator" as one of the editors (Stanley Krippner) discusses his observations of various devices constructed by Czechoslovakian inventor Robert Pavlita. Here also you will meet terms such as "radionics," "cloudbuster," and "psionics." The first two are formally defined when they appear. "Psionics," however, is a word coined in the 1950s by the late John Campbell, editor of *Astounding Science Fiction* (now *Analog*), to denote the science of extrasensory perceptions and abilities, including their machine or apparatus form, called psionic devices. The word has some degree of current usage, so we mention it here.

What specifically do we mean by "the new technology"? The following articles provide many examples: dowsing devices, the Hieronymus machine, the orgone accumulator (which is a functional element in the cloudbuster), the Motoyama device, radionics. We could add the Priore device, the Lakhovsky multiwave oscillator, the Moray free energy device, and Drown radiovision to the list, along with many others. These devices may be spurious or they may be valid; a decision must await further work by researchers who attempt to replicate the original reports. A visual examination of these devices shows nothing sophisticated in the orthodox sense. Rather, they appear to be very simple devices. But their very simplicity may be deceiving to the skeptic, while the open-minded investigator who penetrates their apparent manner of operation will see elegant refinement in their design.

The operation of psionic/psychotronic/psychic technology is as uncertainly understood as is the nature of the X energy, however. Is the human being an integral part of the circuitry? Or can the human factor be entirely removed, leaving only the technology, and still achieve the same results?

Polygraph expert Cleve Backster, who claimed in 1966 to have discovered "primary perception" in plants and other forms of cellular life, devised an experiment to test this question with regard to his position. He constructed an apparatus that was completely automated, with the critical stage under control of a randomizer. Thus, he reasoned, the experiment could be performed without people in the room or even the building, and the time of the experiment would be unknown to anyone until after examination of the recording chart. His findings purportedly confirmed his previous observations of an independent and unknown energy linkage by which psychic communications could take place.

This position is disputed on two fronts. First, one researcher in human–plant communication, Marcel Vogel, reported evidence that plants can be sensitized to psychic-type communications by a human source, but do not have this ability as an inherent part of their nature (see his chapter in *Psychic Exploration,* listed in Appendix III). Two other scientists reported at the 1974 American Association for the Advancement of Science meeting that they had independently replicated Backster's experiment, with negative results. Thus they feel that Backster's work (and presumably Vogel's) demonstrates not plant sentience but pseudoscience, and the issue of human–plant communication remains unresolved.

Plant psychic research aside, the matter of the human element in the new technology needs to be resolved. Researcher James Beal, in his article "How Fields Affect Us," appearing in *Fields Within Fields* (Summer 1974), offered this perspective:

> There is a good deal of interest in what might be called "psychotronic machines." Pipe locators of the "L" shape, the forked dowsing rod, the vibrating rod "aura meter," and more complicated machines of life nature, such as the Hieronymus machine, Abrams' Box, De la Warr radionic diagnostic instrument, or the Pavlita psychotronic generators, are good examples. Rather than go into a lot of detail about these devices and their analytical capabilities (or lack thereof), it is easier to explain that these machines seem to require the man–machine relationship (where the human being is part of the detector circuit), involve variations in the sense of

touch, and seem to act primarily as either amplifiers, resonators, antennas, or psychological transfer mechanisms (placebos). The machines perform no understood function by themselves, based on our present understanding in physics. They appear to have been developed over the years by their inventors in a deductive fashion and definite relationships seem to exist between shape, materials used, texture, arrangement of components, and size of components. Persons using this equipment appear to act as receivers of information on the subconscious level.

This seems to be an enlightened view of the situation, but there are still many questions to be raised and data to be considered. Lawrence LeShan wrote recently of his revised attitude (previously negative) toward radionics, based on just such questions and data. "A Research Project in Psychic Healing" appeared in *Spiritual Frontiers* (Autumn 1974/Winter 1975), the journal of Spiritual Frontiers Fellowship, which sponsors the Academy of Religion and Psychical Research (see Appendix III), under whose auspices LeShan originally delivered the article as an address.

LeShan traced his change of mind about the validity of "strange bioenergetic instruments" such as the De la Warr radionic box to an article entitled "Elastic Surface Waves" in the November 1972 issue of *Astronautics and Aeronautics* by Paul H. Carr of the U. S. Air Force Cambridge Laboratories in Massachusetts. LeShan remarks:

> . . . the article lucidly describes the equipment by which elastic surface waves are produced. These waves travel at the speed of sound along the surface between the input and output transducers; and by using these waves, hardware that could need a kilometer of coaxial cable and huge size and the speed of light can now be reduced to small size and operate at the speed of sound. There is great significance here for missile guidance, secure antijam communications, computer memories and miniaturization.
>
> Furthermore, Dr. William Tiller . . . [has] written a report in quite acceptable scientific language [about] how rubbing the finger over the rubber pad produces elastic surface waves in the pad, and sound in the cavity which is tuned to the condenser; then the finger begins to feel as though it is sticking to the pad when a resonance

is reached between the elastic surface waves and sound
of the tuning item from the patient. The future of radionics will be of great importance, I am convinced, in
our evolving comprehension of paraphysics, and in man's
ability to heal himself.

We have spoken of this technology as new, but that may
not be quite accurate. "Renewed" might prove more precise.
Section II of this book, which dealt with the nature of the X
energy, showed that its character has been recognized since
early times. Not surprisingly, there are also indications that
the ancients had a grasp of technology far more sophisticated
than is generally believed. Hints of this abound in all directions: the 1513 Piri Reis map, based on ancient sources, chart-
ing the Antarctic shoreline apparently prior to the last Ice
Age; a mechanical computer found in Greece and dated 65
B.C.; electric batteries used in Babylon four millennia ago.
Many of these anomalies are explored in Brad Steiger's *Mysteries of Time and Space,* Andrew Tomas' *We Are Not the
First,* and William R. Corliss' *Strange Artifacts* (see Appendix
III).

It is well known that our present technology can appear
magical to naive or primitive people. Might there, by the
same token, be any truth to the stance that some investigators
of the paranormal take—namely, that much today appearing
mythical and fantastic is really the degenerated remnant and
distorted memory of once-real ultrasophisticated technology?
Might amulets, talismans, and scepters, for example, really be
now-misunderstood psychic devices or psychotronic generators used for purposes such as healing, defense against other
psychic energies, etc.?

The UFO phenomenon is a focal point for these mysterious
hints about strange energies, advanced technology, and historical mysteries. Anthropologist Roger W. Wescott points out
that the tradition of prehistoric human flight is global in extent, ranging from air-view ground markings through floating
petroglyphic figures to stories of thunderbirds, angels, and
magic carpets. In examining this record, ufologists have
found instances of UFO sightings and purported contact with
humans in documents of many cultures going back thousands
of years. In the Vedas of India, which are the earliest Hindu

scriptures dating from at least 1500 B.C., there are stories of "gods" who flew through the sky in a type of airship called "vimana."

According to Serge King, in *Mana Physics: A Study of Paraphysical Energies,* the vimana was said to have "rode on a ray and made a tremendous din" very much like a present-day rocket. King, on p. 4, presents a description (and his interpretation) of this ancient device:

> On the underside of the vimana was a device with points of copper sticking out. This apparently had something to do with a levitating effect, for certain vimana were able to stand still in the air or rise straight up, like a helicopter. But the main propulsion was by heated mercury. A rotating flame did something to the mercury that produced energy which was somehow changed into a propulsive force. The wealth of logical detail is such that it is more absurd to dismiss all this as active imagination than it is to suppose such vehicles and such energy actually existed.

One can follow such notions into a wide variety of exciting speculations. Atlantis, for example, is widely regarded as one of the foremost fantasies in the minds of those who delve into archaeological mysteries. Yet a few sober researchers claim to be producing evidence of an inundated prehistoric civilization in the Atlantic basin that matches Atlantis in many respects— a long-vanished society with a high order of technology, just as myth and legend describe.

The psychic Edgar Cayce often spoke of Atlantis while delivering "readings" in an altered state of consciousness. The Cayce version of Atlantis holds that a crystal energy device called the Tuaoi (pronounced "too-oye") Stone—and sometimes referred to as the firestone—provided energy for daily life in Atlantis. It was also the means by which the Great Pyramid in Egypt was constructed. Misuse of this device, Cayce said, destroyed the civilization and the continent containing it.

By carefully following Cayce's indications about the nature of this device, John H. Sutton, a NASA physicist, said that it could have been some sort of laser-fusion reactor-gravity wave generator. He described his admittedly speculative investigation in "The Tuaoi Stone: An Enigma" in the

January 1974 *A.R.E. Journal* (see Appendix III). The firestone, then, seems to be theoretically possible—a remarkable
fact when one considers that Cayce described it psychically
decades before the technology to construct a modern version
of it existed.

At this point, our interest in the new technology has led us
into mysterious vistas that could hugely confound history and
science, if proven. Even more mysterious is the kingdom of
death. Here, too, psychics have much to tell us, and many
have presented a detailed picture of "the life beyond death,"
to use the title of the book by medium Arthur Ford and his
colleague Jerome Ellison. Can the new technology be of use
to science in an investigation of "the final frontier"? The last
two articles in this section answer in the affirmative.

The ramifications of the new technology are enormous.
Consider the theological implications of indisputable evidence
of survival beyond the grave. Consider the effects on drought
and famine if international weather engineering through the
cloudbuster were begun. Consider the energy crisis facing
Western civilization in terms of a crystal energy device which
could tap the planet's gravitational field and turn it into electricity or in terms of the Moray radiant energy device which
apparently taps an unnamed cosmic energy to provide (as T.
Henry Moray, the inventor, claimed to have done in the
1930s) 100,000 watts of electrical power from a 60-lb
package.

In the face of looming catastrophe and global disaster of
many sorts, is it not time to ignore dogmatic voices of resistance which say that these things are pseudoscience, and
mount a coordinated research program? Unconventional
though these devices may be, they may offer enormous hope
to a faltering world up against the limits of its physical and
metaphysical constraints. Thus, we present a variety of devices for consideration here, recognizing their speculative nature and slender claims for authenticity. Yet if only one apparatus of this group is found to be practical, the benefits to
humanity could make the research worthwhile.

In that regard, the words of a British scientific commission,
reporting to Parliament in 1878 on the invention of the incan-
descent light bulb, are worth considering. The commission re-

ported that the new device was "unworthy of the attention of practical or scientific men. It is impossible to adapt electrical lighting to households. Any attempt to do so is futile for it would flaunt the laws of the universe. On this the most eminent scientists agree."

28.

Applications of Dowsing:
An Ancient Biopsychophysical Art

CHRISTOPHER BIRD

Dowsing is an ancient art of *searching*—with the aid of a handheld instrument—for *anything*. This "anything" could be water, oil, or valuable mineral ores below the surface of the Earth. It could be a leak in a subterranean pipe, a break in an underground electric cable, a buried treasure, a ship at sea far beyond the horizon, or a submerged submarine. It could be a lost object, a missing person, even bodily ailments.

In all these cases, the dowser seeks to answer the question, "Where?" The answer is provided by the movement of an instrument. The instrument could be a Y-shaped rod cut from a tree or fashioned from plastic, whalebone, or other tensile material that will snap downward when held immobile in the hands. A pair of L-shaped rods bent from metal coat hangers will also work. When held loosely in each hand, they will cross each other over the spot containing the item sought. Even a simple pendulum made by tying a piece of string to a metal mechanic's nut will suffice. Just let it hang from your hand, and it will swing to-and-fro, rotate clockwise or counterclockwise, or tend to resist as if coming up against an unseen barrier. When a forked rod dips, L-rods cross, or a pendulum swings, none of the movements are random. They are deliberate movements made in answer to your spoken or mentally asked question for information.

The question, understanding or compact between the dowser and whatever is being dowsed, must be as specific as possible. Otherwise the answer that comes through may be

"Applications of Dowsing: An Ancient Biopsychophysical Art" by Christopher Bird is an original article written especially for this volume and is printed by permission of the author.

garbled, just as a radio tuned slightly off the position for a given station will produce a garbled reception of the broadcast.

The radio is only an analogy. It in no way provides a theoretical explanation for dowsing. If this seems frustrating, one may be consoled by Thomas Alva Edison's answer to the question: "What is electricity?" "I don't know," replied the inventor, "but it works."

So does dowsing, and its applications may prove to be more extensive than those of electricity. Of all psychic gifts it appears to be the one most readily teachable. Therefore, almost anyone can learn to dowse with varying degrees of success just as one can learn to ride, swim, or play the violin with varying degrees of success.

Let's look at a few successful cases in which the question "Where?" was given a definitive answer.

The late John Shelley, Jr., former president of the American Society of Dowsers, during a summer tour of duty as a reserve naval aviator at the Pensacola Naval Air Station in Florida, began to get on the nerves of his fellow officers with his constant proselytizing about the dowsing art at which he was a master. They decided to put John into what they thought would be "his place."

On the last day of the tour, the reserve pilots lined up at the paymaster's window to collect their checks. When John stepped up to the window, he was puzzled by the guffaws and snickers of his fellow fliers who began to crowd around him in obvious anticipation of what John felt was going to be a joke at his expense.

The paymaster, a smirk on his face, leaned back in his chair. "John, you've been talking so much about locating things with that silly rod of yours," he intoned sarcastically. "Well, now's your chance. Your paycheck is hidden somewhere in this building and, if you want to cash it, you'll just have to find it."

The building in question had three floors each with a long corridor and rooms branching off from them on both sides. Unhesitatingly Shelley whipped out a small plastic Y-rod which he perennially carried in the breast pocket of his tunic and began silently to ask himself a series of specific questions.

The rod dipped. Trailed by his still snickering companions he went up to the second floor. He walked along the corridor until, just as he was passing the door to one of the rooms, the rod dipped again. Shelley strode to the middle of the room, his witnesses surging through the door behind him. Rod in his hands, he rotated in an arc until it dipped a third time. It was pointing straight toward a black briefcase on the edge of a table.

The snickering suddenly stopped as John began to open the briefcase. He looked inside but it contained nothing. The silence was broken with loud laughing. Undaunted, Shelley held the rod over the briefcase. It dipped downward with a violent jerk. Perplexed, Shelley studied the problem for a moment, then noticed a thin gray-black rubber mat underneath the briefcase itself. After removing the case he gingerly took one corner of the mat between thumb and forefinger and raised the mat upwards. There was a U.S. Government check made out to John Shelley, Jr., lying beneath it.

Louis Matacia, a professional land surveyor, was watching a film at the United States Marine Corps base in Quantico, Virginia, where he was attached as a consultant. Portrayed were Marines in Vietnam helplessly looking over an expanse of jungle terrain for openings of enemy underground tunnels while Robert MacNamara, then Secretary of Defense, appealed for new ideas and suggestions that might help to answer this and other insoluble military problems. A skilled dowser, Matacia grew excited and reported to Marine officers that he believed he could find tunnels by using L-rods which he called his "wire rudders."

The skeptical Marines took Matacia to a mockup of a typical Southeast Asian village—complete with thatched huts, sampans, and pig pens—under which ran an unseen network of tunnels, secret rooms, and booby traps. While the officers watched, stupefied, Matacia roved over the village and in less than an hour had plotted many of the underground anomalies on a map. Though all witnesses were clearly impressed, Matacia's technique was not officially adopted by the USMC high command because Defense Department scientists held that "due to excessive false alarms, the technique would not find ready acceptance by field commanders."

In the meantime, Matacia's success at Quantico had spread along the Marine grapevine all the way to the Vietnam battle-front where individual leathernecks began to use L-shaped rods to disclose Vietcong tunnels and weapons caches. These dowsing feats—and later successful demonstrations of the dowsing technique at Camp Pendleton, the USMC base in southern California—were reported by the *New York Times* military expert, Hanson Baldwin, who put on record that the history of "coat hanger dowsing" among U.S. Marines had indeed originated with Louis Matacia.

A no less fruitful application of dowsing to wartime prob-lems, this time at sea, was made when Captain Vo-Sum, South Vietnam Navy, was in charge of communications dur-ing the fifty-six minute long engagement with Chinese naval forces at the Paracel Islands on 19 January 1974. During the battle he lost contact with a patrol craft escort (PCE).

Using only the name of the ship, *Nhat-Tao HO 10*, written on a piece of paper as an identifying key, he brought his pen-dulum into action over a chart and located a preliminary po-sition for the escort vessel at 16° 18′ North and 111° 16′

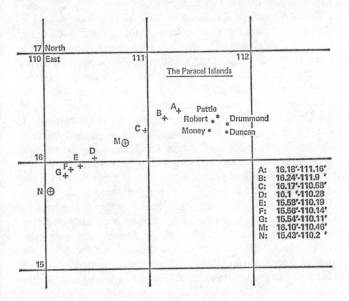

East at 10:00 hours on 20 January (point A on chart). The ship was moving south–southwest.

Having no other information, the operations chief of staff decided to base rescue operations on Vo-Sum's dowsing ability. Twenty-four hours later Vo-Sum's pendulum gave him a second position (point B on chart) with the PCE still drifting in the same southwesterly direction, 240°. Search planes, hampered by overcast skies, at last found the target, disabled by gun fire, right where Vo-Sum had pinpointed it.

On the third day at 10:00 hours the Captain's pendulum gave a reading (point C on the chart). At 18:30 that evening twenty-three crew members, who had abandoned the now-sinking PCE and taken to life rafts, were rescued by the Netherlands merchantman *Kopionella* out of Hong Kong at point M on the chart. They reported that two of their companions had floated away on a wooden raft which Vo-Sum proceeded to dowse, finding its position at point D and heading south–southwest. Vo-Sum gave three more positions (E, F, G on the chart) during the afternoon. At 18:15 hours the raft was sighted by a plane at point N, but the two badly wounded survivors had disappeared.

Scientists such as Dr. Solco W. Tromp, Dutch consultant to UNESCO, Professor Yves Rocard of the University of Paris, and Dr. Zaboj Harvalik, physicist and former Scientific Adviser to the U. S. Army's Advanced Matériel Concepts Agency, have attempted to explain *field-dowsing* as exemplified by Matacia. In their explanations, dowsers' successes are the result of their ability to pick up gradients in the Earth's magnetic field caused, say, by the flowing of a vein of underground water or geological anomalies, be they fissures, faults, deposits of ore, or voids. But such theories fail entirely to explain the *map-dowsing* of a Vo-Sum.

Yet a multitude of proven cases of map-dowsing are on the books going back to the 19th century example of the French clergyman, Abbé Mermet, who located water for monks in Colombia, South America, by using a map of the monastery grounds while sitting in his study in Europe. Another celebrated case of map-dowsing for water was the location on a map of Bermuda—an island which since its settlement in the 1600s had depended on captured rain or imported fresh water

—of successfully drilled points by Henry Gross while in his home town of Portland, Maine. Gross' feats were recorded in three books by the American historical novelist, Kenneth Roberts.

Water has been the principal object of search by dowsing over the centuries. The renowned California dowser Verne Cameron, who learned the art from his grandmother at the age of thirty, spent twenty years trying to get authorities to drill for water in the bottom of Lake Elsinore which had gone dry when the river supplying it was diverted.

State hydro-geologists maintained that no water existed under the former lake. Only after millions of dollars had been spent to pump water into the lake, some of it from as far away as the Rocky Mountains, only to have it subsequently evaporate, were the points indicated by Cameron drilled. Shortly afterwards, yachts and water skiiers were plying the blue surface of Lake Elsinore.

Dowsers and geologists are forever at odds because their theories about the sources of underground water do not accord.

In 1965, Adolph Galli, Chairman of the Water Advisory Committee for Pine Grove, a community in Amador County near the famous Californian "mother lode" country, turned in desperation to a geologist and an engineer to solve his town's shortage of water. The two experts recommended that a nearby hillside could be drilled at a fraction of the cost of importing surface water. But after the drillers had bored down to 157 feet, there was barely enough water for a single family home.

Galli next turned to Jack Livingston, a construction and earthmoving superintendent, who had dowsed for more than a quarter of a century in the difficult hard-rock terrain of the mother lode country, where drilling costs these days are running ten dollars a foot and more.* "It is a lonely task," says Jack, "to have to tell a client that his irrigation water lies two or three hundred feet down because I know that he will waste a lot of money if my prediction is not correct."

Livingston, who has been 98 percent correct and has made

* This is just the drilling cost. Casing a well and other expenses can double the price.

hundreds of water finds, advised Galli to drill down to 130 ft or so in the middle of Pine Grove's park. The drill struck 150 gallons per minute at 136 ft and 200 gallons per minute a little deeper down, which was more than enough for the community's needs at the time.

Livingston's dowsing ability has proved invaluable on construction sites by helping him to avoid cutting expensive cross-country telephone cables. Though assured by telephone inspectors that lines were at a certain depth, Livingston's dowsing has often revealed that the lines were not where the telephone men believed. As proof of his accuracy, Jack reports that there are now several telephone inspectors in California who are dowsers.

Public works employees have used dowsing to save time in many areas. A drainage foreman for the Milford, Conn., Public Works Department told Robert Plimpton, first president of the American Society of Dowsers, that he regularly carried a pair of L-rods in his truck and used them to dowse for underground facilities before calling in his excavation crew.

A few years ago, work at the site of the Pickering, Ontario, nuclear power station had all but come to a halt because power shovels were breaking water pipes and electrical lines lost to memory. Assigned to improvise a way of finding them, field technician, Len Badowich, after unsuccessfully trying commercial adaptations of army mine detectors and gamma-ray radiation devices, heard about L-rods and brought a pair to the site.

While his buddies on the job were laughing their heads off, Badowich worked his way back and forth over the ground and traced the entire length of a subterranean cable. Still laughing, two men grabbed shovels and started digging. At three feet they uncovered the cable exactly where Badowich had predicted it would lie.

Evidence that dowsing is taken with dead seriousness in international industrial circles recently came to light when the worldwide pharmaceutical firm, Hoffmann La Roche and Company, of Basel, Switzerland, devoted an eleven page article to the subject in its own in-house journal, *Roche-Zeitung*, for 1972/74.

Entitled "The Successful Roche Dowsers," the article features the exploits of Dr. P. Treadwell, director of the Roche factory at Sisseln, West Germany, and R. Rupp, an engineer in Roche's headquarters.

Treadwell picked up the dowsing art from a relative who worked for the Zurich waterworks. His first chance to put his skill to a commercially viable test came when he successfully dowsed water for Roche in Basel. On a business trip to India, he discovered that Rupp, then technical manager of the Roche plant at Thana, just north of Bombay, told him that it would be of great advantage if a natural supply of water could be found in this area. When Treadwell's dowsing results were amply confirmed, the previously skeptical Rupp was himself converted to dowsing.

Treadwell, who has found water in Scotland, France, Spain, Japan, Indonesia, Australia, and other countries, says that his Indian success was the most interesting, and spectacular of all. "Conditions were extremely difficult there," he explained, "because subterranean water veins run mainly in extremely narrow rock fissures only 1 to 4 inches wide. One spot I marked had to be drilled through solid basalt, a hard, dense rock. They went down at a rate of only 3 feet per day and after ten weeks made a direct hit at some 215 to 225 feet on a narrow vein which I had previously marked on the surface of the ground. It gave only 4.5 cubic meters of water per hour which is low for industrial use. At Fukuroi, Japan, we got 100 cubic meters."

Treadwell's feats have baffled Swiss scientists and medical specialists. "The pediatrician, Professor Hottinger, once told me, cynic that he is: 'Your dowsing is obviously nonsense!'" said Treadwell. "Whereupon I put a dowsing rod in his hands and walked with him over known dowsing zones. He said: 'I sense the pull of the rod, but I don't know why.' This is about as far as any of us has gone by way of explanation. Though we are assured the phenomenon is real, we just can't get to the bottom of it."

Especially baffling to scientists is the ability of dowsers to traverse the same terrain under which an electric cable, a sewer pipe, a water pipe, and a vein of flowing water might lie and pick up, on each pass, one of the four while not reacting to the three others. In so doing, the dowser is answering not only the question "Where?" but also "What?" as well. When they are "hot"—dowsers have various batting averages just like baseball players—dowsers can also, in the case of water, answer the questions "How much?" in terms of flow per minute or "What kind?" in terms of purity, potability, and other characteristics.

Nowhere in science are the questions "What?," "Where?," and "How old?" more pertinent than in archaeology. From the work of a Scottish general and a Soviet engineer it appears that the systematic recovery of material evidence from man's life and culture may profit by an alliance with dowsing to greatly speed up what traditionally has been an arduous process of search.

Major General J. Scott Elliot, after retiring from the British Army, took up a second career as an amateur archaeologist in his native Dumfriesshire, a Scots border county with coasts washed by the Solway Firth. When he came across Viscount Henri de France's *The Elements of Dowsing,* he decided the art might prove useful and, with the assistance of a local water diviner, taught himself to dowse.

After six months of diligent practice during which he endured condescending smiles from his family and odd looks from his colleagues and friends, he began to get positive results by dowsing at excavation sites where his predictions could be tested.

In October 1965, a year before the general became president of the British Society of Dowsers, the owner of a farm near Dumfries reported to him that in one of his fields a small black patch appeared whenever it was plowed. The general's dowsing investigation in the field itself suggested the presence of an archaeologically interesting remain which led to excavation in the spring of 1966. In his official report, Scott Elliot stated that his dowsing had discovered an early Bronze Age fire pit "not recognizable as a known form."

When news of the general's exploits began to circulate in the United Kingdom, he was soon led further afield. In 1968, the owner of a cottage in Swinbrook near Oxford asked him to check whether there might not have been an old habitation site in her garden as suggested to her by, as the general put it, "what we Scots would call a 'fey woman.'"

Though, during his visit at Swinbrook, Scott Elliot could find nothing visible on the surface of the garden grounds to indicate the presence of an excavatable site, after returning home with a map of the property, he dowsed it with a pendulum and revealed what appeared to be a 35 × 60 foot underground site under the garden lawn. Digs in 1970 unearthed several floors, one, to quote the general's report: "beautifully laid and firm . . . the remains of what is thought to have been a hearth, a line of stake holes well cut into sandstone and accurately spaced, and two sharp-ended ivory tools, beautifully shaped and highly polished." The site, added the general, "was found entirely by dowsing means."

Most recently the general map-dowsed the garden and orchard of a manor house at Chieveley in Berkshire to predict that a road older than those of Roman times, an Iron Age ditch, a series of Roman ditches, and the remains of Saxon and Norman cultures would all be found underground. Excavation in 1973 and 1974 has not only confirmed these predictions but also the presence of specific artifacts carefully plotted, before the digging began, on maps of different scales in the general's workroom.

"The main point of my work at Chieveley," stressed the general, "is that up to the time map-dowsing pinpointed it, this site was completely unknown to archaeology."

Over the past several years Scott Elliot has been training a few students in the art of archaeological dowsing. Similar training is proceeding in the Soviet Union where, according to Alexander I. Pluzhnikov, a docent and Candidate of Technical Sciences (a degree equivalent to the American Ph.D.) dowsing, or the "biophysical method" as it is currently known in the USSR, is being used by him and his colleagues to "search for and describe the contours of subterranean architectural and historical objects, no traces of which show above the surface of the ground."

The difference between the Russian approach to archaeological dowsing and that of General Scott Elliot and his followers appears to be that the Soviets dowse only in the field or at the sites themselves.

Pluzhnikov states that Russian dowsers have found *cavernous anomalies* such as passages and chambers, heating ducts, former ditches and holes, and the hitherto unknown mass graves of French soldiers, the latter at the famous Borodino battlefield where Napoleon's onslaught against Moscow was so bloodily delayed in 1812. *Stone anomalies,* among them the remnants of walls, pillars, and foundations and *water anomalies,* especially those threatening to deteriorate an underground structure, have also been speedily located with the dowsing art.

Soviet archaeological dowsers, says Pluzhnikov, work over extensive terrain while seated in motor vehicles moving at ten to thirty kilometers per hour. When an anomaly is detected in this way, it is then studied in detail on foot.

Pluzhnikov refers to the importance of the "mental convention" when he states that it is "essential that the operator should clearly understand the physical nature of the anomaly he is looking for and concentrate upon it." Cold winds, illness, bad moods, and negative or idiotic remarks or questions from casual observers detrimentally affect a dowser's ability, stresses Pluzhnikov.

At the Iosif Volokamsky monastery near Moscow, the Kruitsky Palace in the Soviet capital itself, the Kremlins in the cities of Serpukhov and Mozhaisk, and other areas dowsing has been used to pinpoint the outlines of former fortifications and towers, moats, and formerly existing passages, buildings, and cemeteries, all below ground.

A dowsing study of the old estate of Tsar Boris Godunov (1552–1605) verified data from Polish sources which up to then had been considered by Russian historians as spurious and came up with what Pluzhnikov terms "startling results." The Russian archaeological dowser adds that the whole dowsing survey of the entire estate took only eight hours, though without the dowsing's assistance, it could have taken weeks.

The Russians also appear to have been the first to give serious recognition to dowsing as a method for speeding up the search for mineral ores. In March 1971, the Central Administration of the Scientific–Technical Society for the Instrument and Appliance Industry sponsored a seminar on the "biophysical effect" (dowsing signal). One hundred twenty-four specialists in geology, geophysics, mineralogy, hydrogeology, geochemistry, physics, radioelectronics, cybernetics, biology, physiology, and other disciplines came from fourteen cities and over forty research institutes to attend.

A summary of the seminar indicated that dowsing had allowed the conventional amount of boring for gold deposits in the northern Caucasus to be reduced by thirty percent. In Karelia, near Finland, areas where dowsers found anomalies produced over sixty percent more indications of rare-earth-bearing deposits than those where no such anomalies were dowsed. In the central Asian Soviet republic of Kazakhstan, reads the summary, "the elimination for boring purposes of areas in which the dowsing effect was lacking permitted a reduction of overall drilling of some thirty-five to forty percent and greatly raised its effectiveness."

Soviet dowsers have been taken up in airplanes and helicopters flying eight hundred to one thousand feet above the ground at speeds up to two hundred miles per hour and have made interesting finds about the macro-geology of hitherto unexplored areas. The seminar recommended that lectures on dowsing as a geological technique be introduced into the advanced curriculum at departments of geology and geophysics in Moscow State University, the Leningrad Mining Institute and the Tomsk Polytechnical Institute. All this while the United States Geological Survey still publishes an informational pamphlet stating that dowsing, as far as scientists are concerned, is "wholly discredited," and American institutes of technology ignore the subject as if hoping, thereby, that it would vanish.

At the First International Congress on Psychotronics held in Prague, Czechoslovakia, in June 1973, Professor Alexander G. Bakirov, a Doctor of Mineralogy, came all the way from central Siberia to review the geological possibilities of the biophysical method. His report stated in part: "In the USSR the biophysical method is used to solve various geological problems in the deposits of polymetals, gold sulfides, gold–quartz, copper–molybdenum, copper–bismuth, rare metals, tin–tungsten, tin–polymetals, monomineral tin, magnetite, sidertics, bauxites, muscovites, and others."

That the Soviets are seriously investigating all aspects of dowsing as a tool for geological prospecting is further illustrated by a special year-long research program launched in

February 1975. The goal of the study is to determine whether dowsers respond differently depending on the time of day or year. This effort to ascertain possible diurnal and seasonal variations in the "biophysical effect" will use some fifty dowser subjects all over the Soviet Union, from Kaunas, in Lithuania, to Magadan, in northeast Siberia, and from Norilsk, on the shores of the Arctic Ocean, to Bukhara, near the Afghan border.

In addition to assisting human beings in their search for clues to man's past and for natural resources, dowsing is slowly gaining recognition as a means to improve the human environment, external and internal. It would seem that healing, or medicine, a word which is only the derivative of the Latin verb, "to heal," will profit immeasurably from an association with dowsing.

In October 1974, a 20th anniversary meeting was held in Paris by the *Syndicat National des Radiesthesistes,* a union of eighty dowsers who earn their living full time by diagnosing the ills of patients and prescribing remedies, all with the help of a pendulum. The union is officially registered with the French Ministry of Labor.

Monsieur Robert Felsenhardt, a Parisian businessman who edits *Radiesthesie Magazine,* the leading French monthly on dowsing, became interested in its medical application when, as advisor to a medical insurance company, he received a letter of complaint from one of the company's female clients. The woman stated that, though the company had paid out hundreds of dollars' worth of doctors' bills for treatment which had failed to alleviate her suffering, it had refused to cover the minimal sum charged by a practitioner, who had at last cured her, because the therapeutist was not a medical doctor, but a medical dowser.

Felsenhardt's interest led to his meeting the Reverend Père Jean Jurion, a Catholic priest, who recently published *La Radiesthésie Médicale,* a book based on half a lifetime of experience as a medical dowser. Jurion's prominence in his field has repeatedly brought him before magistrates at the behest of jealous physicians and he has been fined many times and even jailed. Though hundreds of patients he made well have testified in his defense, his sentences were imposed not, as one judge put it, "for curing people but for treating them." Jurion, undaunted, carries on with the blessing of his ecclesiastical superiors who see in his work God's will being done.

The diagnostic aspect of medical dowsing is performed in a variety of ways. One British medical dowser with a proven record of success, Malcolm Rae, using only a sample of hair from a patient as a key, works over a semicircular pattern with concentric half-rings, each bearing a spectrum of information. The pendulum swings on an azimuth to determine which part of the information applies to the patient. Prescriptions, many of which are homeopathic, as are Father Jurion's, are selected in a similar manner.†

Rae teamed with another medical dowser, Aubrey Westlake, M.D., to write a brilliant pamphlet on the scope and limitations of dowsing in the modern world. Author of two remarkable books, *The Pattern of Health* and *Life Threatened*, Westlake, who looks and acts much younger than his actual age of eighty-five, after practicing standard medicine for thirty years, was put in touch with the British Medical Society for the Study of Radiesthesia founded before World War II by a fellow physician, Guyon Richards. In his home near Fordingbridge, in Hampshire, Westlake stated that he is convinced that, were enough trained medical dowsers available, the hospitals of the world could be emptied of more than half of their occupants, including those with psychiatric maladies.

One of the most far-reaching and intriguing discoveries in medical dowsing is that of harmful radiation coming out of the ground at places where water veins flow, especially where they cross. German researchers have known about such emissions since the work of Dr. J. Walther, a professor of geology, who in the 1920s made correlations between the health of human beings and water flowing beneath those areas over which they spent extended periods of time, either working at desks or in bed. From his study of over 450 persons,

† The French engineer and dowser, André Simoneton, has spent a lifetime dowsing the freshness and health-giving properties of foods which opens up another whole horizon on health. His story is summed up in the book *The Secret Life of Plants* by Peter Tompkins and the author.

Walther came to the conclusion that certain areas were definitely harmful in that they consistently produced cases of degenerative disease such as cancer or arthritis. For such areas he coined the term "geopathogenic zones."

A German-born engineer, Egon Eckert, now retired in Newtown, Connecticut, has written a historical note on the extensive study of these zones. He points to experiments with mice placed in cages over geopathogenic, and neutral, zones, performed in both Germany and Switzerland, which have indicated a link between the dangerous zones and the incidence of disease in the animals.

The research in the German-speaking countries has also been supported by the findings of British dowsers. Over forty years ago the English dowsing expert W. H. Trinder wrote: "There seems to be very little doubt that the rays given off by subterranean water are, if continuous contact is maintained with them, definitely harmful to human beings and plants."

A compatriot, Marguerite Maury, echoes Trinder: "Whatever may be the cause of telluric emissions . . . the effects produced on the health of human beings and animals is nearly always harmful. If there are several streams superimposed, the emission at the surface will be particularly bad."

These conclusions have been supported over recent years by the findings of physicists, Tromp and Rocard, who showed that water flowing underground creates a weak electromagnetic field. Two other scientists, Madeleine Barnothy of the University of Illinois, and A. S. Presman of the University of Moscow, have done research which suggests very weak magnetic fields may cumulatively have greater biophysical significance, over the long run, than strong fields.‡

After becoming acquainted with these findings, Herbert Douglas, a Shaftsbury, Vermont dowser, decided to study persons afflicted with painful and persistent arthritis in the region around his home. Over several years he carefully checked eighteen cases and found, to quote him: "not a sin-

‡ In early 1975, a book, *Geomagnitnoe Pole i Zhizn* (*The Geomagnetic Field and Life*), appeared in Moscow. Written by Dr. Alexander T. Dubrov of the USSR Academy of Sciences' Institute of Earth Physics, it includes over six hundred references dealing with the effect of the Earth's magnetic field on living things.

gle case of arthritis or rheumatism where the person has not substantially or completely improved when they moved to a place that was free of crossing or intersecting of underground veins."

Douglas sent a report of his results to the National Institute of Arthritis, Metabolism and Digestive Diseases in Washington, D.C., only to receive a reply that though his findings "certainly are intriguing and seem to warrant additional investigation," the physicians and scientists at the institute were "in the midst of their own research projects and can spare little time to undertake other studies."

Douglas recently stated that he has begun to check certain cases of cancer in the same region and found evidence that intersecting veins lay precisely under not only the person so afflicted but under the very organ or limb in which the cancer first developed.

The possible applications of dowsing, only partially surveyed herein, seem endless. But in a world faced with annihilation through pollution, contamination, and radiation, unleashed by our eager technologies, dowsing may come up with quick and reliable answers to problems that ordinary scientific methods are incapable of dealing with fast enough to be of real help.

As Dr. Westlake has written: "I believe that the rediscovery of the radiesthetic faculty in these modern times is not fortuitous, but that it has been vouchsafed to us by Providence to enable us to cope with the difficult and dangerous stage in human development which lies immediately ahead, for it gives indirect access to the supersensible world, more particularly to the etheric, thus raising our level of consciousness and extending our awareness and knowledge. The faculty should be regarded as a special and peculiar sense halfway between our ordinary physical senses which apprehend the material world, and our to-be-developed future occult senses which, in due course, will apprehend the supersensible world direct."

Terms Connected with Dowsing

DOWSING a word for the art of searching, with a hand-held instrument such as a Y-shaped rod, a pair of L-shaped rods, a wand or a pendulum—for anything. This word was probably born into the English language where miners were introduced from Germany in the reign of Queen Elizabeth I. In all probability it comes from the German word: *Deuten* for which a good dictionary gives the following meanings: to explain, to expound, to interpret, to point to, to point at, to signify, to bode, to auger —depending upon exactly how it is being used.

SOURCELLERIE an archaic French word for "water finding" stemming from the word SOURCE, or "spring," "source of underground water." Though this word is hardly ever used in contemporary French, the word SOURCIER is commonly used to denote "water diviner" or "dowser."

RADIESTHESIE a word coined in the 1930s by the Abbé Bouly in France. It is taken from a Latin root for "radiation" and a Greek root for "perception" and thus means literally the "perception of radiations." This literal meaning may in fact be misleading but Bouly hoped that by inventing a "scientific" word, the art of dowsing would be more palatable as an object of study by scientists. The word is awkward, hard to convert into a verb in French. It spread into English as radiesthesia. At one time the Journal of the British Society of Dowsers was called *Radio-Perception*. The word has been adopted all over the European continent with the exception of the so-called "socialist" countries which have adopted a newly coined Russian word:

BIOFIZICHESKII METOD or "biophysical method." The old Russian term for dowsing was *lozakhodstvo* or "the art of going with the rod." This ties into the word *rutengänger* in German (from which it probably came) and which means "goer with a rod." The term *radiesthesie* has replaced the longer appellation "Ruten- und Pendelkunde" (The art of the Use of the Dowsing Rod and Pendulum) in Germany.

RADIONICS a word for the art of searching, using a black box composed of dials and circuitry. The term was coined in England by George and Marjorie De la Warr. The term replaced the former "Electronic Reactions" of Dr. Albert Abrams at the start of the 20th century and the "Radiovision" of Dr. Ruth Drown, one of Dr. Abrams' pupils in the period from 1925 to 1950. Radionics boxes are varied, some working with electrical current, some without.

REFERENCES

Bakirov, Aleksandr G., "The Geological Possibilities of the Biophysical Method," *The American Dowser*, August 1974, pp. 110–112 (translated from the Russian by Cyril Muromcew and Christopher Bird).

Barnothy, Madeleine F., *Biological Effects of Magnetic Fields*, 2 volumes, New York: Plenum Press, 1964, 1969.

Bird, Christopher, "Dowsing in the United States of America: History, Past Achievements and Current Research," *The American Dowser*, August 1973, pp. 105–120; "Dowsing in the USSR," *ibid.*, August 1972, pp. 90–96; "Dowsing in Vietnam: The Exploits of Commander Vo-Sum, Vietnamese Navy," *ibid.*, August 1974, pp. 90–96.

"Das Unerklärliche, hier wird's Ereignis: Die Erfolgreichen Roche-Wünschelruten-Wassersucher" (Here the Unexplainable Really Happens: The Successful Roche Dowsers), *Roche-Zeitung*, 1972/4, F. Hoffmann-La Roche and Co., A. G., Basel, Switzerland, October 1972, pp. 65–75.

Douglas, Herbert, "Taking Another Look at the Arthritis–Dowsing Link," *Bennington Banner* (Vermont), 17 December 1973, p. 5 (full page).

Dubrov, Aleksandr P., *Geomagnitoe Pole i Zhizn'* (The Geomagnetic Field and Life), Leningrad, Gidrometeoizdat, 1974.

Eckert, Egon, "Soil Influences and Cancer," *The American Dowser,* November 1974, pp. 142–149.

Harvalik, Z. V., The "Biomagnetic Effect"—*Scientific Studies Showing that Magnetic Fields May Be a Mechanism for the Dowsing Reaction* (*a series of research reports*), The American Society of Dowsers, Inc., Danville, Vermont.

Jurion, Jean, *La Radiesthésie Médicale* (Medical Radiesthesia), Paris: Soprodé, 1973.

MacLean, Gordon, *Dowsing: An Introduction to an Ancient Practice,* self-published, 1971 (obtainable from the author at 30 Day Street, South Portland, Maine).

Maury, Marguerite, *How to Dowse,* London: G. Bell and Sons, Ltd.

Pluzhnikov, Aleksandr I., "Possibilities for and Results of the Use of the Biophysical Method (BPM) in Researching and Restoring Historical and Architectural Monuments," *The American Dowser,* August 1974, pp. 116–118 (translated from the Russian by Cyril Muromcew and Christopher Bird).

Presman, A. S., *Electromagnetic Fields and Life,* New York: Plenum Press, 1970.

Roberts, Kenneth, *Henry Gross and His Dowsing Rod,* New York: Doubleday, 1952.

Rocard, Y., *Le Signal du Sourcier* (The Dowser's Signal), Paris: Dunod, 1964, 167 pp.

Scott Elliot, J. Major General, "An Early Bronze Age Fire Pit at Townfoot Farm, by Glencaple," *The Transactions of the Dumfriesshire and Galloway Natural History and Antiquarian Society,* 3rd ser., Vol. XLIX, 1972, pp. 20–23.

Tomlinson, H., *The Divination of Disease: A Study in Radiesthesia,* Wayside, Grayshott, Hindhead, Surrey: Health Science Press, no date, 209 pp.

Trinder, W. H., *Dowsing,* Guildford, England: Billing and Sons, Ltd., 1939, 1962.

Vtoroi Nauchno-Tekhnicheskii Seminar po Biofizicheskomu

Effektu (Second Scientific Technical Seminar on the Biophysical Effect), 161607, 10 May 1971, order number 2097, printed in 300 copies by the Khozu Typographers of the USSR Ministry of Communications, Gorky Street, No. 7, Moscow.

Westlake, Aubrey, *The Pattern of Health: A Search for a Greater Understanding of the Life Force in Health and Disease,* New York: Devin-Adair, 1961, 180 pp.; *Life Threatened: Menace and Way Out,* London: Stuart and Watkins, 1967, 178 pp.

Westlake, Aubrey, and Rae, Malcolm, *The Radiesthetic (or Dowsing) Faculty: Two Lectures on the Role, Scope and Limitations of the Faculty in the Modern World,* privately printed, Godshill, Fordingbridge, England: Sandy Balls, 1973, 35 pp.

Wethered, Vernon D., *The Practice of Medical Radiesthesia,* London: L. N. Fowler and Co., Ltd., 1967, 150 pp.

29.

Radionics—Science of the Future

EDWARD W. RUSSELL

I.

Radionics, a word coined about 1935, is the modern name for an ancient medical art. It is based on the fact that the human mind can be attuned to detect characteristic emanations from all forms of organic or inorganic matter. Radionics—usually assisted by instruments to help focus the mind of the operator —uses the superconscious mind to diagnose and treat diseases in humans, animals, and crops.

Its development in an instrumented form dates from the basic discoveries of Dr. Albert Abrams of San Francisco just after the turn of the century. We owe these discoveries to a most unusual and fortunate combination of circumstances:

First, Abrams had had an exceptional medical training. After qualifying to receive a medical diploma in California before he was old enough, he learned German and graduated in medicine with the highest possible honors from Heidelberg University.

Second, he had inherited great wealth and could afford to spend a long time doing postgraduate work in Heidelberg, Berlin, Paris, Vienna, and London under the foremost researchers of the day. Later, his wealth allowed him to finance his own researches and contemptuously ignore those who accused him of using his discoveries to make money.

Third, he became the pupil and, later, the friend of Hermann L. von Helmholtz, one of the great scientific figures of

"Radionics—Science of the Future" by Edward W. Russell is an original article written especially for this volume and is printed by permission of the author.

the time, who aroused his interest in the burgeoning science of physics. This stimulated him to try to correlate the laws of biology with the laws of physics.

Last—and perhaps most important—Abrams by nature was an exceptionally perceptive and persistent observer. Little escaped his trained observation and he counted no effort too great in trying to find the cause of some phenomenon he had noticed.

In 1910, while examining a patient with a cancerous ulcer on his lip, Abrams detected a small area of the abdomen which yielded a dull note under percussion with his fingers. After further tests he made the remarkable discovery that the dull note could only be detected when the patient was facing west. This suggested that he was dealing with a phenomenon, perhaps of an "electronic" nature, which was influenced by the Earth's magnetic field.

This led the ever-ingenious Abrams to connect his patient with a wire to a healthy young man, and he made the further discovery that the cancerous "emanations" from the patient induced a dull note in the same area in the young man's abdomen. Later he found that the presence of the patient was unnecessary—a sample of his blood was sufficient to induce a reflex action in the abdominal muscles and to produce a dull note.

Convinced by now that he was on the track of something important which might help him to correlate the laws of biology and medicine, he made test after test, using patients suffering from a variety of diseases. He found that each disease yielded a dull note in one specific area of the abdomen; and he thought that he had found a new tool for diagnosis until he observed that samples from syphilitic patients yielded dull notes in the same area as a sample from cancerous patients.

Undaunted—and believing that the "emanations" from diseased blood were electronic—he introduced a variable resistance box into the circuit. By varying the resistance, he found he could "tune out" different diseases and could assign to each a value in ohms. He named his discovery "the electronic reactions of Abrams" or "E.R.A." and had one of the finest instrument makers of those days make most accurate resistance-boxes. For many years these were used by Abrams and his pupils in the diagnosis of disease.

Some of his pupils found the art of percussing the surface of the abdomen difficult to acquire. For them Abrams found an alternative method: stroking the surface of the abdomen with a glass rod. When the emanations produced a reflex in the muscles under the skin, the rod would encounter resistance and the skin would tend to pucker.

Early in his experiments it occurred to Abrams to try the effects of well-known antidotes for certain diseases. When, for example, he put a sample of quinine into his apparatus along with a specimen of malarial blood, he made another basic discovery: the radiations from the quinine neutralized the radiations from the malarial blood and eliminated the dull note.

This led him to apply E.R.A. to the treatment of disease. With the aid of one of the foremost radio experts of the time, Abrams devised an instrument he called the "oscilloclast." This was connected to the patient by a wire and electrode and produced intermittent negative potentials and radio frequencies. In circuit was a resistance-box tuned to the value in ohms of the specific for the disease, which he had determined with his diagnostic instrument. Abrams and his pupils had great success in treating patients with the oscilloclast and the instrument was in use for many years.

With tireless energy, Abrams worked on his discoveries up to the night before his sudden death in 1924. He made many discoveries, the significance of which have yet to be fully explored. But, despite vast expenditures of time and money, he was never able to find an effective substitute for the human mind and body as a detector. Though substitutes for the abdomen have been found and are in use today, in every case the human mind and nervous system are essential.

Fortunately, imaginative doctors from all over the world came to San Francisco to take postgraduate courses in E.R.A. Thus, Abrams' influence extended far beyond his own clinic and others were inspired to follow in his footsteps. Some of them have made great contributions to the development of what has come to be called radionics. But the present science owes its origin to the basic discoveries described above, which might never have been made but for the exceptionally perceptive genius of Albert Abrams.

II.

Most of the medical doctors who had taken Abrams' postgraduate courses were so successful in diagnosis and treatment and so busy with grateful patients that they had little time or inclination to do much research.

But the publicity given to the "electronic reactions of Abrams" had excited the interest of imaginative people outside the medical profession and had encouraged them to experiment for themselves. Foremost among these was Ruth Drown, who modified Abrams' instruments and was probably the first to use the now-standard rubber detector plate instead of the human abdomen. She eventually discarded resistances and inductances and was the first to rely on a rotary pattern of dials to tune the mysterious energies. She was the first to use in regular practice the distant treatment of patients. She was the first to realize the importance of treating the endocrine glands, and was also the first to obtain photographs of the *internal* organs of her patients by means of her instruments.

After Ruth Drown, radionics owes its next great impetus to a pioneer of radio, Thomas Galen Hieronymus,* formerly of Kansas City, who produced some ingenious instruments which used vacuum tubes for "amplification" and condensers, instead of resistances, for "tuning."

To Hieronymus belongs the honor of being awarded one of the most unusual patents ever granted by the United States Patent Office. This patent—No. 2,482,773 granted in 1949— describes an instrument for the "detection of emanations from materials and measurement of the volumes thereof." This included a radio-frequency amplifier, variable condensers, and a noninductive resistance. But the heart of it was a prism through which the emanations passed. As a detector, it used a rubbing-plate similar to Ruth Drown's, which, by

* See Chapter 30. *Editors.*

this time, many were using instead of a human abdomen. When the plate, usually rubber, is stroked, the fingers encounter tactile resistance or "a stick" when the emanation is tuned in.

In his patent, Hieronymus states that "radiations from each of the known elements of matter produce some form of energy, probably electrons." But his use of a prism by which "the radiations may be refracted, focused, diffracted, or otherwise manipulated in the same manner as the radiations of the visible spectrum" suggested to some who read the patent that the "electronic reactions of Abrams" were not electronic at all in the accepted sense.

To clarify the theory on which the invention is predicated, Hieronymus described an experiment, which any gardener can duplicate. He planted seeds in a darkened basement room from which he led wires to plates outside the building and exposed to light. He reported:

> Such of the known elements as are required to impart normal characteristics to plants were apparently fed thereto by having the radiations of the elements from the light conducted to the plants through the wires and associated electrodes.
>
> The treated plants were relatively healthy but the control plant (to which no wire had been connected) assumed the characteristics of growing vegetation which has been deprived of the elements in natural light. Particularly was the control plant devoid of chlorophyl while the remaining plants were green.

Publication of this patent had two important consequences. When Hieronymus gave a copy to John Campbell, a trained and imaginative scientist and editor of *Analog* Magazine, he duplicated Hieronymus' apparatus, found that it worked and in the early 1950s gave it a favorable report in his magazine. This brought a great demand for copies of the patent and many people started to experiment for themselves.

Another consequence resulted from a hint to John Campbell by Arthur M. Young, president of the Foundation for the Study of Consciousness, which had already carried out extensive investigations of radionics. Young told Campbell that the instrument was merely a device to help concentrate the mind on diagnosis and that: "the true reference is the operator's own organs. The instrument is the human organism."

Acting on this hint, Campbell made a simplified model of the Hieronymus apparatus which consisted *solely* of a circuit diagram with *symbols* of its components—a symbol for instance, of a prism rotated by a dial. He found that this symbolic design worked as well as the actual equipment!

Young, therefore, was probably the first to realize—and Campbell the first to demonstrate—that *mind and pattern are the key to radionics,* and that the type of instrument used is of secondary importance because the instrument only serves to focus the thoughts of the operator.

Essentially, a radionic diagnosis is a measurement of the disorganization of the organism—in part or in whole. It is a measurement of the extent to which the organism deviates from the normal, and this deviation can be represented by the rotation of numbered dials or by a diagram. It is *the position* of the dials, relative to the normal, that indicates to the mind of the operator the degree of deviation, and a diagram can serve the same purpose, depending on the preference of the operator.

Most find numbered dials the easiest way to focus their thoughts, and it does not matter whether the dials operate a resistance or—as in the case of the De la Warr instruments—a helix. All that matters is their position, relative to normal. For those with a mathematical bent, a diagram is preferable.

Over the years Hieronymus has done much other important and interesting work. But perhaps his greatest contribution was to stimulate widespread interest in radionics. Hieronymus was not afraid to admit frankly the importance of the human element; his patent states that his apparatus "preferably relies upon the element of touch and, therefore, the skill of the operator." With this statement, then, and because his patent led John Campbell to demonstrate the true basis of radionics, the Hieronymus patent may be said to mark the beginning of the modern concept of radionics.

III.

Meanwhile another development of the new science—the use of radionics in agriculture—had also been born in the United States. As agricultural radionics can eliminate pests without pesticides and stimulate the growth of crops without fertilizers, it is likely to prove at least as important as medical radionics.

Among those whose imagination had been stimulated by Abrams' discoveries was a young man, Curtis P. Upton, son of an associate of Thomas A. Edison. Upton had inherited his father's inventive mind and when he heard about Abrams' work, it occurred to him that these discoveries must apply to *all* living things and that it should be possible to diagnose and to treat the diseases of plants and crops. So he designed his own equipment and with the help of an electronic engineer, William J. Knuth, he modified Abrams' oscilloclast and substituted a radio-frequency transmitter.

Instead of Abrams' "rates" in ohms and dial settings, Upton used samples of certain chemicals and other "reagents." He seems to have found these mainly by trial and error; he would put a sample of the diseased plant or crop into his diagnostic apparatus and try various "reagents" until one eliminated the "stick" on his detector which showed that it was an antidote to the disease. Some of these were chemically quite different from commercial pesticides.

Instead of the spot of blood that Abrams used with human patients, Upton would take a leaf from the diseased plant and a sprinkle of the selected reagent and put both on the input plate of the transmitter. The leaf linked the curative emanations of the reagent to the affected plant, which could be many miles from the transmitter.

Then he made one of the most remarkable discoveries in radionics—a discovery which even today is one of the most difficult things about the science to understand or explain. To treat a large area of crops he found that a photographic negative, taken from the air, served as effective a link between the transmitter and the crop as a leaf would with an individual plant. He called this negative a "key" and found that it would fit only one "lock."

He would mark out an area in a field with white sheets which would show up on the negative as black spots. Next, on the negative he would cut out and burn all the film outside the marked area. He would then find that only that part of the field represented by the marked area was benefited by his radionic treatment. Everything outside and in adjoining areas continued pest-ridden.

This must be one of the most ingenious "controls" ever devised in science. In hundreds of large-scale experiments it not only proved the efficacy of Upton's treatments to him and also to farmers but also shed some light on the mysterious nature of radionic emanations.

Upton used his instruments in two ways. If he wanted merely to stimulate the growth of a plant or a crop, he would put the leaf, or the "key," on the input plate and switch on the transmitter for five or ten minutes. This was repeated once a week—more often in the growing season. In some mysterious way, the "radiation pattern" of the leaf or the key would be strengthened and transmitted back to the plant or crop. This invigorated them: the green color would become darker and new growth longer than in the case of untreated plants.

If the tree or plant were infested with, say, aphids, Upton would put a leaf on the input plate with a sprinkle of the appropriate reagent and switch on the instrument. This transmitted the "radiation pattern" of the reagent to the plant and the insects were either killed or left the plant, usually within forty-eight hours. The instrument could be operated from a distance of many miles.

If he wanted to treat a field infested with, say, Japanese beetles, he would take an aerial photo of the whole area and trim the negative so that only the area to be treated remained. He would then take a sprinkle of a suitable reagent and place it with the key-emulsion side down on the input plate and switch on the instrument for a few minutes. He found that several of these brief treatments sufficed to kill or drive away eighty to ninety percent of the beetles in the treated area, while they continued to infest the control area or adjoining untreated fields in their former numbers.

It should be emphasized that there is never any physical contact between the reagent and the crop: the connection is purely radionic. It is therefore unnecessary to cover the soil with large and expensive quantities of chemicals which may have unfortunate side effects.

One of the early successes of Upton and Knuth was in the elimination of the plume moth from the crops of forty-four California artichoke growers. They treated these for a modest charge on the basis that if there was no control of the moth, there was no fee. Results were so good that all the growers willingly paid.

In 1947, Upton was visited by his old friend and Princeton roommate, Howard H. Armstrong, of Newport, Pa., also the son of an inventor, to whom he demonstrated his equipment and results. On his return to Pennsylvania, Armstrong aroused the interest and enlisted the support of a member of one of Pennsylvania's best-known people, Brigadier General Henry M. Gross. He in turn interested a friend, Roland M. Benjamin, Executive Secretary of the Pennsylvania Farm Bureau.

Upton, Knuth, and Armstrong had already formed a corporation called UKACO to develop Upton's discoveries. Gross and Benjamin then chartered the Homeotronic Foundation—a nonprofit organization to advance the scientific work of Upton. As the Foundation could not make a profit, General Gross and his friends soon found it necessary to form the Radiurgic Corporation which could operate as a business and treat crops on a commercial basis.

The corporation's treatments of crops were so successful that there was a great demand for its services, always on a basis of no results, no fee. And nominal fees were set at a small percentage of any *increase* in the cash value of crops that resulted from Upton's treatment—an increase that could be measured by comparison with adjacent untreated crops. Most of the hard-boiled Pennsylvania-Dutch farmers felt that they had had good value for money and paid willingly.

Space will not permit a long list of the practical successes achieved by Upton and his colleagues, all of them attested by such independent witnesses as B. A. Rockwell, Director of Research of the Pennsylvania Farm Bureau Cooperative Association. Some of these, however, have been published and are available to the interested reader.†

To summarize a long and eventually sad story, the Radiurgic Corporation was so successful that it aroused the alarm and powerful opposition of the pesticide and fertilizer industries, which the corporation, with its limited resources, was unable to combat. For this and other reasons, including the deaths of Upton and other principals, the work of the corporation came to an end.

But the indomitable General Gross, though nearing ninety, does not give up easily. He still heads the Homeotronic Foundation and has arranged for its scientific work to be carried on by the Mankind Research Foundation of Washington, D.C.‡

With present public uneasiness about pesticides and concern for the environment, with the rocketing costs of fertilizers and with the need to feed an expanding world population, agricultural radionics will be revived in a more sympathetic and receptive "climate." And past successes can not only be duplicated but greatly enhanced.

Meanwhile, the pioneer work of the Homeotronic Foundation has furnished important confirmation of the value of radionics not only to agriculture but also to medicine. It has provided convincing evidence that radionic principles are effective—evidence attested by reliable independent witnesses. It has also disposed of the criticism, sometimes leveled at radionics, that it is "all in the imagination." Indeed, it is unlikely that a large number of practical farmers could have "imagined" the benefits to their crops and even more improbable that millions of Japanese beetles and corn ear worms could have "imagined" some reason for beating a hasty retreat.

† Edward W. Russell, *Report on Radionics—Science of the Future* (London: Neville Spearman, 1973).
‡ See Appendix III for address. *Editors.*

IV.

In the middle of World War II, a lucky chance gave radionics an historic boost. Some of Ruth Drown's instruments had been used in England for several years but, after war broke out, no more could be imported. At this point it occurred to someone who wanted another to ask George De la Warr, just discharged from the Army for asthma, to copy the Drown instrument.

Nobody could have been better qualified. A trained civil engineer with a knowledge of fine instruments, De la Warr had "inventive ability amounting to near genius"—in the words of Judge Christmas Humphreys, Queen's Counsel, who was one of his greatest supporters. De la Warr had already experimented with homeopathy and suspected that there must be subtle, healing forces in nature to be discovered.

With Ruth Drown's permission, De la Warr copied her instrument and while doing so his inventive mind naturally suggested improvements. Thereafter De la Warr, aided by his especially talented wife, Marjorie, picked up the radionic ball and ran away with it. For nearly thirty years, until his death in 1969, he worked ceaselessly, devising innumerable radionic experiments and improvements, which even two books* and numerous papers have not fully described. De la Warr "had an idea a minute," as his wife once remarked to the writer.

Only the highlights of his monumental work can be sketched here. He soon discarded the resistances, inductances, and condensers of previous instruments. Instead, he chose and standardized (for tuning) flat strips of spring metal, formed into a nearly complete circle, over which traveled a sliding contact rotated by a marked dial. He improved the rubbing-plate detector and introduced the use of small bar magnets to sharpen tuning. All these components were stand-

---

* *New Worlds Beyond the Atom* and *Matter in the Making* by Langston Day with G. De la Warr (Old Greenwich, Conn.: Devin-Adair, 1963). Innumerable publications by the Delawarr Laboratories Ltd., Raleigh Park Road, Oxford, England.

ard in his diagnostic and treatment instruments, which were accurately and beautifully made.

With these standardized instruments he developed a book of "rates" representing various parts of the body, most of the diseases to which it is prone and some drugs which might be effective. This book, with over four thousand "rates," was compiled by Mrs. De la Warr, "supreme in her own diagnosis and treatment, on the prephysical plane, of a wide range of human and animal suffering," as Judge Humphreys has written. She established the "rates" with the diagnostic instrument, either from actual samples or by concentrating her mind on the thing for which she wanted a "rate."

At one side of the diagnostic instrument is a panel to carry printed cards with the names of various diseases or parts of the body. A cursor, connected to the detector, slid over the cards and enabled the operator rapidly to concentrate his mind on some specific disease and its location.

De la Warr would not sell his instrument unless he and his wife were satisfied that the would-be purchaser was qualified to use it. But they found that the qualities needed for a radionic operator are not as rare as might be supposed. About six people in ten can get some results and about three in ten —with proper practice and training—can become successful radionic diagnosticians. There is nothing rare or mystical, in other words, about radionics; and its practice does not demand any "psychic" attributes. In the writer's experience, the essentials are an open mind, a capacity to visualize, and a lot of practice with, of course, some medical knowledge.

De la Warr devised various instruments to treat patients. The standard instrument, still widely used, consists of nine tuning dials set on a panel, a magnet set at right angles to the dials, a plate to carry the patient's blood sample and a socket into which to plug a portable detector while tuning. The dials are set to the "complementary rate" which is arrived at by subtracting each digit in the "recognition rate" for the disease from ten.

For treatment, he also used tuned spirals traversed by beams of light, radionic emanations in conjunction with sound and also with fifty-cycle ac current. He invented a colorscope which treated patients with light of different wavelengths. In experimenting with sound of different frequencies, including the subaudible, he discovered that the waveform of sound is altered as it passes through the body and that the waveform of the emerging sound varies with the disease of the patient.

These are merely a few samples of the many things that occurred to De la Warr's restless mind over the years. The flow of ideas exceeded his capacity, in time or money, to explore *fully* their implications and possibilities. But, fortunately, most of them are recorded and, one day, these records will serve as a priceless source of inspiration for future investigators. They are available at the Delawarr Laboratories in Oxford, England.

De la Warr did countless experiments with radionics and photography which led to one of his more amazing achievements, the "camera." This astonishing instrument—about the size and shape of a small washing machine—could tune a spot of blood from a patient and produce a picture of his internals, showing the location and nature of a tumor or a foreign body. It could produce, for instance, a succession of pictures, taken at intervals, showing the development of the embryo in a pregnant woman, hundreds of miles away, merely from a sample of her blood.

From a sample of blood from a sick cow, it produced a clear picture of two objects, one metal and one stone, in the cow's body, which later when the vet operated, were found in the place indicated by the photo.

A doctor confirmed to the writer that the "camera" had given him a clear picture of a large tumor in the brain of one of his patients; and when she died and he carried out a postmortem he found a tumor of the size—and in the position—indicated by the photograph.

There was—and is—however one great and unsolved problem about the "camera": it will only produce good photographs if certain people, with some unknown quality, are present, even if they do not touch the instrument. Experiments with the "camera," therefore, were not "repeatable" in the scientific sense and De la Warr was never able to pin down the elusive human quality without which the "camera" would not work.

At frequent intervals De la Warr experimented with agricultural radionics, usually on a small scale with potted plants or small plots. In the course of these he made the discovery that for each plant there is a "critical rotational position" (C.R.P.) in relation to the Earth's magnetic field in which the plant grows best—something, perhaps, that gardeners with "green thumbs" sense instinctively. Like Curtis Upton, he used photographs as "keys" in some of his experiments but in small-scale experiments he generally used soil samples.

Treating photographs of a farm in Scotland, four hundred miles away, he was able to increase the yield of carrots by twenty percent, as compared with the control plots. By contrast when he treated soil samples from a tobacco farm in Rhodesia with his colorscope, the tobacco plants flowered before those on neighboring farms. Unfortunately, from the farmer's point of view, this was not exactly a success for he wanted leaves, not flowers.

Though De la Warr's agricultural experiments were on a smaller scale than those of the Pennsylvania group and though he used somewhat different methods, they helped to confirm the potential importance of radionic agriculture and to suggest different methods for different circumstances.

As if all this were not enough for De la Warr and his wife, they were also pioneers in veterinary radionics and were particularly successful in treating sick animals—as the Delawarr Laboratories and other British radionic practitioners continue doing today. Their patients have included sick pets, race horses, and circus elephants. "Animals are particularly good patients," one practitioner told the writer, "because they have no hangups." In other words, they do not set up any mental resistance to the treatment.

Early in the 1960s, De la Warr's fertile imagination conceived the idea of using reflected sound waves in conjunction with radionic detectors to detect distant conditions—a kind of radionically monitored sonar. With this he had a spectacular success: he was able to detect the source of a chemical poison that was making cattle sick—a problem which had baffled the British experts because the poison, flouracetamide, is one of the hardest to detect.

To give one more example of De la Warr's contribution to

radionics: in an ingenious experiment (a full description of which is unfortunately too lengthy to include here) he succeeded in establishing a "state of radionic rapport" between a young man in Oxford and his photograph in New York. This historic experiment offered the first attested and *graphic* evidence that:

(1) A state of "radionic rapport" exists between a person and his photograph—as Upton found that rapport exists between a photo and a crop.

(2) Treatment of the photograph can produce *measurable* effects on the person.

(3) Distance makes no difference to radionic "energies."

Fortunately, De la Warr was not only inventive. He was also an enthusiastic promoter with a warm and attractive personality. He was always ready to demonstrate his work to anyone interested, and he wrote and lectured constantly about his work. He aroused widespread interest in radionics, not only in Great Britain but all over the world. Even more than Abrams he stimulated public interest in the new science and encouraged many people to study and practice radionics, with the instruments and instructions he provided.

V.

As early as 1943, the De la Warrs and other responsible pioneers had foreseen the need for some kind of regulation of radionics if it was to be kept in the right hands and to win public confidence. Since there were various kinds of radionic instruments which could easily be copied by unqualified or unscrupulous persons, these pioneers formed the Radionic Association of Great Britain. It was succeeded in 1960 by an incorporated company, The Radionic Association, Ltd, which formally established radionics as a self-regulating profession.

Today the association strives to maintain proper standards of qualifications, training, and ethical behavior. Its offspring, the Radionic Trust, will lease but not sell approved instruments only to practitioners that meet the association's standards, and recalls them if the standards are not met. The association's membership includes not only qualified practitioners but also individuals who are genuinely interested in studying the new science. It encourages research, but because its resources are limited and most of its members busy people, research by the association or its individual members is necessarily on a small scale—a gentle stream compared with the torrent of research that flowed from the Delawarr Laboratories up to the time of George De la Warr's death. Nonetheless, some truly useful and interesting work is still being carried out.

Today radionic diagnosis is a systematized form of the ancient art of radiesthesia, which has been known and used from earliest times. The choice, therefore, of instruments to help to focus the mind of the operator is largely a matter of personal preference; in fact, one or two advanced practitioners use no instrument at all and only require a sample of blood or a snippet of hair as a key to the patient with, preferably, some knowledge of his symptoms in order to narrow down their search.

Some diagnosticians continue to use the De la Warr diagnostic instrument with its rubber detector; others prefer more elaborate instruments, or even diagrams only, and the use of a pendulum as a detector. This, they find, is quicker than the De la Warr detector but its effective use demands even more practice.

A pioneer in the use of pattern or diagrams as the basis of radionic diagnosis and treatment is Malcolm Rae, a former businessman who rose to the rank of Lieutenant Commander in the Royal Navy in World War II. Rae is also the first—as far as the writer knows—to apply mathematical concepts to the science of radionics.

Disease, as Rae sees it, consists of "deviations from perfect structure and functioning" of different parts of the body and radionic measurements of these deviations are best expressed as a percentage of the optimum. To measure these deviations, however, with the highest theoretical accuracy would require a highly cumbrous and expensive instrument. Instead he devised simpler instruments for diagnosis and treatment with twenty-four dials, and for most purposes he now prefers simply to use charts. For he has found that ratio and shape are interchangeable and that "a card bearing a diagram equivalent to any ratio may be energized to produce the same effect as the ratio."

Rae makes a diagnosis by means of a pendulum held over a sample from the patient placed on the chart. Remedies are selected by radiesthetic tests of actual samples, and these remedies can be represented by geometric drawings.

He has found that most of his patients have in common similar deviations from the norm. Using their charts and drawings representing the appropriate remedies, Rae projects these normalizing remedies by energizing the drawings with pulsating electromagnetic energy. Projection to this "repetitive" group is done automatically by an ingenious instrument controlled by a time switch which turns it on for fifteen minutes at the beginning of every fourth hour. To meet the individual requirements of patients, Rae also sends them projections of the appropriate remedy expressed as numerical ratios on a six-dial projector, energized by the ac mains.

No less important for the future of radionics is David V. Tansley, who at this writing is chairman of the Council of the Radionic Association. Tansley is not only a qualified Doctor of Chiropractic but also a knowledgeable student of oriental wisdom.

He believes that radionics can progress faster if it concentrates on what he calls the "subtle anatomy of man"—the prephysical dimension or "etheric body" from which physical symptoms originate—rather than on the symptoms themselves. He has found that defects in this "subtle anatomy" are best treated by working on its force centers or "chakras" as they are known in the East. This, he has found, can simplify and expedite a radionic diagnosis.

Tansley has also found that our chakras are receptive to other forms of energy-electricity: light, sound, and color. Of these lights of different colors and intensities are the most effective and the radionic practitioner can treat the appropriate chakra with light via the blood spot or other sample.

Tansley calls this treatment "center therapy" and has devised a most ingenious instrument—available from the Radionic Trust—which incorporates means not only for radionic diagnosis but also for treatment by electricity, light or sound. In the design of this instrument, Tansley, like Rae, has found that geometry or pattern have great significance, though for somewhat different reasons.

Tansley tells us that the subtle anatomy of man which interpenetrates the physical body is "a web of energy streams, of lines of force" and possesses seven major chakras or force centers, twenty-nine minor chakras, and forty-nine "focal points of energy." He suggests that acupuncture points may be considered additional minor force centers. It is at least possible, then, that in the future radionics may be used to locate and stimulate acupuncture points.†

Most radionic practitioners are by nature imaginative and enterprising—willing to try any new method which shows promise of helping the patient. They do not rely exclusively on radionic treatments per se and do not hesitate to recommend more orthodox remedies, if a radionic diagnosis indicates that they are needed. Some practitioners are also homeopaths and combine radionic treatment with homeopathic remedies, for which radionics can detect the chemically untraceable energies.

In other words, radionics can be an invaluable aid to orthodox medicine, as some doctors have already realized. And orthodox medicine can help radionics. It is possible, and potentially of great benefit to both professions, that in the future they form more of a working alliance.

For example there is one field in which radionics can be especially helpful to the medical and psychiatric professions: mental illness. It can do this in two ways. It can detect obscure physical abnormalities which are sometimes the cause of mental illness. And sometimes it can effectively treat the mind itself, because radionics employs the mysterious forces of mind and thought.

† This brief outline cannot do justice to Tansley's work, but fortunately he has described it more fully in book form (Tansley, David V., *Radionics and the Subtle Anatomy of Man*, England: Health Science Press, 1971).

VI.

In this short account, it is impossible to explain fully how radionics "works" or to examine the various theories that may explain at least some of the science. Nonetheless, some simple clues can be offered which may make radionics seem less mysterious.

For one, there is compelling evidence‡ that the human mind, which is quite independent of the physical brain, is a "unit of pure thought," with properties analogous to the fields of physics. There is an important difference, however, between these units of thought—or T fields, as the writer has termed them elsewhere—and the fields known to physics. This difference is that the waves of thought generated by these T fields do not obey the inverse square law and are unaffected by distance. The mind of the radionic operator, therefore, with a suitable "key," can contact the mind of the patient at any distance and diagnose the trouble.

About this treatment there are various theories. One is that the superconscious mind of the operator instructs the patient's superconscious mind in how to cure the patient. This is supported by the fact, noted earlier, that animals are easier to treat than humans because they do not set up a mental resistance to the suggestions of the operator.

Another theory is that the thoughts of the operator "draw nature's attention" to a disharmony in its organization and thereby mobilize its normalizing forces.

Both theories probably mean much the same thing. Certainly, the second theory at least partly explains the treatment of plants and crops. In this case, however, nature is also "helped" by the introduction of reagents.

However valid these explanations may be, it is at least certain that radionics uses the subtle but powerful forces of thought. And great thinkers, like Sir James Jeans, have suggested that the universe itself seems to be like a pure

‡ See the author's recent book, *Design for Destiny* (New York: Ballantine Books, Inc., 1973). *Editors.*

thought and is the creation of a great mathematician. Radionics, then—concerned with thought and susceptible to mathematical expression—is probably closer to the heart of things than other approaches to healing.

30.

The Incredible Hieronymus Machine

JOSEPH F. GOODAVAGE

Not far from the Pennsylvania Dutch country, a converted military reconnaissance aircraft flew over rolling hills of verdant farmland in the Cumberland Valley. A camera in the wing faithfully recorded the topography, including brown-gray areas where blighted crops were being attacked by hungry insects. The film was developed, shown to a local farmer and the sections he wanted "treated" were outlined. A technician from the Homeotronic Research Foundation in Newport, Pa., clipped out the chosen sections, kept the negative and placed the selected cuts in the small well of a black box.

"Every morning from 8:30 to 11 for a week," the technician instructed the farmer, "turn this large dial on the top all the way to the right."

Several days later every corn borer, Japanese beetle, even the nematodes in the soil of the selected areas, were thoroughly dead—exterminated in some strange way by "something" (but what?) from the box.

In central Florida, Dr. William J. Hale, Chief of Dow Chemical Company Research, photographed a blighted citrus orchard. He daubed a powerful reagent (a chemical deadly to the insects) on the *images* of several rows of infected trees. The slender, threadlike nematodes in this warm climate are among the world's most destructive and ineradicable parasites. They bore into the soil to a depth of fourteen feet and are impervious to the most virulent pesticides.

"The Incredible Hieronymus Machine" by Joseph F. Goodavage originally appeared in *Saga*, September 1972 and is reprinted by permission of the author. Copyright © 1975 by Joseph F. Goodavage.

Dow's chief chemist placed the photograph into a device similar to the one used in Pennsylvania and gave the citrus grower these instructions: "Turn it on for two hours every morning." The "machine" *looked* electronic, but there was no *visible* power source.

A week later, every second row, the "treated" areas of the *photograph*, was free of all parasitic infestation. The insect destruction in the adjacent (untreated) rows had progressed without interruption. In addition, countless numbers of dead nematodes lay underground—killed by some invisible force from the "machine"—in soil that had been their haven and breeding ground.

The Journal of Paraphysics (No. 3, 1969) reports the extermination of termites—*at a distance and without pesticides*—at the Municipal Works in Rosenheim, West Germany. . . . The electrical system of a power plant in California experienced crippling breakdowns with no known cause until a troubleshooter inserted detailed *photographs* of the installation into a mysterious, boxlike "dowsing" device. Within hours, all circuits and malfunctioning relays were back in normal operation.

Similar experiments in California and Arizona resulted in successful treatment of more than 50,000 acres of diseased and infested trees.

Sometimes the leaves or sap from a plant or tree are used as a "resonant point of contact." A blood sample from a human patient, a lock of hair or skin scraping have also been used to establish a "link" to the subject. A photograph is equally effective—if the negative isn't destroyed!

In another experiment in Pennsylvania, a lily *seed* was placed in the well of a psionic device (a device whose mysterious power derives from the affinity between similar matter); when the plate was developed, the *bulb* period of its life cycle clearly appeared in the photograph. Using the same *seed*, the operator concentrated on a later period and, "tuning" to the correct vibrational rate, developed a picture that revealed a flowering, *fully developed* lily!

At a laboratory in Oxford, England, a man put a few drops of a woman's *blood* into the receptacle of an odd looking electronic device. Concentrating intently, he turned a series of dials. A white-coated lab assistant loaded a photographic plate into a side slot. They silently timed the exposure. The developed picture revealed *the profile of a woman's lower vertebrae and pelvic region.* A semitransparent human fetus, as in an X-ray picture, was definitely visible.

"About six weeks gone, I'd say," the assistant remarked. "Let's see if it progresses normally. . . . Set it at four months. . . ."

What's happening here; what do all these various experiments have in common?

"A new force, an energy connected with people, an energy known or unknown that can be directed by mind," wrote Lynn Schroeder and Sheila Ostrander in *Psychic Discoveries Behind the Iron Curtain.* "That's why interest is running high . . . why even the Soviets are trying to find the general laws behind spectacular feats (such as making objects sail through the air, killing living organisms at long-range, tracing and locating foreign agents in distant cities just from their photographs), just as flying a kite to catch a spark of lightning is important only because it led to the discovery of the . . . laws of electricity."

From available evidence, the human race appears to be on the brink of a discovery that dwarfs the combined invention of the wheel, the discovery of fire, electricity—*and* atomic energy!

"My personal hunch," wrote trailblazing editor John Campbell in one of his "Astounding Science Fact" editorials back in 1956, "is that these individuals and groups are prodding at the edges of a new field that will open a totally new concept of the Universe. And that, within the next twenty years, the barrier will be cracked; a reproducible machine will be achieved when a valid theory of operation is achieved—and not before. But I believe that that can be, and will be done before 1975."

And the man most likely to do it is T. Galen Hieronymus, an amazing inventor whose creative history goes back at least sixty years. Hieronymus began working on new methods of broadcast techniques during 1919–1920 when he was in the Army Signal Corps as a radio operator and electrical engineer with the Rainbow Division in France. He's had his own ham radio license since 1913 and was with station KDKA, Pittsburgh, Pa., and took part in the first radio broadcast. He was also trying to develop a wireless telephone in early WW I when he first discovered some peculiar properties of certain metals and minerals. This led him to experiments with psionics, then called radionics, and the work of other early pioneers inspired him.

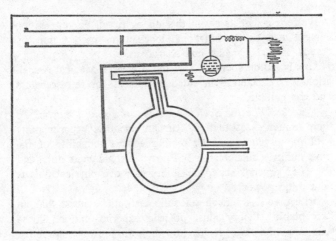

FIGURE 1 *Incredibly, the Hieronymus Machine diagram can also produce provocative effects.*

In 1956, Hieronymus presented Campbell with a copy of his patent for exactly the kind of device the editor wrote about—a patent he had applied for in 1946, which was granted in 1948. Hieronymus was careful to introduce his patent principally as an instrument for detecting new, unknown emanations from inert matter, mainly minerals. For very good reasons Hieronymus deliberately kept any life-affecting abilities of his device a secret.

In London two decades ago, George De la Warr made the startling discovery that the emulsion on a photographic plate was somehow linked to the person whose photograph was taken—or to anything or anyone else in the photograph: Science invariably rejects such *obviously* "impossible" notions.

Scientists *know* such devices are mere figments of the imagination, so why bother investigating when there are much more important fields of inquiry?

If "magic" exists, then the laws of sympathetic magic would come into play, the rule being that "the symbol *is* the object (both in its present actuality and future potentiality), therefore whatever is done to the symbol also happens to the object!"

Western scientists shrug this off as ritualistic superstition camouflaged by nonfunctional mechanisms used mainly by frauds, medical quacks, and charlatans.

"It's based on voodoo," says the American Medical Association. ". . . claptrap invented by quacks for the desperate and the gullible."

"Quacks" like the Soviet Academy of Science, maybe? To their immense satisfaction, Russian scientists experimenting with parapsychology have established the reliability of the most unlikely phenomena: ESP, psychotronic generators, and PK (i.e., psychokinesis, the ability to move physical objects with mind power).

British and American scientific institutions insist that an "acceptable" theory must precede experimentation. Those who know the stakes realize how dark the future could be for the Western nations, particularly in high-risk national security matters, or—as it is now called—ESPionage. It makes relatively little difference whether you establish a link between a man and his photograph or use the picture of, let's say, a foreign agent, to pinpoint his location anywhere on Earth.

In a similar exercise, Hieronymus "eavesdropped" on the flights of Apollo 8 and 11. By tuning his device to the mitogenic emanations (also called odic force, helioda waves, or eloptic radiations) of the American astronauts, he monitored their physiological conditions and changes throughout the lunar voyage and return—even after splashdown and during the ensuing quarantine periods.

Most important, the test data from Hieronymus's device was in complete agreement with NASA's own medical telemetry systems. In this instance, however, Hieronymus is one up on the experts. With his device, he detected the presence of an unknown, mysterious belt of radiation surrounding the moon.

This radiation, he says, is harmful—*possibly deadly*—to human beings!

"We're beginning to find hidden barriers and limitations in unexpected places," Hieronymus claims. "Humans are pretty adaptable creatures . . . *on Earth*. But what kind of energies will we find in other planetary fields?"

Experimenters such as T. Galen Hieronymus, George De la Warr, and Ruth Drown have discovered how people respond to the geomagnetic field, the celestial environment, and . . . to the mental and emotional attitudes of close friends and co-workers.

"Every living thing radiates this odic force," said Baron von Reichenbach (a well-known chemist who invented creosote). He was so impressed by the work of Dr. Henry Abrams, an early radionics pioneer in England, and Austrian physician Dr. F. A. Mesmer (of "animal magnetism" fame) that he devoted his life to the study and practice of radionics.

"No matter how small or diluted it may be, there's a resonance between the whole human body and each of its parts," Ruth Drown, inventor of a radionics receiver–transmitter device, wrote before she died in a California prison. The hostile American Medical Association protested about her methods and devices, and she was charged and convicted for fraud and medical quackery. Her device, of course, was "obviously" a fake, according to the AMA and the authorities. Nothing could *possibly* do what her patients claimed the Drown machine did for them. No point engaging in useless tests, either. Case closed.

There's no resonance, subetheric or otherwise, in blood samples or tissue grafts from different individuals no matter how closely they are typed. In a series of tightly controlled experiments carried out on plants at the Delawarr Laboratories in Oxford, strange new facts began to emerge. The growth and health of plants could be influenced by indirect color irradiation from a distance!

Langston Day, in his book, *New Worlds Beyond the Atom*, wrote: "After discovering that the emulsion of an ordinary photographic plate is somehow linked to the person in the photograph, we found that the same rule applied to plants. Later we discovered that plant growth could be stimulated by irradiating (allowing light to strike) its *photograph* with a device called the colorscope.

"How can there be a link between a plant and its photograph?" he wondered. "The image on the plate is formed by the multiplicity of reflected light rays coming from the cabbage," De la Warr explained. "But in addition to light, other kinds of vital radiations are also emanating from the cabbage; these are received by the emulsion.

". . . Each molecule of matter carries an electric charge which is specific for that particular molecule; this charge acts as an inconceivably tiny radio station which both transmits and receives its own particular signals. When these countless myriads of charged molecules are broadcasting, they build up a generic pattern which is the means whereby form or shape appears in the material world.

"The *combined* signal from a plant or human being, a signal composed of the separate broadcasts of the billions of charged molecules which compose it, is unique. The cabbage in your larder is not quite the same as any other cabbage; 'Mr. Brown,' for example, is a little different in his physical makeup from any other man in the world. In the same way, the signals broadcast from this cabbage, or from 'Mr. Brown,' are different from any other broadcast signals.

"Furthermore, since each tiny molecular charge is also a *receiving station*, the generic pattern of a plant or a human being governs the pattern of signals received from outside. This is where a photograph plays its part. The emulsion retains the generic pattern of the thing which is photographed, and therefore it acts as sort of a tuned transmitter. If a radionic broadcast is projected through it, this generic pattern will transmit exactly the pattern of radiations suitable for affecting the plant (or human being) at a distance."

Probably the most outstanding fact about psionic researchers—according to my own investigations—is that so many are hard, practical, let's-see-if-it-works types, *not* the ivory tower theoreticians lost in dust-covered tradition and completely guided by Authority. The comfortable Establishmentarians naturally won't rock the academic boat; not only do they refuse to investigate, they won't even listen to those who *have* experimented.

That, unfortunately, has been the all too prevalent attitude of the hidebound establishment scientist—more of a corporation man than an honest seeker after truth.

When Ed Hermann, an engineer at McGraw-Hill, Inc., publishing company in New York, requested that Hieronymus treat a caterpillar-infested tree on his lawn, he never expected anything as far out as "long-distance extermination." Everything else had failed. For several years, and in spite of all the pesticides he and his neighbors used, every wild cherry tree in his northern New Jersey neighborhood was under the murderous attack of hordes of voracious tent caterpillars.

Hermann happened to be investigating psionics and was currently collecting information from Hieronymus. The Florida inventor was visiting Brig. Gen. Henry R. Gross's Homeotronic Research Foundation* at the latter's farm near Harrisburg, Pa. Gross, then State Director of Selective Service, was working with psionic devices. (To his neighbors' astonishment, Gross was invariably successful in exterminating insects from a good distance on more than 90 farms in the Cumberland Valley alone!)

"Send me a photograph of your tree," Hieronymus wrote Hermann. "Put some leaves and a few caterpillars in a box and mail them along. *And don't forget to include the negative,*" he added.

This struck Hermann as odd, but he complied with the request. Three hundred miles separated his home from the Gross farm. Yet, a few days later as he pulled into his driveway after work, he hit the brakes and stared in wide-eyed astonishment. Seemingly everywhere he looked there was a "carpet" of many thousands of caterpillars. The furry horde lay in a full circle around the cherry tree and beneath the branches and leaves from which they'd fallen—*struck dead by some mysterious force!*

"For your records," Hermann wrote to Hieronymus later, "I think you should know that whatever you did to the cherry tree on our lawn was good. We don't have a caterpillar in

* The work of the Foundation is being carried on by Mankind Research Unlimited (see Appendix III). *Editors.*

sight! This isn't normal; last year we were still burning off caterpillars in late June and early July with flaming kerosene torches. . . . Something definite and specific was done here. . . ."

Over the years, individual, widely separated researchers in psionics have been discovering and rediscovering that all matter emits radiations. Mesmer's experiments goaded von Reichenbach into studying people who obviously had ESP. With the help of these "sensitives," von Reichenbach accumulated a wealth of data proving the existence of something he called the odic force. He discovered it in crystals, in heat, light, magnets, and in living cells; he also found it manifesting itself wherever chemical reactions were occurring.

Other scientists have reported this mitogenic radiation occurring from the growth of living cells. At Columbia University three scientists, I. I. Rabi, P. Kusch, and S. Millman, developed a new apparatus which conclusively proved that some kind of ray or vibrations pass between one molecule and another. They showed that each molecule, living or inert, is a small radio transmitter (and receiver) that broadcasts continuously. These waves range over the entire electromagnetic spectrum—often *beyond!* The sheer volume of these vibrations is apparently limitless. A single molecule can give off rays of a *million* different wavelengths, but only on one frequency at a time.

When the Hieronymus device operates, the eloptic radiation stimulates the generic pattern of the subject and some kind of psychic bond or link is established between the emanations of the atoms and molecules of matter and the mind of the operator. Even prior to 1946 when Hieronymus (who is a Fellow in the Society of Electrical Engineers) patented his invention, he had learned that any mineral or chemical compound could be identified by placing an ore sample on a tray, *concentrating* on the element he was seeking to identify, and turning a dial. When the fingers of the hand stroking a small plate on the machine "stuck," he knew the dial was tuned to the right frequency. Everything has its own "rate." It makes no difference *who* does the tuning; if the operator concentrates on "copper," the device will detect the presence of copper (if any is present) in the ore sample.

As a detector, it operates in much the same way as a dowsing rod. Everyone who duplicates the experiment will obtain the exact same dial setting (or "rate") for the vibration of copper. Interestingly, neither silver, gold, nor anything else will cause a "stick" unless it is consciously being sought.

All independent psionic researchers are in unanimous agreement (here and overseas) that eloptic radiation of all matter can be caught on a photographic plate and the detector will react to a *photograph* of a mineral specimen as it would to the mineral itself.

Like De la Warr's camera, the Hieronymus Machine also detects emanations from blood samples, minerals, plants, insects—anything at all—that cannot be recorded by any other known method. Moreover, as John Campbell discovered, *the device works even when disconnected from its power source* (regular household electric current); since both devices operate on the same psychic principle—and can be used as receivers *and* transmitters—physical illnesses can be influenced even when the patient is in another town or city. This is the most powerful obstacle to the minds of strictly materially-oriented people. The idea that a bit of saliva on a blotter, a lock of hair, skin, or blood samples (to say *nothing* of a photograph!) could have any connection with a distant patient, is enough to cause the most obstinate reaction even among ordinarily reasonable people.

Yet the emanations from all matter anywhere and everywhere in the universe—as far as is known—can be directed along a wire, like electricity, or transmitted from the subject on light waves. This is why Hieronymus called von Reichenbach's odic force "eloptic radiation." It can be transmitted as an electrical charge, as a radio wave, or as light waves.

To the astonishment of experimenters who sent 50 cents to the Patent Office in Washington and received schematic drawings and a description of Patent No. 2,482,773, the Hieronymus Machine did seem capable of receiving and transmitting eloptic energy. The problem was (and is) that the operator needed some practice to become "skilled in the art." Moreover, some experimenters seemed to have more natural talent (and patience) than others.

When John Campbell built the device and encouraged Ed

Hermann to test it, the "stick" occurred at the right point on the dial every time.

Admittedly, it is a baffling, paradoxical and altogether incredible invention. It can't really be called a machine because it operates as well without connection to a source of power. In this respect, it's a tool. The key to all psionic devices is the *mind* of the operator, which is usually attuned to the emanations of whatever object is under analysis. Man's first really powerful tools for aiding mental activity were the equivalents of paper and pencil. Nearly anyone can perform impressive mental feats with pencil and paper—feats that would be impossible without them. Adding four seven-digit numbers, for example. The paper and pencil though, have nothing at all to do with the function of the mind. *They* don't do the calculating, yet most people couldn't do the job without them.

"Psionics," declared Dr. William J. Hale when he was Chief of Dow Chemical's Research Division, "is the field of human achievement *beyond science*. Only after several thousand years has science been put into some kind of reasonable order. Anyone who thinks this completely new field—at *least* as broad and deep as all known science today—can be thoroughly investigated in just a few decades, is sorely deluding himself."

In his book *Farmer Triumphant,* Dr. Hale demonstrated how thoroughly familiar he was with the beginnings of psionics in the U.S. and England.

"The human mind capable of modulating an energy pattern has a direct connection with *physical* forces," he said. "Universal mind is able to manifest through an energy pattern as matter. The Hieronymus device connects a purely mental function, which we call extrasensory perception, with an image on a photographic plate. These psionic devices provide us with an extradimensional tool which is able to probe the gross material results and to see what is happening a little higher up on the ladder of Causation."

The fact that a psionic device in unscrupulous hands might enable an operator, theoretically at least, *to kill* another human being, has never been squarely faced (publicly at least) by anyone in the field. Yet this apparently unlimited power of life and death resides in the mind of almost any highly skilled psionics operator.

The truth is wholly beyond the comprehension of scientists steeped in traditional attitudes and approaches. Therein lies the margin of safety for the potential killer. He can cause the death of another human in any number of ways and literally get away with it.

Whenever men have dealt with a power beyond human knowledge or experience, no one paid the slightest attention to the fact that "Here's something that *works*, by golly! I don't know how or why, but see for yourself. . . ."

As long as "big science" knows for "sure" that it's impossible to cause any physical effect from 300 miles away with a box, a dial, and a photograph, the guy with the device will get nowhere. It *seems* incredible, but it's true. Any machine that *repeatedly* does what its inventor built it to do, and *predicts* it will do, but whose effect is unexplainable in terms of what we now know, will never get a fair test. The prestigious, lavishly funded National Science Foundation will not look at a practical demonstration of the Hieronymus machine. And the fact that the Soviet Union and other Eastern European countries are developing psionics at a fast pace cuts no ice with corporation executives and government bureaucrats.

"Radiesthesia or whatever you call it," snorted one executive when he heard about it, "is nonsense. It's magic, and grown men know there's no such thing as magic!" Nevertheless, the Pentagon pointedly turned down Hieronymus's offer to test his invention. The brass still seems totally indifferent about learning whether it *is* capable of *more* than just making chemical and mineral analyses.

When John Campbell heard about it, he sent for the patent, built his own device according to specifications, tested it repeatedly and induced everyone who visited his home in New Jersey to experiment with it. For a big, tough-minded, individualistic (often eccentric) science-baiter, he was absolutely fair and scrupulously honest when it came to facts. Here's what he wrote Hieronymus on June 4, 1956:

"If you can kill insect pests by working on a photograph, and at a distance of thousands of miles—*if I accept that*—it implies that *you can kill me with such a machine, despite all I might do to hide, without my having any chance whatever of protecting myself, without my knowledge or opportunity to defend against the attack.* The more you prove that you *can* kill living entities at a huge distance, without any understandable linkage that can be defended—the more you prove that I am helpless to protect myself. The more you make a man know that such forces exist—the less he can feel that he lives in a world of reasonable security, wherein he can, at least, have warning of attack, and prepare to meet it.

"True, you're attacking only insects; you're helping human beings. But—the inherent implications are there, and cannot be denied. You cannot tell me how to defend myself against such an attack; if I acknowledge the reality of those forces—I acknowledge that I am helpless, and know of no defense.

". . . I selected your machine among the many possible psionic machines available because: (1) it was patented; (2) the patent specified simply a mineral analyzer, and *the life-affecting characteristics* could be ignored; (3) it *looks* like an electronic–physical machine—it *appears* to make some sort of almost sense at the purely physical science level.

"A man can learn only at the boundary of the known; your machine *appears* to be right on the boundary between pure electronics and psionics. Therefore, it appears as though this were a learnable–understandable device that can, with a little study, be comprehended with just a little extension of already understood concepts.

"The therapeutic and diagnostic aspects of the machine— the life-force aspects—could be totally ignored, and so physical scientists could attack the problem without stirring deep, and extremely powerful, fears.

"That machine of yours is almost pure magic. In the old, real and potent sense, *it casts spells, imposes death magic, and can be used for life magic.* It operates on the anciently known laws of sympathetic magic; it, like Voodoo dolls, applies the law that 'the symbol is the object, and that which is done to the symbol occurs also to the object.'

"That's a law, too—a real one. The primitive human tribes all over the world, from Eskimos through Hawaiians, Africans, Incas, ancient Greeks, and prehistory European tribes, all independently came to the same fundamental conclusions.

If such independent peoples separately reached the same conclusions—it must be that the laws of the universe are, in fact, involved.

"You're scaring hell out of the people who understand what you've got. You may be using it well—but *release* it, and what *limits* it? If a magician can destroy a man tracelessly—who is safe from threat, from ransom demand, from the vengeful hate of an unjust enemy?

"You're scaring people—and they have reason for their fears, while you can name *no limits* to this powerful technique!

"When I began working with the machine, I learned that it didn't need a power supply. Then I learned that it wouldn't work if a tube was missing or defective. I saw some of the other psionic machines and saw that they worked, despite the fact that their wiring system made absolutely no logical sense. From that, I derived a new concept, a theory, and made a crucial experiment.

"I have a model of your analytical machine, simplified and streamlined to the ultimate. It consists *solely of the circuit diagram;* I have a *symbol* of a prism, not a real prism, mounted on a National Velvet Vernier dial; that, and a small copper loop, alone appear on the front surface of the panel. *Back of the panel, the circuit diagram is drawn in India ink on standard drafting paper; the prism-symbol rotates in its appropriate place in the circuit diagram.* The spiral coil is drawn in India ink on paper glued to the back of the panel; it is connected with the symbolized vacuum tube plate through a condenser-symbol by means of a nylon thread; the other end of the coil-drawing is connected to the symbolized vacuum tube cathode by a second nylon thread from my wife's sewing kit.

"The machine works beautifully; the consistency of performance is excellent.

"We're working with magic—and magic doesn't depend on matter, but on *form*—on *pattern* rather than substance.

"Your electronic circuit represents a pattern of relationships; that is important. The electrical characteristics are utterly unimportant, and can be dropped out completely. The machine fails when a tube burns out because that alters the pattern; it works when there is no power, because the relationship of patterns is intact. My symbolic diagram works because the pattern is present . . .

". . . If you can *do* at a distance through barriers—it is implicit that you could *observe* at a distance through barriers. Clairvoyance means the end of personal privacy. The fact is implicit in the action at a distance without mechanism at the other end. *It's frightening!*"

When Hieronymus filed the patent application for his psionic device in 1946, he was acutely aware of its potentialities. It could be used for great good—or terrible evil. This, he explained later, was why he *deliberately* omitted some critical factors. "Those were crucial times," he said. "There was a realignment of political and military power after WW II, and I was afraid it might get into the wrong hands."

Whatever the extent of his knowledge then, Hieronymus . . . realized that once his device became publicly known, sooner or later, somebody was certain to realize that unlimited power might be available. There are enough intelligent, clever, often unprincipled individuals (as well as nations) who wouldn't hesitate to use his invention for personal gain or power—at everyone's expense. . . .

Anyone with half a buck for the patent, some odds and ends from a workshop or basement, and several hours to spare can build his own Hieronymus device. Or . . . copy the full-page circuit diagram printed with this article, paste it on heavy cardboard and give it the same crucial tests advocated by John Campbell.

"We've never found anything we couldn't analyze chemically or otherwise," Hieronymus said. "Distance is a negligible factor, too. When we analyze our physical world we find practically *nothing* physical, just the manifestation of *energy* when we divide things down to their ultimate particles."

Describing radionics in his book, *Psychical Physics,* Professor S. W. Tromp reported "With an instrument, the etheric energy pattern that corresponds to any given object, substance or condition can be artificially simulated. The process is not on the physical level. It lies beyond the limits of the five known senses and seems to be outside the measurable electromagnetic spectrum."

Nearly every honest report about eloptic radiation is a

mind bender that shatters all precedents. They are so strange, in fact, that Hieronymus and his colleagues were obliged to establish the Advanced Sciences Research and Development Corporation, Inc.

He published a twenty-two-page consolidated statement containing "Vitality Intensity Values" of the astronauts of Apollo 8 and 11—from liftoff to splashdown, and through the quarantine periods.

"Of all the data collected and information uncovered by us during the flight of Apollo 11," Hieronymus wrote, "the most important and startling is that *there is a lethal radiation belt on the Moon,* apparently extending from about 65 miles down to approximately 15 feet from the surface. . . .

"There was a noticeable drop in the general vitality (of the astronauts) and an increase in the carcinogenic readings. The pathologies increased until the men actually stepped onto the Moon, then everything reversed. This situation was similar to all other lunar landings."

Only 500 copies of this report were distributed to interested medical men and scientists willing to study, check, and evaluate the data.

Hieronymus's description of eloptic energy specifically states that "it is in no way related to alpha or beta particles or to gamma rays. It does *not* fit into any part of the electromagnetic spectrum. It operates in an entirely *different* media."

The healing powers of the mind over the body are well documented—as are its negative, destructive abilities. If we have this capacity to control our own health and disease conditions—including that of life and death—the logical extension would be that *some* of us should also be able to exercise control over *others*. If it *can* be done, it almost certainly *is* being done! But without using psionic power, it is almost impossible to determine how sophisticated or powerful a stage the evolution of psionics has reached during the past two decades.

Evidence now available seems to indicate that a powerful effort is being made to keep the facts from becoming widely known. Ridicule, suspicion, and discredit have befallen men who have reached these conclusions. This is extremely difficult to prove, but this writer has personal knowledge of five very suspicious incidents involving the untimely, mysterious deaths—several called "natural" and two listed as "suicides"—of psionics investigators.

Until very recently, this could be done at any distance without the knowledge or consent of the victim—and with absolutely no danger of detection or retaliation. A "psionic shield" is the only conceivable protection against such deadly onslaughts. But such a device would have to be operating all the time—*24 hours a day, 365 days a year!*

Several versions of just such a "psychic shield" are now being secretly developed. Moreover, Bell Laboratories and another electronics corporation are bidding for the rights to produce the Hieronymus device on a commercial basis (for "scientific purposes," it is said).

Before such things are mass produced, we need to learn much more about the strange similarities among the deaths of Dr. Morris K. Jessup (listed as a "suicide" when found dead in his station wagon in Dade County Park, Fla., on the evening of April 29, 1959), the prison death of Ruth Drown, and the suicide and deaths of three other investigators whose researches brought them close to almost complete understanding of psionic powers.

Before he died, a physicist friend of this writer's was a redhot amateur astronomer who analyzed incoming light from nearby planets and distant stars by connecting a psionic device to his telescope.

By concentrating on a mental version of the Twenty Questions game, he was able to learn and report that life exists on two planets (*other* than Earth!) *within our solar system.* One of these is Venus, but Venusian life forms are unlike anything we know. He detected mitogenic radiation resulting from the growth of living cells—"most probably the cell division in the roots of extremely large plants," he claimed.

Other researchers have analyzed the emanations from relics of the past. In this respect, all psionic devices, including the Hieronymus machine, are also *time machines!* With a De la Warr adaptation, radiations from the fossils of prehistoric creatures which existed on Earth millions of years ago have been caught on film and developed!

Using blood samples taken from his wife and himself,

George De la Warr once tuned his camera and concentrated on their wedding day, an event that had occurred nearly 30 years previously! The picture was developed in view of skeptical witnesses and was recognizably that of a young couple in somewhat outdated wedding outfits. He used this same photograph for "positive" identification that the couple were in fact himself and Mrs. De la Warr.

Part of the emerging theory concerning psionics shrinks the significance of time and distance to almost pure illusion. This has many fascinating possibilities. Among practitioners of radionics and psionics, the 18th century concept of the interplanetary ether has replaced astronomy's theory of a "dead vacuum" to explain the properties of empty space. It is from this ether, claim psionics experts, that all life and consciousness comes into material existence—and to which it returns (in a higher state or vibrational plane) after physical "death."

All this makes a compellingly difficult kind of almost sense. Hardly anyone whose views have been shaped by orthodox science is able to cope with it—even the most stubborn materialist. At the same time, it holds forth some hope that all is not chaos after all—and throws a new, excitingly different light on the anciently known concepts of karma and reincarnation.

"As the universe is without beginning and without end, so are all its parts—equally eternal." Or . . . in the words of British cosmologist Dr. Fred Hoyle: "When science begins the study of nonphysical phenomena, it will make more progress *in one decade* than in all the centuries of its existence."

If my own intelligence, information, and hunches are accurate, that decade is upon us.

31.

Orgone Energy Weather Engineering Through the Cloudbuster

TREVOR JAMES CONSTABLE

Existing orgone energy weather engineering techniques, whose efficacy has been demonstrated and documented in the U.S., are a bright new element in the environmental struggle. These techniques permit the solution of climatic problems inaccessible to formal weather modification methods, with their dependence upon deliberate atmospheric pollution—often with corrosive chemicals. Orgone energy weather engineering, through the cloudbuster device, has opened wind abatement, hurricane diversion, rainmaking, precipitation inhibition, and regional temperature control. Smog may be similarly expected to yield to this primary energy engineering when procedures are designed and implemented for its removal.

Severe weather has been a characteristic of world climate in the past few years, as publications and reports of the World Meteorological Organization reveal. With the access provided by orgone energy weather engineering to the energy continuum involved in all weather formation, it has become evident that unprecedented rainfall and spreading drought in recent times are probably by-products—unintentional and undiscerned—of indiscriminate, large-scale, world-wide proliferation of cloud seeding.

Severe weather events of recent times have usually occurred in areas other than those directly under chemical seeding bombardment. This has led to an illusory feeling of innocence among seeding proponents. This overview of orgone energy weather engineering will provide some insight into the

"Orgone Energy Weather Engineering through the Cloudbuster" by Trevor James Constable is an original article written especially for this volume and is printed by permission of the author.

nature of the primary energy continuum that underlies all the weather of the world, and to the ability of that continuum to manifest gross meteorological reactions at sites remote from the application of stimuli. Whether such stimuli are chemical, or the direct stimuli to the continuum that make up the techniques of orgone energy weather engineering, the menace of remote effects remains a major danger.

Cloud seeding with chemicals is no longer necessary or justified. A superior and more versatile technique already exists in orgone energy weather engineering. This means of weather control—in the widest sense of the term—takes account of, and works in harmony with, the underlying primary energy continuum out of which all weather emerges into the phenomenal world.

No chemical contaminants, agents, vaporous infusions, or electromagnetic radiation are utilized in any way in orgone energy weather engineering. This means of weather control is environmentally pure, versatile, and highly effective. The new techniques are also inexpensive when contrasted with the multimillion dollar operational costs of Federal cloud seeding programs.

Simple apparatus undetectable except by direct visual sighting or aerial photography, can easily produce regional weather modification—by no means restricted to mere rainmaking. Such apparatus can be assembled, and has been assembled many times in recent years by the writer, for less than $100. The operational reports covering the use of this apparatus are the most solid evidence of weather-modification-according-to-plan yet published anywhere. The information has been freely supplied to the relevant Federal agencies, in an effort to reduce or eliminate the chemical seeding juggernaut. Ruination of the functioning of the biosphere may well ensue if such action is not soon taken.

History of Orgone Energy Weather Engineering

Orgone energy is the name given to the cosmic life energy by its 20th century discoverer, the late Dr. Wilhelm Reich, psychiatrist and pioneer of orgonomic weather engineering. Dr. Reich was a protege and student of Dr. Sigmund Freud, the distinguished founder of psychoanalysis, and served successively as first clinical assistant and director of Freud's Psychoanalytic Polyclinic in Vienna from 1924–1932.

Dr. Reich called the physical energy he discovered *orgone* to identify it permanently with life, organic functioning, and with the orgasm, which may be termed the root of physical life. The discovery of this energy was the long-term result of the first study ever taken by any scientist of the function of the orgasm. Dr. Reich made this study in the 1920s. Discovery of the orgone energy in living systems and in the atmosphere in 1939–1940 was rooted in Dr. Reich's pioneering investigation into human sexual functioning during the previous two decades.

Orgone energy demonstrably exists in everything living as a pulsatory, specific biological energy of nonelectric character. Externally in nature, orgone energy exists as a primordial mass-free energy in the soil, water, and atmosphere of the Earth. In the latter medium, it is accessible to, and manipulable by, extremely simple mechanical contrivances known as cloudbusters (CLBs). Control of the weather in all its functions is a resultant here-now reality.

Dr. Reich demonstrated the presence of the energy visually, including lumination *in vacuo*, thermically, electroscopically, and at the Geiger–Müller counter. His published experiments are replicable by anyone with training in basic scientific method. Dr. Reich also invented a series of devices for detecting and further objectifying this universal physical energy. These devices include the orgone field meter, the orgonoscope for the visual detection of the energy in the atmosphere, and the orgone energy accumulator for producing concentrations of the energy. The continuous liberation of heat—in and above the orgone accumulator—contradicts the second law of thermodynamics, considered by Einstein to be one of the central pillars of modern physics.

The cloudbuster, with its power to manipulate atmospheric orgone energy potentials, is probably the most potent device ever to come into human ken. This potency has two main aspects:—

(1) Ability to create, shift, and destroy major weather systems.
(2) Simplicity of construction that makes it available to everyone.

A detailed description of the origin of Reich's discoveries, and the years of painstaking work from which they arose, lies beyond the scope of this article. Suffice it to say that the discoveries were made through consistent application of accepted scientific procedures. Reich's biological discoveries were drawn from verified and re-verified clinical findings, and were carried over into repeatable physical experiments. His discoveries were neither happenstance nor sudden, but the yield from organic, unrelenting concentration upon objective facts and processes. All Reich's experiments, save those leading to the development of the orgone motor, have been published for replication by other scientists. The energy itself, as the experiments will demonstrate emphatically, is *physical*.

Current Situation

A small group of professional and amateur workers has continued since Dr. Reich's death to consolidate and extend his discoveries. This cadre of experienced orgonomic investigators and workers, should be a major asset in carrying this work forward with official sanction and official legal support. The orgone discovery has emerged as the universal energic principle underlying all otherwise impenetrable paranormal phenomena that now impinge on the outer perimeters of scientific knowledge. The indecisive theories of paraphysics are functionally unified and solidified by Reich's discovery of the orgone energy, and his establishment of its basic determinism.

Orgone Energy Weather Engineering

While the literature listed at the end of this article will provide the background necessary for understanding the state of the art in orgone energy weather engineering, a substantial investment of time and effort is required for its mastery. Formal knowledge to the highest academic level is no more than a foundation for beginning the study of orgonomy. In many areas of this new field scientific fundamentals are often reversed or negated, as in the case of the negative entropy of orgone energy. Expertise in any formal discipline of science is not by itself a basis for valid criticism of orgonomic science. The books must be studied. The apparatus must be built. The published experiments must be repeated or attempted before criticism is advanced.

To obviate the time problem posed by the long studies required, and to open a new field to open minds, this survey requires only that the reader take for granted certain facts concerning orgone energy in weather control. These facts may be later verified from the literature, and by actual experiment by the reader, if he should so desire. Orgone energy weather engineering may be understood by accepting tentatively the following basic facts:

(1) Orgone energy forms an envelope around the Earth, where its concentration is greater than in extraterrestrial space. This envelope moves around the Earth from west to east, slightly faster than the physical–material planet. The orgone energy envelope may be envisioned as a *bioenergetic torque drive* imparting spin to the planet, such torque arising from the heliotropism of living organisms.

(2) The orgone energy envelope is the agency by which the world's weather is carried on its generally west to east motion around the Earth.

(3) Orgone energy motion takes place in the waveform of the spinning wave or *kreiselwelle*

(KRW). The KRW appears in this form when perceived in the orgone accumulator:

Similar motion on a huge scale in the atmosphere imparts a specific shaping effect to cloud masses that is directly observable as a "KRW signature." This signature is not identified in any cloud atlas or other work on cloud physics known to the writer of this survey, but is objective over thousands of square miles of ocean and can be readily photographed. The KRW signature in clouds is independent of wind movement.

(4) Orgone energy has a powerful affinity for the liquid state of matter, especially water.

(5) Orgone energy is *negatively entropic,* following the law of reversed or orgonotic potential.* Orgone energy flows from low potential states to high potential states. Charged bodies attract bodies of lesser charge, and withdraw that lesser charge to the limit of their own capacity level.

(6) Rows of parallel, hollow metal pipes grounded into water and suitably directed into the atmosphere, have the ability to raise and lower orgonotic potentials in the atmosphere. Such a device is known as a cloudbuster. The formal parameters of meteorology may be manipulated and controlled by such devices through such engineering operations at the primary level.

(7) The orgone energy envelope—the womb of the weather—is highly sensitive, continuous, and responsive on a vast and elastic scale to stimuli from cloudbusters. Because of continuity of this energy envelope, the effects of such stimuli can extend

* In the Reichean tradition, "orgonomic" is used in reference to methodology and "orgonotic" is used in reference to orgone charge or potential. *Editors.*

over millions of square miles. Billions of tons of atmosphere and atmospheric water vapor can be decisively affected in their concentration, distribution, and general behavior.

(8) Orgone energy engineering deals with a living, nonelectric, universal energy to which current formal education, training, and physics give only partial access. A successful orgone engineer in weather control must necessarily be perceptive, sensitive to movements and changes in the atmosphere induced by his operations, and be able to guide his apparatus accordingly. He must be able to both understand and tolerate the extremely powerful corresponding movements of the orgone energy in his own biosystem. He must be a skilled orgonomic observer, with a functioning First Orgonomic Sense, i.e., with the ability to perceive the energy directly.

(9) All the procedures and reactions involved in orgone energy weather engineering are *functional* and not mechanical. A functional mode of mentation is therefore an essential prerequisite for responsible and effective weather control. Persons with no attunement to living processes are not suited to engineering operations of the kind described.

(10) There are at the present time *no real experts* in this field—only a few people whose ignorance is slightly less vast than that of their fellows unexposed to these new principles.

Provided that the above ten points can be taken for granted, we may proceed to discuss basic orgone energy weather engineering and the apparatus employed to effect such engineering.

The CLB consists essentially of a row, or rows, of hollow, parallel metal pipes, one end of which is grounded into water. A rack that will support one end of the pipe row at a suitable height above the ground, while the other end of the row is immersed in water, makes a simple CLB known as a "rack unit." All weather modification operations possible through orgone energy engineering can be effected with such a device. For convenience, however, CLBs are usually designed so that the rows of pipes may be swung on a pivot or turntable.

Variants of the CLB which have been designed and used in practical operations include:

(a) The chambered CLB—featuring a powerful orgone accumulator in series with the pipes and between the pipes and the water ground. There are also subvariants of the chambered CLB.

(b) The tuned CLB. Units of this kind incorporate radionic tuning of the tubes, based on the original discoveries of the late Dr. Ruth B. Drown. Such tuned CLBs have proved their value in original UFO investigation, quite aside from weather engineering.

There are two basic conceptions of CLB functioning:

(1) The classical concept, formulated by Wilhelm Reich, inventor of the CLB.

(2) The modern concept, formulated by the author of this article.

Classical Concept

Reich theorized that the grounded pipes "drew" orgone energy from the atmosphere into the water. External physical manifestations, fully observable, support this concept. A major manifestation is the generation of local wind movement towards the CLB from the direction of its aim. Another manifestation, startling when observed for the first time, is the verifiable and repeatable cloud "busting" or dispersion function from which the device originally derived its name.

Weather control and modification are effected by *lowering* the orgonotic potentials in the atmosphere wherever the CLB is pointed. According to the particular effect desired, regional weather changes ensue from such shifts in orgonotic potential.

Reich demonstrated that the pipes of his CLB drilled holes in the overcast, or in cloud masses, that reproduced the pattern of the "draw" pipes as mounted in his CLB. If the CLB were so designed as to have seven pipes mounted in a three-over-four configuration, then holes would appear in the overcast in a corresponding, three-over-four pattern.

Reich also showed that when the CLB was aimed directly at a cloud, the cloud was rapidly destroyed, i.e., "busted." Aiming the CLB *near* a cloud would cause augmentation of the cloud, i.e., expand the cloud in space.

The core of Reich's concept of CLB functioning is that the moisture-binding, moisture-attracting orgone energy is withdrawn from the clouds—or the atmosphere—into the water in the CLB sumping arrangement, via the draw pipes. Consequent gross effects in the atmosphere were held by Reich to derive from the ensuing orgonotic potential shifts and exchanges initiated by the CLBs action.

While this classical concept of CLB functioning may be subject to revision in the light of extensive engineering experience since Reich's death in 1957, in fairness to him, it should be emphasized that he was given no chance to explore fully and freely the operation of his own invention. His early pioneering in this field roughly coincided with the harassment of Reich and his work carried out by the Food and Drug Administration.

He was thus not permitted, by the unfolding of events, the opportunity to modify his original theories in this area. That he was capable of doing so is well attested to by his brilliant contributions to psychoanalysis, biophysics, sociology, and in the whole panorama of his findings on orgone energy.

So immense was Reich's prestige among those who understood his work, both during and following his lifetime, that until relatively recent times the classical concept of CLB functioning was never seriously questioned.

The Modern Concept

Based upon field experience since 1968, in a broad spectrum of successful weather engineering operations, the author of this article has formulated the modern concept of CLB functioning. This concept envisions the CLB as functioning in the opposite fashion to that theorized by Reich. The history of the electrical sciences confirms the ease with which fundamental polarity errors can be made in a new field. The author emphasizes that without Reich's discovery and theoretical initiative, there would be no modern concept of CLB functioning.

The modern concept holds that the CLB pipes *shoot* coherent beams of orgone energy into the atmosphere and beyond, to a theoretically infinite distance. The modern concept sees each draw pipe as analogous to the generator of a laser beam, except that the projected energy from the CLB is *bioenergetic* instead of electromagnetic.

This analogy gives adequate understanding of the enormous power to modify weather that resides in a CLB. A CLB can be equated with a laser "battery," consisting of an array of powerful EM beams, equivalent in number to the pipes in the CLB.

The CLB pipes, in a presently undetermined fashion probably related to the radial nature of orgone energy, free orgone energy from its physical accretion in water. Atmospheric changes of orgonotic potential are produced by the beams of orgone energy from the pipes *raising* the orgonotic potential in the atmosphere wherever the pipes are directed. This is exactly opposite in concept to the classical approach.

Holes are drilled in overcast because the high potential, coherent beams of orgone energy absorb all moisture within their own discrete location. An identical explanation covers the destruction, or busting, of clouds. Time-lapse motion pictures fail to support the concept that energy is withdrawn from the clouds by a CLB. On the contrary, such films confirm that the clouds are literally blown apart by a CLB.

The modern concept naturally accepts that removal of orgone energy from the vicinity of the CLB will occur as part of the CLB's mode of functioning.

Energy is being shot into space by the CLB and a local lowering of orgonotic potential occurs around the device. The tendency of human beings in the vicinity of an operating CLB to become *bioenergetically overcharged* verifies this situation. Such a condition can only be obtained, under the law of orgonotic or reversed potential, if the environment is markedly lower in charge than the human being.

The classical concept cannot satisfactorily explain the orgonotic overcharge of CLB operators and spectators on the basis of orgone energy being attracted to—i.e., "drawn" to—the CLB site. Such a circumstance would result in the withdrawal or lowering of charge from living systems near the CLB. The opposite actually occurs.

The local region of lowered orgonotic potential around the CLB, furthermore, plays an observably decisive role in diverting orgone energy streams, and in applying this diversional capability to such engineering operations as the production of regional, unforecast rain. Operational reports detailed in the comprehensive survey from which this article has been abstracted, contain two specific examples of this "spillover" effect, as it is known in orgone engineering.

To summarize, the classical concept holds that the CLB draws orgone energy and air to itself, and lowers orgonotic potential in the atmosphere wherever it is pointed. The modern concept holds that the CLB shoots orgone energy into space and draws atmosphere to itself, in a 180-degree reverse flow, from the direction of the shooting beam(s). Orgonotic potential is raised in the regions of the atmosphere to which the CLB is pointed.

Orgone Energy Streams in the Terrestrial Environment

Immanent in the discovery of orgone energy through biophysical, biopsychiatric, and bioenergetic research with human beings are the twin characteristics of pulsation and motion inseparable from life. The streams of energy felt in the healthy and lively human being have their counterparts in the orgone energy streams and motions that sustain the whole life of the Earth. In modern orgone energy weather engineering, the planet itself is approached as a gigantic living organism. Weather engineering, through the appropriate use of CLBs, locally manipulates two currently acknowledged orgone streams. Advanced experimental work, growing out of the modern concept of CLB functioning, indicates that there may be as many as thirty-two individual orgone energy streams involved in the total bioenergetic metabolism of planet Earth. The two streams currently acknowledged by most workers are:

(1) The planetary stream. Flows around the Earth from west to east, slightly faster than the Earth itself.

(2) The galactic stream. Flows generally southwest to northeast, but subject to local variations, especially in littoral areas, and is probably also *seasonal* in some aspects.

The essence of orgone energy weather engineering is its twofold character. There is always a *primary stimulus,* i.e., a direct stimulus to the orgone energy continuum, and a *secondary effect* resulting from that stimulus. Secondary effects occur at the level of ponderable, observable, and recordable meteorological phenomena. The science of meteorology, as presently constituted, is the systematic study of these secondary effects, without any consciousness of the existence of a primary energy continuum. Orgone energy theory and technology bring to meteorology a thus-far-missing primary dimension, and it should be emphasized that the two phases of a synthesized "new meteorology" are mutually supportive and mutually necessary.

From a broad spectrum of weather engineering operations the following operational account has been selected to demonstrate the superiority of orgone energy weather engineering over any other method either in use or envisioned by official sources. A rainmaking operation has not been selected for this presentation because it is not a difficult job of weather engineering, and has been done also—if only in a limited way—by application of cloud seeding.

Operation Kooler is an account of a successful venture into regional temperature control—the decisive countering of a destructive heatwave in the teeth of comprehensive official forecasts to the contrary. The opinion of this writer is that such operations dwarf anything at the disposal of nucleation proponents. Experience such as this teaches the orgone engineer that he has under the control of his will an apparatus of awesome potency. He may wreak havoc thousands of miles away, and unintentionally, through "side effects" to his local goal which are *direct* effects nevertheless.

The orgone envelope of the Earth is a reality to the experienced orgone engineer that is beyond contradiction. Minor stimuli are amplified by its special properties of continuity and elasticity. Aware that he works with a heretofore unapprehended continuum of vast power, he is duly respectful of that power and of the responsibility he bears when he embarks upon his operations.

Operation Kooler is reproduced here as Appendix II with the permission of the editors of the *Journal of Orgonomy*, wherein the account was first published in May 1972.

Five other successful weather engineering operations, planned and executed by the writer, are documented similarly to *Kooler* in the parent survey from which this article has been drawn. The efficacy and value of such weather engineering in the environmental struggle is obvious. Their commercial potential is staggering. All this lies open to human enterprise without the release into the atmosphere of chemicals of any kind. The inevitable question arising is: "Why hasn't this thing been taken up widely and commercially?"

The reasons for the nonuse of this technology are much more complex than the technology itself. Before briefly delineating those reasons, the writer wishes to emphasize that for more than two years such services have been on offer to the American government, foreign governments, and commercial firms with weather-related problems. Services are offered on a strict *no-results-no-pay* basis, and the writer's Merlin Weather Engineering† is the only weather modification contractor in the U.S. able and willing to operate on a basis of complete contingency. Therefore it is impossible for anyone contracting for these services to lose a penny.

The reasons for the nonuse of orgone energy weather engineering in solving pressing environmental problems are highly complex. Human reaction to the new principles in-

† See Appendix III for address. *Editors.*

volved is the core of the problem, and is rooted in two main elements:

(1) Politico-legal;
(2) Technico-neurotic.

The politico-legal problems circulate around the persecution of the late Reich by the Federal authorities, his death in a Federal prison in 1957, and the destruction by federal court order of his scientific books, bulletins, and journals. Should a federal agency now contract for orgone energy weather engineering services, for any reason, the persecution of Reich, the legal decisions against him, and the federal injunction against further work in this field would inevitably come up for review. Thus far, no one in the federal establishment has been willing to lay bare yesterday's mistakes in exchange for the solution of some of today's problems.

The technico-neurotic problems stem from the inability of formal, official science and technology to remotely approach, in efficacy and scope, what is feasible in the here-now with orgone energy weather engineering. One person with a cloudbuster rightly directed can do what battalions of scientists and technicians, backed by massive budgets and armadas of ships and planes, are unable to do.

In this situation, the bearers of officially accepted knowledge and theories inevitably feel challenged, and tend to react neurotically and irrationally. In fact, orgone energy weather engineering dovetails into, and makes whole, all the marvelous matters made accessible through conventional technology. Conventional data-gathering technology and facilities are absolutely necessary to the further development of orgone energy weather engineering, and to its international legal regulation for human welfare.

The technico-neurotic problem tends to reinforce the negative aspects of the politico-legal problems in all their complexity. The solution is straightforward and simple. Admit to the possibility that Reich was right, and the government wrong in ruining his life and career. Make amends, in accordance with fundamental precepts of decency and honor. Honest admission of error is human and upright.

In the technical sphere, open the doors to the wonders of

orgone energy weather engineering, and the comprehensive new concepts of world weather control that it makes possible. Let the new leaven and revivify the old and trusted ways. Objective evaluation of the power and scope of these new methods will quickly and permanently establish their merit. Humanity will be the beneficiary from such a new beginning.

SUGGESTED READINGS

The following publications, preferably studied in the order listed, will give a basic understanding of Dr. Wilhelm Reich's work, including his invention and early use of the cloud-buster. They are available in various editions.

> *The Function of the Orgasm,* Wilhelm Reich
> *The Cancer Biopathy,* Wilhelm Reich
> *Selected Writings,* Wilhelm Reich
> *Man in the Trap,* Elsworth Baker
> *Wilhelm Reich and Orgonomy,* Ola Raknes
> *Cosmic Superimposition,* Wilhelm Reich (available only in the original edition published by the Orgone Institute Press, Rangely, Maine, 1951)
> *Mass Psychology of Fascism,* Wilhelm Reich
> *Murder of Christ,* Wilhelm Reich
> *Listen, Little Man!,* Wilhelm Reich

The following articles in orgonomic periodicals will further illuminate the orgone energy engineering of weather, and some of the legal problems surrounding Dr. Reich's works and discoveries:

> *Journal of Orgonomy* Vol. 1, Nos. 1 and 2, 1967
> *Journal of Orgonomy* Vol. 2, No. 1, 1968

These issues give a full account of Dr. Reich's legal clash with the U.S. government in a two-part article by David Blasband, "The USA vs Wilhelm Reich."

> *Journal of Orgonomy* Vol. 2, No. 2, 1968
> "Mass and the Gravitational Function" by C. Frederick Rosenblum, B.S.
> *Journal of Orgonomy* Vol. 3, No. 2, 1969
> *Journal of Orgonomy* Vol. 4, No. 1, 1970

Journal of Orgonomy Vol. 4, No. 2, 1970
   Contain a three-part article "Problems of Atmospheric Circulation" by Richard Blasband, MD
Journal of Orgonomy Vol. 5, No. 2, 1971
"Operation Backwash #1"—Rainmaking Los Angeles Basin by Trevor J. Constable
Journal of Orgonomy Vol. 6, No. 1, 1972
"Operation Kooler"—Conquest of Southern California Heatwave
"Orop Hurricane Doria" by Richard Blasband, MD (Hurricane Diversion)

These books and professional references will provide a network of cross references into the general literature of orgonomy, which is of considerable scope and still growing.

32.

A First-Hand Look at Psychotronic Generators

STANLEY KRIPPNER

In 1973, during the First International Conference on Psychotronic Research, I met Robert Pavlita, a most enigmatic man. This controversial Czech inventor is the designer of the so-called "psychotronic generator," a device for storing and applying "biological energy."

I don't speak Czech, but with the help of a translator we had a long conversation, after which he demonstrated one of his generators to the people at the conference. His daughter participated by touching her hand to her head in a rhythmic way and then touching her hand to the generator. Within a few minutes the generator started to move. This is very difficult to explain in any conventional way, and I know one physicist who couldn't sleep all night trying to figure out how this happened.

During a more recent visit to Czechoslovakia (January 1974), I was privileged to see ten different demonstrations of psychotronic generators. Dr. Zdeněk Rèjdák and his staff drove me and my associate, Mark Rojèk, to Lazné Belohrad, a town famous for its spa. As we entered the building in which Mr. and Mrs. Pavlita, their daughter, and their son-in-law have their apartment, we noted a large sign. We asked for a translation and discovered that it read:

> This house was built, with the help of the Lord, for myself, for my relatives, for beauty, and for the needs of the city. . . .

> Franz Chernoch, 1899

"A First-Hand Look at Psychotronic Generators" by Stanley F. Krippner is an original article written especially for this volume and is printed here by permission of the author.

We were given a hospitable greeting by Pavlita and his family. Within a short time he produced several of his devices and told us something of their history. Pavlita had been building psychotronic generators for more than thirty-five years. How did he become interested in generators? He studied alchemy books. (Czechoslovakia has always been a center for the study of alchemy. There is a whole street in Prague where alchemists used to live.)

The shape of the items that the alchemists used was very intriguing to Pavlita. What he did was to put together various materials of different shape by trial and error. From this he found that there were three components of the psychotronic generators similar to those that the alchemists used. One is the shape of the device. Another is the material from which it is made. The third and most important is the biological rhythm—the means for getting the biological energy from the living organisms into the device. He says that there are at least sixty-eight centers of biological energy in the human body, and he has invented a generator for each one. Each of these generators is fueled in a different way, and each of them performs a different task.

Pavlita stated that eventually he discovered that the body's biological energy field acts electromagnetically in some experiments, electrostatically in some experiments, and in still other experiments, it acts in ways that defy either an electromagnetic or electrostatic explanation.

What amazed me about Pavlita is that he has obtained all of his information from alchemy books or from trial-and-error experiments. He is not familiar with acupuncture, bioenergetic therapy, dowsing, structural integration ("rolfing"), or any of the other procedures most parapsychologists know about and would naturally correlate with his work. He has gone very deeply into one specific area, and claims to have devised principles and laws by which he has produced these various devices.

According to Pavlita, any person can work with a psychotronic generator because all people possess biological energy fields. However, Pavlita himself was the subject in all but one of the experiments he attempted in our presence, his daughter serving as the subject in the other experiment.

We began to experience the most provocative part of Pavlita's work when we saw the very small and innocuous-looking devices he uses. One appears to be a magician's wand—a small rod with a ball on the end. This was a generator that he claimed to be able to take into a distant part of his house to work on for an hour. He then would place the generator in a room where fruit flies were feeding on rotten fruit. He would aim the generator toward the flies and within a few minutes they would start to drop dead, or so he attested.

After hearing this descriptive account, I asked Pavlita about this device: "If fruit flies drop dead when you point this generator at them, what do you think would happen with a large generator?" Pavlita replied: "This is a generator that has very dangerous implications. I'm too soft-hearted to kill anything but flies, but there is no doubt in my mind that one can kill a cat, a dog, even human beings, with a large enough generator."

In the early days of his work, he said, he and his daughter were working on one of these experimental generators when suddenly her arm became paralyzed. They couldn't decide what to do. If they had taken her to a doctor, Pavlita thought, he would have said that it was psychosomatic. What Pavlita did was to work around the clock for three days, inventing another generator that restored natural movement to her arm again.

After relating the story of his daughter's paralysis and recovery, Pavlita made it very clear that the reason he had not yet revealed his secrets is because he does not know if the world is ready for them. I don't know either, but there is one thing that is obvious: the day may come when psychotronic generators are widely available. According to Pavlita, they are simple and inexpensive to make. Once more people use the generators, their true functions and possibilities can be more accurately assessed.

Demonstration 1

Pavlita placed a compass directly in front of him on a table. He placed a psychotronic generator between himself and the compass. This generator consisted of a steel rectangle covered by a cone. After lifting off the cone and setting it aside, Pavlita passed the rectangular generator over the compass; the compass needle was not affected. Pavlita then began to touch the generator to his right temporal lobe, holding it in his right hand and making the contact with his head in a rhythmical manner. He explained he was "completing a circuit of human biological energy," thus permitting the generator to store the energy. After about two minutes, Pavlita held the generator over the compass; the needle moved five degrees, from south to north. Pavlita then removed three fingers from the generator, placing them under the palm of his hand. As the generator approached the compass, the south-to-north movement of the needle exceeded 15 degrees. By altering the position of his fingers in the rectangular form in other ways, Pavlita was able to increase or decrease the effect upon the compass needle.

Demonstration 2

The second experiment was identical to the first experiment except that Pavlita held the rectangular generator with his left hand and touched it to his left temporal lobe. The compass needle, when approached by the generator, moved the same number of degrees as before, except in a north-to-south direction. Then Pavlita lifted the generator with his left hand and placed it in his right hand. The compass needle moved from south-to-north as the generator approached it. Pavlita moved to the opposite side of the table; trials with the left hand then were accompanied by a south-to-north movement of the compass needle and vice versa.

At one point, the movement of the compass needle was minimal. Pavlita touched the generator to his left temporal lobe several times; thereafter, the movement of the compass needle increased upon the next trial. In commenting on these two experiments, Pavlita said that human biological energy is analogous in some ways to the Earth's north and south magnetic poles. He also noted that the human biological energy field completely surrounded the body and exists within the body as well.

Demonstration 3

Pavlita placed a metal, scaffoldlike stand on the table which resembled an inverted letter "L." A string was tied to the protruding arm of the scaffold and a flat, lightweight bar magnet was tied to the string. A steel psychotronic generator was placed between Pavlita and the stand; the generator was cube shaped with a small protuberance at its top.

Pavlita left the room to demonstrate that he could activate the cube-shaped form from a distance. After about three minutes, he returned. He then brought the cube near the north pole of the bar magnet; the magnet moved toward the cube. However, the magnet was repelled when the cube approached the south pole of the magnet.

Pavlita faced south during the first half of this experiment. He then moved to the other side of the table and faced north. The experiment was repeated with the opposite results. This time he did not leave the room but touched the generator to his right temporal lobe with his right hand, using a different rhythm than in the earlier experiments. He stared intently at the magnet all the while. When Pavlita brought the cube near the north pole of the magnet, it was repelled. However, the magnet was attracted to the cube when the south pole was approached.

Pavlita commented that the eyes are important in this experiment and that the results demonstrate a brain "circuit" which is connected to the hands.

Demonstration 4

The same bar magnet and scaffoldlike stand were used for this experiment, but a different steel generator was utilized. This psychotronic generator was goblet shaped, but topped by a copper and bronze cover shaped like a holly leaf. Pavlita (facing south) touched his right thumb, first to his frontal lobes, then to the cover of the generator, making a rhythmic movement which lasted about one minute. When he approached the bar magnet's north pole, it moved toward his thumb; when he approached the magnet's south pole, it was repelled by his thumb.

Demonstration 5

All the materials were in the same position as for the fourth experiment. At this point, Pavlita (facing south) placed a mirror in back of the generator. Again he approached the magnet's north pole, placing his finger behind the mirror, but this time the magnet moved away from his thumb. When he approached the south pole, the magnet was attracted to his thumb. Pavlita commented that the biological energy field exerted these effects by passing through the mirror. He stated the results were a function of the relationship formed between an object and its image.

Demonstration 6

For this experiment, the mirror was removed, but the stand and goblet-shaped generator remained. Pavlita placed a narrow steel bar on the table. The bar was about three inches long and was placed between Pavlita and the generator so that it touched the base of the generator.

Pavlita (facing south) touched his right thumb knuckle to his right temporal lobe. He then placed his knuckle on the end of the bar nearest to him. Immediately, the north pole of the magnet swung toward the generator. It hovered in the same position until Pavlita removed his knuckle from the bar. At this point, the magnet resumed its original position. Pavlita commented that the magnet resembled the needle of a compass and was reacting to the human body's biological energy field, amplified by this procedure.

Demonstration 7

Again, the scaffold-shaped stand was used. However, the bar magnet was replaced by a narrow, cylindrical-shaped piece of wood, about two inches in length. Before the wood was suspended from the stand, it was placed in a wide, cylindrical-shaped psychotronic generator. Diagonal marks could be seen on the outside of the generator; Pavlita remarked that a "biologically activated energy field" had been burned into the generator. After the wood was placed in the generator, it protruded slightly; a narrow, rectangular steel bar was placed against the wood so that one end rested on the table and the other end rested on the wood itself. Pavlita called this procedure "closing the circuit." After about three minutes, the wood was taken from the generator and suspended by string, from the metal stand.

Pavlita picked up a ferret magnet and brought it toward one end of the piece of wood. The wood was repelled. He brought the magnet toward the other end of the wood; it was attracted. In other words, the piece of wood gave every appearance of having been magnetized. Some observers would claim that the generators are "electrets" which create electrostatic fields, but others would claim that a new energy form is involved.

Demonstration 8

Once again, the scaffoldlike stand was used. Again, a narrow, cylindrical-shaped piece of wood was used that was approximately two inches in length. Pavlita produced a psychotronic generator shaped something like a flashlight. There were holes in the bulbous top of the generator; Pavlita inserted the wood into these holes, first one end of the wood and then the other. He then inserted the entire piece of wood into a long hole on the top of the generator and moved both hands in front of the generator in a rhythmic up-and-down movement with fingers outstretched. After about two minutes of these movements, the wood was suspended to the stand.

As Pavlita held a ferret magnet and approached the wood, one side of the stick was repelled and one was attracted. Again, a piece of wood had apparently been magnetized. Pavlita commented that the hand movements are not absolutely necessary, but accelerate the speed at which the wood is affected.

Demonstration 9

Pavlita's daughter produced a psychotronic generator shaped something like a microphone. A point protruded from the top half of the generator and she touched this to her frontal lobes in a rhythmical manner for about three minutes. The generator was then placed in front of a semicircular solid copper screen. A light metal cone was placed on the top of the generator. She then touched the table lightly with the fingers of her left hand. It began to revolve from left to right. When Pavlita removed her fingers, the cone stopped its motion; when she again touched the table, the cone resumed its movement. She called this procedure "completing the circuit."

After its motion stopped completely, Pavlita's daughter again touched the generator to her frontal lobes. The cone was again placed on top of the generator and once more revolved for a short period of time.

Pavlita commented that this was an "accumulating type" generator. He said that all his generators were "purpose specific" and corresponded to various "biocircuits" of the body of which he claims to have identified sixty-eight.

Demonstration 10

Again the metal stand was used and a flat, rectangular piece of wood (resembling the bar magnet in size and shape) was suspended from it. Pavlita produced a rectangular psychotronic generator which fit easily into the palm of his hand. He held the generator with his thumb on the bottom and the other four fingers on top. As it approached the stand, the wood turned to the right. Pavlita then held the generator between his thumb and forefinger. This time when he approached the wood, it turned to the left.

This phenomenon did not seem to be preceded by any type of body rhythm which would activate the generator.

DISCUSSION

Pavlita told us that he has recorded his experiments in great detail in twenty handwritten volumes, none of which has been published. When he first began his research some thirty-five years ago, he worked by trial and error. Now, however, he knows the basic principles involved. For example, he is aware of the basic bodily biocircuits and how each can be used in a generator. Once the biological energy field is brought into a generator, it stays there permanently. However, a special induction procedure must be used to activate many of the generators. This induction utilizes various bodily "codes."

Pavlita told us that voltmeters and electrometers do not pick up biological energy. During human transmission of this energy, however, some psychophysiological differences were noted. One's heartbeat rate slows down and breathing becomes irregular.

No material has been found by Pavlita which can insulate against the effect of biological energy. Furthermore, it can affect any type of matter to some extent.

Pavlita says he is too "soft-hearted" to work with any type of living creature but insects. When insects are exposed to his lethal generator, their antennae quiver first. Then their feet and legs shake. Soon they appear stunned or paralyzed. Then they collapse and die. However, the effects can be reversed if the insect has not yet collapsed.

Pavlita has done some work with plants, having "shaken" or "physically transported" leaves and flowers at a distance. One type of generator works automatically by absorbing energy from the living organisms around it; this type stimulates growth of plants and enhances seed germination in experiments with pea and lentil seeds. The other type of generator must have biological energy directed into it; this type stunts the growth of plants. The first generator has purportedly been able to purify waste water from a dye factory in small amounts. For this purpose small pieces of stainless steel were treated by the generator, then put into the polluted water—which became clean again. Pavlita has thought of trying to treat stones instead of steel, then attempting to depollute a lake or a river.

Pavlita sees a number of practical uses for his generators. These include biological communication (when other communication systems are nonoperable), medical diagnosis (of the body's biocircuits), the magnetization of material (he claims that any material can be magnetized), testing the contents of unknown material, assessing the healing rate of an injured or sick person (the stronger the field, the better one's health), assessing the deterioration rate of a dying organism, and determining how long an organism has been dead.

Pavlita told us that the right-hand side of the body usually attracts, that the left-hand side usually repels, and that left-handed people are not observably different than right-handed people. He speaks of "plus" and "minus" impulses in terms that remind one of the oriental concepts of yang and yin. From time to time, Pavlita must utilize special procedures to produce the desired balance between "plus" and "minus" impulses; an overabundance of the latter is not uncommon and is not desirable.

By combining several generators, Pavlita can also combine their functions. Some experiments have involved as many as seven generators for a given purpose. The speed at which a function operates depends upon the conduction of biological energy from the organism to the generator. The principle that "form follows function" is basic to the design of the generators, many of which are built to channel energy from two poles to a narrow point.

Psychotronic generators have not yet been used in experiments with the Kirlian photography device, with voltage gradients, with acupuncture points, with altered states of consciousness, with hemispheric brain differences, or with "psychic" healing. However, Pavlita does claim that he can alter a person's movements with his generators, such as making a person pick up an object with the left hand instead of the right hand.

Pavlita claims that he has been able to produce generators which calibrate so well with a person's "biocircuits" that they can be activated at a distance. Once, a generator in Karlsbad was activated by a person in Bradoc Králové, a distance of over 150 miles. For this type of experiment to be successful, the generator must be calibrated with a person's biological energy field, a process which takes from two to three hours.

Pavlita's current project involves the transfer at a distance of biological energy itself. He believes he can make this transfer at a distance of several miles, and may demonstrate it at some point in the future.

After spending three hours with Pavlita, and enjoying the hospitality so lavishly offered by him and his family, I was impressed by his devotion to his work. I am aware that alternative explanations to his demonstrations exist (hidden magnets, electrostatic effects, etc.). It is also possible that Pavlita and his daughter unwittingly have used their own psychokinetic abilities to create the effects, rather than tapping sources of "biological energy" common to everyone. Only future research will indicate whether the psychotronic generators are the scientific breakthrough that his supporters suspect.

33.

Methods of Detecting and Measuring Healing Energies

ROBERT N. MILLER

Instances of paranormal healing are recorded in the earliest historical writings. Ever since the time of Imhotep, the famous sage and physician of ancient Egypt, individuals have been healed by mental and physical methods which are just beginning to be understood by modern science.

However, because the art of mental healing seems contrary to the laws of medical science, it is difficult to understand how healing by mental methods can occur. Also, it is difficult to ascertain the progress of new practitioners because no positive method for measuring the effectiveness of a healer exists at the present time. Such a method, if it could be developed and perfected, would be a powerful tool for accelerating the training process and for instilling confidence in the mind of the practitioner.

The objective of our research program* is to develop practical methods for measuring the effectiveness of healers and to clarify the mental and physical processes involved in successful healing. The most important accomplishment of the past year has been the scientific confirmation of the existence of a healing energy. In addition, several methods for measuring the energy were investigated and perfected. The principal test subject was Mrs. Olga Worrall, a well known healer and lecturer.[1]

"Methods of Detecting and Measuring Healing Energies" by Robert N. Miller is an unpublished article. It appeared in abridged form in *Science of Mind* as "The Energies of Spiritual Healing," January–February 1976.

* Sponsored by the Ernest Holmes Research Foundation. *Editors.*

Cloud Chamber Tests

The cloud chamber experiment, which is described in detail in the July 1974 issue of *Science of Mind*, was the most dramatic of the tests with the healing energies. The cloud chamber is a glass cylinder which has an aluminum bottom and a viewing glass across the top. When methyl alcohol is placed in the chamber and the entire unit is positioned on a flat block of dry ice, a zone of alcohol mist is created in the chamber. High-energy atomic particles generate vapor trails when they pass through the sensitive zone.

By holding her hands around the unit as if it were a patient undergoing treatment, Mrs. Worrall was able to produce a moving wave pattern inside the chamber. Several weeks later, from a distance of six hundred miles, she again caused a wave motion to develop within the chamber. The results of these experiments indicate that "thoughts are things" and visible manifestations in the physical world can be produced mentally from a distance.

Plant Potential Experiments

Cleve Backster and Marcel Vogel claim to have demonstrated that thought can produce changes in the electrical potentials of plant leaves. This phenomenon was used as a means for detecting the energies associated with healing. A philodendron plant was used as the sensing unit. Three silver–silver chloride electrodes were attached to a leaf of the plant. The wires from the electrodes were connected to a preamplifier which, in turn, was connected to an amplifier and a strip chart recorder.

In the normal state a philodendron plant produces an oscillating, low-amplitude electrical signal. When Mrs. Worrall placed her hands about four inches away from the plant, the amplitude of the signal, which was registering on the strip chart recorder, increased greatly. At first it was believed that Mrs. Worrall was functioning like an antenna and the increase was due to normal electrical pickup. However, when other members of the research team held their hands near the plant, only a slight effect was produced.

Several weeks later Dr. Alex Tanous, a healer from Portland, Maine, attempted to influence the plant from a distance of eight feet. When Dr. Tanous mentally tuned in to the plant, the leaf potential trace steadied and then decreased in amplitude. Then, as he mentally directed bursts of energy to the plant, there were corresponding increases in the width of the plant potential trace.

The results obtained so far with the plant potential experiments indicate that plants are good detectors for the energies associated with healing.

Biofeedback Experiments

A series of biofeedback experiments were conducted with both Mrs. Worrall and Dr. Tanous. Mrs. Worrall was asked if she alters her state of consciousness in any way during healing. She said that she does not knowingly do so but merely places her hands on the patient and permits the energy to flow. An Aquarius Electronics biofeedback headset was placed on Mrs. Worrall and her brain waves were recorded before and during healing. Two of the three electrodes were held against her forehead, one over each eyebrow, by an elastic band. The third electrode was positioned against the back of her head on the right side. The left portion of Figure 1 shows the brain wave pattern produced when Mrs. Worrall is in a normal state of consciousness. The tracing has a frequency range of fourteen to twenty-five cycles per second, is somewhat erratic, and corresponds to the beta rhythm.

Mrs. Worrall then administered healing to one of the experimenters by laying-on-of-hands. The right-hand side of Figure 1 shows the brain wave pattern which was produced. The low-frequency, low-amplitude trace is characteristic of the alpha and theta rhythms.

The most remarkable aspect of this experiment was the rapidity with which Mrs. Worrall's brain wave pattern changed from beta to alpha. The time line at the top of Figure 1

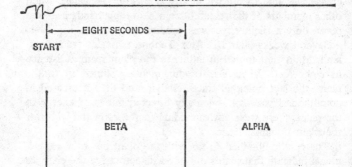

FIGURE 1 *Brain wave trace illustrating Mrs. Worrall's extremely rapid transition from beta to alpha production.*

shows that the change occurred within eight seconds of her initiation of the healing procedure. Meditation research has shown that it takes the average person five to twenty minutes to achieve this state of consciousness. Mrs. Worrall is such a gifted healer that she automatically makes the transition within a few seconds.

Mr. Tanous's brain waves were also recorded while he was in a normal state and while he was mentally projecting energy to a plant. In the normal state he generated a beta pattern but was in the alpha and theta range while he was influencing the plant. It took Mr. Tanous a little more than a minute to make the transition.

Crystallization Effects

It was discovered that solutions of copper salts, under carefully controlled conditions, are sensitive to the energies from a healer's hands. A small pool containing exactly five drops of solution was pipetted onto each of two polyethylene disks. Mrs. Worrall treated one specimen by holding her hands around it for three minutes. The second specimen served as a control. After two days at room temperature (20°–25° C) and 50% relative humidity, the control specimen had crystallized in a jade green monoclinic structure. The treated specimen was also monoclinic but had a coarser grain and was turquois blue in color. The difference in the crystalline structure of the untreated and treated specimens was readily apparent.

Scores of tests were conducted and it was found that copper salt solutions are reliable indicators of energies provided all the variables are carefully controlled. These include the concentration of the solution, the sources of the water, the volume of solution, the relative humidity of the environment, the surface on which the crystallization takes place, and the duration of treatment of the solution by the healer. Both the treated and the control specimens initially crystallize in a green color. After two days at room temperature and 50% relative humidity, the control specimen is still green but the treated specimen is blue.

Surface Tension of Water

It was suspected that the variation in the structure and color of the crystallized copper salts was caused by a difference in the properties of the water. Samples of distilled water which had been treated by a healer and untreated water were tested for viscosity, electrical conductivity, capacitance, refractive index, infrared absorption, and surface tension. There were little or no differences in viscosity and refractive index. There were differences in electrical conductivity and capacitance but no consistent pattern could be established. The most significant differences were in the surface tension and infrared absorption.

A Fisher Model 20 Du Nouy Type Tensiometer was used to make the surface tension measurements. This instrument has a platinum–iridium ring of precisely known dimensions suspended from a counterbalanced lever arm. The ring is immersed in the liquid being studied. The force necessary to separate the ring from the liquid is measured and read directly in dynes/cm. Table 1 summarizes the results of tests in which samples of water were energized and compared with control samples.

EFFECT OF HEALING ENERGY ON SURFACE TENSION OF WATER

| Healer | Water Source | Surface Tension (Dynes/CM) | |
		Control	Treated
Worrall	Atlanta	70.1	62.9
Hill	Decatur	68.3	60.7
Miller	Distilled	74.6	71.1
	8 ppm NaCl	76.7	70.1
	5 ppm NaCl	77.0	70.1

TABLE 1

Effect of treatment by three different individuals upon the surface tension of water. Mrs. Worrall and Kathryn Hill, recognized healers, reduced the surface tension of water 7.2 and 7.6 dynes/cm, respectively. Dr. R. N. Miller, the author, produced a smaller effect upon distilled water and water containing 8 and 5 ppm NaCl. These results indicate that quantitative data may be obtained by measuring the surface tension of water.

For these tests the healers held their hands around a 500-ml beaker of water for exactly three minutes (see photo insert). Subsequent experiments revealed that the maximum transfer of energy is produced when the water is placed in test tubes and the healer holds the test tubes for twenty minutes. The results of the tests summarized in Table 1 indicate that the surface tension of water which has been exposed to a healer's hands is substantially reduced. The most significant feature of this method for detecting the energy from a healer's hands is that, for the first time, a method exists for *quantitatively* measuring the energy.

Properties of Water Treated with Magnets

Baron Karl von Reichenbach reported in the last century that magnets, as well as humans, give off some type of energy.[2] Additional testing disclosed that magnets alter the properties of water in the same manner as do healers. Six Teflon-coated stirring magnets, 3/8 in. in diameter and 2 in. long, were immersed in 500 ml of distilled water for 4½ hours. At the end of that time the control specimen still had its original surface tension of 75.6 dynes/cm but the water which had been treated with the magnets had a surface tension of 60.4 dynes/cm.

Copper salt solutions in a Tygon plastic container were exposed to a magnetic field of 4500 gauss for 15 minutes. After two days at room temperature and 50% relative humidity, the crystals from the solution which had been exposed to the magnet were turquois blue, while the crystals from the control solution were jade green. This same color pattern is obtained when the test solution is treated by a healer.

Additional tests were conducted to determine the effect of water treated by a magnet and water treated by a healer upon the growth of rye grass. Exactly 25 rye grass seeds were placed in each of six plastic cups of potting soil. Holes were punched in the bottom of the cups and each cup was placed on a saucer. The water was placed in the saucer so the seeds obtained their water at a uniform rate by capillary action. Two of the cups were watered every day with Atlanta tap water, two with tap water which had been treated by Mrs. Worrall about 30 days before the tests, and two with the tap water which had been exposed for 16 hours to a magnet having a field strength of 1500 gauss. At the end of four days, 8% of the seeds in the control cups had sprouted, 36% of the seeds in the cups with the healer-treated water had sprouted, and 68% sprouting occurred in the cups with the magnet-exposed water.

After eight days the length of each blade of grass was carefully measured. The average height of the control blades was 2.8 in., the blades watered with the healer-treated water averaged 2.9 in., and the grass blades watered with the magnet-exposed water had an average length of 3.6 in., 28.6% more than the controls. If growth rate may be equated to healing, the results indicate that healing energies emanate from magnets. Indeed, this was one of the claims made by Mesmer in the middle 1800s.[3]

It was anticipated that the healer-treated water and the magnet-treated water would increase growth rate by approximately the same amount. The water which had been energized by Mrs. Worrall was treated 30 days before the grass growing experiment. This raised the question of whether the healer-treated water had lost energy prior to its being used in the experiment.

Stability of Energized Water

Additional experiments with water energized by healers or magnets demonstrated that the water gradually gives up the energy to the surrounding environment. Two hundred and fifty (250) ml of distilled water was energized by immersing two small ceramic ferromagnetic oxide magnets, ¾ in. in diameter and ⅛ in. thick, in the water for 15 minutes. This resulted in lowering the surface tension of the water to 62.2 dynes/cm. The open beaker was then exposed to a normal room temperature (20°–25° C) environment for 70 hours while the surface tension of the water was checked at periodic intervals. Figure 2 plots the change in the surface tension during that time period. By the end of 24 hours the surface tension was back to its normal range of 72–73 dynes/cm. It was found that the energy may be withdrawn from the water in a few minutes by swirling it in a stainless-steel beaker, the mass of stainless steel apparently acting as an energy sink.

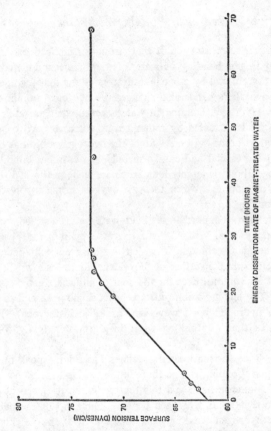

FIGURE 2 Plot showing rate of energy transfer from treated water to the environment. Water energized with ceramic magnets underwent a reduction in surface tension from 75.0 to 62.2 dynes/cm. When exposed to a room temperature environment in an open 250-ml glass beaker, the surface tension of the water changed at a uniform rate during a 24-hour period and then remained fairly constant.

Change in Hydrogen Bonding of Water

Russian scientists[4] report that strong magnetic fields affect the hydrogen bonding of water. Experiments conducted on this program and by other investigators[5] show that the energy from a healer's hands also changes the hydrogen bonding of water. Hydrogen bonding in water occurs when an atom of hydrogen is attracted by rather strong forces to two oxygen atoms instead of only one.[6] Since the hydrogen atom has only one stable orbital and can form only one covalent bond, the hydrogen bond is largely ionic in character with the hydrogen atom oscillating between the two oxygen atoms involved in the bonding.

Specimens of normal distilled water and distilled water treated by Mrs. Worrall were analyzed by infrared absorption, using a technique in which the infrared light beam is reflected from the surface of the water. Figure 3 shows the infrared absorption traces for the control and the treated specimens. The left-hand control trace has a single peak and this is in the hydrogen bond wave length (2.8–3.2 microns). This indicates that all the hydrogen in the water is hydrogen bonded.

The trace for the treated specimen has a large peak in the hydrogen bonding range but has a second peak in the 2.6–2.8-micron band and this represents the presence of hydrogen that is not hydrogen bonded. The ratio of the height of the hydrogen bonding peak to the sum of the heights of both peaks, expressed as percent, shows that only 97.04% of the hydrogen in the treated water is hydrogen bonded. These infrared absorption traces support the conclusion that energy from a healer's hands produces changes in the bond energies and molecular structure of water.

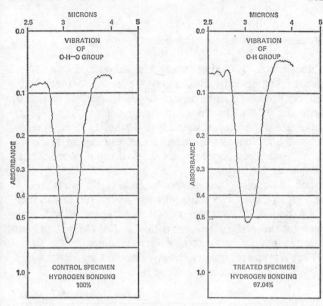

FIGURE 3 *Infrared absorption spectra of distilled water and distilled water which was energized by Olga Worrall.*

Measuring the Energy from a Healer's Hands

The late Ambrose Worrall[7] called the energy from a healer's hands "paraelectricity" because it acts like electricity in flowing from a high potential source to a person or object at lower potential. It is recommended that the unit of quantity for paraelectricity be named a "Worrall" and be defined as the energy required to reduce the surface tension of 100 ml of distilled water from its normal state (72.75 dynes/cm at 20° C) by 10 dynes/cm.

The following procedure has been developed and is now being used to measure the energy from individuals. It may prove to be useful to physicians for measuring the vital energy of patients.

Procedure for Measuring Paraelectricity

Pour exactly 100 ml of freshly distilled water into a 150-ml glass beaker or Petri dish. Allow the water to reach room temperature and then determine the initial surface tension of the water with a Du Nuoy type tensiometer.

Prepare two pieces of stainless steel wire, 1/16 in. in diameter and 8 in. long, by washing, rinsing, and drying. Place one end of each piece of wire in the distilled water, immersing to a depth of 1–1½ in.

The test subject then grasps the ends of the wires, one in each hand, for exactly three minutes. At the end of the energizing period, remove the wires from the water and again measure the surface tension with the Du Nuoy type tensiometer, taking the average of three readings.

The Worralls of paraelectricity absorbed by the water is calculated by the following formula:

$$\text{Worralls} = \frac{\text{Initial Surface Tension} - \text{Final Surface Tension}}{10}$$

Discussion and Summary

Reproducible results from experiments with paraelectricity require strict control of all the variables involved. This energy is absorbed and conducted by various materials in unpredictable ways. The introduction of metal stirring rods or plastic beakers into the experiments cause a variation in the results obtained. The use of glass containers and stirring rods is mandatory.

The results of the experiments described in this paper indicate that a primary energy, different from the energies recognized by modern science, is emitted by magnets and by the hands of healers. The energies from both sources cause decreases in the surface tension of water, change the structure and color of crystals from cupric chloride solutions, change the hydrogen bonding of water, and accelerate the growth rate of rye grass.

Because it is similar to electricity but has its own unique characteristics, the energy has been given the name "paraelectricity." This primary energy is the "life force" of the ancient Chinese, the prana of the yogis, the odic force of von Reichenbach, and the orgone energy of Wilhelm Reich. A procedure for quantitatively measuring paraelectricity has been developed. This procedure and the techniques described in this paper may be used to scientifically study the nature of paraelectricity and determine how it may be generated, stored, transferred, and used with maximum efficiency.

Conclusions

(1) A primary energy, different from heat, light, or electricity, is emitted from a healer's hands and from magnets.

(2) This energy may be detected and quantitatively measured by its effect upon the surface tension of water.

(3) Crystals forming from solutions of cupric chloride will give visual indications of the presence of the energy.

(4) Water which has been treated by a healer or a magnet increases the growth rate of plants.

(5) Water which has been treated by a healer or a magnet undergoes changes in hydrogen bonding.

(6) Energized water is unstable and gives up the excess energy to the environment or to any object in contact with the water.

REFERENCES

1. J. Carlova, *Medical Economics,* 17 September 1973, 99.
2. Karl von Reichenbach, *Letters on Od and Magnetism* (London: University Books, 1968).
3. Jerome Eden, *Animal Magnetism* (Jericho, N.Y.: Exposition Press, 1974).

4. G. W. De la Warr and D. Baker, *Biomagnetism* (Oxford, England: Delawarr Laboratories, 1967), pp. 53–56.

5. B. Grad, *Intern. J. Parapsychology* 6, 4 (1962).

6. A. K. Schmidt and C. A. Marlies, *Principles of High Polymer Theory and Practice* (New York: McGraw-Hill, 1948), pp. 33–34.

7. A. Worrall and O. Worrall, *Explore Your Psychic World* (New York: Harper & Row, 1970).

34.

The Motoyama Device: Measuring Psychic Energy

HIROSHI MOTOYAMA

A yogi is able to experience a deeper and broader range of mental activity than others. The functioning of his mind—manifesting psi-ability—is not of a physical nature: it is non-physical and capable of having a direct effect on the functioning of another person's physical body. . . .

The following is the explanation, according to yoga doctrine, of this nonphysical energy. When the mind is freed from the physical world by loosening its ties with the human body through a process of deep mental concentration, this nonphysical energy (*prana*) is absorbed from the universe through one or more chakras and causes certain transformations in the body. A chakra is a center in a subtle body, a higher dimensional entity, and is seen extraordinarily as a circle of light or an aura. Chakras, situated along the spinal cord in the body's trunk, in the forehead above and between the eyes, and at the top of the head, control corresponding internal organs and nervous plexuses within the body. (See Figure 1.)

This energy is transmitted, on the one hand, through the spinal column and transformed into nervous energy; on the other, it is passed along as *ki* (vital force) to the meridians of acupuncture. These two energy forms are thus distributed to every part of the body, controlling it and keeping the body in a living condition.

The real existence of these chakras and meridians has been

"The Motoyama Device: Measuring Psychic Energy" by Hiroshi Motoyama originally appeared in *Impact of Science on Society*, Vol. 24, No. 4, 1974. Copyright © 1974 by The Unesco Press and reprinted by permission.

FIGURE 1   *Disposition of chakras along the human body's longitudinal axis in their symbolic representations.*

made clear, by myself, in a series of physiological experiments using an electroencephalograph.[1, 2] The nonphysical psi-energy already mentioned radiates from the awakened chakra and the meridian points situated at the tips of the fingers and toes, and this energy is capable of having a strong influence on another person's body. . . .

To see if it could be established experimentally that some form of energy emanates from chakras, I next designed a series of measurements with my recently developed "apparatus for measuring vital energy." In devising this equipment, I had to design and construct a preamplifier with an input impedance of near infinity; this I did by using high-sensitivity integrated circuits which were then connected to a direct current amplifier. I built a sturdy, boxlike frame (2 m high, 1 m wide, and 1 m deep), equipped on ceiling and floor with copper electrode plates (40 × 40 cm) and four more electrode plates (20 × 40 cm) mounted on the inside front, back, left, and right and isolated from a square frame, suspended from four pulley wheels by a system of ropes; the frame was thus free to travel up or down within the box. The entire structure looks something like a telephone booth.

In order to make measurements of the utmost accuracy, this structure was placed inside an earthed (grounded), lead-lined room to assure maximal shielding from extraneous electromagnetic interference. The basic principle in using the electrode frame was that, by positioning the four movable copper plates opposite any of the chakra of the subject standing inside the box, energy emanating from a given chakra would be detected as a slight variation in the electromagnetic field set up across the plane of the electrode plates; if amplified, the variation could be recorded on a highly sensitive strip chart recorder. It was imperative, during the test, that there be no contact between the subject and the electrode plate; otherwise, this would break the preamplifier. Test data were obtained in the cases of (a) no subject inside the box, (b) an ordinary person serving as subject, and (c) a subject manifesting psi-ability. Changes in electrical potential recorded from the vertex of the skull, the forehead, throat, lungs, heart, stomach, navel, abdomen, coccyx, knees and ankles in each case showed, respectively, (a) of course, nil, (b) a slight change, and (c) considerable change. The comparative results of this testing are shown in Figure 2; these data are unique in that they represent the first time anyone has measured, as far as I know, energy of this kind in this manner. It can thus be inferred that a form of energy emanates, in fact, from the chakra of a subject possessing psi-ability.

Next, I carried out a number of measurements with a psychic subject to see what kind of difference appeared in the energy radiating from a fully awakened chakra and that from a lesser, partially awakened one. The data (measurement of the electrical potential and frequency) recorded in the case of electrodes placed in proximity to a chakra easily emitting energy through the subject's will were remarkably different from those data obtained when the electrodes were placed near a

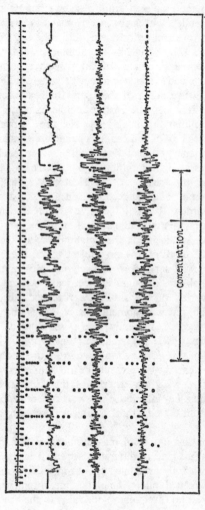

FIGURE 2 *Recordings made inside test structure of bodily reactions for ajna chakra. This chakra is situated above and between the eyes. It corresponds to and controls the pituitary gland, and is fully awakened and controlled by the subject. Before and after mental concentration, at rest and relaxed, the subject is not concentrating on chakra.*

concentration

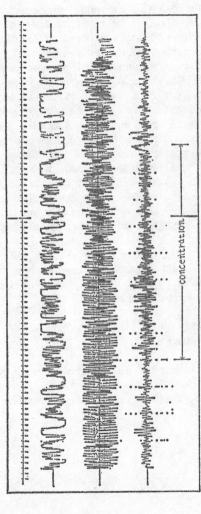

FIGURE 3 Recordings similar to those in Figure 2 for swadhisthana chakra, situated 3–4 cm below the navel, corresponding to and controlling the genito-urinary organs. This chakra is partially awakened by the subject, but here not yet under his control. Both this and Figure 2 were made February 13, 1974 on subject K.Y., in an ambient temperature of 10.5° C., using the "apparatus for measuring vital energy."

chakra not readily emitting energy through the will of the subject (compare Figures 2 and 3). There was also a marked contrast in the data when the subject was in a quiescent state (Figure 2). Thus can be reconfirmed, from the data collected, that a form of energy radiates from the awakened chakra of an individual manifesting psi-ability.

In regard to paranormal phenomena such as those known as psychokinesis, it is clear that psi-energy emanates from the chakra and meridian points of a psychic person; this energy seems to have a significant influence over the psychophysical functions of the person to whom the energy is directed. I believe that further work in this field of research, done in depth, will also resolve the question of mind–body correlation as well as bring to light accurate training methods; with the latter, it will be possible to verify subjectively that the human mind exists not only on the psychophysical plane but that it is capable of evolving to the point where it can exist and function in dimensions beyond those to which we are physically limited at present.

It is my hope, too, that, with time, this research will aid greatly the laying of a solid foundation upon which man will be able to build a peaceful world community where the family of nations can co-exist harmoniously.

REFERENCES

1. H. Motoyama, "Chakras and the autonomic nervous system," *Relig. Psychol.*, **3**.
2. H. Motoyama, "Do meridians exist?" *Relig. Parapsychol.*, **2, 1**.

35.

Paranormal Tape-Recorded Voices:
A Paraphysical Breakthrough

D. SCOTT ROGO

The parapsychological world was stunned when in 1959 and then in the 1960s Friedrich Jurgenson in Sweden and Konstantin Raudive in Germany announced to the world that they had tape-recorded the voices of the dead. Similar work by Attila (Art) von Szalay and Raymond Bayless in the U.S. predated this discovery by several years. Fleeting and often whispering voices seemed to be imprinted directly onto their tapes by some psychic process. Oftentimes Jurgenson or Raudive would sit with a group of people and engage in casual conversation for a few minutes as they ran a tape recorder. When the tape was replayed, extra voices would be heard on the recording. The voices, darting in and out of the conversation, would call the experimenters' names, comment on the conversation, or answer specific questions if some were asked. The voices often claimed to be voices of the dead. (Sometimes the tape recorder would be hooked up to a white-noise band between stations on a radio set, but this method made it hard to filter out extraneous broadcast interference which can get onto the tape and which could be mistaken for paranormal voices.)

What are these voices? Or rather, who are they? Are they actually paranormal voices of the dead or just chance broadcast or shortwave pickups? These are questions which have been baffling parapsychology ever since 1971 when the phenomenon gained international interest due to the publication of the English version of Raudive's book, *Breakthrough*,

"Paranormal Tape-Recorded Voices: A Paraphysical Breakthrough" by D. Scott Rogo is an original article written especially for this volume and is printed by permission of the author.

which chronicled his own experiments and experiences in recording the voices, and his claim that they are the voices of the dead.

Judging from the enormous amount of publicity that followed the book's release and the controversy it engendered within parapsychology, the phenomenon would seem to be a new one. This is not the case, however. The phenomenon of tape-recorded voices is much older than Raudive's or Jurgenson's discovery. (Raudive was introduced to the phenomenon during his experiments with Jurgenson in Sweden and he found that he could pick up voices himself after he returned to Germany.) The true discovery of the voices was due solely to joint endeavors begun in 1956 by West coast psychical investigator Raymond Bayless and his colleague Attila von Szalay, a gifted psychic. I joined them in 1967.

Bayless and von Szalay had been intrigued with the mediumship of Sophia Williams who could produce a tiny disembodied voice. The voice appeared to be physically independent of the medium and often came forth with paranormal information. For example, it once correctly ascertained the cause of Mrs. Bayless' grandmother's death. After several experiments Bayless and von Szalay determined that despite Mrs. Williams' psychic abilities, the "voice" was nothing more than a ventriloquized stage effect. Apparently, Mrs. Williams had a show business background and had learned to ventriloquize with ease.*

Despite this setback, Bayless and von Szalay were still intrigued by the possibility of a phenomenon such as the independent voice, for von Szalay himself had felt that he had produced them on rare occasions. He had even tried to record them years before when making a phonograph disk, but the results were disappointing. So, in 1956 Bayless and von Szalay began a lengthy study to (1) develop independent voices through von Szalay, and (2) isolate the source of the voices completely away from von Szalay's physical proximity. This eventually led to the discovery of the tape-recorded voice phenomenon. Their three year initial study was pub-

---

* Nonetheless, she was so good that the famous American author, Hamlin Garland, wrote a book about her and her "voices" —*The Mystery of the Buried Crosses.*

lished in 1959 in the *Journal of the American Society for Psychical Research*. Coincidentally, only a few months later Friedrich Jurgenson announced his similar discovery of the voices.

The first experiments were conducted in a Hollywood studio rented specifically for the tests. The experimental area consisted of a special wooden cabinet or a clothes closet in which von Szalay would sit trying to produce independent voices. It was hoped that the voices would eventually emanate from the closet *after* von Szalay had left it. A microphone was placed into the enclosure usually resting in the mouth of a speaking trumpet used to amplify the sounds, but the machine itself would be left outside of it along with a speaker. This way people outside the closet could monitor and hear any voices or noises inside and tape record them as well.

Invariably, whether von Szalay was *in or out* of the cabinet, whispering voices, whistles, or raps would be heard over the loudspeaker. The voices were of both men and women and sounded rather mechanical; only a few words were spoken at a time. Still, these voices were heard over the speaker even when von Szalay was outside the cabinet! The tests not only verified the existence of the independent voice but led to the discovery of tape-recorded voices as well. The key experiment was on December 5, 1956. As Bayless reports:

". . . Mr. von Szalay,† for the purpose of this particular experiment, sat in the cabinet alone for fifteen minutes. Believing that nothing was forthcoming, he left the cabinet. We then played back the tape recording expecting to hear nothing, but were surprised to hear a distinct voice say: "This is G." At this time I was sitting on the outside of the cabinet listening to the highly amplified loud speaker and heard absolutely nothing.

"I then decided to make certain tests of the amplifying system and we both stood a few feet from the closed cabinet door and each other in full light while Mr. von Szalay made single whistles at short intervals. I was listening to the loud speaker when I suddenly realized that we were receiving low

† I have used the spelling preferred by Mr. von Szalay, even though it appears as "von Sealay" in the original Bayless reports.

whistles in answer. I then told Mr. von Szalay when to whistle and each time answering whistles were heard. There were at least six or seven answering whistles and at the end of this sequence, double whistles replied. We were standing within three feet of each other and were able to observe each other closely. The room was normally illuminated and fraud, under such conditions, is completely eliminated."

The December 5 experiment demonstrated that von Szalay was able to achieve both disembodied and tape-recorded voice effects. So Bayless decided on a more refined test to prove the "independence" of the voice. For the pilot experiment he used a large upright cardboard box in which he placed the trumpet and microphone. The experimenters then sat a yard away from it, turned on the tape, and replayed it at intervals. Three distinct voices were heard on the tape, but were garbled to such an extent that they could not be deciphered. (I've heard this type of reception with von Szalay very often. The voices will be almost as loud as our own, but so "mush mouthed" that they cannot be understood. Anyone having some experience with a bad quality tape recorder—answerphone system will recognize the similarity!)

In another "box test" conditions were even more stringent. The box with the microphone was completely covered by a heavy, camel-pile overcoat. This in turn was then placed in a larger box and was suspended from the ceiling of the closet while von Szalay and Bayless sat *outside* the enclosure. Again, a cable led from the microphone to the machine outside the cabinet.

As Bayless records:

"During an experiment on July 7, 1957 we placed the upright cardboard 'box-cabinet' previously described inside the closet-cabinet, closed the cabinet door and remained outside in the main room for 45 minutes. One clear human whisper was recorded. . . ."

Later, after Bayless had left, von Szalay recorded a female voice saying: "Hot dog, Art!" This might sound banal, but it heralded another phase of the research. The voice is very loud and there can be no doubt about it. Years prior von Szalay had dated a young woman in New York. Both of them were impoverished and could only dine at the local hot dog stand where they could buy two dogs for a nickel. They often joked about their dinners, promising each other that the "hot dogs" would always be remembered. Von Szalay had not seen nor heard from the woman in years and she was presumably dead so this voice gave a definite hint as to the source of the paranormal voices. Were they recording the voices of the dead?

Actually the voices did show definite intelligence and would answer specific questions. Two examples will suffice. During one test Bayless asked the voice-entities where his brother, who had left town suddenly, was located. A voice on the tape answered: "Bridgeport." Several days later Bayless was informed that his brother was setting up his medical practice in Bridgeport, Conn. In another experiment conducted only two years ago, Bayless asked that the name of his grandmother be given. A voice answered, quite correctly: "Emma." So, we do know that the voices are capable of giving out information of a paranormal nature.

On other occasions they seem to be psychically aware of distant events. Von Szalay keeps detailed notes of all his private sittings. These notes are kept in notebooks that he often turned over to Bayless. On September 30, 1971 Bayless sulkingly told his wife that he would like to cut himself off from the world. His wife, Marjorie, countered by saying that she knew a man who also felt that way and had become a recluse. (That actual word was used.) The same day, 15 miles away, Art was experimenting. He received and wrote into his notes an interpretation of a voice saying: "Bayless is virtually become a recluse." Bayless saw the written records before he told Art of his conversation.

The main research on the voices was published in January 1959 as a lengthy report in letter form to the *Journal of the American Society for Psychical Research*. Bayless and von Szalay hoped that they would arouse the interest of the parapsychological community. But there was not so much as one letter of inquiry! In 1968 I began to contact several parapsychologists in the United States about the von Szalay case and *not one* was willing to investigate it although several have since stated in print that they do not believe in the phenomenon!

In my own tests with von Szalay I have heard both the taped voices *and* independent voices. Here is an account of one sitting held in 1968:

On October 26th I sat with von Szalay at his photographic studio. We used his darkroom for the tests and I supplied the tapes, the recorder, and maintained complete control of the apparatus. A microphone was placed inside the large end of a medium's trumpet which was placed directly next to me. Von Szalay sat over a yard away. Fifteen minutes after we began and while I was looking at the trumpet I heard a tiny airy whistle come right out of it. Von Szalay heard it too for we simultaneously exchanged glances. The whistle was recorded on the tape. An hour later we had gotten no other results so we started asking the voice-entities questions trying to coax voices onto the tape. We replayed the tape at 15 minute intervals. At 9:00 p.m. von Szalay asked who would be elected president during the forthcoming election. When we replayed the tape, a voice clearly answered, "Humphrey"—a definite, though incorrect, answer to the question.

Later that evening von Szalay and I left the trumpet and microphone in the darkroom while we sat outside of it. We were separated from the apparatus by a closed door. Nonetheless at 10:50 p.m. we recorded a clear voice saying: "Hi ya, Art." On another occasion I had been able to hear an audible voice which was also captured on tape. It seemed to pop out of the trumpet and was a distinct male grumble.

Research with von Szalay has been going on now for several years, with Bayless conducting most of the tests when von Szalay is not experimenting alone. The chief finding has been an increase in the *length* of the voices. Von Szalay is now receiving voices that speak up to fifteen words at a time. Second, as we suspected, the voices are acoustical and not electronic in nature. That is, they are not impressed directly onto the tape at all, but seem acoustically produced in front of the microphone and usually at too low an intensity to be heard audibly. Bayless discovered that no voices could be recorded if gum or putty were placed over the microphone.‡

‡ The voices actually constitute only one of von Szalay's psychic abilities. The complete story of his talents can be found in my

Actually only one experimenter has been able to find voices on his recordings which appear to be impressed on an unexposed area of the tape. William Welch, a Los Angeles script writer, discovered the ability to tape record voices after he experimented with von Szalay. The whole story is told in his recent book, *Talks with the Dead*. I have spent only one informal session with Welch and his voices sound very much like those von Szalay gets, but weaker. (Von Szalay's voices are often whispers, but on occasion they explode right over the tape even obliterating our own voices asking questions.) Just once Welch discovered a voice appearing on a section of a tape which he had not used. The quality of the voice rules out the possibility that it was a manufacturing flaw.

1959 also heralded the discovery of the phenomenon in Sweden when Friedrich Jurgenson reported he had received extraneous voices, calling his name and claiming to be the dead, when taping radio broadcasts and when he was taping bird calls.

However, fourteen years later he admitted that the voices were not discovered accidentally at all but that he had an intuitive desire at the time to make electronic contact with the dead via the tape recorder. He didn't know why, and just labeled it an inner urge. At first he was unsuccessful but after months of work he finally achieved his goal. The first voice was of a woman speaking several words and Jurgenson claimed that it was identical to his mother's when she was alive.

It isn't necessary to go into the details of Jurgenson's work, but only to say that for the most part he was ignored by parapsychologists. However, Dr. Hans Bender, who heads a division of parapsychology at the University of Freiburg, Germany, traveled to Sweden and experimented with him, coming to the conclusion that the voices were genuine. Bender has also made voiceprints of the tapes proving that they are definitely human and that *different* voices appear on the tapes. W. G. Roll of the Psychical Research Foundation in Durham, North Carolina, also spent some time with Jurgen-

book, *In Search of the Unknown* (New York: Taplinger Publishing Co., Inc., 1976).

son and was able to record some voices with him. He would not, however, commit himself to any explanation about the voices, although he wrote a private report on them sent out by the P.R.F.

Jurgenson really has become better known due to the late Konstantin Raudive who first worked with Jurgenson and then started to record the paranormal voices himself. This is not odd. While Bayless and von Szalay have always maintained that their results are due to von Szalay's psychic ability, Jurgenson claims that the ability to record these electronic voices is a widespread potential. Both theories might be partially true. Nonetheless, many people who have initially worked with others who can tape the voices develop the ability to do so themselves. For example, Welch developed the ability after working with von Szalay. Even Raymond Bayless has now been able to get voices and raps on tape without von Szalay's presence. Likewise after investigating Raudive, his publisher Peter Bander developed the ability as he records in his *Carry on Talking.*

Raudive published his book, *Breakthrough,* along with a sample record of his voices in 1971. The voices are often whispery but sound identical to some poorer results obtained by von Szalay. Raudive often gives the voices bizarre interpretations explaining that several languages are used in the sentences he receives. In 1969–1970 Raudive's voices were getting much attention and the English publisher of his book, Colin Smythe Ltd., brought him to England for tests. In a shielded room with all the equipment handled by the experimenters, voices were still recorded.

Trinity College, Cambridge, offers a yearly studentship in parapsychology and for 1970–1972 awarded it to a young British chemist, David Ellis, to investigate the voice phenomenon. Unfortunately Ellis had no previous background in parapsychology and was at a complete loss to handle the case. His main finding was that not everybody can hear and interpret the voices the same way. This is hardly surprising since Raudive's voices are faint. However they are frequent and Raudive has almost been able to carry out to and fro conversations with them by asking questions and frequently replaying the tapes. Von Szalay achieves this too, but only rarely.

The voices are also intelligent and even Ellis, who eventually came to no conclusion about the voices, admitted that. Writing in the February 1974 issue of *Psychic* magazine he comments:

> With Dr. Raudive present, the voices sometimes refer directly to the other participants, but at other times they speak mainly to Dr. Raudive (nicknamed "Kosti"). There are some interesting comments when he is absent: the recording may start with "We need Kosti" or "We need Kosti here," or a voice may exclaim, "You have hidden Kosti". . . .

Ellis worked with Raudive sporadically but under all of his controlled conditions Raudive was able to produce the voices on tape. Ellis could never satisfy himself that the voices were paranormal. Raudive's work was cut short by his recent death, though many of his earlier collaborators are receiving the voices on their own.

The whole area of tape-recorded voices has been criticized extensively. So let us take a good look at these criticisms and see if they are valid.

The first criticism usually leveled is that we are only picking up radio broadcasts. This judgment is extremely superficial. For one thing, the voices clearly answer questions, call proper names, and often use profanity. The origin of this fault finding is that Raudive sometimes recorded his voices by taping the white noise of a radio set. This is admittedly a poor way of experimenting, but most voice recordings have been done by using the simple "open mike" technique developed originally by von Szalay.

Another argument against the radio reception theory is that these voices are usually recorded only in the presence of certain people. For example, some people experiment for days and days but will not get one effect on their tapes. Yet as soon as von Szalay or Welch is present, all of a sudden a plethora of voices can be recorded. Why, if these are but radio pickups?

Then there is the criticism that there really are no voices on the tapes at all but we are just imagining that there are voices emanating from the roar of the background white noise. Usually this argument is promoted by people who have never heard tapes of the voices! Indeed, many voices recorded are very indistinct and hard to hear, but others are very loud. Von Szalay's voices are the loudest I have ever heard. Sometimes they are clearer than Art's own, even obliterating it on occasion. In Jurgenson's case, "voiceprints" have been made which absolutely substantiate the "human" nature of the voices.

However, the main criticism against the voices is that many people when listening to the same example interpret it differently. As I said, this is no mystery. Just try having five people decipher an answer-phone message. This was what discouraged Ellis so much. He wrote: "We visited some of Dr. Raudive's collaborators, including Professor Alex Schneider, and discovered that the interpretation of the voices was not a matter of general agreement—except that it was a problem. Professor Schneider told us about a little test which he had helped conduct with Dr. Theo Locher of the Swiss Association for Parapsychology. A tape of voice samples had been sent in turn to ten people, who had been asked to interpret them. Their answers were compared with Dr. Locher's, and agreement was not very substantial."

As I said before, this argument is very weak. Just because the voices are often garbled does not mean that they are not there. The very fact that the voices are on the tapes at all is an immense phenomenon in itself. The actual interpretation of them, although certainly desirable, is not necessary to confirm their paranormality. It is well known in psychology that our hearing is a very indistinct and subjective sense. Even clear tape recordings of human speech will be interpreted differently by a group of listeners. For example, several segments of the Watergate tapes could not be transcribed to the total satisfaction of all the people working on them. But we don't disqualify the Watergate tapes on those grounds.

Actually, I confronted this problem squarely when the *Journal of the Society for Psychical Research* published an attack on Raudive. I wrote the *Journal* the following which was published in the June 1974 issue:

Having followed the controversy over "tape-recorded" voices I would like to point out a fallacy that many critics have been making. It is claimed that because several individuals have different interpretations of a "voice," this disqualifies the possibility that a voice, and not some mechanical or accidental sound, really exists on the tape. This is based on the idea that if a voice did occur on the tape, all listeners would interpret it uniformly. This is a fallacy as I should like to point out.

Some years ago Dr. John Lilly investigating communications in dolphins played the tapes of dolphin sounds to listeners who were supposed to interpret what they heard. Different interpretations were gathered. Lilly then repeated the experiment with a tape of a clearly enunciated human word repeated several times for a period of several minutes. It was discovered that individuals gradually heard different words—in fact sometimes up to thirty. In this case there was no question that a real voice was being heard. This research has obvious bearing on the Raudive and similar taped voices. It is quite clear that listeners must listen to these voices several times before deciphering them, as in Lilly's experiments. Arguing from Lilly's work, it is plainly natural that individuals should vary in what they hear. This seems to rule out the argument that the lack of unanimity among listeners must destroy confidence in tape recorded voices, since similar misinterpretations have appeared where there is no doubt a human voice is repeating a word over and over again. This in fact seems to be a natural phenomenon of our auditory sense perception.

Dr. Charles Tart, a psychologist at the University of California, Davis, wrote a letter making almost the identical points which was published in a subsequent issue of the *Journal*.

If we can agree that voices are being placed on tape, from whence do they come? By far, most people actively experimenting believe that they emanate from the dead. This is certainly the conviction of Raudive, Jurgenson, von Szalay, and Welch. There is some *a priori* evidence of this. The voices often call out their proper names and these indicate people who are dead. (Von Szalay once received a clear voice which he is positive is that of his father. Jurgenson's first voice convinced him that it was his mother speaking.)

The other possible explanation is that the voices are produced psychokinetically by the subjects themselves who are either impressing the voices directly on tape or somehow otherwise creating them. Professor Bender favors this inter-

pretation. We do know that many people can demonstrate PK
on sensitive equipment such as causing random number generators to depart from randomness or by affecting rolling
dice. This may tie in with the fact that so great a number of
people have succeeded in taping voices using electronic equipment. (I know of at least five cases of people with whom I
have worked who can get voices and who are getting them
paranormally to my satisfaction.) Could it be that projecting
voices onto tapes is a minute form of PK ability and one we
all might possess? Raudive and Jurgenson both felt that anyone could get the voices if they worked long enough, but they
still believed the voices were from the dead. A lot more
research needs to be done before this issue is resolved.

Before leaving the subject of tape-recorded voices though,
one further phenomenon needs to be mentioned. Bayless
often noted in his reports on von Szalay that the voices were
sometimes accompanied by "raps," percussive sounds like
wooden knocks that appeared on the tapes. (Of course, raps
are a very common form of psychical manifestation often
heard during poltergeist cases.) Bayless hypothesized that just
as with "low-intensity voices," there might also be "low-intensity raps" which while out of ear range could be a phenomenon in itself. William Welch also notes in his book odd
"clicking" sounds which accompany the voices.

Bayless was fully able to validate his theory in 1975 during
experiments with Mr. Wesley Frank who claimed that he
had been able to pick up tape-recorded voices and also a
plethora of accompanying raps. So Bayless and Frank began
joint experimentation in May 1975. Usually they sat in full
light at a table with the recorder and microphone between
them. Or Frank, who is obviously inducing the raps, sits a
few feet away. They play a tape for a few minutes and then
replay it. The normally blank tape soon becomes filled with
raps if Frank is present. If he sits at the table the raps are
more numerous and louder than when he sits away from the
table. If he sits at the table and invokes his "guide" (a
claimed discarnate who helps produce the PK; in Frank's case
he has arbitrarily chosen Eusapia Palladino who was a famous medium of yesteryear), *the raps intensify*. This authen-
ticates the fact that the raps are paranormal and not just me-

chanical sounds. Not only do they intensify when Mr. Frank speaks to them, but will also rap in a specific rhythm. Bayless, who has now analyzed a number of recordings made with Frank, has made several interesting observations about them:

(1) The sound of the raps does not necessarily match the material upon which they are presumably produced. That is, if the recorder is placed on wood, the raps may be metallic. If placed on metal, the rapping could sound wooden.

(2) The volume of the raps and the quality vary greatly. Sometimes they are feeble "clicks," at other times they sound like a hammer pounding wood in the background.

(3) The raps can be patterned or nonpatterned. The nonpatterned rappings are the most common.

(4) On rare occasions the raps also become audible to the human ear.

(5) Even while taping the raps, some human voices are recorded.

Thus, in this work with Mr. Frank, Bayless has verified the prediction he made during the early von Szalay years. It might also be noted that a similar effect has been discovered during a poltergeist case investigated by Dr. John Palmer and Dr. J. G. Pratt of the University of Virginia which they reported at the 1975 annual convention of the Parapsychological Association. Pratt tried to tape-record the loud raps that assaulted an "infested" house. On replaying the tape he found that there were additional, lower-intensity raps on it which they had not heard audibly.

Many opinions have been expressed about the phenomenon of tape-recorded voices. The common argument that the voices are just misinterpreted mechanical noises or experimenter-produced noises can hardly explain the very loud voices recorded by von Szalay and others. Indeed, although a few experimenters are receiving very faint voices which are hard to hear, some voices of remarkable volume and clarity have been recorded by others. It is sorrowfully true that in several years of work with Mr. von Szalay, neither Bayless nor I were ever able to interest other parapsychologists in the case. They would not even listen to the tapes of the voices, much less carry out their own experiments. Raudive had a similar problem in Europe before his death.

Although the parapsychological establishment is hostile toward accepting the genuineness of the voices, I believe the phenomenon is a breakthrough of the first magnitude. It is to be hoped that as more people begin their own experimentation the phenomenon will eventually force itself to the attention of parapsychology. As it stands now, the phenomenon is one of the most important breakthroughs in paraphysics, yet is a much ignored—if not maligned—subject within parapsychology.

REFERENCES

Raymond Bayless, Correspondence: *J. Amer. Society Psychical Research* **53**, 35 (1959).

Raymond Bayless, "Low Amplitude Tape Recorded Raps," *New Horizons* (in press).

Peter Bander, *Carry on Talking* (Gerrards Cross: Colin Smythe Ltd., 1972).

Konstantin Raudive, *Breakthrough* (Gerrards Cross: Colin Smythe Ltd., 1971).

D. Scott Rogo, "A Report on Two Controlled Sittings with Attila von Szalay," *J. Paraphysics* **4**, 13 (1970).

D. Scott Rogo, *In Search of the Unknown* (Chap. 7, "The von Szalay Affair") (New York: Taplinger, 1976).

William Welch, *Talks with the Dead* (New York: Pinnacle Books, 1975).

David Ellis, "Tape Recordings from the Dead?" *Psychic* **5**, 44 (1974).

36.

Apparatus Communication with Discarnate Persons

JULIUS WEINBERGER

In 1941, after more than twenty-five years of investigation into the question of post-mortem survival of human personality by conventional means (i.e., sittings with mediums), I began a new line of research. This involves apparatus for direct communication with discarnate persons. The ultimate objective was to develop a system over which signals can be transmitted without the need for a "sensitive" intermediary. Part of this work was described in a paper published in 1961.[1] A system has now been developed that is more sensitive and reliable than previous attempts. This utilizes a sensitive plant, *Dionea muscipala* (the Venus flytrap), as a device which is able to respond to signals produced by discarnate persons. In effect, it displaces the medium.

The apparatus has been in almost daily use for more than four years. Thousands of observations have been made with it. It is conceived as applicable to investigations involving contact with discarnate persons, or for other experimental work in which a living organism (the plant) conceivably might respond to energy emitted by or projected from some other living organism (e.g., a human being), as in psychokinesis, dowsing, psychic healing, the "aura," or other paranormal phenomena in which energy apparently is involved.

The apparatus was devised because all methods of mediumistic communication suffer from certain disadvantages. In some cases it is difficult to tell how much of the information came from or was influenced by the medium's own mind.

"Apparatus Communications with Discarnate Persons" by Julius Weinberger is an original article written especially for this volume and is printed by permission of the author.

Other cases—those where a dark or dimly lit room is used for the seance—lend themselves to fraud. Thus, I felt that further progress in this area depended upon the development of a system of communication with discarnate persons that would not depend on the use of a medium, but in which apparatus would be provided that could be influenced by some form of energy available to such persons. If such a system could be developed, then messages could be transmitted, using Morse telegraph code. My present system shows a great deal of promise, even though much remains to be done before the ultimate objective of telegraphic transmission of intelligence from discarnate persons can be said to have been accomplished.

The idea of using a special kind of plant for this purpose came about in the following way. In late 1960, during another sort of apparatus communication experiments, I noticed a peculiar tingling sensation on my scalp. It seemed as though some form of energy was being used which could stimulate sensory nerve endings in the scalp and adjacent areas of the skin. The sensation was not like that which would be caused by an electric current or by an electrostatic field. It had a feeling of vitality, movement and a sort of "granularity," like a rain of tiny particles impinging on the skin. This sensation was rarely felt at other times, and the conclusion was reached that it was not due to some internal neurological disturbance, but arose from an external stimulus. Discussion of the phenomenon with a medium brought the prompt response that it was a well-known effect of the presence of discarnate persons. She said: "It feels like walking through cobwebs."

The force which produces this effect is possibly a manifestation of what has been termed "vital energy," "life force," "elan vital," etc., by philosophers and biologists who have speculated on the possibility of its existence. Their assumptions have been: (1) there exists a universal form of energy which animates living organisms, and (2) discarnate persons not only are animated by the same force as are human beings, but they can project it or utilize it in other ways in the course of their existence. There is now a considerable amount of evidence[2-4] tending to confirm the hypothesis that living organisms not only have associated with them a guiding psychic component, but that this component can make use of a universally available force which we may call "vital energy." It does not seem farfetched to assume that if such energy is common to both discarnate and human life, it could be used to stimulate structures as sensitive as sensory nerve endings or root hair receptors.

Prior to incorporating a plant into the apparatus, I tried to detect electrical changes that occurred in the scalp concomitantly with the unique sensations mentioned earlier. But the methods I devised could not surmount the problems encountered with the pulsation of the blood supply in the scalp as the heart pumped blood up through the arteries and as it diffused through the skin tissue. All sorts of arrangements were tried to balance out these blood pulsations with the aid of a differential amplifier, so as to be able to detect other fluctuations that might accompany them, but without success.

With various forms of animal tissue thus ruled out, I turned to sensitive plants as a possibility, and eventually chose the Venus flytrap. The reasons for this were: (1) it is readily available; (2) it is easy to place electrodes on; (3) its responses to stimuli are rapid and decay quickly; (4) it has been extensively studied and the many references to prior work available in botanical libraries give useful details for experimental procedures; (5) its sensitivity to touch appears to approximate that of human scalp nerve endings. Finally, it was thought possible that it would respond in some fashion to energy from discarnate sources, since it has been shown by Grad that growth of plants can be stimulated by energy emitted from a healer's hands.[5] Such energy was thought to be similar in nature to that which might be available to discarnate persons, and having the characteristics of vital energy.

Experimental Apparatus

Following some years of experiments with various kinds of sensitive plants, work was undertaken in 1966 with Venus flytraps. A vacuum tube amplifier was designed to obtain electrical indications of very minute changes in the bioelectric potential between two points on one of the trap units (a unit is a leaf and trap connected together by a joint which possibly contains some specialized mechanism that closes the trap when the hairs are stimulated). Figure 1 shows the elements

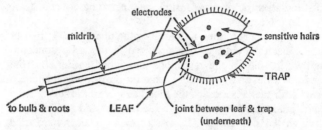

FIGURE 1   *Elements of Venus flytrap unit.*

of such a unit. The points finally chosen for the two electrodes were: a point along the midrib of the leaf (for a "grounded" electrode) and a point inside the trap, close to the little connecting joint (for the "active" electrode). The resting or steady-state dc potential between these two points in a healthy plant is usually between fifteen and forty millivolts. The apparatus could detect changes in this potential of the order of twenty microvolts, that is, less than one part in a thousand.

The extreme sensitivity of the apparatus necessitated certain precautions in order to avoid false signals from artifacts: the plant was placed within a grounded shielding container (a steel box with a movable grill front); shielded amplifier input circuits; battery operation of all tubes; "low noise" tubes used throughout; all sixty cycle power lines kept at a distance of eight feet or more.

Tests showed that starting or stopping of electrical devices in the house produced no responses. Neither did lightning, radio or TV signals, or electrostatic charges on the clothing or bodies of persons. Many observations and tests established the fact that those responses which substantially exceeded the "plant noise" came because of some external stimulus impressed on the trap. (In a selected, healthy specimen of Venus flytrap, having a broad, short leaf and fairly mature trap, the only registrations that are obtained normally are very small, rapid fluctuations which I have called "plant noise.")

The apparatus setup is shown in block diagram form in Figure 2. At the left there is a steel box, about 12 × 16 × 12 in., the front of which is open. A galvanized iron grill composed of ⅛-in. mesh is arranged to slide up and down across the open front, so as to provide access to the interior. Inside the box there is a clamp stand which carries adjustable clamps that hold the electrodes. The latter are of the "wick" type.[6] In these electrodes, a chlorided silver wire is immersed in a 1% solution of potassium chloride, contained in a glass tube with a small orifice (like an eyedropper or hypodermic syringe tube) which is plugged with a wick of absorbent cotton.

A wick electrode is held in a clip attached to a ball and socket joint, carried in a clamp on the clamp stand. The Venus flytrap plant (in a 3-in. pot) is placed on a piece of paraffin (to avoid electrical leakage from plant to ground) on the stand. Adjustment of the electrodes to contact selected points on a trap is simple and quick, and because of the noninjurious nature of the electrodes the same trap and the same contact points can be used over and over again.

From the electrodes connections are brought to a D.P.D.T. switch by means of which either the steady-state dc potential of the plant or its fluctuating output can be measured. It will be seen that three additional boxes of electronic equipment are shown. The first of these is a pulse amplifier, which is used to amplify the fluctuations in potential (that is, the small normal variations which I have termed "plant noise" and the much larger variations which occur as purposeful interventions).

The output of this amplifier goes to one side of a second D.P.D.T. switch, the center of which connects to a vacuum tube millivoltmeter. This instrument is modelled after a design of H. S. Burr.[7] It uses a single 1A7 tube in a Wheatstone bridge circuit. A microammeter across the usual points in the bridge will show a change of one microamp for an input change of four millivolts. In series with the microammeter is another amplifier (transistorized) which increases a one microampere pulse to about three hundred microamperes,

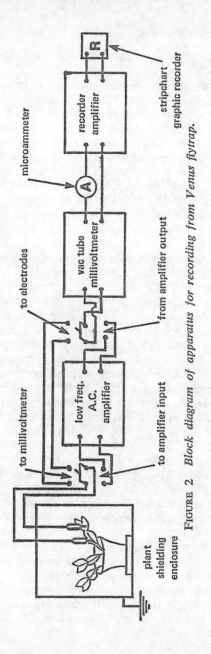

FIGURE 2 *Block diagram of apparatus for recording from Venus flytrap.*

to electrodes

to millivoltmeter

microammeter

from amplifier output

to amplifier input

recorder amplifier

vac tube millivoltmeter

low freq. A.C. amplifier

plant shielding enclosure

stripchart graphic recorder

sufficient to give ample deflection on a one milliamp full scale graphic recorder.

By throwing both D.P.D.T. switches up, the millivoltmeter is used to measure the resting or steady state potential between the plant electrodes—usually of the order of fifteen to forty millivolts. Then by throwing them down, the entire system is ready to record fluctuations.

All units are battery operated. The recorder chart is driven from a clock spring. Thus no power circuits need to be brought near the apparatus.

Procedure

The procedure in using the above equipment was as follows: Each evening at the same time a plant was taken to the apparatus, in the cellar of my house, and the electrodes were placed on it. The plants were grown at a sunny window, or under Gro-Lux fluorescent lamps, depending on the season of the year. The apparatus would be started up, and the plant potential was measured, after five or ten minutes to permit it to stabilize. Then the switches would be thrown to "record."

The next part of the procedure was concerned with making "contact" with such discarnate persons as might perhaps be present and interested in cooperating in the project. This was done by reciting a brief prayer, such as the Lord's Prayer, followed by prayers of a personal nature, then by a request for such cooperation, and a description of the program for that session.

During the prayer period the "scalp sensations" would soon become manifest. These were taken to indicate that discarnate persons were present who were ready to cooperate in the experimental work. The recorder would be run for at least half an hour, or longer if there was a lot of activity. Notes were made of pertinent details: plant potential, plant noise, weather conditions, time of operation and results.

The recorder chart (6 in. wide) can be run at two speeds: 12 in. per hour or 12 in. per minute. Most of the recording was done at 12 in. per hour, and on these records the pulses produced as responses to requests or remarks appear as single lines.

It is well to emphasize that a number of factors appeared to contribute to the successful results obtained. In the writer's opinion these are "essential ingredients" in any attempt to replicate or to carry on further work of this nature:

(1) The presence of a cooperative, qualified group of discarnate persons interested in carrying on work for improving communication between our world and theirs; and a brief prayer session, as described above, for establishing "contact" with them.

(2) A regular daily schedule for experimentation, strictly adhered to.

(3) A quiet place where apparatus can be set up and left undisturbed for months, free from interference.

(4) All possible precautions should be taken to avoid artifacts which might be introduced from any electrical source, and tests should be made to determine effects of operating switches, motors, air conditioners, oil burners, or other appliances in the environment.

(5) Certain precautions and practices need to be observed in obtaining and growing the Venus flytraps so as to assure low-noise plants. These can be discussed with qualified investigators interested in replicating this work, or in applying the techniques otherwise.

Early Experimental Results

After a number of months of preliminary work to develop reliable apparatus, a nightly schedule of observations was begun in June 1968. The writer is satisfied that the phenomena reported herein reflect principally the results of deliberate influence exerted on the sensitive receptors and nervous tissue of the Venus flytrap, and in which some form of energy is employed that is not one of the physical forms known to us.* All possible sources of artifacts were checked repeatedly, and plants selected for use were those which showed the lowest noise. Furthermore, there were other kinds of evidence, which are cited below, to indicate that intelligent, conscious control was being exercised in the production of the signals recorded.

Signals observed were of the following types:

(1) *Plant "noise."* A small amount of fluctuation was always present, arising from the plant itself, and probably due to respiration or sap flow variations. This showed itself as an irregular vibration of the recorder pen, of the order of one quarter to one scale division (s/d) on the recorder chart. One s/d would represent a fluctuation of about twenty microvolts out of a steady-state plant potential of about twenty millivolts—an extraordinarily low noise level.

(2) *Single pulses.* These were the most usual type of signal recorded. They ranged in intensity from one s/d above the noise level to twenty s/d. This would be equivalent to a change in plant potential ranging from twenty to four hundred microvolts.

(3) *Multiple pulses.* These were combinations of two or more single pulses in rapid succession.

Some examples of recordings that were obtained prior to the work reported under the heading of "Experiments Designed for Statistical Evaluation" will be given in the next section. They have been chosen from among many others to illustrate certain points.

In the early stages of the work, no specific requests for responses were made. After making "contact" as described above, the apparatus was run for half an hour, and effects of varying experimental conditions were observed, such as the presence or absence of the observer, variations in his distance

---

* To test whether mechanical force might be a possible stimulus for the plant response, several tests were made at a later date with an extremely sensitive pressure transducer in place of the plant. Responses were requested as usual, but none were ever obtained. If psychokinesis had been responsible for the results, such a transducer would have registered its presence.

from the apparatus, whether or not any recorded pulses were artifacts due to starting or stopping of electrical appliances in the house, etc. Usually during such sessions a number of pulses would be recorded. The question was whether these came from discarnate persons assumed to be present, or whether they were accidental. That is, were they being produced *intentionally* or not?[8]

To settle this question, on one evening I watched a series of pulses being recorded during the first twenty minutes of the half-hour session. At this point I said "Will you please stop transmitting for the next five minutes?" Figure 3 shows the

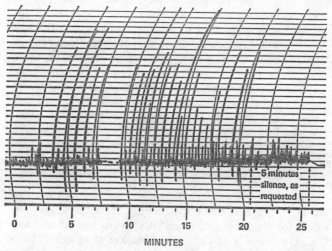

MINUTES

FIGURE 3   *A demonstration of deliberate intention and control. Regularly timed pulses, ending in five minutes of "silence," as requested.*

result. It will be seen that regularly timed large pulses were produced for twenty minutes, and at the moment the request for "silence" was made, these ceased. The next five minutes showed only small pulses, which were obviously part of the plant noise. These can be seen earlier in the record between the "intentional" large pulses.

Further evidence of intelligent control of the phenomena

came from time to time in the form of responses to questions or remarks. That is, the writer might say something, or ask a question, perhaps at a time when there was little activity, and immediately the recorder pen would swing over to a deflection well above the noise level, as though to indicate agreement or to lend added emphasis to what was said.

Figure 4 gives three examples of this, although it was observed many times. The incidents are marked with the time they occurred, and it will be seen that the pulses arose out of an otherwise innocuous background.

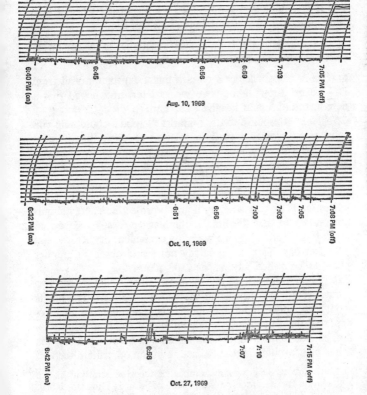

FIGURE 4 *Responses to questions or remarks. See text for details.*

The uppermost record came in response to the following:

6:45 p.m. Probably a "greeting" signal, which was frequently given to indicate readiness for transmission.

6:56 p.m. Response to my remark: "Today is Sunday. We went to church this morning. Attendance was sparse."

6:59 p.m. Response to my remark: "I hope you are giving consideration to my suggestion for a 'code' to be used in communication, such as one pulse for 'Yes,' two pulses for 'No,' and three pulses for 'Don't Know.'" (This suggestion had been made in a previous session.)

7:03 p.m. Response to my remark: "I'm not going to ask you if you think you can do this. No response needed. I take it for granted that you will do the best you can."

The middle record illustrates reactions to a somewhat different type of conversation, thus:

6:51 p.m. Response to a remark that I expected a visit from Dr. Robert Brier† about two weeks later, and hoped that a demonstration could be given for him.

6:56 p.m. Response to my remark: "I wish I could help you solve your problems (i.e., in relation to difficulties in controlling the amplitude of the responses). Apparently what you need is a free-running pulse generator that can be pointed at, or away from, the target."

7:00 p.m. Response to the thought (not spoken) that the pulses might be produced by a group projecting energy simultaneously and that the little preliminary pulses that I saw so often just before a big one were the equivalent of "Ready, set, go!" I wrote this thought in my notes and observed another pulse as I finished writing, at 7:03 p.m.

7:05 p.m. Response to my asking whether a setup using two plants would help in solving the "code" problem. The plants would be connected to a differential amplifier, so that response from one plant would cause a deflection of the recorder pen in one direction, whereas a response from the other plant would cause a deflection in the opposite direction.

† Dr. Robert Brier was a member of the research staff at the Foundation for Research on the Nature of Man in Durham, North Carolina. This staff cooperated in work described in the next section of this paper.

Thus one plant could be used to transmit dots and the other dashes, for Morse code.

The lowest record illustrates responses to a different kind of situation:

6:56 p.m. Just prior to this response I had had to run upstairs to answer the telephone. When I returned I apologized for the interruption, whereupon this response was recorded. *7:07 p.m.* At this point I remarked that I would shut down the apparatus shortly as there didn't seem to be much activity. At once the pen began to move, culminating in a large pulse at 7:10 p.m., as though to indicate that more time would be desirable. The apparatus accordingly was run for another six or seven minutes, but without effects except for a higher noise level. This sort of behavior, namely a response to an expressed intention to shut down, was observed on a number of occasions. Sometimes it was followed by prolonged activity, where previously there had been little or none.

Experiments Designed for Statistical Evaluation

The material presented in the preceding sections of this paper was submitted for comment to Dr. J. B. Rhine‡ in April 1969. He suggested that further experiments be undertaken, according to a plan designed to permit statistical evaluation of the results. The author agreed to this, and Dr. Rhine arranged with Dr. Robert M. Brier, Research Fellow at the Institute, to develop a suitable plan in cooperation with the author. The following procedure was planned and carried out in subsequent work:

(1) The usual half-hour experimental session was first divided into six five-minute sections. Each section was then divided into two halves. A section thus constituted a pair of 2½-minute sectors.

(2) A separate target was prepared for each experimental session. Each target consisted of twelve calls, six requesting a "response," and six requesting *"no*

‡ Dr. Rhine directs the work at the Foundation for Research on the Nature of Man, mentioned earlier.

response." At the beginning of the first half of each pair, there would be a call either for "response" or "no response"; at the beginning of the second half of a pair, the call would be for the opposite of whatever the call had been for the first half. The order of the calls was randomized.

(3) The above targets were prepared at the Institute by Mrs. Carol Schaber Williams, each enclosed in a sealed envelope and numbered in sequence. A total of twenty-five targets was prepared for each experimental series. These were sent to the writer, and each envelope was opened only at the session for which it was designated.

(4) The charted recordings produced in response to each target were sent to the Institute and were evaluated "blind" according to the following procedure: Each "pair" was inspected by a person who did not know the order of calls to decide in which half of the pair one or more responses were indicated. A response was considered to be a deflection of the recorder pen clearly greater in amplitude than the plant "noise," and occurring anywhere within that half. If there was no such deflection in either half of a pair, or if there were deflections in both halves of about the same amplitude, so that no choice was possible as between the two halves, the pair was discarded. If deflections occurred in both halves, but some were of greater amplitude in one half than in the other, the half with the greatest amplitude was chosen as the one to be used in scoring. The *number* of responses occurring within a given pair was not considered in making a choice in such cases.

(5) The above data were tabulated and were then turned over to another member of the Institute staff (usually Mrs. Carol S. Williams), for comparison with the original targets, which had been prepared.

(6) This comparison yielded the total number of usable pairs (trials) and the number of hits, as given in the table in the next section.

Figure 5 illustrates a typical target, with simulated calls, responses and scoring.

Six series were run, as follows:

A pilot series, by the writer alone.

Experimental series 1, by the writer alone.

Experimental series 2, by the writer alone.

Experimental series 3, in the presence of a second observer (Mr. Erlendur Haraldssen).

Experimental series 4, in the presence of a second observer (Mr. William Jack).

Experimental series 5, in the presence of a second observer (Mr. Carl O. Almquist).

In the experimental series numbered 1, 2, and 5, a total of twenty-five targets were used in each series, with three hundred calls for each series. In the other experimental series a smaller number of targets were used, owing to the limited time for which the second observers were available. In the pilot series the same target was used in each of four sessions.

Results

The table gives the results of evaluations of each series, made as described above.

TABLE

RESULTS OF PILOT AND EXPERIMENTAL SERIES

Experiment	Total Usable Trials	Hits	Deviation
Pilot	10	8	+ 3.0
1	25	16	+ 3.5
2	17	12	+ 3.5
3	9	6	+ 1.5
4	15	8	+ 0.5
5	62	44	+13.0
Total	138	94	+25.0

C.R. $= 4.25$, $p = 0.0000107$ (one-tailed)

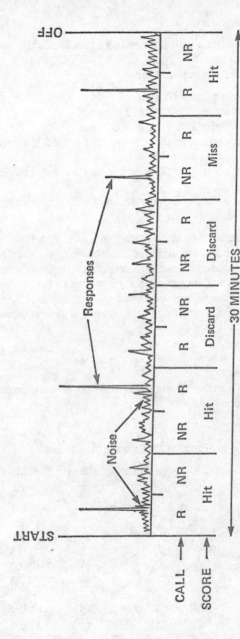

FIGURE 5 *Simulated recording from a target, showing calls, responses, and scoring. R is a call for a response. NR is a call for no response. All calls made at beginning of a sector. One sector is 2½ minutes.*

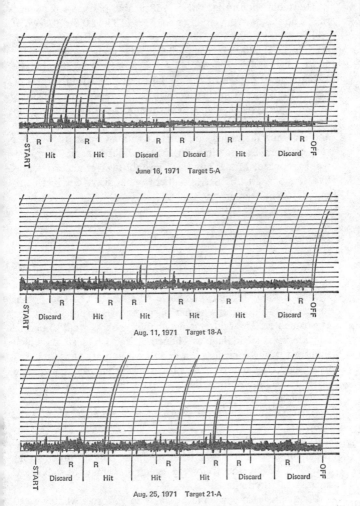

FIGURE 6 *Typical records of responses in three sessions of Series 5, showing calls, hits, and discarded pairs.*

The table shows that out of 138 usable pairs, 94 produced hits. The standard deviation $(npq)^{1/2} = (138 \times 0.5 \times 0.5)^{1/2} = (34.5)^{1/2} = 5.90$. The deviation is $+25$ and the C.R. $= 4.25$, $p = 0.0000107$ (one-tailed). The odds against chance are 1 to 93,000.

Examples of three of the actual recordings from targets of Series 5 are shown in Figure 6. These are reproduced in order to illustrate typical results. The number of hits, misses, and discards varied from session to session, ranging from no hits and six pairs discarded, to four hits with two discards. Misses ranged from one to three in those sessions in which misses were recorded. Misses appeared in only twelve out of twenty-five sessions. In this Series 5 there were forty-four hits compared to eighteen misses.

Discussion

The experimental results given above appear to warrant the conclusion that they were intentionally produced by an agency having freedom of choice whether to respond or not to respond to questions, remarks, or requests expressed by the experimenter. The odds against chance are too great to permit considering the findings as chance artifacts. Questions which require further consideration and discussion are those relating to agency, the nature and source of the energy required to produce responses, and the process whereby such energy is controlled.

At least three hypotheses can be considered regarding the agency:

(1) The stimuli for the plant were produced by the experimenter, as a result of what might be called "unconscious PK." However, the following arguments may be advanced against this hypothesis:

First, the experimenter made no efforts whatever to influence the plants during the regular experimental periods, but maintained a passive attitude as a disinterested observer. Moreover, at various times other than during the regular periods, numerous intense mental and verbal efforts were made to try to produce responses from the same plant which was being used in the experimental work, but at no time were any responses obtained in this way.

Second, all of the PK experiments reported in the literature, to the author's knowledge, have involved conscious efforts on the part of the experimenter to obtain the desired results. If there is such a thing as "unconscious PK" it is certainly a most unlikely kind of unconscious behavior. The unconscious is generally not responsive to a conscious command, particularly where there are no emotional factors involved. It takes long and arduous training, for example, by the practice of one of the yoga disciplines, in order to achieve conscious control of unconscious processes. The author has never had any training of this, or a similar type. Neither has he ever had any evidence of PK ability.

Finally, the very large odds against chance demonstrated herein are much greater than those usually observed in PK experiments. This would indicate much more precise control of whatever form of energy produced the stimuli in these experiments. It is not believed that such precision could occur with a purely unconscious process, which would be much more likely to be erratic and uncontrollable.

(2) A second hypothesis is that the responses were produced intentionally by an independent, intelligent agency, having available to it a form of energy which could be readily controlled and to which the plant could respond directly. Such an agency is conceived as one or more discarnate persons, whose cooperation was solicited as part of the "Procedure." A discarnate agency is considered as most probable, by the author, because of the following: First, the presence of the "scalp sensations" during the experimental periods; second, the appearance of unsolicited and unexpected responses, such as the examples shown in Figure 4, which are like the sort of replies that one might get in a conversation with another person if this person was limited in his responses to manual signals; third, that if we rule out "unconscious PK," then the discarnate person hypothesis is a logical alternative.

(3) A third hypothesis is that a discarnate person or persons was the agency ultimately responsible for the results, but that the energy utilized to stimulate the plants was derived

from the author serving as an intermediary. The process here might be somewhat similar to that reported in investigations of phenomena produced in the presence of physical mediums. Crawford[9, 10] studied and described the process whereby objects were moved in the presence of a nonprofessional medium named Kathleen Goligher. This involved the projection of what he called "psychic rods" from the surface and orifices of the medium's body. The medium was in trance, and the psychic rods were directed toward and adhered to the objects which were moved. Manipulation of the rods was said to be done by the medium's "controls."

The question that arises in this, and with other instances of object movement alleged to be produced by discarnate entities, is that of the source and nature of the energy required, and the process whereby the energy is projected outward from the medium's body. An explanation may be found in the concept of a field of vital energy as forming part of a living organism.

In the literature of psychic research, and in that from many other sources, one can find an extensive amount of material concerning this concept. The field has been called by a variety of names such as "the aura," "etheric or astral body," "beta body," "spiritual body," etc. It is believed to surround and to penetrate into the living body, and it can be perceived by clairvoyants. It may be conceived as a specific, localized organization of vital energy emerging from or concentrated out of a universal, undifferentiated field.[3] It is also believed to be that part of the human organism which passes on at death and constitutes the "body" of a discarnate person.

Since the "body" of a discarnate person may be considered as an energy field, it is conceivable that such a person could penetrate or merge with the "aura" of a human being, and, by some process presently unknown to us, he could utilize some of the human field to influence a sensitive plant. With respect to the work described in this paper it is not necessary to assume that the discarnate person "takes control" of the human, as is the case in trance mediumship. The assumption here is that the discarnate may utilize some of the human energy, if this is more suitable for his use than that which he normally has available in his state of existence, and he may then control it to suit his purpose.

Additional experiments are planned to obtain data which may help to clarify further the questions of agency and process. But I feel justified in saying that, on the basis of the data reported herein, it seems to demonstrate that there exists in nature a form of energy which apparently provides a common bond between at least three forms of living organisms: human beings, discarnate persons, and a certain species of plants which has a rudimentary form of nervous system. Vital energy has long been suspected to exist, by philosophers and by some scientists, but has heretofore not been studied scientifically. Now that a "transducer" has been discovered for registering its presence, it is hoped that further research on the subject may become one of the next great tasks of science.

REFERENCES

1. J. Weinberger, "On Apparatus Communication with Discarnate Persons," *Intern. J. Parapsychology* **3**, Winter 1961.

2. R. S. Lillie, *General Biology and Philosophy of Organism* (Chicago, Ill.: University of Chicago Press, 1945).

3. Gustaf Stromberg, *The Soul of the Universe* (Philadelphia, Pa.: David McKay Company, 1948) (2nd ed.). (A paperback reprint has recently been issued by Educational Research Institute, P.O. Box 4203, North Hollywood, Calif. 10032.)

4. Gustaf Stromberg, *The Searchers* (Philadelphia, Pa.: David McKay Company, 1948).

5. B. Grad, "Some Biological Effects of 'Laying On of Hands': A Review of Experiments with Animals and Plants," *J. Amer. Soc. Psychical Research* **59**, 2 (1965).

6. *Medical Physics,* edited by O. Glasser (Chicago, Ill.: The Yearbook Publishers, 1944), Vol. I.

7. *Ibid.,* Vol. II.

8. T. G. Hamilton, *Intention and Survival* (Toronto: Macmillan Co. of Canada, Ltd., 1942).

9. W. J. Crawford, *The Reality of Psychic Phenomena* (New York: E. P. Dutton & Co., 1918).
10. W. J. Crawford, *Experiments in Psychical Science* (New York: E. P. Dutton & Co., 1919).

VI THE SOCIAL DIMENSION

The Impact of
Science on Society

37

Albert Einstein once remarked that the atomic bomb changed everything except human thinking. He was referring to our perennial aggressiveness, our exploitation of others, our debased sense of values. Nuclear technology was first used for military purposes; the death and maiming—both physical and psychological—it caused are well known. Later, with the cessation of outright hostilities, it was used for political "saber rattling." In its "peaceful" form as atomic power stations, nuclear technology appears to pose an additional danger for humanity. Radioactive wastes present a major ecological threat; likewise, the possibility of a nuclear accident or deliberate sabotage is also a critical security concern.

In other words, opening the atom was a modern enactment of the myth of Pandora's box. Might research into the physics of paranormal phenomena become still another re-enactment?

As this book demonstrates, research into paranormal events and the processes by which they are manifested is growing quickly around the world. It should also be clear that the awesome untapped human potential for both good and harm inherent in this area is a matter of deep significance for the well being of civilization. As research proceeds, what are the political, societal and ethical considerations that should be examined before it is too late? This question and a host of related ones have thus far largely been ignored by the scientific community.

Yet enough evidence abounds in the history of psychic research to raise a serious warning. A glance at the literature shows that renowned psychics were often deficient in one or more of their personality traits. Judging from their character flaws, it would seem that psychic abilities can be developed to a powerful degree without much awareness, if any, of the moral dimension. Accounts of fraud and trickery are not hard to find in connection with famous and lesser-known psychics. One of the best-known American mediums, Arthur Ford, was keenly aware of this, and stated flatly in his biography *Unknown But Known* that being psychic did not at all make one spiritual. Ironically, after his death, Ford himself was accused of fraud by researchers who felt they had found indications, in his papers, that he often collected substantial information on a deceased person whose relatives wanted Ford to contact in a seance.

This lesson has been one of major importance in the teachings of all the world's major spiritual and religious traditions. Yogic philosophy warns against seeking *siddhis* (psychic powers) because they are obstacles to enlightenment. St. Paul spoke at length on this same matter, using different terminology, in Chapters 12 to 24 of his Epistle to the Corinthians. While plainly acknowledging that people have a "spiritual body" separable from the physical body and that there are "diversities of gifts" such as clairvoyance, prophecy, healing, mediumship, and so forth, he emphasized that without a solid moral foundation in one's character, such abilities were "as sounding brass or a tinkling cymbal." His discourse on love (*caritas* or charity) as the essential element in one's behavior ought to be recommended reading for all those entering psychic research either as scientists or subjects.

Even occult traditions such as witchcraft note the difference between the "left hand" or evil path of black magic and the "right hand" or benevolent path of white magic, and emphasize that evil worked on someone will eventually boomerang upon the black magician. The story of the sorcerer's apprentice is a powerful example; paranormal powers can get out of hand and harm the psychic, as well as others, unless there is a sound emotional, moral and intellectual basis from which the psychic applies his powers.

In short, the benevolent use of psychic functioning in general requires a high degree of character development and a balanced, integrated personality. Otherwise the psychic can get into difficulties that cannot be handled easily or wisely.

These difficulties may include delusional belief, uncontrolled telepathy (hearing voices in one's head), poltergeist manifestations unleashed by psychokinetic forces, possession by non-physical entities and a conceited pride in which the psychic assumes the position of infallibility.

In addition, it is remotely possible that a psychic might be employed by unscrupulous parties—civilian, political, or military—to commit clairvoyant "ESPionage," to psychokinetically disrupt an enemy's computers and radars, to assassinate a political leader through PK-induced heart failure, to telepathically implant ideas and commands in the mind of a military or political leader. The ramifications of these and other variations of psychic attack, invasion, and abuse are enormous. Even though there is little solid evidence that the effects can be implemented on a practical basis, to ignore their possibility would be irresponsible and dangerous.

Important as these moral concerns are, there has been little need for society to concern itself with them because of a simple fact: psychic functioning at an observably significant level has been rare until recently. But the emergence of psychic sensitives (some validated by scientific research, others only self-proclaimed) in apparently unprecedented numbers has been coincident with a paradigm shift throughout Western civilization.

A paradigm is the basic belief structure or set of unspoken assumptions underlying a society's world view; it exerts a powerful influence upon what occurs in that society and especially its science. As our belief structures change, as our scientific view of what is possible and impossible in "reality" comes to allow for psychic functioning, many observers believe that latent psychic abilities become increasingly manifest. The psychic talents characterizing a narrow segment of the population in past decades, it is held, could develop in a larger number of people. Supporting this development is a quickened public interest in the paranormal and the spiritual. Psychic functioning is acknowledged as an adjunct to spiritual growth by virtually every major spiritual tradition. In addition to all this, data from the new field of consciousness research suggest new and efficient techniques for enhancing psychic functioning.

What will this mean for the character of public life? How will societal functioning be affected? What is the import for science and the scientific method?

This section attempts to raise significant questions about the consequences of psychic functioning, both human and technological. Willis W. Harman, Michael Rossman, and David Spangler focus on values, attitudes, social and philosophical considerations. Saul-Paul Sirag speaks to the skeptics —many of whom we hope will read this book. Since the articles speak clearly to the issues and their revolutionary implications, we feel it necessary to add only the following two comments:

(1) The consequences of research into the paranormal is a matter of public concern and should be answerable to public control.

(2) It is not premature to consider what procedures could be initiated to defend oneself (or a society) against psychic attack. In this regard, tradition maintains that the best psychic defense is to put on "spiritual armor," i.e., to grow in understanding and to mature in character.

In other words, this section addresses itself to issues that are of practical as well as theoretical importance. Only time will demonstrate whether the warnings voiced by some of the writers are justified, or whether the visions entertained in other parts of this section will be realized.

38.

The Societal Implications and
Social Impact of Paranormal Phenomena

WILLIS W. HARMAN

For at least a century and a half psychic phenomena have held a fascination for some scientists and have been anathema to others. That their scientific study is gaining acceptance may be partly because improved experimentation procedures and new instrumentation have yielded better confirmed results. It is probably even more a consequence of cultural changes that allow these phenomena to "fit in" to a degree that would have been hard to foresee even fifteen years ago.

Thus it will not do to examine the impact of psychic phenomena in isolation from the changing paradigm* of scientific understanding and the cultural movements evident in recent years. The whole social organism moves together, and appears to be fast approaching a metamorphosis in which the field of psychic research is destined to play a significant role. It may have been a sense of this destiny that accounts for the fact of a few scientists having for so long been willing to risk ridicule and ostracism to follow their fascination.

Psychic research and the kindred psychology of consciousness are not just an emerging set of new findings and theories, about which we may conjecture as to social impacts. We have instead to ask: "What new pattern is this a part of?"

"The Societal Implications and Social Impact of Paranormal Phenomena" by Willis W. Harman is an unpublished address delivered to the Eighteenth Annual Convention of the Parapsychological Association, Santa Barbara, California, 22 August 1975. Printed by permission of the author.

* When the word paradigm is used herein it is meant, in the sense made popular by Thomas Kuhn, to refer to the basic pattern of perceiving, thinking, valuing, and acting associated with a particular vision of reality.

Watt's invention of the steam engine provides a parallel. The narrow query as to social impact of the steam engine might have led to the answer that it would make possible the pumping of water out of deep coal mines and hence would facilitate the shift from wood fuel to coal. But the question, "What new pattern?" yields the answer, the Industrial Revolution.

The Discomforts of Scientists

We begin our search for clues as to the form of this new pattern by recalling a few events in the past century and a half of scientific history. All societies have their official or recognized truth-seeking and truth-validating activities and institutions; in the Western world this has been science. Accordingly, what came to be accepted in the scientific community as truth has had important consequences for the basic beliefs of the culture. There are a number of instructive instances where scientists have stumbled for a while over some awkward data, and then recovered from their temporary discomforts and incorporated the new with limited strain.

One of the oldest areas of psychological knowledge has to do with those strange phenomena grouped together under the term "hypnosis." Hypnotism has been studied systematically for over a century and a half, although it has been admitted to scientific respectability much more recently. (Actually, some of the phenomena have been known to esoteric lore for thousands of years, but we will come to that point later.) Among the scientifically demonstrated aspects of hypnosis are that hypnotic suggestion can bring about:

- anesthesia and analgesia, local or general;
- positive and negative hallucinations;
- regression to an earlier age;
- unusual muscular strength, rigidity, resistance to fatigue;
- organic effects normally outside voluntary control.

For example, a hypnotized subject may be induced to perceive an imaginary kitten placed in her lap. She experiences stroking the kitten and hearing it purr; the senses of sight, touch, and hearing seem to corroborate the hypnotist's suggestion. Yet this is a "positive hallucination"—there is no kitty there.

Other examples are familiar. A subject accepts the suggestion that a person sitting in a particular chair really is not there; he perceives an empty chair. A hypnotized person is persuaded that a small wastebasket is fastened to the floor; struggling mightily, he is unable to lift it. A subject's body is rendered rigid by appropriate suggestions; he is then used to bridge the space between two chairs, and one or more individuals mount and stand on top of his unsupported chest and abdomen. Blisters and burned spots can be produced by hypnotic suggestion; or a person may be rendered insusceptible to heat that ordinarily would produce severe burns.

The analgesic and anesthetic potentialities of hypnosis were demonstrated a century ago in hundreds of apparently painless major operations, some witnessed by scores of physicians. Yet the possibility of the phenomenon's existence was denied, and medical journals refused to publish papers documenting the work. Patients were accused of deluding or colluding with their doctors in pretending to feel no pain while limbs were cut off or abdominal operations were performed.

Hypnosis clearly has a long history of irrational opposition. It is less clear just what was so discomforting about these phenomena. Perhaps it is that they so obviously raise doubts that we know what is real. But the important point in our context is that scientists once felt very uncomfortable with hypnosis, and now feel quite comfortable—although they are really not much better off in terms of any sort of "mechanism" or "explanation." The phenomena remain mysterious; however, it is now a comfortable mystery.

The concept of unconscious processes, too, became acceptable to scientists only recently. The initial reaction to the hypotheses of Freud and other pioneers in this area was one of discomfort, rationalized in a number of ingenious ways. To be sure, these are strange ideas—that of mental processes over which I exert no control and of which I have only sporadic or inferred knowledge; the concept of myself repressing information, distorting it or hiding it from my conscious awareness, and lying to myself; the whole sense of one part of myself deceiving or sending cryptic messages to another part of myself. But the strange became familiar, the uncomfortable became comfortable, and unconscious processes became a useful and legitimated concept.

Similarly, the concepts of psychosomatic illness and accident proneness, the power of self-suggestion—the idea that mentally I cause my own headaches and stomach ulcers, or disturb my own kidney functioning, or unconsciously contrive my "accidentally" broken leg, or self-suggest my successes and my failures—were extremely discomforting. They became acceptable only after an initial rejection.

When F. W. H. Myers' *Human Personality* was published in 1903, summarizing preliminary explorations of taboo areas of extraordinary psychic phenomena, included in this forbidden category were not only unconscious processes and hypnosis, but sleep and dreams, and creativity ("inspiration"). The universal testimony of highly creative persons has been that their created projects are the result of higher, unconscious processes over which they have only limited control. Myers' vanguard parapsychological treatise stresses the essential similarities between such psychic phenomena as telepathy and clairvoyance, and the experiences of creative geniuses and of mathematical prodigies. Three quarters of a century ago creativity was part of the domain of "psychical research"—hardly scientifically respectable.

The new tools of biofeedback and related explorations of the past quarter century provided startling revelations. Subjective, inner states have physically measurable correlates—rapid eye movement, changes in skin resistance, muscle tensions, EEG (brainwave) components, electric and magnetic fields around the body. Furthermore, when these indicators are picked up by sensors and returned to the body as input signals, all sorts of involuntary bodily processes and states can be brought under voluntary control. Here was a new basis for legitimation of studies of man's inner world of experience (since at least some aspects of the phenomena are subject to physical measurement) and also a whole new kit of tools. Again the implications are profound. Apparently I do know, in some sense, how I grow my hair and assimilate my food and construct a fetus—except that because of the absence of suitable feedback the processes go on totally outside my realm of ordinary consciousness. And apparently the Indian yogis who claimed control over involuntary processes were onto something Western science has missed. Again, scientists experienced some discomfort over implications, in time becoming comfortable.

Implications of Consciousness and Psi Research

Now, all that preliminary discussion was preparation for the point that there are presently two areas of research about which the majority of scientists still feel some discomfort—discomfort which we may assume will in time go away. One of these is the beginnings of a systematization of knowledge about different states of consciousness, including those inner experiences which have formed the bases for the world's religions and out of which have come man's deepest value commitments. The other is the important testing ground of psychic research.

The latter is a crucial area precisely because it lies midway between and links the objective world of public observation, the domain of "ordinary" science, and the "private" world of subjective experience. The phenomena of psychic research are anomalous—their occurrence is widely attested to, yet they do not "fit in." Still they speak clearly to the point that something is fundamentally incomplete about a world view which cannot accommodate them. They also serve as a sort of reality test for the universe of inner experience. They are not wholly inner—they are characterized by something being publicly observable. Neither are they wholly outer, since some activity of the mind is clearly involved. The following partial list will serve to delineate the territory under discussion:

- telepathy, the apparently extrasensory communication of one mind to another;
- clairvoyance, the apparently extrasensory perception of aspects of the physical world, as in "remote viewing" or "out of the body" experience;
- clairvoyant diagnosis of illness;
- clairvoyant perception of information about a past owner or user of a physical object;

- rapid "faith" healing;
- retrocognition, the "remembering" of events that happened to some other person, or prior to the birth of the "rememberer";
- precognition, the "remembering" of events some time in the future;
- psychokinesis, the apparent influencing of the physical world through mental processes other than by the usual psychomotor processes (e.g., levitation, teleportation);
- unusual control of involuntary processes (e.g., stigmata, firewalking);
- thought photography, the apparent production of an image on a photographic film through mental processes alone;
- unusual mental abilities (e.g., speaking in unknown tongues, mathematical prodigies).

Evidence mounts that these sorts of preternormal knowings and abilities are latent in all persons, but typically highly repressed. One sort of experiment which has been performed in various versions makes use of a stimulus that produces a subliminal effect (e.g., a flashing stroboscopic light which, when the flashing frequency is near the alpha frequency, around ten cycles per second, induces a distinctive component in the EEG wave). The stimulus is applied to one person and the response is picked up from a second person, remote and isolated from the first. The second person typically unable to guess better than a chance basis whether or not the stimulus is applied to the other person during a given time interval—but his subliminal response indicates that unconsciously he knows. (A necessary condition seems to be that the two persons are in some rapport, that one is paying attention to the other—but then we have no adequate explanation for what it means to "pay attention.") The implication, if we extrapolate beyond this particular situation, is that probably we will eventually discover that all persons have the full range of psychic phenomena as potentialities, all unconsciously understood and all thoroughly repressed.

The Extent of the Challenge

It is important to understand both why these two research areas of consciousness exploration and psychic phenomena have caused scientists such acute discomfort, and also why the reconciliation seems now close at hand. The extent of the potential impact of these areas on the scientific world view is suggested by the following list of premises which the scientific paradigm, until recently, has tended to imply:

(1) The only conceivable ways in which man comes to acquire knowledge is through his physical senses and perhaps through some sort of memory storage in the genes.

(2) All qualitative properties are ultimately reducible to quantitative ones; that is, color is reduced to wavelength, hate and love to the chemical composition of glandular secretions, etc.

(3) There is a clear distinction between the objective world, which is perceivable by anyone, and subjective experience which is perceived by the individual alone, in the privacy of his own mind.

(4) The concept of the free inner person is a prescientific explanation for behavior caused by forces impinging upon the individual from his environment, interacting with internal tensions and pressures characteristic of the organism. "Freedom" is behavior for which scientists have not yet found the cause.

(5) What we know as consciousness or awareness of our thoughts and feelings is really only a side effect of physical and biochemical processes going on in the brain.

(6) What we know as memory is simply a matter of stored data in the physical organism, strictly comparable with the storage of information in a digital computer. (Thus it is impossible for a person to

"remember" an event that happened to someone else, in a different lifetime.)

(7) The nature of time being what it is, there is obviously no way in which we can obtain foreknowledge of the future other than by rational prediction from known causes. (Thus it is impossible for anyone to "remember" an event happening three weeks hence.)

(8) Since mental activity is simply a matter of fluctuating states in the physical organism, it is completely impossible for this mental activity to exert any effect directly on the physical world outside the organism. (Thus reports of levitation or other psychokinetic events have to be nonsense or trickery.)

(9) The evolution of the universe and of man has come about through purely physical causes, through random mutations and natural selection. There is no justification for any concept of universal purpose or teleological urge, either in the evolution of consciousness or in the strivings of the individual.

(10) The individual does not survive the death of the organism, or if there is any sense in which the individual exists on after the death of his physical body we can neither comprehend it in this life nor in any way obtain knowledge regarding it.

The reason psychic and consciousness research is such a bitterly contested battleground is that the data in these areas challenge *all* of the above premises. Yet it was on the basis of these positivistic premises that the increasingly prestigious scientific world view was able, in the past, to dismiss as of secondary consequence the religious, aesthetic, and intuitive experiences of man, and hence to erode the value postulates based in those subjective experiences.

The Ultimate Question of Consciousness

Let us put it another way. The reason that all these interrelated research areas—biofeedback, altered states of consciousness, hypnosis, psychosomatic illness, unconscious processes, psychic phenomena—have tended to be discomforting is that they so evidently implicate the ultimate question: "How do I know what I know—and how do I know it is 'true'?" St. Exupery laid down (in *Wind, Sand, and Stars*) the fundamental definition of truth: "Truth is *not* that which is demonstrable. Truth is that which is ineluctable"—that which cannot be escaped.

How do I know what is ineluctable? This question is the heart of the discipline of epistemology, and to one with the stamina to pursue it there, much examination of the subject can be found. Essentially there are two quite different forms of knowing (modern writers are fond of associating these with the left- and right-hand sides of the brain), and we all use both daily. One is "knowing about" things in the manner of scientific "facts"; the other is knowing by intuitive identification with, as in knowing another person.

This second kind of knowing is what the poet Archibald MacLeish referred to when he wrote: "We *really* know a thing only when we are filled with a wonderfully full, new, and intimate sense of it and, above all, of our relation with it. This sense—this *knowledge*—art can give but abstraction (science) cannot." The Indian scholar Radhakrishnan described perception in the higher stages of consciousness thusly: "The conscious division and separation of . . . the object from the subject, which is the normal condition, is broken down. The individual surrenders to the object and is absorbed by it. He becomes what he beholds."

Both kinds of knowing are subject to the possibility of error. The scientific way of "knowing about" involves meticulous testing to ensure that what is claimed as fact can be validated by other scientists making similar experiments or explorations. Intuitive knowing also demands the most careful checking against self-deception. The astonishing extent to which my mental processes are discovered to be out of consciousness sheds doubt on how well I know even that most intimate being, myself. At best I seem to reveal to my conscious self only a small and badly distorted fragment of the wholeness that is "me." Nevertheless, the task of self-knowledge is not futile; from each new vantage point I seem to be able to look back and observe how I have fooled myself in a previous and lesser state of awareness.

Thus in opening up the exploration of consciousness, scientists are forced to confront questions which they have, throughout most of the history of scientific activity, managed to put aside for the philosophers to puzzle over. What are the essential limitations of "knowledge about"? What are the ultimate capabilities of the mind as observing instrument in discerning intuitive knowledge of the universe, and—possibly the same thing—of mind itself? What are the ways in which the latter knowledge is best shared and consensually validated? In some sense all knowledge is ultimately subjective, since the root of all experience is consciousness; consequently, these new explorations that probe the problem of consciousness are fundamental indeed. This is where science, religion and philosophy meet. We can hardly blame the scientists if at this point their resolution quavers and their anxieties become more evident than usual.

In papers currently presented at scientific meetings and in articles published in the most prestigious scientific journals are indications that, with regard to both consciousness research and psychic research, the transition from discomfort to comfort may be at hand. This is only partly because of the psychological effect, noted earlier, of having some physical and physiological correlates to inner experience, serving to legitimize the inquiry into consciousness. More important, it has to do with the growing realization within science that it deals not with reality in some ultimate sense, but with models and metaphors. This has brought a change in attitude and a more promising climate for exploration of inner experience than heretofore.

The precursor to that realization came with the resolution of the battle in physics over the wave or particle nature of light. This was essentially resolved through recognition that both are only metaphors (as is the mathematical equation which incorporates elements of both)—each being useful for expressing certain aspects of the transcendental nature of light. Certain photoelectric effects have no "explanation" in terms of the wave image of light. On the other hand, the electron microscope is "unexplainable" through a particle model of electrons and is understood through a wave image. The resolution of this issue set a pattern for others.

Thus the argument that attempted to resolve in favor of human free will *or* scientific determinism becomes instead a recognition of alternative metaphors for expressing different aspects of a transcendental reality. The old-fashioned warfare between science and religion is rapidly dissolving in a similar way, through the recognition that conventional scientific knowledge is essentially a set of metaphors useful for expressing certain aspects of human "outer" experience. Other facets, especially of deeper inner experience, demand other kinds of metaphors. We have yet to discover what particular metaphors will be most useful for our time; many of those that had the power to move men's hearts in the past seem less useful now.

The New Image of Man

Even though these frontier scientific developments have not progressed very far, it is possible to infer which direction they will push the image of man-in-the-universe. Wherever the nature of man has been probed deeply, in Eastern or Western traditions, the paramount fact emerging is the duality of his experience. He is found to be both physical and spiritual, both aspects being "real" and neither fully describable in terms of the other. "Scientific" and "religious" metaphors are complementary; neither contradicts the other.

Aldous Huxley wrote of the "perennial philosophy," found at the inner core of all the world's religions, East and West, ancient and modern: "(It) recognizes a divine reality substantial to the world of things and lives and minds; . . . finds in the soul something similar to, or even identical with, divine reality; . . . places man's final end in the knowledge of the immanent and transcendent ground of all being."

The esoteric perennial philosophy forms an intermittently visible stream which has had a profound effect on Western civilization. Thales, Solon, Pythagoras, and Plato journeyed to Egypt to be initiated into its then ancient mysteries. Much of it is woven into institutionalized Christianity. In its Hermetic, Cabbalistic, Sufistic, and Rosicrucian forms it affected the history of the Middle East and of Europe. Its Freemasonry symbolism in the Great Seal of the United States (on the back of the dollar bill) testifies to its role in the formation of this nation.

Before brashly attempting to sum up the primary characteristics of the perennial philosophy we should note first that its adherents have always insisted that it cannot be "summed up"—that it is *not* a philosophy, or a metaphysic, *not* an ideology or a religious belief, although others have typically considered it so. Perhaps the flavor of it, but only the flavor, can be hinted at in the following five statements.

Being. The basic experimental proposition is that man can under certain conditions attain to a higher awareness, a "cosmic consciousness," in which state he has immediate knowledge of a reality underlying the phenomenal world, in speaking of which it seems appropriate to use such words as infinite and eternal (divine ground of being, brahman, godhead). From this vantage point one's own growth and creativity, and his participation in the evolutionary process, are seen to be under the ultimate direction of a higher center (atman, the oversoul, the "true self"). The *Upanishad* puts it: "An invisible and subtle essence is the spirit of the whole universe. That is reality. That is truth. Thou art that."

Awareness. The power of suggestion is such that a person is literally and inescapably hypnotized by the suggestions he has absorbed from his culture since infancy. Thus man goes through life in a sort of hypnotic sleep, feeling that he is making decisions, having accidents happen to him, meeting chance acquaintances, etc. With more awareness the direction of the higher self, "supraconscious choosing," becomes apparent. The person finds that decisions he felt he had come to logically or through intuition were really reflections of choices made on the higher level of the self; that his "inspiration" or "creativity" is essentially a breaking through of these higher processes; that experiences and relationships which he needed for his growth were attracted to him by the self and were by no means so accidental as he had assumed. Because ordinary perception, compared to this higher awareness, is partial perception, language built up from ordinary perception proves inadequate to describe the greater reality; attempts often are paradoxical in form.

Motivation. With increasing awareness the pull of material and ego needs is greatly lessened and the person finds his deepest motivation is to participate fully in the evolutionary process, achieving wholeness (haleness, health) through alignment of supraconscious, conscious, and subconscious choices. Evolution is seen not to be a random matter, but directed by a higher consciousness and characterized by purpose—this purpose including development of individual centers of consciousness with freedom of choice, gradually moving toward ever-increasing knowledge of themselves, of self, and of the whole.

Potentiality. It follows from the foregoing that the human potentiality is limitless; that all knowledge and power is ultimately accessible to the mind, looking within itself; and that all limitations (infirmities, illnesses, etc.) are ultimately self-chosen. The great secret of esoteric knowledge is, "I am cause." Such supernormal phenomena as telepathic phenomena, clairvoyant perception, experiencing events that happened to others, "instant" diagnosis and healing, precognition of future events, teleportation and other psychokinetic events, are in general perfectly possible. At some deep level the individual understands them, and at some deep level he chooses the ordinary "physical laws" that preclude them for the most part.

Attitude. With awareness comes a new attitude toward life. One aspect is the desire to consciously participate, to labor and serve, in the evolutionary process, the cosmic drama, the fulfillment of mankind. But the reverse side of this is acceptance, the conscious choosing of what is—since at a deep level of the self one already chooses this. Related to this is a nonattachment, being "divinely impersonal," unattached to specific outcomes, having "impersonal love."

The Case for Social Transformation

No one would claim, of course, that the perennial philosophy has been demonstrated—or ever could be. We may only say that findings in these two fields of psychic phenomena and consciousness research point in its direction, and are compatible with it. However, if the knowledge paradigm of the society is changing to something like the perennial philosophy (which expands upon but is compatible with the scientific paradigm as we have known it), this implies far more—the possibility that the whole pattern of perceiving, conceptualizing, and valuing which has characterized modern industrial civilization may be giving way to a new order. This would involve not only changed folkways and "new age" values, but also changed institutions and power structures and an altered economic and political order.

It must be left to the historians of a later generation to judge whether in fact the last third of the 20th century is indeed such a revolutionary era. There are at this point two basic arguments for asserting it may be so. One is the pull of new cultural beliefs and values. The other is the push of dilemmas of modern industrialized society that may in fact be unresolvable without a fundamental transformation, not just of values and institutions but of the very roots of the culture.

Signs of the "new transcendentalism" are manifest, of course. Evidence abounds of a marked turning inward and of the reacceptance into the culture of those spiritual concerns that had been thrust into the background by the fantastic successes of modern materialist science and technology. These spiritual concerns reappear simultaneously with our growing disillusionment with the satisfactions of an over-materialistic culture. Surveys and polls show clear shifts, especially among such elite groups as students and corporate executives, toward spiritual values and quality-of-life concerns and away from materialistic values. Numerous cultural indicators (e.g., books read, voluntary associations, song lyrics, themes of plays and motion pictures, "new age" subculture) show greatly increased interest in, and tolerance for, the transcendental, religious, esoteric, suprarational, and mystical.

The complementary force, the recognition of need for a new social paradigm to replace that which underlies and shapes modern technological industrialized society, is almost as apparent. The industrial era, that period from the industrial revolution through the present to a few decades hence at most, is a unique period. It is an era in which man has been living off a legacy of virtually unreplenishable minerals and fossil fuels—preceded by long millennia during which man's consumption from this storehouse was small and his impact on the environment was relatively minor. It must be followed by an epoch in which the limitations of the storehouse are recognized, and in which human activity fits into some new set of ecological relationships including modified "natural cycles" with man as a conscious participant. The growth-and-consumption materialist ethic must be replaced by one more compatible with the realities of living on a small planet.

The rapidly approaching climacteric is being brought about by the growing awareness of dilemmas implicit in the industrial-era paradigm and the growing intensity of the conflicts engendered by those dilemmas. It is increasingly clear that unlimited and unguided technological and economic growth —and energy consumption—has to end; yet continued growth is perceived to be necessary to the essential stability of the economic system. Control over the Faustian powers of technological application is vital, yet bureaucratic control of technological options is greatly and rightly feared. More equitable sharing of the Earth's resources with less developed nations seems both intolerably costly and absolutely necessary. The present perception of satisfying work roles being a scarce commodity to be rationed by devious mechanisms—from featherbedding through inflated job-entry requirements to early retirement—is an unacceptable admission of the society's inability to deal with the psychological (as contrasted with the economic) problem of underemployment. These dilemmas are so deeply embedded in fundamental assumptions in the industrial-era paradigm that they will only be satisfactorily resolved if the society evolves toward a new guiding paradigm.

Just what form this new social pattern might take cannot be foretold in advance. Still, we can conjecture what some of the characteristics would have to be if (a) the society were to be compatible with the new transcendentalism, (b) the dilemmas of the advanced industrial state were to become resolvable, and (c) the new social institutions are to be arrived at through a nondisruptive transition (i.e., are continuous with the past).

Guiding Ethic. A new guiding ethic would replace the fragmented materialist ethics (e.g., growth and consumption) which presently dominate the economic system and thence the society. This involves two complementary principles. One is an ecological ethic that fosters a sense of the total community of man and responsibility for the fate of the planet and relates self-interest to the interest of fellow man and future generations. The other is a self-realization ethic which holds that the proper end of all individual experience is the further evolutionary development of the emergent self and of the human species, and that the appropriate function of social institutions is to create environments which will foster that process.

These two ethics, the one emphasizing community caring, oneness, and the other placing the highest value on development of selfhood, are not contradictory but complementary—two sides of the same coin. Together they leave room both for cooperation and for wholesome competition, for love and for individuality. Each is a corrective against excesses or misapplication of the other.

Individual and Social Goals. The two ethics lead directly to paramount goals for the society and its institutions. The first dictates concern for the well being of the human race, all of life on the planet, and future generations. The second implies more specifically the individual goals of life, liberty, and the pursuit of self-realization.

The central activity of self-realization is work-play-learning. Thus an essential goal of the society would be to ensure for each individual access to a satisfying work-play-learning role, performance in which earns affirmation by the society and thus contributes to development of a healthy self-image. In an advanced society in which material goals have become de-emphasized, industrialized production has approached steady state, and routine tasks have been cybernated (for humane as well as economic reasons), it is clear that only a fraction of the work (-play-learning) force will be required to supply material and service wants. The economy will be viewed as the primary mechanism for providing satisfying social roles, and production of desired goods and services will be easily accomplished in the process.

Institutions. It follows that a social institution such as a corporation would have goals compatible with those of the society. Thus prioritized corporate goals would become something like the following: (a) to carry on activities that contribute to the self-fulfillment of the persons involved, managers and workers; (b) to carry on activities that contribute directly to satisfaction of social needs and accomplishment of societal goals; and (c) to earn a fair profit on investment, not so much as a goal in itself but rather as a control signal monitoring effectiveness.

This sounds so utopian that we need to remind ourselves how it might come about. The most powerful force in history for changing social institutions is the power of those who make up the society to grant or withhold legitimacy. Governments have often felt the potency of legitimacy withdrawal (for instance, the post-Watergate Nixon administration, or the post World War II colonial imperialisms). The presently fragmented challenges to the legitimacy of present corporate behavior—consumerism, environmentalism, the civil rights and women's liberation and old people's movements, truth-in-advertising pressures, demands for improved work environment, stockholder revolts—could coalesce into a force for transformation that would be irresistible.

More broadly, the transformation of the institutions of society would be such as to eliminate structured social and environmental irresponsibility. That is, the overall incentive system (economic, community approval, encultured mores, etc.) would foster ecologically wholesome behavior, in the broadest sense. The society would be synergistic—i.e., what the individual *wants* to do would be good for the whole.

Education. Education (as part of work-play-learning) would be a function of every institution in society. Rather than being a segregated activity carried out at a certain place in a certain time period, learning toward human fulfillment would be a recognized aim of all of the various institutionalized activities at which the individual spends his time. The society might be termed a "learning-and-planning society" since learning and planning are the two main kinds of activities (beyond those actually required for the functioning of the society) that are meaningful, nonstultifying, and nonpolluting.

Schools and colleges would still have a place, of course. They would emphasize preparation for a useful role (and "recycling" preparation for undertaking a new career phase); self-understanding and interpersonal skills; ability to gain new skills (over acquisition of any particular skill); having access to knowledge (over having memorized any particular knowledge); dealing with wholes (rather than obtaining only highly detailed knowledge of narrow specialities); and development of an evolutionary and future-oriented attitude.

Science. Under the new transcendentalism, science would be clearly understood to be a moral inquiry. Having a balanced effort of systematic exploration of both the objective and subjective realms of human experience, it could not be, as past science has tended to be, value-empty. It would deal with what is empirically found to promote wholeness—in much the same sense that present-day nutritional science deals with what foods are wholesome for man. It would place particular emphasis on the systematic exploration of various levels of subjective experience, the ultimate source of our value postulates. In this respect it would resemble the humanities and religion, and the boundaries between these three disciplines would become less sharp—as is already presaged in the recent writings of some psychotherapists. The models and metaphors used will be multileveled, corresponding to different levels or realms of experience, and no conflict will be perceived if, for example, mystical experiences are congenial to one of these metaphorical frameworks and operant conditioning to another.

New impetus would be given the biological sciences (with

a whole-systems emphasis) and the psychology of consciousness. The latter will look strongly in the direction of new potentialities suggested by the newly appreciated powers of belief, imagination, and suggestion. To conscious and subconscious choice (repression, projection, sublimation, etc.) will be added what may be termed supraconscious choice (intuition, creative imagination, choosing "better than we know")—possibly with as much impact on our policies regarding education, welfare, criminal rehabilitation, and justice as the Freudian concepts had some years earlier. Social science would be participative, in marked contrast to the "objective" observations of past social scientists. Experimenter and subject explore together, in an atmosphere of mutual trust and with equal status. (The resulting science would be significantly different from the industrial-age social science, since the implicit goals are so different—prediction and control being replaced by the aim of guidance in individual and social development.)

Finally, the new science would be also a sort of "civil religion," supporting the humane value postulates of the culture rather than being neutral or undermining, as was the old science.

Health Care. The new society would have a broadened definition of health, as wholeness of being. As with education, many institutions would share responsibility—medicine, psychotherapy, education, religion, welfare, environmental health. There would be a recognition that the whole society is the environment that affects health—thus, for example, equity in access to economic resources is an aspect of environmental health.

Attitudes toward mental illness and toward death would be greatly changed. There would be a blurring of the distinction between mental and physical illness, and emphasis for both would be placed on the individual's discovering why he caused the illness. Anxiety over the possibility of "losing one's mind" and over death would be markedly reduced (since neither psychosis nor death would be viewed as "permanent"). This changed attitude would especially affect the role of the aged (an area in which the failure of industrialized society is particularly egregious).

The Transition Period

Finally, there is nothing in history to suggest that a social transformation of the magnitude suggested could occur without the most severe economic and social disruptions and system breakdowns. Only widespread understanding of why the transformation is taking place, and of the kind of society that might emerge following our time of troubles, can keep anxiety levels down and transition pains from becoming intolerable.

The forces of societal transformation have gathered impressive momentum. Developments in psychic research and the psychology of consciousness are part of this larger pattern. The next ten or fifteen years will show whether these forces are strong enough to bring about a major societal wrenching, or whether they will somehow quiet down and die away, or whether the confrontation between the new demands and the old rigidities is so violent that the result is destruction without a promising rebuilding. These years will not be one of the comfortable periods of history. It will no doubt be an exciting one.

39.

Parascience and Social Responsibility

MICHAEL ROSSMAN

When Henri Becquerel began in 1896 to investigate the strange fogging of his photographic plates, he did not anticipate that the second wave of researchers into radioactivity would be called upon, as they were, to decide in secret whether it was worth risking a chain reaction that might destroy the entire planet, for the sake of a military victory. Nor did he know how reluctant the third wave would be to confess that the industrial applications of their science had created a pool of poisonous waste, sufficient to exterminate all vertebrate life, which would have to be tended for a million years; and that they were not certain it could be tended safely.

We have the advantage of hindsight, but how should we use it? The parasciences—paraphysics and parapsychology— are rapidly becoming established as legitimate fields of scientific inquiry, and even their earliest researches suggest equally dramatic possibilities of disaster. For example, reports from the Maimonides Medical Center Dream Laboratory in Brooklyn, New York indicate that one human mind can directly modify the subconscious processes of another under certain conditions. There is no reason to assume *a priori* that the forces and energies involved cannot be identified, amplified and directed by appropriate technologies—which might make possible a totalitarianism more subtle, efficient, and massive than any yet envisioned. Is it crazy to imagine

such a possibility—or crazy not to? And what can be done
about it?

These examples dramatize our common experience that
scientific research gives rise to material and social technologies with complex human consequences, and they lead us to
fundamental questions. *What are the social responsibilities of
a new science? Who should care about them, and how can
they be faced?* For the psychic sciences, these questions seem
more complex than they do for nuclear physics, and scarcely
less important. For whatever the theoretical explanation of
psychic powers may turn out to be, anyone abreast of current
research can foresee the advent of technologies with awesome
and complicated potentials for liberation and for tyranny, in
both the psychological and the material domains.

What attitudes are proper to scientist–citizens of an age in
which innocent research into the fundamental nature of physical reality has quickly developed into the unsteadily withheld
capacity to destroy all human life? With the development of
psychic technologies, we are opening a Pandora's box. Perhaps nothing can stop us from meddling with the universe,
but it would be criminal to do so as blindly as we have done
in the past. There is no telling the short and long consequences of our exploration: the uses to which discoveries will
be put by a turmoil of governments, the routine and profita-
ble industrial applications whose mixed blessings will be too
late revealed. I am not simply crying doom. Great wonders
and great human goods may well come from psychic and
paraphysical research, and it is proper to dream them and
seek them. But only the totally irresponsible can fail to recognize the many current examples of technology being routinely
put to the service of humanly disastrous ends.

In this light, the task of establishing paraphysics and parapsychology as legitimate sciences must include the task of
defining what sorts of social awareness and social responsibility are appropriate to their practice. Though no definitive
understandings are possible yet, certain broad conclusions are
obvious and essential from the start. We are dealing with
knowledge that may transform our world. It must be used
morally, for the human good. Its consequence is a matter of
legitimate public concern, and should in the end be answera-

ble to public judgment and control. If we are to have any chance of avoiding past patterns of mistake, we must choose right from the start against the "pure, detached research" view of science, and also, I believe, against the "industry's blind handmaiden" view.

What forms of public knowledge and control are appropriate, and what mechanisms of supervision and regulation are necessary, are still to be discovered. But we can at least declare clearly the necessity and urgency for dealing with these questions. The new field of genetic engineering has recently set an example, in warning the world of the dangers inherent in its research, and in voluntarily taking measures to offset them; and there are groups and societies now working to formulate guidelines for the humane and liberating social employment of science and technology in general, whose advices might be sought—not only to avoid disaster, but to help realize potential good.

Such a perspective of social responsibility is quite foreign to paraphysics and parapsychology as they have been developing, perhaps because the struggle for acceptance in the scientific community has led their researchers to conceive and present their work in the most narrow and conservative ways, blindly imitating the models of research and development which have accounted for our present technological magnificence. But in our time science itself is being called upon fundamentally to reconceive its nature, dimensions and consequences, and to re-evaluate its human responsibilities. *It is vitally important that concern for the social and political aspects of the parasciences not be segregated from concern for them as "sciences in themselves."* Rather, from the start and against tradition, the equal legitimacy of these concerns must be advanced hand-in-hand with the claims of scientific discipline. Let the parasciences create a new example of what a humane and responsible science should be as it declares its emergence. Nothing less is appropriate to the study of the mysteries of consciousness.

To appreciate the complexity of this undertaking, consider one recent proposal from a U.S. government agency for a paraphysics conference that would "formulate standards to identify the potentials for advancing knowledge and its use."

Many thorny problems, both moral and political, are implicit in this innocent project. We know that a science develops as much in response to visions of its usefulness in society, and to pressures stemming from these visions, as it does in response to "intrinsic" forces; and history tells us that on the whole these visions are defined to favor the private interests of those who stand to profit most by technology's application. We must ask, then: *What uses of paraphysical knowledge are to be advanced? What standards should govern the development of parapsychology? And who should determine these matters?*

It may seem indelicate to phrase these questions in terms of economics, power, and justice. But when we consider the example of modern medical science, we can see that the "potentials for advancing knowledge and its use," though nominally neutral, have been interpreted and implemented to produce a medical technology, a medical *industry*, which systematically favors the rich and leaves the poor to suffer; which ignores the effects of our society itself upon our health and refuses to prescribe the prophylaxis of social reform; which progressively reduces its own ability to treat the whole person; which artificially structures the nature and delivery of its services to produce for its practitioners and supporters the highest incomes general in any industry; and which, above all, has taken the power to apply medical science away from the individual, mystified it, and concentrated it in a small elite of specialists. Nor is this example academic, for already each of these tendencies may be seen in embryo in the early development of parapsychological industry.

To imagine that such social distortions of a science's usefulness come about only late in the process of its embodiment in industry is a mistake. Rather they are prefigured, to a great degree, in the character of its basic research, which in turn is largely determined by the cultural context.* A deeply

---

* The present priorities of cancer research, for example, lead directly toward the reinforcement of each of these distortions. It is no accident that the massive funding which ensured their dominance came about as part of the politics of the Nixon administration, and that the "war against cancer" and the Vietnam War both followed the same philosophy of high technology forcing intervention in disease—for such organic entanglements influence the

different social development of medical science might have occurred in a proper climate of public opinion and guidance. In fact it can be argued that a medical science whose practice reverses every clause of the description above is even now coming together in our culture, against considerable opposition; and that it begins with different priorities and methodologies of research. It depends in part upon the understanding and application of psychic phenomena, and its positive characteristics strongly suggest directions in which the psychic sciences as a whole might be developed.

These matters come to focus in a political question: *Is the power of a body of applied knowledge to be distributed among the many, or to be held and controlled by some few?* In this case the fruits of science are not limited to nuclear reactors and spaceships, creations so massive and technical that any individual can hope to exercise control over them only by indirect and political means at best. With the phenomena of the parasciences, it may be quite the reverse: there may be only one Uri Geller or Ingo Swann at present, though I doubt it, but much data suggests that the raw psychic powers are existentially democratic in their essence, a common human birthright, perhaps universal.

If this be so, it may be so also for certain harnessings and applications of these powers that science might achieve. Given the traditional ways of developing science in our society, then, we are faced with a major choice. We can credential, fund and encourage the sorts of parascientific research which will lead to readily industrializable technologies, and to the reinforcement of our society's present structures of power and privilege; or new sorts, which may lead more directly to the personal enfranchisement of every individual in the practical fruits of knowledge. This choice is ultimately a political choice which cannot be avoided, however much it be ignored

---

character of scientific research more than we care to recognize.

A different philosophical approach to cancer—based in the ancient, unprofitable and neglected tradition of medicine as *hygea*, and modern ecological understanding—leads to different priorities of research, which in turn lead not simply to a different "treatment" of the "disease," but toward *a radically different social practice of medicine*, without such social distortions.

—for every attempt to identify desirable directions of research, even for the narrow purpose of legitimizing paraphysics as a science, will contribute in time to determining the implicit politics of an industry's development.

The conflict between these two directions of development is not simply a matter of political theory, but immediately present in the earliest stages of a science's formulation. For example, it seems that certain psychic facilities, such as clairvoyance and "autogenic healing" can be learned, intensified, and taught. Pure research on the nature of psychic phenomena is friendly to research in this direction; but available funding guides it instead towards such projects as the current military experiments in psionics, for the mass alteration of mind states of "enemy" populations. Meanwhile, outside the scientific province, the democratization of clairvoyance proceeds in a familiar industrial fashion, as mind control course franchises and psychic healers stake out their operations among those who can afford to pay. Given such trends, the vision of humanity's enfranchisement by a science devoted to this purpose seems distant indeed.

Who, then, should determine the priorities of paraphysical research? What political standards should be met in setting its goals? How can parapsychology escape the fate of sociology, which has developed not as an unbiased science, but, on the whole, as a tool to enable the managers of society to manage the unempowered more efficiently? Such questions raise the fear that an ideological straitjacket might be put upon research. But beyond where the pure following of question leads, in any science there is always a domain of research, generally the larger, where people seek in response to society's indications of what is interesting, useful, and *proper* to seek. And at this early stage of the parasciences, we perhaps have some choice about whether these indications will come in the usual manner, in the indirect language of governmental and industrial funding; or whether they will come through a different social process.

To imagine a national referendum seems absurd. But there is bold merit to the idea that *a new science, conscious of its broad potential consequences for humanity, should in some way seek public advice as to what its purposes should be, if*

not public determination of these purposes. To proceed otherwise is to persist in a fiction of science's neutrality and in a
curious kind of contempt for the public mind and its sense of
public needs—a contempt so traditional and pervasive in the
practice of science that any questioning of its necessity is
dismissed as irresponsible. For example, the recent, belated
focus of medical research upon sickle-cell anemia has come
about precisely in response to (black) public demand,
backed by political pressure, and has been financed in part
directly by the public. Similar processes directing parascience
research into channels of social responsibility may become
possible, once the public has some idea of how the parasciences might be useful. But to rely on their efficiency seems a
mistake; and it begs the fundamental question of whether the
parasciences can develop in a new way, deliberately responsive and responsible to the public interest.

Our society offers no models for such a development—
though for a time the extension of agricultural science
through the land-grant public colleges embodied its spirit—
and the necessary mechanisms of public interaction can only
be imagined. As matters stand, the most that can be hoped
for now is some form of public dialogue concerning the nature, problems and potentials of parascientific development,
and aimed at guiding it responsibly. Such a dialogue should
involve social critics and planners, theologians, historians of
science, politicians, and so on. In any form, it would still be
an unprecedented social accompaniment to the birth of a science. But most of all it should involve parascientists themselves, not as specialists limited to technical testimony, but as
men and women deeply concerned with the function and
value of their work in society. For the researchers to initiate
the search for responsibility is perhaps the best test of the
genuine newness of a science.

One concrete step in this direction would be for researchers
to conspire in a public declaration of the need for public
disclosure of the nature, scope, and intent of all parascientific
research; and for them to constitute, if necessary, an "underground" to enforce this disclosure. It is widely known that the
militaries of several nations have initiated parascientific researches. That their details and progress are obscure and

mostly rumored should comfort only those who assume *a priori* that the study of paranormal phenomena will produce at best some laboratory curiosities. But citizens of an age in which one generation's curiosity becomes another's Armageddon; in which research is kept secret as much to forestall public reaction as for "security's" sake; and in which governments grasp for imaginative tools of force like weather control and biological warfare, have some reason for paranoia.

In fact, the use of occult science has been a military tradition, from Sparta and Ghengis Khan through Hitler; and we cannot predict how its powers may be enhanced through a modern technologization. Though opportunists could always be found to break it, concerned researchers might do well to promulgate and subscribe to a code of ethics, pledging not to work on projects, military or civilian, which can reasonably be foreseen to lead to destructive ends.† Such a code would serve at least one practical purpose, by providing the moral framework for an immediate effort to assemble the details of classified and unclassified military research now under way, evaluate their implications, and make them public.

Another concrete step would be for researchers, individually or through an organization undertaking this purpose, to begin to describe the social options that follow from their work. For example, certain lore and research suggest that there are privileged places on the Earth's surface, where paranormal forces operate more strongly or accessibly. If paraphysics leads to their identification, understanding, and exploitation, certain predictable questions will arise. Who will control these points and their uses? They may be inconsequential curiosities; they may also prove to be sources of energy as crucial as oil deposits, or to contribute to longevity, or to be good places for schools to be built. Should they be private property or public trust? They will have unknown value; should the nation be prepared, once they are mapped, to hold in reserve the license to develop them, while their significance

† Such a code might have other clauses, including some dealing with the rights of research subjects and the related responsibilities of researchers—an area of social responsibility which has until recently been completely ignored by the human sciences.

is investigated? Are they a rare national resource? Can they be despoiled? This scenario may seem fanciful. But it takes a dim imagination not to recognize that questions like these may well suddenly thrust themselves upon us now, at any time, from any subbranch of the parasciences. Again, what is needed is an instrumentality and a state of mind which scan research and project its social consequences, and act to adjust these for the common good. We should urge their creation as an integral part of the advancement of the parasciences.

A third step, also concrete, would be for the parasciences to become truly visionary, by attempting their work in the context of a clear and integral vision. The ideal that the twin fruits of research—knowledge and power—be placed as directly as possible into as many people's hands as possible, and be shaped for this purpose, should perhaps hold for any science. But it has a special significance for the parasciences. For their early researches seem to restate the literal conclusion of quantum mechanics, in terms of consciousness itself rather than merely its material substrate: we interpenetrate with each other, subtly and irrevocably, the vibrations of each person's most intimate processes resonating directly in every other being, across the boundaries of space and matter which we have assumed to divide us, making us complexly one.

Such is my reading. It may well be premature or misguided, but the parasciences promise to radically reshape our understanding of what it is to be human, and thus our vision of humanity. Such a reshaping is not simply a matter of scientific perspective: it informs our philosophic and spiritual view, and ultimately the politics of our practices. In the scientific tradition, such consequences of interpretation are left to other specialists and to later generations. But it can be argued that we no longer can nor should afford this schizophrenia, particularly in the case of a science that can so directly affect consciousness. Rather, I believe, we should dare the responsibility of casting the practice of the science itself deliberately in terms of the human image we derive from it—choosing our interpretations, as we must, as best and as consciously as we can.

Our culture has done this already, in the cases of Newtonian physics and Freudian psychology, embodying in their social practices the mechanistic, deterministic and authoritarian perspectives which their researches revealed, in addition to reinforcing these more indirectly in society as a whole. These acts were largely unconscious, though perhaps as efficient as had they been deliberate. But given that scientists do exercise their share of such responsibilities in history, consciously or not, the only choice is to be conscious in choice. If indeed the image of humanity and the common good that is latent in parascientific research is of the character I suggest— a deeply democratic and existential fraternity—then it seems a moral imperative to attempt to proceed in terms of this vision.

Thus a parascience discovering the universe to be a radically open information system ought to declare itself against the customary military and commercial practices of research secrecy. It is not so simple to describe in detail the codes of technological practice which are consonant with a vision of our mutual responsiveness and involvement; but I believe that overall they should embody the goal of universal direct enfranchisement in power, and the stance of collective responsibility. Well formulated and well pursued, they would lead to a development of parascientific industry quite different from that which can currently be expected. It is the peculiar opportunity of parascience now, not simply to propose such codes, but to justify them as integrally rooted in the substance of its own research—thus becoming an unprecedented model of a self-conscious discipline in the field of consciousness research.

Thus far I have been discussing the parasciences in terms which might apply to any science whose broad human consequence might be anticipated. But consciousness is a mysterious subject of study, and for all that paraphysics and parapsychology are now dressing themselves in imitation of their namesakes, they may turn out to be quite peculiar sciences, involving quite peculiar and subtle problems of social responsibility. Indeed, dressing up parascience respectably so the scientific community will accept it may be like asking organized science to swallow an innocent pill which will, when digested, blow its mind considerably; and it may be fair, and strategic, to issue some warning.

For it is not unreasonable to surmise that parascientific research will shortly be able to demonstrate, quite rigorously, that much of the entire body of research upon which are founded the present understandings of the human sciences must in the name of scientific honesty be re-evaluated and perhaps discarded and redone, because in innocence it neglected the operation of variables—psychic and paraphysical in nature—sufficient to influence or determine its observations. The parasciences are now recognizing forces which may well play in all human interactions and throughout the material universe, and which add unknown factors to every equation we have construed to account for these. What their quantification may reveal, we cannot tell. Probably electromagnetic theory will still hold in the domain it attempts to describe, but how and why organisms grow and maintain themselves may need revision. And if the parasciences do illuminate a new and significant dimension to the ways that people in general, and hence researchers in particular, project their consciousness and expectations into the world, then almost every research and conclusion of sociology, social and personal psychology, cultural anthropology and medicine may be in peril.‡

Not until acceptable parascientific research conclusively contradicts some theory well established in another discipline will the impact of this strike; and then it will strike chaotically, plunging much of science into the politics of revolution which Thomas Kuhn describes in *The Structure of Scientific Revolutions*. Paraphysicists are generally aware of this, and speculation now grows among them, in circulated papers, about what manner of revision of the framework of traditional relativistic quantum electrodynamics will be necessary to permit the emergence of theory encompassing both physics and paraphysics. It is not too early to begin such speculation about how parapsychology may affect and enlarge

‡ For the parasciences may go much further than modern physics in revolutionizing our understanding of the interaction of observer and observed. When their new concepts and praxes are integrated generally, it is possible that no other sciences may emerge quite as they are today. They may not simply be expanded. Their fundamental characters may change, whether or not such conceptual entities as will and intentionality turn out to be quantifiable.

the traditional human sciences—and for our human ends and responsibilities, it may be more important to do so.

One step is to begin to specify the sorts of research which may prove most immediately and powerfully relevant to the psychological and social sciences. Paraphysics is doing this for physics, as part of winning its respectability. One difficulty in doing this for the softer sciences is that their interaction with parapsychology is not nearly so (ostensibly) value free. For example, parapsychological research may illuminate the ways in which cultural patterns are imprinted and maintained in the individual psyche, and the ways in which people are led to depend on external-authoritative, collective, or inner knowledge and direction. The questions of when, and what kinds of, research is undertaken on these matters may be of considerable social consequence—for the selective consequences, or the avoidance, of such research may powerfully support either the democratic or the authoritarian tendencies in our culture. Here again, then, our values will influence our research, even of the sort which relates the parasciences to the rest of science. And since some value framework will underlie research in any case, we ought as far as possible to see that it be carried out in a visible and humane framework of values. For to some extent the management of society itself may come to hinge on the parasciences, and we would be foolish not to try to provide for this eventuality as early and as well as we can.

It may seem that parascientific researchers have enough to do already, in coping with the domain of problems they have chosen to face, without engaging the cloudy and complex domain of their work's social consequences and responsibilities. But the hard-edged and cautious spirit that tackles only more limited questions which can be more definitively understood, which we imagine to be proper to new sciences seeking to establish themselves, may be inappropriate and untrustworthy here. If I may draw in gentle caricature an image which my friends have presented me with from the pain of their own lives, it is like an engineer confronted with the messy world of personal interplay, in private life and in his work's performance: ill at ease, untrained, and inexperienced in dealing with these realities, he longs to draw back into his work, where he can deal with a world which is simple, mechanical, and clean.

I think the strengths of the present scientific–technological spirit are holy and essential to the adventure of parascientific exploration; but there is some danger that its weaknesses will also come to dominate the style of this enterprise, perhaps fatally. Just as scientist–engineers are in our time being called upon personally to try to open and deepen their human relations, so science itself is called upon to reconceive its nature and adapt to a renewed set of responsibilities. With the parasciences in particular, which may wrench our world, it is blind and irresponsible to ignore the major social and political consequences which may follow from their research. Rather we should try to anticipate them as usefully as we can, to steer consciously and humanely through the chaos of potentials that opens before us.

40.

Science and Illumination

DAVID SPANGLER

For many people, science holds the keys to humanity's future. Looking back, they see a time of hardship, darkness, ignorance, and superstition—from which mankind is well delivered. Knowledge has lifted him and given him dominion over the earth, and science is the best and surest way to acquire knowledge.

If a "new age" is dawning, then it is because the processes of scientific inquiry are bringing us the light of ever-increasing discoveries, insights and knowledge about our world and are laying foundations for new technologies that will transform society. For such individuals, Western civilization, particularly in the United States, represents the pinnacle of human achievement and the hope of the world.

There are others who would differ with this view. Pointing to the ravages of pollution, to the breakdown of traditional forms of human intercourse, and the encouragement of feelings of alienation and isolation within a dehumanized, technological state, they might well say that we are entering another Dark Age. A culture based on paradigms drawn from the atomistic, mechanistic approaches of physics and astronomy places value on knowledge gained by analytically reductive means separated from emotional and intuitive cognition; therefore, in reaching for the symbol of the antiseptic, "cool" laboratory, it loses the sense of the living "presence" within the world. Life, including human life, becomes a collection of objects, of things to be used by a technological imperative

"Science and Illumination" by David Spangler originally appeared in *East West Journal*, May 1974. Copyright © 1974 by David Spangler and reprinted by permission of the author.

that requires parts more than participants. This leads to new superstitions, a new ignorance, a loss of that form of knowledge which is not rational or logical but intuitive, holistic, esthetic, or spiritual. For such individuals, Western culture is less a pinnacle than a pit, a slope leading downward to the degradation of the human spirit.

Naturally, both views represent extremes. The historical tendencies of human consciousness toward polarity insure that its actions and attitudes will reflect both the deific and the demonic in varying degrees. To the extent that our vision is drawn to either end of this "stick" and loses sight of the stick itself in its wholeness, we fail to comprehend the truth. The truth is that transformation is occurring and that whether we see the scales tipping toward Armageddon and apocalypse or toward ascension and apotheosis, science is definitely one of the forces altering the balance.

It is not a cause of transformation; the causes are rooted in the deeper levels of the beingness of humanity and its world which expresses itself in unfolding awareness and self-knowledge. Science is a tool for acquiring knowledge. It is so successful at it within the areas of its competency that it assumes mythic qualities within the popular mind. It is seen as a source of miracles, the true path to knowledge, the yardstick against which experience and information must be measured for validity. Scientific proof becomes the ticket price for entry into recognized and respectable existence; experiences, events, phenomena which cannot meet the standards of laboratory proof are either ignored or often considered illusory or fraudulent.

We recognize that the misuse of science is responsible for many modern ills, yet we look to more science for the answer . . . or, in the reaction that binds us to the thing we oppose, we become antiscience, antitechnology, anti-intellectual. Either way, we remain trapped by the mythic and paradigmatic images of what science is and can be forced into choosing sides and perpetuating a dichotomous consciousness.

The resolution of this challenge and the route to transformation is to acknowledge that the relationship of science to current planetary metamorphosis is an acute one and that it is a primary channel through which the forces of transformation are acting upon and within our civilization. The quality and profundity of that transformation itself, however, do not depend on assigning labels to neutral processes and tools to determine whether they are good or evil, or whether we want more or less of them; they depend on the clarity and understanding with which such tools are used to illumine our knowing.

Of greater importance than whether science is savior or villain is the question of how to transform the transformers, a question which can only be answered by understanding the essential nature and qualities of transformational processes as well as the forms through which they are expressing. It involves a clarity as to what current energies of transformation, of new consciousness and life-awareness, are seeking to create. What lies behind this phenomenon of a "new age?" What new paradigms of civilization, what new qualities and characteristics of culture and of human nature are seeking actualization? Without such understanding and clarity, the new energies of awareness and action can be subtly distorted by the very agencies through which they emerge into human affairs. Caught in the "letter" of the form rather than the spirit, true transformation could thus fail to take place.

As an example of this, the very word "transformation" can be misleading as to the nature of the processes we are discussing. Its dictionary definition is the act of changing the shape, appearance or the *character* of something but its etymological roots suggest the act of going *beyond, across, through,* or *over* the processes of formation. Thus, in common usage, the word means to change a form through which something is expressed. If that is the level of perception and consciousness with which we perform our acts of transformation, then we may likely only deal with changes in form and consider that sufficient. We will envisage planetary transformation as an alteration in forms, such as the creation and adoption of new forms of government, of economics, of art, and of religion. Such change implies a methodology of change, a means by which forms can be manipulated, altered, dissected and recombined. Science is just such a methodology, on one level of its nature; coupled to a manipulative, form-oriented conception of transformation, it becomes limited to that level and will produce the same technological problems that society is challenged with now. No essential change and rebirth has occurred; we alter the outer surface of things but retain the basic paradigms of thought and perception which were creating the limitations we sought to correct.

On the other hand, the roots of the word suggest that transformation takes place by going beyond the forms involved, old and new, to the source of the expression. It suggests a return to the causal center, back to the formlessness that is the womb of formation. A civilization and culture that has reached a point of basic transformation may be likened to a plant that seeks rebirth. Its forms collapse inward, in a sense, toward the genetic center of the seed, the source point which can carry the essence of that plant forward into the organic creation of new forms the following spring. The seed has no roots, stem, leaves, or flowers; yet these do exist in formless reality awaiting a new actualization.

Another analogy may be even more suggestive. A civilization is a constellation of energies, ideas, models, fashions, perceptions, and behaviors revolving around a central field of underlying assumptions about reality; in time, the very weight of psychic inertia generated by this field and its captive expressions begins to collapse inward, to degenerate toward a tight core of self-propagating habits crystallizing and ossifying the dynamic life of the system. This is the creation of the psychic equivalent of a "black hole," a star that has collapsed, creating a gravity well so powerful that light cannot escape it and it becomes invisible.

In an analogous fashion, such an event on a cultural level could lead to a civilization whose basic paradigmatic fields have become "invisible," so bound into the accepted perception of reality that they are taken for granted and are no longer questioned. Such a "black hole" society would take in energies of transformation and remain unchanged, capturing and perverting such energies within the gravity of its own unexamined and crystallized foundations. Yet, at the same time, if this inward collapse is understood and worked with, transformation breaks through that central field of assumptions and can arrive at a still deeper source and center where the being is.

It is this beingness which any given system of expression is designed to actualize. It is the beingness of humanity and of Earth that we now have an opportunity to touch as our society rushes toward degeneration and regeneration; in the presence of collapse, we have an opportunity to see again the essential source from which all human culture originates, the wellsprings of what we are and what we are becoming, the center of knowing from which behavior can spring, truly and creatively transformed.

Science is a channel through which energies shattering the crystallizations of past civilizations are pouring. Yet science is more than that. It is a way of knowing. Ultimately, to know something is to be that thing, to merge with it. Knowing is the progressive unfoldment and actualization of being leading finally to self-knowledge that reveals the one being. Knowing and knowledge, however, need not be the same thing; the former is subjective, born of being and unity. The latter is usually objective, born of a distance between the knower and the known which creates a field of interaction which we call knowledge. Knowledge can be a bridge toward knowing, a means of reducing the apparent separation between aspects of the one. On the other hand, knowledge can be used as a tool, a means of manipulation which maintains and even increases that separation. "Knowledge" can lead away from "knowing."

The evolutionary value of science in the unfoldment of human consciousness is not measured by the technological abilities which it gives us nor even in its accumulation of insights about the universe. Rather, it lies in the essential nature of science as an affirmation of the power to know and thus to be. It is an expression of the universal imperative toward unity: I need not be separated from my world through ignorance. I need not dwell in darkness and superstition. I don't have to simply take things on faith. I can understand.

It will be readily recognized that such a definition of science is far more inclusive than the image usually held by people, for all actions of perception, outreach, assimilation, and apperception can be scientific if they are used to see what is and to increase knowing. On the other hand, science is generally seen not as the art of knowing but as a specific way of acquiring knowledge through objective analysis and research, conducted according to certain standards of detachment, separation, impersonality, and sterility.

Such a view is born not from the nature of science but from the nature of people using science. The mechanistic, atomistic, reductive, impersonal paradigm of technology and science is, in fact, a reflection of a certain kind of human consciousness which has characterized many areas of human activity throughout the past in both East and West.

This is the methodological consciousness of the tool user. Such a consciousness was present in the West long before the industrialization of products, services, knowledge, and people gave it such prominence. The main Christian tradition provides particularly fertile ground for such a consciousness (even while the Christian message is basically one of unity through love) in ways too numerous to elaborate here. As an example, though one could see the roots of the technological attitude toward nature (and toward people, too, for that matter!) as being a resource to be manipulated and used as a collection of objects rather than as a community of interrelated subjects—an attitude which has permitted the excesses which have led to pollution, the rape of the environment, and the disruption of biosystems around the world—planted securely in a concept of the fall of man and of nature and the consequent deliverance of the world and all its kingdoms into the devil's hands. This concept turns the world into a fallen state which it is man's duty to escape from . . . using methodologies of salvation. Such an attitude works against caring for that world and all its members and encourages the perception of them as objects for manipulation.

The methodological consciousness and the technologies that have grown up from it are not necessarily wrong. They are an expression of a divine idea themselves.

The challenge comes when this consciousness stems from a deeper world view or paradigm, that of essential separation from all else, including separation from the source of being. This consciousness of separation is prevalent in East and West and is part of the general experience of humanity. It is mistaken to associate science and technology with the West; the Eastern cultures are every bit as bound within a technological imperative and consciousness. The difference is that there it is turned inward and is expressed subjectively in psychotechnologies, means of overcoming a separation between an individual and reality, a separation which may, in fact not exist anyway.

Whether we call the method science, yoga, technology, or certain kinds of meditation, humanity is dealing with an effort to come to grips with reality, to experience knowing and being, through the use of manipulative techniques. The result is often, as was suggested above, the acquisition of knowledge but the loss of knowing and true transformation.

The correction of this condition is not the rejection of methodologies and techniques but the understanding of the formless yet form-producing essence behind them. Antiscience and a plunge into Dionysian rites of emotional fantasizing over a new age are not going to bring that age into being; emotions are even more form bound than the mind. The need is for an understanding of the nature of science as a global, holistic art of knowing, as well as being a particular approach to knowledge, and for an understanding of how to use that art, how to use knowledge, to reveal and not to obscure.

In this regard, I have three suggestions as to the relationship of science to current planetary transformation and the birth of a new age. First, we must learn to use science as myth and as a means of holistically plugging ourselves back into the formless essence of life into a particular form of knowledge. In this respect, we need to remember that science itself is only one way of perceiving the universe and not always the most accurate. We need to discover the poetic uses of science.

Science can give us new images, new pictures and concepts, new analogies with which to see more clearly other aspects of the one life; it can aid us in our communication and communion with that life. Science becomes the spinner of parables in the marketplace of life; stories which have an outer meaning on one level and multiple meanings on other levels can lead us into profound relationship with the wholeness of creation.

Second, we must learn to use the scientific method more

skillfully. It is essentially a method of validating and clarify-
ing knowledge through experience and through a clear use of
the abilities of the mind. In our time, the barriers of tradition
and routine are breaking down; the collective unconscious
pours in upon us through the gaps.

We are being confronted with mythologies taking flesh,
with avatars, with prophecies of destruction, with flying sau-
cers, with innumerable manifestations of emotion and intuition projected outward into objective consciousness. People
are being swept away by these phenomena.

The scientific method is not one of rejection and skepticism
(that is part of its popular paradigmatic image). Rather it is
a means of holding oneself in a clear light of thought with its
reality emotionally, physically, mentally, intuitively and spirit-
ually. Without the skill of thought and knowing which it can
give, we can be swamped by psychic overflow and overload,
and lose the path of transformation.

If knowing is best done by one who is an integrated
knower, and the scientist is ideally one who is an integrated
being able to face the illusions of the astral and dispel them,
or the thoughtforms of the mind and go beyond them into the
essence of being, then we must learn to be scientists or balanced, disciplined knowers.

Finally, we are witnessing the development of new sciences
and new discoveries. These must be freed from past images of
science and technology, which see people and things as objects to be manipulated. There is already a tendency to turn
toward psychic technologies not as paths to knowing but as
techniques for success, of control, for aggrandizement of self
and so forth.

There is also a tendency to be overly grateful for technological advances which can "prove" data which the race has
already known intuitively. That such intuitive knowing can be
integrated with and allowed to illumine technological knowledge is a good thing, but it is technology that should be grateful for the gifts of the spirit, not vice versa.

To transform the transformers, then, we must know our
source, which is a wholeness and insure that our methods and
technologies reflect that reality and not a reality born of their
own fragmented jurisdiction. Science *is* a transformer, a key

to humanity's future, a portal to the new age, but it possesses this power not because of what its disciplines can enable us to do but because of what it is, an expression of the knowing, self-discovering, self-revealing beingness of humanity.

41.

The Skeptics

SAUL-PAUL SIRAG

"If you're the kind of person who believes that such things are even possible, then I have nothing more to say to you." It was Leon Jaroff, a senior editor at *Time,* speaking to me on the phone in response to an inquiry about Uri Geller, the Israeli psychic. I half expected such a response because I had called Jaroff to find out what was behind his venomous attack on Geller and the physicists at the Stanford Research Institute who had studied Geller for six weeks.

Before I had a chance to commit myself one way or the other on the psychic question, Jaroff launched into his lecture: "Why, if Geller can do those things just by knitting his brows, it destroys everything I hold dear!"

Why this passion? What are these things held dear? Why is the skeptic so sure that the parapsychologist is deluded? It may be that the key to a deep understanding of the paranormal is to pay close attention to the criticisms of those who think that such things are impossible.

The scientific distaste for the claims of the psychic goes back to the Enlightenment era of the 18th century, when experimental science was rapidly emerging from the prejudices and superstitions of the medieval church. The paragon of skeptics in the 18th century was the British philosopher, David Hume. His famous formula on miracles has become part of the credo of the modern skeptic: "No testimony is sufficient to establish a miracle, unless the testimony be of such a kind that its falsehood would be more miraculous than

"The Skeptics" by Saul-Paul Sirag originally appeared in *Psychic,* October 1975. Copyright © 1975 by *Psychic* magazine, 680 Beach Street, San Francisco CA 94109 and reprinted by permission.

the fact which it endeavors to establish." It is one thing to mouth such a sensible dictum, but another to apply it, and there's the rub.

Thomas Jefferson, one of the great minds of the age of Enlightenment, was surely thinking of Hume's formula when he said, in 1807: "I could more easily believe that two Yankee professors would lie than that stones would fall down from heaven." He was castigating a report by two Harvard professors that they had witnessed meteorites. Most men of science in Jefferson's day were loath to believe in stones from the sky because such things seemed too much like medieval superstition so recently eschewed. Isaac Newton had made the heavens into a clockwork where sporadic falls of fiery rock would seem out of place. But really there was nothing in science then that absolutely forbad such falls of rock. One does well to examine the assumptions which paint a thing more or less miraculous.

A large part of the prejudice among scientists against extrasensory perception, psychokinesis, and the like is because of a fear that widespread belief in such things will lead back to an age of irrationalism and superstition. As D. H. Rawcliffe puts it in his book, *Illusions and Delusions of the Supernatural and the Occult:* "The commonsense view of such theories . . . is that telepathy and extrasensory perception are nothing more than thinly disguised attempts to rationalize the occult, or else merely pretentious abstractions from primitive witch lore. Historically speaking, such ideas stem from ancient beliefs in magic and sorcery. The historical traditions can be traced in an unbroken line from the earliest supernatural beliefs to the latest metaphysical theories of the modern ESP experimenter. This is a point which modern occultists, such as Rhine and Soal, do their utmost to ignore; for them the 'supernatural' becomes the more euphemistic but equally question-begging 'paranormal'—a device which may deceive many."

Rawcliffe is logical enough to leave himself a small loophole in case his prejudices turn out to be misplaced: "This factor does not of itself invalidate these concepts."

That's the problem. What if the ESP concepts turn out to be valid? Then, perhaps, the magical is forever with us. Whether that is a good thing or not depends on your view of magic. Charlie Reynolds, an amateur magician hired by *Time* to check Geller out at a private demonstration for *Time*, argued with me about what Geller could do. He complained that if Geller could do what he says he can do—"why then all hell would break loose!" It was more than antagonism between two forms of magic that was being expressed. It was fear!

Many who believe in psi phenomena think that if psi becomes widely practiced all *heaven* will break out. One might well question which view is more realistic. Surely such a question has not been adequately addressed. Perhaps only in science fiction are the problems of the use of psi taken seriously. Willis Harman and his research group at Stanford Research Institute have recently put out a detailed report* on the expected effect of psi on our future technology, philosophy, social structures and such; but it is only a beginning of what needs to be done. Meanwhile, out of fear that his skepticism may be misplaced, the skeptic will contrive to keep the lid on.

The serious skeptic must, however, turn to the experiments of the parapsychologists and find fault with them. Most critics think they detect a complex mixture of incompetence, fraud, and self-delusion in the experiments of parapsychology. Because parapsychology presents a challenge to traditional science, there is a kind of guilty-until-proven-innocent presumption made by the skeptic.

Also, of course, the skeptic will gleefully point out that there has been a long history of fraud and self-delusion perpetrated by spirit mediums; and the story of Houdini, the escape artist, unmasking numerous mediums is an oft-told tale.

What about this charge of fraud? The first thing to note is that it was psychical researchers, some of whom were also magicians (the conjuring type, that is), who first undertook to expose fraudulent mediums. This was many years before Houdini got into the act. Hereward Carrington, for instance, wrote an exposé of mediumship (published in 1907) titled, *The Physical Phenomena of Spiritualism, Fraudulent and Genuine*. It is significant that the fraudulent occupies more than three quarters of the book. However it is also significant

* *Changing Images of Man*, Policy Research Report #4. *Editors*.

that Carrington believed that he had seen things that could not be accounted for by ordinary physical means. For Carrington was a skilled amateur magician, who in 1924 was a member of *Science America*'s committee for the investigation of spiritualist phenomena.

It is perhaps natural that it should be magicians who in the past and at present most loudly cry "Fraud!" at the mention of parapsychology. Magicians know how easy it is to fool the unwary (and even the wary) eye. They untiringly claim to duplicate feats of psychics such as Ted Serios' thoughtography and Uri Geller's key bending (and psychic photography).

It should be clear, of course, that the conditions under which a feat is duplicated should have as much bearing on our beliefs in the magicians' claims as the conditions under which the psychic's feats were performed have bearing on our beliefs in his claims.

Many people seem to believe that Ted Serios was definitively exposed by Charlie Reynolds and Davis Eisendrath, both amateur magicians and professional photographers. They presented their account in a *Popular Photography* piece (October 1967) based on one weekend with Serios and the psychiatrist Jule Eisenbud, whose book, *The World of Ted Serios,* had sparked their ire.

However, the November 1967 issue of *Popular Photography* published Eisenbud's response letter:

"I hereby state that if, before any competent jury of scientific investigators, photographers, and conjurors, anyone chosen by them can in any normal way or combination of ways duplicate, under similar conditions, the range of phenomena produced by Ted, I shall (1) abjure all further work with Ted, (2) buy up and publicly burn all available copies of *The World of Ted Serios,* (3) take a full-page ad in *Popular Photography* in order to be represented photographically wearing a dunce cap, and (4) spend my spare time for the rest of my life selling door-to-door subscriptions to this amazing magazine. No time limit is stipulated."

An article in *Fate,* August 1974, reveals that only one magician has to date responded to this delectable invitation. The Amazing James Randi couldn't resist the bait, but on learning of the conditions, unamazingly enough, he backed out.

Perhaps the word of a parapsychologist who is also a respected amateur magician would be enlightening. William Edward Cox, a member of the Society of American Magicians and a researcher at the Institute for Parapsychology (FRNM, Durham, N. C.), in a privately printed paper, *Mentalism and Magicians* (1972), writes: "I can, however, speak for Ted Serios, a man who in recent years has undergone as great scrutiny as has any alleged physical medium. Being myself the first parapsychologist to give his 'psychic photography' any credence (and knowledge of magic was an asset here, you may be sure), I can testify to the slow, careful study that precedes widened acceptance of a claim such as his. Subsequently Dr. Eisenbud sponsored a host of tests with him, incurred the wrath of a number of magicians, whose arguments I read avidly, but has stood his ground—as have still other parapsychologists since (not withstanding this exbellhop's serious drinking problem, and his apparent disinterest in his ability)."

Magicians have been ready to point out that the researcher's wish to believe in psychic events blinds the mind to fraud perpetrated by psychics. It must be equally the case that the wish to *disbelieve* in psychic events makes many people all too ready to accept the claim that a magician has duplicated a psychic's feats. In fact, so emotionally involved are many magicians in this debunking game, that one has to be wary for fraud on the part of the would-be debunker.

A case in point may be *Popular Photography*'s hatchet job on Uri Geller's psychic photography. This is a piece by Yale Joel accompanied by a piece by Charles Reynolds in the June 1974 issue. Joel claims that he and his son Seth watched Geller "click off 12 or so exposures" on Joel's Pentax with a wide angle Tokamur lens with its lens cap taped on. They left the camera with Geller while they went off to an adjoining room to participate in a telepathy experiment with Geller. The camera was out of their sight for "three to five minutes." Uri clicked off the rest of the roll of film in the taped Pentax in their presence.

Aside from the careless investigative procedure of leaving

the camera with Geller in the first place, there is a serious flaw in their story. The problem is that the picture of Geller holding up the lens cap (which they claim proves Geller a flagrant fraud) occurs at about position 7 on an otherwise blank roll of film—as revealed in a picture of the strip accompanying the story. Joel does not try to explain the discrepancy. He could have said that Geller had rolled the film back but this would have made his story more difficult to believe. Perhaps he did not realize that the strip with its telltale numbers would be printed along with the story.

There are other suspicious things about the piece among which is the fact that the "Geller" in the picture cannot be positively identified as Uri Geller because his face is pushed so far into the upper right-hand corner that he is unrecognizable. And remember, this is a picture Joel alleges was taken by Geller holding up a lens cap and thinking he is photographing himself with an ordinary lens rather than fish-eye lens (which takes in a 180° view). On Joel's supposition Geller should be closer to the center—not pushed up into a corner.

Then of course, Geller has to be given a motive for holding up the lens cap in the first place. It is, after all, rather an odd thing to do. Joel says he supposes that Geller wanted to get a picture of himself mysteriously emerging from a dark region of the picture. Trouble is that none of the other pictures that Geller has supposedly taken through the lens cap have shown this mysterious dark region. However, the Serios pictures which were published in *Popular Photography* in 1967 do show Serios' face and other objects emerging from dark shadowy regions. Now it all fits into a pattern. And I cannot help but suspect that Joel may be the hoaxer here. *Popular Photography* in their September issue published a letter from Alan Vaughan (articles editor of *Psychic*) seriously raising this possibility. To date he has had no response from Yale Joel.

It is a pity that the supposedly definitive proof of fraud by Geller is in fact such a "Keystone cops" affair. Fraud, wherever it exists in parapsychological investigations, cannot be tolerated. Parapsychology needs the fraud squads of nonparapsychologists poking their noses into the psi-pie in the cause of honest ingredients. Yet fraud is a tricky thing. If Geller were really caught red-handed tomorrow, that in itself would not erase the many things he has done that could not have been fraudulent.

True enough, Andrew Weil, M.D., can have his key bent by Geller and then go and have it bent by Randi—as reported in *Psychology Today* (June 1974, July 1974). Weil thus changed from a believer to an agnostic regarding Geller. Weil should have given Geller a more definitive test in the first place, then he could have faced Randi with a true "curve ball." Any magician knows that if you practice at some trick, you can fool most people with it. So why ask Geller to do something he has done over and over before? Geller doesn't necessarily do what you ask him to do, but he can handle curve balls nicely—he likes the challenge.

Among other things, I took him a slinky (a spring-steel coil that kids walk down steps) with the idea that he should try to change its handedness (easy if you can rotate it through another dimension—see Martin Gardner's *The Ambidextrous Universe*). Of course, Geller did no such thing. He was like a boy with a new toy. He played it like an accordian for a few seconds then yoyoed it up and down four or five times whereupon the bottom half of the spring steel coil dropped off onto the floor—all this right before my (and a friend's) eyes. Did Geller have a chance to get at this ahead of time? No, that's the point of bringing a "curve ball" device. He doesn't know what you've brought; can't prepare duplicates, or otherwise tamper with the "props" as Johnny Carson calls them.

I showed Charlie Reynolds another of the curve balls I had thrown Geller—a set of ceramic magnets. Geller had made a crack through one of them and then made half of the broken magnet disappear. Reynolds broke one of the other magnets by hand. It took two distinct movements and made a less jagged break; this had also been my experience. Reynolds' response was that he'd like me to arrange a meeting with Geller. Unfortunately, Reynolds had already accused Geller of fraud at the *Time* demonstration upon which *Time* partly based its scathing March 12, 1973 story. So Geller wanted nothing to do with Reynolds.

The Amazing Randi I never did get to see. . . . But I spoke with him over the phone. Whereas Reynolds had been rational about the whole Geller thing, Randi sounded very emotional. Reynolds and Randi had both seen Geller at the *Time* demonstration (undercover, as reporters). But Randi makes his living as a magician and seemed threatened by Geller's claim to do "real magic." When I told him of the things I had seen Geller do at quite close range, he said: "What about the inverse square law?" So I pointed out to him that not all the forces we know about obey an inverse square law; so why should an interaction we know scarcely anything about be held to an inverse square law?

I asked Randi about the key that Geller had bent at the *Time* demonstration. Reynolds had claimed that Randi and he saw Geller make suspicious movements with the key. I asked Randi why the *Time* story had omitted all mention of the key—was it because he and Reynolds hadn't been able to duplicate the bending? (*Time* had claimed that Randi had duplicated all of Geller's feats.) Randi didn't know. Besides he said Reynolds was going around bending keys for people in bars. I said that the light in the bars must be quite dim, because Reynolds hadn't bent any keys for me. Randi couldn't accept this needling. "O.K. Charlie can't bend keys! I can't bend keys! Only Uri can bend keys!" He sounded as if he was about to burst into tears, and he abruptly hung up.

That was in May of 1973. In 1974, Andrew Weil tells us that Randi bent his key by pushing it against a chair leg when he wasn't looking. More recently, Randi has been posing as a psychic and fooling various people. According to Martin Gardner, Randi has even fooled John Hasted and David Bohm at Birkbeck College and John Taylor at Kings College, both in London. *Psychic News* also in London was apparently taken in as reported in the July 26 issue, which featured an article and picture of "James Zwinge," who looks remarkably like Randi and who claims the powers of bending keys and utensils, etc., through mind over matter. (*Psychic* received a report earlier that Randi was using the name James Zwinge as an alias.) Not everybody is taken in by Randi, however. Charles Honorton of the Maimonides Dream Laboratory told me that Randi succeeded only in scratching his desk top trying to bend a key for him.

Weil does make the interesting point that we tend to see

what we expect to see. He maintains that this also goes for those who claim to see fraud, as well as those who claim to see real magic. "Selective perception of evidence is the basic method by which we construct our basic models of reality." And that reminds me of a thing that Eusapio Palladino said after she had been caught in the act of producing flagrantly fraudulent physical phenomena in a seance. "You don't understand," she said, "when I'm in trance, I'm not in control. If you don't control me and you expect to see fraud, I'll cheat. You have to control me."

Many parapsychologists who have experience working with psychics claim that most people will cheat given half a chance, if there's something in it for them. Accordingly, these researchers believe that experiments have to be designed in such a way that the possibility of cheating can be ruled out. This was the protocol that Stanford Research Institute used with Geller. If they could imagine a way—no matter how bizarre—an effect could have happened by trickery, they ruled it out as evidence. One piece of evidence that passes this test is a balance experiment, in which Geller tried to effect a mass change in a one-gram weight resting on an electronic balance. What is specially convincing about the very small effect that Geller got (in the presence of witnesses, and on camera) is that the paper tracing of the scale movement shows a very peculiar spike that entails a movement above the base line and a rapid return to the base line without falling below the base line. There is no known way to produce such a spike pattern. Balances just don't behave that way. But this one did, and just when Geller was interacting with it. (The researchers attempted to reproduce this spike pattern by various means but were unable to do so.)

There is, a skeptic might say, a way to produce such a spike pattern—that is to *draw* it on a piece of strip chart and claim that this is the record of the weight change event. But this would be fraud on the part of the researchers, and several people would have to collaborate on it. That doesn't seem likely.

However researchers sometimes do cheat. Cancer workers at Sloan Kettering in New York are still trying to recover from the shock of William Summerlin's having fraudulently painted black patches on mice to make them appear to have successful skin grafts. And the Institute of Parapsychology in North Carolina has had to contend with the fraudulent tinkering of Walter Levy. It is noteworthy that in both of these cases, it was fellow researchers who exposed the fraud—and the fraudulent researchers promptly resigned and all their research is in process of attempted duplication.

Having battled the dragons of fear and fraud, the parapsychologist is faced with the skeptic who says: "Oh, there may not be conscious fraud involved, but I'm afraid these results have just got to be artifact—you're just *fooling* yourself!"

As H. L. Mencken put it in 1937: "In plain language, Professor Rhine segregates all those persons who in guessing the cards, enjoy noteworthy runs of luck, and then adduces those noteworthy runs of luck as proof that they must possess mysterious powers."

Martin Gardner repeats the charge in his book, *Fads and Fallacies* (1952, 1957), but he adds: "This alleged 'selection' is not a deliberate process, but something which operates subtly and unconsciously." However, there are so many experiments on record that the selection process must be widespread. And Gardner presses just this point: ". . . let us imagine that one hundred professors of psychology throughout the country read of Rhine's work and decide to test a subject. The fifty who fail to find ESP in their first preliminary test are likely to be discouraged and quit, but the other fifty will be encouraged to continue. Of this fifty, more will stop work after the second test, while some will continue because they obtained good results. Eventually, one experimenter remains whose subject has made high scores for six or seven successive sessions. Neither experimenter nor subject is aware of the other ninety-nine projects, and so both have a strong delusion that ESP is operating. The odds are, in fact, much against the run. But in the total (and unknown) context, the run is quite probable. (The odds against winning the Irish sweepstakes are even higher. But someone does win it.) So the experimenter writes an enthusiastic paper, sends it to Rhine who publishes it in his magazine, and the readers are greatly impressed."

A recent statement of this argument was made by Nicholas Wade in *Science* of 13 July, 1973. "Although the parapsychologists have now amassed an impressive volume of apparently careful experimental literature . . . critics charge that the published work represents an artifact, in as far as it tends to be only the successful experiments that get reported, while the presumably more numerous null results go unremarked."

Happily for the parapsychologist, this "statistical artifact" argument will not hold up under close scrutiny. As Charles Tart, a psychologist at the University of California at Davis, put it in a letter to *Science:* "Aside from the fact that this is true for all branches of science, dismissing ESP results on the ground of selective publication is not statistically valid, as well as being empirically unsupported. If we have only random variation in our experiments (no ESP), then we have to carry out about 20 experiments to get one (presumably publishable) which is significant at the 0.05 level, 1000 to get one significant at the 0.0001 level, and so forth. There are hundreds of published, successful parapsychological experiments with the main analyses significant at the 0.05 level, and of these many have significance levels exceeding 10^{-6} (a million to one against chance). The selective publication hypothesis then predicts that there are trillions of unsuccessful, unpublished ESP experiments, an obviously ridiculous figure, unless one credits the handful of parapsychologists in the last half century with some phenomenal work abilities, paranormal in themselves."

Since Tart is himself a parapsychologist, it may be useful to quote the opinion of an expert in probability theory who is not a parapsychologist. Warren Weaver in his book *Lady Luck* (1963) says: "The Rhine ESP results could be explained on the grounds of selection or falsification of data. Having complete confidence in the scientific competence and personal integrity of Professor Rhine, I find this explanation unacceptable to me. In any very long probability experiment there will occur highly remarkable runs of luck—as in the twenty-eight recorded repetitions of one color at Monte Carlo, or the long runs of 'passes' at craps. But I know of no analysis of Rhine's data, based on such considerations, that makes it reasonable to believe that their success can be explained in this way." Is Weaver a believer in ESP then? No, he remains a very honest skeptic: "As I have said elsewhere, I find this a subject that is so intellectually uncomfortable as to be almost painful. I end by concluding that I cannot explain away Professor Rhine's evidence, and that I also cannot accept his interpretation."

Ah, *interpretation*. Perhaps this is the crux of the matter. The experiments clearly say that something unusual is happening. But what?

The parapsychologist is likely to say that perceptions are being formed in the mind of the subject without the use of the senses and without the usual time relations between events. Of this interpretation Warren Weaver, perhaps typical of most scientists, complains: "On the one hand, we are asked to accept an interpretation that destroys the most fundamental ideas and principles on which modern science has been based: we are asked to give up the irreversibility of time, to accept an effect that shows no decay with distance and hence involves 'communication' without energy being involved; asked to believe in an 'effect' that depends on no known quantities and for which no explanation has been offered, to credit phenomena which are subject to decline or disappearance for unexplained and unexplainable reasons. On the other hand, we are asked not to believe that a highly improbable chance result has occurred. All I can say is, I find this a very tough pair of alternatives."

Two things can be said about this. One is that fundamental ideas in science have been given up before. The other is that physics today is in the process of deciding what fundamental principle to give up anyway. Maybe psi experiments will help decide!

Arthur Koestler in the book *The Challenge of Chance* suggests that beside the smoothing principle that in the long run chance variations cancel each other out, there may be in operation a clustering principle, the exact nature of which he leaves as an exercise to the reader, but the general statement of which is: "Nature abhors randomness." If this reminds you of the medieval statement: "Nature abhors a vacuum," you are on the right track. But this is not necessarily the way out of the woods. If we are to seriously take up *The Challenge of Chance* (and it is a wonderful book, read it) we are going to have to make up theories that can be tested, otherwise we will be fooling ourselves.

Nothing could be better for parapsychology than to pay attention to archskeptic Richard Feynman's prescription. In his commencement address to Caltech in June of 1974, this Nobel prize winning physicist gave a funny rambling speech about the "cargo cult sciences"—methods that mimic the scientific method but seem to be missing something essential —because the "cargo" doesn't come. According to Feynman, parapsychology, along with most of psychology and a host of other things, is essentially a cargo cult.

As I read Feynman's "cargo cult science" (published in *Engineering and Science,* June 1974) I found myself agreeing with the heart of the matter. The essential point in science is not a complicated mathematical formalism or a ritualized experimentation. Rather the heart of science is a kind of shrewd honesty that springs from *really wanting to know what the hell is going on!*

> As Feynman puts it: ". . . if you're doing an experiment, you should report everything that you think might make it invalid—not only what you think is right about it: other causes that could possibly explain your results; and things you thought of that you've eliminated by some other experiment, and how they worked—to make sure the other fellow can tell they have been eliminated.
> "Details that could throw doubt on your interpretation must be given, if you know them. You must do the best you can—if you know anything at all wrong, or possibly wrong—to explain it. If you make a theory, for example, and advertise it, or put it out, then you must also put down all the facts that disagree with it, as well as those that agree with it. There is also a more subtle problem. When you have put a lot of ideas together to make an elaborate theory, you want to make sure, when explaining what it fits, that those things it fits are not just the things that gave you the idea for the theory; but that the finished theory makes something else come out right, in addition."

It may turn out that psychic phenomena are too rare to be understood scientifically. I do not think so. More likely they are too complicated and too far ahead of science's current prevailing concept of the universe. Many people have come to this conclusion and say that the thing to do is just swing with it, experience the strange things in life as they come, and don't try too hard to figure out what is really happening. That seems to be O.K. for lots of people. But my real sympathies lie with those who struggle to understand. There will always be some who have taken it upon themselves to try to figure things out. It is to them I say: "Watch out for the dragons of fear, fraud, and fooling yourself. The skeptic may well be your best friend. And the greatest dragon, yourself."

VII   APPENDIXES

APPENDIX I
THE X ENERGY:
A UNIVERSAL PHENOMENON

In recent years many people interested in the physics of paranormal phenomena have seen the need to investigate the prescientific and esoteric/occult traditions that claim to recognize and, in some cases, control an energy underlying paranormal phenomena. The following compilation has been made in the interests of supporting and advancing such investigations. Special thanks for help with it goes to Laurence M. Beynam and to Christopher Bird.

Because of the large number of ancient traditions and contemporary investigators touching on one of the concepts central to this book—a fifth force in nature—we have attempted to be all-inclusive rather than selective. Thus it will be apparent that terms in this listing are not fully synonymous in all cases. There are varying measures of overlap or convergence among some of them. Prana, for example, is said by yogic tradition to have five forms. Likewise, Rudolf Steiner's presentation of etheric formative forces lists four. One of them—the chemical ether—seems to equate with Wilhelm Reich's orgone energy. It is also apparent that there are major gaps in our knowledge to be filled. In general, however, the terms under "X energy" point toward the idea of a new principle in nature not yet recognized by science.

Discoverer	Name of X Energy	Approx. Date	Reference
	EARLY SOURCES (Before 1500 B.C.)		
Hindu Yogis	Prana	ca. 3000 B.C.	M. Eliade, *Yoga, Immortality, and Freedom*
Chinese	Ch'i (Ki in Japanese)	ca. 3000 B.C.	F. Mann, *Acupuncture*
Hebrews	Ruach	ca. 1000 B.C.	F. Gaynor, *Dictionary of Mysticism*

Hermes Tris-megistus (mythical)	Telesma	ca. 350 B.C. (based on earlier tradition)	F. Yates, *Giordano Bruno and the Hermetic Tradition*
Plato	Nous	ca. 350 B.C.(?)	
Cabalists	Yesod	ca. 350 B.C.	*The Cabala*
Hippocrates	Vis Medicatrix Naturae	ca. 350 B.C.	*Encyclopaedia Britannica*
Aristotle	Formative Cause	ca. 350 B.C.	A. Hardy, R. Harvie, and A. Koestler, *The Challenge of Chance*
Erasistratus	Pneuma	ca. 300 B.C.	*Encyclopaedia Britannica*
Christians	Holy Spirit	ca. 100 A.D.	*Holy Bible*
Germans	Wodan	ca. 100 A.D.	S. King, *Mana Physics*
Galen (Claudius Galenus)	Facultas Formatrix	ca. 170 A.D.	A. Hardy, R. Harvie, and A. Koestler, *The Challenge of Chance*
Sufis	Baraka	ca. 600 A.D.	I. Shah, *The Sufis*
Polynesian and Hawaiian Kahunas	Mana	ca. 600 A.D.	M. F. Long, *The Secret Science Behind Miracles*
Avicenna (IBN Sina)	Anima Mundi	ca. 1150 A.D.	C. G. Jung, *Alchemical Studies*
TRIBAL SOURCES			
Peruvians	Huaca	(Date unrecorded by oral tradition)	S. V. Örnek, *Religion, Magic, Art, and Mythology in the Primitives*
Iroquois Indians	Orenda, Oki	"	"
Algonquin Indians	Manitu	"	"
Sioux Indians	Wakonda, Wakan	"	"
Eskimos	Sila	"	"
Ituri Pygmies	Megbe	"	"
Congolese	Elima	"	"
Kalahari Bushmen	Rlun	"	"
Sudanese	Mungo	"	?
Gold Coast Africans	Wong	"	C. G. Jung, *On the Nature of the Psyche*
Central African Yaos	Mulungu	"	"
Masai (Africa)	Ngai	"	"
Ekoi (Africa)	Njom	"	"
Elgonyi (Africa)	Ayik	"	"

Discoverer	Name of X Energy	Approx. Date	Reference
Australian Aborigines	Arunquiltha, Churinga	"	"
Australian Tribes of the Torres Strait	Zogo	"	"
Malaya	Badi	"	"
Gelaria (New Guinea)	Labuni	"	"
Ponape (Pacific)	Ani, Han	"	"
Palau (Pacific)	Kasinge, Kalit	"	"
Bataks (Pacific)	Tondi	"	"
Maoris (New Zealand)	Atua	"	"
Malagasy (Philippines)	Andriamanitra	"	"
Kusaie (Pacific)	Anut	"	"
Tobi (Pacific)	Yaris	"	"

LATER SOURCES (After 1500)

Paracelsus	Mumia or Munia	ca. 1530	W. E. Mann, *Orgone, Reich, and Eros*
Johannes Kepler	Facultas Formatrix	ca. 1620	A. Hardy, R. Harvie, and A. Koestler, *The Challenge of Chance*
Jan Baptista van Helmont	Magnale Magnum	ca. 1620	S. Ostrander and L. Schroeder, *Psychic Discoveries Behind the Iron Curtain*
Robert Fludd	Spiritus	ca. 1650	Foreword by L. Shepard to K. von Reichenbach, *The Odic Force*
Franz Anton Mesmer	Animal Magnetism, Magnetic Fluid	1775	J. Eden, *Animal Magnetism and the Life Energy*
Luigi Galvani	Life Force	1790	W. E. Mann, *Orgone, Reich, and Eros*
Johann Wolfgang von Goethe	Gestaltung	1800	A. Koestler, *The Heel of Achilles*
Karl von Reichenbach	Od, Odyllic, Odic Force	1845	K. von Reichenbach, *Psycho-Physical Researches*

Charles Richet	Ectoplasm	1850	H. D. Lewis, *The Foundations of Metaphysics in Science*
Henry Bulwer-Lytton	Vril	1872	H. Bulwer-Lytton, *Vril: Power of the Coming Race*
John Worrell Keely	Motor Force	ca. 1880	S. Ostrander and L. Schroeder, *Psychic Discoveries Behind the Iron Curtain*
E. Barety	Neuric Energy, Neuricidad	1887	E. Barety, *Le Magnetisme Animal*
H. P. Blavatsky	Astral Light	1888	H. P. Blavatsky, *The Secret Doctrine*
Georg Groddeck	It	1890	G. Groddeck, *The Book of the It*
Sigmund Freud	Libido	1895	S. Freud, *Collected Works*
Rudolf Steiner	Etheric Formative Forces	1900	G. Wachsmuth, *The Etheric Formative Forces in the Cosmos, Earth and Man*
Prosper Blondlot	N Rays	1903	W. E. Mann, *Orgone, Reich, and Eros*
A. Wendler	Magnetoism	ca. 1920	Z. Rèjdák, J. Paraphysics 5, 1 (1971)
William McDougall	Hormic Energy	1920	W. E. Mann, *Orgone, Reich, and Eros*
Henri Bergson	Elàn Vital	1920	"
Hans Driesch	Entelechy	1920	"
Paul Kammerer	Formative Energy	1920	"
Charles Littlefield	Vital Magnetism	1920	"
Georges Lakhovsky	Universion	1920	G. Lakhovsky, *The Secret of Life*
Radiesthesists	Etheric Force	ca. 1930	E. Russell, *Report on Radionics*
Alexander Gurwitsch	Mitogenetic Radiation	1937	A. Gurwitsch, *Mitogenetic Radiation*
Wilhelm Reich	Orgone	1940	W. Reich, *The Cancer Biopathy*
Thomas Galen Hieronymus	Eloptic Energy	1940	P. Tompkins and C. Bird, *The Secret Life of Plants*
V. S. Grischenko	Bioplasma	1944	V. M. Inyushin, *Bioplasma and its Radiation*
Erwin Schroedinger	Negative Entropy	1945	E. Schroedinger, *What Is Life?*

Discoverer	Name of X Energy	Approx. Date	Reference
J. B. Rhine, Robert Thouless, B. Weisner	Psi Faculty	1947	J. B. Rhine, *The Reach of the Mind*
L. E. Eeman	X Force	1947	L. E. Eeman, *Cooperative Healing*
Gustav Stromberg	The Soul of the Universe	1948	G. Stromberg, *The Soul of the Universe*
Oscar Brunler	Dielectric Biocosmic Energy	1950	O. Brunler, *Rays and Radiation Phenomena*
Carl Gustav Jung	Synchronicity	1951	C. G. Jung, *Synchronicity*
Robert Pavlita	Psychotronic Energy	1955	D. Hammond, *The Search for Psychic Power*
John W. Campbell	Psionics	1956	J. W. Campbell, *Amazing Science Fiction* (Feb. 1956)
Henry Margenau	Quasielectrostatic Field	1959	W. E. Mann, *Orgone, Reich, and Eros*
Abraham Maslow (after Benedict)	Synergy	1960	A. Maslow, *The Farther Reaches of Human Nature*
Andrija Puharich	(1) Psi Plasma	1962	A. Puharich, *Beyond Telepathy*
	(2) Inergy	1973	A. Puharich, *Uri*
Cleve Backster	Primary Perception	1966	J. White, *Frontiers of Conciousness*
George De la Warr	(1) Biomagnetism	1967	G. De la Warr, *Biomagnetism*
	(2) Prephysical Energy		
Nikolai Kozyrev	Time	1967	N. Kozyrev, *Possibility of Experimental Study of the Properties of Time*
Arthur Koestler	Integrative Tendency	1967	A. Koestler, *The Ghost in the Machine*
Ludwig von Bertalanffy (after Woltereck)	Anamorphosis	1967	A. Koestler, *The Heel of Achilles*
L. L. Whyte	Unitary Principle in Nature	1969	L. L. Whyte, *The Unitary Principle in Nature*

Buckminster Fuller	Synergy	1970	B. Fuller, *Operating Manual for Spaceship Earth*
Ambrose Worrall	Paraelectricity	1970	O. Worrall, *Explore Your Psychic World*
Colin Wilson	X Factor	1971	C. Wilson, *The Occult*
Charles Musès	Noetic Energy	1972	C. Musès and A. Young, *Consciousness and Reality*
William T. Tiller	Magnetoelectricity	1973	W. Tiller (see Chap. 23 of this book)

OPERATION "KOOLER": CONQUEST OF A SOUTHERN CALIFORNIA HEAT WAVE*

TREVOR J. CONSTABLE

Orgonomic weather control has contemporary capabilities other than the engineering of rain, dramatically successful though some rain-making operations have been.[1] One purpose of this article is to help dispel the restrictive synonymity that has developed between orgonomic weather control and rainmaking—as though orgone engineering were exclusively confined to this one function. The reasons for this unfortunate "twin think" need not concern us here. Widening our knowledge and comprehension of what is possible in today's orgonomic weather engineering is of far greater importance. This account of Operation Kooler illustrates the contemporary versatility, efficacy, and value of orgonomic weather engineering—the most potent aspect of the new technology brought to human ken by Wilhelm Reich.

Preliminary Notes on Cloudbusters (CLBs)

The objective evidence that may be adduced as to the existence of the orgone energy includes the visual, thermic, and electroscopic manifestations described by WR in his books, articles, and bullctins.[2] These form the classical basis of or-

"Operation Kooler" by Trevor James Constable originally appeared in the *J. Orgonomy* 6, 1, May 1972 and is reprinted by permission of the author.

* The release of this material by the *Journal of Orgonomy* in no way represents approval by the American College of Orgonomy or the Orgonomic Research Foundation of Trevor Constable's theories or practices in weather engineering. *Editors.*

gonomy. Study, interpretation, and understanding of these fundamentals requires a certain amount of apparatus and training. The validity and meaning of this objective material is evident to any scientist with unblocked perceptions who will repeat the experiments.[3] Untrained persons, by contrast, often easily discern orgonomic phenomena and manifestations, but frequently fail to grasp their significance or revolutionary consequences for official science and its philosophical foundations.

The layman who accurately perceives basic orgonomic phenomena can usually do nothing about his perceptions because "authority" negates them, an authority backed by highly trained legions whose world conception and neurotic comfort are anchored to the laws of thermodynamics and other canons that the discovery of the orgone has invalidated. The honorable, clear-seeing scientist similarly encounters the barrier of authority. In our approach to understanding how Kooler was engineered, we seek to bring together scientist, technician, physician, orgonomist, *and* layman—with or without orgonomic knowledge—in such a way that all may grasp basic facts of orgonomic weather engineering.

Finding such common ground is essentially a clearing operation. We clear out of our minds for the time being all thermodynamic, electrostatic, meteorological and kindred theory bearing upon the weather and the cloudbuster. We make our clearing operation extend to the CLB itself. We set in abeyance all theories as to how and why the CLB works. We are now completely free of the burden of current notions of all kinds. There is neither discrimination against, nor enmity towards, the old knowledge in favor of the new.

We approach the CLB with the fresh eyes of a child—WR fashion. We simply want to observe *what happens*. We want to observe directly and clearly, without any theoretical overlay or bias. What happens is easy to see and just as easy to feel. When you point the CLB tubes in a given direction, a light breeze soon develops from that same direction. Once such a light breeze has developed, the CLB may be shifted in its orientation. Within a short time, the breeze will shift correspondingly and begin coming from the new direction. The breeze springs up more readily when we aim to the west, but will follow the CLB in any direction. As an example of a trained observer exposed to this phenomenon of a CLB-generated breeze, we may cite Dr. Ola Raknes and his experience in observing Dr. Reich use the CLB at Rangeley, Maine, in August of 1953.[4]

> One day Reich was experimenting with the cloudbuster, trying to find out in which direction it would be most profitable to point the apparatus. While he was pointing it in different directions, I happened to notice that the wind, a light breeze, over the nearby Dodge Pond, was changing its direction. Not far from the cloudbuster was a weathervane, and I decided to follow its movements. Whenever Reich changed the direction of the cloudbuster the weathervane would show in a few minutes that the wind had changed correspondingly. I was strongly impressed by this observation.

This effect is most easily and ideally observed under conditions of flat calm or light airs. The CLB operator may then switch the wind about literally at will. The effect is not confined, however, to such ideal conditions. Depending upon the strength of the wind under given circumstances, it may be stopped and reversed by appropriately extended operations downwind of the CLB. What is accomplished by the CLB in a few minutes in a flat calm, and may be observed in its totality in a few minutes, may require several hours in the case of a twenty-five-knot wind stemming from a large, regional pressure system. The final result is nevertheless identical. The wind blows back toward the CLB from the direction in which the tubes are aimed. The effect is strongest when the tubes are aimed toward the west.[5]

This is the basic principle behind wind abatement, and it is a highly practical procedure. Aiming a CLB downwind—provided the CLB is of sufficient capacity—will kill any wind in my experience. This includes Southern California's hot, violent, and infamous "Santa Ana"—a regional phenomenon that brings strong, scorching winds from the interior desert to the coastal areas. A single CLB of sufficient capacity will stop a Santa Ana wind once it has started, or, if applied "prophylactically" when these destructive winds are forecast, will abort them entirely. Such operations have been carried out repeatedly by me in Southern California since 1968. The matter is mentioned here because such an abortion of a Santa Ana wind became membered into Kooler which thus demonstrated not only heat wave abatement, but also wind control.

Nothing is said here about how the orgone energy, as manipulated by a CLB, produces this remarkable phenomenon, since this is not directly observable. We confine ourselves to the crucial question of what we can actually see happen. Point a CLB in a given direction and a wind will eventually develop from that direction. This observable and repeatable element of orgone weather engineering was applied in Kooler to a practical climatic problem involving millions of people, thousands of square miles of terrain, and the economy and well being of a vast metropolis.

Background to Operation Kooler

A research program in orgone energy functions and orgonomic weather control was conducted in Southern California in the summer of 1971, funded in part by the Orgonomic Research Foundation (ORF). Over a period of several months spent investigating the engineering of summer rain, it was found that CLBs of much higher capacity are required to effect results in the Southern California summer, than suffice in eastern areas of the U.S. where Dr. Reich did most of his pioneering work in weather control. Southern California is a climatic region virtually unique in the northern hemisphere, with its dry subtropical climate making it a veritable island on the land.

These conditions, combined with a topography favoring the accumulation of atmospheric pollution—plus millions of automobiles for its daily production—make Southern California a challenging environment for any weather control experiments. Official science has been able to offer little in weather control beyond the massive dumping of silver iodide into the atmosphere in rainmaking and hurricane reduction experiments. As the ORF program drew to a close, the basic keys to summer rain were found through new techniques and gradual increases in CLB capacity. Throughout this work, the ability of a CLB to produce wind from the direction of its aim was repeatedly demonstrated. As the capacity of the units was slowly increased, stronger winds could be evoked over wider areas. This opened new and immediately feasible aspects of orgonomic weather control.

The generation of regional winds in accordance with the will of the CLB operator, to override the effects of any extant pressure system, came to hand as a natural result of this field work. Here indeed was the "red thread" of orgonomic functionalism so often mentioned by WR. These findings and personal dawnings came together just as Southern California encountered a major weather problem—a heat wave. The challenge was direct and immediate, like a gauntlet thrown down before a jouster.

Factual Weather Situation Leading to Kooler

On Sunday, September 12, 1971, a cold front which was previously forecast by the National Weather Service (NWS) to enter Southern California from the northwest, with consequent cooling effects, failed to survive its southeastward journey. The sequence of events is shown in maps A, B, and C.

The low pressure area marked "L" and located between Phoenix and Los Angeles was on Saturday, September 11, 1971, already pushing scorching desert air into the Los Angeles Basin and coastal areas by virtue of its basic counterclockwise circulation. The small arrows above the "L" show the direction of this circulation.

The cold front was expected to bring a modicum of relief by Sunday, as forecast Map B shows, but instead, the western portion of the cold front virtually collapsed. The way was thus opened for more hot air to come pouring into the coastal areas from the interior.

The *Los Angeles Times*, Sunday, September 12, 1971, put the situation in practical terms:

> Eye-irritating smog and some of the hottest temperatures of the year plagued many parts of Southern California Saturday, and it may be even warmer today. The sixth smog alert in as many days was called in Riverside County, and in Orange County, where no official readings were available, residents said smog concentrations were extremely high. . . . The highest temperature in Los Angeles County was 107 in Burbank, the hottest reading for the year for that San Fernando Valley community. A high of 97 at the Los Angeles Civic Center equaled the high for the year, and was 14 degrees above normal.

The situation in adjacent Riverside County was even more serious, as a report by M. Dean Hill in the *Riverside Press-Enterprise* on Sunday, September 12, 1971, indicates:

> The mercury climbed to its highest level in two years in Riverside yesterday, while the city was undergoing its

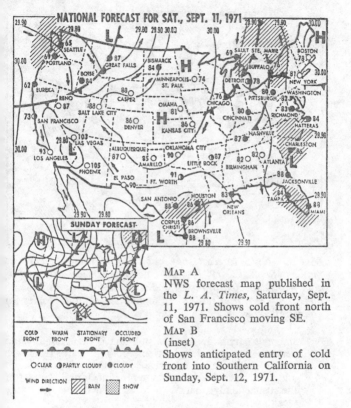

MAP A
NWS forecast map published in the *L. A. Times,* Saturday, Sept. 11, 1971. Shows cold front north of San Francisco moving SE.

MAP B
(inset)
Shows anticipated entry of cold front into Southern California on Sunday, Sept. 12, 1971.

seventh smog alert in eight days, according to the weatherman, who *sees no relief in sight* [emphasis supplied].

The temperature yesterday jumped to 107, the highest reading since the 107 registered on August 22, 1969. . . . The 107 was a jump of six degrees from Friday's reading of 101 and the weatherman says the temperature may get hotter today, possibly reaching 110. . . .

The reason for the unusually hot weather, according to a forecaster for the National Weather Service in Los Angeles, is what he called "a large upper air high centered over the southwestern states." He said there had been little or no movement in the system, which carried with it very warm air. The high, he said, is in a "rather

MAP C   *NWS forecast map published in the* L. A. *Times Sunday, Sept. 12, 1971. Shows collapse of western end of cold front expected to reach Southern California on this same day. This led to decision to launch Operation Kooler to counter heat wave.*

stagnant situation" and the situation is being aggravated because an expected marine cooling trend from the Pacific Ocean failed to arrive in Southern California. In addition, he said, the high system is blocking out most of the usual daily marine breezes, which are generally weak.

The forecaster said *no relief is in sight* [emphasis supplied], because there appears to be no system moving into the area capable of forcing the high out.

This, then, was the practical situation in which to apply *regionally* the basic CLB technique already described. On the morning of Sunday, September 12, 1971, official forecasts anticipated that the Los Angeles Civic Center would top 100 degrees. The circumstances warranted a declaration of war on the heat wave by orgone engineering, since all formal meteorological sources had stated that there was no relief in sight.

The sequence of events and operations making up Operation Kooler are now quoted from the operations log. Date, time groups are employed, in which the first two figures give the date, the last four figures the time in twenty-four hour fshion, e.g., 122200 is 10 p.m. on the 12th. All times are Pacific Daylight Time.

121000   Telephone call to Albert Duvall, M.D., representing the Orgonomic Research Foundation. Practical situation fully discussed as laid out above. Agreement reached on need to intervene with orgone engineering. TJC describes intention to turn entire CLB battery installed near Palm Springs to the west. Objective: Generation of strong onshore breeze from the Pacific, stopping and reversing desert winds and breaking heat wave. Estimated time of placing CLB battery in function: 121700. Estimated time for appearance of first effects: At least 24 hours.†

121600   Depart Orange County for desert base.

121700   Heat in Riverside oppressive, 114 degrees, with heavy DOR concentrations and low humidity. Highway lined with vapor-locked, boiling and crippled vehicles.

121800   Arrive desert base. Air dead calm, heavy, dry, oppressive. Temperature 115 degrees.

121845   Entire battery true west, putting the "draw line" over the middle of Santa Monica Bay and across the heart of Los Angeles.

130800   Heavy cloudbank in the west along the Los Angeles area coast, spreading to cover Los Angeles County and Orange County to about 6/10 by 130900.

131100   National Weather Service forecast high for 13 September for Los Angeles: 108 (actual high 106).

131800   Meteorologist Bill Keene on KNXT-TV: "This is going to go on and on all week. . . . There's no relief in sight."

† Effecting weather changes on the Southern California coast from a base nearly 100 miles in the interior raises the question of the inherent orgonotic delay (IOD) that is inevitably involved. Experience had previously taught that a 24-hour delay would be a reasonable expectation. Since these operations involved the movement of millions of tons of air, and temperature exchanges of phenomenal magnitude, even 24 hours to manifest gross effects may seem incredible. The IOD may be defined as the time lapse between the application of a physical stimulus to any OR system and the appearance of consequent physical effects. The IOD may range from a fraction of a second in the case of a pinprick to the human body, to several days in weather engineering that involves stimulus administered via CLBs.

131855   Bob Hale, KNBC-TV weatherman: "It's going to
         go on and on, continuing hot all week."
         TJC to a Boston guest familiar with orgone en-
         gineering and the Kooler operation: "There is no
         way this can continue as they insist. They will all
         reverse themselves tomorrow."

132000   Small CLB put in function from the Orange Coast
         to reinforce desert battery.
         Conditions in Southern California on Monday fully
         justified the decision to take countering action
         against the heat by orgone engineering. Los Angeles
         had become near chaotic due to high heat and
         heavy power demands. The Los Angeles Depart-
         ment of Water and Power was put close to its gen-
         erating and distributing limit. School closures, smog
         alerts, and imminent power failures were causing
         widespread dislocation of life in the region.
         Every weather source (except the writer) stated
         that there was no relief in sight, further adding to
         the psychological burdens of the populace.

140030   Telephone call from Mary Lee Poe, assistant to Dr.
         Duvall in the coordination of the ORF program.
         She inquires about Kooler. TJC: "The heat wave
         will be cracked today. It is possible we will have
         some rain by the end of the week, due to the huge
         rain accretions in Texas." (See Map D)‡

140900   *Long Beach Independent Press-Telegram* headlines
         describe what the area is to expect this day:
         107! MORE HEAT, MORE SMOG, POWER CRISIS.
         NO RELIEF IN SIGHT FOR TWO DAYS.

140930   National Weather Service forecast for Los Angeles:
         (from *L. A. Times*) "Fair and continued hot
         today. High 102."

141100   TJC crossing Los Angeles for Westwood conference
         with Dr. Duvall. Sea breeze coming in strong and
         cool. Smog clearing out of southern portion of
         L. A. Kooler obviously now taking hold.

141315   Mrs. Jeanette Duvall to TJC before several
         witnesses: "Are you going to be able to do it?"
         Reply: "It's all over."

141500   Los Angeles high reaches only 97 degrees—5 de-
         grees under forecast and down 9 degrees from
         Monday.

‡ The large rained areas are shown on Map D. If the CLB battery continued pointing west, rain could be drawn in from the
opposite direction, a fundamental finding of WR. Thus, in Kooler,
rain was at this stage a possible "side effect."

141800 Bill Keene, KNXT-TV staff meteorologist: "Well, it certainly cooled off today . . . but don't get too excited or cool, because on Thursday there'll be more heat and Santa Ana winds."

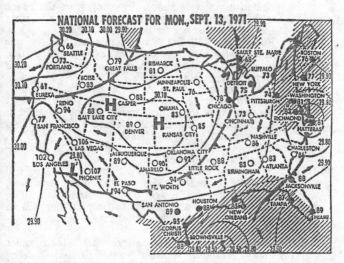

MAP D *Shows rain accretions in Texas due to Tropical Storm Fern. Papaløte, Tex., 25 miles northwest of Corpus Christi, received a monstrous 35 inches of rain on Monday, September 13. The possibility of rain falling in Southern California before the end of the week, i.e., by Friday, September 17, was broached by the orgone engineer in charge of Kooler shortly after midnight September 13–14, 1971. Counter to forecasts, drizzles and light rain hit Southern California on Thursday, September 16, 1971.*

KNXT-TV then provided convincing proof, quite inadvertently, that orgone engineering was doing its job with precision. Sensing a good visual story in the heat wave, KNXT had set up a time-lapse camera above Santa Monica beach, which is on the draw line from the desert base. With the forecast high of 102, the television station intended to make a time-lapse film of the morning arrival of the crowds, shot over a period of perhaps four hours, and then run through in perhaps thirty seconds on TV. The idea was to show Santa Monica beach becoming rapidly buried under the crowds. The idea backfired with great benefit for verification of Kooler. The crowds arrived, then in came a veritable wall of fog and cold air midmorning, and the chilled mobs were shown departing from the beach with lightning rapidity. These pictures were worth a thousand words per frame.

141855   Bob Hale, KNBC-TV weatherman: "Yes, it was down today to 97 but don't get excited or too cool, because on Thursday there'll be *more heat and Santa Anas!*" [Emphasis his.]

141910   Telephone call to Dr. Albert Duvall, advising him of forecast Santa Ana winds for Thursday, now that the "all week long" heat wave has collapsed. Firm commitment to Dr. Duvall: "There will be no Santa Ana winds. Rain is more likely."

142300   Channel 13 TV news: "The heat wave in Los Angeles has been broken."

142310   Bill Keene on KNXT-TV: "That sea breeze will keep the temperature down a little more tomorrow, then we're going to get a Santa Ana wind along about Thursday and Friday, so temperatures will go up again . . . It's only a brief respite today and tomorrow."

150830   National Weather Service forecast: "Much cooler today." National Weather Service Coastal Bulletin, Pt. Arguello to the Mexican Border: "It was fair weather along the Pacific Coast this morning except for coastal fog and low cloud along the coast of Southern California." That is, fair weather everywhere *except where the CLB battery was bearing.* The costly and disruptive heat wave had thus been terminated, with the factual situation of coastal cooling and strong onshore winds substantiated from official reports and *counter to prior forecasts.* Kooler, however, was not yet over. The last life would disappear from the heat wave, and the Santa Ana wind forecasts would be invalidated. The battery was left in function.

151800   Bill Keene, KNXT-TV staff meteorologist: "Almost everywhere, temperatures were down ten to fifteen degrees from what they have been running. With the loss of heat we got a great increase in humidity, running better than 65%. *It now appears that the threat of Santa Ana winds is diminishing* [emphasis supplied]. Temperatures will warm up a little on Friday, but tomorrow they'll stay close to today's." Los Angeles Civic Center was 86.

151855   Bob Hale, KNBC-TV weatherman: "I don't want everybody to get lulled into a sense of false security because it is cool. Don't think this is fall . . . by the weekend I think we're going to have some vicious temperatures, because this just isn't the time of year to cool off. Today we did cool off (sic)."

152300   CLB battery inspected. All OK. Battery left in function.

160800   Entire Los Angeles Basin now overcast and cool. Heat wave smashed. The forbidding Santa Ana could not even begin to manifest against the countering power of the CLB battery. Los Angeles temperatures were pulled down to 75 degrees on Thursday 16 September—the first day since 6 July 1971 that Los Angeles temperature failed to reach 80 degrees.
   Kooler has produced a 31 degree temperature drop from Monday's peak of 106!

161115   Telephone call to Riverside supplementary CLB battery, requesting 15 minutes Zenith Draw to bring rain out of overcast.

161140   Light rain commences in Orange County. Continues until 1300.

161300   Los Angeles forecast high: 85. Actual high: 75.

161800   Bill Keene, KNXT-TV staff meteorologist: "There'll be a lot of drizzle tonight." He blames "Catalina Eddy," a spurious circulation between Catalina Island, off the California coast, and the Los Angeles County shoreline. "Catalina Eddy" is often adduced to explain forecasts suddenly overridden by orgone engineering.

161855   Bob Hale on KNBC-TV: "A lot of people don't realize that the boys at the U.S. Weather Bureau had their fingers crossed the past few days. It's all a matter of high pressure in the center of the nation. Had it gotten close to us, we'd have Santa Ana winds tonight. . . ."

162359   Battery taken down at desert base.
   Operation Kooler successfully completed.

The influence of the CLB battery on the weather situation was further revealed on Friday, September 17, after the units were taken down at midnight Thursday. On that Friday, Santa Ana winds manifested in the mountains and deserts, and, by Saturday, Los Angeles temperatures had climbed from Thursday's 75 and Friday's 76 back to a hotter 85—more typical of Los Angeles in mid-September.

Summary

Kooler was probably the first orgone engineering operation specifically designed to break a heat wave, although it was based on several years' experience in wind abatement and control. Regional circumstances at the onset of the heat wave, both climatic and social, justified orgonomic intervention. Relief from a cruel and extreme weather situation was accorded to a metropolis and millions of people as a result.

Kooler was launched amid the firm convictions of local meteorologists that the heat wave would last a week. Official forecasts, and newspaper and TV reports evidence that conviction. Less than 40 hours after the CLB battery was put in function at 6:45 p.m. on Sunday, September 12, 1971, a 9-degree drop had been effected in Los Angeles Civic Center temperatures from the Monday peak of 106 degrees. By Thursday noon, Kooler had dropped Los Angeles temperatures by a phenomenal 31 degrees from the Monday high. The predicted week-long heat wave had been annihilated, as Los Angeles enjoyed the coolest days in more than two months of Southern California summer.

The local forecasts made on Tuesday, September 14, 1972, when regional cooling was already far advanced, called for hot, dry, Santa Ana winds by Thursday or Friday. These forecasts were also overridden by continued operation of the desert CLB battery through until Thursday midnight. Thursday in Los Angeles was a cool 75 degrees, Friday was 76 degrees. Here again, it was the orgone engineer who firmly stated in advance that the forecast Santa Anas could not manifest while the CLB battery was in function, a statement based on the current engineering situation and on past experience in taming the Santa Ana wind.

The inability of conventional meteorology to cope, in its estimates of the situation, with the intervention of orgone engineering, reflects no discredit whatever upon the professional people involved. They are learned, competent, and diligent experts in their field. With modern data-gathering and processing devices, and such innovations as satellite weather surveillance, their forecasts in Southern California achieve a remarkable level of accuracy—when orgone engineering does not intervene.

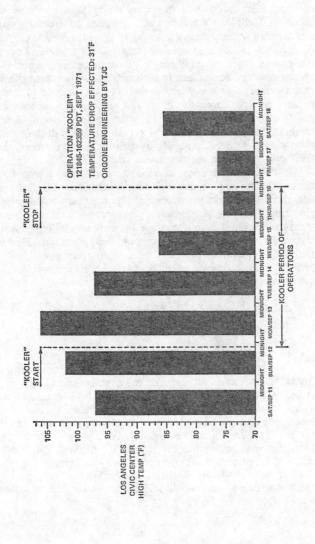

An important factor in verifying and validating the effects of orgone engineering is this consistently high accuracy of Southern California's weathermen. Engineered weather usually stands out as a dramatic anomaly amid the steady stream of accurate predictions coming from official sources. Kooler is a case in point. Since orgone engineering operates upon the primary energy continuum from which known meteorological factors emerge as secondary derivatives, one should actually expect to see forecasts based on secondary phenomena nullified when engineering at the primary level is employed. In short, the weather is ruled by primordial, mass-free orgone energy, and, by working lawfully with the orgone energy, the CLB operator rules the weather.

While Kooler has been described here without reference to the underlying orgonomic engineering functions, the observation should be made in concluding this summary that the engineering aim was not simply to generate a cooling breeze from the Pacific, but to encourage the normal, vitalizing west-to-east flow of the planetary orgone energy stream. This is achieved by pointing the CLB tubes west, making a classical "draw." The secondary effect of an onshore breeze followed this primary stratagem.

Implications of Kooler

Immanent in the success of this operation is a new view of so-called natural disasters arising from rampaging weather. Given an extension of orgone engineering knowledge and sufficient physical resources for its application, man will no longer stand mute and impotent while weather catastrophes overwhelm his life and property. As Kooler demonstrates in one small sphere, there are obviously *laws* by which such catastrophes may be averted, diverted, or diminished. The break-in to this primary energy continuum—the womb of the weather—was made by Wilhelm Reich. Without his genius, operations like Kooler would still be dream stuff for sleeping mankind.

REFERENCES

1. T. J. Constable, "Operation Backwash #1," *J. Orgonomy* **5**, 192 (1971).
2. W. Reich, (a) "The Discovery of the Orgone—Experimental Investigation of Biological Energy," *Intern. J. Sex-Economy Orgone Research* **3**, 108 (1944); (b) "Thermical and Electroscopical Orgonometry," *Intern. J. Sex-Economy Orgone Research* **3**, 1 (1944); (c) "Orgonotic Pulsation," *Intern. J. Sex-Economy Orgone Research* **3**, 97 (1944).
3. R. H. Atkin, "The Second Law of Thermodynamics and the Orgone Accumulator," *Orgone Energy Bulletin* **1**, 52 (1949).
4. O. Raknes, *Wilhelm Reich and Orgonomy* (New York: St. Martin's Press, 1970).
5. W. Reich, *Selected Writings* (New York: Farrar, Straus and Cudahy, 1960), pp. 438–39.

SUGGESTIONS FOR FURTHER EXPLORATION

The following books, periodicals and organizations are offered for their possible interest to those exploring the physics of paranormal phenomena. They are intended for convenience, and should not be construed as implying an endorsement. *Editors.*

BOOKS

Animal Magnetism and the Life Energy, Jerome Eden. Jericho, N.Y.: Exposition Press, 1974.

A Primer of Higher Space, Claude Bragdon. Tucson, Ariz.: Owen Press, 1972.

The Awakening of Kundalini, Gopi Krishna. New York: E. P. Dutton, 1975.

Beyond Telepathy, Andrija Puharich. New York: Anchor Books, 1973.

The Biological Basis of Religion and Genius, Gopi Krishna. New York: Harper & Row, 1972.

Biological Effects of Magnetic Fields, edited by Madeleine F. Barnothy. New York: Plenum Press, 1970.

Biological Transmutations, Louis Kervran. Binghamton, New York: Swan Publishing Co., 1972.

Born To Be Magnetic, Frances Nixon. P.O. Box 718, Chemainus, B.C., Canada: Magnetic Publishers, 1971.

Breakthrough to Creativity, Shafica Karagulla. Los Angeles: DeVorss, 1967.

Consciousness and Reality, edited by Charles Musès and Arthur Young. New York: Avon, 1974.

Consciousness, Radiation, and the Developing Sensory System, William A. Tiller. Stanford, Calif.: Department of Materials Science, Stanford University, 1972.

Cosmic Engineering, Steven Rogers and John Aument. 102 Charles St., Boston, Mass. 02114: Thoth Ltd., 1976.

Cosmic Humanism, Oliver L. Reiser. Cambridge, Mass.: Shenkman, 1966.

Cosmic Humanism and World Unity, Oliver L. Reiser. New York: Gordon and Breach, 1974.

Design for Destiny, Edward W. Russell. New York: Ballantine, 1973.

Electromagnetic Fields and Life, A. S. Presman. New York: Plenum Press, 1970.

Encyclopedia of Occultism, Lewis Spence. New Hyde Park, N.Y.: University Books, 1960.

Encyclopedia of the Paranormal, edited by Rosemarie Stewart. New York: Bobbs-Merrill, 1976.

Encyclopedia of Psychic Science, Nandor Fodor. New Hyde Park, N.Y.: University Books, 1966.

The Energies of Consciousness, edited by Stanley Krippner and Daniel Rubin. New York: Gordon and Breach, 1975.

The Etheric Formative Forces in Cosmos, Earth and Man, Guenther Wachsmuth. New York: Anthroposophic Press, 1932.

Exploring ESP and PIC, edited by Marian L. Nester. American Society for Psychical Research, 5 West 73rd St., New York, N.Y. 10023, 1976.

Exploring the Human Aura, Nicolas Regush and Jan Merta. Englewood Cliffs, N.J.: Prentice-Hall, 1975.

The Fields of Life, Harold S. Burr. New York: Ballantine, 1973.

From Enigma to Science, George Meek. New York: Samuel Weiser, 1973.

Frontiers of Consciousness, edited by John White. New York: Julian Press, 1974.

Handbook of Parapsychology, edited by Benjamin Wolman. New York: Van Nostrand, 1976.

Handbook of Psi Discoveries, Sheila Ostrander and Lynn Schroeder. New York: G. P. Putnam's, 1974.

Handbook of Unusual Energies, J. G. Gallimore. Mokelumne Hill, Calif.: Health Research, 1976.

Health and Light, John Ott. Greenwich, Conn.: Devin-Adair, 1973.

Higher Consciousness, Gopi Krishna. New York: Julian Press, 1974.

The Human Aura, edited by Nicolas Regush. New York: Berkeley, 1974.

The Kirlian Aura, edited by Stanley Krippner and Daniel Rubin. New York: Anchor, 1974.

Kundalini, the Evolutionary Energy in Man, Gopi Krishna. Berkeley, Calif.: Shambhala, 1971.

Letters on Od and Magnetism, Karl von Reichenbach. New Hyde Park, N.Y.: University Press, 1968.

Life Without Death?, Nils O. Jacobson. New York: Delacorte, 1973.

The Loom of Creation, Dennis Milner and Edward Smart. New York: Harper & Row, 1976.

Magic: Science of the Future, Joseph Goodavage. New York: New American Library, 1976.

Mana Physics: A Study of Paraphysical Energy, Serge V. King. 3741 Centinela Ave., Los Angeles, Calif. 90066: Huna Enterprises, 1975.

Man or Matter, Ernst Lehrs. New York: Harper & Row, 1957.

Matter in the Making, Langston Day. London: Vincent Stuart, 1966.

The Medium, the Mystic, and the Physicist, Lawrence Le-Shan. New York: Viking, 1973.

Mindreach, Harold Puthoff and Russell Targ. New York: Delacorte, 1977.

Mysteries of Time and Space, Brad Steiger. New York: Dell, 1976.

New Light on Therapeutic Energy, edited by Mark Gallert. Cambridge, England: James Clark, 1966.

New Worlds Beyond the Atom, Langston Day. Greenwich, Conn.: Devin-Adair, 1966.

The Odic Force, Karl von Reichenbach. New Hyde Park, N.Y.: University Books, 1968.

One, Orest. San Francisco: Strawberry Hill Press, 1977.

Orgone Energy, Jerome Eden. Jericho, N.Y.: Exposition Press, 1972.

Orgone, Reich and Eros, W. Edward Mann. New York: Simon & Schuster, 1973.

Other Worlds, Other Universes, edited by Brad Steiger and John White. New York: Doubleday, 1975.

Physical and Ethereal Spaces, George Adams. Spring Valley, N.Y.: Anthroposophic Press, 1965.

Prodigal Genius: The Life of Nicola Tesla, John O'Neill. New York: David McKay, 1964.

The Probability of the Impossible, Thelma Moss. Los Angeles: Tarcher, 1974.

The Psionic Generator, John P. Boyle. Englewood Cliffs, N.J.: Prentice-Hall, 1975.

Psionic Medicine, J. H. Reyner. New York: Samuel Weiser, 1974.

Psychic Exploration, Edgar D. Mitchell. New York: G. P. Putnam, 1974.

Psychical Physics, S. W. Tromp. New York: Elsevier, 1949.

Psychoenergetics: An Annotated Bibliography, S. F. Fallah. Washington, D.C.: ESPress, 1974.

Pyramid Energy Handbook, Serge V. King. New York: Warner Books, 1977.

Pyramid Power, G. Patrick Flanagan. Glendale, Calif.: Pyramid Publishers, 1973.

The Radiesthetic (or Dowsing) Faculty, A. T. Westlake and Malcolm Rae. Privately printed, 1973. (Available from Mankind Research Foundation—see "Organizations" below.)

Radionics, Riley Crabb. P.O. Box 548, Vista, Calif. 92083: Borderland Science Research Foundation, no date.

Radionics and the Subtle Anatomy of Man, David Tansley. London: Health Science Press, 1972.

Rays from the Capstone, Christopher Hills. P.O. Box 644, Boulder Creek, Calif. 95006: University of the Trees Press, 1976.

The Realms of Healing, Stanley Krippner and Alberto Villoldo. Millbrae, Calif.: Celestial Arts, 1976.

The Reflexive Universe, Arthur M. Young. New York: Delacorte Press, 1976.

Report on Radionics, Edward W. Russell. London: Spearman, 1973.

Researches on the Vital Force, Karl von Reichenbach. Secaucus, N.J.: Lyle Stuart, 1974.

The Romeo Error, Lyall Watson. New York: Doubleday, 1975.

The Roots of Coincidence, Arthur Koestler. New York: Random House, 1974.

The Roots of Consciousness, Jeffrey Mishlove. New York: Random House, 1975.

The Sea of Energy in Which the Planet Floats, T. Henry Moray. Privately printed, 1960. (Available from Cosray Research Institute—see "Organizations" below.)

The Secret Life of Plants, Peter Tompkins and Christopher Bird. New York: Harper & Row, 1973.

The Secret of Life, George Lakhovsky. Mokelumne Hill, Calif.: Health Research, 1970.

The Secret of Yoga, Gopi Krishna. New York: Harper & Row, 1972.

The Secret Power of Pyramids, Bill Schul and Ed Pettit. New York: Fawcett, 1975.

The Secret Science Behind Miracles, Max Freedom Long. Los Angeles: Kosmon Press, 1948.

Selected Writings, Wilhelm Reich. New York: Farrar, Straus, and Giroux, 1972.

The Single Reality, Preston Harold and Winifred Babcock. New York: Dodd, Mead, 1971.

The Source Book Project, edited by William R. Corliss. (Five volumes: *Strange Universe, Strange Planet, Strange Artifacts, Strange Phenomena.*) Box 107, Glen Arm, Md. 21057: Sourcebook Project, 1975.

Space, Time and Beyond, Bob Toben. New York: E. P. Dutton, 1975.

States of Consciousness, Charles Tart. New York: E. P. Dutton, 1975.

Supernature, Lyall Watson. New York: Doubleday, 1974.

Supersenses, Charles Panati. New York: Quadrangle, 1974.

Supersensonics, Christopher Hills. P.O. Box 644, Boulder Creek, Calif. 95006: University of the Trees Press, 1976.

The Tao of Physics, Fritjof Capra. Berkeley, Calif.: Shambhala, 1975.

This Holyest Erthe, Oliver Reiser. London: Perennial, 1974.

The UFO Experience, J. Allen Hynek. New York: Ballantine, 1974.

The Waves That Heal, Mark Clement. Mokelumne Hill, Calif.: Health Research, 1967.

Wilhelm Reich and Orgonomy, Ola Raknes. New York: St. Martin's Press, 1970.

PERIODICALS

American Dowser
American Society of Dowsers
Danville, Vt. 05828
(Articles on dowsing)

American Theosophist
P.O. Box 270
Wheaton, Ill. 60187
(Occasional articles on paraphysics)

A.R.E. Journal
Association for Research and Enlightenment
P.O. Box 595
Virginia Beach, Va. 23451
(Articles on Edgar Cayce, paraphysics and the paranormal)

*Astrologia**
Linear and Circular Permutation
924 Garden Street
Santa Barbara, Calif. 93101
(Articles about time, liberation, and consciousness)

Christian Parapsychologist
1 Devonshire Gardens
London W4 3TW England
(Articles on religion, the psychic and the occult.)

East West Journal
233 Harvard Street
Brookline, Mass. 02146
(Occasional articles on paraphysics)

Eden Bulletin
P.O. Box 34
Careywood, Ida. 83809
(Devoted to orgone research)

ESP Newsletter
ESP Associates
1750 Tower Building
Little Rock, Ark. 72201
(Articles on psychic research)

Fate
500 Hyacinth Place
Highland Park, Ill. 60035
(A popular magazine with general articles on the paranormal)

Fortean Times
P.O. Box 152
London N10 1EP, England
(Covers the full range of fortean phenomena)

Flying Saucer Review
P.O. Box 25
Barnet, Herts.
EN5 2NR, England
(The oldest and most sophisticated journal on ufology)

Human Dimensions
Human Dimensions Institute
4620 West Lake Road
Canandaigua, N.Y. 14424
(Occasional articles on paraphysics)

Imago Mundi
P.O. Box 8
Maximillianstrasse 6
A 6010, Austria
(Articles on religion and parapsychology)

*Journal for the Study of Consciousness**
844 San Ysidro Lane
Santa Barbara, Calif. 93108
(Articles on paraphysics)

Journal of Altered States of Consciousness
43 Central Drive
Farmingdale, N.Y. 11735
(Occasional articles on paraphysics)

Journal of the American Society for Psychical Research
American Society for Psychical Research
5 West 73rd Street
New York, N.Y. 10023
(Articles on psychic research)

Journal of Borderland Research
Borderland Sciences Research Foundation
P.O. Box 548
Vista, Calif. 92083
(Articles on paraphysics)

Journal of Orgonomy
P.O. Box 565
Ansonia Station
New York, N.Y. 10023
(Articles on orgone research)

Journal of Parapsychology
Foundation for Research on the Nature of Man
P.O. Box 6847 College Station
Durham, N.C. 27708
(Articles on parapsychology)

Journal of Paraphysics
Paraphysical Laboratory
Downton, Wiltshire, England
(The oldest and most sophisticated journal on paraphysics)

Journal of Research in Psi Phenomena
P.O. Box 141
Kingston, Ontario K7L 4V6
Canada
(Technical articles on parapsychology and paraphysics theory
and research)

Journal of the Society for Psychical Research
Society for Psychical Research
1 Adam and Eve Mews
London W8 6 UQ, England
(Articles on psychic research)

*Main Currents in Modern Thought**
Center for Integrative Education
12 Church Street
New Rochelle, N.Y. 10805
(Occasional articles on paraphysics)

New Age
32 Station Street
Brookline, Mass. 02147
(Occasional articles on paraphysics)

New Horizons
P.O. Box 427, Station F
Toronto, Canada M4Y 2L8
(Articles on paraphysics and the paranormal)

New Realities—see *Psychic*

Parapsychology Review
Parapsychology Foundation
29 West 57th Street
New York, N.Y.
(Articles on parapsychology)

*Probe the Unknown**
1845 West Empire Avenue
Burbank, Calif. 91504
(A popular magazine with articles on the paranormal)

Proceedings
College of Universal Wisdom
P.O. Box 458
Yucca Valley, Calif. 92294
(Articles on paraphysics)

Psi News
Information Services for Psi Education
P.O. Box 2221
New York, N.Y. 10001
(Guide to educational opportunities and materials on psychic research)

Psychic
680 Beach Street
San Francisco, Calif. 94109
(Recently retitled *New Realities,* it is the best popular magazine on psychic research and the paranormal)

Psychic Observer
P.O. Box 8606
Washington, D.C. 20001
(Articles on psychic and paranormal events)

Pyramid Guide
P.O. Box 176
Elsinore, Calif. 92330
(Articles on pyramid energy research)

Psychoenergetic Systems
Gordon and Breach
1 Park Avenue
New York, N.Y. 10016
(Articles on parapsychology and paraphysics)

Pursuit
Society for Investigation of the Unexplained
Columbia, N.J. 07832
(Articles on unexplained and mysterious phenomena)

Radionics Newsletter
1107 N. Drexel Avenue
Indianapolis, Ind. 46201
(News on radionics research and related topics)

Radionic Quarterly
Radionic Association
Witney Street
Burford, Oxon., England
(Articles on radionic research and application)

Science of Mind
3251 West Sixth Street
Los Angeles, Calif. 90020
(Occasional articles on paraphysics)

Spiritual Frontiers
Spiritual Frontiers Fellowship
10715 Winner Road
Independence, Mo. 64052
(Occasional articles on psychic research)

Theta
Psychical Research Foundation
Duke Station
Durham, N.C. 27706
(Articles on parapsychology and life after death)

Thoth Research Newsletter
102 Charles Street, Suite 20
Boston, Mass. 02114
(Articles on pyramidology and psychotronics)

   * No longer published but available in libraries.

ORGANIZATIONS

Academy of Parapsychology and Medicine
314 Second Street
Los Altos, Calif. 94022

> A nonprofit educational and research organization devoted to the study of all forms of paranormal and unorthodox healing. Publishes a newsletter for members, and offers symposia transcripts for sale.

Academy of Religion and Psychical Research
Spiritual Frontiers Fellowship
10715 Winner Road
Independence, Mo. 64052

> An arm of Spiritual Frontiers Fellowship (see below), the Academy holds public symposia on various topics and publishes the proceedings. Presently available is *Essays in Religion and Psychical Research*.

Advanced Sciences Research and Development Corp., Inc.
P.O. Box 109
Lakemont, Ga. 30552

> Assists man's greater understanding of his environment through research and development of new products (such as the Hieronymus device) and processes in parapsychology, medicine, and electronics.

Aerial Phenomena Research Organization
3910 East Kleindale Road
Tucson, Ariz. 85716
Jim and Coral Lorentzen, Directors

> One of the oldest and biggest ufology research organizations. Open to public membership. Publishes a monthly newsletter.

American College of Orgonomy
515 East 88th Street
New York, N.Y. 10028
Lois Wyvell, Executive Secretary

> Carries on the tradition begun by Dr. Wilhelm Reich, discoverer of orgone energy, by publishing the *Journal of Orgonomy* and pursuing research into orgonomic science through the Oranur Research Laboratories and the

Orgonomic Research Foundation. Also trains physicians in orgonomic medicine and gives courses for the public and qualified professionals.

American Society of Dowsers, Inc.
Danville, Vt. 05828
A nonprofit organization open to public membership. Publishes a quarterly journal, *The American Dowser*, and holds an annual convention in Danville.

American Society for Psychical Research
5 West 73rd Street
New York, N.Y. 10023
Dr. Karlis Osis, Director of Research
An educational and research organization devoted to study of psychic phenomena. Open to public membership. Publishes a newsletter and the *Journal of the American Society for Psychical Research*.

Andhra University
Department of Psychology and Parapsychology
Waltair, Viskhapatam 3, India
Offers M.A. and Ph.D. degrees for work in parapsychology.

Anthroposophical Society
211 Madison Avenue
New York, N.Y. 10016
Promotes the work/world philosophy begun by Dr. Rudolf Steiner under the name of Anthroposophy.

Association for Research and Enlightenment
P.O. Box 595
Virginia Beach, Va. 23451
Hugh Lynn Cayce, Director
Encourages scientific research into paranormal phenomena and healing in the tradition begun by its founder, Edgar Cayce. Publishes the *A.R.E. Journal*. Open to public membership.

Association for the Understanding of Man
P.O. Box 5310
Austin, Tex. 78763
Ray Stanford, Director
Conducts Project Starlight International, an attempt at

contact and communication with UFOs. Publishes a
quarterly journal.

Associazione Italiana Studi del Paranormale
Via Puggia 471/1
16130 Genoa, Italy
Promotes psychic research and college-level education
about it.

Backster Associates, Inc.
645 Oak Street
San Diego, Calif. 92101
Cleve Backster is the investigator of a phenomenon he
terms "primary perception." Originally found in plants,
Backster has since reported observing a primal sentience
in all organic cell life.

Borderland Sciences Research Foundation
P.O. Box 548
Vista, Calif. 92083
Riley Crabb, Director
A nonprofit organization whose chief concern is to make
information available about unusual happenings along
the borderland between the visible and invisible worlds.
Publishes *Journal of Borderland Research* and a catalog
of other publications.

Brazilian Institute for Psychobiophysical Research
Rua Diego de Faria 239
Vila Clementino
São Paulo, Brazil 04037
Investigates phenomena related to "biological organizing
models" of living organisms, e.g., Kirlian photography,
poltergeists, reincarnation reports, unorthodox healing.

Center for UFO Studies
P.O. Box 11
Northfield, Ill. 60093
Dr. J. Allen Hynek, Director
Gathers data about UFOs, then analyzes it using pattern
and content analysis, and statistical study.

City College of the City University of New York
Department of Psychology
Convent Avenue at 138th Street
New York, N.Y. 10031

Dr. Gertrude Schmeidler will accept thesis topics on parapsychology for the Ph.D. in psychology.

C-Life Institute
Box 261
Boulder Creek, Calif. 95006
Dr. Nick Herbert, Director
Carries out theoretical research and field studies in the borderland between objective physics and the experiential disciplines. Offers publications on consciousness research.

College of Psychic Studies
16 Queensberry Place
London SW7 2EB, England
Gives courses on psychic development, as well as public demonstrations by psychics and mediums.

ESP Research Associations Foundation
1750 Tower Building
Little Rock, Ark. 72200
Harold Sherman, President
Conducts an annual public conference on body-mind-spirit healing. Publishes a bulletin, *ESP Newsletter*.

Foundation for Research on the Nature of Man
Box 6847
Duke Station
Durham, N.C. 27706
Dr. J. B. Rhine, Founder
Conducts parapsychological research through the Parapsychology Laboratory and publishes the quarterly *Journal of Parapsychology*.

Genesa
Fallbrook, Calif. 92028
Dr. Derald Langham, Director
A thirteen-dimensional experiential process involving step-into crystals of simple geometrical forms similar to those that life energies move through in nature. An attempt to develop a conceptual model to synthesize, synchronize, and vitalize man's interpretation of universal phenomena.

Group for Psychotronic Investigations
V Chaloupkach 59
Praha 9
Hloubetin, Czechoslovakia
Dr. Zdeněk Rèjdák, Director
Coordinates research in psi phenomena; specializes in psychokinesis, telepathic communication, and psychic healing.

Higher Sense Perception Research Foundation
8668½ Wilshire Boulevard
Beverly Hills, Calif. 90211
Dr. Shafica Karagulla, Director
Conducts research into the aura and physics of energy fields connected with healing and paranormal phenomena.

Human Dimensions Institute
4620 West Lake Road
Canandaigua, N.Y. 14426
Jeanne Rindge, Director
One of the original growth centers, HDI is a nonprofit organization conducting research and educational programs into the psychic–spiritual nature of humanity. Publishes *Human Dimensions* quarterly.

Huna International
2617 Lincoln Boulevard
Santa Monica, Calif. 90405
A nonprofit organization engaged in teaching, application and research of life energy (called "mana" by Huna priests of Polynesia and Hawaii). Membership open to the public. Publishes *Ka Manu* newsletter.

Imago Mundi
P.O. Box 8
Maximillianstrasse 6
A 6010, Austria
Rev. Andreas Resch, Secretary
An organization for elucidating the links between Catholicism and paranormal phenomena. Publishes *Imago Mundi*, a scholarly journal.

Information Services for Psi Education
P.O. Box 221
New York, N.Y. 10001

A clearing house for information about reliable sources and resources in parapsychology. It gathers and disseminates facts about research findings, ideas, and background information for educational programs; names and sources of people and organizations who can help educators, librarians, and others with public-directed programs about psi; and new materials being produced for educational purposes.

Institute for Border Areas of Psychology
78 Freiburg im Bresgau
Eichhalde 12, West Germany
Dr. Hans Bender, Director
Offers courses and graduate degrees in parapsychology; specializes in the investigation of poltergeist phenomena, psychokinesis, and precognition.

Institute of Noetic Sciences
530 Oak Grove Avenue, Suite 201
Menlo Park, Calif. 94025
Dr. Edgar D. Mitchell, President
A nonprofit research and educational organization investigating the nature of consciousness and human potential in order to solve planetary problems. Publishes a newsletter, *Noetic News,* for members.

Institute for Religious Psychology
4-11-7 Inokashira
Mitaka-shi
Tokyo 181, Japan
Dr. Hiroshi Motoyama, Director
Conducts research in psychic phenomena with electrical devices developed by Motoyama and his staff.

Institute of Paraphysics
B.P. 56
75623 Paris Cedex 13
France
Dr. Zbigniew Wolkowski, General Secretary
A nonprofit organization that conducts paraphysical research into the interactions between consciousness, matter, and energy. Current emphasis is paragnostic information retrieval in anthropology through intuitive and nonrational acquisition of knowledge about the past.

Institute of Psychophysical Research
118 Banbury Road
Oxford OX2 6JU
England
Celia Green, Director
    Collects and analyzes cases of out-of-body experience,
    lucid dreams, premonitions, etc.

International Association for Psychotronic Research
43 Eglinton Avenue East
Suite 803
Toronto, Canada M4P 1A2
Dr. Zdeněk Rèjdák, President
    Conducts an International Congress annually for report-
    ing and disseminating information among psychotronic
    researchers. Publishes a quarterly *Journal of Psychoen-
    ergetic Systems*.

International Fortean Organization
P.O. Box 367
Arlington, Va. 22210
Ronald J. Willis, Executive Director
    Continues Charles Fort's work in collecting raw data
    about anomalies in order to build an inclusive phenome-
    nological science. Publishes *Info* and is open to public
    membership.

International Institute of Integral Human Sciences
P.O. Box 1387, Station H
Montreal, Quebec
H3G 2N3 Canada
Prof. John Rossner, President
    Sponsors public symposia on parapsychological and para-
    physical topics. Offers a degree program.

International Society for Religion and Parapsychology
No. 121, 4-11-7 Inokashira
Mitaki-shi
Tokyo, Japan
    Conducts research in psychic phenomena with electrical
    devices.

Japanese Society for Parapsychology
26-14 Chou 4, Nakamo
Tokyo 164, Japan
Dr. Soji Otani, President

Coordinates parapsychological research, especially in the fields of psychokinesis and clairvoyance; sponsors annual meetings.

Kingston Association for Research in Parasciences
P.O. Box 141
Kingston, Ontario
Canada K7L 4V6
Dr. J. Bigu, President
Encourages a multidisciplinary approach to the study of psi. Publishes *Journal of Research in Psi Phenomena*.

Kundalini Research Foundation
10 East 39th Street
New York, N.Y. 10016
Gene Kieffer, President
Sponsors research and public information about the nature of kundalini, the evolutionary energy underlying genius, spiritual experience, psychic abilities, and higher consciousness, as described by yogi–philosopher Gopi Krishna of Kashmir, India.

Maimonides Medical Center
Department of Psychiatry
Division of Parapsychology and Psychophysics
4802 Tenth Avenue
Brooklyn, N.Y. 11219
Dr. Montague Ullman, Chairman
Conducts research into the effects of altered states of consciousness on psychic phenomena through psychedelic drugs, biofeedback, and other methods for voluntary control of internal states. Also conducts educational training programs in parapsychology.

Mankind Research Foundation
1143 New Hampshire Avenue, N.W.
Washington, D.C. 20037
Dr. Carl Schleicher, President
Conducts research, educational and public information activities concerning a wide range of psychic, paraphysical, and mind–body phenomena, including radionics and etherian physics. Publishes *Frontiers of Science*. Open to public membership.

Merlin Weather Engineering
P.O. Box 2664
San Pedro, Calif. 90731
Trevor James Constable, President
> Conducts weather engineering projects on a "no results, no pay" basis. Using cloudbusters, first developed by Wilhelm Reich, MWE manipulates the primary energy (orgone) continuum to make rain, break up cloud cover, abate heat waves and tornado conditions, redirect hurricanes, clear polluted air masses, etc.

Mutual UFO Network
40 Christopher Court
Quincey, Ill. 62301
Walter H. Andrus, Director
> A nonprofit organization interested in resolving the mysteries of the UFO phenomenon. Publishes a monthly journal, *Skylook,* and is open to public membership.

National Investigations Committee on Aerial Phenomena
1536 Connecticut Avenue, N.W.
Washington, D.C. 20036
> The largest ufology research organization.

New Horizons Foundation
Box 427, Station F
Toronto, Ontario
Canada M4Y 2L8
Dr. A.R.G. Owen, President
> Conducts parapsychological and paraphysical research. Publishes a journal, *New Horizons.*

Organization for the Advancement of Knowledge
1406A Northeast 50th Street
Seattle, Wash. 98105
Richard Alan Miller, Director
> A nonprofit organization conducting research in paraphysics and paranormal phenomena.

Orgonomic Research Foundation
P.O. Box 104
Red Hill Road
Ottsville, Pa. 18942
Dr. Richard A. Blasband, President
> Specializes in orgonomic research applied to medicine and weather engineering.

Paraphysical Laboratory
Downton, Wiltshire
England
Benson Herbert, Director
> Conducts paraphysical research into a wide range of paranormal phenomena. Publishes the *Journal of Paraphysics*.

Parapsychology Foundation
29 West 57th Street
New York, N.Y. 10019
Eileen Coly, Director
> A nonprofit organization for supporting impartial scientific inquiry into the total nature and working of the mind and to make research findings available. Publishes *Parapsychology Review* and sponsors an annual conference on parapsychological topics, with proceedings published through the Foundation.

Philosophical Research Society
3910 Los Feliz Boulevard
Los Angeles, Calif. 90027
Manly Palmer Hall, President
> Performs research and educational functions into philosophic, metaphysical, and occult traditions. Publishes a journal.

Psychical Research Foundation
Duke Station
Durham, N.C. 27706
William G. Roll, Director
> Devoted to investigation of the possibility of life after death. Publishes the magazine *Theta*.

Psychologisch Laboratorium der Rijksuniversiteit
Parapsychological Division
Varkenmarkt 2
Utrecht, Netherlands
> Conducts experiments in psychic phenomena; offers courses at the undergraduate and graduate level; publishes the *European Journal of Parapsychology*.

Psychotronics Research Institute
720 Beaver Street
Santa Rosa, Calif. 95404
Daniel Kientz, Director

Manufactures Kirlian photography equipment; conducts public courses in parapsychology and paraphysics.

Radionic Association
Witney Street
Burford, Oxon
England
Holds introductory courses on radionics and publishes *The Radionic Quarterly*.

Rudolf Steiner Institute
2405 Ruscombe Lane
Baltimore, Md. 21209
Dr. Martin Levin, Registrar
Emphasizes renewal of the arts, sciences and humanities through spiritual understanding of man as exemplified in the life and work of Dr. Rudolf Steiner.

Sarasota Research and Development Corp.
1121 Lewis Avenue
Sarasota, Fla. 35577
Dr. Wallace Minto, President
Dr. Minto performed research in the late 1960s to demonstrate that fish generate a previously unknown radiation, termed hydronic radiation, that allows them to transmit signals for long distances underwater at extremely low power. He developed technology to duplicate this communication capacity. Papers describing the research are available.

Society for the Application of Free Energy
1325½ Wisconsin Avenue, N.W.
Washington, D.C. 20007
An independent, nonprofit organization devoted to applying dowsing, radionics, radiesthesia, and healing to meeting and serving the needs of mankind.

Society for Investigation of the Unexplained
Columbia, N.J. 07832
Sabina Sanderson, President
An organization founded by Ivan Sanderson and devoted to the investigation of things and events that are customarily discounted by science. Publishes the monthly journal *Pursuit* and has extensive files available to members. Open to the public.

Society for Psychical Research
1 Adam and Eve Mews
London W8 6 UQ
England

> The oldest psychic research organization in the world, founded in 1882. Publishes the *Journal of the Society for Psychical Research* and is open to public membership.

Space Drive Research Society
P.O. Box 793
Pomona, Calif. 91769
James E. Cox, Director

> Publisher of *The Anti-Gravity Handbook*, which lists more than one hundred different systems of space drive and has a bibliography of more than two hundred articles of anti-gravity.

Survival Research Foundation
P.O. Box 50446
Tucson, Ariz. 85703
Susy Smith, President

> A nonprofit organization to investigate and support research into the conscious survival of the human soul or spirit after death. Publishes a monthly newsletter for members.

Telenoyology Group at Medical Academy
Atanas Smilov
Ivan Rilsky Street No. 55V
Sofia 6, Bulgaria

> Studies unusual states of consciousness as related to healing.

University of California, Davis
Department of Psychology
Davis, Calif. 95616

> Dr. Charles Tart will accept thesis topics on parapsychology for the Ph.D. in psychology.

University of Edinburgh
Department of Psychology
60 Pleasance
Edinburgh EH8 9TJ, Scotland

> Has a parapsychology unit directed by Dr. John Beloff,

who accepts thesis topics in parapsychology for the Ph.D. in psychology.

University of the Trees
P.O. Box 644
Boulder Creek, CA 95006
Christopher Hills, Director

Performs a wide range of investigations in consciousness research and radiational paraphysics (termed "super-sensonics"). Offers courses, literature and paraphysical devices.

University of Virginia
Division of Parapsychology
Department of Psychiatry
Charlottesville, Va. 22901
Dr. Ian Stevenson, Chairman

Performs parapsychological research but offers no courses or degrees.

ABOUT THE AUTHORS

LAURENCE M. BEYNAM lives in Ankara, Turkey, where he is studying electrical engineering at Middle East Technical University.

CHRISTOPHER BIRD is coauthor of *The Secret Life of Plants* and is presently preparing a book on dowsing. He is Deputy to the Vice President for the Western Hemisphere of the International Association for Psychotronic Research, and lives in Washington, D.C.

W. E. BUTLER, a British student of magic, is author of *Magic, Its Ritual and Purpose* and *The Magician: His Training and Word*.

TREVOR JAMES CONSTABLE is a radio officer in the merchant marine, an aviation historian and a consultant in weather engineering. He has authored five books, including *The Cosmic Pulse of Life*, which deals with UFOs.

REXFORD DANIELS is president of Interference Consultants, Inc. of Concord, Mass. He has spent more than thirty years researching electromagnetic compatibility, and has published many articles on the subject. He is presently trying to work in an interdisciplinary fashion by unifying knowledge of natural forces.

LANGSTON DAY, a British author, collaborated with George De la Warr to write *New Worlds Beyond the Atom*, which describes the radionic research conducted at the Delawarr Laboratories in Oxford, England.

ALEXANDER P. DUBROV, Ph.D., is a Russian biophysicist at the Institute of Earth Physics of the USSR's Academy of Sciences, where his studies involve heliobiology and the influence of geomagnetic fields on living organisms. His books include *The Geomagnetic Field and Life*, now being translated into English.

HORACE C. DUDLEY, Ph.D., is professor of radiation physics at University of Chicago Medical Center, and author of *Morality of Nuclear Planning—??*.

JOSEPH GOODAVAGE is a professional writer whose interest is paraphysics. He is author of *Astrology: The Space Age Sci-*

ence, Magic: Science of the Future, and dozens of articles in popular magazines. He lives in Whitefield, Maine.

WILLIS W. HARMAN, Ph.D., is director of the Center for Study of Social Policy at Stanford Research Institute and professor of engineering–economic systems at Stanford University. He has published pioneering articles in humanistic and transpersonal psychology, and has authored several engineering texts.

NICK HERBERT, Ph.D., is a nuclear physicist, teacher and inventor of the metaphase typewriter, an advanced CORE communication device. He founded the CORE Physics Technologium in Boulder Creek, California, to contact and exploit latent structure in "random" quantum processes.

VIKTOR M. INYUSHIN, Ph.D., is director of the Biophysics Laboratory at Kazakh State University in Alma-Ata, Kazakh State, USSR.

SERGE V. KING, Ph.D., is author of *Pyramid Energy Handbook* and *Mana Physics: A Study of Paraphysical Energy,* and is director of Huna International in Santa Monica, Calif.

GOPI KRISHNA, a yogi-scientist-philosopher, lives in Srinagar, Kashmir. He has authored many books and articles, including *Kundalini, The Secret of Yoga, Higher Consciousness* and *The Awakening of Kundalini.*

ERNST LEHRS, Ph.D., was one of the early teachers in the Waldorf School, founded under Rudolf Steiner, where he instructed in physics. He is author of *Man or Matter,* and now teaches at Emerson College in Sussex, England.

W. EDWARD MANN is professor of sociology at York University in Downsview, Ontario. He is author of *Orgone, Reich, and Eros,* and is presently completing a book entitled *Beyond Reich.*

E. STANTON MAXEY, M.D., is a surgeon practicing in Stuart, Fla. His interest is integrating data from various sources, and he has lectured internationally to promulgate such knowledge.

ROBERT N. MILLER, Ph.D., is an industrial research specialist. Formerly a professor of chemical engineering at Georgia Tech, he has authored more than 20 scientific papers and holds two patents. He lives in Atlanta, Ga.

HIROSHI MOTOYAMA, Ph.D., has doctorates in psychology and philosophy. He is director of the Institute for Religious Psychology in Tokyo, Japan.

CHARLES MUSÈS, Ph.D., is a mathematical investigator who enunciated the first theory of consciousness in terms of new mathematical parameters, hypernumbers. He is coeditor of the book *Consciousness and Reality*, and edited the *Journal for the Study of Consciousness*. He lives in Santa Barbara, Calif.

ZDENĚK RÈJDÁK, Ph.D., has worked for more than two decades in psychotronic research. He is coauthor (with K. Drbal) of *Prospects of Telepathy*, and author of *Telepathy and Clairvoyance* and more than eighty articles. He is president of the International Association for Psychotronic Research, and lives in Prague, Czechoslovakia.

D. SCOTT ROGO is a parapsychologist, educator and author of nearly a dozen books, including *The Welcoming Silence, An Experience of Phantoms* and *Parapsychology: A Century of Enquiry*. He is an editor of *New Realities* magazine and lives in Resada, Calif.

STEVEN M. ROSEN, Ph.D., is associate professor of psychology at Staten Island Community College. His article comes from his forthcoming book, *Cosmic Existentialism*.

MICHAEL ROSSMAN left graduate study in mathematics to work in educational innovation. He is author of *On Learning and Social Change*, and is now completing a book about the politics of consciousness expansion. He lives in Berkeley, Calif.

EDWARD RUSSELL has been involved in radionics for decades. A former newspaperman, he is author of *Report on Radionics* and *Design for Destiny*. He also was a friend of the late Dr. Harold Burr, and edited his magnum opus, *The Fields of Life*.

HERMINE SABETAY, born in Czechoslovakia, received her degree from the University of Berlin. She has coauthored *Recent Progress in Organic Chemistry* with her husband, and has published widely in theosophical magazines. She is presently vice president of the Theosophical Society in France.

SAUL-PAUL SIRAG is a research associate at the Institute for the Study of Consciousness in Berkeley, Calif., and a member of the Physics Consciousness Research Group, San Francisco.

DAVID SPANGLER is a director of the Findhorn Foundation in Scotland and was Principal of the Findhorn College. He is author of *Revelation: The Birth of a New Age,* and travels around the planet lecturing and working to assist the processes of planetary transformation.

WILLIAM A. TILLER, Ph.D., is professor of materials science at Stanford University. He has published more than one hundred scientific papers and coedited two scientific books, *Atomic and Electronic Structure of Metals* and *Introduction to Computer Simulation in Applied Science.*

GUENTHER WACHSMUTH, Ph.D., was for the final twenty-five years of his life the secretary to Dr. Rudolf Steiner. He was also his official biographer.

E. H. WALKER, Ph.D., is a research physicist at the Ballistic Research Laboratories of the U.S. Army Aberdeen Research and Development Center in Aberdeen, Md. He has published more than forty technical papers on physics and astrophysics.

JULIUS WEINBERGER retired in 1958, after forty-one years' service with RCA Laboratories, where he directed research in various fields. He holds forty U.S. patents for devices and methods used in radio communication, electric phonographs, acoustics, sound motion pictures, and television. He has been active in psychic research for more than thirty years.

OLIVE WHICHER is a member of the faculty of Emerson College in Sussex, England, where she lectures and gives practical courses in projective geometry and plant morphology.

J. H. M. WHITEMAN, Ph.D., is associate professor emeritus of applied mathematics at the University of Cape Town, South Africa. He is author of *The Mystical Life, Philosophy of Time and Space,* and more than fifty articles on the philosophy of science, physics, mysticism, and parapsychology.